THAT RASCAL FRENEAU

That Rascal Freneau

A Study in Literary Failure

By Lewis Leary

1964
OCTAGON BOOKS, INC.
NEW YORK

Reprinted 1964
by special arrangement with Lewis Leary

OCTAGON BOOKS, INC.

175 FIFTH AVENUE
NEW YORK, N. Y. 10010

LIBRARY OF CONGRESS CATALOG CARD NUMBER: 64-16380

Printed in U.S.A. by
NOBLE OFFSET PRINTERS, INC.
NEW YORK 3, N. Y.

To

M. W. L.

who saw it through

CONTENTS

PREFACE

Philip Freneau failed in almost everything he attempted. It was partly his own fault, and partly the fault of the restless spirit of his time. Nurtured on books and poetry, he found himself at twenty in a world torn by political and economic stress. There was no place in this world for the life Freneau wanted to live; yet the ideals for which blood was being shed and governments overthrown in the late eighteenth century were just those toward which he strove. Caught mercilessly between the necessity of remaining true to his own highest aspiration and the equally compelling necessity of bending often to degrading means for its attainment, his life was a series of alternating compromises with and escapes from activity in revolutionary America. He was not a political philosopher: he was a poet, and too sensitive to personal hurt, too quick to turn in anger on an opponent, to be taken seriously as a measure of the philosophical content of his time. Through all his life Freneau was the young radical who never forgets his quarrel with a world which makes no room for him. As such, he belongs to the twentieth century as well as to the eighteenth, and represents a type of literary failure familiar in almost any age.

But this does not mean that Freneau shall be forgotten. He remains chronologically near the head of every anthology of American verse. "The Wild Honey Suckle" and "The Indian Burying Ground" have become, at least in title, part of the equipment of every man who pretends to knowledge of the pre-Romantic period of English poetry. To students of Washington's administration and to historians of American journalism he is known for his partisan advocacy of Jeffersonian doctrines. His importance as a poet, a journalist, and a political propagandist has been expertly chronicled. Only the details of his life story have remained unknown.

*In this study, therefore, I have emphasized biographical and
bibliographical information, and have purposely avoided speculation on Freneau's sources or his relation to any literary movement.
I have tried not to make too neat a parcel of Freneau's mind (which
was not neat); nor have I attempted to detail exhaustively at any
single moment the influences which made him write as he did. Rather
than create a composite "whole man," who never existed at any one
period of Freneau's long life, I have attempted to show year by
year how one poet in early America tried to adapt himself to an
essentially uninterested public, and how he failed.*

*To do this it has been necessary for me to build with caution on
previous accounts of Freneau's life and to depend largely on newly
discovered manuscript materials and newspaper records. No biographical detail has been admitted unless authenticated by contemporary sources. No bibliographical item has been listed which
I have not examined in the original or in photostat. As a result, it has
been my good fortune to uncover facts in Freneau's life which had
not before been available and to present interpretations which, I
hope, will lead to a more complete understanding of his works.*

*So many tireless friends have contributed to the preparation of
this book that the naming of any of them will be an injustice to
many. I could not, however, have proceeded beyond the preliminary
stages had it not been for the assistance of Miss Edna M. Netter, of
Freehold, New Jersey, who discovered Freneau manuscripts which
everyone else had given up as lost; of Mrs. Edgar Lee Masters and
Mr. Philip Marsh, each of whom graciously turned over to me the
results of years of investigation into the life and writings of Freneau;
and of Miss E. Marie Becker, Librarian of the Monmouth County
Historical Association. An opportunity to follow Freneau's tracks
through the Caribbean and in cities up and down the Atlantic coast
resulted from grants by Columbia University of a George W. Ellis
Fellowship in 1937–1938 and by the University of Miami of a
leave of absence from teaching during the same year. Finally, for
advice and encouragement at every stage, I can here only indicate
the debt I owe to Mr. George A. Osborn, Librarian of Rutgers
University, Dr. Victor Hugo Paltsits, of the New York Public Library, and Dr. Ralph Leslie Rusk, of Columbia University.*

THAT RASCAL FRENEAU

ONE

THE FRESNEAUS

1598–1767

G EORGE WASHINGTON called him "that rascal Freneau," Washington Irving considered him a "barking cur," but Thomas Jefferson said that Philip Freneau saved our constitution when it was "galloping fast into monarchy." [1] Thus between abuse and praise swung the pendulum of Freneau's fame. But he outlived even his notoriety, and died forgotten by the countrymen for whom he had offered most of his life in service. "We had always been accustomed to hear this gentleman spoken of as deceased," wrote a contemporary of his later years, ". . . But on making inquiries . . . we learned that he was still living . . ." [2]

So in large measure it is with Philip Freneau's poetry. Only occasionally, on making inquiries of those whose business or pleasure it is to wander among literary byways, do we remember that the verse which Philip Freneau wrote still lives obscurely on. In vain his apologists remind us that Walter Scott and Thomas Campbell each purloined a line from Freneau, that he is the patriotic "Poet of the American Revolution," the "Father of American Poetry," and the first distinctly poetic voice heard in America. The songs that he sang have outlived their popularity and, were it not for the loyalty of anthologists, would be like the poet forgotten.

But Philip Freneau deserves better than this. He lived through and commented with vigor on the early days of the American republic. Keenly alive to the problems of his time, he saw them with a poet's eye and interpreted them pertinently for all times. He stood squarely against oppression in every form, jealously guarding his poet's vision of a nation in which all men would be truly free. Blindly, savagely, sometimes arrogantly, more often tenderly, he fought with a consuming faith in the rightness of his vision. That he failed, and failed not gloriously, but petulantly and in bitter-

3

ness, is perhaps not as important as the fact that Philip Freneau lived and fought all through his life for an ideal of freedom and democracy in America.

2

The Fresneaus—for so the name was spelled in France and so the spelling was retained until after the death of Philip's father— were of an old family in Oléron, a little island in the Bay of Biscay a few miles west of the ancient city of La Rochelle.[3] There they were known as respectable, hardworking citizens, staunch in allegiance to the reformed faith of the Huguenots. Some, like François, Sieur de la Richauderie, rose to positions of wealth and power. Others followed the sea, building slowly and persistently toward competency. Records in their native province present only an occasional memorial of their activities—here a marriage, there a baptism, and scattered between, a few brief notations to indicate that the Fresneaus often were willing to endure physical and financial hardship for their Huguenot beliefs.[4]

When the revocation of the Edict of Nantes in 1685 forced the Protestants of France to flee from increasing persecutions, members of the old family of Fresneau joined the tide of emigration from the province of Aunis and the coasts of Saintogne. One, Jean Fresneau, attempting to escape by way of Brittany, was captured and sentenced to life imprisonment by the parliament of Bordeaux.[5] Another, Zacarie Fresneau, was successful in flight, but the estate which he left at Oléron was confiscated by royal decree.[6] By the end of the seventeenth century, emigrant members of the Fresneau family had found refuge in the rapidly growing colony which centered about the old Threadneedle Street Church in London.[7] Among them in 1709 was André Fresneau,[8] a vigorous young man of thirty-seven,[9] who prized among his possessions a Bible which had been handed down from father to son in his family for six generations.[10]

In 1590, three years after this Bible was printed in Geneva, Philip P. Fresneau signed his name with a flourish on the flyleaf as he inscribed the volume to his son Jacques. Fifteen years later Jacques placed the Bible in the hands of his son, also Jacques, who in 1630 entrusted it to his son Thomas. The latter, apparently child-less, relinquished the volume to his brother Jean after twenty years. We pause only a moment as we hurry through the generations with the venerable Fresneau heirloom to wonder if this last recipient might not have been the Jean Fresneau who, we have already seen, was captured off the coast of Brittany and condemned to spend the rest of his life in prison. Such a man, martyred for his convictions, would be an ancestor in whom any Huguenot family might take honest pride.

At any rate, the Jean Fresneau who placed his signature pains-takingly below that of his brother passed the family Bible on to his son André in 1680. Twenty-two years went by before André in turn presented it to his son, a second André, who emigrated to London and, having been naturalized as an English subject early in 1709,[11] set sail for America.

3

André Fresneau was a man of energy, adept in practical affairs and preeminently fitted to assume a place of distinction in whatever group he found himself. One account of his coming to America suggests that he first made his way to Boston; [12] but he could not have remained in New England long, because in December, 1709, he was in New York, a member of a syndicate of Huguenot mer-chants who purchased a great tract of undeveloped land in northern New Jersey.[13] Soon, with some capital apparently at his command, he was established as an active trader in West Indian wines and sugar.

Before a year passed he acquired a house on lower Broadway opposite Bowling Green and a warehouse on the waterfront; [14] he was enrolled as a freeman of the city;[15] and, to complete his good fortune, he married Marie, seventeen-year-old daughter of Pierre Morin, a fellow Huguenot emigrant from southwestern France.[16] The future must have seemed bright to André Fresneau. Honored and respected in the colonial seaport community, he was soon called on more than once to represent his fellow merchants as petitioner or administrator.[17] He was elected an elder of the

Church of St. Esprit,[18] and he served for two terms as assessor from the East Ward of the city.[19] As his position became more secure, he invested in lands in New York and in the farming districts of Middlesex and Monmouth Counties in New Jersey.[20] He purchased shares in a copper mining enterprise in Simsbury, Connecticut.[21] His affairs prospered. Invoices from Jamaica, from London, from Amsterdam demanded his attention. Sugar, indigo, snuff and rum filled his warehouse.[22] His home became a place of importance, and his conversation and company sought by visitors of distinction.[23]

During the ten years after his arrival in New York six children were born to André and Marie Fresneau: Andrew in 1711, Marie in 1713, Marguerite in 1715, Pierre in 1718, Thomas Louis who died in infancy in 1719, and Francis in 1720. Each was presented for baptism at the Church of St. Esprit, and the roll of their godparents contains names still venerated among the Huguenots.[24] In the year following the birth of her youngest child Marie Fresneau died. Shortly afterwards André Fresneau married a young woman named Esther, of whose antecedents nothing is known.[25]

But the period of André's prosperity was short. The copper mines in Connecticut produced little revenue, for labor troubles interfered with operation and quarrels among the owners prevented the distribution of profits. After several years of wrangling, the matter was brought to the attention of the colonial assembly, and lengthy litigation ensued.[26] Nor was his business in New York proof against the misfortunes which seemed suddenly to mass against the doughty merchant. There was a question concerning the legality of his possessing a shipment of snuff which had been seized from a Spanish vessel and condemned as contraband. Of the cargo, consigned to Fresneau and stored in his warehouse, many bags were missing when the time for an accounting came. André was hard pressed to explain the matter in court.[27] When he died on August 7, 1725,[28] neither suit had been settled. Two years later the New York case was decided against his heirs, causing the executors to protest that the judgment, if enforced, "would go a great way to ruin the Estate left by sd Andrew ffresneau" and would "induce the widow of sd ffresneau to avoid the misfortune to Depart the province." [29]

This was apparently just what she did; for shortly afterwards Esther Fresneau and her family were found "at their dwelling house at New Hannover in Symsbury." But the copper mines there seem to have been now even less profitable, and soon the greater part of the holdings in Connecticut was sold to satisfy creditors.[30] The future looked dark for the Fresneaus in America. Andrew, the oldest son, was scarcely fourteen; Francis, the youngest, was not yet six.

4

The same misfortune which had pursued André Fresneau seemed to lie in wait for each of his sons. When Andrew, the oldest, reached his majority, he spent several years in Simsbury attempting to reclaim an interest in the copper mines for his father's heirs.[31] Some years later he settled in New York, where he tried to make a place for himself as a merchant in the West Indian trade.[32] But for some reason he failed. In an attempt to stave off disaster he sold most of the property which his father had purchased in New York and in the farming districts of Monmouth County in New Jersey.[33] But nothing helped, and finally young Andrew advertised that he intended to settle his affairs and leave the colony forever. His merchandise, "a fresh parcel of European goods . . . just imported in the last vessel from Holland," was offered for sale "very reasonable for ready money." [34] Thereafter for ten years nothing was heard from him. Even his brother Pierre knew nothing of his whereabouts.[35] In 1758, however, Andrew appeared again, commissioned as an official interpreter of the French language for the province of New York.[36] But there could have been little profit in the position, for early in the summer of the same year he was bankrupt in debtor's prison.[37]

Francis, the youngest son, fared no better. After serving an apprenticeship in his brother's warehouse, he formed a shipping firm of his own [38] and married Helena, daughter of David Provoost, a leading colonial merchant and son-in-law of Jacob Leisler, one of the wealthiest and most influential men in the province.[39] His newly-acquired family connections, however, were not able to save Francis Fresneau from bankruptcy. At the age of twenty-eight he offered his house, his storehouses, and all his possessions at public auction.[40] Forsaking both his wife and his creditors, he fled to the island of Madeira. "He has proved an arent rogue," wrote his brother, "the shame of his country and family." [41] When, some years later, Francis died intestate in Surinam, Pierre Fresneau was appointed to settle his estate.[42]

The second of André Fresneau's sons was only slightly more successful. "I take the oppt . . . to inform you," Pierre Fresneau wrote from Madeira early in 1744, "of my being enter'd into partnership with two Portuguze Gentlemen that by their Skill in Wine, if my friends in America remember me, will Certainly make my Fortune." Thus at twenty-seven he announced the formation of "P. Fresneau & Company," which proposed to export wines "whose Quality we hope will Quite Establish our house." [43] Pierre had already some experience in trade. Two years before he had been "beyond the seas in North Carolina," [44] apparently an agent or supercargo for his older brother. Later he had been briefly employed in some commercial capacity by David Grayson, a merchant of Philadelphia. Whether his recent suffering through an unsuccessful love affair of which he complained, "I have been treated the most ungreatfully of all men," had anything to do with his decision to become a factor in Madeira, we do not know. At any rate, he now set up his own business. "We propose ourselves," he said, "to be the best Shippers in the Island."

On August 1, 1743, shortly after his arrival at Madeira, he sent one batch of letters to America. Now, on February 20 of the next year, a schooner lay moored in the harbor ready to sail for New York. Pierre Fresneau wrote feverishly. "The multiplicity of my letters," he apologized, "obliges me to be brief." His correspondents included some of the first names of colonial America. Among others, he wrote to Abraham Van Courtlandt, Samuel Livingston, Isaac Beauchamp, Brandt Schuyler, Cornelius Van Horne, Abram De Peyster, Gilian Verplanck, Nicholas Bayard, David Provoost, and Anthony Rutgers. From each he solicited custom as the only British trader, "one from Maryland excepted," on the island. He asked for consideration, not "merely for the sake of Country butt because he was capable of Shiping Wines No way Inferiour." To former associates of André Fresneau he submitted his qualifications, his aspirations: "If one whose Father was So well Known can have any affect upon Yᵉ American Gentlemen & his intention to Return among Them and make his Country the better for his own Success he Flatters himself Every Gentleman will give him the Preferance to all heare Established for who riches Nth America is never Like to be the better."

Soon shipments, including beeswax, codfish, nails, cheese, beans, and Indian corn, were sent from New York to P. Fresneau and Company. In exchange pipes of wine were returned from Madeira, including an "excellent parcel of wines of the Jesuits wch every body allows to be the best in the island." Pierre particularly cultivated the New York trade; thus, he said, "we shall have the Less occasion to Ship extraordinary wines elsewhere, wch is not the Case with any of the Factors here, who from an ambitious view of enlarging their correspondence solicit buisness in Engl. Holland, Ireland, the West Indies." In such a situation, he advised his American clients, "your country comes Badly off." "Our wines," he confided with optimism, "begin to show themselves & will in all appearances Turn out Extraordinary this Year."

It took weeks, however, for letters to reach America and as long again for orders to be returned to the island. Foodstuffs did not stand up well on the long sea voyage. Pierre complained to his brother of a cargo the latter had sent: the fish were poor, the cheeses rotten, the beans greatly short of the quantity called for. He suspected the sailors of pilfering, "a practice," he said, "often made use of especially by Ber—dians." Nor did the wines fare better. "My Brother Andrew informs me," Pierre wrote to a customer in New York, "of his having sold you a pipe of wine that prov'd sour wch has given me much Concern But which I hope will never happen for the future." He humbly invited further "tryal of P. Fresneau & Company." "I hope," he concluded, "we will serve you in such a manner as will leave you no Room to complain." Nevertheless, the business did not prosper, and an anxious note breaks recurrently into the correspondence. "Nothing," Pierre asserted, "gives me so much concern as to find several of my best friends (as I thought) give their business to Strangers sooner then to their

Country man after knowing me to be Capable of Remitting them as good wine . . . as any other house can for their lives!"

Yet, though orders lapsed, the young merchant did not forget his friends in America. To William Bradford, the Pennsylvania printer who kept him supplied with newspapers, Pierre sent a large barrel of lemons. Francis Fresneau's bride received a goldfinch which sang charmingly. To his relatives among the Huguenot colony in New York he dispatched a special basket of figs. In return, Pierre solicited "something gay" which he might present to the sixteen-year-old daughter of one of his partners. For himself, he needed three glass lanthorns, a spy glass, and a pen knife. Most of all, however, he wrote despairingly to his brother, he needed trade: "All our fine expectations are come to nothing."

Difficulties were encountered among the islanders as well as with customers in New York. "There is no doing business for a quart of wine without letter upon letter to all our Country Gentry with whom we deal which is the cause of our losing very much." Even when a cargo was ready for shipping, there was often no vessel available. "Your Disappointing us in sending us yᵉ Brig you so long talkd of," Pierre wrote to his older brother, "has been a Prodigious loss to us in yᵉ wines we had prepared for her which we know not how your unfortunate brother can sustain." When Andrew, however, suggested that they become partners in a brig of their own, Pierre replied haughtily, "Your brother does not care to be concerned in shipping . . . therefore returns you his thanks." So, for periods of months at a time the young merchant waited for a vessel to carry his wines to America. "Tis heedless to repeat," he wrote in exasperation to his brother, "what great losses we are at by yᵉ Wastage of our Wines." The situation bred in him "so great a Disgust" that he declared "his Patience after more than four months duration in hopes of business . . . quite exhausted." "We now have nothing to do," he confessed, "but sit with our arms across."

In the meantime he appealed to his younger brother: "We are strongly prepossessed with the notion . . . that was you to take a journey as far as Boston you might create . . . friends throughout New England and thereby get us large consignments from them." When nothing came of this suggestion, Pierre took the matter

in his own hands, announced late in 1747 to his brothers and to
William Bradford that he himself would take the first available ship
home. This he did and, after a passage of fifty-two days, landed at
New York early in January, 1748. "By the beginning of March, I
propose, God Willing," he wrote back to his partners, "to start for
New England, where it will be necessary for me to stay until midsummer." His itinerary would then take him to Philadelphia and
the "western ports," and finally to the Carolinas. His enterprise was
handicapped, however, by the severity of the weather, the condition
of the roads, and an illness which, he was careful to explain to his
associates in Madeira, "My Doctor attributes to my great exercise
. . . on horseback in order to procure business for our house."

Time passed slowly, one delay after another was encountered,
and the correspondence between Pierre Fresneau and his partners
became perfunctory and short-tempered. To make matters worse,
both Andrew and Francis Fresneau owed the company large sums
of money for wines they had taken upon consignment. The partners
despaired ever of collecting any of it. Pierre hid his embarrassment
behind a screen of well articulated anger. It only aggravated the
situation that Francis soon turned up in Madeira where, Pierre complained, "he had the impudence to Settle himself in my house." To
his partners he wrote: "'Tis ye advice of all my friends that you
turn him immediately . . . out of my house and make him pay
rent for the time he lived in it."

But there was a brighter side to the picture. At some time during
the course of his travels through the American colonies, Pierre
Fresneau met Agnes Watson, twenty-three-year-old daughter of a
prosperous Scotch yeoman from Monmouth County, New Jersey.
Her father, David, her uncles, and her brothers all had extensive
holdings in farmlands. They were a steady and industrious people,
active members of the Old Scots church at Freehold.[45] It was not
long before Pierre, archly defending himself against his partners'
accusations that he was neglecting business for personal affairs,
posted the necessary bond with the governor of the province of East
New-Jersey and, on March 12, 1750, married Agnes Watson.[46]

His was an excellent choice. The placid common sense and Scotch
tenacity which his wife brought to their union were to pay high

dividends. More immediately important, however, the established family connections which she placed at Pierre Fresneau's disposal undoubtedly warded off the failure which had overcome each of his brothers.

5

Philip Morin Fresneau, the oldest son of Pierre and Agnes, was born January 2 (O.S.), 1752, at his father's house on Frankfort Street on the outskirts of New York.[47] Had his parents known that the child who lay bundled against the winter's cold was to be a poet, they might have perceived a portent in the brilliant display of the Aurora Borealis, deep red and white and splendidly luminous, which surprised inhabitants of New York just one week after Philip's birth.[48] There was probably, however, little time for pondering over astronomical auguries: the weather was extraordinarily severe; ice so filled the rivers that a sledge could be driven to the Long Island or the New Jersey shore; and shipping was tied up for weeks as vessels crowded beside the wharves waiting for the harbor to clear. By spring smallpox was epidemic through the city,[49] and Pierre Fresneau moved his family to the countryside of Monmouth, where he built a house on property which belonged to the Watsons.[50] Then, leaving his wife and son to be watched over by her people, he set sail once more for Madeira.

6

Monmouth County spread then, as it does now, over a pleasant countryside of fields and wooded hills. Raritan Bay, sheltered by the dunes of Sandy Hook and the higher reaches of the Navesink Highlands, stretches between it and the city of New York. To the south, a hard day's travel over rural roads, lay Philadelphia. Opening into Raritan Bay where the coastline begins to swing northward toward Amboy is Middletown Creek, now choked with marshland, but then a busy inlet leading to Middletown Point, the port of delivery and post town for northern Monmouth County. Here heavy-wheeled carts deposited cordwood or garden truck at waterfront landings where broad, round-bottomed sloops lay ready to carry produce to New York.

Two miles south of Middletown Point was the little settlement of Mount Pleasant. There, on a plot of ground slightly elevated above the surrounding countryside, Pierre Fresneau built his home, and he called it Locust Grove.[51] Upon his return from Madeira early in 1753, he wrote to his former associates, "Finding my crossing of the seas attended with no manner of success . . . I have taken a resolution to give over the wine trade and have established me in the Jerseys where I am now with my family." He entered partnership with Peter Watson, his wife's cousin. "My friends," Pierre explained, "have built me a house near a convenient landing where I carry on a dry goods trade and make returns of country produce to New York." Thus, he submitted, "I hope after a few years to better my circumstances."

But Pierre Fresneau seems never to have been completely happy in the quiet of the Monmouth countryside. Submission to rural retirement was not, moreover, apparently expected of him. "Perhaps," he suggested, "it will surprise my friends." As time went on, he became restless. "It is now near a twelve month since I was in New York," he complained. "I have almost forgot my Portugeze." He hoped "a little time longer will . . . bring some of the Farmers with whom I am daily making acquaintance to venture their produce to Sea." To his friends in Madeira he affirmed: "I am become quite a farmer but despair not (if God assists me) to be concerned once more with my favorite isle." But soon he was forced to admit, "My family is again on the increase . . . I don't know if I shall ever have time to make another trip."

During the next nine years he had little opportunity to gratify either his commercial ambitions or his wanderlust. His oldest daughter, Mary, was born "in her father's house at Mount Pleasant, near Middletown Point, on the 10th of September, 1754." Almost three years later a second son, Peter, made his appearance on April 5, 1757. Andrew, born in 1758, lived only one year. He died "of the small pox at Middletown Point" and "was interred at the old burying ground at Mount Pleasant." Margaret Allaire, the youngest of Pierre Fresneau's children, was born on February 27, 1761.[52]

Trade in Monmouth County moved slowly. Yet, though cash was always a "very scarce Article," the family at Mount Pleasant seems never to have been seriously in want. In 1762 Pierre Fresneau acquired by deed (executed in consideration of love and affection and five pounds cash) all the lands that his brother-in-law David Watson owned in East New Jersey. In addition to the one hundred acres "more or less" on which Locust Grove was situated, there were nine lots in the township of Middletown Point, a tract of one hundred and four acres at the neighboring Boles's Mills, and a sawmill surrounded by thirty acres of woodland on the creek.[53] Some income might be expected from the copper mines at Simsbury in which Pierre now retained the family interest.[54] Rents could sometimes be collected from the great tract of land in northern New Jersey in which André Fresneau had invested years before—though collected not without difficulty, for Pierre was arrested for "making commotion" in connection with the renewing of the leases in 1763.[55]

By the time Philip was ten years old his father's affairs seem at last to have become prosperous. Pierre's activities had been extended to New York, where he was known respectfully as "Peter Fresneau, Gent." [56] He was called upon to act as translator from French to English.[57] He petitioned the Common Council for rights to waterfront property along Rotten Row.[58] He invested in lands in upper New York state.[59] His mill in Monmouth turned out lumber and firewood for the urban market. His fields at Mount Pleasant produced garden truck and grain, enough "blessed bt God," he said, "to carry us the Year Round."

7

Life for the Fresneaus at Locust Grove was devout and simple, with family prayers and Scripture reading part of the daily routine.[60] Of the library, which tradition insists was large and well chosen, only four volumes survive, but these indicate a solid literary fare. *The Book of Common Prayer* was Agnes Watson Fresneau's contribution—a note on the flyleaf tells us that it was "her Booke." *The Works of the Late Reverend Isaac Watts* offered solemn and moralistic nourishment. More battered and, if marginal notes and

checks are any guide to us, of more interest to young Philip were
The Complete Works of William Shakespeare and *The Spectator.*[61]
Scrawled across the end papers of his father's copy of the latter,
he wrote:

> Dont steal this Book My Honest Friend
> For Fear the Gallows will be your end
> And then the Justis will come and say
> Where is the Book you Stole away
>
> Philip Freneau

But of course books did not create the whole background against
which the boy developed. There were his neighbors, the Schencks,
the Van Pelts, the Formans, and the Holmeses, sturdy farm people,
Dutch, Scotch-Irish, and English of wholesome stocks. There was his
mother's honest Scotch family, ambitious and religious people,
leaders in every good work in Monmouth County. Some followed
the sea, some tilled the land, and at least one had settled on the
island of Santa Cruz, far south in the Caribbean.[62] There was his
father, French, mercurial, polylinguistic, who chafed under the
restraint of rural life, who had stories he could tell of long voyages
across the ocean, of travels on horseback through nearly all the
American colonies, of strange lands, and of strange exotic fruits.
Finally, there was Monmouth County, quiet, but already filled with
story.

If Philip followed the hills which rise gently from behind the
Fresneau homestead to where the highlands, grown thick with pine
and juniper and huckleberry, look out over the Atlantic, he might
catch sight of white dots of sail upon the horizon which were ships
on their way to or returning from distant and romantic ports. On
clear days he might even see vessels tacking carefully as they approached the bottleneck entrance to New York harbor. Then, when
his eyes moved southward to the pine barrens which clustered about
the coves and inlets along the Jersey coastline, he might remember
tales of pirates who were said to have made these lonely swamplands
their hiding place. Turning, far to the west, hidden in the haze of
the distance, past mile after mile of farmland and forest, so distant
that he who remained at home knew them only in story, were the
mountains beyond which Indians skulked. There were legends of

captivity and escape, of sudden attack and great braveries. And, as the boy stood on the rugged brow of the Navesink hills looking westward, the green, the white, and the brown of Monmouth County, acres of corn and wheat, timber lands and brush and thicket, the salt meadow and the marshes—all the quiet and the industry of Monmouth County would be spread in abundance before him.

Of Philip's earliest formal education in these pleasant surroundings little can be discovered. We are told that he learned his first lessons from his mother.[63] We are told, again, that he was sent to a boarding school in New York at the age of ten [64]—perhaps it was to the French School at the Reformed Switzer church which promised "to instruct Young Ladies and Gentlemen in whatever is necessary to the finishing of their education;" [65] possibly it was to the less pretentious establishment opposite the Presbyterian church on New Street, which was equipped for "teaching the Latin and Greek languages, with Geography and the Antiquities." [66] At any rate, by the time he was fifteen, Philip was back in Monmouth County, a student at the Mattisonia Grammar School, in Manalapan, fifteen miles from Mount Pleasant.[67] There, under the tutelage of Alexander Mitchell, a young man who had graduated from Nassau Hall at Princeton two years before, and under the supervision of the Reverend William Tennent, acting president of the same institution, Philip prepared for college. He read in Horace, Cicero, the Greek Testament, Lucian, and Xenophon. He proved his mastery of composition in English and Latin.[68] He studied well, for it was Pierre Fresneau's plan that his oldest son should be a clergyman.[69]

8

But failure finally closed in on Pierre Fresneau as it had closed in on his father and each of his brothers. Creditors became "very urgent for their money." "If they once begin to fall upon me," he said, "it must certainly terminate in my ruin." He tried to raise funds among his Huguenot friends in New York. He complained to his cousin, John Morin Scott, that the latter's refusal to lend him one hundred pounds "must inevitably have fatal consequences." He attempted to mortgage the lands he had purchased in upper New

York state. Failing in this, he advertised his holdings for sale.[70] He sent load after load of timber from his sawmill in an effort to stave off disaster. Nothing succeeded.

When Pierre Fresneau died on October 17, 1767, he left his family a rather uncertain income from lands in Westchester, Orange, and Albany Counties in New York, his share in the copper mines at Simsbury, and his property in Monmouth County, together with a debt of thirteen hundred pounds.[71] "Here ends," his oldest son wrote on the last page of his father's letter book, "a Book of Vexation, disappointments, Loss and plagues, that sunk the Author to his grave short of 50 years."

One year later Philip, now sixteen years old and the male head of his family, set out across the hills of Monmouth toward Princeton, forty miles away. His father's wish had been remembered. He was going to study for the ministry.

TWO

PRINCETON

1768–1771

PRINCETON in 1768 was a quiet country village of some fifty houses clustered along the highroad just half way between Philadelphia and New York. Situated on the first high ground which separates the alluvial plain of South Jersey from the hilly regions of the north, it looked in every direction over a countryside of rolling hills and pleasant valleys. To the south an undulating patchwork of meadow and forest stretched as far as eye could see. In the distance the Navesink Highlands curved majestically along the Jersey coastline. Rugged mountains loomed beyond the foothills north of Princeton, while westward plains descended gradually to the Delaware.

Near the center of the village, silhouetted against the sky at the top of a gently rising slope, the college was an outstanding landmark for miles around. A massive stone building, modeled carefully after King's College at Cambridge and just eleven years old when Philip Freneau enrolled, Nassau Hall was the pride of the province. The Reverend John Witherspoon, who the summer before had come from Scotland to assume the presidency of the institution, won all hearts by pronouncing it finer than anything at the University of Edinburgh. Old prints picture Nassau Hall with four tiers of vacantly staring windows overlooking a bare campus. Three solid stone stairways lead to three dark and forbidding doorways. Only a belfry, thrusting above a symmetrical array of brick chimneys, adds a jaunty touch of disproportion to the chaste angularity of the architecture. In this one building more than one hundred and fifty students were lodged and fed, classes were taught, and convocations held. A bust of Homer faced the highway from over the main entrance. A row of young buttonwoods screened the yard from the dust and noise of the thoroughfare.[1]

On proving by examination that his knowledge of Latin and Greek was adequate to the demands made of a second-year student, Philip was admitted to the sophomore class on November 7, 1768.[2] Thereafter for three years he submitted to a rigorous daily program. Summoned from bed at five by the college bell, he made certain that he had his "shoes and stockings tight" according to faculty regulations [3] and proceeded to the chapel for morning prayers. Then, after a period of study, breakfast was announced at eight. One hour later recitations began, and continued throughout the morning.[4] The basis of the curriculum was, of course, the classics. Besides these, however, young Philip as a sophomore began his collegiate studies with an introduction to the "compleat system of Geography, the first principles of philosophy, and the elements of mathematical knowledge." Like every other student, he heard twice over during his junior and senior years the lectures which John Witherspoon delivered annually on chronology and history and on composition and literature. As a senior he sat through the president's favorite course in moral philosophy.[5]

But it was not a harsh routine, nor did it fail in supplying opportunities for creative expression. Every evening at five the collegians gathered in the main hall to hear orations delivered by their fellows. Each stood his turn in regular order, three every evening. In spite of the president's plea that the addresses be simple and entertaining, "that subjects be better chosen, and better suited to the performers," they were, almost without exception, "warm, passionate declamations," colored with flaming periods and swollen with adolescent zeal.[6] Sometimes it was good fun, and not at all serious. Philip composed a rollicking lampoon upon an unfortunate classmate who found his memory failing "in the midst of a public discourse he had got by rote":

> What could be done?—I gap'd once more,
> And set the audience in a roar,
>   They laugh'd me out of face—
> I turn'd my eyes from north to south,
> I clapt my fingers in my mouth—
>   And down I came! [7]

After an evening meal devoid of "luxurious dainties or Costly

delicacies," students often found it more pleasant to congregate in
the taverns of Princeton than to remain at Nassau Hall, where play
at cards or dice was sternly prohibited and where there could be
no "jumping, hollaring, or boisterous noise." In the village, however, arguments could be pursued in warm companionship, and
sometimes, we are told, drinking bouts essayed which ended in wild
pranks scandalous to the "superiority of the college." [8] But when
the curfew rang at nine, each returned to his quarters. "Then,"
wrote Freneau,

> what my thoughts design to do
> My hands with all their might pursue,
> Since Kelsey rum nor wine will sell
> When once they've rung the evening bell. [9]

Among his classmates none appealed to Freneau more than James
Madison from Virginia and Hugh Brackenridge from western
Pennsylvania. The finely balanced young aristocrat, the Scotch
frontiersman, and the slight and vivacious Huguenot boy became
linked in a strong bond of friendship. "Liberty," President Witherspoon told them, "either cannot, or ought not to be given up in the
social state." [10] Liberty then became their watchword. When William Bradford, son of the Philadelphia printer with whom Pierre
Fresneau had corresponded from Madeira years before, entered the
class below them, he became the fourth member of a group which
was thoroughly to enliven the college with its activities.

In its essence undergraduate life in 1768 was little different from
undergraduate life at any other time. "Were you here I could give
you a description of some of the girls, and characters of some of the
lovers, and private anecdotes of both, that would afford you infinite
amusement and diversion," wrote an alumnus on visiting Nassau
Hall. "The college always has teemed with fools of this cast," he
added in dignified disapproval. "There were enough of them when
we were in it, and mercy on me, the breed has increased surprisingly
of late." [11] "Eating, drinking, dancing, and fiddling," to say nothing of "playing for pennies," were among the diversions which
filled leisure hours. [12] And sometimes late in the evening the collegians gathered in their rooms for pious discussions on just such

problems as young men often discuss. More than fifty years later
Freneau remembered

> the midnight prayer,
> Monitions mild, when—free from care,
> When smit with awe, the attentive train,
> Renounced the world, or owned it vain,
> With penitential tear.[13]

Like almost any student at almost any period, Philip's classmate,
James Madison, found the "near approach of examinations" evok-
ing a "surprising amount of study on all sides." [14] But, then as ever,
holidays brought release. As an old man Freneau looked back to
the time

> When *Christmas* came, and floods congeal,
> And fierce northwesters blew,
> As down the ice, on *springs of steel*,
> The sprightly *Juniors* flew:
> They left the page of learned lore,
> Ceas'd nature's wonders to explore,
> At *Morven's* grove they paused—again
> Lost vigour to restore.[15]

2

It would be pleasant to report that Philip's academic career was
replete with student honors and noteworthy for devotion to scholarly
pursuits. Unfortunately few eighteenth-century records remain at
Nassau Hall, and none mentions Freneau.[16] We may be sure, however, that during this period he lived with books. Shakespeare had
already been explored in his father's library. Now Milton became
familiar to him, and the Miltonic Joseph Warton, from both of
whom Philip learned to fashion verses.[17] In the college library he
had access to volumes by Francis Bacon, Montaigne, Bunyan, Cow-
ley, Dryden, and Defoe, copies of *The Spectator* and *The Tatler*,
and of Samuel Butler's *Hudibras*.[18] In the classroom he undoubtedly
heard John Witherspoon recommend Cicero, Quintilian, Homer,
and Lucian as models of eloquence. Addison, Swift, and Pope, who
had succeeded in polishing the English language "of roughness and

improprieties"; Shakespeare, Donne, and Cervantes, whose whip-like strokes of wit had never been excelled; Milton, Marvell, Fontenelle, and Boileau all came in for their share of the president's panoramic praise.[19] Among his own books, however, Philip read longest in Horace and in Pope.

"Don't steal this book," he wrote in Latin on the title page of his volume of Horace, and he inscribed his name and address boldly: "1768 Nassau Hall Nova Ceasarea Philip Freneau his book." He made careful notes on the margins, classifying almost every poem: some he found were Asclepiadean, others Pherecratean, Glyconic, Aristophanic, or Sapphic. The analysis of prosody seemed easy to him as he broke down individual verses to choriambs, spondees, dactyls, and trochees. He was interested, moreover, in literary relationships and sources. "See Salust's history," he reminded himself at the end of Ode 4, Book II. "Gades," he noted at the beginning of the next ode, "is at present called Cadiz situated near the Height of Gibraltor." He made enthusiastic comment on Sappho's "charming lyre," and, like many another neophyte, wondered, "What could have been the reason Virgil never mentions Horace?"

The genial banter, the tolerant yet deep probing lines of Horace appealed to young Freneau. One of the earliest of his collegiate poems, "The Pyramids of Egypt," was to be introduced by the melancholy Horatian motto, *Debimur morti, nos nostraque;* and *A Poem on the Rising Glory of America,* his epic-aspiring valedictory to Nassau Hall, has been found to owe part of its inspiration to the Roman poet's sixteenth epode.[20] Yet, though Philip's college exercises must have included such practice, nothing remains to indicate that he translated from Horace during his years at Princeton. Later he did translate, correctly and freely, and from nearly all the Augustan poets. Ovid, Seneca, Lucretius, and Juvenal, imitated or in quotation, were often to appear in his more mature verses. Like other writers of his time, he found that Vergil was so much a "part of the air that a man of letters breathed" [21] that it was almost impossible to avoid echoes of his poems. But it was Freneau's translations of Horace, "still unsurpassed in our literature," [22] which were among the most popular of his later political satires.

It is no surprise, then, to find that Freneau as a student exhibited more than a casual interest in translations already made by English poets. He copied into his own volume Thomas Creech's rendering of Ode 13, Book II, on the jealous pangs which seize a lover "when Lydia praises Damon's charms," and Philip Francis's translation of Ode 5, Book II, a plaint on the inconstancy of love, was written carefully upon the margins a few pages later. But whatever this choice of sentimental and melancholy themes may signify of Freneau's youthful and sentimental moods, more indicative of his nascent literary ambitions are the two other translations which he copied into the volume: his transcription of Francis's superb rendering of Ode 20, Book II, in which Horace boasts of the poet's superiority to all mundane things, and of Pope's adaptation of Ode 9, Book IV, on the immortality of poetry.

The marginalia in the two volumes of Pope's works which Freneau used during his college years help create even more vividly the picture of an apprentice, serious-minded and reverential, sitting before a master. In the first place, like any other serious student, Philip was interested in biographical details. The dates of Pope's birth and death are jotted on the flyleaf of the first volume. Of Wycherley, whose name appears a few pages later, Freneau notes primly that he died "aged 75 an old debauchee." When Pope states that he wrote the "Ode to Solitude" at the age of twelve, Freneau adds quickly and gets 1699. Beside a letter which mentions Twickenham, he wrote, "A Hog of a fellow now owns all this who will admit no strangers. . . . He is called Sir John Briscoe." At the end of a particularly effusive epistle from the poet to his friend Blount, the reader commented knowingly, "Mr. Pope was immoderately fond of Miss Patty Blount, a daughter of this gentleman . . . and therefore it is no wonder that he seems so interested in the old gentleman's welfare. P. F."

Freneau, however, was most interested in those passages in which Pope explained the ideology behind his writings. He underlined the sentence, "I sincerely wish . . . to contemplate the wonders of God in the firmament, rather than the madness of man on earth." Where Pope expostulated, "Good God! what an incongruous animal is man," Freneau ran his pen forcefully down the margin. "Our whole extent of being," the text continues, "is no more in the eye of him who gave it, than a scarcely perceptible moment of duration." [23] Freneau, who was to be haunted with the melancholy certainty that the life of man consisted of only the "frail duration of a flower," marked the statement for further reading. But perhaps most significant in relation to his own later attempts to find peace in seclusion is Freneau's underscoring of

I doubt not but God's works here, are what come nearest to his works there; and that a true relish of the beauties of nature is the most easy preparation and gentlest transition to an enjoyment of those of heaven: as on the contrary, a true town life of hurry, confusion, noise, slander, and discussion, is a sort of apprenticeship to hell and its furies.[24]

Essentially, it was as a young man who aspired to poetry that Philip annotated his volumes of Pope. "A young scribbler's vanity," he read, "needs no recruits from abroad: for nature like an indulgent mother, takes care to supply her sons with as much of her own, as is necessary for their satisfaction." He underlined the passage carefully, but the stroke of his pen became heavier when he came to the next sentence, for it dealt with fame—a poet's fame: "If my verses should meet with a few flying commendations, Virgil has taught me that a young author has not too much reason to be pleased with them, when he considers the natural consequence of praise is envy and calumny." [25]

3

Freneau tuned his own untried lyre carefully to the strain of melancholy music which then dominated English poetry. All things must pass, sang the poets. Fame and loveliness both must fade. The fairest flower has but its day. The paths of earthly glory lead to one common and inevitable end. In such a mood Freneau at sixteen composed "The Poetical History of the Prophet Jonah." [26] Five sturdy cantos of workmanlike couplets clothe the Biblical story in tattered shreds of eighteenth-century didacticism. For example, in the closing canto, Jehovah speaks to his erring prophet:

> Enjoy thy gifts while yet the seasons run
> True to their months, and social with the sun;
> When to the dust my mandate bids thee fall,
> All these are lost, for death conceals them all—

No more the sun illumes the sprightly day,
The seasons vanish, and the stars decay:
The trees, the flowers, no more thy sense delight,
Death shades them all in ever-during night.

So the poets of England spoke, as they would often speak again, through young Philip Freneau. In his first year at Princeton he was already haunted by the certainty of change, decay, and inevitable death—a melancholy trio that was to remain with him in his poetry always.

Yet, if Freneau's "pensiveness upon the brevity and transiency of life and the certainty of death" was to become his outstanding poetical characteristic,[27] it was his ability to stand apart from life as an observer who reported humorously upon the foibles and incongruities of man which later gave him individuality and popularity as a poet. This second trait reveals itself in "The Adventures of Simon Swaugum," a poem which is also said to have been written during Philip's first year at college. It was not printed for almost a quarter of a century and, as it appeared in 1792,[28] displays a sophisticated subtlety of characterization which can hardly be attributed to an undergraduate. Nevertheless, with "The Distrest Orator," already quoted, and the "Epitaph Intended for the Tombstone of Patrick Bay," written during the next year,[29] it indicates that even as a student Freneau had begun to cultivate a talent for satirical verse.

It was only natural that such talent should sometimes be exercised in prose. In October, 1770, at the end of their junior year, Freneau and Hugh Brackenridge finished a "novel." The first two books of "Father Bombo's Pilgrimage to Mecca in Arabia" have been lost. Book III, with the first chapter written by Brackenridge, the second, the third, and an epilogue written by Freneau, has been preserved in a worn, leather-backed notebook.[30] To something of Don Quixote and a little of Lemuel Gulliver, the two young men added a conveniently distorted display of geographical knowledge and a great deal of youthful imagination. As a result, Mr. Bombo fills their pages with rollicking adventures, ludicrous situations, and an attempt at Irish brogue for which Brackenridge was later to find a place in his satirical *Modern Chivalry*, but to which Freneau never returned. In the second chapter Freneau did, however, resort to an artifice which he was later often to find useful: R. Bombo writes an essay on "Luxury," just as Robert Slender, Tomo Cheeki, and Christopher Clodhopper were later to write essays on any number of subjects in post-Revolutionary American newspapers. The one hundred and twenty-five odd words of this collegiate paper are the forerunners of thousands of words in prose through which Freneau, over various pseudonyms, was to make his subsequent closest approaches to fiction.

At the end of the same chapter the poet wins ascendancy over the young writer of prose as Mr. Bombo suddenly bursts into song:

> Sweet are the flow'rs that crown the Vale
> And sweet the spicy breathing Gale
> That murmurs o'er the hills:
> See how the distant lowing throng
> Thro' verdant pastures move along,
> Or drink the Limpid streams and crystal rills.
>
> Ah see in yonder gloomy Grove
> The Shepherd tells his tale of Love
> And clasps the wanton fair:
> While winds and trees and shades conspire
> To fann with Love the Gentle Fire,
> And banish every black and wanton care.

This is one poem from Freneau's college period which we can be sure comes to us in its original form. The "limpid streams," the "crystal rills," the "gloomy grove," and the "wanton fair" are all phrases stereotyped in eighteenth-century pastoral tradition. Freneau was never quite to escape from conventional forms, but now he made no apparent attempt to escape. He does here present first evidence of an authentic lyric note; but he could not sustain it long, and the exuberant sweep of the first two stanzas changes to a melancholy concern with tombs and tears in the third:

> But what has Love to do with me
> Unknown ashore, distress'd by Sea,
> Now hast'ning to the Tomb;
> Whilst here I rove, and pine, and weep,

Sav'd from the fury of the deep
To find alas on shore a harder doom.

There follow five more dismal stanzas. How his poetical cousins in England would have shuddered over the collegian's closing line:

My Stomach tells me I can sing no more!

But social satire and such pleasantry as "Father Bombo's Pilgrimage" were essentially by-products. Freneau wanted to be a serious poet and to sing of serious things. Sitting apprentice to the poets of England, he wrote in their manner; yet his collegiate verse anticipates each of the major themes which he was later to develop. As "The Poetical History of the Prophet Jonah" had given first expression to the certainty of mutability, so "The Citizen's Resolve," written in 1770,[31] indicates that, like so many others of his time, he had learned to praise rural solitude as a panacea for worldly ills. In "Columbus to Ferdinand," written during the same year,[32] Freneau translated promise of future glory for America from Seneca's *Medea*, thus hinting at the epic theme that was stirring within him. Among his minor collegiate poems, however, three stand out more clearly than all the rest as evidence that Princeton was nurturing a poet.

None of the three is striking for its originality. The first, "The Monument of Phaon," undoubtedly owes its inception to Pope's adaptation of Ovid's fifteenth epistle in "Sappho to Phaon." Freneau, however, imaginatively extends the scene to compose a sequel to the tale told by the older poets. Echoes of Gray have been discovered in "The Monument of Phaon," [33] and the main portion of the poem is in the rhymed tetrameter of Milton's "L'Allegro." [34] The theme is of death and grief, but the situation to which Freneau projected his young sympathy came not from experience but from the books he had read. Yet, "The Monument of Phaon," new in neither form nor manner, exhibits an occasional verbal felicity and a fleeting lyricism which the poet in his later years was seldom to command.

More significant, though none the less imitative, is Freneau's first excursion into blank verse, "The Pyramids of Egypt." [35] Where, he asks, are the glories, the palaces, the powers of "Egypt's mighty lords," the tyrants who drove toiling slaves to erect the pyramids? We are reminded of a similar question implied in Dyer's "Ruins of Rome" and of the gentle humanitarianism which had permeated English poetry since the time of Pope. Where, the poets of England had asked, are the fabled glories of yesteryear? Freneau answers the question in one of his most concrete, most delicately phrased figures:

> —all, all are gone,
> And like the phantom snows of a May morning
> Left not a vestige to discover them.

Only the tombs remain, emblems of death, described in macabre lines that look forward to Philip Freneau's later "The House of Night" and to Poe:

> 'Tis darkness all, with hateful silence join'd—
> Here drowsy bats enjoy a dull repose,
> And marble coffins, vacant of their bones,
> Show where the royal dead in ruin lay!

Yet even death—here is the very theme of "The House of Night"— is not immortal:

> There's nought but God immortal—He alone
> Exists secure, when Man, and Death, and *Time*,
>
> . . .
>
> Are swallow'd up, and like the pyramids,
> Leave not an atom for their monument.

If everything can pass away except God, the implication is that God has no control over the eternal flux of life. What, then, asked Freneau in "The Power of Fancy," [36] is reality?

> What is this *globe*, these *lands*, and *seas*,
> And *heat*, and *cold*, and *flowers*, and *trees*,
> And *life*, and *death*, and *beast*, and *man*,
> And *time*—that with the *sun* began—
> But thoughts on reason's scale combin'd,
> Ideas of the Almighty mind?

Freneau, like any other undergraduate, wrestled with problems of Why and How. He took the materials for his philosophical specu-

lation as he found them. The rationalistic writings of the eighteenth
century supplied him with catchwords that he neither could nor
would withstand.[37] Nor could he have been uninfluenced by the
wave of religious revivalism which swept over Princeton during
his junior year, a movement which disturbed President Witherspoon
because of its idealistic ramifications.[38] When Freneau in "The
Power of Fancy" identifies tangible manifestations of reality as
"ideas of the Almighty mind," we are reminded, then, of Berkeleian
idealism, which has been said to be related, with Locke's mechanical
philosophy, as "simultaneous correspondential dreams are related,"
to the rise of the romantic movement.[39] So this might be. But most
important were the "thoughts on reason's scale combin'd." No modern young thinker might use another phrase. And though the rising
surge of the deistic movement did not carry Freneau with it as an
active participant and articulate champion until many years afterwards, his present attitude was essentially that of his more mature
years. Four decades later he reworked just these speculations into
other poems.[40]

But at best a probing into the philosophical basis of Freneau's
writings is an unprofitable occupation. Sensuousness rather than
rationality will be found to mark Freneau in all his work. What
garb of the latter he donned was of the cloth of his time, cut badly
to fit a poet whose mind was at the mercy of his emotions. Freneau
did respond—as what man does not?—to the influences of his
period. Humanitarianism, perfectionism, deism, naturalism, ro-
manticism, republicanism—all the currents which his generation
or another has found flowing through the late eighteenth century
played upon him.[41] And he took from them what seemed best to
fit the emotional content of the moment, because he wanted to be a
poet.

And so "The Power of Fancy" is more than a proving ground
for philosophical concepts. Beyond what Freneau thought, influencing his thought at every turn, was what Freneau felt. Here
is heard for a moment what is essential in Freneau, what sets him
apart from rather than makes him a part of his generation. Here,
"alert, elastic, full of music," a poem is found which wholly dis-
cards "the sing-song, the artificial phraseology, and the stilted move-

ment then so common in English poetry." [42] It is a poet's manifesto, containing echoes of Milton and promise of Keats—and an invocation:

> Wakeful, vagrant, restless thing,
> Ever wandering on the wing,
> Who thy wondrous source can find,
> Fancy, regent of the mind;
>
> • • •
>
> Come, O come—perceiv'd by none,
> You and I will walk alone.

Only through fancy, through the play of the imagination is man immortal. Fancy may lead him through the harmonious spheres of paradise to the "frightfulness of hell," past "Arcadian rocks" and "desert steeps," over "Ganges' stream," past "Taitis sea-beat coast," to "California's golden shore." "Swifter than the eagle's flight," it beckons to regions far away, to "Norwegia's rocky lands," to "Bermuda's orange shades," to the glories that were in Homer's Greece, and back to America to weep at a maiden's tomb:

> Lo! she leads me wide and far,
> Sense can never follow her,
>
> • • •
>
> Fancy, to thy power I owe
> Half my happiness below.

The fledgling poet spread his wings over regions he dreamed to make his own. So young John Keats, to be born twenty-five years later, sang his song:

> EVER let the Fancy roam,
> Pleasure never is at home:
>
> • • •
>
> Then let winged Fancy wander
> Through the thought still spread beyond her. [43]

Keats was to struggle in an unsympathetic poetic world. Freneau fought through a world that had no time for poetry.

4

The noisy activities of this world awakened echoes among the young men at Princeton. News of the Boston Massacre aroused the students at Nassau Hall to public demonstrations against British tyranny. When a letter was intercepted from the merchants of New York urging associates in Philadelphia to join them in breaking down colonial prejudice against English importations, it was ceremoniously burned in the college yard to a requiem of tolling bells.[44] As a protest against British taxation the whole undergraduate body appeared at college exercises in native homespun.[45] In spite of President Witherspoon's boast that his students, for all their "spirit of liberty," were not defective in "loyalty to our most excellent sovereign,"[46] conservative Jonathan Boucher proclaimed the college a hot-bed of a "Mischievous kind of knowledge."[47]

Some time before Philip's matriculation there had been two literary societies at Nassau Hall, the Plain Dealing Society and the Well Meaning Society. Both, however, had been suppressed because of disturbances created by the bitter rivalry between them. But student controversy could not be suppressed. On June 24, 1769, a group headed by Madison, Brackenridge, Bradford, and Freneau met to reorganize the defunct Plain Dealing Society. Although graced with an innocuous and thoroughly academic motto, *Litterae, Amicitia, Mores*, the American Whig Society, which they formed as a result of this meeting, is said to have been animated by an intense patriotic endeavor. Its members stood ready to defend every liberal and humane ideal. Then, almost immediately, as if in answer to a challenge, former members of the Well Meaning club banded together and called themselves the Cliosophic Society.[48] It was a signal for new skirmishes in an old student war. According to the Whigs, the Cliosophics were Tories and inimical to all good progress. Insulted and angered, the latter retaliated hotly.

Relics of this student war have been preserved in the same manuscript volume with "Father Bombo's Pilgrimage."[49] These, "Satires against the Tories," include ten bitter "pastorals" by Hugh Brackenridge which castigate his student enemies in words of more force than poetic merit, three coarse doggerel diatribes by "J. Maddison,"

and three satires signed "P.F." Freneau was apparently the laureate
of the Whigs, for his clubmates found his satires "piercing strong
and full." When Brackenridge wrote a soliloquy supposed to have
been spoken by a member of the Cliosophic Society "that morning
before he hung himself" in shame, the victim was made to say:

>   . . . in his turn Freneau
> Will send me hedlong to the shades below
> I hear his muse proclaiming from afar
> The thund'ring prologue to the burning war.[50]

These last two lines sound like prophecy. Freneau's satire was
already sharpened to a fine cutting edge. When five years later he
wielded his poetic weapon against adult opponents of American
patriotism, he returned to verses which he had composed as an undergraduate, and "MacSwiggen," written on the eve of the American Revolution, utilizes with very little change such lines from
the "Satires against the Tories" as

> What swarms of Vermin from the sultry South
> Hang in the beard of Warford's dirty mouth
> That sneering villain—father of a Lie
> Cloath'd in the veil of sacred Sanctity
> The base defender of a wretched Crew
> His tongue let Loose on those he never knew
> The Christian spirit & the devil's join'd
> The fiends of Orcus in his soul combin'd;
> The Genius Barren & the wicked heart
> Prepared to take each trifling Scoundrel's part
> The turn'd up nose the monkey's foolish face
> The scorn of reason & the human race.[51]

Evidence of the influence of Churchill and Dryden may be found
in these early satires.[52] Pope, too, must have contributed something
to their acrimonious spirit, and Freneau's reading in the classics to
their forthright denunciation. In spite of pettiness, there is an almost
Juvenalian vigor to the lines:

> Rage gives me wings & boldly prompts me on
> To conquer brutes the world would blush to own,
> No peace no quarter to these dogs we lend
> Death & destruction in each line I send

Call half the taylors that your club supplies
A cloud of nonsense & a storm of lies
Your kitchen wit & Warford's loud applause
That crabhouse rascal with his lanthorn jaws
His cowlike eyes forever on the wink
His soul extracted from the public sink.[53]

The college clubs waged war mercilessly. Some of Brackenridge's contributions hint of physical conflict, of "knocking of heads" and of long fierce discussions over mugs in the taverns of Princeton. Young Philip Freneau was driven to wrath which, at least in his verse, he could not restrain:

I burn, I hasten to engage
To vent my poison with a serpent's rage.

· · ·

A Patriot's flame can meet with no controul
It swells my breast & sends forth half my soul.[54]

5

The "patriot's rage," however, was stilled when he turned to formal poetry. Brooding over his Homer of a theme

More new, more noble and more flush of fame
Than all that went before,

he dreamed an epic of America. A new empire in which every promise of liberty and freedom should be realized, lay clear in vision before him:

I see, I see
A thousand kingdoms rais'd, cities and men
Num'rous as sand upon the ocean shore;
Th' Ohio then shall glide by many a town
Of note: and where the Mississippi stream
By forests shaded now runs weeping on,
Nations shall grow and states not less in fame
Than Greece and Rome of old.[55]

He was to sing the same prophecy four years later in *American Liberty*. After the conflict with England was over, he would continue to celebrate the expanding American frontier. Now, as a student, he thrilled to the promise of an undeveloped land. That he knew the sweep of this land only at second hand did not matter. The books he had read and the tales he had heard spread it all in fascinating detail before him. He was fired with poetic ambition, and he sought the fulfillment of that ambition to the accompaniment of

> ev'ry joyous sound
> Of liberty and life; sweet liberty!
> Without whose aid the noblest genius dies.[56]

In the candle-lit gloom of Nassau Hall, Philip Freneau and Hugh Brackenridge spent exciting hours over a third literary collaboration. "Father Bombo's Pilgrimage" had been a lark, and the "Satires against the Tories" rather a necessary contribution to college activities. Now however the young men were seniors. Both had been deep in books for three years. Both were intensely serious about the project before them. It was to be their poetical valediction to the college, presented at their graduation exercises. So, during the last months of their senior year, they shaped a saga of the new world. The plan was tremendous. Columbus, Cortez, and Pizarro each must have his tale retold in full. The Indian, his origin, his habits, and his character, must be analyzed completely. The colonization, the development, the expansion—the whole impressive story of the Americas must be wrung from history and legend. Of the two authors, Freneau observed more keenly and created more imaginatively. Brackenridge contributed a background of life on the frontier and experience among rugged pioneer colonists. They compressed their poem to dialogue form and, each writing in his turn, completed it.

On September 25, 1771, students, parents, friends, colonial officials, and visiting clergymen, a "vaste concourse of the politest company," gathered in the chapel at Nassau Hall.[57] Brackenridge, who later graciously attributed the greater share of the composition to his classmate,[58] read their production to the delight and admiration of the audience. A patriotic poem in the deepest sense, "The Rising Glory of America" is a prophecy of the time when the standard of England shall wave from the Atlantic to the Pacific. It pictures a

mighty nation of the future whose loyal subjects, "warm in freedom's cause," glory in their English heritage. Commerce, agriculture, and science were the pillars on which colonial prosperity was
to be erected. The Indians were pictured as a savage race whose only
salvation lay in peaceful submission to the wise and kindly rule of
their English conquerors. "Britannia's warlike troops, choice spirits
of her isle," were celebrated with rapt sincerity. General Braddock
and Sir William Johnson are among the principal characters, while
Benjamin Franklin, whom England had already honored, represented the heights to which loyal colonials might rise. Not until years
later did Freneau retouch the poem to make it consistent with a new
patriotic devotion to a new-born country.[59] Then only did Washington take the place which in the original version had been given to
English heroes.

The collegians of 1771 were loyal British subjects. As colonials
they were careless of duties and jealous of liberties; yet there is little
in their poem to foreshadow the events of the next ten years. Though
both young authors had undoubtedly joined in discussions and
demonstrations against British colonial policy, their poem was traditional in allegiance, in form, and in manner—except for the vision
of America. And even that was not entirely new. A year before at
the public commencement at Yale College, John Trumbull had presented his *Prospect of the Future Glory of America*. The theme was
at large in the colonies, but never had it been developed with such
intensity as by the young men at Princeton. Homer and Vergil were
their models in form. Milton, apostle of liberty, was the parent of
their style. Yet "The Rising Glory of America" was more than an
imitative commencement-day exercise. It was more than a mirror of
contemporary ideals. It announced to America that among her
young men she had a poet.

It is particularly fitting that Philip Freneau's part in the graduation exercises was to have been a defense of his favorite classical
writers in a debate, "Does Ancient Poetry Excel the Modern?" But
the program reports him "necessarily absent"; so he did not hear
Brackenridge read their poem from the familiar rostrum in Nassau
Hall. Nor did he hear the polite salvos of commencement-day ap-

plause which greeted his vision of the future of American poetry:

> I see a Homer and a Milton rise
> In all the pomp and majesty of song
>
> .   .   .
>
> A second Pope, like that Arabian bird
> Of which no age can boast but one, may yet
> Awake the muse by Schuylkill's silent stream,
>
> .   .   .
>
> And Susquehanna's rocky stream unsung
>
> .   .   .
>
> Shall yet remurmur to the magic sound
> Of song heroic.[60]

THREE

AMERICAN LIBERTY

1772–1775

WHILE PHILIP thus wove fine poetic fabrics at Princeton, his family in Monmouth faced one after another of small domestic crises. Since her husband's death Agnes Fresneau had been hard pressed by creditors, at whose behest the property at Mount Pleasant, "with the buildings and improvements thereon," was finally advertised for public auction.[1] The sale was apparently a legal dodge by means of which Pierre's widow was able to buy back the property for twenty-five pounds and so wipe out the debt her husband had left. But she was still burdened with problems: in addition to her oldest son at college, there were three younger children for whom she must provide security. Mary, two years Philip's junior, was seventeen; Peter was fourteen; Margaret, the baby, had just turned ten. On June 5, 1771, Agnes Fresneau married Major James Kearny, a widower and a neighboring landowner in Monmouth County.[2] Such a step must have seemed a propitious though, as she was soon to learn, only a temporary solution to her problems.

Major Kearny had five children of his own, and he made hardheaded arrangements to guarantee their rights. Before the wedding took place he drew up a canny agreement whereby he should have no claim on Agnes Kearny's estate, nor she on his.[3] In a codicil to his will he stipulated that, in the event of his death, his wife should retain the personal effects she had brought with her at marriage, and nothing more. Thus sealed and bound with legal strictures, the Fresneau-Kearny wedding was not—if we take the liberty of reading between lines—destined for great happiness. When eighteen months later the Major lay dying, he grudgingly agreed that his wife and "her three cattle" might remain in his house for six months longer. Thereafter, for eight years or until she married again, Mrs. Kearny was to receive three loads of salt grass yearly from his estate.[4]

In this matter-of-fact household there was apparently little room for Philip when he left Princeton. As a college graduate, he might well have been expected to provide for himself. Perhaps because he was unwilling to ask help of his stepfather or perhaps because the Major was unwilling to support his stepson in further study, immediate plans for the ministry seem to have been abandoned. Freneau is said to have toyed with the thought of law,[5] but that, too, demanded leisure for preparation. For seven months following his graduation, then, the young man found time weighing heavily upon him, until forced, as he later intimated, "by the Dame Necessity," [6] he agreed in April, 1772, to become a school teacher on Long Island.

It was not a fortunate choice, either of profession or locale. Even had Freneau's personal qualifications been those of a teacher, he could not long have been satisfied with the situation which he found on Long Island. The industrious Dutch families who had worked their farms there for generations, and the wealthy New York merchants who had recently discovered the advantages of the district for suburban residence, lived simply and conservatively. They looked with disapproval on the increasingly turbulent uprisings against British rule in the colonies. They lived according to rigid standards to which they expected all who lived with them to adhere. If he pleased them, their schoolmaster might supplement his salary (Freneau was to receive forty pounds a year) by acting as town clerk, chorister, sexton, or if his training warranted it, as clergyman. If he displeased them, he left very soon.[7]

Freneau remained in Flatbush for thirteen days. We suspect that he did not give quite all the reasons for his departure when he wrote to Madison:

Long Island I have bid adieu, with all its brutish brainless crew, The youth of that detested place, are void of reason and of grace, From Flushing hills to Flatbush plains, Deep ignorance unrivall'd reigns. I am very poetical but excuse it—"Si fama non venit ad aures" if you have not heard rumor of this story (which by the by is told in various Taverns and eating houses) you must allow me to be a little prolix with it— Those who employed me were some Gentlemen of New York, some of them were bullies, some merchants, and others Scoundrels: They sent me Eight children the eldest of whom was 10 Years— Some could read, others spell and a few stammar over a chapter of the Bible—these were my pupils and over these was I to preside.

There was some trouble over salary. "After I forsook them," Freneau continued, "they proscribed me for four days and swore that if I was caught in New York they would either Trounce or maim me." Promising to punish his tormentors with a "terrible satire," the truant teacher escaped with his goods to Princeton, where he remained until the following September.[8]

Here, thanks to the progressive administration of John Witherspoon, an arrangement had been made which allowed graduates of the college to return for study of "Divinity, Law, and Physic" without payment of tuition.[9] Here, too, there was agreeable company, for Hugh Brackenridge supported himself at Princeton as master of the grammar school while he prepared for ordination.[10] It is just possible that Freneau now began seriously to read theology, but there is a persistent suspicion that he did little during his six months of graduate residence other than devote himself to those pursuits most congenial to a young poet. The occupation could not have been dull, nor the results without gratification, because by the time Freneau left Princeton one small volume of poetry had been printed, another was ready for the press.

During the summer *A Poem on the Rising Glory of America* was issued in Philadelphia as a twenty-four page pamphlet.[11] By August it was advertised for sale in New York.[12] Neither Freneau's nor Brackenridge's name appeared on the title page, but this must have seemed unimportant. That the poem had been printed at all could only be proof to the young authors that they were at least on the road toward fame. And soon Freneau launched a second volume, this one all his own. In November he wrote to Madison: "I have printed a poem in New York called the American Village, containing 450 lines, also a few short pieces added. . . . It is damned by all good and judicious judges & my name is on the title page." [13]

2

Who the "good and judicious judges" were or what they said as they damned the volume has never been discovered, but we may respect them for their acumen, for "The American Village" is neither one of Freneau's most original nor his most successful poems. It is the expression of a young man's desire to escape from noisy affairs to some Elysian retreat where peace and poetry share a quiet reign. Freneau, nurtured on books and visions, found the world struggling over problems which to him owned no validity. In its place he offered an ideal America, rich in beauty and freedom, a refuge where superior minds might find lasting values. Apparently sensing little of the direction in which practical political manoeuverings were turning the colonies, he chose the motto for the poem from Horace's sixteenth epode, which is a plaint on the horrors of civil war and a challenge to search for a new land alike free from tyranny and plagues.

As in his collegiate poems, Freneau followed again in the pathways cut wide by his poetic mentors. Vergil's *Eclogues* and *Georgics* have in common with his poem what they have in common with every eighteenth century pastoral. Horace, too, though the introductory motto may indicate a debt more direct, celebrated over and again the life of man freed from the pangs of jealousy and ambition. Remembering Freneau's admiration for the classical writers, even acknowledging the possibility of an original inspiration from them, we find even more obvious sources for "The American Village" among the poets of England. Where they apostrophized mythical or British heroes, he inserted Cabot and Columbus. Freneau's shepherd and shepherdess are Caffraro and Colma—"euphonious names more suggestive of Covent Garden than of Hudson Bay." [14] As he attempted to fit the new world of America into the pastoral mold of tradition, Freneau still found his models too much with him. The poem is full of echoes; the same things had been better said before.

As we begin to read "The American Village," we suspect that Goldsmith, to whose "deserted Auburn" Freneau pays tribute in the first few lines, may have been the immediate source. Later, when Freneau mentions the "slow wave of silent Acheron," we are reminded of similar phrases in Milton's *Paradise Lost*.[15] Before long we wonder whether Pomfret's *The Choice*, or the American Benjamin Church's poem of the same name, or William Livingston's *Philosophic Solitude* must not also be consulted for parallelisms in thought and word.[16] As we read on, we are tempted to turn to our copy of *The Seasons*, to search for and never quite find passage after passage from Freneau's poem. We note the similarity between the death of Thomson's Amelia and Freneau's Colma, both of the simple shepherdess tradition, and both swept to disaster by the unconquerable forces of nature. Indeed, we might discover the theme of "The American Village" expressed by Thomson thus:

> Oh! knew he but his happiness, of men
> The happiest he! who far from public rage
> Deep in the vale, with a choice few retired,
> Drinks the pure pleasures of the rural life.
>
> .   .   .
>
> The fall of kings,
> The rage of nations, and the crush of states
> Move not the man who, from the world escaped,
> In still retreats and flowery solitudes . . .[17]

And Freneau's lines,

> And nightly chauntings of the fearless dove,
> Or blackbird's note, the harbinger of love,

recall Thomson's more familiar expression,

> The blackbird whistles from the thorny brake,
> The mellow bullfinch answers from the grove;
> 'Tis love creates their melody, and all
> This waste of music is the voice of love . . .[18]

But most surely Freneau's poem reminds us of Pope. In the first lines of "The American Village" the author resolves to picture a bucolic community and its people simply and with gentleness, to forget "ancient woes." So Pope, in the introduction to his juvenile pastorals, urged that the "best side only of a shepherd's life" be exposed and "its miseries" concealed. He admonished the pastoral poet to "write simply and with delicacy." [19] Freneau, the apprentice, followed the dictates, followed, indeed, in the very word tracks of his master.

In "Windsor Forest," after the nymph Lodona makes her speech of farewell, Pope tells the reader,

> She said, and melting as in tears she lay,
> In a soft, silver stream dissolv'd away.

In "The American Village," after the Indian nymph Colma utters her dying words, Freneau writes,

> She said, and downward in the hoary deep
> Plung'd her fair form to everlasting sleep . . .[20]

Pope describes a town "with ease and plenty blest"; Freneau's village is "with fair plenty blest." [21] While Pope's hills "wrapt in clouds" ascend, Freneau writes of rocks "to whose summits clouds eternal cling." [22] Where Pope's fields are "crown'd with tufted trees and clinging corn," Freneau's are "high waving with eternal corn." [23] Pope tells of

> A dreary desert, and a gloomy waste,
> To savage beasts and savage laws a prey,
> And kings more furious and severe than they,

Freneau describes

> The howling forest, and the tiger's den,
> The dang'rous serpent, and the beast of prey,
> Men are more fierce, more terrible than they.[24]

Pope relates the troubles of his country in the past and rejoices in the tranquility of the present; he even hopes for a happy future when again will

> Indians in their sable groves
> Reap their fruits, and woo their sable loves.[25]

What more could Freneau have needed to inspire the creation of Caffraro and Colma, the sentimental aborigines whose "sable loves" and tragic parting clutter one third of "The American Village"?

Freneau accepted the verdict of his "good and judicious judges," for he never reprinted the poem. Yet "The American Village" is not without significance. A young poet was singing of America. Though he saw his country through eyes dulled with reading, there is promise here that he will see more clearly. In the meanwhile, how better might his trade be learned than through the study of Milton,

> Or Shakespeare, Dryden, each high sounding name,
> The pride of Britain and one half her fame,

Or Spenser

who wak'd the fairy muse of old
And pleasing tales of lands inchanted told,

or "heav'nly Pope," or "godlike Addison" who "wrapt the soul of poetry in prose"? [26]

The "few short pieces added" to the volume contain verses less ambitious and more tenuously derivative. "The Farmer's Winter Evening, a Poem," addressed "to a Nymph I never saw," expresses the same desire to escape to rustic solitude that we have found in the longer poem. But now in lighter mood, Freneau gives voice to the no less familiar sentimental longing for the companionship of a sympathetic country maiden. Many lines suggest Milton's minor poems, and once more we are surprised by an occasional almost Keatsian sensuousness and by lyric flashes which die away as suddenly as they appear. Freneau was seldom again to achieve such verbal felicity as

Steep me, steep me some poppies deep
In beechen bowl, to bring on sleep.[27]

Fourteen years later "The Farmer's Winter Evening" was reprinted, "changed almost beyond recognition, and, worst of all, furnished with a new ending," after the model of Horace's second epode, "which mocks at the poet's own sentiment." [28] As he grew older, Freneau became wary of subjective expression: few poets have tried more seriously than he in his later verse to avoid personal sentiment. Perhaps that is the reason he never reprinted the second of the "shorter pieces," for "The Miserable Life of a Pedagogue" is an outburst of juvenile spleen aroused by the unhappy situation in which Freneau had found himself at Flatbush.

The last poem in the volume, "Upon a Very Ancient Dutch House on Long Island," was later republished as "The Deserted Farm House," and as such became one of Freneau's most popular poems, even enjoying the minor distinction of appearing in a London newspaper.[29] In its revised form it has been cited as an instance of Freneau's concern with transience "aggravated by the influence of Gray," [30] but there is little in the original version which evidences such aggravation. As Freneau first presented it, it is a light and laughing poem, extraordinarily free from the insipidity of conventionalized eighteenth-century diction. When reprinted as "The Deserted Farm House," it becomes self-conscious and ponderous, devoid of the buoyant humorous elements of the earlier version. Freneau later used deleted passages from the "Ancient Dutch House" as part of "A Characteristic Sketch of the Long Island Dutch," [31] but the original poem, slight and immature, is superior to either of its derivatives.[32]

During 1772 Freneau wrote another poem which—perhaps because it was not published for fourteen years—displays more poetic polish than any he had yet composed. "Discovery" [33] (generically related to the collegiate "Columbus to Ferdinand" and to "The Pictures of Columbus" with which he was soon to be engaged) is a further attempt to sing the glory of America. The theme is familiar: that the spread of liberty rather than the accumulation of wealth should be the motive for the development of the new western continent. Though evidences of the influence of Churchill have been found in "Discovery" [34] (and though Freneau may have found his interest in the Indian stimulated by such books as Jonathan Mayhew's *Indian Captive*, which was in the Princeton library),[35] the model again, both in idea and expression, is Pope. The English poet in a less inspired moment might have written just such lines as

> Slaves to their passions, man's imperious race
> Born for contention, find no resting place,
> And the vain mind, bewilder'd and perplext,
> Makes this world wretched to enjoy the next.
> Tir'd of the scenes that nature made their own
> They rove to conquer what remains unknown;
> Avarice undaunted claims whate'er she sees,
> Surmounts earth's circle, and forgoes all ease;
> Religion, bolder, sends some *sacred* chief
> To bend the nations to her own belief;
> To their vain standards Europe's sons invite,
> Who claim it as their due to think aright,
> Behold their varied tribes, in proud applause,
> First in religion, liberty and laws,
> And, while they bow to cruelty and blood,
> Condemn the Indian with his milder god—
> Ah, race to justice, truth, and honour blind,
> Are thy convictions to convert mankind—!

Vain pride—convince them that thine own are just
Or leave them happy as you found them first.[36]

Thus, as he set forth bravely in the pursuit of poetry, Freneau
kept his English models constantly before him. His pensiveness, the
sweet, sad desire for escape to simplicity, may have sprung from
Horace and the Roman classics; but the words in which Freneau
expressed this desire were drawn from the overflowing reservoir of
English song. Avarice, pride, and ambition were obnoxious to him,
as they were to Pope and to many another humanitarian of the eighteenth century. Nothing that Freneau had yet sung was new or his
own. But he was only twenty, and his struggle to shape the world to
a poetic ideal had just begun.

3

By the autumn of 1772 Hugh Brackenridge had advanced sufficiently in the study of divinity to secure a license to preach and had
become master of Somerset Academy at Back Creek near Princess
Anne in Maryland.[37] On October 18 of that year Freneau joined
him, after a mysterious and "rare adventure at Annapolis," as
assistant master. "This is the last time," he wrote to Madison, "I
shall ever enter into such a business, it worries me to death and by
no means suits my 'giddy wandering brain'." Only want of money
(Freneau had been destitute "even of a brass farthing" on the
journey from New Jersey) could have led him to attempt teaching
again, for the students, he complained, preyed upon him "like
Leaches."

"It is now late at night," he wrote in November. "Not an hour
ago I finished a little poem of about 400 lines, entitled a Journey to
Maryland—being the Sum of my adventures." When we read the
first three lines of the poem as it was quoted to Madison, we are content that the author never preserved any more:

From that fam'd town where Hudson's flood
Unites with Streams, perhaps as good;
Muse has your bard begun to roam.

"Sometimes," Freneau continued, "I write pastorals to shew my
wit."

Deep to the woods, I sing a Shepherds care,
Deep to the woods, Cyllenius calls me there
The last retreat of Love and Verse I go
Verse made me mad at first and—will keep me so.

"I look," he said, "like an unmeaning Teague just turned out of the hold of an irish Ship. . . . My hair is grown like a mop, and I have a huge tuft of Beard directly upon my chin." Freneau feared that he would never finish his studies. "I would go over for the gown," he explained, "this Time two years—but the old hag Necessity has got such a prodigious gripe of me that I fear I shall never be able to accomplish it." He considered new plans: "I believe if I cannot make this out I must turn quack—indeed I am now reading Physic at my leisure hours, that is, when I am neither sleeping, hearing classes, or writing Poetry—for these take up all my time." Freneau was discouraged: "I want but five weeks of twenty-one years of age," he complained, "and already feel stiff with age."

Although he intended to remain at the academy in Maryland until at least October, 1773,[38] we should not be surprised to find Freneau forsaking this employment almost as quickly as he had forsaken his position in Flatbush. Perhaps he returned to Monmouth County, for his name is on the books of Samuel Forman, merchant in Middletown Point, as indebted to the sum of one pound three shillings and sixpence in June.[39] One persistently repeated story tells us that he severed his connections with Brackenridge to read law in Philadelphia.[40] Another says that he went to sea as a common sailor on the schooner *Mary Howe*.[41] Wherever he was, however, Freneau was restless, and he was with his books. Musing over one of the volumes of Pope, he wrote a translation from Adrian in the margin: [42]

Little pleasing wand'ring mind
Guest companion soft and kind
Now to what regions do you go
All pale and stiff and naked too
And jest no more as you were wont to do.
1774   P. F.

But, if the date which Freneau affixed to "The Pictures of Columbus" [43] is correct, we find him in 1774 seriously at work on one of his most ambitious poems. Though episodic and unarticulated, it was another attempt to develop the theme of the future of the western world. The ground had been broken with "The Rising Glory of America," and "The American Village" had been an attempt to cultivate a pleasant portion of the same field. Then, following the "variety of rebuffs" suffered during his first years out of college, Freneau's emphasis changed until in "Discovery" he revolted against the avarice and bloodshed which accompany the development of new lands. Now, in "The Pictures of Columbus" he seizes upon and further develops the theme. Columbus is made to argue the proportion and eternal plan of nature like a good eighteenth-century rationalist, while among "sweet sylvan scenes of innocence and ease" he finds "children of an early time, basking in the sunshine of the south" before the scourge of avaricious men and the greed of priests brought

> havock, slaughter, chains and devastation
> In every dress and form of cruelty.

As we read "The Pictures of Columbus," we admire the combination of rhapsody and fantasy in the discoverer's scene with the enchantress, his rugged pragmatism in addressing Ferdinand, and the graceful turn of phrase with which he presents his supplication to Isabella:

> As men were forc'd from Eden's shade
> By errors that a woman made,
> Permit me at a woman's cost
> To find the climates that we lost.

The swift-moving anapestics which clothe the homely scene between Thomas and Susan were found "natural and lively" by Freneau's contemporaries [44] and have been acknowledged his "most important contribution to American metrical history." [45] The subtly veiled irony in the monologues spoken by Bernardo the friar and Orosio the mathematician, the mounting elements of suspense in the dialogue with the mutinous sailors at sea, the contrast between Columbus's idealism and the greedy savagery of his followers, and the bitter iconoclastic revery of the defeated adventurer in chains all show Freneau at his dramatic best in the creation of character and mood. The final stanzas, introduced by the memorable lines,

> How sweet is sleep, when gain'd by length of toil!
> No dreams disturb the slumbers of the dead,

complete one of the first original and sustained poems of which America may be proud.

Freneau's humanitarianism had now developed to cogent expression. Transience and freedom run hand in hand through his poetry. Ignorance, greed, and tyranny were the Goliaths which young Freneau set forth to slay. He seldom used blank verse again, and when years later he returned to the theme of the glory of America with "The Rising Empire," his youthful enthusiasm and his optimism had been submerged by disappointment. But "The Pictures of Columbus" reveals Freneau at twenty-two in transition from promise in vision to promise in performance. Never, perhaps, did he again stand more surely on the threshold of poetry.

4

Wherever he was in 1773 and 1774, Freneau did study theology. He kept a careful record of his reading and his more or less random thoughts on divinity, but his notebook [46] gives no indication of just when or where he began his theological studies. The first twenty-five pages of the manuscript volume are missing, and on page thirty we simply find the notation "P. F. 1773."

We may guess that the first twenty-three extant pages of the notebook record Freneau's reading during the time that he was in Maryland with Brackenridge. Only a few books are cited by title—Bucani's and Turettino's *Institutiones Theologicæ*, Burnet's *Exposition of the Thirty-nine Articles*, Patrick's *Mensa Mystica*, and Pearson's *Exposition of the Creed*. Each was a book which a student might have owned, and all were studied in the detail we should expect to find applied to a few books when but few were accessible. In hours undoubtedly stolen from academic duties and poetical exercises, he filled page after page with extracts painstakingly copied from these volumes.

But when he came to page forty-nine Freneau gave up. "It was a vain notion," he wrote, "that a Parson's occupation was the high road to wealth and independency in Life. You have collected a considerable variety of extracts and hints but it was lost Labour: it never answered the trouble." His "giddy wandering brain" was again not suited. "And so," he wrote, "farewell to the study of Divinity—which is, in fact, the Study of Nothing!—and the profession of a priest is little better than that of a slothful Blockhead." Scrawled below this statement is a little problem in arithmetic involving simple division in changing square feet to square miles, just the sort of task which he as teacher might have presented to a class.

It must have been at about this time that Freneau devoted a page of his theological notebook to profane and humorous composition. It must, likewise, have been at this time that he returned to New Jersey, for the doggerel which he scrawled on a blank page of the volume satirizes his neighbors in Monmouth. Obviously in rough draft, the verses were never intended for publication. To us, however, as we attempt to create a picture of young Philip Freneau, the spirit of juvenile tomfoolery in which they are written is in welcome contrast to the sedate sobriety of the rest of the notebook:

> I sing of a wedding that happened of late
> Betwixt two young Lovers nam'd Matty and Kate
> And how in the midst of these nuptials so gay
> The guests fell to fighting and broke up the play
>
> But what was the cause of these quarrels reherse
> Ye muses who govern the regions of Verse—
> Assist me dear Muses Inspire me to tell
> Who conquer'd, who triumph'd, who fought & who fell—
>
> First, Peter Van Pelt, the Sire of the Bride
> To grace his girls wedding all Musick denyd
> The fiddle he thought a superfluous toy
> And meant, being costly, all mirth to destroy.
>
> Some Guests when they found that no fiddle was coming
> Some shuffled their feet and some fell to humming
> Some giving Squire Peter a side looking glance
> Swore they came there not to eat but to dance.[47]

It was not long, however, before Freneau was back at his theological studies. After two blank pages, the notes are resumed and in more abundant detail. Page fifty-five is neatly ruled, as if the young man meant to reserve it and the two following pages for some special and personal listing. It is headed with a translation from Juvenal, "From heaven Descended, Know thyself. P. F. March 29, 1774." Had the student taken new resolution? Perhaps an excursion into law had followed the previous desertion of divinity, and the study of Blackstone had left him even colder than the study of the sacraments. Freneau may have returned to Princeton to continue his studies under John Witherspoon, though it is possible that he would have preferred to remain in Monmouth to read under the direction of William Tennent, in whose school he had prepared for college. Wherever he was, he buckled down to his studies, and the industry shown by the last fifty pages of the notebook belies any thought which Freneau may previously have entertained of abandoning the task.

He now made a complete list of the books which Bishop Burnet had recommended for a candidate for the ministry,[48] he outlined the course of study expected of a deacon,[49] and he carefully formulated his own answers to the first twenty-five of Isaac Watts's questions on divinity.[50] He jotted down thirty-two "Proper texts or Themes for Sermons," [51] including such melancholy passages as "The living know that they shall die" (*Ecclesiastes*, 9: 5) and "The whole creation groaneth and travaileth in pain" (*Romans*, 8: 22). Could he have been thinking of the colonies' troubles with England when he chose the text "But we know that the law is good, if man use it lawfully" (*I Timothy*, 1: 9)? The theme of the future and the glory of America appeared in Freneau's suggestion that *Genesis*, 3: 23 ("Therefore Jehovah God sent him forth from the garden of Eden, to till the ground from whence he was taken") might be used for the text of a "consolatory discourse for the loss of such felicity and incitements to look forward to a better country." In preaching or in poetry Philip Freneau's subjects were to be the same. By May, 1774, the last date in the book, he was able to sign himself confidently as "Ph. Freneau, S.T.S." and he translated the Thirty-nine Articles of the church into Latin.[52]

Most of the notes, however, are of little interest except as they display a young divinity student conscientiously at work among the usual textbooks of his time. Perhaps his interest in the rationalistic elements of the Socinian theology indicates that his mind was continuing to turn, as were the minds of so many others during the late eighteenth century, toward deism. "Where is Hell?" he asked. The answer came succinctly, dogmatically: "I say anywhere in the conscience of a wicked man." [53] As a lover of liberty and reason, it was his pleasure to collect such bits as "May the Pope, or Roman Pontiff, be put into a pillory; and may the Devil pelt him with Priests." [54] Among the scholastic memoranda, however, now and again the hand of a poet is seen. Freneau suggested that "A Sermon on the Spring at the Opening of the Blossoms or fading would be new and useful." [55] He made a careful transcription of John Dryden's translation of the old Latin hymn *"Veni Creator,"* his zeal even carrying him so far that he "improved" Dryden's rendering by changing the last word in the first line of the second stanza from *light* to *heat* to accord with a more modern notion of the pronunciation of the word *paraclete*, with which it was to rhyme.[56]

But the most interesting pages of the notebook are the last, where Freneau wrote his *"Innuenda Sermonibus,"* sketching the general themes on which he would preach. Melancholy and funereal, they show him, like the earlier idealistic Jonathan Edwards, drawn irresistibly to the contemplation of death:

Saladine the Conqueror of Asia who after his return ordered a Shroud to be carried before him on the point of a Spear with this proclamation: That after all his Glories he should carry nothing to his Grave but that poor Shroud, so Adrian caused a coffin to be carried before him in a public Calvalcade— whence this base fear of Death, would you not rather be with the Angels and hear the words of God? . . . Death leaves the body a useless shameful & putrifying Thing, a Dead carcass is a disgraceful thing and becomes burdensome to the Living, the loved. . . . The time will come when even Shakespeare's Tomb will no more attract the world's affection, Nature and her children shall depart.[57]

As we read this, the theme of his earlier "The Pyramids of Egypt" comes to mind—Freneau's ever-absorbing theme of death and decay. We are prepared, then, to find his description of hell the product of a sensitive mind, at once attracted and repelled by the awfulness of the concept. It looks forward to the weird imaginings of "The House of Night" and suggests that Freneau had come under the baleful influence of James Hervey's *Contemplations and Meditations*, a work which, printer James Rivington announced as he issued the first American editions during 1774, had been "more read since it was first published, than any other in the English language, except the Holy Bible." [58]

There is a drowsiness that never slept a wink. There is hunger that shall never be satisfied— There is Revenge with uplifted hand to inflict the Angry blow, which shall fall harmless— There is adulterous Lust which no more meets its object— Love that shall never touch the damask lip— The Soul has lost its wings, it sees God & enjoys it not. Call to mind the burning fever— Thirst that shall never be quenched—a combination of all diseases— The Poetic Soul which departed without hope no more enjoys its meadows & verdant landscapes, Rivulets and Groves— Lost forever &c. There is a fear chased thro hell by shadow— How terribly afraid we are now of Ghosts and Spectres—which of us shall Walk thro' a solitary Grave Yard by Moon or Star Light, who of us would make musings in solitary churchyards our Summer Evening's entertainment? Fear shall reign in hell— What moving lights! What Screams! what shocking phantoms. The original, the first, the best beauty shall hide from the favour of his countenance: Remembrance shall be torment. Many Millions of miserable creatures shall see God forever. [59]

Whether it was a result of genuine sympathy or merely an extension of his own introspective concern with adolescent misery, Freneau further planned to preach that

Pain is no stranger in this world for in this world every Day the Sun looks down on Thousands of miserable creatures who groan in agonies of pain— No wonder that noble luminary so delights to place a veil of clouds mists and vapours between himself and our miseries—he is weary of seeing them and would feign his light were extinguished. [60]

The tragedy of Jesus' life made him wonder if the "Saviour should come upon the Earth in our Days we should be more Humane to him?" Freneau thought not. "Another Traitor would betray him with a kiss," he wrote, "a second Pilate would condemn him, though innocent." The abuse which the man from Nazareth suffered aroused the student to complain, "Every base fellow had a blow at him." [61] "The rabble," said Freneau, "is the Same in all Ages!" [62]

5

The "rabble" of the American colonies was soon to make its courageous stand at Lexington and Concord, disorganize attacking masses of contemptuous red-coats at Bunker Hill, and trap General Gage and his trained forces in Boston. "This does not seem to be the proper time for poetry," William Bradford had written Madison, "unless it be such as Tyrtaeus wrote." [63]

By the late spring of 1775 Philip Freneau had thrown aside any immediate thought of divinity, law, or physic and from New York heaped line after mocking line upon the unhappy British general who was finding that he could not govern Massachusetts. If the verses were not quite like those which Tyrtaeus had written to spur the Spartans on to victory two thousand years before, the ridicule with which Freneau covered Gage and his subordinates was well determined to break down any dignity with which the British cause in America had been invested.

Freneau had been slow to join the patriot party. Two years before, after the townsmen of Boston had banded together to destroy shiploads of English tea, he had been chiefly impressed by the ridiculousness of a situation in which Americans compounded "Ginseng, Catnip, Sage, Balm Carolina Yoppon and what not" as substitute for the imported beverage. Almost fifty years later he reported that "on the occasion of the before-mentioned event in Boston" he had published a "colloquial conference" entitled "Margery and Patty. A Boston Dialogue." A humorous satire in Freneau's characteristic manner, it was printed, he tells us, in a "New York Half sheet weekly Paper of those days called *The American Whig*, now long since forgotten, and perhaps shot away in cartridges during the Revolutionary war." [64] "Plague on all who keep a king!" cries Margery, who loves her tea but who has been convinced by Patty that she must not drink it " 'Till the Yankee ships are free . . . to trade with whom they please." For—

> Englishmen, of all mankind,
> Are the bravest and most blind.

But by 1775 events had taken a more serious turn. Ticonderoga and Crown Point had been captured by the colonists, and the Continental Congress had sent additional forces from Virginia and Pennsylvania as reinforcements for the New England militiamen. Washington was busily whipping untrained troops into fighting trim. The citizenry in every colony was aroused. In April, Freneau wrote, a giant liberty pole, "upwards of eighty feet in height, including its topmast," was set up in New York. One month later a "gang of the disaffected to the American cause approached the unguarded Pole at midnight, hacked it down, and separated it with their axes into *thirteen* different portions." Had the perpetrators of this outrage been discovered, said Freneau, "it would have fared badly with them," for the deed "produced a spirit among the whig populace and their leaders almost bordering on frenzy":

Instantaneously a party of ax men were despatched up the North River beyond *Haverstraw* Bay, to cut a *new Pole* which was speedily brought down; a beautiful stick of *Red Hickory*, about 75 feet in length. No sooner had the mast maker done with it, than a Mr. Boyd, a first rate democratic master Blacksmith, was engaged to arm the Pole against future insults. Iron bars, case hardened, were prepared, about sixteen feet in length. These were perforated with many spike holes, and then spiked on to the Pole, so as completely to enclose its whole circumference, and present an adamantine face on every side, to the edge of any tool or force whatever. The Bars extend about four feet down into the earth, and twelve above the surface. Those provisions rendered it, with the addition of a nocturnal Guard, and two three pounders (called bull dogs) perfectly secure, and iron proof against all invaders and assaillants.

When the new pole was ceremoniously dedicated, the following verses, said Freneau, "were read to the surrounding multitude. They were also printed in a hand-bill, and circulated in all directions, and carried thro' every street, and thrown into every door in the City."

THE NEW LIBERTY POLE.—*Take Care!*

Seized from the woods, this honored TREE
We dedicate to LIBERTY:
Here may it stand while Time remains,
Or Liberty, with reason, reigns.

May no vile hand again presume,
In midnight storms, to work its doom;

In Blacksmith's shops no tool be found
To bring *Red Hickory* to the Ground.

This to prevent, with bars of steel
We fence it round, that can repel
The traitorous stroke that *some* would give,
Who, to be slaves, were born to live.

Let them advance, by night or day,
Let them attempt a new affray,
And speedy vengeance will ensue,
—*At least their hides beat black and blue.*

Reflect, repent—nor frown dislike
  On these, our plain, our humble rhymes;
For some *advise,* while others *strike,*
  Such is the humor of the times!

Some acts are passed he must annul,
Or, woe to them who serve JOHN BULL;—
The ASIA, now, protects them not,
Nor all the force of VANDEPOT.

Though we respect the *Powers that be,*
We hold *him* an non-entity,
Who would not stir in our good cause
And rise to spurn *despotic Laws.*[65]

At this time there was not, however, among the American colonies
any general wish for independence. Members of the Congress in
Philadelphia objected strongly to the name of rebel, and still thought
of themselves as subjects to whom constitutional rights were due.
John Dickinson was allowed to draft a petition begging George III
to interpose and bring about a permanent reconciliation by repeal-
ing the statutes against which the colonists rebelled. It was still as
unhappy and increasingly angry subjects in defense of their liberties
that the American militiamen opposed attempts of the English to
enforce laws which seemed unjust.[66]

Such, too, was apparently Freneau's attitude. His forthright
"Libera Nos Domine," which he tells us was published in June,
1775,[67] has often been cited as evidence that the young poet urged

separation from England more than twelve months before the Declaration of Independence.[68] But no copy of the poem as it was originally printed has been produced. We know it only as Freneau published it twenty years later when he was anxious to capitalize his reputation as the "Poet of the American Revolution." In view of the changes which we shall find him making in many of his antebellum poems, it seems unwise to base an estimate of Freneau's attitude in 1775 on a text which is found only in his collected works. Nor do the other satires which he wrote during this year justify the conclusion that Freneau was anxious for separation. On the contrary, though his pen sputtered angrily, he looked forward with hope to a time when "war's red lamp" would "cease to burn" and "Britannia rule our hearts again." [69]

Now, when war's red lamp did spread its horrid rays over America, the "patriot rage" of which Freneau had boasted at Princeton could not be restrained. "Allow me to tell what I have heard"—he scrawled the motto from Vergil on the title page of the new poem. By July 6 *American Liberty* was published and advertised for sale by John Anderson from his shop at Beekman's slip. The poem, announced the *New-York Journal* on the same day, is "humbly addressed to all true lovers of this once flourishing country, whether they shine as soldiers or statesmen. In it Ciceronian eloquence and patriotic fire are happily blended." [70] With this introduction Freneau made his appearance as an articulate champion of freedom in America.[71] Reprinted in Philadelphia as *The Present Situation of Affairs in North America, A Poem,* the verses rang a clear call to all patriotic countrymen.[72] Readers could not have been disturbed because many lines were reminiscent of Churchill and more of Pope— the matter and the satiric characterization were Freneau's own, and the theme belonged to every free man.

But *American Liberty* is not a poem by a participant in great struggles. It is rather by an observer who follows a contest the results of which will prove or disprove the validity of his most cherished convictions. The war was many miles away in New England. It was safe, therefore, to sit in New York spurring distant countrymen on to valor. As the Continental forces rallied against the English, Freneau wrote:

What breast but kindles at the martial sound?
What heart but bleeds to feel its country's wound?
For thee, blest freedom, to protect thy sway,
We rush, undaunted to the bloody fray;
For thee each province arms its vigorous host,
Content to die, e'er freedom shall be lost.[73]

It was inspiring to cheer as a spectator for a cause in which one believed. Praise for New England, scorn for all Tories—the "pension'd fools of slavery," ridicule for Gage and his futile proclamations, loathing for the wilful obstinacy of the king, and faith in the wisdom of the Continental Congress ran together breathlessly as Freneau envisioned the future of the western world. The oppressed of all lands were invited to make America their home and her cause their cause. Freneau looked forward to a time

when strangers rule no more
Nor cruel mandates vex from Briton's shore;
When Commerce shall extend her shorten'd wing,
And her free freights from every climate bring;
When mighty towns shall flourish free and great,
Vast their dominion, opulent their state;
When one vast cultivated region teems
From ocean's edge to Mississippi's streams;
While each enjoys his vineyard's peaceful shade,
And even the meanest has no cause to dread;
Such is the life our foes with envy see,
Such is the godlike glory to be free.[74]

A month later, when Freneau published *General Gage's Soliloquy*, the clarity of his vision was obscured beneath the harsh broad strokes with which he then satirized the English commander.[75] Like the collegiate "Satires against the Tories," this poem proceeds directly to its immediate object—the defamation and ridicule of a despised opponent. Written during the early days of the Boston siege, it represents Gage as a vacillating puppet torn between duty to his king and his own suspicion that he wasted British blood in an unrighteous cause. Even our enemies, Freneau told his readers (and reminded himself), believe that our cause is just.

So Philip Freneau, a young man of twenty-three, fresh from years of study and vacillating plans for a professional career, found occupation as a lampooner. To those of us who read him only as a patriot burning for his country's cause, the publication of so facetious a poem as *The Expedition of Timothy Taurus* in August, 1775,[76] seems, therefore, particularly anomalous. We need remind ourselves that Freneau was simply a young man of poetic talent who happened to live in colonial America on the eve of a revolution. When he could fit the details of his poetic vision into the welter of contemporary unrest, he did so; for the pressure of opinion bore heavily on him. When he could not, he wrote verses anyway.

And one day late in the summer he happened to visit the falls of the Passaic. The Hogarthian portraits which he drew of the assembly gathered at this fashionable watering place in New Jersey show at once the acuteness of Freneau's observation and the development of the flair for characterization which he had shown in "Simon Swaugum" and "The Pictures of Columbus." Scapella—the innkeeper's wife, Lawyer Ludwick, Parson Pedro, and Brigadier-General Nimrod live as proof to whoever stops to read of their misadventures that Lowell and Holmes, though more kindly and more penetrating, were not the first to pierce sham and pretense with versified sketches of American people as they really existed. Freneau was always to write most effectively when he thus knew his subjects; so we detect in the portraits in *The Expedition of Timothy Taurus* an authenticity which we look for in vain in his satires based on what he had heard of British activity in Boston.

Early in October the correspondence between Generals Gage and Washington was published in patriot newspapers by order of the Continental Congress.[77] Americans could afford to chuckle now over the bumptious demands of the British leader, because, bottled helplessly in Boston, Gage was powerless to enforce his threats. Nevertheless, it was scarcely a laughing matter that the general damned them all as rebels and threatened summary execution to every captured militiaman. That was carrying things too far. Freneau, like most of his patriotic countrymen, resented the word and its implication of treason. In "Reflections on Gage's Letter to General Washington, Aug. 13," printed in the New York *Constitutional Gazette* on October 18,[78] he wrote:

"Rebels you are," the hopeful Gen'ral cries,
Truth stand thou forth and tell the wretch he lies.

. . .

If to controul the cunning of a knave,
Our freedom love, and scorn the name of slave;
If to protest against a tyrant's laws,
And arm for battle in a righteous cause
Be deem'd rebellion—'tis a harmless thing,
This bug-bear name, like death has lost its sting.

The alarm of war had long since sounded in America, and the sword had long been unsheathed in New England. Now, belatedly, but none the less with intense rhetorical effect, Freneau sounded his call:

To arms, to arms, and let the trusty sword,
Decide who best deserves the hangman's cord.

While the royal troops remained at Boston, Freneau continued the barrage of words with which he joined the attack upon them. No poem of his had apparently ever been more popular than *A Voyage to Boston*, in which he next ridiculed the ineptitude of the tyrants from England. From October 21 it was advertised for more than a month in New York.[79] By the middle of November newspapers of Philadelphia announced a second edition, which soon warranted an advertisement in the *Pennsylvania Evening Post* larger than any which had been allotted to any single literary production in that paper before.[80] Like Freneau's other publications of 1775, *A Voyage to Boston* was issued anonymously. His reputation, however, had so far advanced that he could now identify himself on the title page as the "Author of American Liberty, a Poem, General Gage's Soliloquy, &c."

A Voyage to Boston was not only the most ambitious and the most popular of Freneau's early satires, but also the most forceful. Made invisible by a magic vest given him by a friendly genius, the poet journeys to Boston, where he boldly slips past British guards to listen to a midnight consultation of enemy leaders. "High in a dome a dire assembly sat," composed of Gage and Graves, Wallace, Burgoyne, Percy, and Howe. Like Milton's apostate angels, each speaks in his turn: each blames the other for the failures of His Majesty's troops, and each looks with wonder and awe at the brave stand which the colonial militiamen have made. Gage is pictured as an equivocating blockhead, haunted with tantalizing visions of roast beef; Burgoyne is an impotent scribbler writing to keep his courage up, a dilettante, confused and horribly afraid; Graves condemns himself as a blunderer who only half believes in the cause for which he fights; and Percy squirms in embarrassment when called on to explain his failures at Bunker Hill.

Not satisfied with exposing the enemy's ponderous ineptitude, the poet turned to a dissection of the American Tory. Never had Freneau been more blunt in expression, never more pointed in characterization: it was all first rate and effective satire. His workmanlike couplets, alternating mockery, defiance, and aspiration, must have set liberal men to chuckling as they read *A Voyage to Boston* over their mugs in the taverns, must have forced many an advocate of reconciliation to take new and patriotic resolution as he pondered them before his hearth. It was not poetry at all, but it did its work well.

When word was finally received that the British Ministry had recalled Gage from New England, Freneau sped his departure acidly. *General Gage's Confession,* eight pamphlet pages containing the "Substance of His Excellency's Last Conference with his Ghostly Father," appeared on October 25.[81] Representing the culmination of Freneau's early satirical attack, it is directed both against the unfortunate commander and against the spirit of papistry which to the free-thinking young poet seemed equally a menace to America. In this poem Gage makes free confession of his sins against a "faultless country," of the murder and devastation he had there wrought, of his cruelty to captive patriots, and of his lies and vile invectives. As he departs in sorrow from the guiltless land he has wronged, the general acknowledges that pride, and pride alone, has been the cause of all his sins.

Then, the arch-fiend having left America, Freneau's political satire ceased.[82]

6

Feeling ran high in New York: violent partisans lived and fought together with all the malevolence bred of propinquity. Even solid and influential men like the Rev. Samuel Seabury upheld the loyalist side of the controversy. Myles Cooper, the learned president of King's College, after page on page of political polemics in prose, descended to doggerel satire against the rebellious among his countrymen. Though young Alexander Hamilton issued impassioned prose replies to the Tory pamphleteers, there was no one to withstand the coarse, unpolished, but disarmingly logical special pleading with which Cooper attacked the patriots in verse. Epithets which would now be unprintable and suggestive omissions even more vile were published boldly.[83] In truth, it was not "the proper time for poetry." Propaganda was understood, and acid verse that burned any doubt of the justice of the American cause from vacillating minds, but not poetry which promised something more than the bolstering of fierce contemporary prejudice. In this turmoil of conflicting opinion where ideals of freedom were buffeted carelessly to vulgar ends, Freneau was bewildered:

> Alone I stand to meet the foul-mouthed train
> Assisted by no poets of the plain.[84]

But it was more than the burden of producing political propaganda without assistance that disheartened Freneau. It was not the ridicule to which the patriot cause was subjected that discouraged him. Rather it was personal abuse directed against him as a poet which made Freneau "quit the Mean conquest." His valedictory, "Mac-Swiggen," he tells us, was written "in Answer to a Hostile Attack." Reworking lines which he had composed five years before as part of the "Satires against the Tories," the poet delivered staccato blasts of scorn at his critic:

> If thus, tormented at these flighty lays,
> You strive to blast what ne'er was meant for praise,
> How will you bear the more exalted rhime,
> By labour polish'd, and matur'd by time?

For it was, after all, to poetry that Freneau's aspiring, though often wavering eyes were directed. He yearned for a "safe retirement from all mankind," for solitude where his muse might cheer him with "gay poetic Dreams," for time to pursue his vision of the future of America:

> BLESS'D be our western world—its scenes conspire
> To raise a poet's fancy and his fire,
> Lo, blue-topt mountains to the skies ascend!
> Lo, shady forests to the breezes bend!
> See mighty streams meandering to the main!
> See lambs and lambkins sport on every plain!
> The spotty herds in flowery meadows see!

How familiar to Freneau were the details of this fanciful world of poetry! "But what, ungenerous wretch," he asked of the unknown critic who had attacked him, "are these to thee?" Now, as he saw his poetic vision distorted by the shadow of war, Freneau confessed:

> LONG have I sat on this disast'rous shore,
> And, sighing, sought to seek my passage o'er
> To Europe's towns, where, as our travellers say,
> Poets may flourish, or, perhaps they may . . .

Five years had been devoted to the celebration of freedom and liberty. Ever since he left college Freneau had sung courageously of his own concept of personal liberty and individual freedom, the possibilities for the attainment of which were rich with promise in America. When, during the last six months, he had paused to satirize the enemies of his ideal, Freneau had not directed his attack against England, but against individuals in England and in America who misused their powers or who acted as instruments of tyranny. His mockery aimed at Gage, Burgoyne, and North was that of a Swift or a Defoe who would expose evil in order that his country might turn from it. His raillery against George III was more bitter, because on the king Freneau heaped the invective that literary tradition had always reserved for tyrants. But toward England his attitude was that of a subject abused, but a subject still:

> O Britain come, and, if you can, relent
> This rage, that better might on Spain be spent.[85]

He was puzzled, bewildered:

> What madness, heaven, has made Britannia frown?
>
> . . .
>
> Who should have thought that Britons bore a heart,
> Or British troops to act so base a part?
>
> . . .
>
> Can they whom half the world admires, can they
> Be advocates of vile despotic sway? [86]

The England which had won its way to Philip Freneau's heart was the cradle of the ideals of human progress on which he had built his poetic creed. His America was but to grow in realization of poetic hints sprung from English minds. Pope had declared for freedom; Goldsmith had mourned the decay of old standards in England and called upon posterity for their return; Thomson had celebrated the possibilities of the triumph of personal freedom in the calm of simple living; Addison's *Cato* personified ideals of unyielding resistance to tyranny; and Milton had worn his life away struggling for human liberty. Freneau, too, as he prayed, "Oh heavenborn peace, renew thy wonted charms," looked forward to a time when liberty, the personal liberty of individuals to seek their small share of happiness, would be established through the courageous, Roman-like stand of its loyal votaries, their "injur'd claims" blessed by victory, and freedom triumphant:

> So shall past years, those happy years return,
> And war's red lamp in Boston cease to burn:
> Hear and attest the warmest wish I bring,
> God save the Congress and reform the King!
> Long may Britannia rule our hearts again,
> Rule as she rul'd in George the Second's reign,
> May ages hence her growing empire see,
> And she be glorious, but ourselves be free . . .[87]

The England of armies and tyrants seemed false to the England which had sired fine poetic ideals of freedom. Turning from dreams to reality at twenty-three, Freneau stumbled awkwardly over unfamiliar ground. There were adjustments to be made before he could again move forward with assurance. "Sick of all feuds," he wrote,

"to reason I appeal." But reason was seldom to be a satisfactory
ally: Freneau's difficulties were of the emotions. He longed for time
and quiet to fit the jagged edges of his vision together again:

> In distant isles some happier scene I'll choose,
> And court in softer shades the unwilling Muse,
> Thrice happy there, through peaceful plains to rove,
> Or the cool verdure of the Orange grove,
> Safe from all miscreants that my peace molest,
> Miscreants with dullness and with rage opprest.[88]

In the deepest sense it was not escape which Philip sought as he
"to the sea with weary steps" [89] descended. There was escape involved, escape from the turmoil of conflicting opinion in the colonies, and escape from the divided allegiance of his own mind, too
intelligent to be led by the shouting of mobs, but too sincere in sympathy to do anything but support them. As a patriot, Freneau's retirement on the eve of the American Revolution leaves him exposed
to malevolent glances from those who read history as a record of
waving flags and parading pageants. As a poet, however, he did
what a poet must do—follow the beckoning finger of his own vision.

FOUR

AMERICAN INDEPENDENCE
1776–1778

ALMOST twenty years later Freneau is reported to have admitted in casual conversation that "upon the commencement of hostilities, being averse to enter the army & be knock'd in the head," he left America to follow the sea.[1] But in old age, when it was to his financial advantage to forward claims of patriotic service, he insisted that from the "breaking out of the Revolution . . . till some time in the year 1778, he was engaged in the West Indies, principally on board of American privateers."[2] Perhaps the truth is that Freneau could not find in contemporary America a place for the kind of poetry which he wished to write; so, when opportunity to leave presented itself, he left. It seems fair to remember that, like his own later "Highland Sawney,"

> His belly was not over-full,
> His jerkin would not bear a pull;
> Dejectedly he walk'd along,
> His noodle meditating song.[3]

The desire to escape from the raucous political uproar of colonial America had not burst suddenly upon Freneau. Even in the preceding July he had written:

> Bear me, some power, as far as winds can blow,
> As ships can travel, or as waves can flow,
> To some lone island beyond the southern pole,
> Or lands round which pacific waters roll,
> There shall oblivion stop the heaving sigh,
> There shall I live at last with liberty.[4]

"But honour," he explained, "checks my speed and bids me stay."[5] So during the summer and early autumn, he had remained in New York, contributing to pamphlet warfare. In October he was still restless to be gone and away, if not to "Europe's towns" where "poets

may flourish," at least to the peaceful seclusion of which he had been
dreaming for three years:

> How curs'd the man whom fate's unhappy doom
> Confines, unluckly, to his native home,
> How doubly curs'd by cross-grain'd stars is he,
> Whom fate ties down, tho' struggling to be free! [6]

A mysterious interval separates Freneau's quitting of New York,
probably by November, 1775, and his departure for the West Indies.
For nearly three months he was apparently at loose ends, though
there is a constantly recurring, seemingly unverifiable suspicion
that he was engaged in some commercial capacity. Any one of his
father's former associates, the Livingstons, the Schuylers, the Van
Courtlandts, or his cousin John Morin Scott, all men prominent in
colonial trade, could have provided a position in which a young man
might earn a living. Yet Freneau apparently did not find it necessary
to remain in New York. On January 16, 1776, he was in Monmouth,
a witness to an indenture wherein his mother was appointed attorney
for her cousin, John Napier, mariner, of the island of Santa Cruz.[7]
At some time during this winter Freneau is said to have been in
Philadelphia and there to have met a Captain Hanson, a Danish West
Indian plantation owner who sailed as master of his own vessel.

According to Freneau tradition, the captain took an immediate
liking to the young man and invited him to make his home in the
West Indies. In the face of such an opportunity, there could be no
refusal. During the voyage, Hanson's first mate is said to have died,
and Freneau—fortified, we discover, by a manual which his uncle
David Watson had given him [8]—studied navigation with such success that he was able to take the deceased officer's place at once, and,
eventually, to advance to the post of captain.[9] The story is perhaps
too simple to be entirely apocryphal, but those of us who would
question so artless a hospitality or so rapid a mastery of nautical
skill may prefer a less widespread variant which explains that Freneau sailed for the Caribbean as agent of a New York shipping firm.[10]
Others may suspect that his mother's cousin, who, we have seen, was
a seafaring resident of the islands, may have had something to do
with the formation of Freneau's plans. By whatever means, however,
and on whatever terms, Freneau did enjoy, he tells us, an "agreeable

residence" in Santa Cruz "for above two years off and on during the wars in America." [11]

It could not have been easy for him to leave America. It could not have been easy to explain his departure to himself. But for a young man whose dream of poetic glory got in the way of his ability to strike openly against the "bloody army" which threatened the colonies, there was only one thing to do. Reaching deep within him, "midst grief in exstacy of woe run mad," Freneau wrote a poem of death. Revolted by the horrors of civil war, though that war was for freedom, he cleansed his mind of the doubt and irresolution which kept him vacillating on the verge of activity in the colonial rebellion. He saw death rampant in America. And in "The House of Night" Freneau killed death: he had to if he were to enjoy peaceful and poetic solitude while his country suffered.

Thus we may find "The House of Night" Freneau's true vale-dictory to war and to America. [12] As he walked in dream by the shore of the Chesapeake, the poet came upon a dismal mansion. Mounting several flights of winding stairs, he entered a high chamber where, attended by jealousies and cares, "Ghosts, imps and half the black Tartarian crew," Death lay dying. Nothing was immortal, not even death. Nothing mattered, except that every man anticipate mortality by grasping in to himself all that he could of happiness. It was transitory enough, this happiness; soon, even as death passes, it would pass. Gathering up the shattered fragments of his vision, Fre-neau escaped into himself. With one tremendous stroke he broke through a tangle of indecision and psychological turmoil. What mat-tered it that war scarred America?

> O Hudson, Hudson, dreary, dull and slow,
> Seek me no more along that mountain stream,
> For on its banks is heard the sound of woe. [13]

2

The appearance of the island of Santa Cruz as you approach it from the ocean, Freneau tells us, "is inexpressibly beautiful." The water a mile from shore appeared to him "as blue and bottomless as any part of the main ocean," but nearer land it became suddenly shallow and transparent: sponges and seaweed seemed to sway in an undulating mirror. Looking over the side of the vessel, he could see "fine bright sand, and various kinds of fishes sporting above it." They were more beautiful than any he had ever seen, "particularly the angel fish, which is streaked over with circles near a half an inch in breadth, which glow with all the lustre of the most brilliant diamond." As he raised his head, the island seemed patterned with cultivated fields "cutting each other every way at right angles." The verdure of the sugar cane, "a most lively green," gave him pleasure such as he had never experienced in "any northern country."

Everything was "inexpressibly charming." Headlands rose precipitously from the sea, but beyond them, sloping "with a gentle descent" to the south "as far as eye can reach," stretched "enchanting plains and little vallies" where planters' houses were surrounded by groves of mango and orange. Even a hurricane which whipped through the island soon after his arrival could not dampen Freneau's enthusiasm. "A continual solitude and silence reigns here," he wrote. "The noise and tumult of the world is far removed from this peaceful abode." Simplicity and grandeur and physical well-being made it seem the Elysian paradise of which he had dreamed poetic dreams. "Happy the Man," he exclaimed, "who could pass his days in these extremities in peace and retirement."

Only the plight of the West Indian negro cast a "shadow over the native charms of the country" and spoiled the "beauties of eternal spring which Providence . . . here ordained to reign." "No class of mankind in the known world," wrote Freneau, "undergoes so complete a servitude." Not even the "profusion of nature," the "brightness of heaven," and the "mildness of the air" could compensate for the cruelty which they suffered. "It leaves me melancholy and disconsolate," Freneau admitted, "convinced there is no pleasure in this world without its share of pain."

And the moral to be drawn from this? Nature in all her works, though harsh and demanding, was just. The eternal plan of the universe was fitted, piece by piece, with elements in harmonious proportion. So Pope had said before him. Only man, and man's insatiable greeds, disturbed the eternal plan:

And thus the earth, which were it not for the lust of pride and dominion, might be an earthly paradise, is, by the ambition and overbearing nature of mankind, rendered an eternal scene of desolation, woe, and horror; the weak goes to the wall, while the strong prevails, and after an ambitious phrenzy has turned the world upside down, we are contented with a narrow spot, and leave our follies and cruelties to be acted over again by every succeeding generation.[14]

Pride, avarice, cruelty, lust—Freneau was always to be a bold knight who broke his lances against them. As he sailed through the Windward Passage and saw the island of Saba rising "like an immense cone" from the surrounding ocean, he turned to the theme again. Here on this little island Dutch settlers lived simply, "equally strangers to the luxury and the tyranny of the Sugar Islands." Here there was no slavery, no greed. But instead of the lyric rhapsody which we might expect from a more romantic poet, the melancholy young mariner wrote a dramatic monologue upon the evanescence of such harmonious tranquility. "The Hermit of Saba" is an expansion of a theme Freneau had developed in the fourteenth of "The Pictures of Columbus": three seamen are wrecked upon the rocky shores of Saba where lives a friendly hermit who brings them aid; the hermit, however, has the misfortune naïvely to boast of the rich bounty which living has given him; and the sailors, to whom richness can only mean gold, misconstrue his meaning and straightway murder him for the treasure. Selfish, wilful cruelty—and to what ends but desolation, horror, and woe? Lest the moral remain obscure, Freneau intensified it by calling "Perdition on those fiends from Europe, whose bloody malice, or whose thirst for gold . . . lays the world in ruin!" [15]

When he wrote "The Jamaica Funeral," Freneau's gloomy cynicism had expanded to encompass love, faith, friendship, and religion. Bitter, iconoclastic, and febrile, this poem snarls petulantly, not at any particular individual but at a world in which the young poet could find no room. Freneau was singing through mental darkness to keep his courage up. "Live while you may, be jovial while you can," he makes the besotted preacher advise in "The Jamaica Funeral." Nothing much matters, for

> Like insects busy in a summer's day,
> We toil and squabble to increase our pain,

Night comes at last, and, weary of the fray,
To dust and darkness all return again.[16]

Nothing must seem important. He had to make himself believe that; because if he could not believe it, he could not remain idly in the Caribbean. Though his vision of America gnawed persistently at his conscience, Freneau sang himself into assurance that nothing was important, even that.

It was inevitable that he should attempt to weave the warmth and lush beauty of the tropics into poetry. When he did, he found few models among his English literary masters. Such inherited phrases as "sylvan haunts," "crystal waters," and "sad retreats" were no longer adequate; so in "The Beauties of Santa Cruz" he strode manfully along untravelled paths of poetic description. There is much of Gray in the poem—even Freneau must have recognized the ancestry of such a stanza as:

The drowsy pelican wings home its way,
The misty night sits heavy on the sea,
Yon lagging sail drags slowly o'er the main.
Night and its kindred glooms are nought to me.[17]

Yet the imagery is not from Gray, nor is the sensuousness which flows through "The Beauties of Santa Cruz" derived from any source except Freneau's attempt to create new phrases for the products which "Nature's liberal hand" had strewn on this "envy'd isle." Every sense was called into play as he described "cooling acid limes," the "conic form'd cashew," "sweet spungy plums," the "happy flavored pine" and the "uncloying sugar cane." Freneau delighted in "cool, woodland springs" about which grew the "lowly mangrove," the "white-bark gregory," the guava, the pomegranate, the plantain, the pawpaw, and the coconut. Fishes and birds, blue skies and clear waters were pictured vividly. Never, perhaps, had tropical luxury been spread so profusely through poetry.

It is just this fervent phrase-mongering, however, which makes "The Beauties of Santa Cruz" a museum piece of baroque landscape rather than a poem which we read with pleasure. Freneau attempted to adapt the technique of the miniature painter to the gigantic canvas of the muralist, and failed. It must have been pleasant diversion, though, thus to luxuriate amid a thrilling, new, and peaceful scene. It was so logical. All nature was bound together in a close-knit skein of logic—its beauty, its harmony, its amazing proportion. Only man remained outside the orderly plan; and man need not remain outside.

Come, Freneau seems to say, come join me in my island paradise, Shepherd of the North, that you, too, may experience these voluptuous delights. Here, he promises, you will find neither war nor bloodshed, only splendor and languid ease. Yet, if you cannot join me, then I beg you to exert yourself and drive the tyrant from your own shores. As for me, I will "trace the vales of Santa Cruz, and sing with rapture her inspiring shade." Freneau must have recognized the evasion implicit in his song. "Fain would I view my native climes again," he admitted. But he thrust responsibility resolutely behind him: "Absence and death . . . why should they cloud the sunshine of my mind?" [18]

As he climbed the hills of Santa Cruz, "high mountains bordering on the sea covered with wood," he was reminded of majestic lines from Milton. "Even those who have no taste to admire the beauties of nature," Freneau asserted, "would at the view be forced to confess that the vales of Paradise were now displayed in their primeval beauty." It was an "inchanted island . . . such as we read of in romance." Brisk, dry winds from the east alleviated even the midday heat. Nights were cool and refreshing. The moon and stars shone "with an extraordinary brightness, owing to their reflection on the water of the ocean, which surrounds these happy lands." On a clear day one might look across the sea to Cape Malapasco on the east end of Porto Rico, or to Crab Island, or Tortola, or the Virgin Gorda. The ocean seemed full of islands, each one an earthly paradise. "Every saint in the Popish calendar," Freneau noted, "has his island here." Captain Hanson's estate on Butler's Bay ("a beautiful little bay" with a "sandy shore and an excellent landing") was charming. When, after two years, Freneau had to leave, he looked back upon his residence there in much the way that "Adam did after he was banished from the bowers of Eden." [19]

Nature in all her works enchanted Freneau, and not the least of these was the sea. As supercargo of the sloop *Liberty*, he made

several voyages to Bermuda during 1777.[20] In July of the same
year we find him for a moment idling on the island of St. James
while the vessel was being loaded with coral rock.[21] He sailed to
Demerara, south of the Orinoco; to the island of Curassoe, among
the Lesser Antilles, and to Comana, on the mainland; to Maracaybo,
in the Gulf of Mexico, and to Porto Cavallo, on Honduras Bay.[22]
From Yucatan to Trinidad, from Jamaica to the Virgin Islands, the
sloop seems to have plied comparatively untroubled and neutral
waters. The record of voyages which he has left presents little justification for Freneau's later statement that during this period he
sailed "principally on board of American privateers."

On April 1, 1778, Freneau embarked on a final voyage to Bermuda. Seventeen days spent in passage were followed by six weeks
ashore,[23] time which the young supercargo is said to have filled
with a poetic courtship addressed to one of the daughters of the stern
and loyal British governor.[24] He wrote with light abandon verses
"On a Lady's Singing Bird, a Native of the Canary Islands, Confined
in a Very Small Cage." [25] Playfully and deftly he embroidered a
pretty tale—of a melancholy maiden, mad through grief and love,
who mourns her absent swain; and of a half mad poet who spoils the
trees of the forest with whimsical inscriptions as he woos the maiden
in vain. Alas for lovelonging, alas the poet! The maiden sorrows
and sickens and dies.[26]

So poignantly does Freneau tell the story that it is hard for us to
remember that in the traditional love elegies of the eighteenth century many melancholy lovers walked at midnight through many
gloomy groves and pined with monotonous regularity through sickness to death for unrequited love. What could be more pleasant to
a young poet, bronzed by the sea and with his head full of fancies,
than an appreciative female audience? What more flattering to a
young lady than facile verses chiding her for false constancy? How
could an impecunious supercargo woo more safely than by teasing
his "Fair Solitary" about her faithfulness to another? Nothing that
he said could be taken seriously, but how charming the diversion!
It was pleasant to play the poet-courtier, and with no responsibility.
"And I was once a merry lad," [27] he sang—in very much the same
spirit which later in Tom Moore delighted the ladies of Bermuda.

It was perhaps at this time that Freneau received news of the war in America, news that aroused him from his poetical languor. Howe had driven Washington from New York, across the Hudson into New Jersey. The American troops, victorious at Princeton, had been defeated at Brandywine and Germantown. Though Burgoyne had surrendered his army in the north, Cornwallis, at the head of the British line and aided by a contingent of German mercenaries, had routed the patriots from their capital at Philadelphia.

Leaving Bermuda on May 24, Freneau arrived at Santa Cruz two weeks later. From there, on June 15, he engaged passage on a vessel bound for home. After an exciting voyage during which the ship was captured by a British privateer off the Carolina coast, Freneau stepped ashore on July 9 at Shrewsbury, five miles from Mount Pleasant.[28] Not two weeks before, a disorganized British army had fled, plundering as it went, across Monmouth County. The ravages of war were everywhere to be seen. "From every mouth," Freneau cried, "some doleful tale I hear." [29] Later, he admitted sadly:

> Returned, a captive, to my native shore,
> How changed I find the scenes that pleased before! [30]

3

War had suddenly become a reality. Stories of pillage, of destruction, of rapine, of arson greeted him on every side. The fields where he had wandered as a boy were deep stained with patriot blood. Beyond Monmouth Court House, seven miles from Mount Pleasant, a great battle had been fought in which Washington and his army had been victorious—but at what cost! Monmouth County lay desolate. "Pests of mankind, remembrance shall recall . . . these horrors," Freneau vowed.[31]

On July 15, 1778, six days after he returned from Santa Cruz, Freneau enlisted as a private in Captain Barnes Smocks's company of the First Regiment of the New Jersey Militia. Assigned to service as a "scout & guard along the shore," covering about twenty miles of seacoast between South Amboy and Long Branch, he was "on duty day and night." At some time during the period of his enlistment (Freneau was on the militia rolls until May 1, 1780) [32] he was promoted to the rank of sergeant.[33] "He was in no battle on shore but in several skirmishes." [34] His dog Sancho, however, who kept watch with him, "was wounded in the head with a sabre in a midnight assault and robbery near the Neversink Hills." [35]

Who could "tell the conflicts of these stormy days," express the wrath, picture the dreadful scenes of war? Only a poet inspired by heaven, said Freneau as he set himself to the task. Boldly and with extravagant zeal he began to tell of what he had now seen of war and what he dreamed of conquest for his homeland. When *American Independence, an Everlasting Deliverance from British Tyranny* was published in the autumn of 1778 by Robert Bell in Philadelphia, it was attributed to "Philip F——————, Author of the American Village, Voyage to Boston, &c." Introduced by the ominous lines from *Hamlet* in which the Ghost warns his son of the necessity for vengeance, its plea is forthright:

> Americans, revenge your country's wrongs;
> To you the honor of the deed belongs.

Freneau called upon his countrymen, formed in God's image to be free, to force the tyrant from their shores. Freedom was dead in Europe; it had even died, he admitted sadly, in England. In America, however, shorn of the cankers of greed and ambition, it might bloom to beauty never known before. What had been America's crime, except that she had raised her arm to stay an assassin's knife? Hasten to the foe, Freneau exhorted. Drive him homeward in defeat. Then may our country grow gloriously, through freedom, to liberty and peace. It was a shrill, clear cry of hatred and sudden resolution, a public pronouncement and a private vow that no longer would England or her baneful influence distort his vision of a free America. It was not a new song. Coming upon scenes of carnage and desolation after idle poetic years in the West Indies, Freneau only added a fresh and a passionate new voice to the chorus which had been chanting bravely of freedom since the Declaration of Independence two years before.

All up and down the Atlantic coast patriots were setting out to sea in small boats, prepared to brave the British blockade and smuggle arms and supplies into the country. Enemy vessels might be captured in the process, and prize money obtained. "Privateering," wrote a contemporary, "was never more in vogue than at the present. . . . Men seem as plenty as grass-hoppers in the field; no vessel being detained a day for want of them." [36] From New England John Paul Jones issued a broadside plea for "gentlemen Seamen and able bodied Landsmen who have a mind to distinguish themselves in the glorious cause of their country, and make their fortunes." [37] Freneau joined enthusiastically in the effort to recruit men for naval service by writing spirited stanzas on "Captain Jones's Invitation." [38] When he read of the courageous stand which the Continental frigate *Ranger* had made against the British twenty-four gun ship *Yarmouth,* he composed "Verses to the Memory of Capt. Nicholas Biddle" in honor of the intrepid American commander.[39] Later, when a continental frigate was ready to sail from Boston Harbor for British waters, he sped her voyage with a lively ballad "On the New American Frigate Alliance." [40]

In the intervals between his tours of duty as a militiaman Freneau himself joined the increasing band of mariners who dared the privateer-infested waters of the lower Atlantic and who guided their vessels by night into shallow inlets along the Jersey coast with cargoes of arms, or rum, or dry goods for the Continental forces. On October 25, 1778, he sailed from the Shrewsbury River, captain of the schooner *Indian Delaware,* for Philadelphia and St. Eustacia in the West Indies.[41] Four months later his log contains invoices for almost two thousand dollars worth of merchandise which he had landed at American ports.[42] In July of the next year he set out from Philadelphia, master of the sloop *John Couster,* again for St. Eustacia.[43] Freneau took part in "several privateer sea fights," he tells us, and carried a British bullet in his knee to the end of his life as a memento of one of these engagements.[44]

Late in September, 1779, he shipped as supercargo on the brig *Rebecca,* Captain Chatham, bound for the Azores. Still apparently a novice at navigation, Freneau compared his observations daily with those of the captain. He had difficulty getting his meridian distance to check with his longitude. "By my reckoning, which I find to be wrong," he confessed after they had been three weeks at sea, "I find I am as far west as the Island of St. Mavis, which is not the case."

Twice during the course of the voyage the brig was pursued by British vessels. Not until early in November did she arrive at Santa Cruz on the island of Teneriffe. It was a mean town, but, said Freneau, "makes a handsome appearance at a small distance." The houses were so white that they transformed even the narrow streets into bright and enchanting avenues.[45] It was strange and exotic, not to be compared with the Santa Cruz in the Caribbean, but, even so, filled with new wonders for a poet.

When, on December 30, 1779, a gale whipped down the Jersey coast, driving the rich British privateer brig *Britannia* upon the ice floes near Middletown Point, Private Freneau was a member of the detachment of the Monmouth County militia under Colonel Asher Holmes which fought its way through wind and whirling snow to capture her.[46] Eighty of her crew (fatigued, said the Tory newspapers of New York, by their exertions in attempting to save the vessel) were taken prisoner by the boarding party.[47] The cargo was carried ashore to await distribution by the Court of Admiralty: sails, rigging, and huge strips of copper from the brig's bottom were offered at public auction; "Blunder Busses, Muskets, and Pistols, Cutlasses, Fire Arrows" were sold throughout the township; Irish beef, bread, coffee, and sugar from the ship's larder were divided among the citizens of the county.[48] When the prize money was allotted, Freneau's share (the only pay, he tells us, that he received for his Revolutionary services) was $800 in Continental money. Of this, he said, "$120 was shortly paid for a pair of shoes." [49]

In all, Freneau's participation in military or naval exploits was brief and relatively unimportant. He apparently covered himself with no particular glory as a soldier or as a sailor, though after 1778 he did not evade service. One may be at least as tolerant of his martial activities as he was himself of the military record of his friend, Francis Bailey. "I am sensible," Freneau wrote, "he never cut off the heads of giants or drove hosts before him as some have done; at the same time . . . I believe he never acted otherwise than became the character in which he acted." [50]

4

In the meantime Freneau's classmate Hugh Brackenridge, after a varied career as army chaplain and patriotic publicist, had launched a brave new literary enterprise in Philadelphia. In partnership with Francis Bailey, a printer recently come to the city from western Pennsylvania, he established in January, 1779, *The United States Magazine,* a monthly publication which promised to serve equally belles-lettres and politics.

Freneau, of course, was called upon for contributions. The first issue contained an "Account of Some of the West India Islands by a Young American Philosopher and Bel Esprit, just Returned from Several Small Voyages amongst those Islands," in which were detailed the charms and disenchantments of Bermuda. In the February issue was presented an "Account of the Island of Santa Cruz, Containing an Original Poem on the Beauties of that Island." Brackenridge thought the poem "truly beautiful." He published his friend's prose "Account of the Island of St. James" in March. Thereafter almost every number of the *United States Magazine* contained contributions from Freneau, "a young Gentleman," the editor acknowledged, "to whom in the course of this Work we are greatly indebted." [51]

In May appeared "King George the Third's Soliloquy," a poem in which the British ruler is made to tremble in rage and fear at the thought of his failures in America. In June, Brackenridge published "The Dying Elm. An Irregular Ode" and "Columbus to Ferdinand," both of which Freneau had written some years before. The July issue of the magazine contained "The Loyalists," contributed by a correspondent in "Shrewsbury, East-Jersey." Although Freneau included the first nine lines in *The British Prison-Ship* a year later, he never reprinted "The Loyalists" as a whole.

Perhaps it told too much. After nineteen bitter lines directed against the Tories, "blood hounds of some murderous line," who prey "like famished wolves upon their country," the attack is turned toward

> Sylvan Bards who deal in flow'ry themes,
> Who sing the meadows and the purling streams,
> Who yet remote from blood and murder stray.

Once, Freneau confessed, his Muse had also strayed to "quiet groves"

> And sung the pleasure of the plantain shade;
> Sweet was the toil, and sweetly passed the time;
> Soft was the verse, and easy was the rhyme;
> But when she saw your blazing turrets fall,
> Your slaughter'd friends in vain for mercy call,
> Your captive sons with British poison die,
> Your fields laid waste and total conquest nigh;
> Griev'd at the view she rais'd a bolder strain,
> Expos'd the tyrant and deny'd his reign.

Now Freneau looked scornfully upon those who, like himself only a few months before, had evaded service. "The Loyalists" explains the transition between "The Beauties of Santa Cruz" and *American Independence*. It represents Freneau's apology to himself for his earlier failure to take an active part in the Revolutionary struggle. It is another, and perhaps the most straightforward, of his expressions of new-found resolution.

Perhaps, too, it explains the lines with which he opened "The House of Night" when that poem appeared in the August issue of the *United States Magazine*. "Let others draw from smiling skies their theme," Freneau said then. "I sing the horrors of the house of night." We can only guess how closely the version of the poem which Freneau now published approximates the version which he first had written four years before. He apparently worked over it carefully, adding, deleting, changing its too revealing passages to suit a new attitude. Yet in spite of Freneau's puttering and the revision he subsequently made for almost every new edition of his collected poems,[52] we may regret that he never preserved the first version of "The House of Night," written amid the mental turmoil which resulted in his leaving America. Turgid and confused though this writing would probably be, it might illumine for an instant the melancholy vision which was almost transformed to great poetry. For "The House of Night" as Freneau printed it in the *United States*

Magazine just misses. Rising toward poetic heights, it wavers before its goal. A sternly vindictive and purposefully didactic Freneau attempted to turn the poetic product of a more mystic, less earthbound mood into a vehicle for war propaganda. It could not be done. Nor was the earlier mood ever again to be recaptured. The "caverns measureless to man" which he had started to explore were closed to him forever.

"Psal. cxxxvii. Imitated," signed by the author's name and dated "Monmouth, September 10, 1779," appeared in the *United States Magazine* in September. Again Freneau presented a forthright dedication of his poet's might to the sorrowful cause of his country. In October he contributed "The Sea Voyage," a versified account of his passage from Santa Cruz the year before. No longer, however, did he dwell on the beauties of the "gay island green and fair." War now engaged him completely. He hurled defiance at the foe, he stormed, he laughed, he ridiculed. *Sir Henry Clinton's Invitation to the Refugees,* a rollicking lampoon on the treatment which Tory fugitives might expect from the English, was distributed as a ballad sheet through the streets of Philadelphia.[53]

George III was a moral weakling with an eye for other men's wives, a badly frightened poltroon who desperately sought advice which would guide him from the avenues of defeat through which his greed and ambition had led him. So Freneau pictured the king in "A Dialogue between His Britannic Majesty and Mr. Fox," which appeared in the December issue of the *United States Magazine.* As the craven ruler cringed abjectly, the Whig minister counselled peace and immediate recognition of the new United States. Paraphrasing the speeches which Fox had made in Parliament, Freneau insisted that if England would abstain from futile aggression and meaningless oppression in America, she might then turn her full attention to enemies in Europe:

> When France and Spain are thund'ring at your doors,
> Is this the time for kings to lodge with whores?
> In one short sentence take my whole advice,
> (It is no time to flatter or be nice)
> With all your soul for instant peace contend,
> Thus shall you be your country's truest friend.

> Peace, heavenly peace, may stay your tottering throne,
> But wars and death and blood can profit none.

There was, however, no peace in the struggle against the red-coated army from England, nor in the constant internal bickerings which sapped the strength of America. The *United States Magazine* foundered perilously upon the turbulent sea of Pennsylvania politics. Soaring prices and depreciating currency, and political bickering bred of the intensely partisan attitude of citizens in Philadelphia finally drove Brackenridge to announce in December that the publication would be discontinued. At the same time he reported that a group of patriotic American ladies had expressed a desire that the author of "The House of Night" "employ his poetic and descriptive vein in like manner, on the *prison-ship* at New York." [54]

5

Less than six months later Freneau had just such an opportunity. Soon after quitting the New Jersey Militia in May, 1780, he "entered on board a Pennsylvania Letter of Marque, called the Aurora." [55] She was a new twenty-gun ship, loaded with a cargo of tobacco for St. Eustacia,[56] and dedicated to the service of her country. "Grant that this pile," wrote Freneau in poetical invocation, "may travel safely . . . seize pirates on the watry way . . . and alter for our port their destined course." [57] "I was enrolled," he recorded in his diary, "as third mate." [58] After the rigors of a northern winter, he "fondly promised" himself once more to visit the "fragrant groves and delectable Plains of Santa Cruz, to enjoy the fruits and flowers of that happy clime." [59]

What hardships might have been avoided, Freneau later suggested, had not the *Aurora*, setting out from Philadelphia on May 25, sighted, pursued, and captured an enemy sloop in Delaware Bay. Was it not avarice again—even so small and patriotic an avarice—at work undermining the happiness of men? The encounter "hindered us," he said, "from standing out to sea that night." The next day was sultry and little wind blew. At three o'clock in the afternoon the lookout on the foretop sighted a British frigate bearing down from the northeast. Soon it was visible from the quarter-

deck, and Captain Sutton of the *Aurora,* perceiving that his vessel
would stand small chance in open combat, ordered all sails set as
he stood back for the bay. Freneau suggested that they take the
shorter route to "Egg Harbor or any part of the Jersey shore and
run the ship on the flats rather than be taken." But this advice was
disregarded.

As the enemy frigate came nearer, they could see that she was
His Majesty's ship *Iris,* of thirty-six guns, and with two American
prizes in tow. Crowding on all sail possible, the *Aurora* fled toward
Cape Henlopen. "Our design," Freneau explained, "was, if possible, to get within the road around the point, and there run the ship
on shore, but want of wind and the tide being against us, hindered
from putting this into execution." A half hour before sunset the
wind died completely, and the ebb of the tide drifting out from the
bay drove the vessel toward the enemy. At a distance of three hundred yards firing commenced. "The frigate hulled us several times,"
Freneau wrote. "One shot went betwixt wind and water, which made
the ship leak amazingly."

"We found our four pounders but were trifles against the frigate,"
he reported. Only slightly better were the results obtained when the
one nine-pounder aboard the *Aurora* was directed from a cabin
window against the enemy. The American ship was clearly out-
classed:

At last a twelve-pound shot came from the frigate and, striking a parcel
of oars lashed upon the starboard quarter, broke them all in two, and
continuing on its destructive course struck Captain Laboyteaux in the right
thigh, which it smashed to atoms, tearing part of his belly open at the
same time with the splinters from the oars; he fell from the quarter deck
close by me and for some time seemed very busily engaged in setting his
leg to rights.

"Every shot seemed now to bring ruin with it," until, finally, "finding the frigate ready and in a position to give us a broadside," the
Aurora struck her colors, "after having held a very unequal contest . . . for about an hour."

When the British prize master came aboard, Freneau insisted
that he was a passenger sailing upon private business and, therefore, not subject to capture. Unfortunately, however, his name was

discovered on the ship's books as a member of one of the gun crews. In vain he insisted that it was a mistake. "Cruelly seized" and driven "amid a torrent of cursing and blasphemy" aboard the frigate, he was ordered handcuffed between decks with ordinary seamen, "the stench of whom was almost intolerable." It was "a cursed disgrace," he said, "which I hardly knew how I should get clear of." "Pray," he protested to the master-at-arms in charge of prisoners, "is it your custom to handcuff passengers? The Americans, I am confident, never used the English so."

Only after he had been identified by a Tory member of the frigate's crew, was Freneau allowed to "come over among the gentlemen." Even there, however, he was miserable, for he was in his "common ship clothes" and, not having been allowed to bring his sea chest from the *Aurora* with him, suffered "mortification" at being unable to dress "so as to appear decent for want of it." He comforted himself with the thought that he would be immediately released when the *Iris* reached port.

Three days later in New York Freneau was refused parole, though he insisted that his friends in that city would offer security "even to £10,000." Still protesting that he was a noncombatant who had paid for his passage, he was sentenced on June 1 to the prison ship *Scorpion*, which lay anchored just off shore in the Hudson River. "The best lodging I could procure this night," he said, "was on a chest, almost suffocated with the heat and stench. I expected to die before morning, but human nature can bear more than one would at first expect." He wished that he had never seen a ship in all his life.

Nothing which Freneau experienced made a deeper impression upon him than his six weeks of incarceration aboard the prison ships. Nothing so mirrors his sensitive poet's nature as his reaction to his imprisonment. He who had written lachrymose verses on a canary shut fast in a cage was now crowded with three hundred men into an evil-smelling hold. He was filled with bitter hatred by the brutality of the guards, who clubbed mutinous prisoners to submission and who punished an attempt to escape by firing at random among the Americans huddled below decks. "No usage seemed to them severe enough for us," he said. "We had water given us to drink that a dog could scarcely relish; it was thick and clammy and had a dismal smell."

After twenty-two days on the *Scorpion,* Freneau succumbed to fever and was removed to the hospital ship *Hunter,* which lay in the East River. Here conditions were even worse:

She was miserably dirty and cluttered. Her decks leaked to such a degree that the sick were deluged with every shower of rain. Between decks they lay along struggling in the agonies of death; dying with putrid and bilious fevers; lamenting their hard fate to die at such a fatal distance from their friends; others totally insensible, and yielding their last breath in all the horrors of light-headed frenzy.[60]

The dead were carried without ceremony to shallow graves on the Long Island shore. The living, subjected to "damnable draughts of a German doctor" ("a dog of a Hess"), suffered agonies which reminded Freneau of the lazar-house in *Paradise Lost.* Bread and meat was their only diet—"Our fresh beef was generally heads and shanks, and would just answer for soup."

> Such food they sent, to make complete our woes,
> It looked like carrion torn from hungry crows,
> Such vermin vile on every joint were seen,
> So black corrupted mortified, and lean.[61]

The fever fortunately proved to be of the "remittent kind." "Had it turned to putrid, as it did with numbers, in all probability," said Freneau, "I must have died as well as the rest." A large blister placed upon his back helped him somewhat, but when released on July 12, he was so weakened and so afflicted with pains in the joints that he could scarcely walk.[62] His friends found him a "perfect skeleton" when he arrived home two days later.[63] Indeed, as he approached Mount Pleasant, Freneau turned from the main road into a roundabout path through the woods for fear of terrifying the neighbors with his ghastly looks.[64]

6

At last war had touched Freneau personally. He knew its horrors at first hand and had suffered its brutalities. As a result of his experience on the prison ships, hatred of British tyranny hardened to flint from which the recollection of his confinement struck glowing sparks. Amorphous visions, of which songs might be sung, gave place to dogmas to which every talent must be subjugated. Vague humanitarian impulses were transformed to one mighty resolution —the extermination of English influence from America forever. Henceforth Freneau was to be truly the poet of American independence. Embittered and personally hurt, he made his vow:

> Weak as I am, I'll try my strength today
> And my best arrows at these hell-hounds play,
> To future years one scene of death prolong,
> And hang them up to infamy in song.[65]

During his convalescence at Mount Pleasant he wrote a detailed prose account of the capture of the *Aurora* and of his weeks of imprisonment. Then, turning to poetry while the memory of his torment was still hot within him, he composed the first draft of *The British Prison-Ship*.[66] No such hymn of hate had ever been produced in America. He heaped invectives on the "gorg'd monsters," "infernal miscreants," "foes to the rights of freedom and of man," who, "flushed with the blood of thousands," spare "no age, no sex from lust and murder"; on "hell-born Tories," "traitors to every sense of shame," "who leave no art of cruelty untried"; and on the tyrant king "whose murderous acts shall stamp his name acurst." With sincerity bred of bitter hatred he called on his countrymen to "glut revenge on this detested foe." "See," he challenged, "how they pant to stain the world with gore." Out with them. "Defeat, destroy, and sweep them from the land." Thus only might America be free.

When late in September the newspapers of Philadelphia announced that, "lost to every sentiment of honor, and disgraced by the inordinate thirst for gold, General Arnold has gone over to the enemy," [67] Freneau found a new subject for his belligerent muse. Was no one free from the curse of ambition? Even Benedict Arnold, the hero of a score of battles, had fallen. In what contrast to the infamy of the American traitor was the conduct displayed by young Major André, whose courage was tried by death but still remained secure and honored by every man of sentiment. In the same notebook in which Freneau had written the account of his captivity and the poem on the prison ship, he began a drama in five acts. Only fragments of "The Spy" have been preserved and these, because of the penstroke deletions and interlineations with which Freneau covered the manuscript in revision, are almost indecipherable.[68] The prose spoken by the minor characters is flexible and idiomatic, and the blank verse in which the principals speak is a workmanlike imitation of classical tradition. But there was no time now to complete anything so purely literary as a drama, even so patriotic a drama as "The Spy."

On December 13, 1780, when the "Verses to the Memory of Capt. Nicholas Biddle" appeared in the *New-Jersey Gazette*, Freneau had already left Mount Pleasant for Philadelphia, where on December 10 he had bought a copy of Beccaria's *Essay on Crimes and Punishments* at Robert Bell's bookstore for eight shillings specie. The bookseller "at that time," explained Freneau, "would not take paper money; he said it was not worth a straw." [69]

FIVE

THE FREEMAN'S JOURNAL

1781–1784

NDAUNTED by the failure of the *United States Magazine* sixteen months before, Francis Bailey now launched a new
periodical in the maelstrom of political and financial unrest
in Philadelphia. This time he proposed a weekly newspaper which
would be "open to all parties but influenced by none" and which
would strive to "encourage genius, to deter vice, and disrobe tyranny
in every plumage." [1] Thus announced, the first number of *The Freeman's Journal: or North American Intelligencer* was issued on
April 25, 1781. Burdened, however, with the increasing demands of
his printing business, Bailey was soon glad to turn for assistance
to the "young American Philosopher and Bel Esprit" who had contributed to his former periodical enterprise. So Freneau "went to
Philadelphia & became the Editor of a wig paper there called the
Freeman's Journal in which," he said, "he supported the cause of
the Revolution all the more." [2]

At no period had patriot endeavor in America more needed encouragement. The Continental Congress was bankrupt. Washington
had not fought a battle for two years and could hold together barely
enough men to maintain a strategic position along the Hudson Highlands. Thousands of Americans were playing a waiting game, watching cautiously which way the victory would turn. One great traitor
had been discovered in Arnold, but lesser traitors grew wealthy
through illegitimate traffic with the British in New York. Cornwallis
preyed relentlessly on the South, where he established a reign of
menace and corruption. In the North whole regiments of Continen-
tals rose in mutiny: thirteen hundred soldiers of the Pennsylvania
line marched toward Philadelphia to enforce demands for back pay.
Meanwhile, prices continued to rise, while money depreciated to
such an extent that business was demoralized. To many the Revolu-

tion seemed over. The best that could be done was to wait patiently and attempt to build some measure of security from the chaos war had brought.

Although it has been suggested that Freneau composed the prospectus published in the first issue of the *Freeman's Journal*,[3] the new editor apparently took no active part in the management of the newspaper until late in the summer. During April and May the printer seems to have been without any inspired editorial assistance: the paper was sedate and prosaic, almost entirely concerned with reporting events of the past week or the week before. The first issue contained an advertisement of *The British Prison-Ship*, which Bailey had published in March as a twenty-four page pamphlet, but nowhere in the columns of the *Freeman's Journal* was there yet any echo of the ringing words with which Freneau had expressed his denunciation of all things English.

By June, however, there was evidence of a more spirited editorial control. Commentary became more frequent and more acrid. When, on June 20, an article on American prisoners was reprinted from a Charleston loyalist paper, someone wrote a paragraph on the "slaughter houses called prison-ships" and quoted the same lines from *Paradise Lost* which Freneau had used in his unpublished account of the capture of the *Aurora*. By July there was definite indication of a new hand supplying copy to the compositors. News was no longer merely reported: it was embellished with outspoken patriotic sentiments. Phrases that sound a familiar note are found on July 11 in an account of a Tory raid in Monmouth, wherein the action of the loyalist leader was described as the "monstrous barbarity of this DOG OF HELL."

On August 8 the newspaper carried a report that General James Robertson, the Royal Governor of New York, had decreed that two-thirds of the fodder produced in that city must be contributed to the British army. "Huzza for BRITISH LIBERTY," chortled the editorial writer of the *Freeman's Journal*.

There you have it,—neat as imported.—Ah, you rebel rogues! why will you suffer yourselves to be deluged by tyrannical assemblies and congresses, who give you no security for your property, and do not protect you in the enjoyment of it? Fly to the standard of the best of kings:—go to

New York, and old Mr. Robertson, who represents his majesty, will be very glad to see you.

In the same issue Freneau printed "A Poem on the Memorable Victory Obtained by the Gallant Capt. Paul Jones." Thereafter for more than a year his verse and prose appeared in nearly every number.[4] He followed the events of the war with intense and patriotic comment, he lampooned the Tories and mocked the British, and he set forth again his ideal of a free America. It was an exciting, disappointing, and very productive period.

2

There was much to do, much to counteract. The *Royal Gazette* in New York printed exaggerated accounts of British successes and took every opportunity to scoff at the efficiency of "rebel commanders." It insisted that a "vast and immense majority" of Americans were loyalists. Brazenly it asserted that popular opinion was against the continuance of war.[5] Freneau fought back point for point. If the Americans were as disaffected as the British were informed by their good friends the Tories, why, he asked, had the war not ended long ago? Why did the British not march from New York, join the loyalists of New Jersey, and sweep on down to Philadelphia? Why, in particular, did the *Royal Gazette* print such lies?

The truth is—the Americans, as a body of men, notwithstanding all their misfortunes and distresses begin to taste the sweets of independence, so that all ranks of men are convinced of the necessity of supporting it, which with the view of what must inevitably happen upon its overthrow . . . will more and more firmly establish the minds of men on this point.[6]

Soon, however, it was no longer necessary thus to encourage the patriots of Philadelphia. Late in August the *Freeman's Journal* surged upward on a gigantic wave of popular enthusiasm as Washington and Rochambeau entered the city at the head of their combined forces. The streets were lined with cheering crowds, and salutes resounded from all the vessels in the harbor. "Every class of citizen," said the *Pennsylvania Gazette*, "seemed to vie with the other in shewing marks of respect to this illustrious pair." [7] As the French forces passed in parade, Freneau reported, "The appearance

of these troops far exceeds any thing of the kind before seen on this
continent, and presages the happiest success to the cause of America." [8] Four days later joy in Philadelphia was complete when
Colonel John Laurens arrived from France with money and supplies for the Continental army. "The bells of Christ Church were
rung and joy appeared on every countenance" when news was received that Admiral de Grasse and a French fleet of twenty-eight
warships had arrived at the mouth of the Delaware. Then, a dispatch
from South Carolina reported that General Greene had driven the
British forces into Charleston and held them there in a state of siege.
Philadelphia seethed with excitement. After two years of bickering
and depression, something was about to happen. Troops, money, and
heartening news all poured into the city within the space of a few
days.

As his part in the jubilant celebration Freneau on September 5
printed verses "To His Excellency General Washington":

> Accept, great chief, that share of honest praise
> A grateful people to your merit pays:
> Verse is too mean your virtues to display,
> And words too weak our meaning to convey.

Only France and her glorious king could share in the homage show-
ered upon the American commander. All citizens of Philadelphia,
said the editor of the *Freeman's Journal*, "were impressed with the
most lively gratitude to the brave, noble and virtuous prince who
so happily governs the French nation; whose shining reign and
magnanimous acts place him on a line with the most illustrious
princes of modern times." Anti-monarchial feelings were forgotten
in the emotional release of the moment.

How ludicrous now seemed the garbled reports in the loyalist
press! Freneau ridiculed the bumptious confidence of the British by
printing what he represented to be a "Copy of an Intercepted Letter
from a New York Tory, to His Friend in This City." [9] The tables
were turned—at least, they were turning. What mean and contemptible cowards the enemy were: they even plundered their own
subjects who lived (and who were becoming prosperous through
energetic trading with the Americans) in the neutral Dutch West

Indies. Following a quatrain reprinted on September 12 from a London paper "On Admiral Rodney's Allowing the Governor of St. Eustatius Only One Hour to Consider Surrender," Freneau published the "Reflections of an American on the Above Lines":

> This hodge-podge chief, compos'd of all that's base,
>   Trembled to look a Frenchman in the face;
> To him, forgetful of his master's fame,
> De Grasse and fifty devils are the same:—
>   Yet poor in purse, and hungry for his prey,
> To Statia's isle the fiend makes haste away,
> And found it safer, as his actions show,
> A friend to plunder, than attack a foe.
>
> Weep, Britains! weep, degenerate, pilfering race,
> And brand this plundering villain with disgrace;
> The time has been, you may recall with tears,
> When deeds like *this* had cost him nose and ears.

As the combined armies of France and America moved southward, Freneau turned his attention to lampooning British activity in Virginia. Cornwallis, confident of victory, had inspired the Colonial Minister in London with a silly expectation that the war might soon be concluded. If this should be, taunted Freneau on September 19 in the "Dialogue between Lords Dunmore and Mansfield," then good Lord Dunmore could return to Virginia and again make himself wealthy by confiscating rebel estates. No American could hope for mercy if conquered. Therefore, America had to win. And it looked now as if she might, for the English army which had been plundering cruelly through Virginia was finally trapped in Yorktown by Washington. Could it be the end? On October 8 Freneau addressed lines full of scorn and triumphant hatred "To Lord Cornwallis":

> Hail, great destroyer (equall'd yet by none)
> Of countries not thy master's nor thy own!
> Hatched by a demon on a stormy day,
> Satan's best substitute to burn and slay,
> Confin'd at last—hemm'd in by land and sea,
> Burgoyne himself was but a type of thee.
> Wouldst thou at last with *Washington* engage,
> Sad object of his pity not his rage?

See round thy posts now horribly advance
The chiefs, the soldiers, and the fleets of France!

One week later, on October 17, Freneau published "An Epistle from Lord Cornwallis to Sir Henry Clinton," in which the beleaguered commander, seeing disaster before him, was made to appeal servilely for assistance to his superior in New York. Cruelty, cowardice, and resignation to defeat were outstanding traits of the English. Fortitude and resilient strength were characteristics of the American soldier. Verses such as these were effective reminders to the citizens of Philadelphia that their cause was just.

Then, on October 24, the news arrived. Tench Tilghman galloped through the streets of Philadelphia with word of Cornwallis's surrender. The populace went wild: "People of all ranks seemed to contend who should distinguish themselves most in demonstrating their joy on this important event." [10] The artillery in the State House yard sounded all through the day, and every ship in the harbor hoisted her colors in triumph. Torch-light processions and fireworks lasted long into the night. It was an event never to be forgotten. The *Freeman's Journal* carried a streamer across the whole top of the first page:

BE IT REMEMBERED
THAT ON THE 17TH DAY OF OCTOBER, 1781, LIEUT.
GENERAL CHARLES EARL CORNWALLIS WITH ABOVE
5000 BRITISH TROOPS SURRENDERED THEMSELVES
PRISONERS OF WAR TO HIS EXCELLENCY GEN. GEORGE
WASHINGTON, COMMANDER IN CHIEF OF THE ALLIED
FORCES OF FRANCE AND AMERICA.
LAUS DEO!

Freneau's verses commemorative of the surrender did not appear until two weeks later, and "On the Fall of General Earl Cornwallis," printed on November 7, was not a jubilant song of celebration. It was a chant of war, of revenge, of abomination. It rings with the spirit of the inexorable battle hymns of the Old Testament warriors. It promises to forgive nothing, nor forget. But its wrath, if not righteous, is sincere. The "arch-butcher of the times" had fallen,

the wolf who wrought by night his prey
And plunder'd all he met with on his way,

> Stole what he could, and murder'd as he pass'd
> Chanc'd on a trap, and lost his head at last.
> What pen can paint, what human tongue can tell
> The endless murders of this man of hell!
> Nature in him disgrac'd the form divine;
> Nature mistook, she meant him for a—swine.

Between expressions of wrath and triumph, the poet turned sadly to the desolate scene presented in America. He could no longer invite true lovers of freedom to seek on her shores release from a tyrant's grasp. Instead, he now advised:

> Thou, who resid'st on those thrice happy shores,
> Where white rob'd peace her envied blessings pours,
> Stay, and enjoy the pleasures that she yields;
> But come not, stranger, to our wasted fields,
> For warlike hosts on every plain appear;
> War damps the beauties of the rising year:
> In vain the groves their bloomy sweets display;
> War's clouded winter chills the charms of May;
> Here human blood the trampled harvest stains;
> Here bones of men yet whiten all the plains;
> Seas teem with dead; and our unhappy shore
> Forever blushes with its children's gore.

Yet, as Freneau's rage was directed toward those who were responsible for the prostration of his country, so his sympathy reached most tenderly to those who sacrificed themselves to defend her. Rather than celebrate General Greene's victory at Eutaw Springs, the poet composed stanzas "To the Memory of the Brave Americans, who Fell in the Action of September 6, 1781." Freneau never wrote a poem more sincere, more restrained, or more effective in its simplicity. Walter Scott is said to have called it the finest poem of its kind in the English language,[11] and paid the author the compliment of borrowing a line from it for *Marmion*.[12] Freneau's emotion was never more controlled than when he mourned:

> At Eutaw Springs the valiant died;
>   Their limbs with dust are cover'd o'er—
> Weep on, ye springs, your fearful tide;
>   How many heroes are no more!
> If in this wreck of ruin, they
>   Can yet be thought to claim a tear,

O smite thy gentle breast, and say
   The friends of freedom slumber here!
Thou, who shalt trace this bloody plain,
   If goodness rules thy generous breast,
Sigh for the wasted rural reign;
   Sigh for the shepherds sunk to rest!
Stranger, their humble graves adorn;
   You too may fall, and ask a tear:
'Tis not the beauty of the morn
   That proves the evening shall be clear—
They saw their injur'd country's woe,
   The flaming town, the wasted field;
They rush'd to meet the insulting foe;
   They took the spear—but left the shield.

.   .   .

Now rest in peace our patriot band;
   Tho' far from nature's limits thrown,
We trust they find a happier land,
   A brighter Phoebus of their own.

The surrender of Cornwallis did not mean to Freneau and his contemporaries an end to the struggle for independence. The British army was still firmly established at Charleston and New York. The British fleet maintained an effective blockade of the Atlantic coast. But England was carrying on heavy wars elsewhere, in widely separated portions of the globe—with the French, the Spaniards, the Dutch, and the native tribes of India. By the beginning of January, 1782, it became evident that America, in spite of her almost incredible losses, might expect to receive conciliatory overtures. Thus, when Freneau was asked to write a prologue to the dramatic entertainment given in honor of General Washington at the Southwark Theater on January 2, the poet, flushed with the hope of peace, again reviewed his dream of the future glory of America:

Even here where freedom lately sat distrest,
See, a new Athens rising in the west;
Fair science blooms where tyrants reign'd before,
Red war reluctant leaves our ravag'd shore—
Illustrious hero, may you live to see
These new republics powerful, great and free;

> Peace, heaven born peace, o'er spacious regions spread,
> While discord sinking veils her ghastly head.

Until this time should come, however, Freneau continued his poetical assaults against the enemies of freedom. His verse was crude and coarse, inspired by a deep patriotic spirit, but leveled to the understanding of the multitude. It made no pretense to literary finish. Yet his productions, said a contemporary, "were celebrated as masterpieces of ingenious satire—in which the poignancy of the attick salt was allayed by a plentiful proportion of genuine good humour." [13] We look in vain for the "genuine good humour," however, when on January 20 Freneau presented "The Royal Adventure." Reminding the Tory citizens of New York of the "joy ineffable and universal" with which they had greeted the arrival of Prince William Henry, he derided them for their shamed silence on his precipitous flight from America. What in the world, asked Freneau, is there for a Prince to do when he has no armies to command? The satire was obvious, the verse was doggerel, but "The Royal Adventure" became immediately popular. Within three weeks of its appearance, it had been reprinted by the *New-Jersey Journal*, the *New-Jersey Gazette*, the *Connecticut Courant*, and the *Boston Gazette*. From this time on, Freneau's poems, which had hitherto been confined to the *Freeman's Journal*, were regularly reproduced by other patriotic periodicals. [14]

Particularly successful were the verses in which Freneau ridiculed the alleged attempts of English leaders to reestablish themselves in the favor of Americans. "Lord Dunmore's Petition to the Legislature of Virginia," printed on February 13, was a smashing denunciation of "that silly old fellow, much noted of yore," who, having been driven from Virginia in 1775, was now with the British at Charleston. The former Royal Governor was pictured presenting to his former subjects an humble plea for reinstatement:

> Though a brute and a dunce, like the rest of my clan,
> I can govern as well as most Englishmen can;
>
> .   .   .
>
> Give me lands, whores and dice, and you still may be free;
> Let who will be master, we shan't disagree;
> If King or if Congress—no matter to me.

When news was received of the speech George III had made at the opening of Parliament three months before, the blood of citizens in Philadelphia rose hotly, for the king stubbornly insisted on a continuation of hostilities against his "deluded subjects in America." Had he forgotten Yorktown? Freneau took pains to supplement "His Majesties Most Gracious Speech" with "A Speech That Should Have Been Spoken by the King of the Island of Britain to His Parliament." Doggerel lines exposed the threat of continued warfare as pompous bombast. What of Washington and his valiant army? Did England never know when she was beaten?

American patriotic spirit needed such injections of sanguine confidence during these tedious months, for peace seemed long in coming. Clinton's forces in New York were a constant threat to the Northern states. As long as the British remained in stronghold there, the Continental army was powerless to attack or to disband. Idleness bred discontent, and after the triumph at Yorktown, depression settled again over the country. Though Greene was said to be making progress in the South, English troops still remained at Charleston. Trade was paralyzed. Waiting became tedious and unrest a compelling incentive to national disorganization.

During this whole dreary period the editor of the *Freeman's Journal* remained manfully at his task. On March 27 he printed a poetical prophecy which foretold the end of the war by 1786. On April 3 he devoted the whole first page to a long poem, "The Political Balance," in which he attempted to prove, by argument and ridicule, that Britain's period of supremacy was drawing to a close. On April 24 he presented "A Dialogue at Hyde Park Corner," in which Burgoyne and Cornwallis lamented their defeats in America. Most particularly, however, he kept up a running attack upon James Rivington, the Tory printer in New York, whose *Royal Gazette* had been the principal medium of British propaganda since the beginning of the war. Through February and March appeared in rapid succession the "Epigram Occasioned by the Title of Rivington's Royal Gazette Being Scarcely Legible," the "Lines Occasioned by Mr. Rivington's New Titular Types," and "On Mr. Rivington's New Engraved Kings Arms." Crude and coarse with journalistic propaganda, the lines were edged with an excellent sharp humor. Taking cue from a prose satire on the Tory printer which Francis Hopkinson had written several months before,[15] Freneau published "Rivington's Last Will and Testament." Because he had read in Scripture that "worms on the dead shall deliciously feed," the King's Printer was represented as having decided to leave his carcass to "be made into cakes of a moderate size, to nourish those Tories whose spirits may droop." Bound copies of the *Royal Gazette* were to be sent George III in order that he might rejoice over lying reports of provinces taken and victories won. The fiddles, flutes, and guitars which Rivington advertised in his paper were left to the British officers who, Freneau suggested, had better proved their skill on the stage than on the battlefield. The printer's stock of brandy was to go to General Clinton, to "give him fresh spirits for battle and slaughter." The burlesque was spirited throughout. People liked that sort of thing. Rivington replied to Freneau's taunts only once.[16] There really was little that he could say.

Only seldom did patriot activity in America give Freneau an opportunity to turn from the viciousness of satire to clearer songs of hope or triumph. When in April the merchants of Philadelphia fitted out a privateer under the command of Joshua Barney to protect the ravaged shores of Delaware Bay, he did compose "Barney's Invitation" which, like his earlier "Captain Jones's Invitation," was a plea to all brave men who would seek honor or wealth in the service of their country. Then when the little vessel put to rout the predatory British sloop of war *General Monk,* Freneau's "Song on Captain Barney's Victory" was sung through the streets of Philadelphia.[17] Inspired by the success of the Pennsylvania privateer, Freneau on April 17 wrote in prose over the signature "Pylades" to suggest the necessity of developing a large and organized coastal defense. One week later as "Orestes" he proposed the establishment of a fleet of small, swift craft to protect our shores. But this could not be accomplished, he told his readers, until the common seaman could expect a more humane treatment from his superiors. America, insisted Freneau, must not only achieve great victories; she must prove herself worthy of the admiration of all mankind.

During the spring and early summer he kept up his barrage of ridicule against England and English influence. He scoffed disdainfully when the new Whig party in London withdrew General Clinton from America to make room for Sir Guy Carleton, a more moderate man. In the poem "On Sir Henry Clinton's Recall," Freneau addressed the departing commander:

> Now Carl'ton comes over to give you relief,
> A knight like yourself, and commander in *chief*,
> But the *chief* he will get, you may tell the *dear honey*,
> Will be a black eye, hard knocks, and *no* money.

Ineffectual doggerel? Not quite that, for it was pertinent to the moment. Selected by the new ministry because they hoped his reputation for humanity and kindness would placate the Americans, Carleton proceeded immediately to negotiate for terms of peace. The Congress, however, would have nothing to do with any proposals not made in concert with France. Carleton then addressed himself to the governors of separate states. They, too, turned him down. Then the new commander appealed directly to the people. England, he told them, was an amiable parent, ready to forgive, anxious for reconciliation, and prepared to welcome her wayward children with kindness. Look to your safety, warned Freneau. He printed a versified parody of "Sir Guy Carleton's Address to the Americans." "With a sword in one hand & a branch in another" the new commander pled with the rebels:

> the war is now alter'd, and on a new plan;
> By negociation we'll do what we can—
> And I am an honest, well meaning old man;
>
> .   .   .
>
> Then lay down your arms, dear rebels— O hone!
> Our king is the best man that ever was known,
> And the greatest that ever was stuck on a throne:
> His love and affection by all ranks are sought;
> Here take him, my honies, and each pay a groat—
> Was there ever a monarch more easily bought?
>
> .   .   .
>
> So quickly submit and our mercy implore,
> Be as loyal to George as you once were before,
> Or I'll slaughter you all—and probably more.

War continued to press heavily upon the poet's spirit. France, Spain, Holland, India, America, and England—all the world seemed locked in conflict. Freneau saw little promise of peace or happiness when, over the signature "Philomeides," he wrote "Philosophical Reflections" for the *Freeman's Journal* of July 17:

> Still round the world triumphant discord flies,
> Still angry kings to bloody conflict rise;
> Hosts bright with steel, in dreadful order plac'd,
> And ships contending on the wat'ry waste . . .

No matter what the result of the contest, death smiled alike on victor and vanquished. Passion was aligned against reason, and humanity suffered. Deep at the root of all the fierce disorder of his age Freneau found one horrible canker:

> Curs'd be the day, how bright soe'er it shin'd,
> That first made kings the masters of mankind;
> And curs'd the wretch who first with regal pride
> Their equal rights to equal men deny'd;
> But curs'd over all, who first to slav'ry broke
> Submissive bow'd and own'd a monarch's yoke,
> Their servile souls his arrogance ador'd
> And basely own'd a brother for a lord;
> Hence wrath and blood, and feuds and wars began,
> And man turn'd monster to his fellow man.

Yet even worse than the pride and ambition of kings was the grovelling servility of subjects. This had not been true in that ancient age of innocence and ease when social man had lived in happy simplicity under the benign rule of reason. Murder and fear had been then alike unknown. But now, mistaking power for happiness, ambition ruled mankind. Fierce passions—vanity, revenge, and avarice—tempted to martial folly. Disaster grew on disaster; war bred war. The common man searched vainly through darkness:

> All urg'd alike, one phantom we pursue
> But what has war with HAPPINESS to do?
>
> .   .   .
>
> Thou happiness! still sought but never found,
> We, in a circle, chase thy shadow round . . .

By midsummer it became evident that some terms would be reached in negotiations for peace. The prospect thoroughly alarmed loyalist Americans, who were not happy in the thought of being abandoned to the reprisals of patriot neighbors. Many who had fled to the enemy when American success seemed impossible, now made every overture to be readmitted to the good graces of their countrymen. Even James Rivington became more temperate in the *Royal Gazette*. On July 10 he published an editorial in which he admitted that "his zeal for the good success of his Majesty's arms, his sanguine wishes for the good of his country, and his friendship for individuals" had led him to print accounts which had not always been fully authenticated. He now hastened to assure the public that, if they would overlook his errors of the past, he would be more scrupulous in the future. What arrant nonsense! "From hence it is to be assumed," said Freneau on July 31 when he reprinted Rivington's apology, "that Satan, Rivington & Co. have thoughts of breaking up partnership."

Finally, on August 2 Sir Guy Carleton informed General Washington that England had consented to negotiate for a general peace at Paris. Loyalists of New York became frantic: they had gambled the whole future on British success. Freneau ridiculed them gleefully in "The Refugee's Petition to Sir Guy Carleton" and in "Sir Guy's Answer," both printed on August 14. In reply to their petulant cry, "What have we to expect?" the English commander was represented as offering four suggestions. The Tories might, he said, enlist in the British army, join the British navy, make their own peace with the victors, or—go to the devil.

As a journalist engaged in propaganda, Freneau deliberately turned his back on literary aspiration. He plunged whole-heartedly into the task of sustaining patriotic feeling, and he left poetry behind him. Now, at thirty, he was world-weary and discouraged. Happiness was a dim phantom which was sought in vain. His collegiate assurance of the transience of all things changed to an assurance of the vanity of all worldly desire. He found America transformed from a land of promise to a land desolated by conflict sprung from avarice and ambition. The tinsel stripped away, he found life cold and cruel, dominated by brutal passions. Freneau's realism was born of his pessimism, and we shall find the two nowhere better shown in conjunction than in "A Moral Thought," four quatrains which he had printed in the *Freeman's Journal* on October 24, 1781, just when the Revolution was reaching its climax:

> In youth, gay scenes attract our eyes,
>   And not suspecting their decay
> Life's flow'ry fields before us rise,
>   Regardless of its winter day.
>
> But vain pursuits, and joys as vain,
>   Convince us life is but a dream.
> Death is to wake, to rise again,
>   To that true life you best esteem.
>
> So nightly on some shallow tide,
>   Oft have I seen a splendid show;
> Reflected stars on either side,
>   And glittering moons were seen below.
>
> But when the tide had ebb'd away,
>   The scene fantastic with it fled,
> A bank of mud around me lay,
>   The sea-weed on the river's bed.

The particularized realism in the last stanza, bred of his observation as a sailor, marks Freneau's break with conventionalized literary tradition. But, more important in our understanding of the author as an individual, the intense expression of disillusionment marks his abrogation of the poetic ideals which had fired him in his youth. The scope of his vision had narrowed, but, within the limits which his disillusionment set, he was to see more keenly. The glory of America was now something worth fighting for, to which poetic talent must be subjugated, and in the defense of which caustic verses must be written. Reality broke his dream to a thousand pieces, and Freneau was the rest of his life trying to put them together again.

As the Revolution dragged through its last weary phases, Freneau remained in the deep darkness of despair. During the first year of his connection with the *Freeman's Journal*, he printed only four poems which did not deal with some aspect of the war, and one of these, "On a Lady's Singing Bird," [18] had been written in Bermuda three years before. The others, "A Moral Thought," "Plato the Philosopher to his Friend Theon," [19] and "Stanzas Occasioned by the Ruins of a Country Inn," [20] all sang of the certainty of change and inevitable ruin. Emptiness, vanity, desolation, and despair were all that the poet could find in the gloomy scene that surrounded him. "Joy," he mourned, "has to grief the heart resign'd." It was more than Freneau's country that was despoiled by war. Less tangible than the British bullet he carried in his knee, but more important, was the wound that never healed in the poet's mind:

> Constrain'd to dwell with pain and care;
>   These dregs of life are bought too dear,
> 'Tis better far to die than bear
>   The torments of another year.[21]

3

During this period of intense occupation with events of the American Revolution, Freneau projected a series of informal essays. He observed that, among the periodical publications of America,

there is scarcely one which ever presents the reader with any other essays than such as immediately relate to politics, and the transactions of the times, or local and domestic matters, arising from a variety of circumstances in the constant intercourse of men and business. Morality and refined sentiment are painfully neglected.[22]

To remedy this defect he proposed a collection of sentiments "worth the notice of men of taste." He assumed, therefore, the character of a learned and benevolent traveler who for thirty years had wandered over the world observing men and manners. Attracted by the opportunity for freedom in America, he had taken up residence in a lonely cave not far from Philadelphia. Here he pondered in solitude and worked on his great treatise, *De Anima Mundi*, in which he planned to explain the "great invisible *Soul of the World*, which most incomprehensively animates the various productions of nature." At moments stolen from more serious labors, the traveller promised to submit random jottings, drawn from the fund of his experience, for the entertainment and instruction of the people of

Philadelphia.[23] In such character Freneau contributed nineteen essays, which he called "The Pilgrim," to the *Freeman's Journal* from November 21, 1781, to August 14, 1782. As his verse during this period has exhibited him as a conscientious, vitriolic patriot who followed the events of the war in highly charged lines, so these informal papers present the poet himself, struggling in prose to express what he had no time to work into poetry.

In spite of his promise to eschew political matters, it is not to be expected that the Pilgrim could entirely evade issues of the day. Rather than direct his observations upon any particular event of the war, however, he limited his remarks to the character of the English people. In the course of his travels the Pilgrim observed no nation in the world more conceited or credulous. He found Englishmen proud, ambitious, ungenerous, self-seeking, inhospitable, impolite, intolerant.[24] They were boasters, flatterers, poltroons.[25] There were more gluttons and drunkards among them than among any people he had ever visited. They were faction-ridden, malevolent, contradictory in argument, idolatrous, and cruel.[26] "After a criminal is suspended to a gibbet, no nation but this takes him down when half dead, rips up his bowels, tears out his heart, and throws it reeking with blood into his face!" [27] No crime was now too great to impute to the enemy.

Freneau had effectively wiped from his mind all memory of freedom loving Englishmen. Only six years before it had been his "warmest wish" that "Britannia rule our hearts again." [28] Now hatred burned bitterly in him. No adjective was too lurid with which to describe the British: they were the arch-hypocrites of the world, lovers of discord and enemies of peace. "The people at large are the slaves of the great; are saddled with kings, royal families, lords temporal and spiritual and myriads of their dependants, who subsist wholly upon the labours of the industrious." [29]

Such misapplication of power, whether it was charged to the enemy in England or to the aristocratic junto which Freneau saw rising in the United States, was the theme which he wove through the essays. The Pilgrim was a foe to special privilege and a champion of natural rights, with an "innate love for *republics*." Driven from his boyhood home in Switzerland by the avarice of a wealthy landowner, he had never since then been able to live at ease "in the vicinity of kings, emperors, kingdoms or aristocracies," which to him "were but different names for tyrants and tyranny." His conduct was determined by the ideal of man returned to an original state of innocence. He held the nervous hurry and artificial pomp of cities in abhorrence. Woods and solitudes were more congenial to him, and simple living among the bounties of nature.[30] To Freneau the Pilgrim represented the ideal toward the expression of which he had fumbled in "The American Village," in "The Pictures of Columbus," and in his own febrile escape to an island paradise in the Caribbean. He was man alone, dependent upon none of the artificialities of civilization, man uncorrupted by avarice, pride, or ambition. He was the passive observer whose only desire was to be allowed to live his own life fully and to comment on the raucous strivings and picayune jealousies of his corrupted fellows.

"What simpletons," the Pilgrim said, "are mankind to surrender so many of their natural rights forever." "Nature, the mother of all men, and all things," [31] called for a different solution of human problems. The observation of natural phenomena should convince all rational men that life is fleeting, that the glamorous pretense of the world is ephemeral, that the days of darkness shall be many:

What misery then must these men endure when that thin partition is thrown down, that fine thread broken, that curtain drawn which divides us from the world unseen; when they must depart into those regions of immateriality where so many generations of men have gone before them, and where the disembodied spirit must be wretched indeed, unless in this life inured and habituated to those sentiments of virtue, upon which the soul must in some sense subsist, and which must constitute the ground work of her felicity through everlasting ages. . . . For life is not valuable, unless as a season for that which shall be more permanent.[32]

Life, Freneau said in effect, could only be lived to the full when each individual explored deep within himself to discover what was essential and what was merely the result of the unnecessary complications with which avarice and ambition had corrupted mankind. It was not a new creed. The influence of the Bible and of Freneau's theological studies was probably as strong as any direct effect of the teachings of Locke, Shaftesbury, or Rousseau.

New or not, such was the doctrine which Freneau developed throughout "The Pilgrim" essays. He attacked negro slavery as an institution unworthy of civilized man.[33] He came to the defense of servants who were forced to long hours of labor in order that their masters might enjoy worldly pleasures.[34] He wrote against cruelty to animals, particularly execrating a clergyman for driving his horse to exhaustion in order to further his own professional reputation.[35] He derided the citizens of Philadelphia both because of their inability to appreciate fine drama, and because of their desire to spend time at the theater while their country struggled for existence.[36] He did not always write seriously. Sometimes he passed frivolously over subjects which meant much to him, as when he advised an impecunious bookseller to trade his stock of literature for a few casks of sugar, indigo, hides, tallow, soap or candles, because, he said, Americans were not yet convinced that the mind was as important as the body.[37]

Toward the ladies Freneau exhibited an easy tolerance: with proper masculine indulgence he even condoned their concern with dress by rebuking a citizen who complained that virgins and married women alike should be dissuaded "from the dangerous practice of exposing their naked bosoms to every licentious eye." [38] His tolerance, however, could not be stretched to include the young beaus of Philadelphia. "This hermaphrodite species of mortals" received some of his most bitter comment. Like politicians who lived by large tyrannies, the fops, pretending to greatness, exercised small tyrannies in their overwhelming arrogance.[39] In fact, Freneau inveighed against "all fantastical politeness, ceremony, and insincerity." [40] Lawyers were derided for their insistence upon the letter rather than the spirit of the law.[41] Doctors, he suggested, might soon become so eager for gain that they would pray for plagues and pestilences. Clergymen were called to account for the ostentation of their discourse.[42] To Freneau, as to Chaucer, the happy man was the simple parson who went his way quietly, shepherding his little flock of country parishioners, satisfied with simplicity, and envying no one.[43]

Beneath the gentle raillery, the sympathetic humor, and the often very pointed sarcasm of "The Pilgrim" essays, there is a seriousness, an apparent coherence of purpose which had not been manifest in Freneau's earlier social satire in verse. Brushing aside pretense and false values, he was feeling his way toward some dogma upon which to base his social philosophy. He must have read Rousseau— at least he had read someone who accepted Rousseau's theories of equality. A thinking man could hardly have lived then in America without having read Thomas Paine and having discussed or heard discussed his exposition of natural rights. But, chiefly, Freneau had lived, sensitively aware of the broad social currents of his own time. Ten years' experience, at sea, as a soldier in the militia, thrown among men of all ranks in the prison ship, rubbing shoulders with printers and men of the streets in Philadelphia, had destroyed whatever aristocracy he had acquired at Princeton. The rabble, at which he had scoffed as a student, was drawn to the center of his dream of freedom. He had become the champion of the common man, the simple man of toil who would not be ashamed to take "his great grandsire Adam by the hand, where he was labouring with his spade" and cry, " 'Good morrow, sir!' " [44] Learned ostentation was unworthy of the natural man. Like Wordsworth almost two decades later, Freneau pled for simplicity in language. "Remember," he urged,

it is possible to display an elegance of language, and a true dignity of stile, and solid sentiment . . . which yet, without giving offense, shall be easily comprehended by the lowest vulgar, as well as by the middling class, and be received with real pleasure, and improvement by those of more elevated tastes.[45]

As such a champion, Freneau turned, as Rousseau had turned, to a consideration of education. How foolish were parents of moderate circumstances, he said, who yield to the "weak and ridiculous ambition of having their children educated at unavoidable expence for the learned professions!" On the other hand, "if the children of the rich are alone initiated into the sublimer mysteries of literature, the world would quickly be overrun a second time with monkish ignorance and Gothic barbarity." What to do? Freneau had sincere contempt for the man who owned the title but not the content of education:

It is observed that youths born to great riches are upon that account generally idle and averse to study; and for the most part turn out, after many years at schools and universities to little purpose, mere town and country gentlemen, or in other words, very great blockheads, whose education no one would suppose to have been superior to that of their coachmen, were it not that they have a collegiate diploma ready in their pockets, and a library in an open thoroughfare, called their Study, to convince the visitor of a mistake he would otherwise be in danger of falling into.

Education does this sort of man no good, said Freneau. Nor can it insure success for men of any rank. Why, then, so much emphasis on education? The poet, perhaps, looked back with suspicion on his own adventures in learning, when he wrote:

An advancement in the world merely from merit is so precarious, that it is cruel for a father to drive his son through the thorns and briars of a collegiate course, upon so uncertain a prospect.—If a lad possesses real genius, it will blaze out at one time or another, notwithstanding the want of what is called a learned education; if he is not blessed with that choicest gift of nature, science will only render him vain, impertinent, and a monster of self conceit.

"It is astonishing," said the Pilgrim, "how little the world is indebted to the schools and colleges for the several useful inventions that have benefited mankind." On the other hand, consider the "illiterate man of invention." He is a Columbus who boldly "launches out into the immense ocean of ideas, and brings to light new worlds." Compared to him the scholar is a "timorous and cautious pilot, who creeping along shores already discovered, by the help of his lead and line, makes shift, in a bungling manner, to get from port to port." True wealth and true happiness, the Pilgrim continued, can only be realized through simple living, far from thronged city ways:

If any man be said to possess an independent fortune, it is he whose industry draws immediately from the earth the necessary supports of life. . . . Who would exchange the situation of the simple husbandman, enjoying the fruits of his labours by his winter fire side, or under the shade of his summer's retreat, for that of the idle scheming citizen, who sits perpetually behind his counter, like a spider in his web, watching his commodities, and sedulously observing the steps of every passenger, hoping he may come in to purchase: since upon this casual visit depends his existence from day to day.[46]

The perpetual hurry of business allowed city men no time to develop the "self knowledge which it ought to be their constant study and greatest ambition to acquire." [47] The natural attendants of a rural life, on the other hand, were health, cheerfulness, and a contented mind. "If there remain on this earth any traces or resemblances of the first paradise," said Freneau, "they exist among the forests, mountains, and vallies of this western world." So it was the common man, the Columbus of invention, who would lead America onward. Freneau drew word pictures of regions beyond the Western frontier, where trees of the forest were stately and tall, where meadows and pastures were spacious, and where rivers no longer bent their courses eastward toward the Atlantic. "Nature does nothing in vain," he insisted. America, with her lakes and streams, her fertile plains and boundless forests, was her gift to reasoning man.[48] Not to the man softened by the corruption of urban life or the ephemeral reaching of education, but to the honest man of toil was the opportunity and the glory.

But war still clouded Freneau's vision. He called it the "savage profession of war which has constantly vitiated the morals of mankind, misled their understandings." Yet war seemed inevitable "till the interests of all nations are the same, and till all men are drawn to one way of thinking." Would the time ever come? Freneau thought not. His experience prompted him to confess that

discord and disorder are interwoven with the nature and constitution of the human race, and I am well convinced that we may as reasonably expect to see an ocean unruffled by tempests, or the sky perpetually clear of the iron glooms that so often infest it, or to find individuals without private quarrels, jealousies and bickerings, as the world delivered from rapine, dissention, tyranny, discord, violence and bloodshed.[49]

But, oh, the irrationality of war:

O reason, where art thou fled!—one man is compelled to drive another violently into eternity, that he himself may subsist a little longer, and nations to extirpate nations that the survivers may enjoy a little peace; is not the earth spacious enough for all? but so it is that madness gets the better of reason and folly of wisdom. What multitudes were a year ago full of life and vigour, and had flattering prospects before them of many joyous seasons to come, who are now sleeping with the dust of their ancestors;

perishing in hopeless captivity on some foreign shore; or floating pale and bloodless in the bosom of the ocean! [50]

While war raged through America, striking heavily on every side, there was no time for a poet to follow the beckoning of his vision.

Instead, Freneau turned often to prose. On July 10 he assumed the character of Christopher Clodhopper, a simple rustic who complained of the "ridiculous gewgaws" on which Philadelphians squandered money. He suggested a tax on fripperies like high-heeled shoes, outlandish bonnets, tye-wigs, gilt buttons, and all the other such "jiggumbobs" which made Americans preposterous. Even country people were becoming infected with the fantastic notions of the town. Christopher's own son sprinkled his hair with powder, wore ruffles from the end of his sleeve down to his fingertips, circled his neck with a stock large enough to be a winding sheet, and, like the coxcombs of the city, dangled a long sword at his heels. "The silly fellow," said his father, "had put more on his back than would pay our taxes for a year."

On July 17 Freneau replied to the complaint as Priscilla Tripstreet, a Philadelphia belle. To her, Christopher was simply a wretch, too niggardly to supply his own family with even the littlest luxuries. How would the poor of the country live, she asked, if it were not for the generous spending of the rich? Tax hats, indeed! Would America enrich herself at the expense of women's heads? Rather tax inconsequential things like watches or umbrellas. Better yet, turn all the male tailors and clerks to more manly occupation. Let the needle be sacred to the female world. Let girls be trained to cipher and transcribe. Thus thousands of able-bodied men would be free to serve their country in more useful occupations. Christopher Clodhopper, ruffled at the vehemence of Priscilla's reply, offered a short rejoinder in the issue of July 24. The exchange was inconsequential—except that it indicates that Freneau was turning now from national affairs and philosophical generalities to the practical problems which disturbed Revolutionary Pennsylvania.

On August 7 he published a letter which pretended to be from one Jacob Whissel, a farmer from New Castle, who complained in broad country dialect that the state did not afford efficient protection to the countryman from predatory Tory bands. On August 14 Freneau printed, again in prose, "A Short Catechism for Those Whom it May Suit," in which Titus Taxgrumbler, a citizen who spent more in a week at taverns than he did for taxes in a year, was exposed as a miscreant unwilling to shoulder the responsibilities incumbent upon him as a member of an independent state.

4

In the meantime, political struggles in Pennsylvania were becoming increasingly violent. Judge George Bryan, leader of the radical party, struggled to defend the State constitution of 1776 against attacks of conservatives who demanded a more vigorous and responsible government. Their insistence upon the establishment of what Bryan considered an undemocratic upper chamber of the legislature, seemed to him seriously tinctured with a proprietary or, at least, an aristocratic social and political philosophy. The unicameral Pennsylvania Assembly, controlled by the Constitutionalists since its establishment, had the power not only to make laws, but also to appoint executive and judicial officers. As a result, the party in power, unhampered by any system of checks and balances, had been able to build a powerful political organization.

Now, as the disturbances of the war years submitted to the comparative calm which resulted from the cessation of active hostilities, intelligent public sentiment shifted to the conservative party, which was identified with the group supporting the Bank of Pennsylvania and the Bank of North America, both recently founded through the efforts of Robert Morris and the commercial community of Philadelphia. Many prominent citizens who had formerly been active in the national crisis now turned their attention to state politics. If commercial interests were to be protected and credit established, the present constitution must be withdrawn. The issue became one between visionaries, supported by those politicians who saw their best interests bound with the popular appeal of the democratic doctrines of Bryan's Constitutionalist party, and the mercantile and propertied classes who, with more practical sagacity, demanded assurance of economic and political stability.[51] In such a controversy, in which the rights of the common man seemed threatened by restrictions imposed by a powerful and wealthy minority, there was only one side for Freneau to choose. By word and conviction he was committed to the radical party.

By the end of 1781 the turn of the political tide in Pennsylvania became evident. Though General Joseph Reed, who had been chief executive of the commonwealth since 1778, relinquished his office to William Moore, a much more moderate man, the present system of government began to seem incompetent to friend and foe alike. John Dickinson, steady, sane, and universally respected, was recalled from retirement to campaign as the conservative candidate for president of the Supreme Executive Council. Radicals and doctrinaires, under the leadership of Bryan and Reed, rallied valiantly to defend their party against accusations of graft and corruption. As the election of November, 1782, approached and a frank discussion of public affairs deteriorated into an even franker discussion of public personalities, the *Freeman's Journal* was drawn to the midst of acrimonious political controversy.

Although Francis Bailey boasted a free press in which political issues would be dispassionately reviewed, his newspaper, since its inception, had openly championed the Constitutionalist party. Neither the *Pennsylvania Packet* nor the *Pennsylvania Gazette*, which attempted to maintain a judicious attitude in defense of the Dickinsonian group, were any match for the slander and abuse with which contributors to the *Freeman's Journal* attacked them. Freneau and his fellow writers were capable of invectives to which the more sedate journals would not stoop to reply.

Once, however, Francis Hopkinson, Judge of the Court of Admiralty and a member of the Supreme Court of Pennsylvania, who had neither agreed with nor admired the methods of Bailey's paper, showed his disapproval by publishing in the *Pennsylvania Packet* on April 2, 1782, a parody of the witch scene in the fourth act of *Macbeth* which he called "The Rise of the *Freeman's Journal*." Three scribblers met in a garret to prepare the "infernal ink," "fraught with Mischief, Discord, Care," with which Bailey's newspaper was printed. Devoid of all honor and manly pride, they planned to sow seeds of dissension by publishing libels against a public character renowned for wisdom, prudence, and truth. Stirring their inky brew, they sang:

> His deeds to infamy we'll turn all
> And murder in the FREEMAN'S JOURNAL,
> Where malice sets her venomed tooth,
> Virtue's made vice and falsehood truth.

The unsavory ingredients used to prepare the ink were cataloged as the scribblers crouched about their steaming kettle:

> SLIME, discharg'd from maw of snake,
> Mantled on putrescent lake;
> Gangreen, yellow, venom fraught;
> Rankling spleen and gloomy thought
> Engendering.

During this same month the *Freeman's Journal* found itself confronted with a new opponent who was to take its measure more effectively. Colonel Eleazer Oswald, a vitriolic gentleman who admitted none as his superior in hurling epithets, established the *Independent Gazetteer* in Philadelphia on April 13, 1782. The colonel, an Englishman by birth, had served under Arnold at Quebec and had been commended for bravery at the battle of Monmouth. In 1779 he had become associated in the management of the *Maryland Journal*, but had so incurred the enmity of the Whigs of Baltimore by publishing an article in which General Charles Lee attacked Washington, that he had been forced to move his press to Philadelphia. He was a man of great courage in the discharge of what he thought his duty. By October he had been arrested for libel and had challenged Francis Bailey to a duel which might have had serious consequences had not the latter evaded it by an over-meticulous observance of the formalities of rendering and accepting such an invitation.[52] Oswald was ready and willing to match insult for insult with the *Freeman's Journal*, and by the end of the summer had drawn Freneau into a quarrel which recognized few rules of decency or restraint.

Oswald centered his attack upon General Reed who, though only a little more than forty years old, was probably the most influential member of the Constitutionalist party. A man of unquestioned ability who had served his country and his state in military and civil capacities, Reed, though no longer in office, was a constant threat to his political opponents. They proceeded, therefore, mercilessly to tear down his reputation. On August 24 Oswald printed verses from a correspondent who signed himself "A Foe to Tyrants." The lines were addressed to a "most infamous Tyrant—and to a noted Speculator when high in office." After quoting lines from Churchill's "Epistle to William Hogarth," the writer accused "Pale Joe" (General Reed) and his associates of malfeasance in office, and charged that the former President had retired on money pilfered from the state. In contrast, "Honest Jack" (John Dickinson) was represented as a man ready to right every public wrong. It was the first shot fired in a scurrilous battle.

Four days later, in the *Freeman's Journal* for August 28, Freneau answered the accusation as "A Foe to Malice." When the howling tempest, he said, raves about a barque tossed upon a thousand waves, the lubber landsmen weep, lurking in the hold, fearing every moment will be their last. They rely on the pilot to carry them safe through the storm; but when the storm is over, up they come, at once grown brave, to tell the pilot that he has done no more than they themselves could do. The implication was obvious: Reed had guided the ship of state through the storm of war years; now, the tumult over, the people he had safely piloted turned against him. How scurrilous the accusation made by Oswald's scribbler: it demanded a reply. Thus, in spite of the fact that "A Foe to Tyrants" had been careful to supply quotation marks to his lines from Churchill, Freneau accused him of having stolen "wreathes to shade his barren scull" and suggested that, if he could do no better than borrow rhymes, it would be safer to sneak back into prose, for

> REED'S patriot fame to distant years shall last
> When these base reptiles to the dogs are cast.

"A Foe to Tyrants" lost no time in answering Freneau's attack. "Mr. Oswald," he wrote in the *Independent Gazetteer* on August 31, "Please to give the following lines, addressed to the Foe to Malice a place in your useful Paper: in Order to convince this great Poet (who never borrowed a line in his Life) how easy it is to take his battery, and turn it against himself." Using Freneau's figure of a vessel in a storm, he accused the pilot of having been found incapable of duty and driven from the helm by free-born landsmen who refused further to rely on him. Then, turning, as Freneau had turned, from the general issue, he attacked "A Foe to Malice" directly:

> What wondrous fancy urg'd thy genius bright,
> To speak of Churchill,—as if thou coud'st write;
> To shine in *borrow'd plumes,* with base design,
> And to oblivion worthy men consign.
> Reptiles and Dogs, and all those dreary things,
> Bespeak the mind from whence such slander springs:
> Dirt thou may'st throw—the dunce's last retreat,
> For none but dunces will thy lines repeat.
> Not Churchill's wreathes, but hick'ry withes will do,
> To twine thy brows, and lace thy jacket too.

Freneau made a tactical blunder by descending to personalities. He laid himself open to attack. Now, he was hit in a vulnerable spot. The original issue of the quarrel was forgotten. Wounded where it hurt him most, in his literary vanity, his poetry exposed to the jeers of every man, Freneau gathered together all his power of invective. We may be sorry that he did it; but he did do it well. In the *Freeman's Journal* for September 4 he wrote "To the Foe to Tyrants":

> Vile as they are, this lukewarm tory crew
> Seem viler still, when they are prais'd by you.
> By you adorn'd, in *yellow* robes they shine,
> Sweat through your verse, and stink in every line.
>
> .   .   .
>
> Scribbler retire—what madness would it be
> To point a cannon at a mite like thee!
> Such noxious vermin crawling from the shell,
> By squibs and crackers might be kill'd as well.
>   But if you must torment the world with rhimes,
> (Perhaps thou were sent to scourge us for our crimes)
> In stupid odes indulge your smoky wit
> Dull lyrics would your happy genius fit;
> With your coarse white wash daub some scoundrel's face,
> Blockheads in power, or traitors in disgrace,
> To gain immortal praise I leave you free,

> Go scratch and scribble unchastis'd by me.
> Haste to the realms of nonsense and despair,
> The ghosts of murder'd rhimes shall meet you there;
> Like rattling chains provoke incessant fears,
> And with eternal jinglings stun your ears.

If, however, Freneau had intended to have the last word in the exchange, he reckoned without his opponent. "A Foe to Tyrants" was capable of following up his advantage and meeting blow with blow. On September 7 "To the Foe to Malice. The Farewell" appeared in the *Independent Gazetteer:*

> When men will prostitute the power of rhime,
> Their dirt and malice jingling out of time;
> When men the sacred shrine of truth forsake,
> And deal in slander just for slander's sake;
> 'Tis time to quit plain reason, common sense,
> And in their stile Correction to dispense.

> Our Theme first pointed to your *pale-fac'd* friend
> Whom you forsook—unable to defend;
> To save his fame, you thought it best to fly
> To vile abuse, and low scurrility;
> Then feel the Weapons you yourself have us'd,
> And blame not those you've dirtily abus'd.

Freneau was then subjected to a personal attack so vile that even he "blush'd for the wretch that could such filth display." Or, at least, that is what he said when four days later he answered the attack with "To the Foe to Tyrants on his Farewell." "Such an odour," he protested,

> scented from your song,
> I stopt my nose, and quickly pass'd along

Abuse, then, was to be the only reward for service in the cause of the common man? Freneau seemed to forget that his had been the first blow. Now again, as he had seven years before in "MacSwiggen," he vowed to escape from an atmosphere of bickering and slander. "Bear me, ye gods," he said,

> to some sequester'd place,
> Where never rascal shew'd his brazen face;

Remove me far from all the rascal kind
(Dullness with insolence forever join'd)
To some retreat of solitude and rest—
Nor let another pang disturb my breast,
When I have wept to think the world shall know
I had to combat with so mean a foe.[53]

After his "Farewell" on September 7, "A Foe to Tyrants" was silent for more than a month. But the political quarrel in Pennsylvania continued to rage with unrestrained virulence. "Calumny and slander," reported Francis Hopkinson, "were carried to a greater extent than was ever known, perhaps, in a civilized city." [54] "A Foe to Dirty Fellows," in the *Freeman's Journal* for August 28, accused John Dickinson of having attempted to persuade a battalion of the militia to declare against the independence of their country. The *Gazetteer* retaliated on September 7 by charging General Reed with having entertained pro-British sympathies during the early days of the Revolution. Back and forth the charges went. There seemed no stint to anonymous defamation. Even the finest minds of the state entered the controversy: Bryan and Chief Justice John McKean contributed to the *Freeman's Journal;* the conservatives were aided by such eminent men as Dr. Benjamin Rush and Judge Hopkinson.[55] Liberty, charged the *Pennsylvania Packet,* was openly extended to licentiousness.[56] "The road to honor in Pennsylvania," write a correspondent in the *Gazetteer,* "is to be abused by the Freeman's Journal." [57] "It is a disgrace to us," said the *Pennsylvania Gazette,* "to have such a paper printed in this City. It is called a sink of scandal, and it has lately got the name of Bailey's Chamber Pot." [58]

Though Freneau was probably still editor of the paper at this time, he was apparently not taken very seriously as a political force by his contemporaries. In listing the members of the "Skunk scented association," by which unsavory appellation writers for the *Freeman's Journal* were known to their opponents, the *Pennsylvania Gazette* named George Bryan; Jonathan Dickinson Sergeant, an active Constitutionalist lawyer and former Attorney-General of Pennsylvania; William Calijon, at one time secretary to General Gates; George Osborne, an Irish lawyer who rose to some prominence in Philadelphia before he was forced to flee the country to escape charges of bigamy; and last, mentioned contemptuously, "one Freneau, a poet." [59] Arthur Lee is elsewhere spoken of as "Peter Paragraphist for the Freeman's Journal, and principal scribe to the Skunk Confederation." [60]

In fact, Freneau seems to have been counted only an intelligent hack, bound to the service of a party. To his opponents he was "little Fr-n-u, Poetaster to the Skunk-scented association, and successful imitator of Sternhold and Hopkins." Thus were stanzas "in humble imitation of his own doggerel" addressed to him in the *Independent Gazetteer* on October 15:

> Fr-n-u, great man! 'tis thee I sing,
> And to thy shrine just incense bring
>   The attribute of praise;
> To thee, who scorn'd all common rules,
> Supreme of dunces, chief of fools,
>   I dedicate my lays.
>
>   .   .   .
>
> Thy verse, but ah! my powers are vain,
> To tell the wonders of thy brain,
>   Where mists of dulness sit;
> *Cimmerian* darkness round thy head
> It's sable mantle long hath spread,
>   To veil thy *wooden* wit.
>
> Thy satire, mystic type of *lead*,
> Keen as a dart *without a head*,
>   And vigorous as *age;*
> 'Twould almost make a *mill-stone* cry
> To have thy muse its enemy,
>   When cloathed in her *rage.*
>
>   .   .   .
>
> Thy eyes, the index of thy soul,
> With mad, poetic fancy roll,
>   In eager search of fame;
> Thy face, ye god! ah! what a face!
> Thy air, thy port, thy quaint grimace,
>   Add honor to thy name.

To one who had not followed the quarrel very carefully, the verses must have seemed mysterious, because Freneau had certainly not published in the *Freeman's Journal* any "doggerel" in this stanzaic form. Of what could it be in imitation? Of Freneau's manner in epithet, certainly. He was represented as the favorite son of the Queen of Dullness, praised only by the wretches who contributed to Bailey's newspaper. This time, however, Freneau refused to answer. For two months he went quietly about his routine work as a journalist.

During all this later controversy, Freneau's occasional prose contributions to the *Freeman's Journal* avoided local politics. Over the signature "Hawser Trunnion" he suggested that the national government seek out "new and transmarine countries in the distant part of the globe," to which the Tories, the "scum, the off-scouring, the refuse and the eternal scandal of America," might be transported. As "Harpax" he printed "A Short Account of the Bermuda or Summer Islands, and Some Hints of Reducing them to the Obedience of the United States," and his melancholy "Midnight Soliloquy in the Market House of Philadelphia" was signed "W. H." Though attacks in the *Freeman's Journal* did not cease when John Dickinson was elected chief executive of the commonwealth in November, Freneau had little to add to the partisan warfare. Instead, as "Catholicus" he wrote about the publication of the Bible in Philadelphia. "With what pleasure," he said, "will each patriotic mind reflect on this event. . . . The very paper was manufactured in Pennsylvania, the whole work is therefore purely American." A month later he contributed a short prose burlesque of a sacerdotal military commander who so disturbed his troops concerning their assurance of salvation that, rather than risk death and damnation, they fled the field in terror. At the same time he again turned his attention in verse to the Tory printer in New York whom he had attacked earlier in the year. "Rivington's Reflexions" simply restates what Freneau had said before: the King's Printer looked with alarm and terrified dismay at the failures of the English army; like all frightened Tories, he was ready to make any sacrifice to be received again into the good graces of his American countrymen.[61]

The Revolution was virtually over, and Freneau saw a group ascending to power who seemed worthy of no public trust. Men who had stood on the sidelines to watch which way the victory would turn now threw their wealth and their influence to the support of measures which threatened the rights of free men. War profiteers, their sense of importance as swollen as their purses, controlled the national coffers. Natural rights, menaced on all sides, were again in danger of being surrendered, this time to a selfish aristocracy. On December 11 Freneau published "The Prophecy of King Tammany," in which the Indian chief, driven westward by colonial adventurers, foretold a time when other tyrants would come to ravage the lands which the white man had taken from the Indian. The colonists, he said, would repulse the attack, but

> When half your foes are homeward fled,
> And hosts on hosts in triumph led,
> And hundreds maim'd and thousands dead,
> A timid race will then succeed,
> Shall slight the virtues of a former race,
> That brought your tyrant to disgrace,
> Shall give your honours to an odious train
> Who shunn'd all conflicts on the main,
> And dar'd no battles on the bloody plain,
> Whose little souls sunk in the gloomy day
> When VIRTUE ONLY could support the fray.

So America seemed now. There were few among those in power who held to the principles of liberty for which Freneau believed the Revolution had been fought. Sordid quarrels and even more sordid scrambling for political spoils dominated the national capital. There was little for a poet to admire, little for him to defend except the ideals which he believed lay at the root of all successful living. And no one seemed to care for such ideals.

In spite of disillusionment, Freneau continued as a workaday journalist. On December 11 he offered an essay, signed "R.," against what he considered the barbarous practice of encumbering cities with burial places. Surely, he suggested, America was large enough to make it unnecessary to place reminders of mortality where men must see them every day! In the same issue he printed over the pseudonym "Plus Ultra," an article in answer to an anonymous attack against the *Freeman's Journal* which had appeared simultaneously in the *Pennsylvania Gazette* and the *Pennsylvania Journal* on December 4, and in the *Independent Gazetteer* on December 7.

"Some ass in a squire's skin," said Freneau, had attempted to stigmatize the writers for the *Freeman's Journal* by inventing scurrilous names for them. Nothing, he insisted, sooner betrayed a vulgar man than such a practice. The mind which invented such a "low-lived simile" as "Bailey's Chamber-pot" must have spent a large part of his life scouring the "necessary utensil." "The Freeman's Journal," he said, "does not pretend to immaculate purity." But, surely, what of its enemies?

Finally, on December 18, Freneau replied to the attack which had been made upon him in the *Gazetteer* almost two months before. In lines to which he did not even bother to supply a title, he washed his hands of the whole dirty controversy:

> Shall Oswald's scribblers call you all that's base,
> Abuse your stature and blaspheme your face,
> Make you the worst and vilest of your kind,
> With not a spark of reason in your mind,
> Who would to Oswald's rancorous page reply,
> So fam'd for scandal, and so prone to lie?
>   Still may those bagpipes of sedition play,
> For fools must prate, and dogs must have their day;
> Still from that page let hoarse mouth'd whelps defame,
> And madness rave and malice take her aim,
> May scribes on scribes in verse and prose combine,
> And one dark chaos glow, through every line!
> Long may they write unquestion'd and unhurt,
> And all their rage discharge, and all their dirt:
> Night owls must screech by heaven's severe decree,
> And wolves must howl, or wolves they would not be.
>   From empty froth these scribbling insects rose;
> What honest man but counts them for his foes?
> When they are lash'd, may dunce with dunce condole,
> And bellow nonsense for the tortur'd soul!
> When they are dead, and in some dungeon cramm'd,
> (For die they will, and all their works be damn'd)
> When they shall belch their last departing groans,
> May dogs and doctors canonize their bones,
> And the last horrors of their souls to calm,
> Fallon, the priest, console them with a psalm!

It was Freneau's farewell to the political squabbles of Philadelphia. On December 22 the *Independent Gazetteer* printed two paro-

dies in which each accusation was turned against the "Skunk-Associ-
ation" or its "poetaster." Freneau, however, refused to be goaded
further to reply. By the end of the year he had apparently given up
any official connection with the *Freeman's Journal*.

5

Sometime before November 8, 1782, Freneau found employment
which made it possible for him to retire from the unsavory political
quarrel into which he had been drawn; for on that date he was able
to sign himself "Philip Freneau, Clerk, Postmaster General of the
United States." [62] His contributions to the *Freeman's Journal,* which
had been voluminous since August, 1781, were printed less frequently after September, 1782. In October he apparently contributed nothing in verse or prose. In November and December his
essays and poems appeared again, but irregularly. From this evidence, it may be assumed that he was first employed in the Post
Office sometime during the autumn. His subsequent contributions to
Francis Bailey's newspaper were written after his day's work was
over.

He was apparently known in Philadelphia as a versifier who
could be counted on to turn out rhyme at will. During the first week
of 1783 he supplied three sets of New Year's verses, to be distributed
as broadsides by the news carriers of that city. The first, dated January 1, was addressed to the "Gentlemen who have been pleased to
favour Francis Wrigley . . . with their custom"; the second, January 4, to the "Customers of the Pennsylvania Evening Post"; and
the third, January 8, to the "Customers of the Freeman's Journal."
Each reviewed the incidents of the past year and humbly expressed
the carrier's wish that he might serve his customers in the year to
come.

Freneau also continued to submit an occasional manuscript to
the *Freeman's Journal.* Early in January as "Heraclitus" he blandly
discussed the relation between barbers and Sabbath observance. The
satire was obvious and goodnatured, but the fops of Philadelphia
came rather badly off. At the same time he turned to the consideration of another Tory rogue, a second New York printer, in "Hugh

Gaine's Life." There was no good humor in Freneau as he again viciously attacked the policy of moderation toward loyalists which he saw springing up among his countrymen. The time is approaching, he warned, when the "false hearted tory" shall "rise to take hold of the helm of affairs," while the "honest poor soldier," the patriot, the common man of America, "like a dog in the dirt shall be crushed and held down." A month later, however, when he printed "Stanzas Occasioned by the Departure of the British from Charleston," Freneau's ominous prophecy was stilled for a moment beneath a glad cry of triumph. The fight for independence was clearly drawing to a close. Only New York now remained in British hands. Everyone suspected that in a short time she, too, would be free. Meanwhile, one could only wait, help as he could, and hope for the best.

Ebenezer Hazard, the Postmaster General, was proud of the talented young man who was employed in his department. On February 12 he wrote to the Rev. Jeremy Belknap of New Hampshire, "I send you the 'Prison Ship.' The author of it is now a clerk in my office. He has wrote several other things, such as the Voyage to Boston, Rivington's Reflections, Hugh Gaine's Life, &c." Freneau's forthright denunciations did not, however, appeal to the New England clergyman. "He has a good practical genius," Belknap admitted, "and there are some curious strokes in his Life of Gaine; but there is one thing which, perhaps, it would be a kindness to mention to him. I think he plays rather too freely with Scripture in some of his allusions and comparisons." [63]

This criticism probably indicates fairly accurately the reputation which Freneau now enjoyed. He did have a "good practical genius," was a facile wielder of rhyme, and verses came easily to him; but conservative readers must often have been shocked by the vindictiveness with which he pursued his victims. Freneau's appeal was to the masses whose passions were easily stirred. Men like Francis Hopkinson, an established writer and known for his culture and refinement, were said to have looked upon him as a young scape-grace.[64]

It was among men like Peter Markoe and plump Robert Bell that he found most congenial companions. Markoe, who divided his time among law, poetry, and conviviality, was like Freneau of Huguenot descent, and the two young men had many interests in common.[65]

Together they must often have attended the auctions which Bell, the "Provedere to Sentimentalists in America," held almost every week at his bookshop. It was as good as a play, because Bell kept everyone in an uproar by drinking humorous toasts from a giant mug which he habitually kept at his side, and there was scarcely a literary character in Europe or America of whom he could not tell some pertinent anecdote.[66] Books were Robert Bell's life, and he was known through Philadelphia for his encouragement of young talent.

At one of these sales in February Freneau spent six shillings sixpence for a two-volume edition of Guillaume Derham's *Théologie physique ou démonstration* and the same author's *Astro théological* in one volume.[67] The poet was apparently able to read French almost as easily as English. He translated "for the satisfaction of the curious" a long article which he called "Sketches of Republics" when it appeared, in two installments, in the *Freeman's Journal* on March 12 and 29. On April 29 he contributed "Strictures on the Poem Paradise Lost," which he had translated from the *Mercure de France* of January, 1779.[68]

But there seemed little opportunity in Philadelphia for a young man to establish himself securely in a literary career. Poetry aside, there were printers and booksellers enough—perhaps too many. The same situation prevailed in almost every city along the Atlantic seaboard, except possibly at Charleston, and one scarcely knew what to expect there, because the city had been demoralized by two years of British occupation. Late in December, 1782, Peter Freneau, now twenty-five and already experienced in commerce, set sail for South Carolina. "I believe," he wrote soon after his arrival, "I shall shortly get into some advantageous position here." Meanwhile he investigated prospects for his brother. "I think," he advised, "there is a fine opening for a Printer." Only lack of equipment seemed to stand in the way. "As soon as I got here," he wrote to Philip, "I made a diligent search for types, and soon learned there was none for sale." Nonetheless, he promised, "I will make further inquiry about them and give you what information I can collect in my next." [69] Within three months, however, four weekly newspapers sprang up in Charleston. Competition there was as keen as anywhere else. It seemed wisest to remain a clerk in the Post Office Department.

When a transcript of the speech which George III had delivered at the opening of Parliament on December 5 reached Philadelphia, Freneau seized upon it avidly. It was better even than he had dared hope. The monarch who attempted to subject free men now made public admission of failure as he offered to allow his former colonies in America to become free and independent states. Freneau delighted in the opportunity thus given him. In prose, over the pseudonym "Lucullus," he contributed "A Few Reflections on Reading the King's Most Gracious Speech to his Parliament" to the *Freeman's Journal* for March 5. Warning Americans always to remember the perfidy, the cruelty, and the insane lust for blood and power which had animated the British ruler, Freneau cautioned against an easy acceptance of terms. America must stand her ground. Addressing the king directly, Freneau charged:

O Pharaoh! how is it possible that you can hope or expect what you so much flatter yourself with, *i. e.* an entire cordial reconciliation and intercourse with America; when, after being so long called upon, by the good and wisest part of your nation, to let the people go, and your hard heart would not consent to it, continuing maliciously to spill their blood, and to deluge their land with the blood of its inhabitants. O Nero! the blood of thousands calls aloud for vengeance on your guilty head. Repent! repent! and humble yourself in the dust, murderer, if you wish to obtain mercy; and make all restitution in your power whilst you continue to exist.

In the next issue, on March 12, Freneau considered the same speech in verse. Less sternly, more gleefully he taunted:

> Grown sick of war and war's alarms
> Good GEORGE has changed his note at last—
> Conquest and Death have lost their charms;
>   He and his nation stand aghast
> To see what horrid lengths they've gone,
> And what the brink they stand upon.

News that a general treaty between England and France had been signed on January 20 reached Philadelphia early in April. Thousands of Tories, realizing now that the end had come and that little mercy would be shown them by the countrymen they had deserted, embarked at New York for Nova Scotia or the Bahamas. To Freneau this was as it should be. In "A New York Tory's Epistle to One of

his Friends in Philadelphia—Written Previous to his Departure for
Nova Scotia," which appeared over the signature "Tantalus" in
the *Freeman's Journal* for May 7, he both mocked the departing
loyalists and attacked those who, with "double face," dared attempt to insinuate themselves again into the ranks of their countrymen.

During the summer of 1783 Freneau contributed nothing to the
Freeman's Journal: now that the war was virtually over, he could
afford to engage in new literary endeavors, just as patriotic, just as
useful, but perhaps a little more dignified. The year before, Abbé
Claude Robin, military chaplain to the Count de Rochambeau's
troops, had published in Paris the *Voyage dans l'Amérique septen-
trionale*. The author had accompanied the French army on its
marches through the Northern and Middle states just previous to the
battle of Yorktown. He described the military campaigns of the war,
noted the peculiar natural phenomena of the western continent, and
commented on the inhabitants. Robert Bell, a "truly philanthropic
book-seller," [70] announced on July 30 the publication of Robin's
New Travels through North-America. Freneau had translated the
work faithfully: "Some pains have been taken," he said in introduction, "to retain . . . the style and philosophical manner of the
French original." To be sure, many of the Abbé's ideas on religion
and politics were at variance with those popularly held in America.
"Yet," Freneau suggested,

there is certainly more satisfaction in discovering what opinion a foreigner
entertains of us, although only from a casual acquaintance . . . than in
reading the best accounts and narratives of our own, which, in such matters,
may be suspected of being too ready to humour our local prejudice, or flatter
our vanity.

The *New Travels*, though reprinted in Boston in 1784, was apparently not a popular book.[71] Ebenezer Hazard found it a "paltry
performance." "There is a genuine French vivacity in the style,"
he wrote to Belknap, "but the man has miserably mistaken his
facts." [72] Freneau did what he could to correct Robin's misstate-
ments by supplying footnotes to the most flagrant. For example,
he explained:

The author seems not to have known, that there are two sorts of maple in America, very nearly alike in external appearance, but of different properties. That here taken notice of is called the Sugar Maple, and grown in great quantities in the northern and western parts of New York and Pennsylvania.[73]

Sometimes he supplied explanatory notes—on the migration of the Acadians from Nova Scotia, or an eyewitness's account of the overbearing insolence of the English on submitting to surrender at Yorktown. But to Freneau the work achieved essential validity because it displayed the natural beauty of America and the natural simplicity of her inhabitants. The *New Travels,* he said, would not appeal to those who "saunter over half the Globe to copy the inscription on an antique column, to measure the altitude of a pyramid, or describe the ornaments on the Grand Seignior's State Turban." None but admirers of simple nature could travel through America with pleasure themselves or read the travels of another with profit. The French chaplain won his way to republican hearts by treating even the Indians, not "as mere beasts of burden, calculated solely for the grandeur, wealth and omnipotence of Great Britain," but as "men and Free-Men." [74]

Meanwhile the war ended very slowly. New York remained in the hands of the British all through the summer. Though Sir Guy Carleton received orders in June for immediate evacuation, he was delayed for months by the necessity of providing for the loyalist Americans whom he felt obliged to protect against reprisals threatened by the victors. On September 5 the *Freeman's Journal* announced that the "most authentic accounts agree that between 12 and 1500 refugees are to be deported at New York . . . for Nova Scotia." In spite of Carleton's orders that property was not to be molested, the departing Tories are said to have destroyed everything which they were forced to leave behind. "New York from all appearances will be left bare," the *Freeman's Journal* warned, "the refugees showing a disposition to carry off not only their effects, but the very buildings of the city to their new settlements in the north." [75] Freneau, on September 12, published a long and mournful poem dedicated to "New York." All of America was free, except his native city. There, because of the depredations of departing loyalists, were only to be found

> dirt and mud, and mouldering walls,
> Burnt domes, dead dogs, and funerals.

Finally, however, Carleton prepared to leave New York. As the last British transport departed from the harbor on December 2, General Washington and Governor George Clinton made public entry into the city. That evening there was a display of fireworks such as never had been seen in the country before. Two days later, after a ceremonious farewell address to his officers, Washington started for Annapolis to present himself to the Congress and resign the commission which he had held for eight years. As he approached the outskirts of Philadelphia, he was met by John Dickinson at the head of a committee of state officials who escorted the commander into the city to the accompaniment of artillery salutes and the joyful ringing of church bells.[76] Citizens lined the streets, and Philadelphia rang with cheer after cheer as the triumphal procession passed. Freneau's "Verses Occasioned by General Washington's Arrival in this City on his Way to his Seat in Virginia" in the *Freeman's Journal* on December 8 echoed the popular sentiment:

> The great unequal conflict past,
> The Britain banish'd from our shore,
> Peace, heaven descended, comes at last,
> And hostile nations rage no more;
> > From field of death the weary swain
> > Returning, seeks his native plain.
>
> In every vale she smiles serene,
> Freedom's bright stars more radiant rise,
> New charms she adds to every scene,
> Her brighter sun illumes our skies;
> Remotest realms admiring stand,
> And hail the HERO of our land.

Washington, grown immortal by his deeds, "despising pomp and vain parade," was a second Cincinnatus who, "not less in wisdom than in war," would continue to bestow his counsel upon the new nation he had rescued from tyranny.

Deserted by the British, those Tories who were forced to remain in New York now made new overtures to the patriots. Among them was James Rivington, who did everything that he could to reestablish himself. On December 31 Freneau contributed to the *Freeman's Journal* the first part of "Rivington's Confession Addressed to the Whigs of New York"; one week later the second part appeared. It was the poet's last satirical poem of the Revolution, and though more carefully composed, it was merely an amplification of attacks which he had often made before. Rivington petitioned the patriots:

> Even swine you permit to subsist in the street;—
> You pity a dog that lies down to be beat—
> Then forget what is past—for the year's at a close—
> And men of my age have some need of repose.

During the early part of 1784 Freneau continued to be a literary jack-of-all-trades. He translated Boulanger's "L'Origine de Despotisme" for the *Freeman's Journal* of January 9. He is said to have written the "prophecies" for *Bailey's Pocket Almanac*,[77] and his "Verses on General Washington's Arrival" were reprinted in that publication as "Verses on General Washington's Retirement." He wrote New Year's verses for the carriers of the *Freeman's Journal* and the *Pennsylvania Gazette*. Shaking the weariness of conflict from him, he composed a hymn of thanksgiving which he called "The Happy Prospect":[78]

> No more the vales, no more the plains an iron harvest yield;
> Peace guards our doors, impells our swains to till the grateful field:
> From distant climes, no longer foes (their years of misery past)
> Nations arrive, to find repose in these domains at last.

Now as Freneau settled down to the promise of quiet in free America, his old inclination to dwell on the certainty of death reexpressed itself. "The Dying Indian; or the Last Words of Shalum," appeared in the *Freeman's Journal* on March 17. In it a warrior, mortally stricken, reviewed evidences of immortality. For him life after death was only a shadowy reproduction of the pleasures which he had enjoyed among the lakes and mountains of his youth. As he bade a plaintive farewell to earthly joy, he resigned himself to the forbidding darkness of endless sleep. Life, which Freneau had dismissed as a dream in "A Moral Thought" two years before, reasserted itself. Death, rather than an awakening to "that true life you best esteem," became in "The Dying Indian" again the eternal mystery and the center about which Freneau's most serious poetry was to revolve. As the Revolution ended, the poet prepared to return once more to his vision of literary glory.

On Monday, May 10, 1784, the sheriff of Philadelphia, attended by officers of the city and state, made public proclamation that a definitive treaty of peace had been concluded between England and America. Again the bells of Christ Church pealed triumphantly. The state flag was ceremoniously hoisted over the Market Street wharf. After a day of celebrating, thousands of citizens crowded that evening about the exhibition of transparent paintings which the patriotic artist Charles Wilson Peale designed for the occasion. A triumphal arch over thirty feet high was gayly festooned with flowers. Fireworks again lighted the city streets throughout the night.

The American Revolution was over, and with "Lines Intended for Mr. Peale's Exhibitions," in the *Freeman's Journal* of May 19, Freneau offered his benediction:

> Born to protect and guard our native land,
> Victorious virtue! still preserve us free;
> Plenty—gay child of peace, thy horn expand,
> And, Concord, teach us to agree!
> May every virtue that adorns the soul
> Be here advanc'd to heights unknown before;
> Pacific ages in succession roll,
>   'Till Nature blots the scene,
>   Chaos resumes her reign
> And heaven with pleasure views its works no more.

SIX

CAPTAIN FRENEAU

1784–1790

FRENEAU left Philadelphia soon after peace was publicly declared. On June 24, 1784, he sailed from Middletown Point as supercargo of the brig *Dromelly*, bound for Jamaica.[1] For five weeks the voyage was slow and uneventful, until on July 30 a hurricane, more severe than any which had struck the West Indies for forty years, drove the brig perilously among the reefs and shoals just below Kingston. "Such a conflict of elements I never saw before," reported an observer. "The clouds rolled along in thick and murky volumes . . . branches of trees were darted through the air; and loud and frequent was the noise of falling buildings." [2] Only eight of one hundred and fifty vessels in the harbor survived, and when the battered *Dromelly* limped into port the next morning, she was found damaged beyond repair.[3]

Death had been very close as the brig skirted the coral reefs of Jamaica. Mountains of water broke on every side as she pitched defenseless before the fury of the storm. The experience was new and terrifying to Freneau. In "Verses, Made at Sea, in a Heavy Gale" he wrote:

> Happy the man who, safe on shore,
> Now trims, at home, his evening fire;
> Unmov'd, he hears the tempests roar,
> That on the tufted groves expire;
> Alas! on us they doubly fall,
> Our feeble barque must bear them all.
>
> Now to their haunts, the birds retreat,
> The squirrel seeks his hollow tree,
> Wolves in their shaded caverns meet,
> All, all are blest but wretched me . . .

129

Nature had no compassion for man in his helplessness. Nothing assuaged her all-consuming wrath:

> Thus, skill and science both must fall,
> And ruin is the lot of all.[4]

While he waited for eight weeks in desolated Kingston for passage back to America, Freneau sank deeper and deeper into the morass of melancholy which had engulfed him during the war years. Across the bay stood the ruins of old Port Royal. "Of all the towns that grac'd Jamaica's isle," Freneau wrote, "this was her glory." As a result of an earthquake two centuries before, there now remained only a sandy spit of land supporting a few poor houses, an ill-kept church, and an ancient fort. Sagging roofs, mouldering walls, and courtyards overgrown with weeds were dismal reminders of former splendor. The awful hand of time had descended once more upon the creations of man. Fourteen years earlier Freneau had developed such a theme in "The Pyramids of Egypt." Now in "Lines Written at the Pallisades, near Port Royal," [5] he rebelled against the hold which the concept of death and decay had upon him:

> Where shall I go, what *Lethe* shall I find,
> To drive these dark ideas from my mind!

"Talk not of blossoms and your endless spring," [6] Freneau wrote, for in his present mood the tropics held no glamor for him. Beneath the lush exterior which had made the West Indies seem a terrestrial paradise eight years before, he now found only corruption and avarice. British inhumanity had never been more plainly evidenced than when the officer in charge of the Royal Reservoir refused to give the shipwrecked Americans even one puncheon of fresh water. Freneau punished him with a scorching pasquinade "To the Keeper of the King's Water Works." [7] Cruelty ruled the islands. No torments of Hell could be worse than the treatment meted to slaves on the Jamaica sugar plantations—and all for the greedy ambition of their masters! "What have they done," Freneau asked in "The Island Field Negro," "to merit such a fate!" [8] Was not the suffering black man a symbol of the oppressed among mankind everywhere?

These then were the "joys that flow from vaste domains." [9] Freneau engaged passage on the brig *Mars* which sailed from Kingston on September 23.[10] Somewhere he might find—perhaps in America after all—a land where man, secure in freedom and firm in allegiance to natural rights, might build his life on rational and benevolent principles.

Returning to Philadelphia on November 4,[11] Freneau again applied himself seriously to writing. But the temper of his verse was changed. He had tried traditional poetry, and his volume had been "damned by all good and judicious judges." He had delivered blast after blast against the enemies of his country, only to be subjected to violent personal abuse by the party which rose to power when the English were routed. Now his verse became more lightly caustic, even flippant, as he allowed his talent to grow as the small breath of popular approval bent it.

"Humanity and Ingratitude," printed on December 8 over the signature "K.," is a translation of the old French story of a fisherman who in rescuing a neighbor from drowning accidentally puts out the latter's eye. Demanding remuneration for his loss, the neighbor takes the matter to court, where a wise judge decrees that the plaintiff be thrown back into the sea: then, if he manages without aid to save himself, the defendant will be severely punished; if, however, the plaintiff perishes, his former rescuer will be handsomely rewarded for having saved him the first time. The thankless neighbor, of course, leaves the court in confusion. The analogy was clear; General Reed and his associates, brought to trial in the contemporary press, deserved similar exoneration. But simply as a tale well told, "Humanity and Ingratitude" could not have failed to appeal to the least poetic of readers. An easy colloquialism replaces the obvious literary diction of Freneau's earlier and more serious poems. The verse is fluent, the rhyme ingenious.

Freneau was writing for his audience. The "Sketches of American History," the first installment of which appeared on December 15 over the signature "K.," is a travesty on his former poems in praise

of the western continent. Instead of celebrating the bucolic life of
the aborigines in traditional phrases as he had done in *A Poem on
the Rising Glory of America*, he now drew a more obviously realistic
picture in rollicking anapests:

> In a mere state of nature, untutor'd, untaught,
> They did as they pleas'd, and they spoke as they thought—
>
>   •   •   •
>
> The toils of the summer did winter repay,
> While snug in their cabins they snor'd it away.
>
> If death came among them his dues to demand,
> They still had some prospects of comfort at hand—
> The dead man they sent to the regions of bliss,
> With his bottle and dog, and his fair maids to kiss.

The "Sketches," however, won an immediate popularity. In less
than a month they were reprinted in the *New-York Packet,* the New
Brunswick *Political Intelligencer,* and the Charleston *Columbian
Herald.*[12] A second part appeared in the *Freeman's Journal* on
December 29. As a modern young man of the world, Freneau said
of the inhabitants of early New England:

> Ah, pity the wretches that liv'd in those *days,*
> (Ye modern admirers of novels and plays)
> When nothing was suffer'd but musty dull rules,
> And nonsense from *Mather,* and stuff from the schools!
>
> No story, like Rachel's could tempt them to sigh,
> Susanna and Judith employ'd the bright eye—
> No fine spun adventures tormented the breast,
> Like our modern Clarissa, Tom Jones, and the rest.

A practical poet now, and anxious to be read, Freneau found his
subjects dictated by the interests of his public. Philadelphia in 1784
amused itself with experiments in aeronautics. What the Mont-
golfier brothers and Jean de Rosier had accomplished in France
could surely be accomplished as well in America. As a consequence,
paper balloons were released almost daily "to the great astonish-
ment of the Populace." [13] "The name of Congress," wrote Francis
Hopkinson, "is almost forgotten—& for every person that will men-

tion that respectable body, a hundred will talk of the Air Balloon." [14] A public subscription was solicited to finance an "elegant
Air Balloon, capable of raising great weights, of carrying up men
and other living animals into the regions of the atmosphere, and
returning them with safety to the earth." [15] Even the possibility of
air communication and the use of balloons in military manoeuvres
attracted attention. Thomas Jefferson wrote to Hopkinson:

This discovery seems to threaten the prostration of fortified works unless
they can be closed from above, the destruction of fleets and what not. The
French may now run their laces, wines, &c to England duty free. Inland
countries may become *maritime* states unless you chuse to call them *aerial*
ones as their commerce is in the future to be carried on through that element.[16]

When, therefore, Freneau (again using the signature "K.") contributed "The Progress of Balloons" to the *Freeman's Journal* for
December 22, he was only following popular speculation in suggesting that

> The man who at Boston sets out with the sun,
> If the wind should be fair, may be with us at one,
> At Gunpowder Ferry drink whiskey at three,
> At six be at Edentown, ready for tea.
>
> . . .
>
> Yet more for its fitness for commerce I'm struck;
> What loads of tobacco shall fly from Kentuck,
> What packs of best beaver—bar-iron and pig,
> What budgets of leather from Conococheaque!
> If Britain should ever disturb us again,
> (As they threaten to do in the next George's reign)
> No doubt they will play us a set of new tunes,
> And pepper us well from their fighting balloons.

People seemed to like facile verses of this sort—at least, no one
could ridicule them or the poet who made them. And sometimes
perhaps a needy young man who rhymed easily might turn his
talents to cash. Freneau wrote the New Year's verses which the
carriers of the *Freeman's Journal* presented to their customers on
January 1, 1785, and contributed two poems to Bailey's annual
Pocket Almanac. "The Seasons Moralized" was a conventional

analogy between the passage of time through spring to winter and the life of man through youth to old age, tagged with a familiar gloomy reminder that, though the seasons replenish themselves, "youth returns to man no more." In the "Stanzas on the Emigration to America, and Peopling of the Western Country," however, he once more looked optimistically toward lands beyond the Alleghenies for the source of a new spirit. There, where nature's works outdid the boldest pattern art could frame, brave settlers might establish states where reason would be triumphant over discord, and freedom reign supreme.

But Freneau was not well, and what employment he could find in Philadelphia was of necessity temporary. On January 15 Patrick Rice, who was later to become a bookseller of some importance in the city, wrote to his fellow printer, young Mathew Carey, "Mr. Freneau is gone home sick, & I have no one to assist me." Because Rice asked that Carey lend him the services of the latter's apprentice, we assume that it was in some very practical capacity, as compositor or pressman, that the poet now attempted to earn his living.[17]

Handicapped by illness during the next two months, Freneau contributed only infrequently to the *Freeman's Journal*. For the issue of January 19 he submitted "The Literary Plunderers," which told of the depredations made by mice on the contents of a bookseller's library: with excellent good taste the rodents gnawed most persistently upon Freneau's favorite books—Homer, Horace, Shakespeare ("the only genius I adore"), Montesquieu, Milton and Swift. Why could they not, he complained, have limited their ravage to books by "brainless authors" who "in snivelling rhimes . . . at folly's door submissive wait"? Then it was four weeks before the now familiar "K." appeared again on February 16 appended to "Elegiac Verses on the Death of a Favorite Dog." The icy dangers of a Philadelphia street in winter were described on February 25 in "Pewter Platter Alley." Finally, on March 9 were presented verses to the memory of General Joseph Reed, who had died four days before. Then, leaving his manuscripts for Bailey to use as he saw fit, Freneau set out for Pacolet Springs in South Carolina "for the recovery of his health."[18]

His poems appeared occasionally in the *Freeman's Journal* during the spring and early summer of 1785, but none shows any evidence of having been written at the time of publication. "The Four Ages," printed on March 23, simply discusses the possibility of a fifth age of paper. "To the Great—the War-like—the United—the Independent Americans," published on March 30 is just the sort of doggerel satire which Freneau had written freely more than a year previously. The "Verses Made at Sea, in a Heavy Gale," on April 13, had been written in Jamaica nine months before. On May 18 appeared the "Epitaph Intended for the Tombstone of Patrick Bay," a collegiate production, and "The Deserted Farm House," which had first been printed in *The American Village* volume. "The Monument of Phaon," on May 25, had been composed during the poet's junior year at Princeton.

Freneau never tells us what the ailment was that took him to the mineral springs of Pacolet. Situated near Spartanburg in the northern part of South Carolina, the waters were highly esteemed during the eighteenth century for their curative powers. Especially efficacious in "alleviating all feverish complaints," they were also said to be "remarkably serviceable in most inflammatory cases, the hot scurvy, and in all tendencies to consumption from inflamed lungs." [19] All we know of Freneau's case is that while at Pacolet he wrote a poem called "The Invalid," which describes a sickly blade who filled himself with grog to forget his misery rather than with health-restoring draughts of water.[20] The young blade could not have been Freneau, but the robust sly humor of the characterization indicates that the poet was becoming quite himself again.

Late in the summer Freneau visited Charleston, where his brother Peter was now counted a substantial member of the mercantile community. On September 14 stanzas "To the Author of Some Late Extraordinary Poetical Pieces" appeared in that city over the signature "K." in the *Columbian Herald:*

> Say, mighty Bard, what songs of praise,
> To thee shall every poet raise—
>   Chief of the sevenfold scull:
> Thy lays are sharp as any wedge,
> So razors cut without an edge,
>   Or hatchets when they're dull.

'Tis sung great poet at thy birth,
Thy mother *Dulness*, rose from earth
    By love parental led:
And clad in all somnific state,
She o'er thy thick unmeaning pate,
    Her sacred opium shed.

Hence at thy verse, so much like prose,
With ev'ry line, we nod, we doze;
    At length we fall asleep.
Tho' common sense by thee is shun'd,
Hail genius of the vast profound!
    Hail master of the deep!

Such an attack so precipitously disturbing the calm of newspaper correspondence in Charleston must have been confusing to
readers of the *Columbian Herald*. Who had contributed "poetical
pieces" in any way "extraordinary" to any newspaper in the city,
except perhaps the popular young physician, Joseph Brown Ladd?
As "Arouet" he wrote patriotic verses in the heroic couplet, translated from the Bible and from Homer, paraphrased Ossian, and
wrote lugubrious stanzas under the influence of Goethe's Werther.
His verse was derivative, sentimental, and extremely well received;
but there was no harm in Dr. Ladd or in anything he wrote. Indeed,
he admired Freneau and celebrated him among the chief of American poets:

Hark! FRENEAU's voice attunes the solemn air,
He sings to freedom, and he sings of war;
With noble warmth shows man created free,
"When GOD, from chaos, gave this world to be." [21]

What the readers of the *Columbian Herald* could not have known
was that the verses by "K." were in exactly the same stanzaic form
as those which had been addressed to "little Fr-n-u" in the Philadelphia *Independent Gazetteer* just three years before. We have the
advantage of remembering that the earlier attack was said to have
been written in "humble imitation of *his own doggerel*" and of
knowing that up to that time Freneau had published nothing in the
particular form which the writer in the *Independent Gazetteer* purported to imitate. Therefore, perhaps we may conclude that the

stanzas which Freneau now published in Charleston were written
in 1782, and circulated in manuscript as part of the former newspaper quarrel of Philadelphia. We remember that Freneau had
then been abused as a child of Dullness and an imitator of Sternhold
and Hopkins; so now he offered a similar accusation:

> Thus shall thy name be aye renown'd,
> And thou and Sternhold still be found,
> Two blocks forever dull.

When Freneau's satire appeared in the *Columbian Herald*, the
editor of that paper promised that a reply would be shortly forthcoming; and on September 21 either someone came to the defense
of Freneau's supposed present victim or Freneau himself contributed verses which had formerly been directed against him during the political squabble in Philadelphia. With his tongue very
evidently in his cheek, the editor introduced this rejoinder by saying:

We flatter ourselves, our correspondent K, on considering the delicate keen-
ess of the satire, the sublimity of the sentiment, and the beauty and harmony
of the versification, of his antagonist's reply, will decline the continuance
of a contest, for which he must confess himself totally inadequate.

Then in shoddy couplets which struggled to keep their measure,
appeared an attack upon "K." by a versifier who signed himself
"Satiricus":

> Thou mighty Bard! forger of songs of praise!
> Who late borrowed—strove thy fame to raise;
> Arm'd with a wedge, hatchet, and razer dull,
> Tools I found scented from thy tainted scull;
> Which happily rent thy hull enough
> To ease thy upper story of its *green stuff:*
> Flimsey infected of each fell disease,
> Infernal destroyer of mirth and peace! . . .

These were accusations conspicuously like those which the *Independent Gazetteer* had formerly heaped upon Freneau. He was
reproached, as he had been before, as a calumniator inspired by
malice. The charge of plagiarism which Freneau had first made
against "A Foe to Tyrants" in 1782 and which was then thrown

back against him, here made its appearance again. In the earlier
stanzas to "little Fr-n-u" the poet had been accused of such dullness that "e'en L-e" would yield first place to him; in the attack
now printed in the *Columbian Herald* he was accused of association
with "great L—," undoubtedly Arthur Lee whom we remember
described as the "principal scribe to the Skunk Confederation." [22]
Though the verses by "Satiricus" may have been a spontaneous rejoinder written by some Charlestonian in answer to the attack which
Freneau made upon the "author of some late extraordinary poetical
pieces" in the *Columbian Herald,* it bears a suspicious resemblance
to the satires which had been directed against "A Foe to Malice"
in the Philadelphia newspaper war: it is characterized by the same
heavy-handed use of epithets, and it took Freneau's own words and
turned them back against him.

In spite of the editor's suggestion that the exchange of insults be
terminated, an answer "To Satiricus" appeared on September 30
in the next issue of the *Columbian Herald:*

> Nonsense precipitate, like running lead;
> That split thro' cracks, and zigzags of the head.
> Saw—see—saw
> See—saw—see.
> *Farewell K.*

Freneau was apparently determined to have the last word in the
quarrel which had harassed him in Philadelphia—even if he had to
go to another state to do it. After his derisive farewell it was four
years before he entered again into controversial matters. Of his
poetry he said, "Most of those who attended to it, would not allow
my verses to be good. I gave credit to what I deemed the popular
opinion, and made a safe retreat in due time, to the solitary wastes
of Neptune." [23] Thereafter for a long time it was as Captain Freneau, a crusty and singularly perspicacious tar, that he was known
to his contemporaries.

2

On November 24, 1785, he sailed from Middletown Point, master of the sloop *Monmouth,* a staunch vessel of forty tons newly

built for the coastal trade.²⁴ As he rounded Sandy Hook southward, the captain closed his mind to the cacophonous squabbles of
the Middle States and looked to new poetic opportunities:

> From Hudson's cold congealing streams
> As winter comes, I take my way
> Where other suns prompt other dreams
> And shades less willing to decay,
> Beget new raptures of the heart,
> Bid spleen's dejective crew depart,
> And wake the sprightly lay.²⁵

Two weeks later, the sloop arrived at Charleston, where she was
advertised on December 9 "for freight to any part of the State of
Georgia, or Charter to any free port in the West Indies." Terms
would be arranged by Philip Freneau, master on board the vessel,
or by Peter Freneau, at his office at 102 Church Street.²⁶ Six weeks
passed before a cargo was acquired; but meanwhile, the poet was
not inactive. He wrote the New Year's verses for 1786, "addressed
to the Customers of the Columbian Herald, by the Printers Lads
who carry it," and as "K." contributed occasional verses to the
same newspaper.

"The Poetaster," published on January 12, was an angry valedictory to literary pursuits. What opportunity was there for poetry
in America, where the writer struggled in sordid competition with
the man of trade?

> The wight that keeps a tippling inn,
> The red-nosed boy that deals out gin,
> If aided by some paltry skill
> May both be statesmen, if they will.
>
> The man that mends a beggar's shoes,
> The quack that heals your negro's bruise,
> The wretch that turns the cutler's stone—
> Have wages they can call their own.
>
> The head that plods in trade's domains
> Gets something to reward its pains—
> But *wit*, that does the world beguile,
> With pain attracts an empty smile.

Criticism was represented by men like Robert Morris, "great *Robert* of mercantile skill," who had gratuitously informed the Pennsylvania Assembly that "America has produced nothing like a poet" and, said Freneau, who had publicly stated that

> all the sing-song of our clime
> Is only nonsense—tagg'd with rhyme.

Yet what did it matter? Whether he rhymed to please those in power or whether he rhymed for bread and cheese, one common lot awaited the man of letters:

> To all that write, and all that read,
> Death shall with hasty step succeed;—
> Even *Shakespeare's* scenes of mirth and tears
> Shall sink beneath this flood of years.
>
> *Ned Spenser's* doom, shall *Pope*, be thine!
> The music of each moving line
> Shall bribe an age or two to stay,
> Admire thy strain, and flit away.
>
> The people of old *Chaucer's* times
> Were once in rapture with his rhymes;
> But time that over verse prevails
> To other ears tells other tales.

What did America appreciate? Instead of rising steadfastly toward greatness in pursuit of the ideals which had inspired her during the Revolution, she was settling back to an easy reliance upon the methods and institutions of England. Would America ever be free? asked Freneau in "Literary Importation" on January 19:

> Can we ever be thought to have learning or grace,
> Unless it be sent from that damnable place?

Lip service was paid in America to ideals for which Freneau was proud to devote his talent. But it seemed now only lip service. Hardly anyone acted as if he believed what he said. Browsing through his copy of *The Works of J. J. Rousseau*, Freneau came upon lines which made many of his own seem a paraphrase:

> Shame on the fierce and haughty soul,
> Whose odious insolence of place,

Whose damn'd ambition, would controul
And keep in chains the human race . . .

How well it was said here; how well many among his contemporaries had said the same thing! Yet verses such as these were
merely "sentiments," tellingly expressed, easily parrotted, "Sentiments," Freneau thought bitterly, "in the mouth of every one but
in the heart of very few." [27]

At least he might retire from quarreling and find some quiet
solace at sea. On January 21 the sloop *Monmouth* cleared for Sunbury, Georgia; two weeks later, on February 6, she returned to
Charleston.[28] During her absence the "Lines Written at the Pallisades, near Port Royal" appeared on February 2 in the *Columbian
Herald*. Then while the vessel remained in port at Charleston
through the next month, "The Prisoner," on February 16, "The
Newsmonger," on February 20, and "The Lost Adventure," on
March 6, all were printed over the signature "K." Freneau described the jaunty irresponsibility of an American debtor who, snug
in jail, watched care-worn men hurry by in pursuit of gain; he
related the troubles of a newspaperman busy with types and shears;
he told the story of an old mariner happy on a tropical island—held
by the spell of the sea, though his days of usefulness were over. The
Monmouth, which had for several weeks been advertised ready to
sail, finally left Charleston on March 7. Arriving at New York
sixteen days later,[29] she proceeded to Middletown Point, where she
remained at anchor until June.

Meanwhile in Philadelphia Francis Bailey was preparing for
publication the manuscripts which Freneau had left in his care. By
May 16 a correspondent to the *Charleston Morning Post* prema-
turely included the "collection of poems, just published at Philadelphia, written by the ingenious Mr. Philip Freneau," among the
original American literary productions which "must excite pleasing emotions in every philanthropic breast." It was not, however,
until June 7 that Bailey in the *Freeman's Journal* formally announced *The Poems of Philip Freneau, Written Chiefly during the
Late War*, "just published and to be sold" at his bookstore at
Yorick's Head on Market Street at one dollar the volume.

"The true poetic flights of imagination—the ease, the wit, the elegance of expression, which mark the writings of our author, are such," promised the publisher, "as cannot fail to give pleasure to the sentimental reader." Nevertheless, lest the public be misled, Bailey admitted in the "Advertisement" with which he prefaced the book:

A considerable number of the performances contained in this volume, as many will recollect, have appeared at different times in Newspapers, (particularly the Freeman's Journal) and other periodical publications in the different states of America, during the late war, and since; and from the avidity and pleasure with which they generally appear to have been read by persons of the best taste, the Printer now the more readily gives them to the world in their present form, (without troubling the reader with any affected apologies for their supposed or real imperfections) in hopes they will afford a high degree of satisfaction to the lovers of poetical wit, and elegance of expression.

This first collected edition of Freneau's works contains much of his most spirited and spontaneous writing. The poems are arranged approximately in the order of their composition, beginning with the collegiate "History of the Prophet Jonah" and ending with the verse contributed to the *Freeman's Journal* during the spring of 1785. *A Poem on the Rising Glory of America* and the satires of 1775 were made consistent with the more patriotic temper of his later Revolutionary poems; "The House of Night" and "The Beauties of Santa Cruz" were both presented in much enlarged versions; *American Independence* (now called "America Independent") and *The British Prison-Ship* were reprinted with only minor changes; and except for an occasional variation in title, the verse from the *Freeman's Journal* appeared as it had first been printed. Of one hundred and eleven poems included in the volume, all but twenty survive in some previously published form; and many of these twenty, such as "MacSwiggen," "Stanzas on the New American Frigate Alliance," "Captain Jones's Invitation," "Truth Anticipated," and "The Sailor's Invitation" had undoubtedly been circulated in manuscript or run off as broadsides or ballad sheets long since lost.

In spite of Freneau's poor opinion of the literary taste of his contemporaries, the collection was reasonably popular. Bailey advertised it regularly in the *Freeman's Journal* until the first of the next year. Beginning on July 26, Robert Hodge listed it as the first item in his regular book notice in the New York *Daily Advertiser*. Soon booksellers in Charleston were announcing it among their literary wares.[30] The records of James Muir, a Philadelphia bookbinder, show that five hundred and thirteen copies were bound in his shop from June 7, 1786, to April 27, 1787. During June one hundred and three volumes were delivered to the printer: twenty-one on the 7th, thirty-one on the 9th, nine on the 24th, and forty-two on the 27th. In July two lots were finished: twenty-two volumes on the 3rd, and fifty on the 10th. During August sales were more vigorous, and Muir billed Bailey for one hundred and thirty-seven volumes. Thereafter the demand fell off. Orders of fifty volumes each were listed on November 22, December 5, January 30, and April 27. The binder himself seems to have appreciated the book, for he accepted twelve copies in partial payment of the sum Bailey owed him.[31]

But Freneau himself did not think very highly of the collection of 1786. It was published, he said, "in a strange way, while I was wandering over the gloomy seas." [32] On June 3, just four days before the volume was announced, he sailed again from Middletown Point with the sloop *Monmouth*.[33] He was many days at sea before lines "To Mr. Philip Freneau, on his Volume of Excellent Poems," appeared on June 14 in the *Pennsylvania Herald*. Though fulsome and heavily turned, the praise was at least more than Freneau had ever publicly received before:

> Your name to bright honor, the spirits shall lift,
> That glow'd in the bosoms of Boileau & Swift.
>   And when you are number'd, alas! with the dead,
> Your works by true wits will always be read,
> Who, pointing the finger, shall pensively shew
> The lines that were written, alas! by Freneau.

Alas, indeed! Freneau had turned his back upon poetry. It was an ephemeral thing, like a flower that soon must wither and die. When the sloop *Monmouth* entered the port of Charleston on June 28,[34] the *Azalea Viscosa*, known as the White, the Wild, or the Swamp Honeysuckle, was already in bloom in the moist sandy regions along the seacoast and river banks of South Carolina. Beauty among the swamplands, yet doomed like everything else to extinction. All man's striving was vain, the flower was doomed, but the foreboding of that doom made poetry:

> Fair flower, that doth so comely grow,
> Hid in this dreary dark retreat,
> Untouch'd thy honey'd blossoms blow,
> Unseen thy little branches meet;
>   No roving foot shall find thee here,
>   No busy hand provoke a tear.
>
> By Nature's self in white array'd,
> She bade thee shun the vulgar eye,
> And planted here the guardian shade,
> And sent soft waters murmuring by—
>   Thus quietly thy summer goes,
>   Thy life reclining to repose,
>
> Smit with these charms that must decay,
> I grieve to see thy future doom—
> (They died—nor were those flowers less gay,
> The flowers that did in Eden bloom)
>   Unpitying frosts, and autumn's power,
>   Shall leave no vestige of this flower!
>
> From morning suns and evening dews
> At first thy little being came—
> If nothing once—you nothing lose,
> For when you die you are the same—
>   The space between is but an hour,
>   The empty image of a flower.

These stanzas, printed as "The Wild Honey Suckle" in the *Columbian Herald* of July 6 over the signature "K.," placed Freneau, beyond the reach of calumny or special pleading, chronologically at the head of America's procession of poets. Written during the same year that the Kilmarnock edition of Burns's poems appeared, some years before Blake's *Songs of Innocence*, and antedating the *Lyrical Ballads* by twelve years, they live to testify that in America a poet did leave the pathway cut wide by Pope and his imitators to sing in the spirit of the renaissance of wonder. Yet "The Wild Honey

Suckle" was seldom reprinted, except in Freneau's own collected editions, during the poet's lifetime. It was copied within a month of its first publication by the *Pennsylvania Packet* and the *Freeman's Journal*, and four years later it appeared in the *Massachusetts Centinel*, but does not seem to have been reprinted again until 1814, when it is found in the *New-York Weekly Museum*. Even astutely critical Joseph Dennie, who in 1807 published a list of those poems by Freneau worthy of preservation in a selected edition, omitted "The Wild Honey Suckle." [35]

"The Drunken Soldier," which Freneau contributed to the *Columbian Herald* on July 10, was more popular. The coarse doggerel in which a besotted veteran and his harridan of a wife carried on their domestic quarrels was reprinted in newspapers from Savannah to Hartford. Equally trivial and almost as well received by Freneau's contemporaries when it appeared on July 13 was "The Roguish Shoemaker," a parody of Watts's "Indian Philosopher." Was it burlesque, then, that America wanted? Very well, Freneau could give her burlesque.

Meanwhile, however, he had to earn a living. The sloop *Monmouth* was advertised for five days in the Charleston newspapers before she left on July 11 for the North. She entered at New York eight days later,[36] but thereafter nothing more is heard of her. In October a letter for Captain Freneau went unclaimed for weeks at the New York Post Office.[37]

3

In spite of all his protestations, Freneau could not keep away from the small literary opportunities of Philadelphia. On October 4 he contributed verses "On the Honourable Emanuel Swedenborg's Universal Theology" to the *Freeman's Journal*, which newspaper had been advertising a proposed edition of the mystic philosopher's works for almost a month. Freneau's verse could readily be turned to the advantage of Bailey's book trade. The lines "On the Legislature of Great Britain Prohibiting the Sale, in London, of Doctor David Ramsay's History of the Revolutionary War in South-Carolina," printed on October 11, were also apparently an attempt to encourage the sale of a volume in the publication of which the printer had an interest.[38]

But Freneau had projects of his own to advance. The rancor which had been growing within him as a result of his failure to find sympathetic encouragement broke into expression in untitled stanzas printed also in the *Freeman's Journal* on October 11. Disappointed at the lack of response to his 1786 volume, he found refuge in ridicule against his critics, ridicule which became querulous when Freneau asked:

> Was all my work a barren waste—
> Was not one bright idea sown,
> And not one image of my own?

Of course there was merit in the *Poems*. Swollen with Horatian scorn for all little men who traduced his verse, Freneau exclaimed:

> Give me a cane of mighty length,
> A staff proportion'd to my strength,
>
> .   .   .
>
> Arm'd with a staff of such a size
> Who would not smite this man of lies;
> Here, scribbler, help me! seize that pen
> With which he blasts all rhyming men:
> His goose quill must not with him go
> To persecute the bards below.

The reception of his first collected volume, however, was satisfactory enough to encourage Freneau to plan a second. On October 18, 1786, the *Freeman's Journal* proposed "printing by subscription an Additional Collection of Entertaining Original Performances in prose and verse by Philip Freneau, author of a volume of poems lately published by the printer of this newspaper." "Such persons as are disposed to encourage American authors, (particularly at a time when we are surfeited with state publications retailed to us from British presses) and are not unwilling to be known as promotors of polite literature & the fine arts, in these republican States," were invited to lend their assistance to the undertaking. A volume of more than four hundred pages was promised, printed on a good paper in a clear type, and priced at one dollar. It was to be issued when five hundred subscribers were secured. Printers, book-sellers, and stationers in all parts of the country were invited to solicit subscriptions from their customers. The advertisement ran bravely in the *Freeman's Journal* for more than three months, until the end of January, 1787.

Meanwhile Freneau continued to assist Bailey. To the printer's *Pocket Almanac* for 1787 he contributed verses subjoined to a prose account of the West Indies, again contrasting the cruel tyranny of man with the beauties of nature in the tropics. When the verses were reprinted in the *Freeman's Journal* of January 31, they were said to be "wrote by Mr. Freneau," but when his less consequential "Stanzas on a Young Lady in a Consumption" were contributed to the same newspaper on February 7, they were identified only with the ominous signature "T.B." "The Almanack Maker" appeared on February 14, and "Thomas and Susan, An Irish-Town Dialogue" and lines "Occasioned by the Death of Mr. Robert Bell, the Cele-brated Humorist, and Truly Philanthropic Bookseller of this City," two weeks later.

Beginning with the issue of February 28, 1787, a new advertise-ment, which ran almost without interruption till June 3, 1789, appeared in the *Freeman's Journal*. It announced that "Poems on Several Occasions written during the late war by Mr. Philip Fre-neau, Now collected & neatly printed in a Handsome pocket vol-ume" were "to be had at Francis Bailey's Printing Office." Fine copies were offered for eight shillings sixpence, and coarse copies for seven shillings sixpence. On March 14 Robert Hodge in New York reinserted his advertisement for "Freneau's celebrated Poems —satirical, humorous and entertaining." On April 4 announcements identical with those which were running in the *Freeman's Journal* began to appear in four other Philadelphia papers.[39]

Either a new printing had been run off or the publisher, perhaps encouraged by the poet himself, had been roused to new efforts in getting rid of a stock already on hand. The change in title from *The Poems of Philip Freneau* to *Poems on Several Occasions*, however, is baffling, because no copy of a volume by Freneau with the latter title has been found. It is unlikely, even if Bailey had only prepared a new title page for sheets which he had already printed, that all trace of the edition, which the extent of the advertising indicates to have been large, should have disappeared. As first announced, the *Poems* of 1786 was priced at one dollar, and no distinction was made between volumes printed on fine or coarse paper. However, among the copies of this edition which have survived, some are found on excellent stock which has stood up well and is today almost as clean and white as when first issued, while others are found on a soft, thick paper which has yellowed and torn. Each variety is identical throughout, in title page and pagination. In each, page 337 is misprinted 537, and each contains the same typographical signatures. We may perhaps, therefore, safely conclude that the change in title appeared only in the newspaper advertisements, and that the volume advertised in 1787 (though Bailey may have run off additional copies on cheaper paper to encourage its sale) was the same volume which had been first printed in 1786.

When after a silence of almost two months Freneau contributed "The Insolvent's Release, or Miseries of a Country Jail" to the *Freeman's Journal* of April 11, so realistic in detail is his description of a debtor's prison that we cannot help wondering if the poet had not himself fallen victim to his creditors. The same issue of the newspaper contained "St. Preux to Eloisa," inspired by Rousseau's *Nouvelle Héloïse,* and one week later, on April 18, appeared "May to April," popular as a seasonal poem until the turn of the century, and "The Departure," which Freneau had written two years before when he set out on his career as a seaman.

On April 25, 1787, Bailey announced that he had just published "A Poetical Narrative of a Journey from Philadelphia to New-York, by way of Burlington and South Amboy" which had been written by "Robert Slender, A Stocking Weaver." A pamphlet of twenty-eight pages, it might be purchased for one shilling at Bailey's bookstore on Market Street. There was, said the printer, "some truth in the occasion, and a good deal of fancy in the colouring." "The stile," he promised, "is smooth and easy, and the pleasureable air that is diffused over the whole piece, will certainly render this poem acceptable to such as choose to read it." Robert Slender was, of course, Philip Freneau, and the tale told in *A Journey from Philadelphia to New-York* is evidently an amplification of his own experiences. Robert Hodge warned, when he advertised the pamphlet in New York, that the story though founded on fact, was "intermixed with a good deal of Fancy, and some Satire." [40]

Hodge did not exaggerate. The poem recounts the adventures of Slender, the weaver, who, "tormented with critics, and pester'd with care," decides that, since he has "got a few shillings to spare," he will leave his loom and the heat of the town to enjoy fresh air, new faces, and strange scenes on a jaunt to New York. Not being content to travel alone, he sets about recruiting a party to accompany him. First, he convinces Will Snip, a crotchety tailor, and his red-headed, freckled wife, Susanna Snipinda that they need a vacation from Philadelphia, that "gravest of towns on the face of the earth." Then, blustering Captain O'Keef, a "killer of men, and a lover of beef," and his ward, a young milliner who is called Cynthia because of the shape of her face, are induced to accompany them. Next are added to the party, Monsieur Touppee, a fashionable barber from Paris; young Bob, a balladmonger; and one O'Bluster, a crusty tar who sailed the seas on British boats because he found conditions on American vessels intolerable. Finally, a New Englander named Ezekiel, an attorney and a cantankerous man "as cunning as Satan," joined the group. The series of misadventures which overtake this company as they make their way by water to Burlington, overland to South Amboy, and by stage-boat to New York, is detailed in lusty doggerel. Like "The Expedition of Timothy Taurus," written twelve years before, the *Journey* contains caricatures of familiar American types, but little poetry.

Then, after ten months, which apparently were divided between his old haunts among the printshops of Philadelphia and the more peaceful environment which surrounded his home at Mount Pleasant, Freneau again set out to sea. On May 20, 1787, he arrived at Charleston in command of the sloop *Industry*, which had sailed from New Jersey loaded with corn. His stay in South Carolina was short, and he contributed nothing to the newspapers there except an advertisement offering the cargo for sale.[41] By June 7 he cleared outwards at the Custom House and headed again for New Jersey.[42]

Two weeks later "The Indian Student, or Force of Nature" appeared in the *Freeman's Journal*. Freneau's Indian, like his vision of America, had undergone a metamorphosis. Endowed with all the virtues of Rousseau's "noble savage," he spurned the false criteria of the white man's culture and returned to the simpler faith and more idyllic existence of his ancestors. So would Freneau himself return to simplicity were he not entangled in the mesh which competitive civilization wove about him. An humble votary, he made obeisance "To Misfortune" in the *Freeman's Journal* of July 18:

> Dire Goddess of the haggard brow,
> Misfortune, at thy shrine I bow,
> Where forms uncouth betray thee still,
> A leaky ship, a doctor's bill,
> A poem damn'd, a beggar's prayer,
> An empty purse, a load of care,
> The critic's growl, the pedant's sneer,
> The urgent dun, the law severe,
> A smoky house, rejected love,
> And friends that void of friendship prove.

It was not only lack of appreciation that Freneau lamented, but lack of intelligent criticism of any sort. In "The Author's Soliloquy," [43] he said of the reception of his first collected volume:

> What most torments my boding mind
> Is that no critic will be found
> To read my works and give the wound!
>   Thus, when one fleeting year is pass'd
> With dead men's works my book is class'd;
> With some to praise, but more to blame,
> The soul returns from whence it came,
> And I must wear the marks of time
> Who hardly flourish'd in my prime.

Yet whatever Freneau's personal misfortunes, and however he grumbled at the lack of appreciation shown by his contemporaries, his poetry was becoming increasingly popular. His newspaper verse was reprinted by editors from Savannah to Boston. The New York *Daily Advertiser* extracted "The Desolate Academy" from the *Poems* on October 26, 1786. Charleston newspapers abandoned the anonymity under which most contributions to their poetical departments were presented by identifying selections from the collected edition as "From Capt. Freneau's Poems" or "From the much admired Poems of Philip Freneau." [44] In Connecticut, when a political rhymster wished effectively to silence an opponent, "The Retort" was paraphrased as "Advice to Wits and Poets, from Freneau's Poem to Spectator, with Variations for the Latitude and Longitude of Connecticut." [45] On August 16, 1787, when the *New York Journal* reported Prince William Henry's visit to the exiled Tories in Nova Scotia, "The Royal Adventurer" was reprinted as comment upon the "abusive, illiberal, and ungentlemanly" aristocrat. In the next issue of the same newspaper, on August 23, a correspondent asked that "Prince William Henry's Soliloquy" be reprinted from Freneau's *Poems* without comment, for, said the correspondent, "ample opportunity is offered, by that pragmatic tar, for the Severist Satire and Retort." Not least indicative of the poet's growing fame was the inclusion of two of his poems in the third edition of the school reader with which Noah Webster was flooding America.[46]

Most important, however, Freneau's verses were recognized in England. "The Deserted Farm House" and "The Prayer of Orpheus" appeared in the *European Magazine* for July, 1787, attributed to "Mr. Freneau, an American Poet." On July 12 the *London Morning Herald* printed the former poem which, it explained, had been "written in America by Mr. Freneau, whose poetical productions tended considerably to keep alive the spirit of Independence during the late civil war." Bailey, with pardonable pride and anxious, perhaps, to further the sale of the *Poems,* reprinted "The Deserted Farm House" and the laudatory sentence with which the English newspaper had prefaced it on the first page of the *Freeman's Journal* for November 14. At the same time he took the opportunity to announce: "A new volume of the original miscellaneous productions, by the above mentioned author is now in the press, and will be published by the printer of this paper." Bailey apologized for the delay in its appearance. "An unusual hurry of business," he said, "has unavoidably delayed . . . its publication to so late a period."

When Mathew Carey established the *American Museum* late in January, 1787, Freneau's poems began to reach an increasingly growing audience. During the winter and spring the publisher included poems assigned to Philip Freneau in almost every monthly number of his new magazine. Indeed, Carey was so conscientious in attempting to give credit for lines he thought Freneau had written that "The Death Song of a Cherokee Indian" was mistakenly attributed to the poet in the first issue of the *Museum.* As far as we know Freneau neither denied nor acknowledged the authorship.[47] When, however, Carey announced in the *Pennsylvania Herald* on August 29 that he intended to include Freneau's poem on Washington in the magazine for that month, the poet, who had just arrived in Philadelphia from North Carolina as master of the sloop *Goodluck,*[48] this time wrote immediately to the editor:

I see by this days paper that my verses on Genl Washington's arrival &c are to appear in your next Museum. If it is not too late, I would request the favour of you to rectify an error (which was entirely of the press) in the 5th line of the 13th stanza, as it materially affects the sense— Instead of *whom* please to read *who.*[49]

During the late summer and early fall of 1787, occasional verses by Freneau appeared in the *Freeman's Journal,* and on November 10, he sent Carey two more poems. "If you will honour them with a place in the poetical department of your Museum," he said, "you will confer an additional obligation on . . . your very humble servant." [50] Both were printed in the November issue of the *American Museum:* the first, the elegy on Laurens which had already appeared in the *Freeman's Journal* and which Freneau submitted in a clipping from a "Virginia newspaper"; [51] the second "an original poem in manuscript," the "Lines Occasioned by a Visit to an Old Indian Burying Ground." The latter has been compared with Schiller's "Nadowessian Death Lament" and found to lose little by the comparison; [52] Campbell attested to its worth by borrowing from it a line for "O'Connor's Child"; [53] and with "The Wild Honey Suckle" it is the poem quoted most often as representative of Freneau in modern American anthologies:

> And long shall tim'rous fancy see
> The painted chief, the pointed spear,
> And reason's self shall bow the knee
> To shadows and delusions here.

The shadows and delusions which had haunted Freneau for the past six years were about to be dispelled. "I am at this moment about leaving Philadelphia," he wrote Carey. "I expect however my new volume to be published in about a month." [54] The new volume did not appear for several months; but Freneau, as he sailed the sloop *Industry* into the harbor of Charleston on December 17,[55] was about to begin his most profitable period as a sea captain. Before leaving Philadelphia he had written the New Year's verses for the carriers of the *Freeman's Journal*.[56] Thereafter for more than two years he apparently wrote little. He was busy at sea.

Three days after her entry at Charleston the *Industry* cleared for Savannah, where she arrived on December 27.[57] On January 7, 1788, having returned to Charleston four days previously, the packet set out again for the Georgia port.[58] Late in the month Captain Freneau moored her at Charleston for the last time; [59] he had acquired a larger, faster vessel.

While arrangements were being made with Adam Gilchrist, merchant of Charleston, for cargo on the new schooner *Columbia*, Freneau contributed verses to the daily *City Gazette*. "A Parody on Sappho's Ode, Addressed to Old England," on January 28, re-expressed the poet's plaint that America was not yet free from British domination. Playful stanzas written "to a young Quaker Lady, that went passenger in his Vessel to Georgia, to reside in the Western parts of that State" appeared on January 30. "The Exile," a versified paraphrase of Lord Bolingbroke's essay on the same subject, was printed on February 2, and on February 9 "The Invalid," which Freneau had written on his first visit to South Carolina almost three years before.[60]

The *Columbia*, a fast sailing schooner, capable of carrying five hundred barrels and having comfortable accommodations for passengers, was quite the finest vessel that Captain Freneau had commanded. Advertised for New York from February 21, she cleared at Charleston five days later with an assorted cargo of indigo, tobacco, tallow, myrtle wax, and peanuts. Heavy winter seas made the voyage slow, and it was March 24 before she was ready to sail southward again. Almost a month later, on April 22, she entered at Charleston, twenty days from New York, loaded with saltpetered hams, cider, rum, tea, window glass, bar iron, and windsor chairs.[61]

On April 23, one day after the poet returned to Charleston, Francis Bailey advertised in Philadelphia that Freneau's "Miscellanies, Consisting of performances in Prose & Verse" was finally ready and would be offered for sale on Monday, April 27. The price was set at seven shillings sixpence. "Those gentlemen in Philadelphia, New-Jersey, & Maryland," advised Bailey, "who honored this volume of the lucubrations of our American author with their subscriptions are desired to send to the printer for the same as soon as possible." [62] One month later Robert Hodge in New York announced the sale of *The Miscellaneous Works of Philip Freneau*. "This second volume of our American Author," he said, "is replete with the highest sentimental entertainment. Humour, wit, and satire flow in copious strains. It requires only to be read to be admired." [63] Soon the ingenious Mathew Carey, apparently with a supply of the 1786 volume still on his shelves, announced that at his bookstore "Freneau's Poems and Miscellanies" might be had in a set of two volumes for fifteen shillings.[64]

4

More than four hundred subscribers had been secured before the volume was published—forty-five from Pennsylvania, New Jersey, and Delaware; forty-two from Maryland; one hundred and twenty-five from New York; and almost two hundred from South Carolina. Freneau's friends, Mathew Carey, Ebenezer Hazard, Peter Markoe, each put down his name for one copy. Robert Hodge ordered twelve for his bookstore in New York. His Excellency Governor Moultrie of South Carolina purchased six printed on "fine" paper. Aedanus Burke, DeWitt Clinton, Charles Pinckney, and the Hon. David Rittenhouse lent solid distinction to the list of patrons.

The *Miscellaneous Works* is perhaps the most representative volume that Freneau ever published. Composed of almost equal parts of verse and prose, it based no portion of its claim to popular success on the author's service as the "Poet of the American Revolution." "The Pictures of Columbus," written in 1774, opened the volume, followed by "The Hermit of Saba," a product of Freneau's first excursion to the West Indies; but most of the verse was that which had appeared in the *Freeman's Journal*, the *Columbian Herald*, and the *City Gazette* during the past three years. Many of "The Pilgrim" papers were reprinted as "The Philosopher of the Forest," and new essays on a variety of humane and humorous subjects were included in the volume. By far the most conspicuous contributions were attributed to "the late Robert Slender," a stocking and tape weaver who cared little for wealth or fame, and whose executors had found hidden away in a strong box the bundle of manuscripts ("penned in a very antiquated, obscure and perplexing hand") which were now presented.[65]

Among these, the "Tracts and Essays on Several Subjects" contain, in addition to "An Oration on Rum," "Rules and Directions How to Avoid Creditors, Sheriffs, Constables, &c.," and "Directions for Courtship," the cursory thoughts of Robert Slender on a variety of subjects, such as "The Market Man," "The Man in Business," "The Man out of Business," "The Debtor," "The Private Tutor," and "The City Poet." Under the heading of "Essays, Tales and Poems" the late weaver discussed "The Power of Novelty," pictured the misery of "The Sick Author," told of "The Voyage of Timberoo-tabo-eede, an Othaheite Indian" to Philadelphia, presented a humorous "Report of a Law Case," talked darkly of "The Academy of Death," became sharply satirical in "Robert Slender's Idea of a Visit to a Modern Great Man" and in "A Discourse upon Law." "Light Summer Reading" detailed the melancholy musings of a mad young poet enamored of a Bermudian maid. Many of the stocking weaver's contributions were only fragments, random thoughts and short passages of solid moralizing, gathered together as "Narratives, Observations and Advice on Different Subjects" or "Reflections, Narratives, and Ideas of the Late Robert Slender." His trenchant "Discourse upon Whigs and Tories," however, was fully developed in its condemnation of all unpatriotic men. Finally, at the end of the volume appeared the "Journey from Philadelphia to New-York," which Bailey had printed as a pamphlet the year before.

Robert Slender controlled a deft and deep-biting humorous style. In the "Idea of the Human Soul" [66] he suggested that the inanimate body of man be represented by a glass of pure water. Then, he said, but pour in a little old Madeira wine, and the water becomes diffused with life—wit, generosity, and benevolence. Add rum, and it becomes like "one of your hot headed touchy fellows, who is in a violent passion of rage three fourths of his time." Stir in some heavy mead, and the mixture is "dull and spiritless, and typifies one of your stupid fellows." "Put some vinegar into the water, fellow—ah! what sad trash it is—this tumbler of water has a sour soul indeed —an ill natured, squabbling soul, the very quintessence of acidity itself!" Beer added makes a "soft and milky soul, equally fitted to be the dupe of the nurse and the priest." A dash of high proof brandy in the mixture and "enthusiasm is instantly kindled into being, upon the dregs of dullness, insipidity, and nonsense." But whiskey, American whiskey, infuses the whole with generosity, bravery, benevolence, and good nature in excellently good proportions.

Nor was Robert Slender uninformed on the literary situation of America. "There are few writers of books in this new world," he said, "and amongst these very few that deal in works of imagination, and, I am sorry to say, fewer still that have any success attending their lucubrations." It could not be otherwise, for the United States was a commercial nation, and the counting house her temple. "Authors (such I mean as are not possessed of fortunes) are at present considered as the dregs of the community: their situation and prospects are truly humiliating." What was more, the writers of America quarreled incessantly among themselves. To Robert Slender such animosity was stupid and unnecessary. "Any other sett of men in a similar state of calamitous adversity would unite together for their mutual defence instead of worrying and lampooning each other for the amusement of the illiberal vulgar."

What then must American authors do? In the first place, advised Robert Slender, they must sedulously avoid "epistles dedicatory," because such fawning hostages to favor were the claptrap of aristocracy and monarchy. In the second place, they must keep away from learned men: "A mere scholar and an original author are two animals as different from each other as a fresh and salt water sailor." Furthermore, it is a dangerous practice for a writer to propose a subscription for his works, because the public will inevitably be disappointed when they receive what they have paid for in advance. Nor must authors despair at poverty: "Fortune most commonly bestows wealth . . . upon fools and idiots." America, however, was not alone in her lack of encouragement to letters. "Few authors in any country are rich, because a man must first be reduced to a state of penury before he will commence author." Yet whatever his circumstances, the writer should never borrow money. Let him work: "It is far more honourable to be a good bricklayer or a skilful weaver than an indifferent poet." Above all, "do not forget that there is such a thing in the world as a decent pride." If the author cannot make a living with his pen, cautioned Robert Slender, he must

never engage in any business as an inferior or understrapper. I cannot endure to see an author debase his profession so far as to submit to be second or third in any office or employment whatever. If fortune, or the ill taste of the public compels you even to turn shallopman on the Delaware, let it be your first care to have command of the boat. Beggary itself, with all its hideous apparatus of rags and misery, becomes at once respectable whenever it exhibits the least token of independence of spirit and a single spark of laudable ambition.

Never, continued the weaver, give your works away; if they are not worth buying, let them die. Finally, "if fortune seems absolutely determined to starve you . . . retire to some uninhabited island or desert, and there, at your leisure end your life with decency." [67] Such must be the fate of American authors. "Poetry, gentlemen," said Robert Slender, "I am fully convinced, is at best but a poor trade." And especially poetry in Philadelphia; "Barbers cannot possibly exist, as such, among a people who have neither hair nor beards. How then could a poet hope for success in a city where there are not three persons possessed of elegant ideas!" [68]

But it is in "The Picture Gallery," one of the few miscellaneous essays not presented under the pseudonym of "Robert Slender," that Freneau most candidly expressed the disappointment which made him turn from literary projects to the simpler and more satisfying life of a seaman. Hung in a fashionable gallery were the portraits of mean men who had built fortunes at the expense of the common man during the American Revolution. How characteristic was such a display of a country where "real merit and virtue, the maimed and unrewarded soldier, and the honest and disinterested patriot, hung back in the rear of the throng; while impudence, avarice, selfishness, ignorance, cowardice and villainy were foremost!" [69] The sea with all its hardships offered life arranged more rationally upon Nature's plan.

5

Captain Freneau and the schooner *Columbia* were busily engaged during the spring and summer of 1788. Leaving Charleston on May 5, they entered at New York eight days later with rice, indigo, tallow, and wax for the northern markets.[70] After loading a cargo including Madeira wine, New York rum, peach brandy, ham, sugar, and herring, they sailed again for Charleston, where they arrived on June 16.[71] There Freneau contributed "Modern Devotion" to the *City Gazette* on June 23 and "The Virtue of Tobacco" on June 25. Both were slight, humorous poems, for the captain had now apparently little time for any but commercial ventures. On June 26 he cleared at the custom house with the usual freight of rice and indigo, to which he had added for this voyage orange juice and candle "week." Arriving at New York on July 7, the *Columbia* was at once advertised ready to sail again within ten days.[72]

There was some delay before the schooner left port on July 21 with a cargo of iron. Then, two days later, while in sight of land off Cape Henry, she ran into a violent gale. She was swept from her course, dismasted, and thrown three times on her beam ends. Her heavy cargo shifted perilously; every article loose upon her deck was washed into the sea. "All my people," wrote Freneau, "except one, an old man who stuck fast in one of the scuttles, were several times overboard." A passenger from Charleston and one member of the crew were drowned, notwithstanding every effort to save them. "As for myself," Freneau reported,

I took refuge in the main weather shrouds, where indeed I saved myself from being washed into the sea, but was almost staved to pieces in a violent fall I had upon the main deck, the main-mast having given way six feet above the deck, and gone overboard— I was afterwards knocked on the head by a violent stroke of the tiller, which entirely deprived me of sensation for (I was told) near a quarter of an hour.—Our pumps were now so choaked with corn that they would no longer work, upward of four feet of water was in the hold, fortunately our bucket was saved, and with this we went to bailing, which alone prevented us from foundering in one of the most dismal nights that ever man witnessed.

The next morning Freneau rigged a make-shift sail and steered as best he could for land five miles away. "Nothing," he wrote, "could exceed our distress—no fire, no candle, our beds soaked with sea water, the cabbin torn to pieces, a vast quantity of corn damaged and poisoning us to death." The crew kept up their spirits with grog, while the captain, he said, resorted to his "old expedient of philosophy and reflection." Two days later the crippled vessel was overtaken by a ship from London and towed into Hampton Roads. By July 29, assisted by the Potomac pilot, the *Columbia* and her weary crew made port at Norfolk. They were so forlorn that Freneau imagined, "The very dogs looked at us with an eye of commiseration—the negroes pitied us, and almost every one shewed a disposition to relieve us."

A week later, on August 6, Freneau wrote to Francis Bailey in Philadelphia:

I have unloaded my cargo, partly damaged, partly otherwise— This day I also begin to refit my vessel, and mean to proceed back to New-York as soon as refitted, which cannot be sooner than the 25th, perhaps the 30th of this month. It is possible, however, that I may be ordered to sell the vessel here; if so, I shall take passage to Baltimore, and go to New York by way of Philadelphia, to look for another more fortunate barque than that which I now command.[73]

Repaired, the *Columbia* was back in New York by September 20, advertised for freight or passage to Charleston.[74] Then, leaving port early in October, she made her way slowly southward. It was November 6 before she arrived in South Carolina,[75] and eight days later she set out again through heavy winter seas for Baltimore.

During a tedious voyage of thirty-three days, the schooner was again twice driven from her course before she reached her destination late in December.[76] Dejectedly her captain wrote:

> Sorrowing I reef the sail, while slowly creeps
> The dull Columbia o'er the length of deeps,
> Her northern course no favoring breeze befriends,
> Hail, storm and lightning on her path attends;
> Here wint'ry suns their scanty light restrain,
> Stars dimly glow, and boding birds complain,
> Here boisterous gales, the rapid gulph controul,
> Unpitying breakers near my Argo roll,
> Here cloudy, sullen Hatteras, restless, raves,
> Scorns all repose and swells his weight with waves.

> . . .

> Lost are my toils, my longing hopes are vain,
> Yet midst these ills permit me to complain,
> And half regret, that finding fortune frail,
> I left the Muses to direct the sail.[77]

Philip Freneau was a bachelor about to celebrate his thirty-seventh birthday. Among the stories popularly told of the "longing hopes" which bothered him at this period, one details his protracted courtship of Eleanor Forman, a beautiful young neighbor in Monmouth, whose family is said to have looked with small favor upon the impecunious poet. Advised to establish some measure of financial security before he further pled his suit, the story continues, Freneau turned to the sea.[78] But time went quickly on, and his fortune was not yet made. Eleanor Forman was twenty-six now, and the proposed marriage seemed remote as ever before. As he struggled to bring his crippled schooner into the Maryland port, Freneau composed "Lines Written at Sea, Addressed to Miss ———, New Jersey":

> Driven from my course by cold December's gale,
> As near your shores I spread my weary sail,
> From bar to bar, from cape to cape I stray,
> From you still absent, still too far away:
> What shall repay me for these weeks of pain,
> These weeks of absence on this restless main.[79]

Weeks of absence stretched to months. Early in January the *Columbia* was locked by ice in the harbor at Baltimore.[80] Again Freneau wrote of the subject which now seemed uppermost in his mind:

> Now fetter'd fast in icy fields
> In vain I loose the sleeping sail;
> The frozen wave no longer yields
> And useless blows the favouring gale.
>
> Yet still in hopes of April showers
> And breezes moist with morning dew,
> I pass the lingering lazy hours
> Reflecting on the spring—and you.[81]

Not until early in February was the *Columbia* able to leave port.[82] Weeks later she entered the harbor at Charleston, and proceeded almost immediately to Yamacraw in Georgia,[83] where she took on a cargo of lumber. Now in better humor, Freneau passed lightly over his misfortunes:

A *schooner* is confided to my care, humble, indeed, when compared to those lofty piles which I have seen you so much admire, but which is, nevertheless, really capable of an European, nay of an Indian voyage. Read all history, ransack libraries, examine a million of manuscripts on vellum, on parchment, on paper, on marble, on what you please, and I defy you to find the most distant hint of any *poet* in any age or country, from Hessiod down to Peter Pindar, having been *trusted* with the controul or possession of anything fit to be mentioned or compared with the same barque, which, you say, *I have the misfortune to command.*

To be serious: misfortune ought to be only the topic of such men as do not think or reason with propriety, upon the nature of things. Some writer says, it is but another name for carelessness or inattention: Though that may not at all times be the case, it is in the power of every man to place himself beyond *assuming* a dignity of mind, (if it be not the gift of nature) that will, in the end, get the better of untoward events, that may frequently cross out best purposes.—Indeed the *sea* is the *best* school for philosophy (I mean the moral kind); in thirteen or fourteen years' acquaintance with that element, I am convinced a man ought to imbibe more of your right *stoical* stuff, than could be gained in half a century on shore.

The "right *stoical* stuff" which Freneau had imbibed left him, however, still cynical:

Poets and Philosophers shall ever travel with me at a cheap rate indeed—not because they are generally men of this world, but because, even supposing the barque that bears them; should make an eternal exit to the bottom of the ocean; the busy world, as things go, will regret the loss of most of them very little, perhaps not at all.[84]

On March 19 the *Columbia* cleared for Charleston, where she was advertised "completely fitted for sea" and ready to sail within a few days.[85] In the meantime Freneau indicated his present complete disavowal of political partisanship by submitting to the *City Gazette* of April 10 a poetical tribute "To John Dickinson, Esq.," who had recently retired from public life in Philadelphia. Four days later the schooner sailed for New York.[86] On the morning after his departure from the southern port Freneau's "Lines Written at Sea. Addressed to Miss ——, New Jersey" appeared in the New York *Daily Advertiser*, and on the next day, April 16, the same poem was printed in the Charleston *City Gazette* as "A Yankee Epistle. Written at sea, December, 1788, Addressed to Miss ——." After a voyage of eight days the *Columbia* entered at New York on April 23 with, in addition to her familiar cargo of rice and indigo, a pair of "South American Ourang-Outangs." The day after Freneau's arrival George Washington crossed the harbor from Elizabethtown to take over his duties as the first President of the United States, and the schooner *Columbia*, "dressed and decorated in the most superb manner," was one of the vessels which stood by to welcome him.[87]

On May 4 the schooner left again for Charleston, where she arrived on the 21st of the same month.[88] She sailed for New York on June 1. Entering the harbor there eight days later,[89] she was advertised for Charleston and Savannah until June 16. Then the shipping notices in the New York dailies announced that, having been completely repaired, the *Columbia* was ready "for freight or charter" to any free port in the West Indies.[90] On June 23, however, she cleared for Wilmington, Delaware.[91] Again the voyage was tedious. Delayed at Cape Hatteras for sixteen days "with strong winds ahead," Captain Freneau amused himself with verse: the fractious gods who ruled the stormy cape, he explained in "Tormentia's Complaint," [92] were punishing him for once having ventured to remark "that Hatteras maidens are not fair"; and in "The Pilot of Hatteras" [93] he drew the character of an ancient seaman whose wife worried fretfully every time her husband put out to sea.

Finally, on August 6 the *Columbia* returned to New York from Wilmington.[94] There was more delay before the captain advertised that his schooner would sail for South Carolina on September 20.[95] She arrived in Charleston on October 6, and three weeks later cleared for Sunbury, Georgia.[96] There, while the vessel was again detained, Freneau considered the contentment which a weary sailor might find in some simple island retreat such as St. Catherine's off the Georgia coast.[97] When he returned to Charleston on November 18, Captain Freneau's last voyage as master of the *Columbia* was over. He was to be married. One week later the schooner sailed again, but under the command of a Captain Billings.[98] Freneau at thirty-eight was prepared to return to his interrupted career as poet and journalist.

His reputation had been growing during the years at sea. "On the wit, satire, and pleasantry of Freneau," said Benjamin Russell in the *Massachusetts Centinel* on July 18, "an eulogium is not now necessary . . . and we cannot but lament his mistaking the 'popular opinion'—which we can assure him was very far from considering his verses bad." Again on August 1 Russell sincerely praised

Captain Freneau—who is considered the Pindar of the United States—and perhaps as nearly related to the poet of Thebes, as his English relation, Peter. To those who have seen his pleasantries during the war nothing need be said of his satirical, humorous and yet chaste abilities.

On November 14 "The Pilot of Hatteras" appeared in the New York *Daily Advertiser*, attributed to "Capt. P. Freneau." When Russell reprinted the poem in the *Massachusetts Centinel Extraordinary* on November 2, he noted that "this celebrated Genius, the Peter Pindar of America, is now Master of a Packet, which runs between New York, Philadelphia and Charleston." Freneau's collected editions, too, were apparently still in demand. Messrs. Hodge, Allen, and Campbell in New York advertised that "a few copies of Capt. Philip Freneau's Celebrated Poems" and a fresh supply of his *Miscellaneous Works* had come to hand and could be purchased by their customers.[99]

But for two months during the autumn and early winter Freneau remained at Charleston, a regular contributor to the *City Gazette*. In "A View of Columbia," on November 28, and "The Procession to Columbia," on December 14, he ridiculed the removal of the state capital to a small town in the interior. Printed on November 30 were stanzas "To Harriot," in which the poet pled that the fair recipient of his verse be at least as kind as Neptune who, though he had frowned severely, had spared his servant's life. "Lines formerly Written in a Tavern at Log Town in the Pine Barrens of New Jersey," on December 8, and untitled verses which Freneau later called "The Bird at Sea," on December 10, were both light and inconsequential.

Soon Freneau's verse also began to appear with some regularity in New York, in the *Daily Advertiser*. Stanzas "Translated from the Greek of Bion," [100] in which the poet voiced his conviction that every earthly delight is dimmed by age, were printed on December 16, and "Stanzas Written at St. Catherine's, an Island upon the Coast of Georgia" was attributed to Captain Freneau on January 2. "On the Present Situation of the Theatre in Charleston" appeared simultaneously on January 8 in the *Daily Advertiser* and in the *City Gazette*. Finally, in the Charleston paper appeared "Father Dobbin's Complaint" on January 15, and "A Columbian Dialogue" one day later.[101]

Freneau left South Carolina, a passenger on the brig *Betsey*, late in January.[102] While he was at sea, "A Characteristic Sketch of the Long Island Dutch" appeared in the *City Gazette* on February 2 as a portion of "The Rising Empire, a Poem." Two days later, on February 4, "A View of Rhode Island" was printed in the *Daily Advertiser*, extracted, it was said, "from a new Poem, entitled the Rising Empire, not yet published." Freneau had turned again seriously to verse-making. The brig *Betsey* docked in New York on February 12.[103] "We are told," said Benjamin Russell in the *Massachusetts Centinel* on January 27, that Captain Freneau, "from a long succession of calamities and misfortunes at sea, has determined once more to try the powers of his pen in his native city of New

York." It must be the wish of "every friend to genius and merit," said the New England editor, "that the future success of this American bard—this genuine son of NEPTUNE and CLIO—whose writings in verse and prose have rendered such eminent services to his country—may be greater than he has hitherto experienced."

SEVEN

THE DAILY ADVERTISER

1790–1791

NEW YORK, the capital of the United States, was larger and more prosperous than it had ever been before. It was growing every day, boasted its citizens, "into symmetry, elegance and beauty." [1] The old municipal building on the corner of Broad and Nassau Streets had been remodeled at the expense of twenty thousand pounds to a "convenient and elegant structure worthy of being the permanent residence of the Federal legislature." [2] Already plans were completed for the demolition of Fort George, the last reminder of English occupation, and for the leveling and landscaping of the whole Battery. Bowling Green was to be cleared of debris, made ready for whatever ceremonious use should be demanded of it. Eight thousand pounds had been granted by the state for the construction of an "elegant mansion" for the president of the republic.[3] New York was a quiet, clean, industrious city of thirty thousand inhabitants: its rivers were filled with vessels, its wharves with merchandise, its streets with busy merchants and important statesmen. Money changed hands quickly when the Congress was in session. Business boomed for every class. It was good indeed to live in the "peaceful seat of the happiest empire in the universe." [4]

By 1790, however, almost everyone understood that the government would soon be moved elsewhere—to Philadelphia, said those who gauged the temper of the Congress most closely. New York made increasingly attractive overtures in vain. Its conservative commercial newspapers, the *Morning Post,* the *Packet,* and the *Daily Gazette,* emphasized the financial advantages to every class of citizen of the present situation. The *Weekly Museum,* a miscellany of interesting and entertaining anecdotes, had little to say on the rumored removal, and Thomas Greenleaf in the *New York Journal* was torn between interest in the good-will of the non-commercial common man of America and loyalty to his city. It was generally conceded that John Fenno in the *Gazette of the United States* would faithfully mirror the opinions of his sponsors among the leaders of the Federalist party, even that he might pack up his types and follow them to a new capital. The *Daily Advertiser,* published by Francis Childs and John Swaine in their shop at the corner of Wall and Water Streets, viewed all questions judiciously. Cautiously anti-Federalist in policy, it was the most reliable of New York's seven newspapers, and the oldest of its dailies.

Bronzed and toughened by his years at sea, Freneau made his debut as a journalist in New York in the employ of the *Advertiser.* His poems, which had been attributed to "Captain Freneau" when they had not infrequently appeared in the New York paper during the past few months, began on February 18 to appear anonymously or over some simple initial appropriate to a professional newspaperman. Many of the contributions to the *City Gazette* during his last weeks in Charleston were republished, but changed ever so slightly to suit the predilections of Northern readers.[5] Not until early in March, however, did Freneau contribute new verses to the *Daily Advertiser.*

Crossing over to Monmouth soon after his arrival in New York, he apparently spent some weeks among familiar old surroundings, and happily in the company of Eleanor Forman. It could have been no secret among Freneau's friends that his retirement from the sea was closely linked with plans for marriage. It was fitting, then, that the first of the new poems which he submitted to the *Daily Advertiser* should be "Lines Addressed to Some Young Ladies, who were Detected in Attempting to Cut Pieces from an Old Great Coat of the Author's, that he Might be under the Necessity of Buying a New and More Genteel One," [6] for the young ladies so addressed are said to have been Eleanor Forman and her friend Fanny Ledyard (whose brother Benjamin had married Eleanor's oldest sister). Seldom again did Freneau write with more light-hearted abandon:

> Caitiffs forbear, and let me urge my plea!
> Tho' this be sport to you—'tis death to me—
> Stop, stop the fatal scissors—no such fun;

This reverend coat through many climes has run,
Stuck to my hide, and never left its master,
Thro' frost, snow, sunshine, puppies & disaster.

May—now I swear, if you're determin'd on it,
May you be punish'd with a homespun bonnet:
When married, may a spendthrift be your son,
And each a widow ere she's twenty-one—
Yes, if it falls a victim to your shears,
I'll mourn it longer than you will your Dears.

Oh, Jades, why have you scollop'd out the tail!
I guess your meaning, but you shan't prevail,
Its owner is a weather beaten Bard
Who would be sooner feather'd, hang'd, or tarr'd,
Than lose one tatter of his faithful friend
Which (take it as you please) you'd better *mend.*

You ask me what I see in this old rag
That makes me look so proud and talk so big;
Why, madams, 'tis a very honest coat
That now has been at least seven years afloat
Has stopt a window when a pane was broke,
And serv'd some travelling ladies for a cloak,
Has saved me often from the wintry blast,
And kept the deck when Neptune took the mast.

In this have I pass'd many a tedious night
Content'd, tho' the land was out of sight,
In *this,* have I met many a bloody nose,
Have fought, scratch'd, squabbled, scribbled verse and prose;
And tho' some sad mischance too often tore it,
I thought it might out last the wight who wore it.

In *this,* have I been lugged before the squire,
And sweat'd well—without the help of fire;
In short, it has through such adventures gone,
So many times put off, so many on,
If prayers or tears can o'er your shears prevail,
Fair ladies, let me hang it on this nail,
By your consent henceforth to stay on shore,
And safe from clipping, tempt the seas no more.

By the end of the first week in March Freneau was back in New York, contributing to almost every issue of the *Advertiser*. Controversial matters were avoided. Even "On the American and French Revolutions," printed on March 7, was cautious in its approbation of the nascent republic in France. Freneau preferred to submit for the same issue a humorous sketch, like "The Boatman of Indian River" or, two days later, a versified comment on some safely popular subject, like "On the Proposed Demolition of Fort George." "A Descriptive Sketch of Maryland," evidently intended as another portion of "The Rising Empire," appeared on March 10. "Federal Hall," March 12, describes with acid humor the types of men, the cobblers, barbers, tailors, and debtors, who neglect their proper responsibilities to listen to the proceedings of the Congress. In the "Philosophical Sketch of America," March 13, Freneau discussed the Indian, not as a natural man perfect in simplicity, nor as the degenerate offspring of Asiatic or Greek antiquity, but as an ordinary human being subject to the same faults and the same aspirations as any other man.

To have been called, as Freneau was called by Benjamin Russell, the "Peter Pindar of America," was high praise. Few poets were more popular in the United States than John Wolcot, the English satirist whose verses were copied regularly in contemporary newspapers. His combination of malicious wit and ingenious satire appealed to the American public, who found Wolcot an oracle of social criticism. And Freneau had been writing in much the same manner in such poems as "The Prisoner," "The Newsmonger," "The Drunken Soldier," "The Roguish Shoemaker," and "Federal Hall." Now, on March 15, in the "Epistle to Peter Pindar," [7] he indicated his complete sympathy with Wolcot's satiric purposes:

> Peter, methinks you are the happiest wight
> That ever delt in ink, or sharpen'd quill.
> 'Tis yours on every rank of fools to write—
> Some prompt with pity, some with laughter kill;
>
> . . .
>
> But, Peter, quit your dukes and little lords,
> Young princes full of blood and scant of brains—

Our *rebel* coast some similes affords,
And many a subject for your pen contains
Preserv'd as fuel for your comic rhymes,
(Like Egypt's gods) to give to future times.

But whatever his debt to the English satirist, Freneau's idiom
was now his own. There was an easy colloquialism in "The Sabbath-
Day Chace," which was printed on March 16 to burlesque Yankee
hypocrisy. And his long poem, "The Rising Empire," was to be in
a distinctly native style—"The American Village" rewritten more
concretely and freed from dependency on English models. Two
more portions of the poem now appeared: "A Description of Pennsylvania" on March 17 and "A View of Massachusetts" on March
29. Apparently each state was to be described and the character of
her people discussed. But it was never completed. Freneau was
busy with other things. "On the Sleep of Plants," March 20, was
much like other poems which he had composed during the past six
years, particularly in its analogy between the life of man and the
life of a flower. In fact, of the verse now contributed to the *Daily
Advertiser,* only "On the Demolition of Dartmouth College," which
on March 22 described a mutiny among the undergraduates at Hanover a few months before, had reference to any contemporary event.

On April 15, 1790, Freneau was married to Eleanor Forman in
her father's house at Middletown Point by Hendrick Hendrickson,
Justice of Peace.[8] Shortly after the wedding the couple moved to
New York, where the first census of the United States found Philip
Freneau living in the East Ward of the city, the head of a family
consisting of one free white female and no slaves.[9] By May he was
a member of the New York Society Library,[10] and settled to the
routine of a newspaperman.

2

But for two months after his wedding few contributions by Freneau appeared in the *Daily Advertiser.* "Stanzas Occasioned by the
Death of Dr. Franklin" was published on April 28, six days after
the statesman's death was announced in the New York newspapers.
On May 1 appeared "Constantia," a playful recitation of a bluff
and hearty tar who wooed and won a serious young maiden in order

to save her from life in a nunnery. After an uncomplimentary "Description of Connecticut" on May 10, nothing by Freneau is found in the newspaper until May 24, when "Verses from the Other World by Dr. Fr-k-n" took to task those panegyrists who had been too facile or too fulsome in eulogizing the deceased patriot.

By the middle of June, however, the newspaper was enlivened by an energetic and imaginative editorial direction. But though most of the poetry and much of the prose from this time until late in the following winter was undoubtedly Freneau's, he acknowledged only a portion of it by inclusion among his collected works or by republication over one of his familiar pseudonyms. "A Descriptive Sketch of Virginia," on June 11, is certainly his, for he included it in two of his later volumes; but such characteristic poems as "The Country Squire's Exit" and "The Origin of Lee Boards," [11] though both were attributed to Freneau by his contemporaries, were never collected. Similarly, though many of the prose essays in the *Advertiser* are in Freneau's informal style, [12] the only ones surely identified as his are "A Speech on a New Subject" on June 29 and the later "Opay Mico" papers, which were subsequently incorporated in the "Tomo Cheeki" essays.

Freneau tried now for no high standard in his verse; he was a journalist. Timely, deft, and humorous, his lines illumine the period in which he lived more than they enhance his literary reputation. For example, when workmen engaged in tearing down Fort George came upon deposits of human bones in the old ramparts, Freneau celebrated the discovery with "Lines Occasioned by the Skeletons Dug up at Fort George." Can man, he cried in mock despair, not sleep in peace when life is fled? He cautioned the ladies of New York to have their teeth pulled at once rather than risk exposing them to decay in some mouldy grave. It was good newspaper verse, but poor poetry.

Perhaps true poetry could not be written amid the hurry of city life; at any rate, Freneau came to think that it could not. Bound by necessity to the editorial desk, nearing forty and with few of his youthful ambitions realized, he hid his disappointment beneath the light lilt of his verses. Only occasionally, as in "The Orator of the Woods" on June 29, did he express such sentiments as:

> Alas, no joys on age await
> *Retirement comes a day too late.*

The sale of his first two volumes [13] encouraged him to consider the publication of a third. On June 24 the *Daily Advertiser* announced that "Mr. Freneau proposes publishing a volume of original poems to contain about 250 pages. . . . As soon as there appears a sufficiency of subscribers to defray the expence of paper and printing, the collection shall be put to press." The price would be seventy-five cents; subscriptions would be received at the newspaper office or by Messrs. Hodge, Allen, and Campbell, at their bookstores. On July 2 the announcement appeared in the *New-York Journal,* and on July 14 Francis Bailey, in Philadelphia, informed readers of the *Freeman's Journal* that subscriptions for the new volume would be received at the office of that publication. Later in the month the editor of the *Maryland Journal* presented a prospectus of the volume to the citizens of Baltimore. [14]

Meanwhile the discussion of the proposed removal of the government from New York to Philadelphia provoked a series of new satirical poems. After extended debate the Senate voted that the capital of the United States should be located on the Potomac, some sixty miles from Baltimore. Until such a site could be prepared, however, the Congress would meet after December, 1790, in Philadelphia. [15] It was a blow to New York and her plans for civic advancement which Freneau treated lightly by printing on July 1 a poetical epistle from "Nanny, the Philadelphia House Maid, to Nabby, her Friend in New York." Said the servant in Pennsylvania:

> I plainly forsee that if once they remove
> From morning to night we shall drive and be drove,
> My madams red rag will ring like a bell
> And the hall and the parlour will never look well;
> Such scowering will be as has never been seen,
> We shall always be cleaning, and never be clean
> And threats in abundance will work on my fears
> Of blows on the back and of slaps on the ears.

While the bill for the transfer of the capital was being discussed in the House of Representatives, Freneau printed on July 5 "The River Delaware to the River Hudson." Philadelphia was jubilant:

What honour on our town awaits!
Lift up your heads, ye Dutchmen's gates,
Fame says, they now are on the wing,
They're welcome—*for the wealth they bring.*

On July 12 Freneau sang of the contentment of "The Bergen
Planter" who, unworried by the artificialities of town life, watched
his harvest come and go with humble pride. "Nabby, the New York
House-Maid, to Nanny her Friend in Philadelphia" appeared on
July 15. The bill for the removal of the seat of government had
passed both houses: therefore Nabby wrote ruefully:

Well, Nanny, I am sorry to find, since you writ us
The Congress at last has determin'd to quit us:
You now may begin with your brushes and brooms,
To be scouring your knockers and scrubbing your rooms;
As for us, my dear Nanny, we're in such a pet,
And hundreds of houses will be to be let;
Our streets, that were just in a way to look clever,
Will now be neglected and nasty as ever.

On July 31 Freneau reprinted the verses "On Tobacco" which
had first appeared in the Charleston *City Gazette.* Then, returning
to the subject of the Congress, he contributed "The Removal," not
to the *Daily Advertiser,* but to the *New-York Daily Gazette* for
August 10. The first legislators of the United States appeared in no
glamorous light:

From Hudson's banks, in proud array,
(Too mean to claim a longer stay)
Their new ideas to approve,
Behold the *generous* Congress move!

New chaplains, now, shall ope their jaws,
New salaries grease unworthy paws:
Some reverend men, that turtle carves,
Will fatten, while the soldier starves.

The bombast, the pretense to aristocracy, the chicanery of men
high in power were in disquieting contrast to the principles which
the common men of America had been led to believe actuated the
American Revolution. The small heroes whose united effort had
made independence possible seemed forgotten. Finally, after re-

printing the "Stanzas Written at Baltimore, January 1789," in the *Daily Advertiser* for August 25, Freneau published his last sarcastic poem on the Congress. Both houses had adjourned, to reconvene later in the year at Philadelphia. The "Lines Occasioned by a Visit to Federal-hall" on August 31 were plain-spoken:

> To see the men that preach'd for pay,
> In vain we stretch our eyes—
> And, Mister Spaker, where are you,
> That *look'd* so wondrous wise!

What humbug was the desire of mankind for wealth! "A Strict attention to trifles," wrote the author of "On the Advantage of Steadiness" on August 31, "is the best way I know of to become rich." And yet, he cautioned, "the habit of steadiness is not originally in the nature of mankind. It is a child of society, the effect of constraint and necessity. It is one of those cumbrous, artificial, subordinate virtues to the tyranny of which we submit because we cannot help it." All savage races, all noble primitives happy in their innocence, were erratic. In fact, he said, "Opay Mico (one of M'Gillivary's Indian Kings lately departed from this city) told me one day . . . that he would be miserable confined to a town."

Andrew McGillivary, a half-breed chief of the Creek Indians, had been causing trouble for years among the settlements of the Southwestern frontier. Born of a Scotch father and a French-Indian mother, he had been educated at Charleston and become associated in business with his father, a prominent trader in Georgia. During the Revolution he had been a loyalist, his property had been confiscated, and he had gone to live among the Creeks, whom he organized for service with the British forces in the South. After the war, he helped Spain in her effort to subdue American competition in the Indian trade by carrying on guerrilla warfare against frontier settlements from Georgia to the Cumberland. Early in 1790, however, an emissary from the Congress succeeded in persuading McGillivary to consider a treaty of peace. With thirty "Kings, Chiefs and Leaders of the Creek Nation," the half-breed arrived in New York late in July to be greeted with ceremony by the President of the United States and fêted by the Society of Saint

Tammany. Promised a substantial pension by the government, Mc-Gillivary signed the treaty and, with his attendant chiefs, left the capital early in August.[16] The Indians, solemn and inarticulate, made a tremendous impression upon the citizens of New York, and especially upon Freneau.

On September 1 he printed in the *Daily Advertiser* "A Short Discourse upon Drunkenness," said to be written by "Opay Mico one of the Indian Kings from the little Tallasee country, lately departed from this city." "Several papers of this savage," Freneau informed his readers, "have been discovered since his departure, written in the Tallassee language. They will be translated for the satisfaction of the curious." The Indian, like the "Pilgrim," would comment upon men and manners. "The end and design of man is happiness," he said, but Freneau developed the theme with no high seriousness. Instead, he had Opay Mico discuss the pleasure to be derived from the "strong spirit of the juice of the grape." Admitting that some men became irresponsible under the influence of alcohol, nevertheless he reminded the reader that nature, too, had "her passions and her whims, her fits of anger and her seasons of moderation." In fact, he said,

I was ever greatly afraid of that man who was never known to transgress the bounds of strict sobriety in drinking. Such a man is cold and unfeeling. His whole happiness is centered in himself continually. He never relaxes the severe brow of care, but like a certain animal in our forests, is continually anxious to collect a hoard which it is most likely he will not long exist to enjoy— To be always serious is not true wisdom. Life should, in a certain degree, be chequered with folly, otherwise we disguise the feelings of nature, and under the severe mask of wisdom lose those pleasures which folly, when sensibly indulged, never fails to inspire.

The second of the Opay Mico essays appeared on September 8, when the Indian chief presented "Reflections on my Journey from the Tallassee Towns to the Settlements of the River Hudson." His thoughts were melancholy, because they were concerned with the fate of his people. The Indian, he mused, had been driven from a life of pastoral simplicity bestowed by a benevolent mother, Nature, to a state of war and, finally, to threat of extinction because of the cruelty of the white man. Opay Mico saw a dismal future for his race: nothing could overcome the natural antipathy between the Indian and his conquerors.

What is to be the fate of our posterity; a feeble race who will become weak and spiritless by the extravagant use of these poisonous liquors which you supply us with in so fatal an abundance? Doubtless both they and we, and our progenitors, will be reckoned among the lost things of the world; if remembered at all, it will only be in song or fable—possibly too in the page of some fortunate historian!

The last of the Opay Mico essays, "A Discourse upon Horse Shoes," was printed on September 17. The chief compared Indian superstitions, upon which the white man looked with such disdain, with the absurd faith his conquerors placed in the powers of so insignificant an object as a horseshoe.

Under Freneau's direction the *Daily Advertiser* became a lively commentary upon contemporary events and human foibles. But it was journalism, and pretended to be no more. Of his contributions during the autumn of 1790 he rescued for later publication only "The Banished Man," printed on September 1, "Tormentia's Complaint," September 7, "Palemon to Lavinia," November 17, "The Blessings of the Poppy," November 18, and, in prose, "The Discourse on Barber's Poles" which appeared on November 1.

When the Congress reconvened in December, the *Daily Advertiser* followed its proceedings with suspicion. Men like Freneau, who looked forward to a time when principles of freedom should animate all mankind, found little encouragement in reports from the new capital. Dominated by the conservative mercantile class of the Northern states, the Congress seemed to be forgetting its obligations to the volunteers who had fought to make freedom possible. Or was freedom in America possible? It did not seem to Freneau that it was, when on January 24 he published "The American Soldier":

> Sold are those arms which once on Britons blaz'd,
> When flushed with conquest to the charge they came,
> That power repell'd, and FREEDOM's fabrick rais'd,
> She leaves her soldier—FAMINE and a NAME!

When the fulfillment of ideals could not be accomplished, a man might retire to himself, to enjoy simple living among simple things.

So Freneau had found twice before, in Santa Cruz and during his years at sea. Now again in "Stanzas Written on the Hills of Neversink," printed on January 26, he expressed his desire for the quiet of personal seclusion. Apparently written soon after he quit the coastal trade, the lines present Freneau's most felicitous expression of his recurrent longing to be away from noisy competition:

> These heights, the pride of all the coast,
> What happy genius plann'd;
> Aspiring o'er the distant wave
> That sinks the neighbouring land:
> These hills for solitude design'd,
> This bold and broken shore,
> These haunts, impervious to the wind
> Tall oaks, that to the tempest bend,
> Half Druid, I adore.
>
> . . .
>
> Proud Heights! with pain so often seen,
> I quit your view no more,
> And see, unmov'd the passing sail,
> Tenacious of the shore:
> Let those who pant for wealth or fame
> Pursue the wat'ry road,
> Soft sleep and ease, blest days and nights,
> And health, attend these favorite heights,
> Retirement's safe abode!

So, too, in a portrait of "The Market Maid," published on January 28, Freneau asked the hard-working young girl who rowed over the East River at dawn with kail and cabbage for the city markets, "Sweet nymph, why all this useless pain?" Find some alert young man, he advised her. Retire with him to a country home, abjure the city and its ways, and in quiet find happier living. There was little to be admired in avaricious mankind. On February 1 Freneau printed his most severe indictment of negro slavery in "The Island Field Negro. (Written some years ago, on a Sugar Plantation in Jamaica)."

Even when someone had a useful scheme which might benefit all men, he had little opportunity to succeed. Such seemed the situation in which John Churchman, the Quaker mathematician and surveyor, found himself. Having published a chart on which he set forth the magnetic variation of the compass from the true north for every part of the globe, Churchman petitioned the Congress for a subsidy which would allow him to test the accuracy of his compilations. His application for funds had been before the Congress since 1789; but in spite of hearty recommendations from men like James Madison, nothing was being done about it.[17] Freneau advised, therefore, on February 2 in "Lines on the Failure of Mr. Churchman's Scheme of Going to Baffin's Bay, to Ascertain the Truth of his Variation Chart":

> The men, whom you petition for some dollars,
> Tho' willing to be thought prodigious scholars,
> Yet care no more for variation charts
> Than ace of spades, or king of hearts.
>
>   .   .   .
>
> Rather attach yourself to Caesar's wing
> You'll find it better—better, Sir, by half,
> To tell him Yankee jokes, and make him laugh:
> Then shall you, mounted in a coach and six
> Ride envoy to the country of the Creeks;
> Then shall you visit Europe's gaudy courts
> And see the polish'd world at public charge,
> Come back, and spend your life in sports,
> Be air'd in coach, and sail'd in barge,—
> Pursue this track, thou man of curious soul,
> Nor, like the whale, go puffing to the pole.

Lines such as these could not make Freneau popular—at least, not popular with influential people who might help a poet to fortune. When he avoided controversial matters, however, Freneau found his audience ready to welcome him. No poem that he had ever written was received with more applause than "The Tea Drinker," which he published on February 5. Reprinted in newspapers and magazines again and again during Freneau's lifetime, it struck the public fancy as none of his more serious poems had done. And this is the way it began:

> Let some in Grog place their delight
> O'er bottled Porter waste the night,
>   Or sip the rosy Wine;
> A dish of Tea

> More pleases me;
> Yields softer joys
> Provokes less noise
> And breeds no bad design.

Four stanzas followed, none better than the first: tea revived the soul, warmed old maids, charmed widows, attracted beaus, and put sprightly life into the female tongue! This was verse that America enjoyed.

On February 8 Freneau published "The Shelbourne Threat," a humorous tale of a Scotch fisherman who tried to outwit the canny Yankees of New England by smuggling a load of fish into Boston—of course, he could not do it. Then on February 11 Freneau printed "The Jug of Rum." It even eclipsed "The Tea Drinker" in popularity; nothing that he ever wrote was to be more widely copied. To many of his contemporaries he must, indeed, have been known solely as the author of "The Jug of Rum" or, as it was sometimes called, "The Jug of Whiskey." It was rollicking doggerel, without a single spark of poetry:

> Within these Prison-walls repose
> The seeds of many a bloody nose,
> The clattering tongue, the horrid oath,
> The fist for fighting nothing loth,
> The nose with diamonds glowing red,
> The bloated eye, the broken head.

Freneau's plans for retirement from urban life now reached a definite stage. A broadside dated "New-York, February 15, 1791" announced that he proposed—if sufficient encouragement was given him—to edit a weekly newspaper entitled *The Monmouth Gazette, or, General Magazine of Information and Amusement* at Mount Pleasant, New Jersey. The publication would be a quarto of eight pages, and would be delivered to subscribers by a rider engaged especially for that purpose. Because of the editor's former connections with printers in all parts of the United States, the *Monmouth Gazette* would be inferior to no newspaper published in New Jersey. Subscriptions were to be received by the editor's brother-in-law, Major Benjamin Ledyard, at Middletown Point, or by Philip Freneau at his residence at Mount Pleasant.[18] "Mr. Freneau—the

Pindar of America—is about establishing a news-paper in New Jersey," wrote Benjamin Russell in the *Columbian Herald*. "He has also prepared for the press a third volume of his Miscellanies." [19]

Some weeks were to pass, however, before Freneau left New York. He was increasingly discontented, and his contributions to the *Daily Advertiser* became even more acid than before. To what length would the Congress not go? How inept it seemed in the management of national affairs! In order to ease the burden upon the mass of the people, a bill was introduced to repeal duties placed upon distilled spirits and substitute others in their place. But what to tax? A representative from North Carolina suggested newspapers. Freneau howled derision in lines "On the Proposed Taxation of Newspapers." Was the freedom of the American press to be jeopardized? Were newspapers to become court organs? In disgust at the proposal, he wrote:

> The well-born sort alone, should read the news,
> No common herds should get behind the scene
> To view the movements of the state machine:
> One paper only, filled with courtly stuff,
> One paper, for one country is enough,
> Where incense offered at Pomposo's shrine
> Should prove his dog-house and himself divine.

To Freneau the United States seemed headed toward disaster. The very elements of tyranny against which the free men of America had fought in the Revolution were gaining new footholds. Avarice and ambition seemed to dominate the national councils. Men in responsible positions were said to take advantage of public trust to build large personal fortunes. Speculation in public lands ran unchecked. Leaders like John Adams and Alexander Hamilton were suspected of advocating, if not monarchy, at least a very selective aristocracy. Revolutionary soldiers, small farmers, hard-pressed country merchants, and courageous settlers on the frontier were victimized by what seemed a vicious system of taxation and by manipulation of public securities. The voice of popular opinion was heard only faintly above the busy din of legislators. To republican members like bluff Senator William Maclay of Pennsylvania even

President Washington appeared highhanded in his treatment of the Congress.[20] There seemed little room for ideals in the hardheaded busyness of the national capital, for, said Freneau on February 26 in "The Useful only in Vogue at Court":

> Whoe'er at court would hope to cut a dash,
> He must go loaded with some *useful* trash:
> Something sage *dullness,* to assist your reign:
> All fancy-stuff, all ornament is vain.

3

During the last months of Freneau's association with the *Daily Advertiser* an undercurrent of personal controversy ran through the columns of the newspaper. It began when "A.B.," irritated at a poem too fulsome in its praise of Thomas Jefferson, contributed on November 11 "Rules How to Compliment Great Men in a Proper Manner." Never, wrote "A.B.," flatter a republican like Jefferson by saying that he is fit for a throne. Do not address him as though he were a dictator. Remember that he is chosen by the people and is paid by the people to do his work well. It ill becomes a poet to seek personal advancement through flattery.

Five days later an unsigned satirical essay "On Epic Poetry" appeared. What must one do to write an epic? First, one must "borrow or purchase Pope's Homer's Iliad, the Odyssey, Pitt's or Dryden's Virgil." When these volumes have been studied by day and placed lovingly under the pillow at night, the "complete sing-song Heroic" will soon be established in the aspiring poet's mind. Then, he must find a fable; because "you might as well make pumpkin pye without a pumpkin . . . as make an Epic poem without a fable." Ancient Jewish history perhaps supplied fables most plenteously, because bloodthirsty and butchering deeds were there discovered in abundance. Next, much "ancient nonsense" must be used; God is to take sides in every quarrel. Above all, there must be no such thing as realism in the epic. A sailor in a storm, for example, must be "dissolv'd in terror" as he lifts "ardent prayers" for delivery from the "angry elements." "I appeal to any man," wrote the author of the essay (and it is difficult to imagine that he could have been anyone but Freneau), "if sailors are not rather at such times employed in sending down yard arms and top gallant masts, bringing the ship to the wind, or scudding before it under bare poles."

Enough, however, for the pretensions of epic poetry. But what of the fame of men who wrote it? No poem during the Revolution was more read than *McFingal,* written by John Trumbull of Connecticut. Since the war, three patriotic epic attempts had come from the same New England state, and each had raised its author's name in popular esteem. In 1783 when Colonel David Humphreys published *The Glory of America,* few remembered that eleven years before Freneau had published *A Poem on the Rising Glory of America.* Four years later Joel Barlow presented *The Vision of Columbus,* and the theme of his poem was not unlike that of Freneau's "The Pictures of Columbus." In 1785 the Reverend Timothy Dwight had published *The Conquest of Canâan,* which compared the struggles of the Israelites under Joshua with the victorious campaigns of Washington.

The poets of New England flourished, Freneau's *A Poem on the Rising Glory of America* had fallen still-born from the press. What then of poetic fame? The question was answered by an essay "On the Power of Chance in the Production of Great Characters" which appeared in the *Daily Advertiser* on November 27. Had not Milton, Shakespeare, Corneille, Molière, and Rousseau all owed their renown to a fortuitous interrelation of events? Did chance not play an equal rôle in determining the popularity of an American poet?

Yet Freneau could not feel that it was chance alone. "There are more wonderful things brought to light in Connecticut," announced a correspondent to the *Daily Advertiser* on December 9, "than in all the rest of the United States." What are these wonderful things? asked "D. Doubtful" three days later. We suspect that it was Freneau who entered the discussion on December 14 to suggest that Connecticut produced mammoth pumpkins and cabbages, a great many children, psalm tunes, a fine grade of onions, and epic poems. On the next day another correspondent wrote indignantly:

While other states have been publishing volumes of scraps *gathered together from old newspapers,* under the title of poems, Connecticut has given the world a *M'Fingal,* a *Conquest of Canaan,* and a *Vision of Columbus,* three poems which are the admiration of Europe and the boast of America.

The gauntlet was down. A gesture of scorn had been made toward Freneau—at least, he thought it had. On December 16 in "Reflections on Sundry Subjects" he defended himself: "By *the admiration of Europe* nothing more is oftentimes understood than the venal admiration of the London Reviewers." As Dwight was from Greenfield and Humphreys from Fairfield the implication of the following charge was obvious:

Fairfield and Greenfield (it is whispered) since the war have had the happy knack of writing encomiums upon the poetical productions of their sons, and sending them to England to the Reviewers, with a little of the NEEDFUL in order to procure a quantum of this *boasted admiration.*

On the other hand, Freneau averred, "the author of *'the Poems gathered from old newspapers'* " has adopted none of these pitiful measures of attracting notice. Unlike Dwight who had dedicated *The Conquest of Canâan* to "His Excellency George Washington, Commander in Chief of the American Army, the Saviour of his Country, the Supporter of Freedom, and the benefactor of mankind," or Barlow who had addressed *The Vision of Columbus* to "His Most Christian Majesty Louis the Sixteenth," Freneau boasted that he dealt "neither in court sycophantism, nor in sublime dedications." He had been gratified, however, he said, "in observing a constant unsolicited republication of most of his writings in the periodical works of both America and Europe; and frequently by those who strut in their *borrowed* plumes, without the generosity to give the least credit for them to their original owner." Finally, in a last outburst of resentment against the New Englanders, he complained:

It cannot but excite sentiments of indignation in every man of a liberal spirit to see a sett of heavy moulded pedants coming forward from the *Eastward,* and, with the extremity of arrogance, affecting to dictate in matters of polite literature to the other nine States.

On December 17 a correspondent reminded Freneau that "there is a very great difference between making *verses* and writing *poetry.*" Freneau retreated scornfully with a sarcastic rejoinder on the next day. "*Your* disapprobation," he said, "will *certainly* injure the sale of the two volumes I have already published, and possibly of that which is to make its appearance in the spring!"

Freneau was glad for every evidence of the popularity of his work. Early in February he printed an "Extract from a Letter from London" which said of one of the prose sketches from the *Miscellaneous Works:*

An American production, entitled, "A law case between Soloman Dash and Frederick Flute," has been lately delivered with great eclat in the British theatre, owing to that fund of satyrical humour with which it abounds, and yet is of such a nature as to please without offending.[21]

Could any writer from New England exhibit higher commendation? In Philadelphia Mathew Carey printed the "Sketches of American History" and the "Stanzas on the Emigration to America and Peopling of the Western Country" in a splendid anthology called *The Beauties of Poetry, British and American.*[22] But in the same collection Dwight and Barlow, even young Joseph Brown Ladd of Charleston, were more handsomely represented than Freneau. Finally, subscribers were found wanting for the new volume of Freneau's poems, and nothing more is heard of it.

Almost a year previously the poet's friends had recommended him for a government position, but no post had then been available.[23] Freneau struggled as a workaday newspaper man—the best, James Madison was soon to say, in the whole country.[24] To another poet, however, one who had dedicated his works well, had come recognition of a far more practical sort. Late in February a dispatch to the *Daily Advertiser* announced that Colonel David Humphreys had been appointed representative of the United States to the court of Portugal.[25] Freneau commented bitterly:

> For Lisbon's port has sail'd our man of song,
> And trust me, *Bards*, the Muses went along:
> Since that bright morn he stepp'd on board his brig,
> No Muses here—no Muses are with pig,
> Nor, 'till his barque shall heave in sight once more,
> Can one true Muse grow pregnant on this shore.

He compared his own humble rôle with that of the new envoy:

> Did I the smiles of fortune still pursue,
> And Memmius, wish to rise to fame like you—
> Were this my scheme, I'd quit at once the mob,
> And haste to court with pendulum and bob,
> Quit all the gains the finer arts bestow,
> The fields of fancy, and the flowers that blow;
> Indulge some potent *something* in the skull,
> That makes us famous while it makes us dull,
> To that best place prefers its steady claim—
> The road to fortune, and the road to fame.[26]

Freneau had come to a crossroads. Perhaps the situation had not yet arisen, but, at any rate, he must determine for himself what he would do if he were confronted with an opportunity such as had been presented to Humphreys. "Can love of Fame the gentle Muse inspire?" he asked in untitled lines on March 4. The answer, of course, was negative, and of his own verse Freneau vowed:

> Yet while it walks the page, let no one say
> It flatter'd knaves, or help'd to puff the vain.

Of his own plans for the future he wrote:

> Sick of the wasted hours, some toil, some play;
> Half pleas'd, I seek my barren fields again,
> Look back on years, that can return no more
> And fools at sea, that might have stay'd on shore.

A correspondent in the Philadelphia *Independent Gazetteer* of March 5 answered Freneau's attacks on Humphreys with an "Epigram on a Certain Satyrist":

> PHIL, why so angry at a brother Poet—
> And with the snakes of envy sting thyself?
> It is a fact—and well the public know it,
> While *his* works sell—*yours* rust upon the shelf.

Insult again! Was there no respite from infamous defamation? Five days later in the *Daily Advertiser* Freneau replied:

> Poet whoe'er you are, you do me wrong,
> I envy not, the least, your man of song;
> Envy should rankle in my breast as soon
> As Frogs that croak on Schuylkill's shores in June;

My works in *Bailey's* shop for sale are shown
And if not *bought*—are *borrow'd* through the town.

4

Meanwhile Freneau's friends again busied themselves in his behalf. Aedanus Burke of South Carolina called James Madison's attention to the financial difficulties under which the poet struggled.[27] Both Madison and Henry Lee recommended their former college mate to Thomas Jefferson,[28] who late in February wrote to Freneau:

The clerkship for foreign languages in my office is vacant. The salary indeed is very low, being but two hundred & fifty dollars a year; but also it gives so little to do as not to interfere with any other calling the person may chuse, which would not absent him from the seat of government. I was told a few days ago that it might perhaps be convenient to you to accept it—if so, it is at your service. It requires no other qualifications than a moderate knowledge of the French. Should anything better turn up within my department, that might suit you, I should be very happy to bestow it as well. Should you conclude to accept the present, you may consider it as engaged to you, only be so good as to drop me a line informing me of your resolution.[29]

"Upon receiving this letter," said Freneau, now resident at his home in Monmouth, "I consulted several of my friends, who advised me to accept Mr. Jefferson's overture." But the salary seemed inadequate, and plans for the future were already made.[30] Freneau was going to establish a country newspaper and live quietly at Mount Pleasant. He apparently sent no answer to Jefferson; and during the next two months remained in New Jersey, submitting occasional poems to the *Daily Advertiser.* "Marriage a la Mode" on March 22 told of the courtship and elopement "occasioned by a quarrel between a weaver and a ditcher; the latter having supposed his family consequence disgraced by the clandestine marriage of his son with the weaver's daughter." On March 24 appeared verses "On Putting a Dog Ashore on the Island of Sapola for Stealing," which had been written in 1788. Three weeks later, on April 13, Freneau contributed a versified complaint "On the Prohibition of Spirituous Liquors in the New York and Albany Jails."

Except that his sympathy rose to the defense of all men oppressed

in whatever manner, Freneau, however, was apparently little concerned with contemporary affairs. On April 16 was printed "Charity
a la Mode," a poetical description of the hardships encountered by
the captain of a trading vessel. On April 20 appeared the verses
"To the Keeper of the King's Water Works," which had been written
five years earlier in Kingston. And on April 29 Freneau presented
lugubrious verses "Written on a Beau Drowned in a Mill Pond."
The poet found contentment among his fields at Mount Pleasant.
He had been invited to Philadelphia. But, he wrote in "Kay-Grove,"
which appeared on April 15:

> To crowded courts and would-be kings
> Where fawning knaves are most carest
> Who would, tho' oft invited, go,
> While here so many charming things
> By Nature to perfection dress'd
> To please the man of science grow.
>
> The native of this happy spot
> No cares of vain ambition haunt;
> Pleas'd with the partner of his nest
> Life flows—and when the dream is out
> The earth, that once supply'd each want,
> Receives him, fainting, to her breast.

Back in New York by April 20 and hearing that some settlement
might be made to descendants of those men who years before had
invested in lands in northern New Jersey, Freneau made application in behalf of Agnes Kearny, who had inherited interest in the
Ramapo tract which André Fresneau's syndicate had purchased
in 1709. Land titles were confused. Proprietors of New Jersey
claimed the original purchase void because the land had belonged
by patent to the Proprietors, not to the individuals who had sold it
to the Huguenot merchants. Freneau threatened litigation to retrieve
his grandfather's investment. Nothing came of it.[31]

On the first of May Freneau was in New York again, to confer
with friends on the offer of employment which Jefferson had made.
Madison quieted Freneau's qualms concerning qualifications for
the position of translating clerk by insisting that a knowledge of
French really was all that was necessary. A newspaper published in

a thriving city like Philadelphia would be, he suggested, much more likely to succeed than one printed in rural Monmouth County. Furthermore, a "free newspaper, meant for general circulation, and edited by a man of genius of republican principles would be some antidote to the doctrines and discourses circulated in favor of Monarchy and Aristocracy." Freneau's forthright republican talents would be wasted if they were buried in the obscurity of a country town.[32] Madison acknowledged that his friend was a "man of literary and retired tastes, knowing nothing of the world." [33] Yet, he reported to Jefferson, "it is certain that there is not to be found in the whole catalogue of American Printers, a single name that can approach towards a rivalship." [34]

Convinced for the moment, Freneau set out for Philadelphia with a letter of introduction to the Secretary of State. "It is not improbable," Madison warned, however, "that he may halt in New Jersey." [35] Released from the pressure of his friends' encouragement, Freneau's enthusiasm waned. After waiting the poet's arrival for almost a week, Jefferson wrote, "I suppose . . . he has changed his mind again, for which I am really sorry." [36]

Jefferson had occasion to be sorry that Freneau had given up the plan, for there was no newspaper in Philadelphia powerful enough to combat the "doctrine of monarchy, aristocracy, and the exclusion of the people" which the Secretary of State found in John Fenno's openly Federalist *Gazette of the United States*. Republican newspapers, such as Benjamin Franklin Bache's *Pennsylvania Daily Advertiser* and John Dunlap's *Daily American Advertiser*, opposed Federalist policies, but neither was capable of prolonged editorial controversy. "We have been trying," Jefferson wrote to his son-in-law, "to get another weekly to set up here, but failed." [37]

From Monmouth Freneau continued to send verse to the *Daily Advertiser*. While he had been in New York "Lines Written Some Years ago on the Death of a Fiddler" had appeared on May 2. Now he contributed a satirical picture of "The Rural Bachelor" on May 13, "Stanzas to the Memory of Mrs. Gertrude Burnet" on May 17, humorous animadversions "On the Crew of a Certain Vessel, Several of which Happen'd to be of the Same Name with Celebrated Clergymen" on May 20, and on May 26 "The Invalid," which had been written in South Carolina five years before. The simplicity of country life seemed to be no more conducive to the production of poetry than the turmoil of city ways.

When the occasion demanded, however, Freneau could still write with vigor. Appearing serially in the *Daily Advertiser* from May 6 to May 27 was Thomas Paine's *The Rights of Man,* the first publication of which had caused Thomas Jefferson to rejoice that "Something is at length publicly to be said against the political heresies that have sprung up amongst us." Printed at the end of the final installment, Freneau's "Lines Occasioned by Reading Mr. Paine's Rights of Man" attest to the poet's continued abhorrence of monarchial tyranny, "the curse, the scourge, the ruin of our race." The vision of an America builded firmly on the natural rights of every man was again clear before him when he wrote:

> COLUMBIA, hail!—immortal be thy reign;
> Without a king we till the fertile plain;
> Without a king we trace the encircling sea,
> And travel round the globe in each degree,
> Each distant clime, our gallant flag reveres,
> Nor asks the monarch to support new STARS;
> Without a king the laws maintain their sway,
> While honour bids each loyal heart obey.
> Be ours the task, the ambitious to restrain,
> And this great lesson teach, That kings are vain,
> That warring realms to certain ruin haste,
> That kings subsist on war, and wars are waste;
> So shall our nation (form'd on Reason's plan,)
> Remain the guardian of the Rights of Man,
> A vast republic, fam'd thro' every clime,
> WITHOUT A KING, TO SEE THE END OF TIME.

Natural man needed no hereditary ruler to guide him along the paths of reason. No more did nature need the artificial restrictions which man would place on her. Therefore, when the Common Council of the City of New York voted to include among its ordinances one which stated that after June 10, 1791, no tree was to stand within the city limits, the common people of New York rose clamorously in protest. A petition for the preservation of the trees was directed to the Mayor and the Aldermen; letters condemning the ordinance poured into the newspapers.[38] On May 31 Freneau contributed to the *Daily Advertiser* two columns of prose "Strictures on the Late Law for the Removal of All Trees Standing in the Streets of this City." Following in verse was "The Landlord's Soliloquy," in which a disgruntled homeowner is represented in the midst of a mournful farewell to the boughs which so long had shaded him from the noonday sun. Spare them, he begged, at least until winter comes and their slaughtered trunks can be used in our fireplaces! Few poems by Freneau achieved their purpose more quickly. Early in June a Philadelphia newspaper reported, "The Trees in New-York have lately been in jeopardy, through an ordinance of the Corporation—but agreeable to a poetical hint in a poetical supplication to procrastinate their fate till next winter, the law has been suspended till the first of December." [39]

Though Freneau apparently thought little of it, Madison and Jefferson did not abandon their plan for a republican newspaper in the national capital. When the Secretary of State passed through New York early in the summer, a meeting was arranged with Freneau.[40] Negotiations were begun with Childs and Swaine whereby the printers would underwrite a Philadelphia publication.[41] But Freneau could not be pinned down. He now considered the establishment of a paper of his own in New York. Madison informed Jefferson:

I have understood that Mr. Freneau is now here & has abandoned his Philad[a] project. From what cause I am wholly unable to determine; unless those who know his talents & hate his political principles should have practiced some artifice for the purpose.[42]

Some days later Jefferson replied:

I am sincerely sorry that Freneau has declined coming here. Tho' the printing business be sufficiently full . . . yet I think he would have set out on such advantageous ground as to have been sure of success. His own genius in the first place is so superior to that of his competitors.

The Secretary of State acknowledged that he would have done all in his power to assist Freneau:

I should have given him the perusal of all my letters of foreign intelligence & all foreign newspapers; the publication of all proclamations & other public notices within my department, & the printing of the laws, which added to his salary would have been a considerable aid.[43]

But by the end of July Freneau had changed his mind again. From Monmouth he wrote to Madison:

Some business detains me here a day or two longer from returning to New York. When I come, which I expect will be on Thursday, if you should not have left the city, I will be glad to give you a decisive answer relative to printing my paper in the Seat of Govt. instead of N. York. If I can get Mr. Childs to be connected with me on a tolerable plan, I believe I shall sacrifice other considerations, and transfer myself to Philadelphia.[44]

Very shortly thereafter an agreement was entered into with Francis Childs in which the printer agreed to finance the publication of a newspaper in Philadelphia and to stand responsible for any loss which should be incurred in its publication. Issued twice a week from the branch shop of Childs and Swaine in Philadelphia, where John Swaine had been carrying on a printing business since the Congress had removed from New York, the newspaper was to be under the editorial control of Freneau, who was to be free of financial responsibility, but was to share as a third partner in the division of profits.[45]

The poet's decision having been communicated to Jefferson, the following document was filed among the papers of the Secretary of State:

Philip Freneau is hereby appointed clerk for foreign languages in the office of the Secretary of State with a salary of two hundred & fifty dollars a year, to commence from the time he shall take the requisite oaths of qualification. Given under my hand and seal this 16th day of August 1791. Th. Jefferson.[46]

Freneau, however, did not proceed to Philadelphia until early in October. During the summer he sent an occasional poem to New York for publication in the *Daily Advertiser*. "The Drunkard's Apology" appeared on July 9, "Minerva's Advice" on August 4, and "On a Painter, who was Endeavouring to Recover from Memory the Features & Portrait of a Lady, who Died at Sea," on August 24. In the meantime a prospectus for the proposed newspaper was drawn up. On August 24 the Philadelphia *Freeman's Journal* contained an advertisement of the forthcoming publication of "The NATIONAL GAZETTE, a Periodical Miscellany of News, Politics, History, and Polite Literature, by Philip Freneau." One day later the same announcement began to appear in the New York *Daily Advertiser*.[47] The first issue was promised for November 2, "or sooner, if a sufficient number of Subscribers are procured."

Freneau's last contribution to the *Daily Advertiser* was "The Parting Glass" on September 17. Then, shortly after the birth on September 20 of his first child, Helena,[48] he set out for Philadelphia. He did not know and, he said, he did not care particularly whether the clerkship in the Department of State was still open or not. His first object was to establish a newspaper. When informed by Jefferson, however, that the position of translator was being held for him, Freneau immediately took the requisite oath of office.[49] The *Daily Advertiser* on October 24 reported:

We hear from Philadelphia that the Hon. Thomas Jefferson, Esquire, Secretary of State for the United States, has appointed Capt. Philip Freneau Interpretor of the French Language for the Department of State.

At forty Freneau was about to step into a hornet's nest.

EIGHT

THE NATIONAL GAZETTE
1791–1793

B Y the autumn of 1791 Alexander Hamilton, the brilliant and audacious young Secretary of the Treasury, had proved himself the most forceful political figure in the United States. "Mr. Hamilton," grumbled Senator William Maclay, "is all-powerful, and fails in nothing he attempts." [1] Visualizing the United States as one interdependent, efficient economic unit, free from the diverting opinions of separate states or recalcitrant individuals, Hamilton advocated a concentration of national power in a strong centralized government. He had little faith in democracy. To him it was a virulent poison that threatened the life of a nation.[2] Man in fumbling for security needed direction and intelligent control.

To political opponents like Jefferson, Madison, and Maclay, each of Hamilton's measures seemed to threaten the rights of the common man of America. For example, Hamilton proposed to fund a national debt of more than fifty million dollars by replacing depreciated public securities with new government bonds at par.[3] As a result, speculators received one hundred cents on the dollar for bonds they had bought from original holders for fifteen or twenty cents. Veterans who had been given debt certificates in payment for services during the Revolution were victimized by money-dealers. Even members of the Congress were said to have joined in the riot of speculation.[4] Republicans were shocked at rumors of immense personal fortunes made at the people's expense. To them Hamilton's plan seemed only to increase the profits of men already wealthy.

Moreover, it was proposed that state debts amounting to more than twenty-five million dollars be assumed by the national government. This meant more taxes. And who, asked the republicans, bore the weight of Hamilton's tax measures? The common people! Among the masses throughout the country a murmur of protest arose at the proposed tax on whiskey. "Had we not gone to war with England on a tax?" [5] Then it was tea, now it was whiskey.

Yet each of Hamilton's measures was approved by the Congress. Having redeemed the national credit by his funding system and having inaugurated a system of direct taxation to put federal finances on a sound foundation, Hamilton now proposed a national bank. It would supply capital for private enterprise. It would add to the resources of the government. Many considered the plan a frank bid for the cooperation of monied interests. Like previous Hamiltonian measures, it meant a concentration of financial power in the already wealthy North, and at the expense of the agricultural South and the undeveloped western country.[6] To Anglophobes like Freneau one of the most obnoxious features of the bank was that it was obviously modeled on the Bank of England. But, in spite of grumbling in republican ranks, so powerful was Hamilton's influence that even Senator Maclay thought it "totally in vain" to oppose the Bank Bill.[7] Jefferson objected to it hotly, but it was quickly approved by both houses of the Congress.

Hamilton now seemed omnipotent. All the wealth and the power of the nation seemed bound in one small group. But what of the rights of man? What of the doctrine that all men were created equal and endowed with certain inalienable rights which a government could disregard only at its peril? What of the spirit of the American Revolution, which had been fought to establish just such a doctrine? Republicans questioned petulantly, but there was small strength among them. So it was that Thomas Jefferson, fresh from the influence of agrarian France, welcomed Thomas Paine's *The Rights of Man* as an antidote to the "political heresies" which he found among leaders in America. The nation seemed headed straight back to monarchy.[8]

Indeed, had not the manners of London and the fashions of Paris been transferred to the drawing rooms of Philadelphia? "I should spend a very dissipated winter," wrote Abigail Adams, wife of the Vice-president, "if I were to accept one half the invitations I receive, particularly to the routs, or tea and cards." [9] "Ye Gods," expostulated Senator Maclay, "with what indignation do I review the late attempt of some creatures among us to revive the vile machinery" of "royalty, nobility, and vile pageantry, by which a few of the human race lord it over and tread on the necks of their fellow mortals." [10] Nothing made an American happier, remarked a visitor from abroad, than to be exalted above his fellow citizens.[11] Youthful Chateaubriand on his visit to the United States was scandalized by the elegant dress, the luxurious carriages, and the frivolous entertainment in the republican capital.[12] "Democratic gentlemen," reported another observer, "no matter how high their social qualifications, were rigidly ostracized." [13]

Yet Philadelphia the city had changed little. Wide cobblestone streets flanked with willows, buttonwoods, and poplars crossed each other at right angles to make tidy rectangular blocks on the borders of which stood squat houses of brick with well-scrubbed entranceways.[14] Though its waterfront was cluttered and odorous, Philadelphia was on the whole a clean city and well planned. Noah Webster, of New England, complained of the monotonous regularity of its streets and the depressing sameness of its buildings.[15] But the Duc de la Rochefoucault thought it one of the most charming municipalities in the world. He was particularly impressed with the pumps of fresh water placed along all the principal thoroughfares. Nothing better could be met with in all Europe! He thought that if Philadelphia had more ornamental parks and fewer burial places, it would be an ideal city.[16]

Second in importance only to the great public market which stretched for nearly half a mile down High Street was the State House, fronting on Chestnut Street just below the intersection of Sixth. Here the state assembly met, and here—in a wing extending to the north—the city carried on its official business. Congress Hall, a commodious building newly erected for the national government, stood just to the south. Behind it spread a quiet garden shaded with buttonwoods and maples. Just below it on Chestnut Street was Oeller's Hotel, with the best table and the most comfortable beds in the city. The landlord was famous for his punch and pineapple juice, which enlivened many a sultry afternoon. "Papered after the French taste" with "imitation festoons, pillars and groups of antique drawings," the assembly room of the hotel was the scene of balls and public receptions at which no gentleman was admitted "in boots or colored stockings." [17]

Philadelphians were proud of the attractions their city offered. The Franklin Library, open from two o'clock till sunset, contained more than twelve thousand volumes.[18] Plays were given nightly at the old Southwark Theatre, and John Ricketts, late of Blackfriar's in London, offered daily equestrian exhibitions at his circus on High Street. Bowen's wax works and Peale's museum tempted the curious, but the more learned gathered in the reading room of the Philosophical Society, where Dr. Benjamin Rush, David Rittenhouse, or even Thomas Jefferson might be found in conversation with other members. But in Philadelphia the accepted standard for all things was European. "Nine tenths of our American ideas and prejudices," said a visitor some few years later, "are English." After leaving the city, he admitted, "I could see no difference between Philadelphian and English manners. The same style of living, the same opinions as to fashions, tastes, comforts, and accomplishments exists." [19]

Such was the capital to which Philip Freneau came in October, 1791, to establish the *National Gazette*. The free spirit of the American Revolution seemed to have vanished from the people, and democracy was held in contempt. Yet throughout America, and even in Philadelphia, there were many staunch republicans. They were poorly organized and they fought clumsily—though even Federalist Oliver Wolcott admitted, "If they were a compact, uniform body of people . . . they would be formidable." [20] It was Thomas Jefferson's plan to shape republican opinion into a political weapon of force, and Philip Freneau and his newspaper were to be among the Secretary's instruments.

Although Philadelphia already supported twelve newspapers, none but the Federalist *Gazette of the United States* achieved more than local influence. The *National Gazette*, therefore, was to reach beyond the bounds of city or state. Its function was to be the education and organization of republican opinion in all parts of the country. James Madison solicited subscriptions in Culpeper and Fredericksburg.[21] Henry Lee spoke of the project to his friends in Richmond.[22] Aaron Burr wrote enthusiastically of it to his wife.[23]

Jefferson did what he could to further the circulation among his partisans everywhere.[24] Freneau's paper was to be read from Boston to Georgia, and in the frontier towns of Kentucky. It was to be the focus from which republican ideas would radiate, and was to be dedicated to the "great principles upon which the American Revolution was founded, and which alone can preserve the blessings of liberty." [25]

When the first issue appeared on October 31, 1791, bold letters below the masthead on the first page announced that the publication was "By Philip Freneau": no doubt was to exist on whom responsibility for policy was to be placed. In his address "To the Public" the editor promised to include all important foreign news, not only from European journals, but from personal correspondence which came to his attention. Domestic news would be printed fully and "all decent productions of entertainment in prose and verse" and "such political essays as have a tendency to promote the general interest of the Union." In a "Poetical Address to the Public of the United States" Freneau offered his salutatory:

> Thus launch'd as we are in an ocean of news,
> In hopes that your pleasure our pains will repay,
> All honest endeavours the author will use
> To furnish a feast for the grave and the gay;
> At least he'll essay such a track to pursue
> That the world shall approve—and his news shall be true.

2

During the first four months of its existence there appeared little violent partisanship in the *National Gazette*. Each issue contained a detailed official account of the proceedings of the Congress. Hamilton's "Report on Manufacturers" was printed complete, and Freneau even published a notice of the subscription which was being solicited for a special portrait of the Secretary of the Treasury. The editor's former classmates Hugh Brackenridge and James Madison each contributed pithy disquisitions on national affairs, but neither wrote with animus at which Federalists might take serious offense. Freneau himself was restrained and judicious in expression. The

National Gazette was establishing itself as an intelligent, thoroughly impartial organ of public opinion. Its articles were directed to the "best hosts of public liberty and the strongest bulwarks of public safety," the common countrymen "who provide at once their own food and their own clothing." [26]

If anything indicated a political bias in the journal, it was the anti-British and pro-French tone which dominated it from the beginning. "Americanus," for example, derided the English for their refusal to restore property which had been seized during the American Revolution. Prominent position was given to extracts from Robespierre's speech to the National Assembly of France. The whole first page of the issue of November 17 was devoted to Thomas Paine's "Thoughts on the Establishment of a Mint in the United States." On the whole, however, the early *National Gazette* was non-controversial and intensely patriotic. Republican leaders were well satisfied with Freneau's progress. The newspaper, Madison wrote Henry Lee, "justifies the expectations of his friends and merits the diffusive circulation they have endeavored to procure it." [27]

Freneau's poetry appeared regularly, but most of it was reprinted from former contributions to the *Daily Advertiser*. Besides the "Poetical Address" in the first issue, the only new poems which he published during the first four months of the *National Gazette* were "A Mistake Rectified," November 14, "The Prudent Philosopher," November 17, "The Debtor's Soliloquy," December 8, and "The Country Printer," which ran in four installments from December 19 to January 5. During this period, however, Freneau identified himself with a new pseudonym: "The Mistake Rectified," a nautical tale, was signed "Sinbat the Sailor"; poems of the sea reprinted from the *Daily Advertiser*, such as "The Pilot of Hatteras," January 19, "Lines Written at St. Catherines," February 16, and "Charity a-la-Mode," February 20, were all published over the shorter "Sinbat." The name was well chosen for the poems to which it was appended, but there was no anonymity to it. Soon, to Freneau's embarrassment, "Sinbat" became a weapon which his political opponents used unsparingly against him.

By the end of February, 1792, the *National Gazette* had begun to make its influence felt: "It is rising fast into reputation," Henry

Lee reported to Madison.[28] Now, more strongly established, the journal became openly polemic. A correspondent who signed himself "Continentalist" attacked the new excise laws as unfair to the common man.[29] At the same time an editorial charged the funding system with being responsible for the rise in speculation, the desire to amass fortunes rapidly, and the thirst for rank which seemed to affect the whole country. On March 1 "A Farmer" wrote that the "accumulation of that power which is conferred by wealth in the hands of a few is the perpetual source of oppression and neglect to the rest of mankind." Hamilton was accused of giving open preference to the demands of the wealthy at the neglect of public welfare. This was the gravest of all evils, and something should be done about it. "Though the American Aristocrats have failed in their attempt to establish titles by distinction of law, yet the destructive principles of aristocracy are too prevalent amongst us."

But it was "Brutus" who in a series of attacks "On the Funding System" dealt the earliest telling blow against Hamilton's influence. The whole plan of funding and taxation, Brutus warned, was but a plot to increase the influence of the Treasury Department and to coerce voters to the support of whatever measures Hamilton might propose.[30] The national bank, moreover, was an offspring of the funding system, therefore damnable. Seats in both houses of the Congress were filled with stockholders, and public creditors were erected into a body politic with exclusive privileges.[31] But who suffered? The victims were the "industrious mechanic, the laborious farmer, and generally the poor and middling class." [32] "Principles subversive to the equal *rights of man* are in rapid succession introducing themselves into our system of government, our political bark seems to be gently gliding down that stream leading from freedom to slavery." On March 26 "A Farmer" warned that the private actions of free citizens were being subjected to arbitrary laws, more of the "spirit and regulations of a military camp" than the humane legislation of a republican government. "Let the Secretary of the Treasury and his adherents beware," warned Brutus.[33]

Freneau, as an editor, was, of course, responsible for what appeared in the columns of his newspaper and, therefore, was subject to attack by opponents of its policies. But when he was first attacked, it was neither as an editor nor as a controversialist. He was ridiculed as a poet! The politically active Hartford *American Mercury* published on March 12 as part of number seven in "The Echo" series:

> Sinbat the Child of Clio and of Trunnion
> Who reels off verses as he reels off spun-yarn,
> Sinbat, whose ardent soul mistook a sail,
> For the broad feathers on a Muses tail;
> Who really tho't the boatswain's whistle sound,
> Pegasus whinnying on Parnassian ground,
> His quarter deck the song inspiring mount,
> And cans of grog the pure Castilian fount;
> Who held for years the pitch poetic rudder,
> Came home from sea, kill'd Death, and wed the widow.[34]
> Sinbat, alike well skill'd in either trade
> To flush the vessel's or his master's head,
> Sinbat the author, captain, printer, tar,
> The News-boys Poet, and the Dog of War,
> The blackguard's pattern, and the great man's fool,
> The fawning parasite, and minion's tool.

Such an attack could not pass unnoticed. On March 29 the "Receipt to Make an Echo Writer" appeared in the *National Gazette:*

> Two bushels of meal and three gallons of water,
>   (Rain water or river is held to be best)
> The guts of a swine just warm from the slaughter,
>   And a pumpkin boil'd up with a gallon of yeast.
>
> Six quarts of strong *bogo,* that stinks from the still,
>   A jill of molasses, and swichell three pints,
> With malice and scandal—as much as you will—
>   And a *quantum* of bear's grease, to supple the joints.
>
> Old Midas's ear, and the sweatings of brass,
>   The tongue of a goose, and the husk of an onion,
> The liquor that chills in the hoof of an ass,
>   Some verses, *slight-banded* from Pope or from Bunyan:—
>
> Work these up together, and let them ferment,
>   In the space of a day the *serrago* will *rise;*
> Eight more must elapse, and the eighth being spent,
>   On the *ninth* the spruce puppy will open his eyes.

He'll then be completed for *epic* or *lyric*,
　　To plunder from Butler, and call it his own,
To scribble on dunces some dull panegyric
　　Or whine out his poems in sorrowful tone:

He'll then be completed, to publish his jokings,
　　To furbish up psalms, or to cobble damn's stuff,
In poems called ECHOES, with pitiful croakings,
　　To snuffle out lies, and expire in a snuff.

Nor was this enough. Two blows must be given for one. Therefore on April 2 Freneau presented the "Ode to the Echo Writer":

In Echo's caves, with shrill-voic'd conchs hung round,
　　And pumpkin shells, responding all they hear,
A Bard, call'd *Whaacum*, catches every sound
　　Governs their tone, pricks up his lengthy ear:
In putrid ink then dips his pen of lead
And scribbles down what prattling Echo said.

Bard of the lengthy ode! whose knavish paw
　　Ne'er grasped the helm, *besprent* with odious pitch,
'Twas better far, (you know) to *practise* law,
　　Whine at the church or in a court-house screech;
No heart had you to face the wintry blast
Fight with the storm, or climb the tottering mast.

Then why so wroth, thou bard of narrow soul,
　　If *Sinbat*, tir'd of puppies sought the brine?—
He drank no swichell from your white-oak bowl,
　　Nor from your poems *filch'd a single line*:—
　　　When he does this—then echo from your caves,
　　　"Who robs a beggar, is the worst of knaves."

This, however, was only a skirmish, far off on one flank, while the main forces were manoeuvering into position. For several weeks writers for the *National Gazette* had been sniping at the Federalists in Philadelphia. The House of Representatives was engaged in lengthy debate over one paragraph of Hamilton's "Act for Establishing a Mint," in which the Secretary proposed that a representation of the head of Washington be stamped upon all coins of the United States. What are we coming to? cried the republicans. It is the "practice of monarchies to exhibit the figures or heads of their kings upon their coins!" [35] "Shall Washington, my fav'rite child be ranked 'mongst haughty kings?" asked Freneau on March 29 in stanzas "Occasioned by the Debate this Day." The same issue of the *Gazette* found "Valerius" attacking Vice-president Adams as unfit for office. And on April 2 Madison contributed an article entitled "The Union. Who Are Its True Friends?" They were not, of course, speculators or those who favored measures which pampered the spirit of speculation. Neither were they those who fostered the spirit of aristocracy or monarchy in opposition to the republican spirit of the people. Friends of the Union were those who opposed every public measure which led to hereditary government and every move made to enslave the common man by burdening him with a large public debt.

Then the papers of "Sidney" really brought the opposing forces into open battle. "Let us suppose, for the moment," he wrote on April 23 in an attack on Hamilton's "Report on the Excise," "that the Secretary is perfect in wisdom, immaculate and infallible with respect to integrity." The censure was back-handed, but soon Sidney became more pertinent. Hamilton, he accused, opposed public opinion and embraced the interests of one class in preference to the interests of all other classes. His methods of influencing deliberations of the Congress were as flagrant as any practiced by Prime Ministers in England. His measures, particularly his excise tax, were "injurious to the liberty and enslaving to the happiness of the people." Sidney spoke bluntly.

John Fenno in the *Gazette of the United States* for May 2 replied by growling about "mad Dogs" and "audacious scribblers" with "disordered imaginations," who "rave about monsters because they are out of their wits." "Such," replied Freneau on May 10, "is the hue and cry raised . . . against every man who writes on the measures of government without dipping his pen in molasses." "Centinel" on May 3 warned that the "fate of the excise law will determine whether the powers of government . . . are held by an aristocratic junto, or by the people." "It is downright despotism," added Freneau, "when a public officer, drawing an arbitrary line of separation between his own interest, and those of the people, enriches

and aggrandizes himself by cheating and betraying his employers."
"Cackling sentinel!" derided Benjamin Russell in Boston. "When
the printer of the National Gazette is dead, the patriotick people of
these States will fall asleep!" [36] But Freneau kept on. "It is worthy
of notice," he said, "that no direct denial has ever appeared of the
. . . multiplied accusations that members of the government have
carried on . . . speculation." [37]

On May 7, at the end of its first six months of publication, Freneau rededicated the *National Gazette* to the people of the United
States. The circulation, he said, "exceeded beyond the Editor's most
sanguine expectations." He hoped that subscribers would find the
paper at all times "truly republican in its principles and tendency,
as well as instructive and entertaining to every denomination of
reader." It would, he reminded them, continue to welcome every
sort of decently conducted political discussion, with no partiality
to parties or opinions.

John Fenno scoffed at this pretense of impartiality. For every
sentence printed in the *National Gazette* in favor of the government,
there were, he asserted, whole columns devoted to opposition.[38]
Nor is Freneau's boast of impartiality completely justified by succeeding issues of the newspaper. "Sidney" continued to contribute
articles "On the Injustice of the Excise Law and the Secretary's
Report." [39] "The people," insisted Freneau, "are still asleep." He
called attention to "poverty in the country," "luxury in the capi-
tals," and "corruption and usurpation in the national councils." [40]
Excerpts from the second part of Thomas Paine's *The Rights of Man*
were printed, because, said Freneau, "there is no American newspaper but might, with credit to itself, now and then occupy part of
a column with extracts from a work that so forcibly inculcates the
genuine principles of natural and equal liberty." [41]

"The abusers of government," retaliated Fenno, "pretend that
they are only exercising a right given them by the constitution."
As a matter of fact, he informed anxious Federalist readers, "a
majority of them are persons from other countries who having
lately escaped from bondage, know not how to enjoy liberty." [42]
"Oyez! Oyez! Oyez!" bandied Freneau. "Hear! Hear! hear, and
attend! . . . attend, ye *foreigners,* from every country, and from

every clime!" Freneau was openly playing for support from the
immigrant population. "Here is *John Fenno* come all the way from
Boston to lodge informations against you. . . . He swears (and
who dares disbelieve him when he swears?)—that you *foreigners*
are a set of rebellious turbulent dogs!" [43]

Fenno saw the trap into which he had fallen. There were too many
Irishmen, Scotchmen, Frenchmen, and Germans in Philadelphia to
make his position comfortable. He insisted that his meaning had
been mistaken.[44] "Once more, Ye foreigners, attend!" cried Freneau. "The aristocratic printer," "Pomposo's printer," "J———
A———s's printer" had insulted and slandered all foreigners in his
"court gazette." [45] Thus were the common people effectively to be
united under the standard of republicanism. The fight was fair on
neither side, and it raged furiously into the summer of 1792.

The funding system and the speculation which had risen from
it continued, however, to be the center of attack in the *National
Gazette*. John Fenno accused the republican newspaper of being
supported by a faction who planned to use its columns for elec-
tioneering purposes.[46] Freneau admitted that the Federalist editor
was correct—if he meant by a faction "a very respectable number
of the anti-aristocratical and anti-monarchial people of the United
States; whom we shall be proud to serve at all times." [47] But Freneau could not be diverted long from his favorite indictment. Members of the Congress, he charged again, were deeply concerned in
speculation, were even combined with money-dealers in order to
gull their uninformed constituents of government securities.[48]
"Knaves!" cried John Fenno, "propagators of calumny!" [49] "Stop
calling names," suggested Freneau, for "such a judicious evasion of
arguments, instead of answering them, has always been a nice point
among *twisted characters*." [50]

The editor of the *Gazette of the United States* challenged Freneau
to name one member of the Congress who victimized the people.[51]
That, retorted Freneau,

reminds us of the impudence of a noted prostitute of London, who, having
a difference with a young man, was by him reproached for her profligacy,
and called by the plain name of her profession . . . 'I'll make you prove
it or pay for it,' said she. Accordingly, she sued the young man for defama-

tion of character, yet nobody could prove her incontinency without owning himself an accomplice, and the defendant was lost for want of evidence and obliged to pay heavy damages. Thus it is when any man talks of speculators —'prove the fact, sir!'—as if, indeed . . . the brokers who negociated the securities would come forward to expose their employers and *themselves*.[52]

John Fenno and the Federalists were losing ground. Even a correspondent in the *Gazette of the United States* reprimanded its editor for his "scurrilous reproofs" and his attacks upon foreigners: "Peace, Brawlers! Peace!" [53] Finally "Crito" began a more orderly assault against the policies of the *National Gazette*. Freneau's paper was established, he said, by a junto of jealous politicians. Every charge leveled against speculation was but dust raised to cover their main design, which, said Crito, was "to *oust* from the government almost every man now in the administration." [54] "Court paragraphs," sniffed Freneau.[55] He did not bother to reply. Meanwhile, however, the Hamiltonians marshaled their forces. "Now, Mr. Fenno," advised a correspondent to the *Gazette of the United States*, "I hope the writers in your paper will adopt a different line of conduct—and as they have begun, will go on to set in a conspicuous point of view the principles and representations contained in that NATIONAL paper." [56] Freneau's journal should change its name, suggested a contributor to the Boston *Columbian Centinel*: "its title ought to be the *Anti-National Gazette*—unless the publisher means to begin with a lie, to make his paper consistent throughout." [57]

In addition to the political discussion which had enlivened the *National Gazette* during the spring and summer of 1792, Freneau presented his own verses whenever space permitted. Many of them, still, were republished from the *Daily Advertiser*, for editorial duties apparently left him with little time for the cultivation of poetry. When he reprinted "The Landlord's Soliloquy" on March 8, he prefaced it with a new prose introduction, a little essay of six paragraphs which he called "On Trees in Cities." "Tormentia's Complaint" was included in the issue of March 16, signed "Sinbat." "The Shelbourne Threat," perhaps because it was an excellent slap at his Yankee opponents in New England, appeared on April 5. "The Parting Glass," May 10, "The Market Girl," May 28, and "The Dish of Tea," July 7, were all reprinted just as they had appeared before. "The Demolition of Fort George," in the issue of June 21, was introduced by a prose passage on "New-York," which described the pleasant park which had been constructed on the site of the old battery.

The publication of hitherto unprinted poems was less frequent, but until late in the summer they, too, had little to do with contemporary affairs. "The Village Merchant," which ran serially in six install-ments from May 17 to June 28, was the poem which Freneau later called "The Adventures of Simon Swaugum" and which, he said, had been written in 1768 when he was a student at Princeton. "The Fair Buckle Thief," a character sketch in the manner of "The Market Girl" and "The Almanac Maker," appeared on June 4. Curiously enough, stanzas written to the memory of Robert and William Sevier, twin brothers who had been killed during an Indian raid in North Carolina, were printed on June 27, not in the *National Gazette*, but in the New York *Diary*. It was not until a month later, on July 28, that they appeared in Freneau's paper, and then not until four days after they had appeared in the Philadelphia *Federal Gazette*.

After the *National Gazette* had been established for eight months, Freneau began to produce finished verses on more timely subjects. On July 4, 1792, he printed "Independence," a warning to his countrymen jealously to guard their liberties:

> Peace to all feuds!—and come the happier day
> When Reason's sun shall light us on our way;
> When erring man shall all his RIGHTS retrieve,
> No despots rule him, and no priests deceive;
> Till then, Columbia!—watch each stretch of power,
> Nor sleep too soundly at the midnight hour,
> By flattery won, and lull'd by soothing strains.

France, in tearing aside the bonds of ecclesiastical and mo-narchial misrule, was setting an example to the free men of America. France, who had been so instrumental in America's victory over tyranny, was now establishing a commonwealth built securely on principles which protected the rights of the common man. To many Americans the developments of the French Revolution seemed to portend anarchy and terrorism, but to Freneau the rebellion of the people of France represented the beginning of a world-wide recognition of democracy. For the second anniversary of the fall of the Bastille he presented "On the Fourteenth of July" as the first of a series of "Odes on Various Subjects." He spoke for the republicans of America:

> Bright Day, that did to France restore
> What priests and kings had seiz'd away,
> That bade her generous sons disdain
> The fetters that their fathers wore,
> The titled slave, a tyrant's sway,
> That ne'er shall curse her soil again!
>
> Bright day! a partner to thy joy,
> Columbia hails the rising sun,
> She feels her toils, her blood repaid,
> When fiercely frantic to destroy,
> (Proud of the laurels he had won)
> The Briton, here, unsheath'd his blade.
>
> By traitors driven to ruin's brink
> Fair freedom dreads united knaves,
> The world must fall if she must bleed;
> And yet, by heaven! I'm proud to think
> The world was ne'er subdued by slaves—
> Nor shall the hireling herd succeed.

For the common man of America, Freneau proposed, "Fill the generous goblet high; *Success to France* shall be the toast." Again speaking for his republican countrymen, he dedicated the second of the "Odes on Various Subjects" to "Crispin O'Conner, Esq. a backwoods planter." He, an Irish emigrant who had gone westward to develop a homestead on the frontier, prospered by the toil of his hands. Now rich harvests sprang from fields which once had been overgrown with briars. Of such was the opportunity in America. O'Conner, and all men like him, though abused by John Fenno in the Federalist "court journal," would determine the fate of liberty in the United States.[58]

3

By midsummer it had become evident that there could be no peace to the feud which the *National Gazette* had started with adherents of the Secretary of the Treasury. Hamilton was alarmed.

The attacks against him were reaching to all corners of the United States. "Let any impartial man peruse all the numbers down to the present time," Hamilton wrote, "and I never was more mistaken if he does not pronounce that it is a paper devoted to the subversion of me and the measures in which I have an agency." The Secretary in his anger perhaps credited Freneau with too many of the articles: "Whenever the editor appears," he said, "it is in correspondent dress." And who supported him? "It is reduced to a certainty," Hamilton exclaimed, "that he was brought to Philadelphia by Mr. Jefferson to be the conductor of a newspaper." [59] The Secretary wrote to New York to see what could be learned of the circumstances of Freneau's coming to the capital.[60]

The summer was unusually warm in Philadelphia. Tempers were stretched to the breaking point. Congressmen returned to their homes to hear from liberal constituents who subscribed to Freneau's paper. If Hamilton was to maintain his control of the Congress, the *National Gazette* would have to be discredited before national elections were held in the autumn. Though Washington retained his popularity, it was already rumored that the opposition planned to unite on George Clinton for the vice-presidency. "The plot thickens," wrote Hamilton to John Adams, "and something like a very serious design to subvert the government discloses itself." [61]

Thus with his back to the wall, Hamilton began a counter attack against the most articulate of his opponents. On July 25, hiding his identity behind the signature "T.L.," he presented this note to the *Gazette of the United States*:

The Editor of the "National Gazette" receives a salary from government:— *Quere*—Whether this salary is paid him for *translations*; or for *publications*, the design of which is to vilify those to whom the voice of the people has committed the administration of our public affairs—to oppose the measures of government, and, by false insinuations, to disturb the public peace?

In common life it is thought ungrateful for a man to bite the hand that puts bread into his mouth; but if the man is hired to do it, the case is altered.

The fat was on the fire. Freneau reprinted the "*Quere*" on July 28. "The above," he said, "is beneath reply." Nevertheless, he did suggest:

It might be queried, however, whether a man who receives a small stipend for services rendered as French translator to the department of state, and, as editor of a free newspaper, admits into his publication impartial strictures on the proceedings of government, is not more likely to act an honest and disinterested part towards the public, than a vile sycophant, who obtaining the emoluments from government, far more lucrative than the salary alluded to (by undermining another who was in possession of the employ) finds his interest in attempting to poison the minds of the people by propagating and disseminating principles and sentiments utterly subversive of the true republican interests of this country, and by flattering and recommending *every* and *any* measure of government, however pernicious its tendency might be, to the great body of the people.—The world is left to decide on the merits of each.

All this was involved and rather rhetorical. Not suspecting the true origin of the charges against him, Freneau saddled them on John Fenno, with whom he dealt again on the same day in the third of the "Odes on Various Subjects":

> Since the day we attempted the NATION'S GAZETTE
> Pomposo's dull printer does nothing but fret;
>> Now preaching
>> And screeching,
>> Then nibbling
>> And scribbling,
>> Remarking
>> And barking,
>> Repining
>> And whining
>> And still in a pet
> From morning till night with the Nation's Gazette.

Fenno was jealous. Freneau was sure of that. The Federalist editor, who flattered and lied, palavered and puffed—who, like a spaniel, submissively licked the shoe of his master—was worried, said Freneau, because of the success of his republican rival. An "Advertisement Extraordinary" was printed in the same number of the *National Gazette:*

WANTED. A Place in a Public-Office in this city— No objections to acting as French Translator to the Department of State, should the present encumbent be ousted or resign.

N.B. Times being hard, the duty will be done at extraordinary low wages, besides soul, body, and conscience surrendered to the absolute disposal of government. A line addressed to T.L. at Mr. Fenno's, No. 69, High-street, will be thankfully attended to.

Perhaps, said "A.Z." in the *Gazette of the United States* on July 28, the author of the *"Quere"* wished to announce his own small talents for sale, and at a low price. Fenno, however, assured his correspondent that "T.L." was "neither the editor, publisher or printer of any newspaper whatever, nor directly or indirectly concerned in any." Then "Detector," a new and equally vigorous assailant, entered the quarrel. "It is high time," he wrote, "that the mask were torn from the faces of these professed friends, but real enemies of the United States." He demanded the exposure of "those hypocritical republicans, those pretended advocates for the liberties of the people" who made the *National Gazette* a nest of sedition, "the tool of faction, and the prostituted vehicle of party spleen and opposition to the great principles of order, virtue and religion." How could they dare call others hirelings? Was not their principal editor, he asked, professedly retained under a department of the very government which he opposed? [62]

"The same insolent language against the real whigs of America now fills the pages of the court gazette of the United States," scoffed Brutus in the *National Gazette* of August 1, "as appeared in the gazette of St. James during our arduous struggle for liberty." Freneau, on August 4, devoted the fourth of the "Odes on Various Subjects" to a review of the policies of his newspaper:

> Nine months have now laps'd, dear rambling paper,
> Since first on this world's stage you cut your caper
> With spirit still of democratic proof,
> And still despising *Whaacum's* canker'd hoof—
> What doom the fates decree, is hard to say,
> Whether to live to some far distant day,
>   Or sickening in your prime
>   In this news-taxing clime,
> Take pet, make wings, say prayers, and flit away.

What of the accusations made by Detector in the *Gazette of the United States?* Freneau laughed at them:

> *"Virtue, Order,* and *Religion,*
> Haste and seek some other region:

Your plan is fix'd, to hunt them down;
Destroy the mitre, rend the gown,"
And that vile b-tc-h—Philosophy—restore—
Did ever paper plan so much before!

He shook off his calumniators with scorn:

For nine months past, a host of busy foes
Have buzz'd about your nose
White, black, and grey,
By night and day;
Garbling, lying,
Singing, sighing:—
These eastern gales a cloud of insects bring
That fluttering, snivelling, whimpering on the wing,
And wafted still as Discord's demon guides,
Flock round the flame, and yet must scorch their hides.

On August 4 Fenno printed the attack on "Sinbat the child of Clio and Trunnion," which had appeared in the *American Mercury*. Three days before, Hamilton as "T.L." had contributed a second accusation against Freneau. How much, he asked, is the republican editor paid for his dirty work? "We must wait with patience 'till the treasury accounts are published . . . and then, perhaps, the mystery will be explained." But the Secretary of the Treasury was after a scalp more important than an editor's. On August 4, as "An American," he dismissed Freneau contemptuously as the "faithful and devoted servant of the head of a party," and launched his attack upon Jefferson directly. It was plain to any intelligent reader, he said, that the principles of the *National Gazette* were the principles of Mr. Thomas Jefferson. Why, then, if the Secretary of State so opposed every measure of the government, did he not resign his position? "Can he reconcile it to his own personal dignity and the principles of probity to hold an office under it, and employ the means of official influence in opposition?" Hamilton established his point boldly. Jefferson supported the *National Gazette*, he thundered. Jefferson dictated its policies. Jefferson used it to advance his own party. Jefferson, behind the scenes, pulled every wire.

But now Freneau began to suspect the direction from which the charges came. "The melancholy howlings that have for some time past been heard through the dreary regions of the Gazette of the

United States," he said four days later, "are full and clear proof that *all is not right* with certain lofty minded persons that fondly imagine their ambitious career was to proceed, without check or interruption, to the summit of their wishes." "The devil rageth," he added, "when his time is short." Hamilton's attacks had apparently been based entirely upon assumption. Freneau decided to put a stop to them. He went to the mayor of Philadelphia and swore to an affidavit:

Personally appeared before me, Matthew Clarkson, Mayor of the City of Philadelphia—Philip Freneau, *of the City of Philadelphia, who being duly sworn, doth depose and say, That no negociation was ever opened with him by* Thomas Jefferson, *Secretary of State, for the establishment or institution of the* National Gazette: *that the deponent's coming to the City of Philadelphia, as the publisher of a Newspaper, was at no time urged, advised, or influenced by the above officer, but that it was his own voluntary act; and that the said Gazette, nor the Editor thereof, was ever either directed, controuled, or attempted to be influenced in any manner, either by the Secretary of State, or any of his friends; nor was a line ever, directly or indirectly, written, dictated, or composed for it by that officer, but that the Editor has consulted his own judgement alone in the conducting of it— free—unfettered—and uninfluenced.*

It was a blanket denial of all charges. It seemed water-tight. Freneau submitted it, with a review of the circumstances of his coming to Philadelphia, to the *Gazette of the United States* on August 8.

"Facts," scoffed Hamilton, again appearing as "An American" on August 11, "speak louder than words, and, under certain circumstances, louder than oaths." He examined Freneau's affidavit clause by clause. He came close to the truth when he suggested that, though the Secretary of State had kept in the background during negotiations which brought Freneau to the capital, "a *particular friend* of that officer" had "openly urged, advised, and influenced him." Then, addressing the editor of the *National Gazette* directly, he said:

the circumstances of your having come from another State to set up and conduct a *new paper;* the circumstance of the *Editor* of that *new paper* being appointed a Clerk in the department of State—the *coincidence* in point of time of that appointment with the *commencement* of your paper, or to speak more correctly, its *precedency*—the conformity between the com-

plexion of your paper and the known politics of the head of the department who employs you—these circumstances, collectively, leave no doubt
of your true situation—the conviction arising from them is too strong to
be weakened by any of those bold, or even solemn declarations, which are
among the hackneyed tricks employed by the *purists* in politics, of every
country and age, to cheat the people into a belief in their superior sanctity,
integrity or virtue.

But the editor was only incidental to Hamilton. "These strictures," he concluded, "though involving Mr. Freneau, it shall be
confessed, have been drawn forth principally with a view to a character of greater importance in the community." The Secretary of
the Treasury wrote again to New York for affidavits concerning all
the particulars of Madison's negotiations with Freneau. "A friend,"
Hamilton naïvely informed his correspondent, had asked him to
secure the information! [63]

"Personal charges from an anonymous writer," parried Freneau,
"deserve no answer, and shall have none." But what, asked a correspondent to the *National Gazette,* of the *"immaculate* Mr. John
Fenno?" Was he not printer to the Senate of the United States? Did
he not enjoy exclusively the printing for the Treasury Department?
Had he not been promised the contracts from the Bank of the
United States? Did he not receive ten times more from the government than the translating clerk of the Department of State? If two
hundred and fifty dollars made Freneau a knave, what did twenty-
five hundred dollars make John Fenno? [64]

So the quarrel dragged on, back and forth, through the summer.
"The enemies of genuine republicanism," complained "Cato" in
the *National Gazette,* "are constantly buzzing in our ears." [65] A
contributor to the *Gazette of the United States* made merry over
Freneau's affidavit. What, he asked, had the poet sworn upon, the
Bible or Jefferson's *Notes on Virginia?* [66] "If the Republican party
patronize Mr. Freneau," temporized the *Boston Gazette,* "it is
equally evident that the Aristocratic party befriend Mr. Fenno." [67]
The editor of the *Connecticut Courant* found the *National Gazette* a
"disgusting paper," published by "professed grumbletarians." [68]
But the liberal Boston *Independent Chronicle* recommended it
wholeheartedly to all true friends of liberty, particularly as it was

said "to be printed under the eye of that established patriot, Thomas Jefferson." [69] So! answered the *Columbian Centinel*, republicans did admit that Jefferson pulled the strings! [70] Soon Hamilton, over the pseudonym "Civis," began a defense of the funding system.[71] "Mercator" answered him valiantly,[72] and the controversy raged on. Freneau continued to laugh at his assailants:

> Three well-fed lads, in solemn junto met,
> Swore to destroy the National Gazette;
> One *smelt* a *bribe,* that never did exist,
> One scrawl'd some nonsense with his mutton fist,
> One, swoln with fancied state and fancied power,
> Reported lies, that scarcely lived an hour:
> Bold were their aims (even envy might confess)
> But *paunch* alone can never crush *this press,*
> Their breadth of *belly,* or their—*length of nose.*[73]

Late in August Washington did what he could to effect a reconciliation between his two principal cabinet members. "How unfortunate," he wrote to Jefferson from Mount Vernon, "and how much it is to be regretted . . . that, while we are encompassed on all sides with avowed enemies and insidious friends, internal dissensions should be harrowing and tearing our vitals." [74] To Hamilton he advised "charity in deciding on the opinions and actions of others." "My earnest wish," said the President, "is that balsam may be poured into *all* the wounds." [75]

Jefferson, who, during the whole controversy, had been in retirement at Monticello, answered with a long explanation of his arrangements with Freneau. He had employed the poet upon the recommendation of mutual friends. He had, he admitted, been glad to see his translating clerk establish a newspaper, and had taken it for granted, from what he knew of Freneau's principles, that the editor would "give free places to pieces written against the aristocratical & monarchial principles" which had been advanced by Federalist writers. The Secretary of State acknowledged that he had supplied his clerk with copies of the *Leyden Gazette* and that he had solicited subscriptions to the *National Gazette* among his friends. "But as to any other direction or indication of my wish how his press should be conducted, what sort of intelligence he should give, what essays encourage, I can protest, in the presence of heaven, that I never did by myself or any other, directly or indirectly, say a syllable, nor attempt any kind of influence." Nor had Jefferson written for this or any other gazette. He thought it unseemly that a high public official should enlist himself as an anonymous newspaper writer.[76] Hamilton was equally forthright in his reply. He had, he admitted, had "some instrumentality of late in retaliations which have fallen upon certain public characters." Furthermore, he said, "I find myself placed in a situation not to be able to recede *for the present*." [77]

Meanwhile Freneau had been going earnestly about his work as a liberal editor. He rejoiced to report that "republican sentiment was fast rising" in all parts of the country. Soon, he forecast, it would "reassume its former elevation in the political thermometer." [78] He reprinted "The Island Field-Negro" on July 21, "Constantia" on August 11, and "Farmer Dobbin's Complaint," now changed in title to "Farmer Dobbins to the Buck-Suitors," on August 25. He ridiculed the aristocratic pretensions of wealthy Philadelphians on August 11 with a versified burlesque, "A Curious Dialogue (Occasioned by the Emblematic Devices on a Certain Travelling-Coach)." On August 20 he presented the poem which had appeared four years before in the Charleston *City Gazette* as "A Parody on Sappho's Ode," now rewritten and renamed "Rinaldo's Complaint to the Fair Shopkeeper." It began:

> Curs'd as a beggar's dog is he,
> The unlucky man who deals with thee.

The opportunity for parody was too much for the editor of the *Gazette of the United States* to resist. On August 25 he printed the following stanzas addressed to "The Nation's Gazette":

> Dup'd as the greatest fool is he,
> The man who pins his faith on thee;
> Whose columns lies and slander swell
> And a long list of woes foretell.
>
> Whate'er you touch, its rue is chang'd—
> The order of the world derang'd—
> And wretched trash, from ——'s pen,
> Would bring old Anarch's reign again.

'Tis this that makes your page so sad—
At times—your readers say you're mad—
They're sure you do not count the cost,
Subscribers gone—and money lost.

The world grows tir'd—your carping crew,
Alas, presents them nothing new;
Old lies, new vamp'd, alone abound,
Lies smok'd by all the country round.

With antifederal stuff they're vext,
With dismal prophecies perplext;—
For this your readers will not pay—
You'll fret—then quit—alack-a-day!

It was poor stuff—even for a parody. Freneau laughed again, scornfully and a little impatiently:

Hark ye, my dogs—I have not learn'd to yelp,
Nor spend my breath on every lousy whelp,
Much less to write, or stain my wholesome page
With puppies lingo—answering their rage—
Home to your straw!—such contest I disdain,—
　　　Learn this,
　　　('Tis not amiss)
　　　For men
　　　To keep a *pen*,
　　　For dogs—a cane.[79]

On September 19 the poet contributed to the anti-Hamiltonian campaign with stanzas descriptive of "The Speculator," who dashed from town to town swindling old soldiers and widows. But soon, on September 28, he was to write more angrily of a "dirty attempt to prevent the circulation of the National Gazette in the Eastern States." The *Columbian Centinel*, of Boston, had reported on September 12 that the "Clergy of this country are constantly vilified, and Religion ridiculed through the medium of the National Gazette." But, answered Freneau, what of that? Clerical opposition to the principles of the French Revolution led him, as it led many republicans, to distrust organized religion. Theocracy was as baneful to him as monarchy. Formalities of any sort restricted man's spirit, which should be free:

What if this heart no narrow notions bind,
Its pure good will extends to all mankind—
Suppose I ask no portion from your feast
Nor ride to heaven behind *your* parish priest,
Because I wear not Fenno's Sunday face,
Must I for that be loaded with disgrace?

In France the higher clergy of the Catholic church were said to have allied themselves with monarchy. During the American Revolution many leaders among the loyalists had been enlisted from clergymen of the colonial Anglican church. Now, Freneau rejoiced for all true republicans in America:

In this new World our joyful hymn we sing
That even a Bishop is a harmless thing.

Though the quarrel between Hamilton and the Jeffersonians who espoused the principles of the *National Gazette* continued through September and October, Freneau had now little part in it. "Aristides" printed a detailed defense of the Secretary of State in the *Gazette of the United States.* Hamilton was now known as the author of the original attacks. "It has been said," charged "Aristides," "that a certain head of a department is the real . . . instigator of this unprovoked and unmanly attack on Mr. Jefferson." [80] A contributor to *Dunlap's Daily American Advertiser*, however, refused to believe that either secretary had so lowered himself as to enter the controversy. "The truth," he said, "should be told." The real authors were "Grubs who wanton in the salaried sloth of public office, where they come at the knowledge of sundry little stories half told, and now dress themselves in the attire of their betters, to retail those chamber-maid-wares tortured and manufactured for that purpose." [81] "Mischievous calumniator," retorted "An Enemy to Detraction" in the same newspaper, "name the officers!" [82] Let us have an end to this "very unprofitable as well as very unseemly controversy wherein two exalted characters . . . have been traduced," suggested "A Foe to Idlers." [83] But the quarrel went on. Hamilton, as "Catullus," printed a series of replies to "Aristides" in the *Gazette of the United States.*[84] He repeated his assertion that "Mr. Jefferson is the institutor and patron of the National Gazette." "Can any attentive reader of that Gazette doubt," he asked, "that it has been systematically devoted to the calumniating or blackening of public characters?" [85]

The Secretary of State refused to be drawn personally into public conflict. Only in letters did he express the bitterness of his feeling toward his younger colleague. "The indecency of newspaper squabbling between two public Ministers," he wrote Edmund Randolph, "has drawn something like an injunction from every quarter. Every fact alleged . . . as to myself is false. . . . But for the present lying and scribbling must be free to those who are mean enough to deal of them and in the dark." [86] Madison considered Hamilton's charges "as impotent as they are malicious." [87] He too, for the present, remained out of the quarrel.

Meanwhile *Dunlap's Daily American Advertiser* came stalwartly to Jefferson's defense. It surveyed his character and reviewed his career of service to his country. It vindicated him of all charges.[88] "I trust," wrote a correspondent to the *Federal Gazette* early in October, "that the people of the United States are too much enlightened to pass judgement upon him as an enemy of good order and a promoter of sedition, because he happens to be opposed . . . to the favourite measures of another Member of the Cabinet." [89] Hamilton seemed to be losing the battle. "With the greatest deference to his abilities and respect to his character," the same correspondent said, "I do not wish to see the day when it will be deemed a crime to differ with him in a mere matter of opinion." As the *National Gazette* approached the end of its first year, its editor was again attacked in the *Gazette of the United States*,[90] and ardently defended in *Dunlap's Daily American Advertiser*.[91]

Freneau himself only suggested that it "be left to every candid person to decide whether it is probable that a salary of 250 dollars a year . . . can be supposed to influence the Editor in the publication of the National Gazette." [92] He stated openly "that the Gazette of the United States was set up . . . under an anti-republican patronage." [93] He printed on September 28 a humorous poem which offered "Advice to the Ladies Not to Neglect the Dentist." He reprinted "The Bergen Planter" under the title of "The Pennsylvania Planter" on October 3, "Marcella in a Consumption" on October 13, and "The Sixteenth Ode of the Second Book of Horace's Odes,

Imitated," on October 24. He was apparently content to let the quarrel rage on without him. It seemed to do his newspaper little harm. By the end of the first year of publication, he boasted "upwards of thirteen hundred subscriptions from honest and independent citizens of the United States, through every part of the Union." [94]

Republicanism was gaining ground. "The slander and retraction" of men like Jefferson seemed to the Boston *Independent Chronicle,* "convincing proof of the badness of the cause behind it." [95] Partisans of the Secretary of State seemed to have increased, and partly because of Hamilton's attacks. The *National Gazette* became more popular. It was "rising fast into reputation" through the South.[96] It was even, said Jefferson, "getting into Massachusetts under the patronage of Hancock and Sam Adams" to counteract the "hymns and lauds chaunted by Fenno." [97]

4

The newspaper entered its second year with a fanfare of rededication. Although the editor had experienced "no small share of calumny and misrepresentation from interested or designing characters," he promised to maintain a free publication, open to all liberal discussion.[98]

But on November 5 Freneau made the mistake of printing a laudatory poem in French, "from an unknown correspondent," addressed "À Monsieur Philipe Freneau, Éditeur de la Gazette Nationale," which began:

> Plus je vois tes écrits, plus je lis ta gazette;
> Plus je me sens saisi d'une flame secrètte
> Que m'inspire leur verité.

The author praised Freneau's attacks upon speculation and upon the monarchial tendencies of his anti-republican foes. He railed against the monster Law which bound free men. He foretold its overthrow and looked forward to the time

> quand l'histoire
> Nous instruira, qu'un en fut le chasser

A coup-de-pieds au cul, pour précipiter
Au fond de l'Onde noire.

"Why," asked a contributor to the *Gazette of the United States*, "was not the elegant French Sonnet, addressed to Mr. Freneau . . . translated for the delight of common readers?" Did the editor of the *National Gazette* mean it just for the pleasure of an enlightened few? Or was he too modest to print it in English? He could translate, could he not? Was he not employed by Mr. Jefferson for that purpose? Who, then, could better do the service than Mr. Freneau, the poet, who poured forth his genius so often for the amusement of the public? "Perhaps," suggested the contributor, "after all, the *many* may yet hope to be favored with a translation." [99]

Freneau refused to be drawn to the trap, for it was a very poor poem, perhaps too daring for any but the most liberal, and much better left in the original. He did, however, prove his linguistic ability a month later by publishing on December 8 a translation of stanzas addressed "To the Americans of the United States, by the French Patriotic Society of Charleston, S.C." And on December 15 he translated patriotic Latin verses which had been contributed to the *National Gazette* three days before.

In the meantime, Freneau continued his onslaughts against the arch-foes of republicanism. The Vice-president was exposed as an Anglophile by quotations from an English journal which had paid tribute to the conservative political notions of "the learned Mr. Adams." "Mirabeau" contributed strictures on "Forerunners of Monarchy and Aristocracy in the United States." He inveighed against the titles, the pomp and parade, and the high salaries of public officers. He derided the adulation with which "certain department heads" loved to be treated. He viewed with grave alarm such monarchial ceremonies as the public receptions held by President Washington. Monarchy seemed to have gained a foothold everywhere. Philadelphia was a little court. Someone even suggested public celebrations to honor the birthdays of important officials. [100]

Fenno met each attack, blow for blow. Bache, whose paper John Adams considered "nearly as bad as Freneau's," [101] stood valiantly by the republican cause, and Dunlap's daily refused any quarter to the Federalists. Finally, John Adams was reelected, but not without considerable loss in prestige. Five states had gone over to the Jeffersonians. The Vice-president had small joy in explaining that one of the contributing causes was that "there is no other newspaper circulated in the back country of the southern states than Freneau's National Gazette, which is employed with great industry to poison the minds of the people." [102]

For several months France had been becoming increasingly important in the pages of the *National Gazette*. Freneau continued to print extracts from Paine,[103] and presented a long essay "On the Military System" from Joel Barlow's *Advice to the Privileged Orders*.[104] Now that the French Revolution was entering its most dramatic stage, he offered translations from the writings of Condorcet [105] and featured a warmly sympathetic "Letter from Thomas Paine to the People of France." [106] The issues precipitated abroad were inevitably those which disturbed American republicans. That Hamilton looked with fierce disfavor upon the revolutionists and refused to admit that free Americans owed any debt of gratitude to the nation which had helped them gain liberty,[107] only whetted republican appetite for the cause. That Adams said, "Dragon's teeth have been sown in France and come up monsters," [108] only increased liberal sympathy for the common men of France.

Freneau, of course, was a vigorous champion of the French Revolution. To him it was a justification of the ideals for which America had struggled in her war for independence. He chided the Senate for allowing portraits of Louis and Marie Antoinette to remain upon the walls of their assembly chamber.[109] He composed a long, versified "Present View of France and her Combined Enemies" for the issue of December 19. He held Edmund Burke in scorn, and he openly championed the doctrines of Thomas Paine. He gloried in the name of "Jacobin" and looked forward to the time when principles of liberty would encompass the world. He called for the assistance of all right thinking men:

> O FRANCE! the world to thee must owe
> A debt they ne'er can pay:
> The rights of man you bid them know,
> And kindle reason's day!

COLUMBIA, in your friendship blest,
Your gallant deeds shall hail,
On the same ground our fortunes rest,
And flourish, or must fail:
But should all *Europe's* slaves combine
Against a cause so fair as thine,
And *Asia* aid a league so base,
Defeat would all their aims disgrace,
AND LIBERTY PREVAIL!

With France taking such splendid strides toward freedom, the least that sympathetic Americans could do was to purge their own country of every monarchial tendency. "Mirabeau" had mentioned birthday celebrations. On December 19 "G.G." wrote more pointedly on the subject for the *National Gazette.* "Every good citizen of government *really* and not *nominally* republican," he said, "will not only carefully avoid countenancing innovations of a more serious nature, but even those apparent trifles . . . birth-day odes." It might have been foreseen that such a suggestion printed in a newspaper whose editor was known as a poet would leave that editor subject to attack. On December 29 Fenno took advantage of the opening. Freneau was again roundly abused in the *Gazette of the United States:*

The party writers have used the words monarchy, aristocracy, anti-republicanism, corruption, ministerial influence, &c. till their own ears seem to be tired of the sound. To relieve the dullness of prose, their poet strings rhymes together. He has served them up hot in French—he has hashed them into English. But the same sentiments even in verse, have become by repetition, as trite as Sternhold and Hopkins. For the sake of variety, it is recommended to the artificers of calumny on the government, to get it set to music. . . . To bring the good work about, no means should be left untried— Accordingly, it is asserted that the Poet Laureate of the faction is hammering out the verses of certain songs, which have a tendency to abolish Birth-day odes.

Poet Laureate! Freneau siezed upon the phrase. The time would come, he asserted, when "some sycophant and toad-eater" *would* be appointed poet laureate to pester the people with "long splay-footed odes." He inserted an advertisement in the *National Gazette* of January 5, addressed "To the Noblesse and Courtiers of the United States":

Wanted against the 21st of February, a person who is well skilled in the trade of versifying, and who is willing to offer up his talents as a Poet Laureate. As this is somewhat a new trade in the United States . . . it is intended to write the poet laureate of his Britannic majesty for a few lessons. One thing, however, will certainly be required, a dexterity in composing *birth-day* odes.

He outlined the qualifications necessary: "A certain *monarchial prettiness* must be highly extolled, such as *levees, drawing rooms, stately nods instead of shaking hands, titles of office,* seclusion from the people." Such a poet, concluded Freneau, would be rewarded well, either at home or—the reference to Humphreys is evident—abroad.

The capital was stunned. "Even the President's character," Oliver Wolcott informed his father, "no longer remains inviolable." [110] Mrs. Adams was scandalized: "The President has been openly abused in the National Gazette," she wrote.[111] It had never been done before. The Hartford *American Mercury* found new opportunity for satire. All this talk about poet laureates could only mean that Freneau was jealous:

> O were the favor'd aera come
> When we might laureates have at home!
> Bards who should pour the lyrick strain,
> Not in small streams, but plenteous rain;
> Not sprinkle us with little drops,
> But fairly souse us to the chops!
> Then Sinbat glorious might arise
> *Wiping the cob-webs from his eyes;*
> His eyes long closed in dolorous night
> Since Echo frantick made the wight.
> In him some *ancient powers* combine,
> Dull fool, and rhimster, he would shine! [112]

Meanwhile everything French continued to receive commendation in the *National Gazette.* Thus, when Jean Pierre Blanchard, the celebrated balloonist who had made the first aerial crossing of the English Channel in 1785, arrived in Philadelphia, he was warmly greeted. Freneau printed a detailed history of aeronautics, reviewing the exploits of other valiant Frenchmen, the Montgolfiers and de Rosier,[113] and he followed every development of the plans Blanchard made for a "grand aerostatic experiment" in Philadelphia. He reprinted a portion of "The Progress of Balloons" [114] in honor of the event. To liberal Americans Blanchard typified the modern Frenchman, intrepid and daring. Crowds jostled about him at Oeller's Hotel and thronged to see his apparatus in the prison courtyard. But to staid John Adams, Blanchard was a menace. The Vice-president wished "H. would . . . send him back to Europe." Petulantly, he complained that Blanchard set "all the world upon a broad stare at his balloon." [115]

On January 29, ten days after Blanchard made the first ascent in America, Freneau presented readers of the *National Gazette* with long prose "Reflections on Balloons," followed by stanzas inspired by the Frenchman's daring exploit. France led the world in political reform, and she led the world in scientific adventure. M. Blanchard, popular, affable, and a pensioner of the French Republic, did the republicans of America no harm by his presence among them. For weeks after the flight Freneau kept his readers informed of the aeronaut's activities.

But again all this was skirmishing, a mask to the real advance of the republican forces. As Hamilton had attempted to force Jefferson from the cabinet during the previous summer, now the adherents of the Secretary of State turned their full arsenal loose on the Federalist leader. In June, 1792, the Secretary of the Treasury had subscribed two million dollars for five thousand shares of capital stock in the Bank of the United States. He had also immediately borrowed two million dollars from the bank at six percent interest. Thus, the United States government was the largest stockholder in the national bank, and it had the loan of a sum equal to its whole investment.[116] Hamilton, the republicans thought, had been a little high-handed in his financial arrangements. The Congress demanded an accounting. When a bill was introduced which would authorize the President to float a loan at five percent in order to pay the two million dollars owed to the Bank of the United States, republicans protested vigorously. Such a procedure would increase the national debt, mean more taxes. It would be better to sell the stock right back to the bank.[117]

Madison fanned the flame in Congress by announcing that he

wished that some candid explanation might be given by the Secretary of the Treasury in regard to public finances. Was there not, he asked, unappropriated money in the treasury? Was it not owed to France? Had it been paid to France? If so, to whom in France? He wished that it might be sent there on the wings of the wind, in order to support the cause of liberty! [118] Representative William Giles offered a resolution that Hamilton be instructed to submit intelligible reports immediately. "We have been legislating for years," he charged, "without competent official knowledge of the state of the Treasury." [119]

What of the state of the country under Hamilton's dictatorial reign? asked Freneau in the *National Gazette.* "Poverty still reigns triumphant over her thousands; and thousands after every effort of œconomy and industry, still shrink into the cheerless hut of want and misery, as before." And why? Because "speculators and ministerial favorites" receive "vast blessings" under the "operative influence of the federal government." From such sycophants came all praise of fiscal measures. On the other hand, Freneau submitted mirthfully:

> Since federal-sway hath been exerted here
> What numerous blessings to our country flow!
>   Whales on our shores have run aground,
>   Sturgeons are in our rivers found;
> Nay—ships have on the Delaware sail'd,
>   A sight most new!
>   Wheat has been sown—
>   Harvests have grown—
> On coaches, now, gay coats of arms are bore
> By some who hardly had a coat before—
>   Silk gowns instead of homespun, now are seen,
>   Instead of native *straws*, the leghorn hat:
>   And Sir, 'tis true
>   (Twixt me and you)
>   That some have grown prodigious fat
>   That were—prodigious lean! [120]

But Hamilton maintained his hold over the Congress. He was accused by Giles of malfeasance in failing to give official information of money borrowed from Europe, and because he did not consult the public interest in negotiating a loan with the Bank of the United States.[121] The Secretary hurriedly drew up more complete reports. Did he dare meet a full and fair inquiry? asked "Franklin" in the *National Gazette*.[122] Hamilton did, and he was vindicated.[123] But such a vindication! said Franklin. The Secretary had apologized, not justified himself.[124] An analysis of the votes in his favor showed too many of his adherents directors or shareholders in the bank.[125] The Jeffersonians still needed to struggle for supremacy.

Freneau continued to do his share in undermining Federalist prestige. He laughed uproariously at the aristocratic beaus of Philadelphia in a poetic squib entitled "Short Canes" on January 12. A month later, on February 2, he derided those Federalists, who blamed every untoward event on their republican rivals, by printing mocking verses on the absence of shad, which "winter, that antifederal knave," had kept from the rivers. More seriously, he reprinted from Bache's *General Advertiser* an extended defense of Jefferson by "Mirabeau." [126] As editor, Freneau continued to receive some credit, but much abuse as a political writer. "I will venture a conjecture," said "A New England Republican" who was attempting to establish the identity of "Mirabeau" for readers of the *Connecticut Courant*, "that it is none other than the famous Capt. Sinbat." [127] Bache came to the rescue. "Mr. Freneau is not," he stated, "the author of the papers signed Mirabeau; and I further declare, that he had not either directly or indirectly any part in furnishing their matter." [128] Freneau laughed again at the aristocratic pretension of Federalists, particularly Federalists from New England:

A new *Titular Dictionary* is said to be composing at Hartford. . . . It is conjectured that when this work is accomplished, the claim of the above place to the old assumed name of the *American Athens*, will be renewed. Two Epic poems, one Mock-Heroic, The Triumph of Infidelity, and a Spelling Book had previously given some colour of right to this title. But the addition of A DICTIONARY will disarm Envy herself, should she attempt to dispute their claim to Parnassus.[129]

Furthermore, he suggested, that the "impudent effusions of aristocracy" which "The Echo" writers foisted upon the public, annually be burned "in a heap by the common hangman." [130]

"What a nose for sedition has 'Sinbat,' " retorted the *Connecticut Courant*.[131] And "The Echo" writers were well able to take care of themselves. They spared no words in their answer in *American Mercury* of February 4:

> Sinbat, the smutty link-boy of the muse,
> Who blacks himself to clean his master's shoes—
> Sinbat, who sells his dirty soul for pay,
> Then tries in vain to swear the bribe away.
> Sinbat, who steals fair freedom's holy name,
> The favorite sons of Freedom to defame—
> Spits his dull venom at the wise and good,
> And stabs the hand that kindly gives him food.
> Sinbat, bright nymph, thy charming music blames,
> And fain would yield thee to the hangman's flames,
> Thus thieves protected by the shade of night,
> Curse the warm radiance of returning light.
> Yet heed not Echo, Sinbat's venal lays
> Whose *praise* is *slander*, and whose slander praise.

As the winter drew to a close, prejudices were excited and passions enlisted in Philadelphia. The Hibernian Society organized a special fête for France, and the Pennsylvania militia, headed by Governor Thomas Mifflin, met at the City Tavern to exchange toasts to the new Republic.[132] France and liberty were bound close together in the heart of the common man. But as popular feeling rose, the Hamiltonians let fly the whole store of their invective. The writers for the *National Gazette,* said Fisher Ames, "have, like toads, sucked poison from the earth. They thirst for vengeance." [133] The anti-Federalists, charged a writer in the *Connecticut Courant,* had "enlisted a new set of writers to complete the failing crew of Capt. *Sinbat.*" They were said to be Irish emigrants, ignorant fellows, unused to liberty, who abused their privileges in the radical newspapers of Philadelphia.[134] "The long sought for *'Perpetual Motion,'* " wrote the *Columbian Centinel,* "may be found in the nibs of these grumbletarians' pens, for the 'more they write the swifter move their quills.' " [135] Freneau answered with reference to the "aristocratic, speculating faction at Hartford" who, "in favour of monarchy and titular distinctions," openly profess the same principles as the "old defunct Tories of 1775." [136] "The Echo" writers came back at him angrily:

> Alas! 'tis strange that not a sigh
> Can pass that babbling creature by;
> To give true answers he'll pretend,
> Yet almost lie to gain his end.[137]

Washington's birthday was publicly celebrated on February 22, 1793. A detachment of artillery and three light infantry companies paraded by the State House toward the Artillery Grounds, where cannons fired a federal salute of fifteen guns and musketry rent the air with a *feu-de-joie*. All the shipping in the harbor displayed colors, and the bells of Christ Church rang peals every half hour of the day. The President and Mrs. Washington held open house. Crowds gathered about their doorway for a glimpse of the distinguished persons who called to offer felicitations. In the evening a grand ball was held at Oeller's. The *Gazette of the United States* reported it as a dazzling affair,[138] and the next day printed two odes which had been written for the occasion. "Valerius" in the *National Gazette* was surly. "Even Cincinnatus," he said, "received no adulation of this kind." Birthday Odes! He did not mean to intimate, "Valerius" assured his readers, that such a man as Washington would succumb to flattery—but what of precedent? It would certainly lead to monarchy.[139]

But republican opposition all seemed useless. Hamilton was finally vindicated by the Congress. Adams was reelected Vicepresident. The Jeffersonians, after a valiant stand, seemed once more to be driven backward. "The attack made upon the Secretary of the Treasury," reported Oliver Wolcott, "is, I believe . . . held in universal detestation." [140] Freneau continued to flay "men of exorbitant ambitions" who "under the garb of humility . . . conceal the cruel tyrannical heart." [141] But his diatribes seemed now to have little effect. When news reached Philadelphia that Louis XVI had been beheaded by order of the French National Assembly, the *Gazette of the United States* immediately published extended accounts of the "assassination" from London papers and printed sentimental eulogies to the late king.[142] Though Jefferson admitted to Madison that the death of Louis did not produce "as open condemnations from the Monocrats" as he had expected,[143] a reaction among the American people was perceptible. Louis had sent his troops to aid America. Louis had been killed by an angry mob. Where did rational republican sympathies lie? There was a pause. Even Freneau had little to say.

5

When in April it became known, however, that France had declared war on England, republican spirit revived. George III, the ancient enemy, was once again the opponent of liberty. His soldiers, gathering on the French frontier, again threatened the rights of free men. It was monarchy against democracy, and American public sentiment rallied to the cause of France. England must be wrong. The revolutionists of Paris were, therefore, right, and the good will of every honest man must go out to them. The atmosphere became electric. Little would be needed to rouse public feeling to the point where it would demand that America join in a European war for freedom.

Washington hurriedly called the cabinet together. There was the treaty with France to consider, because America had pledged herself in the event of war to open her ports to prizes captured by French privateers, and to close them to all others. Hamilton wrestled with a delicate problem. With whom had the United States made the treaty? The old government of France was overthrown: what was America's duty to the new government? [144] Treaties are made, suggested Jefferson, not with kings, but with people. The people of France might, therefore, still demand that America keep the terms of her agreement.[145] On the other hand, the United States was in no position to risk war. She had no navy capable of protecting her shipping. Her Western territory was virtually undefended. War would increase the public debt, mean more taxes. No one wanted it.

But the question of recognition of the new French Republic had to be met immediately, because Edmond Charles Genêt, her minister plenipotentiary, was even now on his way from Charleston. How was he to be received? As an official representative of a sister republic, said Jefferson.[146] We must receive him, agreed Hamilton, but receive him with qualifications which will leave us free to consider more leisurely the binding force of our treaty with France.[147] Secretary of War Knox agreed with Hamilton. Attorney General Randolph agreed with Jefferson. So the matter stood.

Soon another question vexed the cabinet. The French frigate *L'Embuscade*, in which Genêt had landed at Charleston, had brought two captive British vessels to port with her. English vessels scudded out of Southern waters in alarm. Then Genêt fitted out two more privateers in South Carolina—manned by American seamen and supplied with American arms. It was almost an act of war. England would never stand for it. Washington met the situation with a proclamation of neutrality which forbade citizens of the United States to take any part in privateering, with or against either belligerent power. He warned Americans against carrying contraband, enjoined them to refrain from any act inconsistent with the neutrality of a friendly nation.[148]

Genêt, meanwhile, traveled slowly overland toward Philadelphia. He seemed in no hurry to arrive with his credentials. Pausing often in his journey to receive the plaudits of republican citizens, he made arrangements for the purchase and transport of supplies to France. He was thrilled with the reception he found everywhere, and he observed among all Americans a "grateful attachment to those, who like themselves at a former period," struggled in the cause of liberty.[149] He was a charming young man. His "fine open countenance, and pleasing, unaffected manners" made him immediately popular.[150] Though just past thirty, he had been successful in many diplomatic positions—at Berlin, Vienna, Rome, and Amsterdam. Born an aristocrat, he had early become an ardent republican, and his path of conduct lay clear before him: he would do everything in his power to enlist America actively at the side of France. While Hamilton and Jefferson argued over how he should be received, Genêt charmed his way into the affections of the people of America.

Philadelphia awaited his arrival with impatience. When he comes, promised "A Pennsylvanian" in the *National Gazette* of May 4, the celebrations in his honor "will at once demonstrate the patriotic character of our citizens, and the interest they take in the noblest of causes, the success of our French allies, who are giving up all that is near and dear to them for the general interests of human nature." Republicans rejoiced in reports of Genêt's reception in the South. "The example of France," said Freneau, "has struck terror into the hearts of all governments." [151] Inspired by the "most liberal and benevolent motives," the Patriotic French Society of Philadelphia solicited funds for the purchase of provisions for France. Subscription books were opened in the City Tavern and in the printing offices of Citizens Benjamin Bache and Philip Freneau. "Every gentleman who feels himself animated by . . . liberal and humane principles" was urged "to deposit such a sum as he is willing to bestow for the furtherance of the noble endeavours of that nation." [152]

On May 2 *L'Embuscade*, which had been searching the Atlantic coastline for British packets, sailed up the Delaware. As she came opposite the Walnut Street wharf, she fired a federal salute which was returned by two field pieces at the foot of High Street. Crowds gathered along the water-front gave rousing cheers "to testify their joy at the sight of this first visit of a ship of war from the free and independent republic of France." Seldom had a vessel been more gallantly decorated. Her topmast, her figurehead, and her stern were crowned with liberty caps. Across the top armors of the foremast swung the motto, "Enemies of Equality, Reform or Tremble!" From her mainmast she proclaimed, "Freemen Behold, We Are Your Friends and Brothers." Her mizzenmast boasted, "We Are Armed for the Defense of the Rights of Man." [153] When the waiting throngs saw that the frigate had British vessels in tow, "when they saw the British colours reversed & the French flag flying above them, they rented the air with peals of exultation." [154] The stage was set for a splendid show. "I anxiously wish," wrote Madison, "that the reception of Genêt may testify what I believe to be the real affections of the people." [155]

Two weeks later, the French Minister arrived. Crowds flocked to see him from all parts of the city. Again his charm won everyone. Sentiments of gratitude toward the generous allies, the "defenders of the rights of man and real friends to America in the dark days of war and desolation," reported Freneau, swelled every republican

breast.[156] Though there was dissension among the President's coun-
selors concerning Genêt, the people were determined to receive
him.[157] Nor were they, by any means, people of little importance.

The patriotic citizens of Philadelphia, headed by Charles Biddle,
former Secretary of State for Pennsylvania, met in the State House
yard to draw up congratulatory resolutions to present to the new
minister. Led by Dr. David Rittenhouse, president of the Philosophical Society, and Chief Justice McKean, a committee of thirty
marched three abreast to the City Tavern, where, when the shouts
and cheers had been quieted, they presented a ceremonious welcome. Again the streets rang with huzzas. Genêt replied "in terms
which touched the heart of every auditor." He seemed generous,
spontaneous in everything he said. He and his listeners were
genuinely moved.[158] Later in the day, the French Benevolent Society
paid its respects and, on the day following, the German Republicans called upon him in a body. That afternoon, accompanied by
Thomas Jefferson, Genêt produced his credentials and was officially
received by President Washington as minister plenipotentiary from
the Republic of France.[159]

In the evening a banquet was given in his honor at Oeller's, by the
French and French-American citizens of Philadelphia and the officers from the frigate *L'Embuscade*. It was a convivial occasion.
French and American flags were draped throughout the hall; the
tree and the cap of liberty surmounted every table. When the dinner
was over, fifteen toasts were proposed, each more impassiond than
the one before. Then, Citizen Peter Duponceau read an ode to France
composed by young Citizen Pichon. It was greeted with cheers. The
gathering voted unanimously that Citizen Philip Freneau be commissioned to put it into English verse, and that both the original and
the translation be printed in the *National Gazette*. It was a service
to France that Citizen Freneau accepted with gratitude.[160] Hardly
had the applause died down when Citizen Genêt rose in his place to
sing verses of his own composition. It was a charming and fervent
expression of his devotion to the freedom of all men. The cap of
liberty traveled from head to head around the table as each wearer
in turn rose to deliver patriotic sentiments. As a climax, everyone
joined in singing "The Marseillaise Hymn." Never perhaps since

1776 had a group of Americans been more ardently excited. When they left the hotel to escort the young ambassador to his lodgings, they found the streets lined with curious citizens of all degrees, to whose huzzas Genêt responded with a gracious "God save the United States!" [161]

Such demonstrations were to Freneau both a justification of all he fought for in the *National Gazette* and an indication that the people of America willed him to fight on strongly. The whole country seemed again to be united in ardent republicanism. Democratic clubs sprang up everywhere. *The Rights of Man* became the book of the hour. Joel Barlow's *Advice to the Privileged Orders* and *The Conspiracy of Kings* became popular overnight. In taverns and theaters, on the streets and in fashionable drawing rooms, France was honored. Toasts were drunk, songs were sung, and republican vied with republican in expression of patriotic fervor. It seemed impossible that America remain neutral. Freneau published an open letter to Washington from a correspondent, who said, "I doubt much whether it is the disposition of the United States to preserve the condition you enjoin." [162] France must be helped, wrote Mirabeau, because "should France, alas! be the victim of tyranny, America will not have a friend on whom she can cast herself for protection." [163] Public opinion demanded action. Was the President "so much buoyed up by official importance as to think it beneath his dignity to mix occasionally with the people?" [164] Emotion more than ever ruled the columns of Freneau's paper. The editor became more outspoken, more daring.

Washington was exasperated. "Sore and warm," he summoned Jefferson to suggested that the latter interpose in some way, perhaps withdraw Freneau's appointment. "But I will not do it," said Jefferson. "His paper has saved our constitution which was galloping fast into monarchy. . . . It is well & universally known that it has been that paper which has checked the career of the Monocrats." [165]

On May 25 Freneau published the "Ode—à la Liberté" which had been sung at the dinner in honor of Genêt. In the next issue, on May 29, he presented his translation. Not for five years had he written verses over which he had apparently taken more care. The flame which had burned brightly during the American Revolution flared once again as he wrote for the freedom of France. But it was now a quivering flame, not as intense, not as vigorous as it had been ten years before. Something of poetry had been consumed in Freneau, until only the stout spirit of liberty remained. Then, on June 1, at another dinner for Genêt, the spirit was revealed again, as Freneau's ode, "God Save the Rights of Man," was presented in the assembly room at Oeller's. For more than six months it was the anthem of republican America: [166]

> God save the Rights of Man!
> Give us a heart to scan
>   Blessings so dear;
> Let them be spread around
> Wherever man is found,
> And with the welcome sound
>   Ravish the ear.
>
> Let us with France agree,
> And bid the world be free,
>   While tyrants fall—
> Let the rude savage host
> Of their vast numbers boast—
> Freedom's tremendous host
>   Laughs at them all.
>
>   .   .   .
>
> If e'er her Cause should fail,
> Ambitious fiends assail,
>   Slaves to a throne—
> May no proud despot daunt—
> Should he her standard plant,
> Freedom shall never want
>   Her WASHINGTON.

On June 1 Freneau began to print "The Probationary Odes," described as "By Jonathan Pindar, a cousin of Peter's; and a candidate for the post of Poet-Laureate." The odes attacked Hamilton and Adams unmercifully, and derided every Federalist activity. They were trenchant satires, almost as good as any Freneau had ever done, better than he had composed since 1783. Almost all of his opponents thought that he had written them. When the first appeared, a correspondent to the *Gazette of the United States* replied: [167]

> tho' hungry be thy maw,
> Thy suit will be rejected;
> For who should heed his lies of straw,
> Whose oaths have been detected.

Later, after the odes had been appearing for more than two months, a writer for the same paper suggested: [168]

> P—, in spite of all your puffers say,
> Your Odes for th' reading do not compensate.

When Benjamin Russell copied these lines into the *Columbian Centinel*,[169] he filled in the blank so that the line read, "Philip—in spite of all your puffers say." But Freneau had not written the odes. Only a few then knew that "Jonathan Pindar" was astute St. George Tucker of Virginia, whose family the editor had undoubtedly known years before in Bermuda. "The Probationary Odes," Jefferson informed Madison, "are saddled on poor Freneau, who is bloodily attacked about them." [170]

Freneau also presented on June 1 the first of a series of papers addressed "To the President of the United States" and signed "Veritas." Accusing Washington of double-dealing in issuing the proclamation of neutrality, the writer reminded the President that he was, after all, simply a temporary magistrate of a free country, and not an hereditary ruler. "Whatever favours of monarchial mystery or court intrigue . . . ought surely be rejected with abhorrence." The people of America, he said, desired no neutrality.[171] "Let me caution you, sir," he suggested to Washington, "to beware that you do not view the state of the public mind at this critical moment through a fallacious medium." Beware of "court satellites," the "mushroom lordlings," who have deceived you. "Let not the buzz of the aristocratic few and their contemptible minions of speculators, tories, and British emissaries be mistaken for the exalted and generous voice of the American people." Remember, he continued, that the "spirit of 1776 is again aroused" and that the "American Whigs of 1776 will not suffer French patriots of 1792 to be vilified with impunity." [172] Redeem yourself in the eyes of your people, Veritas demanded. Remember, sir, that you are great. Do not be led. Defy your Tory advisers. "Take all upon your shoulders at this critical juncture." [173] Finally, he concluded, do not forget that the people of America are beginning to realize "that *principles and not men*, ought ever to be the objects of *republican* attachment." [174]

Such outspoken opposition to the President created an uproar. "Uriel" and "A Friend to Peace" wrote heatedly in *Dunlap's American Daily Advertiser*, and "A Freeman" came to Washington's defense in the *Federal Gazette*.[175] Hamilton, as "Pacificus," wrote a series of articles for the *Gazette of the United States*, upholding the neutrality policy and the right, even the duty of the President to issue the proclamation.[176] He wrote very convincingly. "For God's sake," Jefferson begged Madison, "take up your pen . . . and cut him to pieces in the face of the public." [177] Obediently, Madison prepared a series of papers signed "Helvidius," which he, too, contributed to the *Gazette of the United States*.[178] So the quarrel which had begun in the *National Gazette* went on, but Freneau avoided the intricacies of debate. He played loud and long on a single string. "Let republican patriotism revive," he said, "and let every individual reacknowledge those great principles upon which our revolution was founded." [179]

Washington was troubled. "In what will this abuse terminate?" he asked Henry Lee. The publications in the *National Gazette* seemed to him "outrages on common decency." [180] "That rascal Freneau!" he exploded in a cabinet meeting.[181] The President's feeling was shared by many honest partisans. Whatever Freneau's popularity among republican readers, the Federalists, particularly those in New England, spared no words in expressing their opinion of him. To young Charles Adams the *National Gazette* was merely a "mint of defamation." [182] "No art, however vile—no plan however wicked—no attempt, however base and unjustified," said a correspondent to the *Connecticut Courant*, "is left unessayed." [183] Timothy Dwight, the poet-teacher, wrote to Oliver Wolcott, "Freneau, your printer, linguist, &c., is regarded here as a mere incendiary, or rather as the despicable tool of higher incendiaries, and his paper as a public nuisance." [184]

But attacks continued to rise most bitterly in Philadelphia. "Who then is the Editor of the '*National Gazette*,' " wrote "Justice" in the

Gazette of the United States, "that takes the liberty upon every occasion . . . not to examine with candor and decency into the conduct of our first magistrate, but to cast at him the most illiberal and unwarrantable abuse?" Must Washington be made to wait upon

the Editor of the *National Gazette*—that great reformer of law and government—the appointed censor of the rulers of the people—the colossus of learning and jurisprudence.—Can this infatuated man suppose that the boldness of his impertinence and abuse, will deserve or acquire the applause of the people more than the inestimable services of their old, approved, patriot and fellow-soldier, *Washington?* What remarkable events appear in the annals of the Editor's life—what great or useful actions has he performed, upon which he founds his claim to attention and applause— Let us look a little into his merits— Is he a great politician, and has he assisted the counsels of your cabinet, either in peaceful or in perilous times?—No!—but he is a *Poet*— Has he commanded your armies or fought your battles?—No!—but he can describe a more sublime battle than Washington ever fought.—Did he ever risque his life amidst the horrors of a naval war? No!—a Poet's person is too precious for such exploits— but he wrote a very pretty account, in verse too, of a *sea-fight*— And also published in all the newspapers and magazines on the continent, a "most musical, most melancholy" *Ode Written On an Evening at Sea*— As he has such fine *ideas* of those things, it is a pity he did not reduce them to practice.

Finally, after more abuse and further ridicule, "Justice" concluded:

Go poor creature, I am done with you; your heart is embittered with disappointment, and you are driven to scurrility, the usual and last refuge of the rejected suitors of the Muses—after many unsuccessful attempts to gain an honest living, you have engaged in one more infallible, though less honorable—I mean a professed slanderer of good men and good government.[185]

It was not all true, but it was partly true, and that made it hurt the more. However Freneau's actions and opinions are to be judged, he did believe in what he was doing. That he had failed before, that he must have known he was failing now, made the abuse harder to bear. So perhaps Freneau may be pardoned for the truculent scurrility of his reply "To Justice" in the *National Gazette* on July 31, wherein he said, "A blockhead's venom ever spits in vain." He spoke hotly of "white-washed squires," of "little apes," and of blundering "elephants." "How profuse! How prodigal!" derided the *Gazette of the United States,* "are some men of their genius." One would suppose that Freneau's verses had all been written at sea, because they rocked so from one incongruity to another! [186] Freneau struck out blindly in a second reply "To Justice" on August 7:

> Because some pumpkin shells and lobster claws
>   (Thrown o'er his garden wall by Braintree's Duke)
> Have chanc'd to fall within your meagre jaws,
>   A dose at which all honest men would puke:

> Because some treasury luncheons you have gnaw'd
>   Like rats that prey upon the public store,
> Must you for that, your crude stuff belch abroad
>   And vomit lies on all that pass your door!

Then, more reasonably, he expressed again his patriotic determination:

> Why should you then with hangman-hand destroy
>   A wight that wastes his ink in freedom's cause;
> Who, to the last, his arrows will employ
>   To publish freedom's rights, and guard her laws.

By now Freneau may well have thought that his ink truly was wasted, for Citizen Genêt over-played his hand, and public opinion turned precipitously against him. Over-confident of the temper of the American people, Genêt dared defy and, in spite of Jefferson's patient admonition, continued to defy the government of the United States. When the frigate *L'Embuscade* captured an English merchantman and brought her as a prize to Philadelphia, Genêt refitted her, enlisted a large native crew, and prepared to send the vessel on a privateering expedition as the *Petit Democrat.* When remonstrated with, the French Minister threatened that "he would appeal from the President to the people." In defiance of all restraint, he ordered the vessel put out to sea.[187] Even Jefferson was disgusted. "Never," he wrote to Madison, "was so calamitous an appointment made, as that of the present Minister of France here." He lacked judgment. He was hot-headed and disrespectful. By the middle of August the cabinet had drawn up charges which were to be submitted to Paris in substantiation of its demand for Genêt's recall. The American government, said Jefferson, "had been insulted and set at defiance by Mr. Genet." [188]

All over the country liberal men reversed their opinions of the personable young Ambassador. Merchants of Philadelphia met to draw up resolutions against him.[189] The city, Fisher Ames was glad to report, became less "frenchified." "Citizen Genet is out of credit; his rudeness is as indiscreet as it is extraordinary and every one is provoked with him." [190] By mid-September even Jefferson reported, "His conduct has become that of a madman. He is abandoned even by his votaries in Philadelphia." Worst of all, he had "ruined the Republican interest in that place." [191]

But Freneau, foolishly and blindly, remained loyal to the young Frenchman. Except for lugubrious "Reflections on the Death of a Country Printer" on July 6 and a humorous "Dialogue between Whaacum and Whiffle" on August 3, his poetry in the *National Gazette* during the summer had all been devoted to the cause of France. On July 13 he had printed "The Marseilles Hymn, Attempted in English." On July 17 he had presented his own "Patriotic Stanzas on the Anniversary of the Storming of the Bastille."

Now though public opinion was swinging swiftly away, he published on August 17 the first installment of a long poem celebrating the running battle which had taken place between the *L'Embuscade* and the British frigate *Boston* off the Jersey shore earlier in the month. The poem, "On a Late Memorable Naval Engagement," was continued in the issue of August 24. In it Freneau tried valiantly to recapture the spirit which had enlivened his early naval ballads. Indeed, the Boston *Independent Chronicle* proudly commended the poem, even suggested that it be set to music "as a counterpart to the noted song called 'Britannia rules the Sea.'" But little merit could be found in the lines by any but the most prejudiced republican. At forty-one Freneau seemed to have lost his old ability to transmit action into stirring words. He had fought in too many causes. But, though the burden of his song was weakened through repetition, and though his countrymen turned away from the cause he celebrated, he still fought on. A contributor to the Norwich *Weekly Register* suggested:

And thou poor Sinbat, lay thine harp aside
For lo! against thee wit and verse allied
Move dreadful onwards, bid thee cease thy lays
And threaten vengeance to thy saucy press:
To Treasury shelter, swift as wind can waft ye
Like brother Fenno, fly for Ark of safety.[192]

6

By the end of August, 1793, citizens of Philadelphia began to be thoroughly alarmed at the number of deaths in their city from malignant fever. There seemed to be no treatment to which the disease responded. It was spreading everywhere. President Washington was ordered out of the city, Secretary of War Knox fled in alarm, and Hamilton was himself seized with a fever which threw him into a panic.[193] As the epidemic raged on, everyone suspected everyone: houses were shut up tight; no person walked abroad without a sponge or bottle to his nose; friends were avoided; business was suspended; and "universal stillness prevailed day and night." Daily the death-cart rumbled with its awful load through silent streets. Brigands plundered the houses of those who had fled: the city was lawless, terrified.[194] By the middle of September deaths had mounted to ninety daily.[195] Never, said the doctors, had such a plague visited North America.[196]

On September 11 the *Pennsylvania Packet* announced that it would suspend publication till the epidemic subsided. Three days later *Dunlap's American Daily Advertiser* ceased to appear. Next, Fenno, of the *Gazette of the United States*, abandoned his press; [197] and Bache, of the *General Advertiser*, "sharing with his fellow-citizens the dread which the raging disorder naturally inspired . . . thought it his duty to put a temporary end to his business." [198] The plague thus effectively ended newspaper controversy in Philadelphia. But Freneau stayed on. He wrote laughingly of "Orlando's Flight":

On prancing steed, with spunge at nose,
From town behold Orlando fly:
Camphor and Tar where'er he goes

Th' infected shafts of death defy—
Safe in an atmosphere of stink,
No doctor gets Orlando's chink.

. . .

Blame not Orlando if he fled—
So little's got by being dead.[199]

In fever-ridden Philadelphia Freneau continued to support Genêt. John Jay and Rufus King heard the reports that the minister had openly threatened to appeal from Washington to the people of America. Friends in New York asked them if the reports were true. Jay and King replied with a public affirmation in the New York *Diary.*[200] Freneau, however, scoffed at them and their accusations. The evidence against Genêt was hearsay. It was a Federalist fabrication, a plot to vilify staunch republicans and destroy the allegiance to France of the people of America. In "A New Way to Tell an Old Lie" Freneau attacked Genêt's detractors:

Come, says King—Justice Jay,
Let's return—come away
    I long to relate this fine story.
If true—it is well—
If not, it will tell—
    To a whig—like myself—or a tory.

By the aid of your name,
I'll raise a hell flame;
    For stockholders, fools, and addressers
Each township will vie,
To conform this da—d lie,
    And we, shall be gorg'd with caresses.[201]

Just a week before he shut up shop and fled the city, Fenno reported that "some reasonable persons have expressed their surprise and indignation, at the stinking lies which appeared in the National Gazette." Then the Federalist editor had presented a last diatribe against his republican rival:

But why express the least surprise?
It is in *course* such fumes arise;
The fund and endless source supplies!

The "Nation's Gazette" is a sink—
Whose atmosphere as quick as wink,
Reminds you there's no time to think.[202]

Stinking lies! What could not be justified in the war for freedom? Freneau commented no further. Perhaps he had learned that
Knox and Hamilton were ready to sign affidavits attesting to the fact
of Genêt's statement.[203] The editor could not afford to scoff at affidavits. While Jefferson and Governor Mifflin, who knew all the details of the incident, remained silent, there was little that Freneau
could say. Many less stalwart republicans turned against the French
minister. The *National Gazette,* his defender, became a victim of
their reaction.

Though Freneau continued publication through the epidemic,
there was little more of controversy in his paper. He suggested in a
leading article on September 7 that "if there be any office . . . perfectly superfluous, it is surely that of Vice-president." On August 13
he lashed heavily against "British sea tyrants" who impressed American seamen. In the main, however, he was jocular, high-spirited,
and noncommittal. On September 18 he printed an "Elegy on the
Death of a Blacksmith." One week later appeared humorously
satirical "Lines Addressed to a Very Little Man, who was Fond
of Walking with a Very Large Cane." "Quintilian to Lycidas" on
September 25 advised a ten-year-old boy not to neglect his play.
Only the publication of "The American's Prayer for France" on
September 25 attests to the editor's continued devotion to the principles of the French Revolution.[204]

Freneau refused to submit to the depression which shrouded
Philadelphia. He did his best to revive sinking spirits by printing
on September 28 a humorous prose "Dialogue between a Citizen
of Philadelphia and a Jersey Farmer (Ten Miles from Town)."
The farmer would have nothing to do with the refugee from a
diseased city. No shelter or assistance from him! The Philadelphian
pled in vain. And Freneau, instead of condemning either, laughed
at both. Such an essay must have been good medicine for his disconsolate, fear-crazed neighbors.

Soon Freneau was happy to inform his readers that the "con-
tagious fever in this city bears a much milder aspect, and yields

much sooner to medicine than it did some weeks ago." He assured them that there could be no possible risk in receiving his paper, as it was printed "towards the upper end of Market-street, which street has been, and still continues uncommonly healthy." Moreover, "no person employed in the typographical, or other work of the National Gazette has been or is indisposed." [205] This was too much for his Federalist opponents at Hartford. Vulture-like, they seized on his notice. Of course, they said, there can be no danger in receiving the paper

for the editor and his paper have both had the plague for more than a year past, and yet no mortal has caught it from him. And as a rogue often attempts to pass a single counterfeit dollar, among a thousand good ones, he is advised to cease writing ridiculous dialogues on a subject infinitely serious—resign up his treasonable press to those who gave it to him, and then mix with the crowds of honest but unfortunate people who are falling fast around him, shrink from infamy in this world, and endeavour to palm himself upon death for an honest man.[206]

In spite of the advice of his New England opponents, Freneau lived on. But the *National Gazette* was dying. Even before the fever crippled Philadelphia, the editor published a request that subscribers make "punctual and speedy remittances," [207] and had especially pled with "distant subscribers" [208] to bring their accounts to date. Indeed, from the very beginning, Freneau later asserted, so many obstacles were placed in the way of delivery of his paper that more complaint was received than payment. Many months earlier Henry Lee had warned that the "precariousness in the reception of the paper will cramp the circulation of it." [209] Freneau admitted that he would have had to suspend publication at the end of the first year, "had it not been for the complaisance and good will of Messrs. Childs and Swaine, who furnished me with the necessary sums for carrying it on." In September, however, Francis Childs informed the editor that he could no longer finance a paper that lost money. Freneau published another plea for subscribers to bring their accounts to date,[210] and, "from some little money that was collected in," continued to issue the *National Gazette*. It had, he asserted proudly, "become an object of terror to the enemies of liberty and equality." [211] Once more he pleaded for "speedy remittances," because, he told his readers, "Punctuality of payment in subscribers is the first requisite in undertakings of this nature, and without which it is impossible that any publication, depending merely on subscription, can long exist." [212]

Freneau also experienced difficulties as clerk in the Department of State. Papers were sent in, he said, from "Russia, Holland, Prussia, Germany, and elsewhere." Being unable to translate from any modern language but French, Freneau was obliged to hire others "at an exorbitant rate of charge" to do the work for him. "The place," he said, "was beginning to be rather a loss than a matter of emolument." In characteristic manner, he further explained:

Apprehending therefore that official dispatches might soon arrive from, perhaps, his very sublime majesty, Kien-Long, the emperor of China, written in Chinese characters, of which not a soul in Philadelphia had the least knowledge; from the brother of the sun and moon at Constantinople, in Turkish—or from the dey of Algiers, in Arabic, with which sort of people or their writings I wished to have no concern, I resigned the translator's office . . . as well from the aforementioned reasons, as to put an end to the clamor that was raised against me in several New England papers of a particular cast, in which I was basely aspersed by men of illiberal and malignant minds, and whom I wish never to think of again.[213]

Accordingly, on October 11, he submitted his resignation, to be effective from October 1, 1793, to the Secretary of State.[214] He left the position convinced that he had been no man's hireling. More than ten years later he was able to boast "that Mr. Jefferson did not, at any time, establish, support, or patronize the National Gazette, and that I was neither his pensioner nor confidential agent." [215]

But scarcely any of his Federalist opponents believed him. For years thereafter Freneau was remembered as the tool of faction. Nothing that he or Madison or Jefferson said changed that opinion. The controversy became as vicious as it was (except as a very practical political bludgeon) pointless. Of course, Freneau's opponents were neither correct nor unprejudiced in their accusations. No more was he in his defense. From a republican point of view, Jefferson was guiltless, for he openly encouraged and supported the National Gazette just as any other politician would support a newspaper which staunchly supported him. From a Federalist point of view, he was equally guilty—for was not his approval implicit in every word Freneau printed? Both Hamilton and Jefferson were practical men who played their game boldly with whatever pawns came to hand. Freneau was a poet who embraced the cause of freedom for its own sake, and with little regard for personal consequences. His appointment to a clerkship in the Department of State was a political blunder for which both he and Jefferson have been made to pay. Yet, if the Secretary had really wanted to control a newspaper, how much better he could have managed it with a personal subsidy to an editor!

The point about which the solution of the whole bitter controversy revolves is that Freneau needed no bribe to publish a republican newspaper, for he went even further than Jefferson in his expression of radical doctrine. He had planned to publish anyway— in New York or New Jersey. When he did settle in the capital, he spoke perhaps too boldly. He refused to watch which way the wind was blowing, but headed directly for a visionary land where all mankind might be free, where ambition and avarice were forgotten, and happiness secure. That Freneau made mistakes as a journalist is evident to the most casual reader: he quarreled so often about minor matters that the force of his argument was lost when a major issue arose. He was too sensitive, too easily hurt personally, too much wrapped in his own ideal of freedom to compromise. That he was uncontrollable must have been equally evident to republican leaders of his time: even when it was considered politically inexpedient to support Genêt, Freneau supported him. And for these reasons he failed. But never before in America had there been such an editor. He is first in a line of liberal crusaders who have made journalism a force, not always admirable, but vital and tremendously efficient.

As the second year of publication drew to a close, an editorial notice in the *National Gazette* reaffirmed the principles on which the paper had been founded.[216] By this time, rain and cool weather had settled upon Philadelphia, and the spread of the fever seemed under control.[217] But on October 27 Freneau announced that his paper would be discontinued. "Having just imported, on his own account, a considerable quantity of new and elegant printing types," he informed his subscribers, however, that he intended to resume publication when the Congress reconvened early in December. In the meantime, he earnestly asked all delinquent subscribers to bring their accounts to date. The continuance of the *National Gazette*, he said, would depend upon their cooperation. The *Connecticut Courant* received the news with glee:

Your correspondent congratulates the Clerk of *Foreign Languages,* that he has become his own man, and able to import "types *on his own account.*" It is presumed he will now feel more independent of his great, wise and wonderful master; and therefore when that wonderful master again gets himself into deep trouble, the clerk will be very cautious of swearing him out.[218]

What of the "great, wise and wonderful master"? "Freneau's paper is discontinued," Jefferson wrote to his son-in-law. "I fear it is want of money. . . . I wish the subscribers in your neighborhood would send on their money." [219] The Secretary informed his daughter: "He . . . promises to resume again. I fear this cannot be till he has collected his arrearages." [220] But there is no evidence that Freneau cried for help. On the other hand, John Fenno wrote a pitiful letter to the Secretary of the Treasury, explaining that he, too, had been experiencing difficulties, and that he needed money if he were to continue. Hamilton communicated immediately with Rufus King in behalf of "poor Fenno." "If you can," he wrote, "without delay raise 1000 Dollars in New York. I will endeavour to raise another Thousand in Philadelphia. If this cannot be done, we must lose his services." [221]

Freneau remained in Philadelphia until early December, collecting what debts he could. Then, having determined on a "final discontinuance of the National Gazette," [222] he packed his "new and elegant types" and retired once more to Monmouth.

NINE

THE COUNTRY PRINTER

1794–1796

FROM beneath the shade of the locust trees which his father had planted at Mount Pleasant more than forty years before, Philip Freneau could look out over rolling hills to the Navesink Highlands and the blue haze which hung over the sea. From the mouth of Middletown Creek a sail might be seen in the distance as it rounded Sandy Hook and stood for Manhattan. Miles to the south, more than a day's travel over country roads, lay Philadelphia, recovered from her sickness and embroiled once more in controversy. But neither the commerce of New York nor the politics of the national capital further concerned the poet. He was tired. "I mean to pass the remainder of my days," he wrote Madison, "on a couple hundred acres of sandy patrimony." [1]

Agnes Kearny and her eldest daughter, Mary Freneau, had lived alone at Mount Pleasant since 1788, when Margaret, the younger of the poet's sisters, had married John S. Hunn and gone with her husband to New York.[2] Peter, after a visit of several months in 1792, had returned to his home in South Carolina.[3] There was plenty of room in the old house for the poet, his wife, and their two-year-old daughter, Helena. And there, on June 14, 1794, a second daughter, named Agnes for her grandmother, was born.[4] "My two little girls and books," wrote Eleanor Freneau to her brother in Cayuga, "are my chief comforters." [5]

The Freneaus were proud of their books. "I wish it was in my power to send you out as good a collection as we have here," Mrs. Freneau continued. To her, too, life in Monmouth must have seemed doubly pleasant after the hectic years in New York and Philadelphia. "We must endeavour to make ourselves as independent of the world as possible," she wrote, "and let our own minds furnish us with that pleasure which too many of us go in search of abroad." [6]

For now Philip Freneau apparently wanted nothing more than to be allowed to live quietly with his time divided between his library and the supervision of the family farm. He wrote to Madison to recommend Francis Bailey as printer to the House of Representatives.[7] For himself, he solicited nothing. He was content to rest. "Remember, however," Madison encouraged him, "that as you have not chosen any longer to labour in the field of politics, it will be expected by your friends, that you cultivate with more industry your inheritance on Parnassus." [8]

But Freneau, at forty-three, had climbed as high as he would ever climb on that fabulous peak. His verses were faintly damned in New York by young John Blair Lynn as "pretty" productions.[9] His best songs had been lost in the welter of controversy, and he was tired.

A sixteen-page pamphlet had been issued by Hoff and Derrick, printers in Philadelphia, which contained "The Village Merchant" and "The Country Printer" just as they had formerly appeared in the *National Gazette*. The "Verses Written at Sea, in a Heavy Gale" had been included the year before in the first anthology of American poetry—and printed in Connecticut, at that.[10] The same poem, together with the "Sketches of American History" and "On the Migration to America and Peopling the Western Country," was attributed to Philip Freneau when published in *The Columbian Muse, a Selection of American Poetry, from Various Authors of Established Reputation*.[11] Freneau himself, however, was happy to court contentment among the quiet hills of Monmouth.

2

Yet he could not remain inactive long. By the middle of June his friends were informed that Philip Freneau "has built a printing house and now spends his time in printing and farming." Crossing to New York, he visited old acquaintances with whom he chatted of the stormy days of the Revolution. He ordered engravings made in type metal for his press at Mount Pleasant. In no manner, remarked a young friend, does his appearance "bespeak him to be the real Poet he is." [12]

Late in the spring the plan for the establishment of a country newspaper was again suggested to Freneau. On July 4, 1794, he issued proposals for *The Monmouth Gazette, and East Jersey Intelligencer* which would be published weekly and circulated among the townships and settlements of the county. The newspaper, printed in the "elegant new type," would begin to appear on the first Tuesday in October. Subscriptions would be a dollar and a half for fifty-two issues, and at least five hundred subscribers would be needed to make the undertaking possible. The paper would contain "freshest foreign and domestic intelligence," gathered by the publisher, Philip Freneau, through a constant correspondence with the news-printers of New York, Philadelphia, Trenton, and New Brunswick, from whom he could expect information with the arrival of every stage coach that passed through northern Monmouth County. "The advantages to be derived to the inhabitants of this large and populous country from an impartial and judiciously compiled Newspaper," advised Freneau, "are too obvious to need particularizing." [13] But a sufficient number of subscribers were apparently not found, and the *Monmouth Gazette* never appeared.

Nevertheless, by the end of 1794 Freneau was established as a country printer. He then issued *The Monmouth Almanac, for the Year M,DCC,XCV* and placed it for sale with "most of the Store-Keepers in Monmouth, and adjacent counties." It contained an illustrated table explaining the signs of the zodiac; a notice of the eclipses of the sun and moon; charts anticipating moveable feasts, equinoxes and solstices, the rise and fall of the tide, and the sessions of the Supreme Court in New Jersey during 1795. The yearly meetings of the Quakers and the roads leading eastward and westward from Middletown Point were listed carefully. The weather, of course, was forecast for each day.

Tired of information so baldly detailed, the reader might turn in the almanac to short didactic articles on such subjects as the "Advantage of Using Oxen on Farms," a "Method to Preserve Peach Trees from a Destructive Species of Worms," or—roaming farther afield— the "Strict Discipline Observed in the Prussian Armies." Of verse he would find little—only a few lugubrious lines "supposed to have been written by a young prisoner the night before his execution" and a doggerel astrological catalog of "The Names, and

Order of the Twelve Signs." As a matter of fact, he would discover most of the material included in the collection the common property of almanac makers the world over. Only two contributions, both of them essays, present any pertinent evidence of having been written by Freneau. Both the "Discourse on Barber's Poles" and the "True and Faithful Account of the Ugly Club of Charleston" had been printed five years before in the *Daily Advertiser*, and neither of them represents Freneau at his best.

3

Soon, however, the press at Mount Pleasant was to issue a more ambitious production. On April 17, 1795, Freneau secured a copyright from the clerk of the District Court of New York for a volume entitled *Poems Written between the Years 1768 and 1794.* He described it as a "new edition, revised and corrected by the author, including a considerable number of pieces never before published." [14] It was a thick book of more than four hundred and fifty pages, "printed at the press of the author at Mount-Pleasant, near Middletown-Point." New York newspapers immediately announced the volume for sale at all principal bookstores. But it did not seem to go well. By the end of the summer Thomas Greenleaf was the only bookseller in New York who still advertised it regularly, and he was content to list it merely as one of many books which might be purchased at his shop.[15] Freneau, however, had a maker's pride in the collection. Late in November he presented a copy to John Motley of New York, requesting that it "never be lost mislaid or abused but be Reserved in his family forever." [16]

Remembering that Freneau later complained that his first two volumes had been published "in a strange way" while he was "wandering over gloomy seas," [17] we might expect to find sweeping revisions in this new collection. Changes were made: scenes one and two were omitted from "The Pictures of Columbus"; the long song of Ismenius was dropped from "The Monument of Phaon"; "The Power of Fancy" was broken into two lyrics, the "Ode to Fancy" and "Fancy's Ramble"; "Female Frailty" was shortened and renamed "The Northern Soldier"; and "The Jamaica Funeral" and

"The House of Night" were presented only as fragments. Most of the two hundred and eighty-seven poems in the collection, however, were printed as they had appeared in the 1786 or the 1788 editions and in the *City Gazette*, the *Daily Advertiser*, or the *National Gazette*. Punctuation was improved, more forceful adjectives were sometimes chosen, and faulty lines were omitted or rewritten. Some titles were abbreviated and others rephrased; Latin mottoes were deleted and footnotes abandoned. Each poem was edited carefully, but few underwent essential change. "The British Prison Ship" was divided into eighteen cantos instead of three, but only four lines were cut from the version that had previously appeared. "The Rising Glory of America," "The Wild Honey Suckle," "The Indian Burying Ground," and even "The Jug of Rum" were very little revised. "Santa Cruz," "The Poetical History of the Prophet Jonah," and "The Village Merchant" were as long as they ever had been. Though "The Sailor's Invitation" and the "Song on Capt. Barney's Victory" were omitted from this volume, other verses of the American Revolution were reprinted just as they had appeared in the earlier editions.

Freneau's purpose seems to have been to edit just as simple and clear a text of his poems as he possibly could. The puerile attempt at sophistication in "The Jamaica Funeral" must have seemed inadequate either as poetry or exposition. The great misty promise of "The House of Night" belonged to a period the poet had long since passed. Its amorphous suggestion of sublimity might easily have been lost upon the older man whose early dreams of poetic conquest had been shattered by the variety of rebuffs he had encountered. The mood wherein his spirit had adventured into the awful chambers of death and dared attempt to translate mysteries from the nether world had left Freneau. Perhaps it was better that he simply shortened "The House of Night," though he robbed it of its subtlety. He could not go back. Looking forward, he prepared his volume in the spirit of the common man whom he had vowed to serve. Latin mottoes were the baggage of erudition. He omitted them. Grandiose titles applied to individuals were not republican; so the verses "To His Excellency General Washington" were renamed "An Address to the Commander in Chief, Officers, and Soldiers of the American

Army" and the phrase "the renowned and illustrious General George Washington" was omitted from the poem "On the fall of the General Earl Cornwallis."

Arduously, carefully, and, we may imagine, happily, Freneau worked over his verses at his press at Mount Pleasant. He puttered at little changes in form and make-up, but his lines remained essentially as he had first presented them. Twenty-nine poems were added which had never been previously printed, but each was a variation on some theme Freneau had often treated before. He had little new to offer except correctness in form.

4

On May 2, 1795, Freneau's plan for establishing a country newspaper finally materialized with the publication of the first number of the *Jersey Chronicle*. It was to be a weekly, issued early every Saturday morning and delivered at the subscriber's expense. Those who had formerly subscribed to the *Monmouth Gazette,* and who had not subsequently made other arrangements, were advised that copies would be sent to them immediately upon application.[18] Furthermore, the printing shop at Mount Pleasant was prepared to turn out advertisements and hand bills "at the shortest notice, and on the most reasonable terms." [19]

Soon the office of the *Jersey Chronicle* became a bookstore and the poet became a country printer complete. He advertised as "just received from New York" Samuel Throckmorton's *The Stranger's Assistant, and Schoolboy's Instructor,* a marvelous compendium containing "many useful and valuable rules in Arithmetic with explanations." [20] Later, Francis Bailey sent a shipment of books from Philadelphia: three copies of *The Cavern of Death: a Moral Tale,* six copies of *A Collection of Treaties between America and several Nations in Europe, with a copious Appendix,* six copies of *The American Remembrancer,* and—indicative, perhaps, of the taste of Freneau's rural clientele—one hundred two-volume sets of Richard Brother's *A Revealed Knowledge of the Prophecies and the Times,* which attempted to predict political and social developments through scriptural revelation.[21]

In addition to these volumes, Freneau also announced a further supply of books "just received from Philadelphia." One might purchase Johnson's *Rasselas*, Mackenzie's *Man of Feeling*, or the anonymous *Voyages and Adventures of Captain Robert Boyle*. The shop was well stocked with poetry, for Cowper's *Poems*, which were all the rage in Philadelphia, could be bought there, or Goldsmith's *Essays and Poems*, Watt's *Poems and Hymns*, Humphreys' *Poems*, and, of course, the *Poems* of Philip Freneau. Those interested in more serious entertainment could have Patrick Brydone's *Tour through Sicily and Malta*, the instructive *Juvenile Miscellany, in Prose and Verse*, or Edward Young's satirical *The Centaur not Fabulous*, six letters to a friend on contemporary manners. Hugh Blair's *Sermons*, Soame Jenyns's *Free Inquiry into the Nature and Origin of Evil*, or Luigo Cornara's *Treatise on the Benefits of a Sober Life* supplied meaty thought to pious customers.[22]

Freneau now seems to have settled comfortably into living for the first time. "Amongst grubbing and ditching," [23] he edited his small country paper, and he enjoyed no small repute in the community. His ode, "God Save the Rights of Man," was sung at Middletown Point as part of the public celebration of the nineteenth anniversary of the independence of the United States.[24] He was elected secretary of a committee from the townships of Middletown and Freehold to draw up resolutions to Congress on the pending treaty between America and Great Britain.[25] He was apparently a solid citizen to whose views the local leaders who met at Major Thomas Hunn's tavern, just off the main highway at Mount Pleasant, listened with respect.

5

"Never was there a more interesting period than the present," Freneau told his readers in the first issue of the *Jersey Chronicle*. Nor, he said, had mankind ever been so united in "emancipating themselves from those shackles of despotism which . . . so long impeded the happiness of the human species, and rendered the rights of the many subservient to the interests of the few." New republics were forming, new empires bursting into birth, and the family of mankind was advancing from the shadow of tyranny to the sunlight of democracy. At such a time the editor was proud "to *renew* his efforts for contributing, in some small degree, to the general information of his fellow citizens in the present history, and politics of the world." [26]

For the satisfaction of those readers who were not informed on recent political affairs, the first issue of the newspaper included a brief retrospect of events which had occurred in Europe since the beginning of the year, for the *Jersey Chronicle* was preeminently a voice crying in the wilderness of Monmouth County. It was devoted to the education of its rural subscribers. It taught patriotic republicanism, the right of the common man to fight his way out from under whatever despotism attempted to crush him. To this end Freneau published extended extracts from the leading anti-Federalist journals: the *Aurora* of Philadelphia, the *Argus*, the *Journal*, and the *Patriotic Register* of New York, the Boston *Independent Chronicle*, the *Maryland Journal*, the Charleston *City Gazette*, the *Albany Register*, and the *New-Jersey State Gazette*. He had a message to deliver and he sought an efficient simplicity which his country readers might understand. "I will not make high promises of what it will contain," he wrote apologetically to Madison of the *Jersey Chronicle*. "It will scarcely be expected that in a crude barbarous part of the country I should calculate it for the polite taste of Philadelphia." [27]

There was no mistaking the trend which the paper would follow. Freneau called attention to public debts. "With some people," he accused, "*national debts are national blessings!* a system borrowed from the wretched policy of Great Britain." [28] England was America's most malicious foe: "Ever since our Independence she has manifested the most inveterate hatred to these states, and contemplated their misery and subjugation." Why, then, should the United States make a treaty with her? Why particularly was an aristocratic Anglophile like John Jay allowed to represent America in negotiating such a treaty? It was known by every impartial observer that England depended on the shipping of the United States. Why, therefore, should not the latter dictate terms? Were the commercial advantages which Federalists claimed the treaty secured "to be deemed a compensation for national injury, injustice, and dishonour?" What satisfaction would be given "for the shameful spoliations upon our commerce, the invasion of our territory, and the detention of the western posts?" What of France? "It is far from being impossible," wrote Freneau, "that the object of Britain in Mr. Jay's much talked of treaty, is to excite the jealousy of France against us, and to produce misunderstanding between the two republics."

The attitude of the *Jersey Chronicle* toward England could not be misunderstood: "Shall we invite the serpent to our bosom, that when cherished by our vital heat, she may sting us to death! Forbid it Heaven!" Freneau did not mean the men of Monmouth to forget the nation which had plundered its way through New Jersey seventeen years before. In a final burst of rhetoric he charged:

Citizens, Freemen of a favoured and happy land, arouse from your slumbers! Storms and tempests menace your peaceful dwellings, prepare to avert them! Your inveterate and implacable enemy is seeking to obtain a footing among you, chase the conspirator away! Remember that where despotism and corruption obtain an establishment, there liberty is insecure; and let it never be effaced from your minds, that Great Britain sought to enslave you, that she is the enemy of freedom, that she is at this moment waging a cruel warfare against it, and that no effort of hers will remain untried to exterminate it from the Earth.[29]

The leading article in the second number of the *Jersey Chronicle* was an essay "On Monarchy" which pointed out the dangers inherent in monocratic rule.[30] But one week later "Observations on Monarchy" spoke out even more sharply against hereditary government. "When men prostrate themselves before an individual or individuals of their fellow beings, no wonder that they are trodden under foot by them." [31] Despots were, however, doomed. The free citizens of the United States had fought their way from bondage. Never would they return. Freneau drove the point home with verses "On the Approaching Dissolution of Transatlantic Jurisdiction in America": [32]

> From Britain's grasp forever freed,
> COLUMBIA glories in the deed:
> From her rich soil, each tyrant flown,
> She finds this fair estate her own.

Even in Europe, as France and Holland had demonstrated, tyranny bowed to the demands of free-born individuals. Eventually the common man everywhere would win his way to power. So Freneau, in "The Republican Genius of Europe," [33] chanted derisively:

> Emperors and kings! in vain you strive
> Your torments to conceal—
> The age is come that shakes your thrones,
> Tramples in dust despotic crowns,
> And bids the sceptre fail.

It was America that must lead toward the "immutable perfect system of government" which would follow the dictates of reason, avoid sophistry and custom, and develop toward a realization of general human needs. "To be . . . creatures to the selfish dogmas of insatiable power, ill comports with the character of enlightened republicans." [34] Now that the United States had proved her independence and established her power as a commercial nation, the poet explained in "The Rival Suitors for America," [35]

> Like some fair girl in beauty's bloom,
> To court her, see what suitors come!
> An heiress, she, to large estate,
> What rivals for her favours wait!

First, the haughty Briton came to prefer his suit. Then, the Dane, the Dutchman, and the Swede, the "Russian bred in frost and snow," the "Spaniard grave, with cloak and sword," and the Turk from Asia offered their hands. All were rejected. But when came the gallant, martial Frenchman, Columbia succumbed:

> Smit with his lofty generous mien,
> She admires the Gaul, as soon as seen,
> Grants him her commerce—yields her charms,
> And takes a hero to her arms!

By the end of the first month of publication, readers of the *Jersey Chronicle* had been subjected to their first lesson: England was traitorous and not to be trusted, France was a loyal friend to whom allegiance was due, and freedom was the sword and the shield of the common man. Then Freneau, in the best pedagogical tradition, purposed to instruct the people of Monmouth in the terms and catch-

words of republicanism. During the next month he printed a series
of "Political Extracts" which, whether written by him or not,[36]
indicate what he, as editor, wished to bring before his readers. "On
the Despotic Form of Government" appeared as the leading article
on June 6. Despotism, of course, was explained as the simplest, the
lowest, and the worst possible kind of rule. Plutarch and Homer
were both quoted against it. Nero was held up as a horrible example
of its evils. Monarchial governments were, almost without exception,
"tyrannies, impostures, violations of the natural rights of mankind,
and worse than anarchies." On June 13 was presented "On the
Aristocratic Form of Government." This might be even worse than
despotism, for there were benevolent despots, but no unselfish aristocrats. "The yoke of this species of government is so galling that
whenever people have got the least power, they have shaken it off
with the utmost indignation." A week later, on June 20, appeared
the third of the series, "On the Democratical and Mixed Forms of
Government." The history of Athens and of Rome was sketched,
because each had been subjected to tyranny when one man became
popular and powerful. A mixed government, such as England
boasted, was dismissed with contempt as a bastard form, inheriting
all the faults and none of the virtues of the other three.

Only an *"improved Republicanism,"* based on popular representation and a frequent rotation of men in office, could succeed. The
text was firmly driven home on July 4 in an essay "On Some of the
Principles of American Republicanism." Power under this system
derived from the people, was vested in elected representatives of
the people, and was exercised for the benefit of the people. Hereditary dignity, aristocratic pretense, religious bigotry, and restraint of
free expression had no place. What then did not the future hold for
America? Leaders would be chosen for their virtue and their
ability, but they would not be left in office long lest they become
tyrannical. Every honest occupation would be considered respectable, and the acquisition of wealth would be curbed. Education
would be improved, flattery discouraged, and, soon, "even the mischievous spirit of warfare and conquest would cease." As artificial
distinctions broke down, the rights of every individual would be
respected and man would cease to be the oppressor of man. But

republicanism, in its truest application, went even further than this: it would "extend itself even to what is called the *brutal creation,* and their comfort and good usage, will undoubtedly, soon become an object of legislative concern."

On the nineteenth anniversary of American independence Freneau printed an editorial in which he rejoiced at the spread of republican principles. "The flame that was kindled here," he wrote, "is expanding through Europe . . . and in the course of one or two centuries . . . will probably embrace the world." [37] Among the citizens of Monmouth such sentiments were received with enthusiasm: as the day wore on, the militia made the hillsides ring with shouts and salvos; enthusiastic toasts were offered to the rights of man, the Republic of France, the downfall of kings, the American countryman who "never blushed at the plow nor trembled at the sword," and to the eternal friendship of France and America. [38]

Meanwhile the *Jersey Chronicle* was filled with letters, reports, and "American Advices" telling of British attacks on American merchantmen. The accounts were written in strong, hot language which hinted piracy, spoke of "bare-faced and impudent" [39] breaches of the law of nations, and growled of revenge for British "insolence and rapacity." [40] "The conduct of the Federal Executive of this country toward the Republic of France," Freneau reported, "has given great and general disgust to the citizens of the United States." [41] On July 11 and 18 the citizens of Monmouth found prominent place in their newspaper given to a complete transcription of the "Treaty of Amity, Commerce & Navigation, between his Britannic Majesty, and the United States of America." The terms were outrageous! "Was ever a nation," asked Freneau, "treated with such indignity? Were we worse off as English colonies?" [42] During the remaining months of its existence the *Jersey Chronicle* became little more than a medium for the collection, organization, and expression of opinion against Jay's treaty.

Column after column was reprinted from other republican newspapers as the inhabitants of Monmouth were subjected to every argument which Freneau, busy with pencil and shears, could find. The terms of the treaty were in direct opposition to the agreement made in 1783 with England. It broke faith with France. [43] It made

America a puppet of the British Parliament.[44] It offered no compensation for property which George III had confiscated during the Revolution.[45] It was silent on neutral rights and on the very grave problem of the impressment of American seamen.[46] "Mr. Jay's treaty meets with general disapprobation," Freneau explained.[47] He encouraged citizens of Freehold and Middletown townships to meet for the purpose of drawing up "their full and unbiased opinion." "Almost every town and parish in South Carolina," he told them, "were publishing proceedings inimical to the treaty. Savannah and several other places in Georgia have done the same." [48] He reprinted a series of ten provocative articles by "Valerius" from the Philadelphia *Aurora*.[49] In the face of such a partisan bombardment, the rural districts of eastern New Jersey could have been nothing but republican.

In the autumn a "Political Watchman" contributed a documented discussion of Washington's attitude toward American relations with European powers. Every instance showed that the President had favored England over France. As a result, the Political Watchman said, "the nation has been secretly, I will not say treacherously, divorced from France and most clandestinely married to Great Britain." [50] The figure of speech is so similar to that which Freneau had used in "The Rival Suitors for America" that we suspect the editor of appearing, as Hamilton had formerly accused him, "in correspondent dress." A week later, "Timothy Turnpenny," a Tory of 1776, rejoiced that the United States was "solemnly betrothed and married to Great Britain." Now, he said, the country may revert to that monarchy for which John Adams has been working for so long! "An Old Soldier" defended Washington, and the Political Watchman changed his point of attack. "Mr. Jay," he said, "has dishonoured his country." The British "smote us on one cheek and we turned the other—they took from us our cloak—we gave them our coat also." [51] But now Freneau fought a losing fight. The treaty was ratified by the Senate and signed by President Washington. "If we can have confidence in such an administration," grumbled the Political Watchman, "we deserve to be slaves." [52]

During these months there was room for but few contributions which did not treat of the subject of American relations with France and England. Freneau printed an essay "On the Ingratitude of Republics" on August 29 and a humorously satirical account of the yellow fever epidemic of 1793, entitled "The Devil upon Two Sticks in Philadelphia—A Fragment," on September 5. Verse appeared very infrequently. "Lines Written Several Years ago, and Intended to Have Been Engraved on a Tomb Stone under an Oak Tree, where a Despairing Lover Had Hanged Himself," were published on June 6. The ode, "God Save the Rights of Man," was reprinted on July 11 as the "Hymn to Liberty." Except for these, and the three poems that Freneau had published in May, no other verse in the *Jersey Chronicle* ever appeared in the poet's collected editions. The "Lines, Written by a Young Gentleman, during a Tedious Consumption, of Which He Died in his Twenty-second Year," August 1, "The History of Monarchy," August 15, and the "Stanzas Written Some Years Ago to the Memory of Miss Field, a Young Lady of North Carolina," March 26, 1796, were all in his manner. Occasional short rhymes, such as "An Imitation of Spenser," September 5, the "Epitaph on Doct. Monsey," December 5, "An Epitaph on a Hermit," December 19, 1795, and "A Simile—To a young Lady," January 16, 1796, may have been written by Freneau, but the only justification any of them could have for existence was that each apparently just fit into a vacant space at the bottom of a column. The *Jersey Chronicle* contains little to recommend it to a student of early American belles-lettres—except the "Tomo Cheeki" essays.

6

Freneau had been interested in attempting a treatment of an Indian's reaction to the complexities and sophistries of the white man's civilization ever since Andrew McGillivary had brought his thirty Creek sachems to New York in 1790. The "Opay Mico" essays which appeared at that time in the *Daily Advertiser* constituted his first adventures with the theme. It does not seem possible, however, that the poet could have supposed the concept original. He must have read Montesquieu's *Lettres persanes,* either in the French original or as translated for publication in Edinburgh in 1773. Goldsmith's *Citizen of the World: or, Letters from a Chinese Phi-*

losopher Residing in London to his Friends in the East, must have been available to him in the bookshops of Philadelphia and New York. He certainly had read the *Spectator,* in the first volume of which appeared Addison's "Account of London by Four Indian Kings." [53] Such a theme was a favorite during the eighteenth century. Jonathan Swift was vexed that Addison's essay had deprived him of the opportunity of writing a book which he had contemplated on the subject.[54]

It was probably a desire to achieve, at the same time, historical verisimilitude and the sanction of literary tradition which made Freneau change his hero from "Opay Mico" to "Tomo Cheeki." The latter, in addition to being an historical personage, had already been celebrated in anecdote, poetry, and drama. He was a *mico,* or chief of the Yamacraws, of the Creek Confederacy, who, in 1734, had been brought to England by Oglethorpe, presented to the king at Kensington, and feted in the British capital.[55] John Henley had devoted three issues of his periodical, *The Hyp-Doctor,* to "Memoirs of Tomo Chachi." [56] An ode had been composed in honor of "Tomacha-chi" on the occasion of Oglethorpe's second voyage to Georgia. In 1758 a play had been published in London entitled *Tombo-Chiqui: or, the American Savage.*[57] A contemporary account describes it as "a satire on the foibles of those European nations, who deem themselves superior to the rest of the world, on account of their polite accomplishments." These, "in the opinion of the honest American savage," were "only vicious derivations from the original simplicity and integrity of nature." [58] This might have been the text for the essays which appeared in the *Jersey Chronicle.*

Tomo Cheeki, as Freneau described him, was an Indian set apart from his fellows. While other chiefs amused themselves by shooting arrows at half pence set perpendicularly in hitching posts or caroused in taverns and dramshops, he spent his time in lonely strolls through the fields and woods and in noting down observations on the character and customs of the white man. Like Freneau's Pilgrim, he was a recluse, fond of melancholy contemplation. The publican at whose house he lodged in Philadelphia reported him a singularly unsociable individual who drank only cider and small beer, slept five hours each night, and rose at the first break of dawn for long, solitary walks. Tomo Cheeki expressed "great disgust at the manner of civilized society,—and danced a whole hour, the evening before his departure, with a favourite squaw." [59]

After the chief had returned to the land of the Creeks, his landlord discovered a sheaf of manuscripts, written in the Tallassee language, hidden in a hamper in the corner of the room in which the Indian had lodged. It could hardly have been merely a literary coincidence that Addison had used the same device in explaining his acquisition of the material he used in the "Account of London by Four Indian Kings" in the *Spectator*—or that Washington Irving, many years later, purported to have come upon the papers of Diedrich Knickerbocker in much the same manner. At any rate, Freneau pretended to have purchased the manuscript from the landlord. As no translator could be found, he said, the bundle was laid aside and for a long time forgotten, until, finally, a white man who had spent twenty years prisoner among the Creeks was engaged to turn the Indian's observations into English. They would be inserted, Freneau explained, in the *Jersey Chronicle* "for the amusement and information of the curious." [60]

"Tomo Cheeki, the Creek Indian in Philadelphia" appeared as a series of essays from May 23 to October 31, 1795. Three of the papers had already been published five years before in the *Daily Advertiser*, as the first and the third of the "Opay Mico" essays on September 1 and 17, and as "A Speech on a New Subject" on June 29, 1790. Now the series became immediately popular. The *New-Jersey State Gazette* and *Wood's Newark Gazette* reprinted it complete. The *New-Jersey Journal* used the first eight essays, the New York *Argus* and the Philadelphia *Aurora* the first three, and single papers were presented in the *Independent Gazetteer* and the *Columbian Herald*. Whatever national recognition Freneau's country weekly received appears to have been through the republication of the "Tomo Cheeki" essays.

Fundamentally, this series is little different from "The Pilgrim" essays which had been published more than ten years before. The Indian, as a man of the forests, disliked the cobblestones which covered the earth at Philadelphia and he scorned the small, dark rooms in which the white man dwelt.[61] He made fun of the picayune collections of the Philosophical Society. He marveled at the egoism which allowed men to believe that they could control, or even understand, the great laws of nature.[62] He lamented the spirit of cruelty which had sprung up among the Indians and the white men alike. The laws of reason had been abandoned, and the lust for wealth and power seemed to animate all men. But, at least, he pondered, how happy the Philadelphians must be to live in a town where each man dared trust himself to the barber's knife without fear! [63]

Tomo Cheeki was amazed that the men and women of America were "fond to distraction of their own images." Not content with looking glasses, they had their resemblances engraved on copper or painted on canvas:

Wherever we pass through these streets and narrow ways, we are not only gratified with a sight of the originals, but we see the copies also, in profuse abundance, suspended by way of a sign from the houses; fixed over the doors as an invitation to come in; fastened to the walls in the nature of ornament; or attached to glass-windows as an article of sale. This is the sort of vanity or folly, that gives disgust to my heart. . . . Can the great white men do nothing for their country but the little people must be compelled to become minutely acquainted with the width of their faces; the length of their noses, the rotundity of their cheeks, the depression of their chins, or the elevation of their foreheads? . . . O Vanity! I find thee existing here in every shape, and under every guise.[64]

Artificiality of every sort displeased the Indian. He chuckled over the formal pretensions of city gardens. Could these "tawdry productions of art," he said, these "little foppish trees, these shrubs, and bearers of fruit, that have been transferred from another country," hope to vie with the "wild genius of the forest"? The venerable oaks, "towering with all the contempt of sovereign dignity," would reproach the audacity of man for "defacing the amiable reign of nature." [65] The keynote of the "Tomo Cheeki" essays was a plea for natural simplicity.

In such a state had the Indian lived before the advent of his white conquerors. In such a state he might still remain on terms of friendship with the invaders. "When the red men shall no longer see in you a race of murderers and plunderers," Tomo Cheeki promised his readers, "you may travel all day, and in the night lay down in our forests in perfect safety." Far to the west, in lands no white man had ever found, were tribes who lived happily still. They had not been made "monsters of revenge" by the rapacity of avaricious adventurers. There one might travel in safety and live harmoniously with the children of the forest.[66] The Indian was a stranger to the cruel passion of jealousy. No tax collector clamored at his doors. He lived upon the bounty of nature and repaid her bounty with worship.[67] Yet the Indian was doomed. Contact with the white man's civilization, its barter, its treachery, and its strong drink, was effectually destroying the red man. Christian missionaries had been sent to him, but their teaching could not atone for the treachery of their lay compatriots. "I wish those gentlemen," said Tomo Cheeki of the missionaries, "had been as assiduous in inculcating the practice of the moral and social virtues as they were busy in pestering us with mysteries." Were not the rights of the Indian the rights of man? [68]

The more Tomo Cheeki considered the condition of the white race, the more fixed became his opinion that they had lost rather than gained "by subjecting themselves to what they call the laws and regulations of civilized societies." Endless cares were the natural results of endless wants. The white man "had enslaved almost the whole creation of living things, in order that they, in their turn, might become the slaves of all." Wants had been so multiplied that it was no longer possible to find their gratification. Goods must be brought for their pleasure from all corners of the earth. Great canoes must be built, rigged, and furnished with sails to bring new stimuli for jaded tastes. Millions of unfortunate slaves must labor under broiling suns to produce sweets for the gratification of blunted appetites. Many must work for long hours to satisfy the wants of a fortunate few. Happiness had been misdirected by avarice. Even love had been degraded by sordid interests. Man by his wants had become the slave of the very animals he abused. The spirit of man was debased. No longer was he the lord of all creation.[69] Tomo Cheeki found nothing but misery among the white men. "Perpetual jealousies of all around them, and a suspicious eye cast upon futurity, damp all their pleasures, and embitter the most joyous bowl." [70]

Finally Tomo Cheeki dreamed a dream. The Genius of the World appeared to him, angry and disgusted at the greed and cruelty of man. "Is all this order and beauty to be disturbed and defaced," he asked, "by a creature that has neglected and perverted the divine faculty of reason?" Because of its sins, therefore, mankind would be destroyed, and the Genius would choose a new species in its place. It was done, and the "inferior animals" passed before the god in review. Who should be the new lord of the creation? The elephant was rejected as too heavy and unwieldy for a governor. The horse was admired for his swiftness, strength, good nature, and generosity, but would not do in man's place because even a monkey might spring on his back to direct him.[71] The monkey, in turn, was rejected because of his cunning, the dog because he had once been a deity in Egypt and might yearn again for divine power, and the lion because of his cruel lust for blood. In desperation, the Genius created a new species, like man in intellect, but motivated by benevolence. These built no towns, sailed no seas, and fought no wars. They dwelt in simple security on the verdant banks of rivers. They subsisted upon the results of their own honest toil and the bounty of nature. When their labors were over, they gathered in quiet groups to discuss the characteristics of Deity, the origin of the universe, and the eternal perpetuity of felicity among men.[72]

Thus, Freneau, living quietly upon his acres at Mount Pleasant, saw the green hills of a far away Utopia. A new race, perfect in every good and simple virtue, was necessary for the peopling of his vision, for he found his compatriots unworthy. He no longer found refuge in his old faith in the natural goodness of primitive man. Perhaps it was not, as the Pilgrim had insisted, the simple man in simple surroundings on whom rested the rational salvation of the world. Freneau found man brutal, selfish, and slightly ridiculous.

7

As the *Jersey Chronicle* approached the end of its first year, Freneau continued his attacks upon the monarchial and aristocratic factions which he saw menacing freedom throughout the world. "The liberal, the rational, and the virtuous," he said, must rejoice that the revolutionary activities in France and in America have proved a "liberating of all the powers of men, from the variety of fetters, by which they have hitherto been held." A new age was dawning:

The generality of governments have hitherto been little else than a combination of the few against the many; and to the low passing and mean cunning of these few have the great interests of mankind been too long sacrificed. Whole nations have been deluged in blood, and every source of future prosperity has been drained to gratify the caprices of some of the most despicable, or the most execrable of the human species. . . . How glorious then is the prospect, the reverse of the past, which is now opening on the world. Government we may now expect to see, not only in theory and in books, but in actual practice, calculated for the general good, and taking no more upon it than the general good requires; leaving all men to the enjoyment of as many of their natural rights as possible, and no more interfering with the matters of religion, with man's notions concerning God, and a future state, than with philosophy or medicine." [73]

England was the black beast which snarled defiance at liberties in America. "Who can be so weak as to believe that the present government of Britain is sincere when it offers friendship to America?" challenged Freneau. He warned that the consequence of such amity might easily be foretold. "It will bury in the same tomb the American treaty with France and the popularity of our first magistrate." Republican America had come to a turning point. Speculators who had made immense fortunes through the funding system and the administration of the national bank were impressed with the belief that their wealth was in danger and had become convinced, said Freneau, "that nothing less than erecting a monarchy upon the ruins of the republic" could ever "give them security against *popular principles.*" No one in his proper senses could believe that such men, who had made great fortunes at the expense of the people, could ever be friendly to a government based upon popular authority. Freneau's prejudices were sincerely intense. Every man who opposed the principles of French democracy was a knave, a rascal influenced by England, and a monocrat. There was no middle ground. Therefore, Freneau could inform his readers:

There is something wrong and rotten in our affairs; and no stronger proof of it could be desired than to see the British, those idolators of royalty and hereditary aristocracy, so feverishly eager to push the President and his power higher and higher, over the head of law and constitution. The political ship is indeed leaky, from rottenness in some of her planks, or the weakness of her timbers.[74]

On April 23 he printed a "Parody on the Attempt to Force the British Treaty on the People of the United States." "Americans!" he exhorted,

> behold the fruits,
> The end of all your vain pursuits,
> Whole years in blood and warfare spent
> To save this injur'd continent.—
> How must it mortify your pride
> To take once more the British side.

The public debt grew alarmingly and taxes increased. The common man seemed bowed under a burden from which he could never be released. Money meant power, and the wealthy drained their substance from the pockets of the poor. That age, when avarice and ambition might be subjugated to simple human virtues, seemed far in the future. The many remained prey to the few. Though Hamiltonians explained that a public debt was a public blessing, Freneau scoffed at the phrase as sophistry:

> Public debt's a public blessing—
> O the blessing
> Past confessing,
> Never ending, still defending—
> What a blessing
> To be fleecing
> All the nation, without ending.[75]

During the controversy over Jay's treaty the Federalist newspapers were vehement in denunciation of its opponents. The republican press was equally noisy, and a journalistic battle royal kept every spectator aroused. Names were called and accusations flung heavily by both sides. But Freneau took little part in the quarrel, except faithfully to reprint trenchant anti-treaty arguments which would keep the people of Monmouth uncontaminated by pro-British propaganda. After the treaty was ratified and the republican press deprived of much of its ammunition, he warned his readers:

Men of Republican principles in this country are frequently denominated *Jacobins* by the leaders and printers of the aristocratic party. At other times they are stigmatized as *disorganizers*—aliens by birth—enemies to America in principle—Genet's mob—institutors of democratic clubs, *where darkness and drink make them shameless,* &c., &c.—Such is the abuse that men of integrity must put up with from the hireling tools of a disappointed British faction and their venal press—

> Should Shylock publish you had stabb'd your brother,
> Lampoon'd your father or debauch'd your mother,
> Say what revenge on Shylock could be had?—
> Too dull for laughter, for reply too mad—
> On one so poor you cannot take the law,
> On one so old your sword you scorn to draw;
> Uncurb'd—then, let the harmless monster rage,
> Secure in madness, dullness, want, and age! [76]

But the *Jersey Chronicle* had been a financial loss to its editor from the beginning. After it had been published for six months, Freneau inserted a plea that the subscribers pay "their several dues." By the end of the year it was evident that the newspaper could not be continued. On April 30, 1796, Freneau announced in a final editorial that a "necessary number of Subscribers having not yet appeared, scarcely to defray the expenses of the undertaking, notwithstanding the very low rate at which it has been offered, the Editor, with some regret, declines a further prosecution of his plan at this time."

Ten days later the Federalist New York *Minerva* chided: "Mr. Freneau has discontinued the publication of the Jersey Chronicle. . . . We suspect the paper failed, because Mr. Freneau and the PEOPLE of New-Jersey do not think alike." [77]

8

The last two issues of the *Jersey Chronicle* contained proposals for a weekly newspaper to be published in New York by the editors of the *Diary*. It was to be a "gazette for the country" and to be entitled the *Register of the Times*. Subscriptions would be received at the printing office at Mount Pleasant and papers would be forwarded from New York to Middletown Point "by the earliest water opportunities." [78] We suspect that Freneau was to have been more than just a subscription agent in this new project, because some months later he told DeWitt Clinton that he had recently abandoned a "mercenary plan" in connection with the *Diary*.[79] But the *Register of the Times* never appeared, and Freneau subsequently experienced "one or two disappointments" in finding employment with other liberal editors in New York.[80] He even considered establishing there a daily of his own, but remembered in time that such an undertaking was dependent on commercial notices and that merchants of New York were wary of advertising in too liberal a newspaper. "What can be done in that line," he explained, "Mr. Greenleaf seems already to have engrafted." Freneau was more cautious now than he had ever been before. He was even ready to make small compromises. "Interest has never been my ruling motive," he wrote, "but with years and experience it appears to me to be an important ingredient in composing our little feast of life that should not be neglected." [81]

Finally, DeWitt Clinton suggested that he enter partnership with Thomas Greenleaf, who published both the *New-York Journal*, a semi-weekly, and the *Argus,* a daily. Freneau pursued the plan avidly. Greenleaf's papers were noted, he wrote Madison, "for a steady attachment to Republican principles." What was more, they were both firmly established.[82] Personal interest and political convictions might equally be served. "One could wish," he told Clinton, "to be consistent."

Greenleaf was interviewed early in November. Freneau presented an outline of his qualifications, both in the book printing and the newspaper departments. When it became evident that a new partner would be expected to present some capital as an investment in the business, Freneau even went so far as to write Clinton: "Upon good prospects my delicacy will not be so great as to prevent me from asking favours of my friends." Meanwhile he wondered if Clinton would not use his influence to arrange a loan of £91.1.11 upon security of a note which Thomas Greenleaf owed Freneau.[83]

By December 1 the poet was able to inform Madison that the partnership was almost certain to be formed. "Something in the spirit of the National Gazette" would be revived. "As I consider the bargain the same as completed," he continued, "my next object is to make all the friends here that I decently can among men of eminence and ability." He asked that Madison mention the projected partnership to Robert R. Livingston, Chancellor of the State of New York.[84] Six weeks later Madison wrote Livingston:

Having been acquainted with Mr. Freneau from our Youths, and being sensible of his private worth, his literary talents and his steady application to the true principles of liberty displayed in our Revolution & republican form of governments, I feel an interest in the success of his laudable pursuits, which will I hope apologize for the freedom of recommending him to your esteem and countenance. You can appreciate much better than I can the particular undertaking he has in hand; but if it merits the encouragement which I hope it does, the value of your favorable attention to it, justifies the ambition he feels to obtain it.[85]

For some reason, however, arrangements with Greenleaf were apparently never completed. By May 13, 1797, Freneau was associated in New York with Alexander Menut, a printer recently from Canada. Together they planned the publication of a new periodical, *The Time-Piece; and Literary Companion*. It would be issued three times every week, "early Monday, Wednesday and Friday mornings." In it republicanism would again be served through devotion to the interests of the American common man.[86]

TEN

THE TIME-PIECE

1797–1798

"OF what use are the richest of treasures," asked Freneau, "which, while they are concealed in the deep abysses of the earth, can be attained only by privileged companies?" Free men could maintain their liberties only through knowledge of the rational basis upon which those liberties were founded. How better, then, might they be instructed than by a "judiciously managed" periodical? Through such a publication, edited fairly and with contempt for "partial, mercenary, or altogether selfish views," man might realize the "exalted character, and . . . real pre-eminence which he was evidently designed to hold in the scale of animated nature." The influences of ambition might be obviated, the cause of virtue advanced, and society be brought to that state of harmonious felicity of which the philosophers had dreamed.[1]

So Freneau, at forty-five, still a knight in shining armor, leveled his battle-worn lance once again. *The Time-Piece; and Literary Companion* was to be more than a newspaper. It was to be a medium of instruction which would, at the same time, prove and promote the dignity of man. Its columns would be open to all "political, moral, or other interesting discussion, from any quarter whatever." Contributions would be "written with candour, decency and liberality" in order to "promote the general good of our great Commonwealth, or the common interest of man." Controversy would be avoided. News would be summarized, the proceedings of Congress abridged, and advertising kept at a minimum in order to make room for more interesting and helpful material.[2] The new publication was to be a miscellany, "intended for the diffusion of Useful as well as Ornamental Knowledge, News and Liberal amusement in general."[3] Freneau sped the venture with a "Poetical Address" in which he predicted:

Wherever our pages chance to be read
For the feast of good humour a table we spread—
Let each bring his dish, and whoever may eat
Shall have no just cause to complain of the treat.

Not only were subscribers to be instructed in the principles of freedom, but, in order to render the periodical, in point of variety, acceptable to every taste, the editor proposed to supply his readers with selections of merit on all subjects, above all, with original contributions from "persons of literary character." [4] "The general plan upon which the TIME-PIECE is meant to be established," he said, "is Literary amusement." [5] Furthermore, he promised, "Every endeavour will be used to promote the rising genius and literary ability of this country, and of the flourishing capital of New York in particular." [6]

New York was the busiest, the wealthiest, and, some said, the gayest city in the United States. "The bustle in the streets; the perpetual activity of carts; the noise and hurry on the docks, which encircle three sides of the city; the sound of saws, axes, and hammers in the ship yard" [7] all attested to the industry of its citizens. Barges brought produce to its wharves and warehouses from New Jersey and Long Island, and from the upper regions of the Hudson. Wines from Madeira, rum from the West Indies, coffee from South America, and curious spices from the Orient arrived at its waterfront in odorous abundance. Factors and super-cargoes hurried about with manifests and letters of credit, and the stock exchange at Tontine's Coffee House hummed with activity. If Philadelphia was the London of America, said an observer from England, New York was the Liverpool.[8] It was a cosmopolitan city whose inhabitants prided themselves on their worldly breadth of mind. The new Vauxhall Gardens on upper Broadway served refreshments and presented open air concerts in the British manner.[9] At the Indian Queen, on the Boston Post Road, aristocrats and democrats alike wore the tri-colored cockade of France.[10]

Nowhere in the United States, not even in Charleston, was richness and brilliance of costume, particularly among the ladies, more noted than in New York,[11] nor was public entertainment anywhere more enthusiastically supported. At Baker's Museum, near the

Battery, one might view illuminated transparencies of Washington, Franklin, and La Fayette or pick out familiar landmarks on a brilliantly colored panorama of Manhattan.[12] Musical clocks, which played whole concerts, and a "beautiful representation of human and animal automaton forms" were exhibited on Water Street.[13] For two shillings an African lion might be seen at the Fly-Market, near the Ferry Stairs,[14] or a baby elephant which was shown on Front Street. The Menagerie, just off the Battery on Pearl Street, was open to the public every day except Sundays. There wolves, monkeys, owls, eagles, and a "remarkable Mexican wild hog from the forests of South America" were kept, each in its separate cage.[15] Zest was added to the bear baiting on the outskirts of the city when one contest "terminated most unfavorably to the sporters" as the bear escaped and hugged some of them "most fraternally." [16]

Perhaps the most popular entertainment of all, however, was to be found in the new amphitheater on Greenwich Street where Mr. Ricketts, formerly of Philadelphia, housed his equestrian circus. There horsemanship and pageantry were combined in a splendid show.[17] Those interested in science might visit the enclosed ground off Ball Alley, where M. Blanchard, also recently come from the national capital, performed aerostatic experiments with balloons and parachutes.[18] In the evening the John Street Theater presented a repertoire of comedy, farce, tragedy, and opera with astounding versatility.[19]

The merchant of New York was known as a stalwart individual, fond of hard work and vigorous play. By nine o'clock he was in his counting house laying out the business of the day. An hour later he was on his wharf, with an apron about his waist, rolling hogsheads of rum and molasses. Noon found him at market, "flying about as dirty and as diligent" as a porter. At two, he was "back again to the rolling, heaving, hallooing, and scribbling." At four he dressed for dinner, at seven attended the playhouse, and at eleven, says a not very sympathetic observer, he repaired to supper, "with a crew of lusty Bacchanals who would smoke cigars, gulp down brandy, and sing, roar, and shout in the thickening clouds they created, like so many merry devils, till three in the morning." "Certainly," he remarked, "few men throughout the Union worked harder for their enjoyment." [20] Reading, except for an occasional volume of history or travel from the Society Library or Literary Coffee House, had little place in his scheme of living. His leisure was better spent at the racing grounds at Harlem or Hempstead, and in hunting grouse or deer among the fields and woods of Long Island.[21] Literature was left to the women, to clergymen, or to young men who would probably amount to little anyway.

Among the women of New York, however, there were many who were "studious to add to the brilliant external accomplishments, the more brilliant and lasting accomplishments of the mind," and whose conversation was said to have been "as inviting as their personal charms." [22] All the ladies, said an English traveller a year later, declared that the circulating library of bookseller Hocquet Caritat on Pearl Street was charming! "Novels were called for by the young and the old; from the tender virgin of thirteen whose little heart went pit-a-pat at the approach of a beau; to the experienced matron of three score, who could not read without spectacles." [23]

2

So it was that the "persons of literary character" who answered Freneau's call for contributions to *The Time-Piece; and Literary Companion* were largely recruited from among the ladies of New York. "Anna," "Clara," "Cynthia," "Scriblera," "Caroline" and many another correspondent under a similar pseudonym exchanged poetical compliments and presented lachrymose lyrics on slavery, hope, or the evils of war. Soon "Philander," attracted by the sensibilities of "Anna," began a poetical courtship with the sentimental bluestocking. Later "Mr. L.," a love-lorn poetaster who sighed in vain for his maiden, exposed his heart in verse and received in return very unsound, but thoroughly sentimental advice from a legion of female scribblers. So doleful did their lines become that Freneau was soon called upon to suggest:

Our poetical correspondents have hitherto been too generally lifted on the gloomy side of things; owing perhaps to the succession of dull weather that has prevailed for some time past. As the genial month of May is now scattering the clouds and dispensing the blessings of sunshine, it is hoped, we shall be favoured, particularly from the ladies, with poetical communications of a more cheerful . . . nature.[24]

Nevertheless, until October, the *Time-Piece* was spattered with sentimental effusions, the only virtue of which is that they sketch a poetical background against which Freneau's most careless verses stand out as sane and workmanlike. Finally, however, "Duncan Downright," whom we suspect of voicing an editorial opinion, silenced the poetical exchange with caustic doggerel verses "To the Lovers." [25] At the same time Freneau announced, "The printers decline proceeding any further in the poetical controversy between L— and his opponents." "Caroline" made a smart retort and "Scriblera," piqued that her replies had not been published, wrote tartly to Freneau: "I beg leave to give them place . . . as they may serve to show Duncan, that his having the last word, was, more owing to the indulgence of the Editors . . . than to his own knock 'em down arguments." [26] Thereafter, however, the belles and the beaus of New York wept less frequently through the columns of the *Time-Piece*.

In the meantime Freneau offered his subscribers an inviting miscellany of more manly literature, including extracts from Goldsmith, Swift, and Smollet; anecdotes of Pope, Young, and, of course, Dr. Johnson; translations from Lucian, and a song from *Cymbeline*. He reprinted serially his own translation of the *New Travels through North America* as "The Travels of Abbe Robin," and he presented a revised arrangement of the "Tomo Cheeki" essays. Old poems appeared again, sometimes reworked to suit a new attitude—from the *Freeman's Journal*, the *National Gazette*, the *Poems* of 1795, and the *Jersey Chronicle*.[27] Occasionally he presented new poems, laughing poems, never very serious, lest he be laughed at in turn. Such was the doggerel "On a Young Lady who Wore in her Cap, Iron Conductors, on the Plan of Dr. Brydone, to Guard against the Effects of Lightning." [28] Such, too, was the farcical account of the misfortunes of a henpecked mariner which Freneau blandly called "Thetis; or the Heroine." Perhaps the "Reflections on Dr. Perkins's Metallic Rods," however, is most characteristic of the level to which Freneau's own poetic aspiration reached at this period. The Connecticut physician who had patented two simple metal strips, one of iron, the other of brass, the application of which on an afflicted part was said to relieve rheumatism, inflammations, aches, bruises, or burns,[29] was ponderously satirized:

> Perkins! what verse is equal to your praise
> Whose hocus-pocus from sick beds can raise!—
> Pains in the head, or palsies of the joints
> Henceforth shall yield to your Metallic Points;
> Ricketts and rheums shall at your presence fly
> Like Satan's self when holy water's nigh;
>
> .   .   .
>
> Touch'd by your magnet, dead men shall revive,
> Old Bachelors for Hymen's blessings strive—
> Maidens, averse to men, be taught to love,
> And wives—long barren—now prolific prove.

Early in May Freneau published verses on the "Equestrian Exercises at Mr. Rickett's Circus," because, he said, the horseman and his company "certainly deserve great credit for their exertions to entertain the town." "A Remarkably Dull Discourse, of near Two Hours in Length, from a Rambling Lay-preacher in the Backwoods of North-Carolina" supplied material for satire equally didactic. During the summer, the editor of the *Time-Piece* treated his readers to workmanlike disquisitions on such subjects as "On a very Small Garden Belonging to a Citizen of N.Y." and "On a Sea Captain that Shot Himself." Only in September with the publication of the stumbling first version of "On a Bee Drinking from a Glass of Wine," was there indication that a poet directed the policies of the paper. Though very evidently modeled on Thomas Gray's verses "On the Death of a Favorite Cat, Drowned in a Tub of Gold Fishes," this latter poem reveals again for a moment the lyric impulse which in Freneau had been dormant for nearly ten years.

But these "literary productions" were widely popular. The "Poet's Corner" of many a contemporary publication proudly displayed extracts of sensitive or satirical verse "From the Time-Piece." Of Freneau and his achievement said Benjamin Russell in Boston, "We were ever admirers of the talents and fancy of this gentleman, although we detested the politics . . . and still hope to enrich the Centinel with native gems from his rich cabinet." [30]

Freneau's literary reputation was secure, but secure at a level far below that to which he had once aspired. He wrote pleasantly of trivial things, sometimes lightly of things more serious. When in 1797 *The Columbian Songster, or Jovial Companion, Being a Collection of Two Hundred and Twenty Choice Songs* was published in Philadelphia, three of his productions were included. But each of them—"Father Dobbin's Complaint," "The Indian Student," and "The Rights of Man"—was a smartly lilted song, not really a poem at all. That sort of verse was expected of him. Something more serious, like "The Last Words of Shalum," was so little associated with Freneau's name that a New England editor could include it among the posthumous works of an obscure Yankee poet.[31] Even though the collection published at Mount Pleasant two years before was still advertised in Philadelphia,[32] it brought attention of only the slightest sort. "Caroline," one of the most prolific female contributors to the *Time-Piece*, however, thought it splendid. She told Freneau so in verse:

> Deign to accept the humble lays
> Your charming book inspired:
> I send you nought but heart-felt praise,
> I read and I admired.[33]

And another literary bluestocking attested:

> You do with just poetic-skill
> My mind with pleas'd ideas fill.[34]

Was this fame? Freneau was plagued by the ladies. They wrote him poetic letters, sensitively critical, very conscientiously literary.[35] His office was thronged with female visitors "mostly wanting favours of one kind or another." [36] At some time during this year Freneau says that he printed six copies of a pasquinade directed against an anonymous female critic, an English actress, who had written "a very satirical and biting attack" upon him. The "dear, defeated Amazon," who braved the gracefully feigned fury of his doggerel, offered no reply and, said Freneau, "there the correspondence ended." He suggested that his fair opponent thereafter

> Leave it to men to snap and snarl—
> Be you the sweet engaging girl.[37]

3

When we remember the brave introductory remarks with which Freneau launched the *Time-Piece*, we wonder why during the first six months of publication he himself engaged in so little of his wonted snapping and snarling. For, in spite of the attractive miscellany of literary material it offered, the newspaper was primarily concerned with instruction in what its editor was fond of denoting "genuine republicanism." To this end he reprinted political essays from the *Jersey Chronicle:* "Observations on Monarchy" appeared in the first issue; "On the Despotic Form of Government" and "On the Democratical and Mixed Forms of Government" followed in successive articles a month later; and "On Some Principles of American Republicanism" was the leading article for May 5. Nor was this enough. Thomas Paine's "First Principles of Government" ran serially from May 8 to May 12. "Agrarian Justice" by the same author appeared in four installments from July 21 to July 28. Rousseau's "Dissertation on Political Economy" was featured from August 25 to September 13, and his essay "Of Political Religion" appeared on December 8. No reader of the *Time-Piece* was to be left in any doubt of the rational basis on which its editor based his complaint against despotism in all its forms.

But active controversy was avoided—during the first six months. No names were called. No opponents were baited. And why? Perhaps Freneau did intend a literary periodical which would avoid politics. Yet we know too much of his intense and fiercely belligerent nature to believe that he really would. Perhaps he could not afford to antagonize any of the first few subscribers to the newspaper. Profit from publishing was precarious enough without that. By the end of two months the office of the *Time-Piece* was moved from Alexander Menut's printing shop on Beekman Street to 123 Fly-Market, where Freneau and his family occupied quarters.[38] Not three months later the editor was forced to remind his readers that "pecuniary engagements . . . must be immediately answered" if the publication was to continue.[39] But never before had financial danger deterred Freneau from speaking his mind bluntly. We suspect that neither was that the reason for his comparative silence now. Early in 1797 it simply was the better part of political expediency for a republican to have as little as possible to say.

Though Hamiltonian Federalists suffered a set-back in the election of John Adams as President and the old arch-enemy Thomas Jefferson as Vice-president, the political pendulum was slowly swinging back again. James Monroe, the liberal Minister to France who had shocked conservatives by too cordial an acceptance of Jacobin doctrines, was suddenly recalled, and staunchly Federalist Charles Cotesworth Pinckney was sent to Paris in his place. Then, when the French Directory not only refused to accept Pinckney as minister, but advised him to leave the country immediately, sensitive national pride rose hotly. Was the incident to lead to war? Many among American leaders suspected that it would. Moderate men advised a commission to conciliate France. But almost everyone agreed that she had acted churlishly. She and those who upheld her cause in America were in disrepute. Reports were received regularly that France seized American ships, just as England seized them. What more, asked the Federalist press, could we expect? American commerce was really crippled, and everyone would suffer. Even a Jacobin might turn in anger at a threat against his own purse. Again there was little that Freneau could say.

When, therefore, he reprinted "The Rival Suitors for the Favour of America" on March 20, he made cautious changes in the context. The Frenchman was no longer a dashing lover who would overcome fair Columbia with his "lofty generous mein." He came now, talking "much and loud of favours past," "with leering eye." And now Columbia refused to yield her charms to him:

> She dropt some tears at what he said,
> But thought it was no time to wed:
> Then thus to all her suitors cry'd,
> I wish not yet to be a bride—
> Whoe'er would in my eye excell,
> The secret is,—to treat me well.
>
> · · ·
>
> Take not my ships—seize not my men,
> As some have done—and you know when.

Four days later, on March 24, Freneau printed stanzas "On the Too Remote Extension of American Commerce." War seemed to be threatening again. Could it not still be traced to avarice and ambition? American ships, plying distant waters to advance the wealth and power of their owners, were seized by French or British privateers. Merchants, made powerful by the money they had already acquired, demanded retaliation. War would naturally result, and not to the benefit of the common man. Yet war might be avoided:

> Americans! why half neglect
> The culture of your soil?
> From foreign traffic why expect
> Sure payment of your toil?—
> At home, a softer harvest springs
> From mutual intercourse of things,
> Domestic virtues to fulfill—
> Vast seas *within* your realm abound
> Where commerce soon shall spread her sail,
> Nor Europe's wrangling race be found
> To bend you to her will.

Reason, the only true oracle of Freedom, would undermine every one of the once powerful doctrines of tyranny. Thus Freneau, when he came quietly to the defense of France in a poetical address "To the Americans" on March 29, suggested that his countrymen review the situation dispassionately. He explained of Europe and her conflicts:

> In these new wars new views we trace;
> Not slavery for the human race:
> And France!—where'er you spread your blaze,
> Lo! superstition's reign decays.

Can it be possible, he asked, that free citizens of the United States will join the minions of despotism and attempt to interrupt the progress of a world-wide republicanism? Can Americans ever take such a "vile ungrateful part" against their former allies in France? War in such a case was unthinkable. Who would lead America in such a war? Leaders would fail, for the cause was not righteous, honorable, or just. Freneau pled with his countrymen:

From Britain's yoke so lately freed
Wouldst thou, new legions basely lead,
To crush that power, whose valour gain'd
And once her sinking cause sustain'd.

From each true heart be banish'd far
The thought of so profane a war—
A curse would on her arms attend
And with that war your honours end.

This was not the "spirit of the National Gazette" which Freneau had promised to revive in the *Time-Piece*. It does not seem true to the fiery spirit of controversy which had once dominated the poet. Freneau was an older man, but not much older. He was still intense in his republicanism. He was more cautious now, because France, too, had fallen prey to ambition. Sympathy had to be stretched far in order that even he overlook her faults. Therefore, no member of the war party in Congress was attacked in the *Time-Piece*. Even John Adams, a favorite victim for satire, remained unscathed. Freneau walked quietly beyond the fringe of hostile public opinion, waiting for an opportunity to strike effective blows for liberty.

Reason became more than ever before the catchword of his political and social philosophy. When it was rumored that Thomas Paine was returning to America from France, Freneau, on June 23, suggested to readers of the *Time-Piece*: "It is intimated he has made many enemies in this country on the score of his Age of Reason. Let us therefore receive him cordially . . . in the name of common sense." When Elihu Palmer, who preached a religion derived from the unperverted nature of man, came to New York to organize the Deistical Society, Freneau was one of ten who petitioned the Common Council to allow Palmer to deliver an address from the large court room in the City Hall on the ensuing July 4th. The petition was denied and Palmer was branded "An Infidel" in the municipal files; [40] but the oration was delivered elsewhere and was published entire for the enlightenment of readers of the *Time-Piece*.[41] Through the autumn Freneau was glad to carry advertisements of Palmer's public lectures on "Natural Religion Opposed to Supernatural." [42]

Though no records of the organization exist, it may be supposed that Freneau was a member of the Deistical Society, which, according to its opponents, was a "combination of treachery, of indulgence, of frenzy, intemperance and every species of polluted baseness, for the purpose of combatting religion, virtue and wisdom." [43] To Palmer, as to Freneau, it seemed thoroughly rational that education and reason might bring about freedom from degrading religious superstition in the same way that the American Revolution and the republican movement had accomplished political emancipation. To liberals at the end of the eighteenth century it seemed perfectly evident that man should soon be free of every shackle which had bound him. And reason would light the way.

It was probably at about this time that Freneau joined the Tammany Society, or Columbian Order,[44] which had been active as an organized Anti-federalist group in New York since 1789. Though instituted immediately after the Revolution as a social and fraternal organization, the Tammany Society soon became, in the words of one of its founders, a "political institution founded on a strong republican basis, whose democratic principles will serve in some measure to correct the aristocracy in our city." [45] Freneau would have been very much at home in such a group. He certainly must have been a member by July 4, 1797, when the society marched in a body from the Battery to the new Dutch Church on Cedar Street as part of the ceremony commemorating the twenty-first anniversary of American independence. Citizen George James Warner delivered an oration on "Means for the Preservation of Public Liberty," after which an ode, composed for the occasion by Philip Freneau, was sung by the Uranian Musical Society: [46]

> Once more our annual debt to pay
> We meet on this auspicious day,
> That shall through every coming age
> The feelings of mankind engage;
> Red war will soon be chang'd for peace,
> All human woe for human bliss,
> And nations that embrace again
> Enjoy a long pacific reign.

Warner's oration and Freneau's ode were printed by Thomas Greenleaf in a twenty-two page pamphlet which was offered for sale at the office of the *Argus* for one shilling and sixpence. The publication, however, did not go well: Freneau advertised it in the *Time-Piece* for months after Greenleaf discontinued notices of it in his newspapers.[47]

Meanwhile he made plans for still another book, noncontroversial and full of exciting adventure. On July 26 he announced that he had obtained the manuscripts of John Ledyard, the celebrated American traveller who had sailed around Cape Horn with Captain Cook and who, after experiences in many lands, had died in Cairo nine years before. Letters, journals, and notes written by the explorer had been gathered together by his cousin, Dr. Isaac Ledyard of New York, a brother and former business associate of Major Benjamin Ledyard, who had married Catherine Forman, the oldest sister of Eleanor Freneau. Now Freneau proposed to arrange the materials for a volume of two hundred and fifty pages, if a subscription could be obtained adequate to the expense of the undertaking.

"We are happy to announce," said Noah Webster, editor of the New York *Minerva*, "that Mr. Freneau has obtained the manuscripts of the late adventurous traveller, Mr. John Ledyard, and proposes to prepare them for publication." [48] Similar encouragement appeared in other New York papers,[49] and on August 30 Freneau printed an extended prospectus in the *Time-Piece*. As progress was made, however, it became evident that at least four hundred pages would be necessary and that the price could not be twelve shillings or a dollar and a quarter, as first announced, but two dollars. The volume was to be a handsomely bound octavo, illustrated with a full length portrait of Ledyard as he appeared upon taking leave for his last voyage into Africa.

But now the *Time-Piece*, after four months of placid existence and cautious republicanism, first raised its back in anger. On July 12, 1797, more than a hundred liberal citizens of New York met at a congratulatory "Feast of Reason" to honor James Monroe, late Minister Plenipotentiary from the United States to France. Presiding was General Horatio Gates, the conqueror of Burgoyne; Aaron Burr and Edward Livingston offered patriotic toasts. When glasses were drained to the President of the United States, the company responded with three cheers. But when someone proposed the Republic of France, nine huzzas rent the air.[50] When news of the celebration reached Philadelphia, John Fenno, in the *Gazette of the United States,* was disdainful: the gathering, he said, was composed of Jacobins, enemies of order, and promoters of sedition.[51] The charges were so familiar that Freneau's reply was almost a reflex. He dashed off doggerel "Stanzas Occasioned by Some Late Illiberal Remarks in Fenno's Gazette" for the *Time-Piece* on July 24. The Federalist editor was a "petulant cur," who, "riding the air" on a "broomstick from hell" could appreciate no company which lacked apostates. A schoolboy might have composed these verses with which Freneau now attacked his old opponent. His satire had lost its sting, and his invective had been dulled through much use.

The editing of a republican newspaper seemed indeed a thankless task. Freneau reminded his readers again that subscription fees must be paid promptly if publication was to continue. Finally after six months his partnership with Alexander Menut was dissolved. Thereafter creditors were advised to send their accounts to Philip Freneau at 123 Fly-Market.[52] Soon the living quarters there, including a kitchen, a cellar, yard room, and a large room on the ground floor "well calculated for a grocer's, or any other retail store," was advertised "To be Let." [53]

Freneau had found a new and more energetic partner in Matthew L. Davis, a young man of twenty-four, a politician of republican interests, a member of the Tammany Society, and, later, campaign manager, defender, and literary executor of Aaron Burr. From September 15 the newspaper was printed at Davis's shop on Moore Street. Its title was shortened to *The Time-Piece,* and it displayed a new and more outspoken vitality.

As he changed partners at the end of six months of publication, Freneau thanked those who had supported him, asked for a continuance of their favor, and reasserted his journalistic creed:

For a periodical paper to be of general utility, and to support those principles on which the American Revolution was founded, and which interest every man as a free citizen of the globe, something more is required than the bare commercial or political intelligence of the times. Such a paper would constantly be engaged in bringing home those great truths to every one's reflection that most nearly concern the rights and liberties of man, and which, while they speculatively enlighten the understanding, may be reduced to practice with more facility from these compendious vehicles than as they stand dilated in the voluminous publications of philosophers, which few have leisure to peruse with the necessary attention. It is an easy matter to fill the columns of a Gazette, as the world now goes, with the history of military marches, details of battles and sieges, storms, shipwrecks, murders, and that endless variety of events that are continually rising and floating on the surface of human things; but all these do little more than gratify curiosity and leave the mind benighted as to the interests of humanity and bettering the condition of human nature. These casual events undoubtedly should not be forgotten in any publication that makes pretenses to record the history of its own times, but should not occupy so great a space as to operate to an almost rejection of those ideas and observations, those hints and sketches of information, those lights and disquisitions, at the view of which tyrants tremble, and every description of the invaders of the rights of man sink back into annihilation and insignificance.[54]

Shall America go forward to liberty or shall she retreat to despotism "by British arts, or gold, or titles reconverted?" he asked in a poetical "Address to the Republicans of America." The answer, of course, rested with the free men of the United States. Freneau laid the challenge before them:

> Here, on this virgin earth the soil unstain'd,
> Where yet no tyrant has his purpose gain'd,
> Keep bright the flame which every bosom fir'd
> When Hessian hirelings from these lands retir'd,
> When, worn and wasted, all that murdering crew
> And Britain's squadrons from the Hudson flew
> When, leagu'd with France, you darts of vengeance hurl'd,
> And bade defiance to the despot world.

4

Then, for twelve weeks during the autumn of 1797, Philip Freneau guided the *Time-Piece* through a lively series of sorties against the enemies of republicanism. On September 21 Noah Webster, formerly of Connecticut but now editing the sedately Federalist *Minerva* in New York, announced to his readers:

The Time Piece published in this city, at *first* appeared in a decent dress, as a "Literary Companion," but has lately been copiously bespattered with filth like the National Gazette formerly. An old book says "the dog returns to his vomit and the sow that was washed, to her wallowing in the mire."

Freneau's newspaper, said William Cobbett of Philadelphia was a "miserable filthy thing," and its editor was a mere "understrapper" to that malcontent, the philosophical Vice-president, Thomas Jefferson.[55]

In all his experience Freneau had not met two men better suited to take his measure than Webster and Cobbett. The former, calm and judicious, enjoyed the respect of both the clerical and the mercantile classes. He hammered steadily, but with tempered strokes, against every vestige of non-conformity to Federalist principles. He was a conservative and wrote conservatively, with little malice. Subscribers to his newspaper were proud that he seldom stooped to scurrility as was the "low bred custom of low bred Editors." [56] Cobbett, of Philadelphia, on the other hand, blustered and ranted. He pulled none of his punches. He libeled without a blush, and truth had little room in his philosophy.

William Cobbett was one of the most fiery figures in early American journalism. Coming to America from England in 1792 as a radical too outspoken in opinion to be safe in his native country, he applied without success to Thomas Jefferson for a place in the government service. Subsequently he became, first, a tutor to French *émigrés* and, then suddenly doing a political about-face, a pamphleteer who denounced Jacobism and democracy in all their forms. As violent a defender of British policy as he had formerly been a violent critic, he began early in 1796 to produce a periodical called the *Political Censor*, which commented acidly upon proceedings of the Congress. Finally on March 4, 1797, he launched over the pseudonym of "Peter Porcupine" a daily newspaper which he called *Porcupine's Gazette*.[57] He wrote freely and vented whatever opinions he chose. Thereafter John Fenno's *Gazette of the United States* was second among anti-republican newspapers. Peter Porcupine, riding rough-shod over every form of decency, trumpeted loudly and with apparently no fear. For many months Benjamin Bache and the Philadelphia *Aurora* were his favorite victims.

As the *Time-Piece*, however, became more articulate in the expression of republicanism, Cobbett turned his attention northward. On September 8 he treated his readers to an exposé of its editor's career:

Freneau conducted a jacobin gazette at Philadelphia, but it expired with the office of his patron. He then took a sort of trading tramp through the Jerseys, where he endeavoured to barter his *patriotism* for bread; but the Jerseymen, with their usual justice and good sense, refused to a literary vagabond what they never refuse to unmerited distress. At last, after hard travelling, and hard fasting, he took shelter in New-York, and once more set his press and his types to grinding sedition. He is hard at work at it, but he'll not do much mischief . . .

Notwithstanding all this, it must be remembered that the fellow's a CAPTAIN. How he came to be thus dubbed, I know not, if it was not in consequence of his serving his master Jefferson in the quality of what is called in England a LED CAPTAIN; that is, a tool, a toad-eater, a lick-spittle, &c. &c. &c. for which post he was undoubtedly, extremely well qualified.

To Freneau this, of course, called for a response. "Among a despicable mass of scurrility in one of Porcupine's Gazettes of last week," he wrote on September 13, "he mentioned that he was plagued with the Time-Piece for several months'." Of course he was plagued. "It has also been a plague to some others of his brethren, and will go on to be so," its editor promised, "till they are hustled into their native dog-kennels." Then, Freneau explained:

> From Penn's famous city what hosts have departed,
> The streets and the houses are nearly deserted,
>   But still there remain
>   Two Vipers, that's plain,
> Who soon, it is thought, yellow flag will display;
>   Old Porcupine preaching,
>   And Fenno beseeching
> Some dung-coat to wheel him away.

Two days later, on September 15, Freneau printed "Melancholy Reflections on Passing a Burying Ground in the Neighborhood of Philadelphia." Another yellow fever epidemic raged in the capital, but it seemed scarcely as dangerous as the anti-republican activities of Cobbett and Fenno:

> Pensive, on these green sods I cast my eye,
> But why torment myself, and grieve and sigh,
> Because, perhaps, beneath some scoundrels lie?
>
> Who knows if these, who here so soundly sleep,
> Alive, would not have stolen my flock of sheep,
> Or, failing, plung'd me headlong in the deep?

Perhaps below this turf in silence rests
Those, who when living were of men the pests,
Patrons of titles, ribbons, crowns, and crests.

What though made sacred by a parson's whine,
Why sorrowing on these *tombs* should I recline,
Sheltering some *Fenno* or some *Porcupine:*

Wretches, who breathing, poison'd freedom's air,
Brethren in villainy—a goodly pair—
But now are gone to print—the Lord knows where.

Not content with a single, or even a double reply, Freneau prepared a third attack for the issue of September 18:

The uniform share of abuse and scurrility thrown out by Mr. Porcupine, towards every character that becomes obnoxious to him, or has not fallen in with his policies, has long been notorious to the public. His scurrility and abuse, however, has always fallen harmless; it is only his praise that people are afraid of. Mr. Pitt had too mean an opinion of American Republicans, if he thought their cause was to be shaken by ribaldry, and blackguardism. The sooner, therefore, he withdraws his agent the better; or, perhaps, a *dismissal* will take place, without much formality, especially, as there is scarcely an Englishman in this country but what detests Porcupine, and the cause in which he is engaged.

Since he worships king LOG
    With strenuous devotion,
They should keep him at home
    To give him promotion:
But if sent to this station
To seek elevation,
To shew what we think of the HOG
    We'll break up his quarters,
    Without gun or mortars;
    And some are prepar'd
    (Who by owls are not fear'd)
To kick him down stairs
With a clip at his ears,
And drive him to hell in a fog.

Freneau's prose was now more forceful than his verse. His satirical rhymes had lost the "attick salt" which had made them such a caustic years before. He wrote freely, even ferociously, but a note of petulance, almost querulous, creeps into these later attacks. Freneau had wielded the pen in controversy too long. He had been too often on the losing side. He snapped angrily still, but his bite had little force.

The life of a newspaper publisher in America at the end of the eighteenth century was not easy, especially that of a democratic editor who refused to submit to the increasingly powerful mercantile class. No writer of the time has left a clearer or more sympathetic picture than Freneau of the vicissitudes of a journalist during the early years of the American republic. For example, the essay on "The Ridiculous Distress of a Country Newsprinter," on September 20, presents a good-humored account of a rural editor's troubles both in collecting news to fill his columns and money to pay his debts. On September 22 the stanzas "On the Death of a Country Printer," which had appeared four years before in the *National Gazette*, were republished in the *Time-Piece*. Leaving the subject for a moment on September 25, Freneau proved his continued devotion to republican activity in France by reprinting the "Ode on the Fourteenth of July":

> Bright Day, that did to France restore
> What priests and kings had seiz'd away!

At the same time he candidly repudiated Federalist charges that republican editors in America were minions of France:

The Democratic printers, and editors of patriotic papers in this country, are not unfrequently reproached by the typographers and editors of *another cast*, with being bribed by French gold. One day they are made so rich with this same gold that they can build printing houses and carry the world before them: the next they are all in the suds; the gold melts, or turns into a sort of devil's gold, such as John Faustus, of wizzard memory, was wont to deal in. In fact, gentlemen federal editors, it is difficult to say what end the French republic could have in bribing American printers, any more than in setting fire to Albany, as is basely and cruelly laid to their charge. The French have long set the Americans down in their books as an ungrateful nation; and with sovereign contempt leave us to pursue our own plans and line of policy. As to the printers, it is a truth, that a few in the United States, from the influence of sentiment only, are attached to France and her cause. Observe these men, and there will be found nothing in their characters or

circumstances, that will countenance the charge of bribery on the part of
the French, or others.

> Yes! they are brib'd—that's clear;
> And paid French millions by the year;
> And prov'd most plainly, by the coats they wear:—
> They are the lads that live in houses grand,
> And own vast tracts of fertile land;
> With so much self-denial in their natures
> (They are such good, obliging creatures),
> That shunning pleasure and the glare of wealth,
> They for the public good waste time and health;
> Sit up all night,
> Compile and write;
> One day a shilling from Kentucky get—
> Then stay a week to starve and fret.
> Why, Mr. Fenno, if this be French gold,
> No wonder that you federalists look so bold.

Yet the lack of support given to his undertakings depressed Freneau. All reason seemed to be on his side, and every ideal of human
freedom, but men inclined their ears to other prophets. Mammon
seemed to whisper, and America listened with unfeigned interest.
The rights of all men appeared to be forgotten as the right of each
individual to secure his own mercenary salvation became increasingly manifest. On September 25, Freneau asked in "Reflections on
the General Debased Condition of Mankind":

> What is this world, this sun, this skies,
> If heaven's bright lamp on man must rise
> Deject'd and distress'd?—
> Why blazes round the mid-day beam?
> Why, reason, art thou call'd supreme,
> Where virtue sinks oppress'd?—
>
> What are the views of Nature's laws—
> What is the deep unfathom'd cause
> That does her plagues prolong?
> Nature, on earth, confus'd appears;
> On little things she wastes her cares,
> The great she models wrong.

The task of supporting the principles of the American Revolution
seemed thankless indeed. "Strangers arriving in this country," said

Freneau on September 29, "generally expect to find, from what they have read of the American character, openness, plainness, and sincerity in dealing." Yet how different the situation! Almost every man was "upon the watch to take advantage in business and trade." The United States had become a "mere Chinese kennel of sharpers." Never, in all the annals of history, Freneau charged, had love of wealth "gained so much upon any people, in the same short space of time, as upon the Americans." He admitted that wealth was valuable and that no wise man would despise it. "At the same time," he continued, "he will not make it the *primum mobile* of all his actions." He suggested that the money dealers of New York chant the following hymn:

> O Satan! I thy aid implore,
> That thou wouldst yet increase my store,
> For much does always covet more.

> Thou first inventor of all coin,
> Of BANKS who plann'd the great design,
> Give me but gold, and I am thine.

> I crave no blessings parsons prate on,
> My bags are what I most debate on,
> Then fill them up—and take me Satan.

Many of the leaders in the war for independence had succumbed to the blandishments of wealth. Their affection for the people and their republican interest had cooled. On October 2 Freneau quoted the familiar allusion to a camel passing through the eye of a needle. "The same may be almost said," he suggested, "in respect to an overgrown rich man being a good republican." Yet the plutocrats were fond of answering, "When I was a child, I spoke as a child." They meant, Freneau explained, "while I wanted the assistance of the people I courted their favour and interest, but the moment I found I could do without them, I turned my back upon, and despised them." Do not look to men of wealth for the protection of your interests, he advised his fellow republicans. "What is called the middle and lower classes, have always been the guardians of this deposit, and with them it appears it will eventually remain." At the foundation of every state were the people. Above them, blown by

every wind, were the continually fluctuating great. He amplified the
figure in verse:

> Thus, in yond' steeple towering high,
> Where clouds and storms at random fly
>   The weather cock is plac'd,
> Which only while the gale does blow
> Is to one point of compass true,
>   Then veers with every blast.
>
> But things are so appointed here
> That weather cocks on high appear,
>   On pinnacle display'd,
> While sense, and worth, and preaching wights,
> And clerk, that times grave Music's flights,
>   Sit humble in the shade.

But the wealthy seemed to control national policy. The merchants of the United States had, for a long time, insisted that some
means be provided for the protection of their ships at sea. Radical
republicans in Congress were equally consistent in opposition: "It
is the design of the Court party," William Maclay said in 1790, "to
have a fleet and an army. This is but an entering wedge of a new
monarchy in America. . . . It is another menace to our republican
institutions." [58] Nevertheless, in 1794, the Congress ordered six
frigates built to protect American commercial vessels from Algerine
corsairs. When peace was effected with the Algerines in 1796, so
much money had already been invested in shipbuilding that it was
considered wasteful not to continue. Now in 1797 it seemed to the
merchants that protection was more necessary than ever, because
France preyed mercilessly on American shipping. Three hundred
vessels were reported lost. As a result, the Congress ordered that
work be continued on three of the frigates. The *Constellation* was
under construction at Baltimore, the *United States* at Philadelphia,
and the *Constitution* at Boston. Expenses mounted, however, and in
June, 1797, Congress was asked for a further appropriation for the
completion of the ships of war.[59]

Republican members rose in protest. For what would the frigates
be used? asked Albert Gallatin of Pennsylvania. Would they act as

convoys for fleets of merchantmen, would they cruise through the West Indies in search of privateers, or would they simply patrol the Atlantic coast? Let the President decide, answered the Federalists. Our duty, they added slyly, is only to provide the money. Republicans became suspicious, because President John Adams was known to have so little love for France that a navy under his control might well be used to lead the United States into war. Would France negotiate with representatives of a nation arming against her? Besides, said Gallatin, the money needed for outfitting the frigates could be raised from the people only by oppression. The plan was useless, expensive, injurious, and unfair to the common man.[60]

The appropriation bill, however, passed with an overwhelming majority. By the first week in September the first two frigates, the *United States* and the *Constellation*, were launched. The *Constitution*, the largest and the most costly of them all, was still under construction at Boston. The Federalist *Columbian Centinel* announced on September 20 that she was a splendid vessel, comparable to the constitution of the United States in strength and security. "That Heaven may long preserve both the *original* and the *type*," said the Boston newspaper, "is the hearty prayer of all—save Jacobins and worms." The comparison was unfortunate, for two days later at the elaborately planned official launching of the frigate, it was discovered that she had settled into the ground and could not be moved. Republicans chuckled. It was an omen. "What will be the eventual fate of our *Glorious Constitution*, conducted by such bungling pilots?" punned Thomas Greenleaf in the *New York Journal*.[61] Freneau commented on September 29:

It is sincerely to be regretted, that this fine ship stuck on her ways, particularly as thousands must have been severely disappointed who came from a long distance with their families to witness the launch; and some of them at a very considerable expense.

> Some with their airs aristocratic
> And some with honors diplomatic,
>   All came to see the show—
> This frigate, Constitution call'd,
> In vain the builders pulled and hawl'd,
>   Alas! she would not go—!!

Each antifederal, with a smile
Survey'd this gallant glorious pile,
   As if he meant to say,
Builder! no doubt you know your trade,
A *Constitution* you have made,
   But should her *ways* have better laid.

Well—now to heave the ship afloat,
And move from this unsettled spot,
Take our advice, and give her soon
(What should have long ago been done)
AMMENDMENTS—You know what.

Meanwhile John Fenno in the *Gazette of the United States* derided Freneau's attempts to revive the spirit of the American Revolution. Who was the editor of the *Time-Piece*, he asked, to present himself as an exponent of that spirit? During the struggle for independence, the Jacobin poetaster, Freneau, "was idly chaunting in fulsome and leaden strains, the horrors of the prisonship, or inditing lazy-lagging rhymes for newsboys and hawkers." On the other hand, every male member of the Fenno family had borne arms in defense of his country.[62] "Thereby hangs a tale," answered Freneau, "of *tar and feathers*, appendages very inapplicable to American patriots of 1775." Once a tory, always a tory.[63] Benjamin Bache gleefully reprinted the accusation against the Federalist editor in the *Aurora*.[64] John Ward Fenno, in his father's absence, defended the family honor with vigor:

Nothing that the poor despised bard of the *Time-Piece* is capable of saying could possibly excite anger; nor in the present instance, any notice, had not a falsehood from his paper been transferred into the Aurora. The author of the paragraph in which "tar and feathers" are spoken of . . . is *a liar* and *a scoundrel.*[65]

"If fame says true," Freneau retaliated a few days later, "there are a few lines in Trumbull's M'Fingal, that owe their origin to this *dark affair.*[66] Should Fenno, the great *"federal patriot,"* one of the *"typographical pillars of the government,"* who had been "enabled to 'wallow in wealth' by an *easy compliance"* be, like Cato's wife, above suspicion?

This pitiful wight
Shall be dragged into light;
All his plans, and his schemes,
And his *monarchy* dreams,
Be brought to the ear of the nation.—
Your mighty Gazette,
Is too little, *old Sweat,*
Too scanty, by far
To wipe off the TAR
That stuck on a certain occasion.

But even Fenno and Peter Porcupine were unimportant to Freneau. They were irritating gad-flies, small in comparison to the patriotic ideals of the *Time-Piece.* "Among the great events which time is unfolding," he said, "and which will claim the attention of posterity, the American revolution will hold an exalted place in the history of man." [67]

For several days an advertisement had been appearing in the New York newspapers, calling for subscribers to a new patriotic work, an epic poem, to be published in twelve installments and called "The Columbiad." [68] "If this work should succeed, and receive the stamp of public approbation," said Freneau, "no doubt the poem will be immortal, and go down to posterity with the fame of the revolution itself, and waft the author's name along the stream of fame." [69] It deserved to succeed, for it was "a REPUBLICAN POEM, at once comprising all that is pleasing in poetry, and yet responsive to the views and interests of truth and liberty." [70]

Little of Freneau's literary creed has survived. The following paragraph, however, contains much of the ideal upon which he had built his own literary career and toward which he had worked with so much fervor a dozen years before. Now he applied it to the work of another man, as he said:

Perhaps no other event in the history of man, as a subject of epic poetry, has equal claim on the exertion and animation of genius, with the emancipation of the western world. Poems of the epic strain that have been handed down from the remote periods of antiquity, are founded on a comparatively narrow basis. The Rape of Helen; the Return of Ulysses to Ithaca, from the siege of Troy; or the transferring of an insignificant colony in a few barques from the Lesser Asia to the western coasts of Italy, have been the subjects of those great masterpieces of poetry penned by Homer and Virgil, which stand at the head of all poetic excellence, and have commanded the attention of mankind for hundreds of centuries back, and been preserved as the most precious of all reliques, when in danger from the devastations of war, Vandalism, and conflagration. If the genius of such authors as Homer and Virgil, could aggrandize events, even in those limited times, of no great moment in the eye of the historian, so as to render them immortal in the memory of mankind, by the "magic of song," how much the more should this sublime incident of our own times, the AMERICAN REVOLU-TION, awaken genius, and enable it to transmit to posterity . . . this STORY OF FAME, this *real Revolution,* which, in its consequences, includes no less in the general condition of man, than a transfer from tyranny to slavery, and subjugation, to the benignity of rational government, equal liberty, and the advancement of that temporal felicity designed for man by Nature, while a resident in this sphere of her creation.[71]

Freneau himself had long deserted the epic ideal. He was a man of action now who found his subjects in the life he observed about him:

> To seize some *features* from the faithless past;
> Be this our task—before the century close:
> The colours strong!—for, if we deem aright,
> The *coming age will be an age of prose:*
> When sordid cares will break the muses' dream,
> And COMMON SENSE be ranked in seat supreme.[72]

From October 16 to November 15 he published in rapid succession "The Book of Odes" in twelve installments. The first, a parody of Isaac Watts's translation of the first of the Psalms of David, derided that type of aristocratic sycophant who shunned the company of Democrats, but who

> in the glare of splendid halls
> Doth place his whole delight,
> And there by day eats force-meat balls,
> And roasted hogs by night.

The *Connecticut Courant* called it a profane parody and pointed out that the aristocrat in Freneau's version corresponded to the saint in the original psalm, and the democrat to the impenitent sinner. With feigned seriousness, the editor of the New England newspaper proceeded to a discussion of the poetical value of the parody:

Although some emendations might be made in the phraseology, yet where the intention is right the critic should be lenient. Where a *youth* has genius we should wish to see it fostered—and, although in the present production, there appears to be a peculiar *luxuriance of expression,* and an unusual *sublimity of idea* which does not perfectly accord with the nature of his subject, yet we cannot but think from this *puerile effort,* that, by a due attention to rhetorical rules, and a dispassionate study of fine writing, together with *practice* he may, *in time* attain to that degree of perfection, at which he should be able to dress up *trite ideas in smooth verses.* On the whole the production is such as will not discredit his *heart,* though it may not reflect much lustre on his *head.*[73]

Freneau, always ready for a set-to with his Connecticut opponents, replied:

These gentlemen writers ought to consider that the parody in question . . . was not meant to be sung through a deacon's nose, to the sound of the organ; nor yet to the timbrel of seven strings: it was merely intended to be *harped* upon out of doors, for the benefit of all good democrats, and the utter confusion of the *contrary character.*[74]

The gentlemen from Connecticut, however, were right. None of the odes in the *Time-Piece* can be recommended for their poetical content. Each is facile in rhyme and rhythm. Each satirizes some phase of contemporary life of which the poet disapproved. Each is interesting, but none is essentially important except in relation to the times in which it was written.

During the last week in October and the first weeks of November Freneau presented a second series, this time of informal essays written in the character of "Hezekiah Salem," a defrocked Connecticut parson who was forced to make his living as a basket weaver on Long Island. Hezekiah Salem was didactic, pragmatic, and more than a little ridiculous. His first essay on October 23 was a discourse "On the Culture of Pumpkins": nowhere did pumpkins grow larger or more delicious than in his native New England. The second contribution, "A Sketch of Biography," on October 25, was so long and rambling that Freneau stepped out of character for a moment to admonish as editor, "We shall be happy of a more intimate acquaintance with our correspondent, Hezekiah Salem; but, in the future, he will adapt his pieces to the limits of our paper." [75] Thereafter the essays were less lengthy: each was written with excellent good humor and each helped make the New Englander more ridiculous. On October 31 Hezekiah Salem explained in "Rules How to Get through a Crowd" that a mouthful of garlic and a strong pipe clutched between the teeth would cause any assembly to open a way. On November 1 appeared an extract "From Hezekiah Salem's Last Basket," a plaint on the zeal of the housekeeper who insisted upon cleaning Salem's study. On November 10 he presented "A Few Words on Duelling," and on November 13 a dissertation on "The Howling House." Finally, on November 17, he contributed "A Scrap from a Keg, of Hezekiah Salem's Sermons," a pompous and repetitious discourse in "his former manner of preaching." The essays were fragmentary, humorous, and sly with satire, but Freneau had written better before; soon as "Robert Slender" he would write better again.

By the end of November contributions to the *Time-Piece* became less intense. Freneau published doggerel "Elegiac Verses on a Man Killed by a Cow" on November 29. Robert Goodloe Harper who, both because of his name and because of his Federalist activities in Congress, lent himself readily to satire, was exposed in verse on December 1:

> When a Harper a harping doth tune up his harp,
> For fear of a harpy let people look sharp.

On December 4 Freneau printed a poetical plea to Congress on behalf of Deborah Gannet, "the American heroine," who had served through the Revolution as a common soldier.[76] In the same issue he presented acid editorial comment upon royalty, followed by these lines:

> When at the altar a new monarch kneels,
> What conjur'd awe upon the people steals!
> The chosen, he adores the precious oil,
> Meekly receives the solemn charm—and while
> The priest some blessed nothing mutters o'er,
> Sucks in the grease at every opening pore.
> He seems at once to shed his mortal skin
> And feels divinity transfused within;

> The trembling vulgar dread the royal nod,
>   And worship God's annointed—more than God.

It was Freneau's last attack as a controversial newspaper editor.

5

The *Time-Piece* was floundering. "My attempt to establish a Newspaper in New York," Freneau later admitted, "was the wrongest step I could possibly have taken." Anti-French feeling was rising and a republican editor might well have been uncomfortable. "In a few months," said Freneau, "I almost literally found myself trampled upon by some Mean sneaking devils of that place." [77] Perhaps he was in danger of being physically assaulted as Benjamin Bache was assaulted in Philadelphia four months later.[78] More likely he was pressed by creditors, for the *Time-Piece* was steadily losing money.[79] There was the matter of a troublesome note which he had signed with his landlord and which was subsequently "rascally manoeuvered." In fact, Freneau wrote: [80]

I have reason to think certain political hypocrites and Liberty-Mongers wished me to have a seasoning in their lousy prison, as it was conjectured I was too haughty; and a summer or two passed there might render me fitter and more pliant for a cats-paw.

By the end of the first week in December Freneau's contributions to the *Time-Piece* had become so restrained and moderate that we suspect he had either become reconciled to the futility of opposing contemporary feeling or had given up active control of the newspaper entirely. On December 6 he presented "The High-Minded Apprentice," the story of a dull-witted boy who, when he considered the hardships involved in every other trade, decided that he would be happiest bound over to a king. Two days later, on December 8, stanzas "On a Fly, Fluttering Round a Candle" were printed. Freneau's own high-flown idealism had suffered another defeat and he wrote with feeling:

> Attracted to the taper's rays,
>   Thou busy, curious fly,
> Come not too near the quivering blaze,

For if you do, you die—
  This little sun destruction brings,
  Destroys your coat, consumes your wings.

Thus man, like thee, ambitious still
  Some dangerous course to run,
  Aspires to drive with fancied skill,
  The chariot of the sun,
    And while to mount the seat he tries,
    Like Phaeton, he falls and dies.

On December 11 Freneau printed stanzas which told "Of Thomas Swaugum, an Oneida Indian, and a Missionary Parson"; on December 13 he printed "A Modern Tale," satirical verses on a penny-pinching lawyer; and on December 18 he printed "A College Story," which recounted the misadventures of an intoxicated undergraduate who ended a night of carousing in a graveyard with a tombstone for his pillow. He wrote the New Year's verses which the carriers of the *Time-Piece* were to present to their customers on January 1, 1798. In none of these, however, was there anything political or anything which might arouse the most thin-skinned of opponents to retaliation. When Benjamin Russell of Boston remarked late in December that the *Time-Piece* was "fairly tinctured with Jacobism," [81] he must have referred to those twelve weeks during the autumn when the poet had snarled and snapped in courageous imitation of his younger, more ferocious manner. By the end of the year Freneau had again tired of controversy and of the ever mounting pile of unpaid bills which seemed to be its only reward.

On January 3, 1798, he sailed from New York as a passenger on the sloop *Caty*.[82] Arriving at Charleston after a tempestuous voyage of thirty-one days, he remained with his brother Peter until March. Eleanor Freneau and the two children had returned to Mount Pleasant, where during the father's absence, a third daughter, Catherine, was born on February 25.[83] Three weeks later, on March 14, Freneau landed again at New York on the ship *Maria*, seven days from Charleston.[84]

He apparently had not been idle during his absence from the city. Two days after his arrival the *Time-Piece* announced that the completed manuscript for "The Interesting Travels of John Ledyard, with a Summary of His Life" had been received by the printer. The volume would be issued, it was promised, just as soon as a sufficient number of subscribers had been secured. The advertisement ran through August, but the volume edited by Freneau never appeared.[85] Fortune had not been kind to the poet in his efforts to make a living. Literature had failed him, the sea had been a stern master, and journalism had brought him almost to the gates of a debtor's prison. It was probably of little financial advantage that the verses "On the Honorable Emanuel Swedenborg's Universal Theology" were reprinted as an introduction to an ecclesiastical pamphlet presenting *A Compendium View and Brief Defence of the Peculiar and Leading Doctrines of the New Jerusalem Church*.[86] On March 21, 1798, Freneau's name was dropped from the masthead of the *Time-Piece*. Thereafter, the public was informed, the newspaper would be conducted by M. L. Davis & Co.

6

By the spring of 1798 war seemed inevitable. The American commissioners to France had been treated with contempt by Talleyrand, who demanded a cash price for negotiations. French diplomacy, he reminded the envoys, was powerful. It might reach even to the internal affairs of the United States, arouse the French party there against the British party and overthrow the American government. Even military invasion was mentioned.[87] The Federalists press in America boiled with indignation. Democratic editors were accused more heatedly than ever before of being tools of France. "Peter Porcupine" opened wide every stop on his tumultuous organ. Irish Democrats in the pay of Talleyrand, he said, were inciting negro slaves to insurrection. Blacks would be pitted against whites, and no man's wife or daughter would be safe. Rape, pillage, and incendiarism would sweep across the country when France had her way with America.[88] In the House of Representatives, Robert Goodloe Harper spoke excitedly for war. Bills were introduced to suspend commercial intercourse with the French Republic and to void every treaty the United States had ever made with her.[89] Clergymen thundered from pulpits and judges stormed in courtrooms against

France.[90] Mob spirit was aroused among the people. Republican editors were assaulted in their offices.[91] "All the passions," said Jefferson, "are boiling over." [92]

It was not, therefore, without some courage that Freneau stood out against popular opinion during that hectic spring. On June 15 he contributed an "Ode to the Americans" to Thomas Greenleaf's New York *Argus*. He appealed again to reason, because war with France was war against human freedom. It would be a step backwards into the arms of England. America would be combating her own destiny were she to take such a step, for, Freneau explained in introduction, "the present progress of liberty in the world, considering the present state of things, cannot be long impeded, or its complete establishment prevented." Man had risen from barbarism "by reason's secret aid." Monarchs and priests had been thrust aside. Every assault of despotism had been repulsed. Much had been accomplished and the rising sun of liberty smiled upon her people.

> But struggling now to quench her flame,
> Britain's amphibious legions aim
> To chill the blossom in the bud,
> And retrograde to chains and blood.

Yet Nature would have her way. Appeal to force of arms was vain. Liberty, now but a splendid glow on the horizon, would soon mount high in the skies to shine on all men. It ill comported with the spirit of America that she, who had been present at the birth of freedom, should attempt to interrupt its progress. War bred despotism. Peace was the heritage of liberty.

> Americans! could you unite
> In putting out this growing light—
> Could you, so late from fetters freed,
> Join, party in so base a deed?
>
> Would you dear Freedom sacrifice,
> Bid navies on the ocean rise,
> Submit to military laws,
> And all, to aid a despot's cause?
>
> Oh NO!—but should all shame forsake,
> And *Gratitude* her exit make,

> Could you, as thousands say you can,
> Desert the common cause of man?

Freneau's most cherished beliefs were at stake now that the Tories of 1775 seemed once more abroad in the land. On June 16 he presented "The Republic and Liberty" in the *Argus*. Seldom had he written with more feeling. Seldom had his words been more stirring. Arranged in the rhythm of the popular melody "Anacreon in Heaven" which Francis Scott Key was later to use in "The Star Spangled Banner," Freneau's song was a rallying cry to all the free men of his country:

> Americans! rouse at the rumours of war,
> Which now are distracting the hearts of the nation,
> A flame blowing up by a race you abhor—
> That aided so lately Old England's invasion,
>   When with heart and with hand,
>   And a murdering band
> Of vagrants, she plunder'd and ravag'd our land.
> In LIBERTY's cause we are ever array'd,
> But yield not her substance to feast on her shade.

Then Freneau turned his attention again to "Peter Porcupine" with verses on "Democracy" in the *Argus* of June 25. "Prejudiced foreigners," he said in an introductory prose paragraph, "are continually barking and growling against Democracy, without even understanding the word." It was the subject of all their conversation and it was evident to any unprejudiced observer that these foreign, English-bribed critics wished to "destroy, banish or proscribe every man of democratic principles in the United States." Yet what was democracy but an attempt on the part of a nation to govern itself "upon principles of reason, liberty, and equality"? And what did an Englishman know of these? Turning to verse, Freneau derided the "cocknies from London" who, he said, were paid by the British government to arouse feeling against France in America. "Corporal Cobbett, the Knight of the Blade" was treated to the poet's most timeworn invective. He was a "blackguard," a blockhead," who crammed his gazette, "a sink of scurrility" with "vile libels" in order to curry favor with the court party in the United States. True

patriots, however, would pay no attention to his egotistical chatter-
ing. Freneau advised Cobbett and all his kind:

> We Americans, far from your king-ridden isle,
> Do humbly beseech you, all Democrat haters,
> That you may not your souls or your bodies defile,
> Pack off with your printers, your lies, and your satires;
> The monarch you love is in want of assistance,
> And how can you help him at such a great distance?
>   'Tis an Englishman's creed,
>   And they long have agreed,
> That out of Old England there's nothing (they swear)
> That can with what's English, true English, compare;
> So away to Old England, or we'll send you there.

Whence came the ills of man? What was the origin, Freneau
asked on July 7 in lines "On the Causes of Political Degeneracy,"
of the ills which prostrated America? Little men, swollen with the
sense of their own importance, were aping the monarchial traditions
of Europe. The common man, oppressed and perplexed, knew small
happiness this side of the grave. As in ages past, he was driven to
war against his fellows in order that a few wealthy men might reap
a rich harvest. True freedom, however, bred peace:

> Left to themselves, where'er mankind is found,
> In peace they wish to walk life's little round,
> In peace to sleep, in peace to till the soil,
> Nor gain subsistence from a brother's toil,
> All but the base, designing, cunning few,
> Who seize on nations with a robber's view,
> With crowns and sceptres awe the dazzled eye,
> And priests, that hold the artillery of the sky;
> These, these, with armies, navies, potent grown
> Impoverish man and bid whole nations groan.

All through the United States the Federalist press churned public
opinion into an uncompromising solidity against France. The war
party in Congress passed bill after bill for strengthening the national
defense. The progress of freedom through peace was threatened.
Freneau appealed to the people:

> Shall views like these involve our happy land,
> Where embrio monarchs thirst for wide command?
>   .   .   .

Americans! will you controul such views!
Speak—for you must—you have no time to lose.

Not until July did Freneau again contribute to the *Time-Piece*.
Meanwhile Matthew Davis had withdrawn from the publication,[93]
which was now edited by John Daly Burk, an Irishman as noisily
republican as William Cobbett was noisily anti-republican. Noah
Webster's *Commercial Advertiser* on June 11 compared Freneau
and Burk by suggesting, "The late Editor was a more fit inhabitant
for Botany Bay than for any place on this country; but his successor
without his discretion in mischief, has ten fold his malignity." Under
Burk's control the *Time-Piece*, said Federalist rivals, "even exceeded the infamous *Aurora*" in abuse and defamation.[94]

When the Alien and Sedition laws were passed by the Congress,
Burk was immediately prosecuted for libel because of insinuations
of forgery which he had directed against President Adams. In verses
addressed "To an Alien," printed in the *Time-Piece* on July 13,
Freneau expressed his sympathy for Burk and his disapproval of
the oppressive statutes under which the editor suffered. Where in
the United States did liberty survive? Nowhere. Freneau advised
new settlers in the western world to seek instead western Louisiana
"where freedom doth her flag display." His America was no longer
a refuge for the oppressed.

It seemed particularly ironical that an anti-French opponent
should suggest that Freneau was a "fit inhabitant for Botany Bay,"
the English penal colony in Australia. What more proof was needed
that Great Britain directed the hysterical furor against France?
Freneau drove this point home in the *Time-Piece* of July 16 with
doggerel lines on "Botany Bay" which reminded his detractors that

This Bay of bays, that makes such noise
Is own'd we're told by British boys.

Meanwhile the yellow fever, with no respect for men or parties,
swept again over the cities on the Atlantic seacoast. By the end of
the summer both John Fenno and Benjamin Franklin Bache had
been carried away by the disease in Philadelphia. In New York it
had taken Thomas Greenleaf. The *Time-Piece* expired on August
30, 1798, when John Burk went into hiding to escape imprison-

ment.[95] William Cobbett continued to publish without fear, for he was on the winning side. Philip Freneau, defeated again, returned once more to his family and his "sandy patrimony" at Mount Pleasant.

ELEVEN

SLENDER *REDIVIVUS*

1799–1814

T HE Sedition Laws effectively curbed expression of republican opinion in the American press. Even editors of established newspapers, like Thomas Adams of the Boston *Independent Chronicle*, William Duane, who had succeeded Benjamin Franklin Bache on the Philadelphia *Aurora*, and David Frothingham, who assumed control of the New York *Argus* soon after Thomas Greenleaf's death, were prosecuted for publishing "libels" against Federalist policy.[1] Printers of less important republican journals were silenced when advertisers shunned their columns, subscribers refused payment, and fine, imprisonment, and even physical assault threatened any man who dared speak out against governmental measures. No one was safe. Congressman Matthew Lyon, the free-spoken democratic leader from Vermont, spent four months in a country jail. Dr. Thomas Cooper, an Englishman by birth, a physician of culture, but a Jeffersonian, was convicted of sedition for criticizing President Adams's naval plans.[2] In such a situation it was just not good sense that Freneau, without money or popular support, should expose himself to his creditors or to his victorious political opponents.

The combat, however, was not lost. Freneau was proud that he had been able to disappoint the "mean sneaking devils" who had wished to chasten him with a term in jail. He boasted that neither Federal courts nor threat of debtors' prison had silenced him. Nor had he, like some others, accepted freedom at the price of promises of more docile behavior in the future.[3] Freneau had not run away: he had retired in order to rally for another attack. Soon after returning to Mount Pleasant, he sold fifty-five acres to his brother-in-law, John S. Hunn, for one hundred and fifty pounds in New York State currency.[4] Then, doubly secure in his newly acquired capital and in his country retreat, he began a fresh sortie against the enemies of the common man.

By the spring of 1799 opposition to the Sedition Laws was increasingly bold in Pennsylvania, and William Duane's *Aurora* became the rallying ground for those who would speak openly and without fear. On March 25 Freneau contributed to the Philadelphia newspaper an essay signed "A Monarchist," in which he attacked with apparent great seriousness the "very erroneous principle that princes or presidents ought always to act fairly, openly and ingenuously." He quoted authorities—Pliny, Plato, Tacitus, and Plutarch —to prove that rulers were subject only to laws of their own choice and making. He lauded the Alien and Sedition laws. He chided the people of America for objecting to taxes, because, he said, no prince or president could be truly supreme without money to insure his supremacy. Each of Freneau's arguments was so ridiculously exaggerated that the dullest reader of the *Aurora* could have turned the essay inside out to make it testify against itself. Yet there was no word in it that might be construed as seditious.

Four days later the first of a series of letters by "Robert Slender," a simple countryman, appeared in the *Aurora*. Freneau had begun to skirmish again. Robert Slender had read the essay by "A Monarchist" and had been naïvely surprised at the information it contained. Indeed, he was surprised at the whole newspaper, because he had always considered the *Aurora* a *"French* paper" and had picked it up only through curiosity. He had been forced, some time before, to discontinue his subscription to *Porcupine's Gazette* because it "taught the children to *curse* and speak *bawdy."* Now, though his neighbors accused him of being a turn-coat, he just could not for the soul of him keep from reading the *Aurora* which made "everything appear *so fair, open,* and *so like a history."*

As for princes and presidents who abused their powers, he wondered if they had not been heathen princes and presidents. "I am sure," he said, "Christians could not be guilty of such crimes." But one of Slender's friends, a quiet, serious man and a democrat, had assured the countryman that Christian rulers were often worse than pagans. God preserve us, said Robert Slender, where then shall we look for help. If depravity is allowed to the great, if some wickedness is counted laudable, and every species of wickedness winked at, what hope can there be for the world?

The answer was obvious, explained his friend. The common men, "our American farmers" who were honorable in name and in reality, who had not been enticed from the "standard of VIRTUE, INDE-PENDENCE, and FREEDOM," were the bulwarks of the United States, the guardians of her rights, the supporters of her dignity, and the pillars of her constitution. Through the influence of this common man, liberty would triumph—

The mist of darkness, ignorance, and error, begins to dissipate; party-spirit will soon, like a fretful child, cry itself to rest; the seeds of reform that are sown in our constitution, will bring forth fruit; the storm indeed may awfully growl and grumble at a distance: but . . . the sun will arise with tenfold glory; the demons of war, discord, and desolation shall be disappointed —true religion shall banish pretence and hypocrisy, and AMERICA SHALL BE STILL FREE.[5]

Robert Slender, the stocking weaver, he who had chronicled *A Journey from Philadelphia to New York* in burlesque verse in 1787 and from whose papers Freneau had culled essays for the *Miscellaneous Works* in 1788, was dead. The new Robert Slender was a much more simple man. By his own confession, he stood "unnoticed among the swinish herd, as the poor are generally called by the great and well born." He could not understand the events which had taken place during his lifetime, or the high-sounding words with which politicians and clergymen clothed their thoughts. He detested quarreling of any kind. He had trembled with fear and skulked in his corner when the people of America had dared to go to war for their independence. When the Revolution was over, he slipped from his hiding place to prate of "Liberty, Independence, Freedom, and such like things," just as did all the rest of his neighbors who had hidden during the struggle. He marveled to see old Tories slipping little by little into places of prominence and trust. He was awed to silence by such terms as "funding systems" and "banking systems," and he puzzled in vain over the expression "public debts are public blessings." He did not understand the Alien Laws, but he supposed that they were good things. He laughed at intimations that he might be influenced by French ideas, for he knew no word in any language but English, and even some words in his native tongue were difficult for him.[6] In short, Robert Slender was a distinctly American character who did not comprehend very much, but who wondered about the mysterious events of which he read in his newspaper.

He kept up a running comment upon contemporary affairs through the spring of 1799. He could not understand why the people of Pennsylvania should vote for James Ross of Pittsburgh for governor when they might vote for Republican Thomas McKean, whom they all knew very well and liked very much.[7] He had heard of such things as votes being forged and voters being bribed, but he hardly credited the reports. When glancing over his newspaper one morning he noticed an essay two columns long, he was prepared to pass it over, because, he said, "My head could never, even in my youngest days, know the meaning of so long a tale." But when he saw that the essay was signed by a clergyman, he decided, "It would be a sacrilege not to read it." He read, he misunderstood, he commented. His friend the republican explained that Thomas Paine's *The Age of Reason* would not have been nearly so popular had the clergy not written tracts against it. But Robert Slender still could not understand. He was fearful of argument, and his own pastor frightened him.[8]

The countryman was found of repairing in the evening to a tavern for a pint of ale and an hour over his newspaper with a "seegar." He was a quiet man and seldom entered into disputation, and the scraps of conversation which he overheard sometimes filled him with terror. "Peter Porcupine" so alarmed him with warnings of a French invasion that he barred his doors at night and lay quaking in his bed. "If you think a sea tyger a strange beast," one traveler said to another in the tavern, "I wish you could but get a sight of an aristocrat." Poor Robert's sleep was broken with tortured dreams of monsters for weeks to come. He begged the editor of the *Aurora* to come to his aid, to tell him whether such an animal as an aristocrat really did exist.[9] Newspaper reports caused him untold apprehension. When he heard that William Duane had been set upon and beaten by a group of United States cavalry officers who were angered at the editor's criticism of their methods of quelling mob disturbances in western Pennsylvania, Robert Slender hastened to pack his belongings for instant flight. He was terrified, for had not President Adams said that the country was in danger of being turned into bedlam because of French principles? [10]

The satire of the Robert Slender essays was not subtle. No reader could mistake the innuendo behind the countryman's naïve comment. The language was colloquial, the humor broad, and characters were sketched in crude but unwavering strokes. In prose which often seems more effective than his satirical verse had ever been, Freneau exposed the weakness and laughed at the pretension of all foes to republicanism. He mentioned names and cited instances, but he chuckled rather than stormed at his opponents. A Federal prosecutor would have been made ridiculous in attempting to prove sedition by the words of the simple-hearted Robert Slender, who admitted that he knew nothing, but only wondered.

However successful the essays may have been in goading Federalists and giving fresh courage to republican readers, they apparently did not supply any adequate source of income to the author. The old problem of acquiring a means of livelihood still confronted Freneau. On May 26, 1799, he sailed from New York as a passenger on the schooner *Rambler*. Eleven days later he disembarked at Georgetown, South Carolina, and continued his journey overland to Charleston.[11]

There his brother had prospered. Five years before, in partnership with Seth Paine, Peter Freneau had bought the *City Gazette and Daily Advertiser,* one of the outstanding newspapers of the South.[12] Though an ardent Jeffersonian and one of the leading Republicans in South Carolina, he had been appointed by Secretary of State Timothy Pickering, along with Federalist Benjamin Russell of Boston and the conservative firm of Hopkins and Company of New York, as one of the printers commissioned to publish the Acts of Congress.[13] He had also invested in real estate and acted as a broker in land and merchandise.[14] Peter was a large man, over six feet in height, clever, affable, and industrious, whose generosity had become a tradition among the members of his family in New Jersey.[15] What aid he was able to afford his older brother at this time is not, however, known. On July 22 Philip left Charleston on the schooner *Ann*. He arrived in Philadelphia seven days later, went by stage to New York, crossed over to New Jersey, and returned on August 9 to Mount Pleasant.[16]

During Freneau's absence Robert Slender had appeared twice in the *Aurora*,[17] and "Simon Simple," a cousin of the loquacious countryman, had submitted a letter in which he advised his relative to avoid too intimate a concern with public affairs.[18] On July 6 was published an untitled ode on the anniversary of American independence which Freneau had apparently left in manuscript with William Duane. But by the end of July, the regular appearance of Robert Slender was missed by Republican readers. A contributor who signed himself "Slender Thomas" and who also claimed cousinship with the countryman, inquired concerning the continuance of the "shrewd and sapient observations." "If my dear and faithful cousin Robert," he said, "flew into the country to avoid dangerous assaults it is now time for him to take up his lodging again in Philadelphia, and once more resume his pen, for the storm is blown over." "Our correspondent is informed," replied the editor of the *Aurora*, "that we have a favor of his cousin's some time in hand." [19]

From August 1 to December 4, 1799, then, eighteen more letters from Robert Slender appeared in the Philadelphia newspaper. The countryman compared kings to horse thieves to the advantage of neither.[20] He admitted that every man was subject to error, but wondered why the Federalists seemed to make so many. He commented with some heat upon the incomprehensible action of President Adams in turning poor Jonathan Robbins, an American seaman, over to the British simply because they charged that he was a deserter from the Royal navy.[21] Slender campaigned vigorously for Republican Thomas McKean.[22] He discussed state politics, the relation of religion to politics, national politics, and European politics.[23] He denounced war and bloodshed, and he pleaded with increasing fervor for the return of true republican principles.[24]

On December 28, 1799, William Duane announced that the *Letters on Various Interesting and Important Subjects; Many of Which Have Appeared in the Aurora,* "corrected and much enlarged by Robert Slender, O.S.M.," would be collected into a volume, which might be purchased bound for sixty-two and a half cents, unbound for half a dollar. Two days later, it appeared, "Printed for the Author, from the Press of D. Hogan," and sold by all republican booksellers of the city. No publication of Freneau's had been more popular. The first printing was exhausted in a few days. On January 4, 1800, the *Aurora* announced that the "Letters of Robert Slender are now received in sufficient numbers, to answer the demand." From January 11 to March 10 the volume was advertised in the *Aurora* for sale "by all the Booksellers." A liberal discount was promised to those who purchased quantity lots.

The collection was dedicated by "Robert Slender" to his fellow citizens, the free men of the United States. The author explained that, unable to use a more high sounding title, he had thought to gain reputation for his work by appending "O.S.M." to his name. To his friends he confided that the initials simply stood for "One of the Swinish Multitude." At least, however, they afforded him dignity suitable to authorship. In an "Advertisement" at the end of the volume Robert promised:

SHOULD these Letters meet with a favourable reception in their present form, a second volume will shortly be published; containing, besides those that have since appeared separately, a variety of original ones, upon such interesting subjects as may hereafter claim the public attention.

2

No sooner had the *Letters* been issued than Freneau found it necessary to make another trip to Charleston. There on January 10 he contributed to the *City Gazette* over the signature "Myrtilla" the "Stanzas Occasioned by the Death of General Washington." Five days later in the same newspaper he presented a second poem, "To the Memory of General Washington," dated "Orangeburgh, January 8, 1800" and signed "Sylvius." In spite of earlier opposition to many of the first president's policies, Freneau still admired the man who had led American armies to victory over England. The "share of honest praise" with which he had greeted Washington fifteen years before at the close of the Revolution had not been more sincerely offered than the expression of national gratitude which he now presented:

> Thou, WASHINGTON! by Heaven design'd
> To act a part in human things,

That few have known among mankind,
  And far beyond the lot of kings—
    We hail thee, now, to heaven receiv'd,
    Your mighty task in life achieved.

·   ·   ·

Those monarchs, proud of trophied spoils,
  With nations fetter'd in their train,
Returning from their desperate toils,
  With aspect lofty, fierce, or vain—
    In all they did, no traits are known,
    Like those which mark'd our WASHINGTON.

Freneau's friendships in South Carolina seem to have tran-
scended party lines. He is said to have enjoyed intimate acquaintance with Republican Charles Pinckney and with such Federalists
as Charles Cotesworth Pinckney and Governor Edward Rutledge,
and with many others among the Southern leaders, at whose residence he was "as much at home as at his brother's." [25] One of the
volumes of the poet's library is a copy of Ovid's *Opera,* inscribed
"a present from Aedanus Burke, Esq., at Charleston, South Carolina, January 8, 1800." [26] When Governor Rutledge died late in January, Freneau immediately composed "Elegiac Stanzas" for the
City Gazette.[27]

Early in April the poet returned to New York, and thence to his
farm at Mount Pleasant. When creditors brought suit against him
in the Mayor's Court of New York, he hurriedly borrowed one
hundred dollars from his brother's partner, Seth Paine. "A con-
currence of unfavourable circumstances," Freneau explained, "has
for several years past laid me under a pressure of difficulties, chiefly
arising from an ill grounded confidence I had in designing or malicious individuals." He complained of "disappointment and vexation" in a land "inhabited by sharpers and ruffians." But he was resigned to misfortune, he said, for "reflection tells me that Mankind
are every where pretty much alike."

"Every day of my life convinces me," he wrote to Paine, "that
while I live I must be active. A sedentary dull life has a strange effect
on me. I must be in motion to be happy." During the summer, then,
he laid "plans and schemes once more to get charge of a vessel in
some southern trade where there may be a chance of making some-

thing." He hoped, he said, to arrive sometime that autumn once more "upon the friendly and hospitable shores of South Carolina." But he received small encouragement in his nautical yearnings. "People here think I am mad," he reported, "in again attempting the water. I have persuaded some of them that my real view is to establish a Printing office on the East Side of South America, on the coast of Patagonia, near Cape Blanco, for the benefit of the natives of that country." [28]

While he waited for employment as master of a coastal packet, Freneau contributed occasional letters to the *Aurora* over the old signature of "Robert Slender." He wrote a humorous description of the troubles of a republican editor.[29] He twice chided clergymen for mixing politics with religion.[30] He attacked Federalists as speculators and ballot-box-stuffers.[31] He considered possible difficulties in moving the national capital from Philadelphia to the city of Washington,[32] and he discussed with mock seriousness the Federalist threat of civil war and secession if the Republicans won in the coming national elections.[33] The promised second volume of the *Letters*, however, never appeared. In New York, Freneau's *Poems* of 1786 and the *Miscellaneous Works* of 1788 were still offered for sale at the office of the *Argus*,[34] and the revised edition of 1795 was advertised regularly in the *Weekly Museum*,[35] but the demand for none of them could have been great. Mathew Carey published an extract from "America Independent" in a miscellany volume.[36] But Freneau was not satisfied. "There is no taste in this place," he wrote, "for any thing good or philosophical. The vilest trash has here a currency above all the eloquence of Plato." [37]

Late in the autumn of 1800 Freneau again appeared in Charleston. Peter Freneau, who was at the state capital managing Jefferson's campaign in South Carolina, wrote hurriedly to Seth Paine, "Tell my brother by no means to think of returning Northward before my return, I will try to get back to do something better for him than going on the wretched plan he has embraced." [38] But the poet was restless. He sent Peter an urgent letter. "Beg my brother to wait my return," the latter again wrote to Paine. "I will endeavor to do something for him." [39]

Meanwhile Philip Freneau continued to contribute to the Charleston *City Gazette*. "Lines on the Federal City" appeared on December 18 and "On a View of the Planet Jupiter and His Moons through a Large Telescope" on December 20. "Reflections on the General Debased Condition of Mankind," which had first appeared in the *Time-Piece* three years before, was rewritten and entitled "On False Systems of Government, and the Generally Debased Condition of Mankind" for the issue of December 24. The humanitarian basis of Freneau's republicanism was never more clearly expressed than when he asked:

> How can we call that system just,
> Which makes the FEW the high, the first,
>   The lords of all that's good;
> While millions, robb'd of all that's dear,
> In silence drop the ceaseless tear,
>   And leeches suck their blood.

"Our Country is yet safe," Peter Freneau wrote to his partner at Charleston. "I flatter myself that Mr. Jefferson is secure." [40] The presidential campaign progressed with feverish activity by both parties. Names flew and accusations were hurled from all sides. President Adams was a monarchist, the "Duke of Braintree"; what sensible man would vote for him? Thomas Pinckney had been educated in England and was supported by British sympathizers; out with him! Thomas Jefferson, on the other hand, was a deist, an infidel, a trifler who menaced order and religion. Through the agency of the *National Gazette* he had attempted to bring the young American republic to anarchy and ruin.[41] The campaign developed into just the sort of pitched battle which Freneau in his younger days would have relished. But now he had little to say. His only contribution was a letter in the *City Gazette* of January 5, 1801, in which he again emphatically denied that Jefferson had in any way sponsored the *National Gazette*.[42]

Two weeks later, after the poet had returned to Mount Pleasant, another "Robert Slender" letter appeared in the *Aurora*. The farm in New Jersey now, however, demanded all of Freneau's attention, and he had no time to indulge in the luxury of extended newspaper controversy. "The place is as well as could be expected after my four months absence," he wrote to Peter. "I have been and shall be for some time busy in repairing old fences, and making new ones, a new garden and some other small improvements as far as I prudently can with the money you let me have."

The five hundred dollars which Freneau was able to secure from his brother did not, however, go far. When debts were paid and a sum set aside to provide for Agnes Kearny, who now lived in New York with the Hunns, little remained for the poet's family in Monmouth. His oldest daughter, Helena, attended school in New York, and plans were already being made for Agnes, his second, to join her sister there in the spring. Catherine, the youngest, had just passed her third birthday. A fourth daughter was born a few weeks later, on June 10, 1801. "Thus," wrote Freneau, "are new cares and vexations coming on." [43]

Friends did what they could to help him. Aedanus Burke wrote to Madison, "I am sorry to have to say that Freneau is still in embarrassed circumstances. He is an honest man, and an undeviating Republican; yet utterly incapable of soliciting for himself." [44] Two years later Francis Bailey recommended the poet for the position of postmaster of New York. [45] But Freneau seems to have accepted overtures pridefully, sensitive perhaps because he was placed in the position of a suppliant. If tradition is to be believed, he repulsed an offer from the new Republican administration by haughtily declaring, "Tell Thomas Jefferson that he knows where Philip Freneau lives, and if he has important business with him, let him come to Philip Freneau's house and transact it." [46]

"I suspect," Freneau confided to Seth Paine, "I am doomed to end my life among the very enlightened, disinterested, and philosophical folks of Monmouth." During the spring of 1801 there had been some talk of sending the poet to the New Jersey state legislature. "This was rather better," he admitted, "than being sent to Jail for editing Newspapers." But he refused to consider becoming a candidate, and vowed never again "to meddle with the public or their business." As a private citizen he chuckled over the defeat and discomfiture of the Federalists. In his personal correspondence he ridiculed John Adams, who, he said, sulked at Braintree writing political dissertations and hoping some day to be reelected president. Now that America was made safe for the common man by

Jefferson's victory at the polls, Freneau found little incentive for expressing himself on political questions. He who had done so much to enliven late eighteenth-century American journalism now found the "public papers barren and insipid." He was content to "deceive the summer heat" beneath his trees at Mount Pleasant and, as he wrote Paine, to "see as few people as possible, except there should come any worth seeing." [47]

His leisure hours were spent with his books and manuscripts, "in writing poetry, answering and receiving letters." [48] "Mr. F. and the children," his wife complained some time later, "are always scribling and never fail to spoil both pen and ink." [49] "Stanzas on South Carolina" appeared in the New York *Weekly Museum* on August 1, 1801, and "The Third Epistle of the First Book of Ovid's Tristia, Translated from the Original Latin," was printed on October 24 in the same periodical.

Freneau's literary reputation had settled to a low, but apparently stable level. His poetry was known, if not admired, in all parts of the United States. The *Poems* of 1786 and the *Miscellaneous Works* were still advertised in the Philadelphia *Aurora.* [50] Verses like "The Jug of Rum," and "The Dish of Tea" were occasionally reprinted in the poets' corner of some small country weekly. [51] The editor of the Poughkeepsie *American Farmer* found the style of a didactic poem entitled "A Branch of the Maple" familiar enough to attribute it to "P. Freneau," [52] although it appears in none of the poet's collected editions. A parodist in Georgia imitated "The Roguish Shoemaker" in "Shavings, a Freneauic Ode," for the Savannah *Columbian Museum.* [53] "The Indian Student" and "The Indian Burying Ground" were quoted with approbation in William Priest's *Travels in the United States of America.* [54] "The British Prison-Ship" was reprinted as an "etching from the hand of a master" in the *Life of Silas Talbot.* [55]

But Freneau's reputation as a political partisan overshadowed his reputation as a poet. His name was associated with republicanism, and he received little criticism divorced from that association. "Where did he get his rhymes?" asked a contributor to the Federalist *New-England Palladium.* "Out of the dictionary," was the answer. "Where the spirit and originality? There isn't any!" [56] On the other hand, the *Aurora* hurled charges of "literary swindling" when Freneau's verses were reprinted without a line of credit in political periodicals like the *Port-Folio* of New York and the *Washington Federalist.*[57]

"What think you of Freneau?" John Davis, the prolific *littérateur* from England was asked. *"Freneau,"* Davis replied, "has one good ode: *Happy the Man who safe on shore!* But he is voluminous; and this ode may be likened to the *grain in the bushel of chaff!"* [58] When erudite Dr. Samuel Miller of New York prepared a survey of American literary achievement for his *A Brief Retrospect of the Eighteenth Century,*[59] he was hardly less severe. Freneau was listed among those who "manifested talents honourable to themselves and their country" and who were "noticed with respect by foreign as well as domestic critics," but he was not, like Timothy Dwight, John Trumbull, and Joel Barlow, "among the first class" of American writers. Freneau had made the mistake of trying to earn his living with his pen. "Authors by trade," advised a correspondent to the New York *Commercial Advertiser,* "are yet unknown in this country." [60]

Unsuccessful as an author, Freneau seems to have been equally unsuccessful as a farmer. Though "he loved to see the work going on" and "was fond of feeding poultry and all dumb animals, when the season came for slaughtering the porkers, he generally managed it so as to have some business in New York to be absent." Even when chickens were wanted for dinner, Mrs. Freneau is said to have been forced to order the slaves to kill them secretly, so that her husband would not be upset by the sight.[61] An anecdote handed down among Freneau's descendants, though perhaps apocryphal, is apparently true in spirit:

One day the poet and his wife, who had walked together into the field to inspect the work, found a slave asleep in the young corn. Mrs. Freneau seizing his hoe declared that she would show him how to work. At the very first attempt, however, she cut down a hill of corn, whereupon the slave remarked gleefully: "Ho, ho, Missie Freneau, if that's the way hoe, the corn'll never grow." She threw down the hoe in disgust, declaring that, "No wonder the farm doesn't pay when even the slaves talk in rhymes." [62]

Country life, which had seemed such a magnificent ideal to Freneau ten years before, now was fretted with cares and practical difficulties of which idyllic poets had never told. "Probably I shall have to embark on some new expedition or plan before long," Freneau confided to his brother, "wherever or to whatever the devil shall see fit to drive me." [63]

3

His "plans and schemes to get charge of a vessel in some southern trade" finally were realized. On November 13, 1802, the schooner *John*, of seventy-three tons burden, newly built, and owned by Peter Freneau of Charleston, entered New York Harbor with a cargo from Richmond.[64] Two weeks later, with Captain Philip Freneau at her helm she headed south towards Fredericksburg with a cargo of salt. After an exceedingly difficult voyage, the vessel returned to Manhattan on January 12, 1803, loaded with twelve hundred bushels of wheat, which Freneau was able to sell for only slightly more than two hundred dollars.[65]

Profits were slim and cargoes scarce. While he awaited a new consignment, Freneau returned to his books and papers at Mount Pleasant. There late in February he wrote verses "On Walking over the Ground on Long Island, near New York, where Many Americans were Interred from the Prison Ships during the War with Great Britain." [66] By the time the poem appeared in the New York *Weekly Museum* on April 16, however, Captain Freneau was again at sea. On April 23, ten days from Perth Amboy, the schooner *John* entered the port of Charleston carrying an assortment of "stone red and black earthenware assorted, the best racked red streak New-Jersey cyder, apples in barrels, and butter in firkins." Two days after her arrival, however, the vessel was advertised for sale.[67] The Freneau brothers had made plans for a more enterprising and, they hoped, a more profitable investment.

The brig *Washington,* fitted for the Madeira wine trade and newly purchased by Peter Freneau, sailed from Charleston on May 8 under the command of Captain Philip Freneau. Her voyage across the Atlantic was long, and weeks were spent in Madeira before she was loaded to return. Not until four months after his departure, was Freneau again in South Carolina.[68] After lying there in port until October 15, he sailed for New York with a cargo of cotton, rice, and hides.[69] Six weeks later his vessel, now loaded with produce, turned southward again, and arrived late in December at Charleston.[70]

Almost a month passed before Captain Freneau and the brig Washington once more left port, on January 21, 1804, for Madeira.[71] Hardly had the shores of South Carolina dropped below the horizon when a gale arose which drove the vessel helpless before it. Freneau must have remembered the hurricane which he had encountered twenty years earlier at Jamaica. Now, as then, he compared the overpowering forces of nature with the futile attempts of man to stand before them. He was older and more resigned as he wrote stanzas on "A Midnight Storm in the Gulph Stream": [72]

> What ruling force, what active power
>   That bids the winds and waves obey,
> Will now appear to sooth the roar
>   Of nature, in her agony?
>
> Does lightning's flash announce our doom!—
>   Do thunders, rattling through the sky?—
> Strange fires the watery wave illume,
>   That inlet to eternity!
>
> .   .   .
>
> How feeble are the strongest hands,
>   How weak all human efforts prove!—
> He who obeys, and who commands
>   Must wait a mandate from above.

The vessel finally reached Madeira on March 7, having been driven by a "hurricane of wind all the way." [73] His recent experience with the unpredictable power of the elements reawakened Freneau's concern with the transience of all human institutions. Some months earlier the city of Funchal had been partially destroyed by a flood of "unprecedented torrents of water which had collected from the mountains." "What works of pride in one short hour were swept away," wrote Freneau as he viewed the ruins of the island city. Man's aspiration and all his works were as nothing when confronted with nature in her less benign moods. Freed from the compulsion of controversy, Freneau's poetical musing returned to those channels which had been cut deep during his formative younger years. All would pass, the fairest of man's handiworks was vain. Of his countrymen, Freneau wrote, "I left them in wrangles, disorder, and strife." The sea bred quiet and an opportunity for contemplation, for, said Freneau, "I was sick of their quarrels." [74] Leaving Funchal on April 12, the *Washington* called at Teneriffe on April 15, at Aratava on April 22, and on May 11 sailed for Charleston, where she arrived on June 19 after a voyage of thirty-nine days. [75]

Freneau had not been inactive during these last periods at sea. He later published "On the Peak of Pico; One of the Azores, or Western Islands" and "A Bacchanalian Dialogue. Written in 1803," [76] both of which were probably composed during his first voyage to Madeira. The "Answer to a Card of Invitation to Visit a Nunnery at Garrichica, on the North Side of Teneriffe," "On Seniora Julia, Leaving a Dance under Pretence of Drowsiness," "Lines on Seniora Julia, of Port Oratave," and "On a Rural Nymph, Descending from One of the Madeira Mountains, with a Bundle of Fuel Wood on Her Head" [77] all seem to have been written during his final voyage. In the last named poem, in which he again celebrates rustic contentment, Freneau achieves a simplicity of expression much like that which Wordsworth was advocating in England:

> Six miles, and more, with nimble foot
> She came from some sequestred spot,
> A handsome, swarthy, rustic maid
> With furze and fern, upon her head:
> The burthen hid a bonnet blue,
> The only hat, perhaps, she knew,
> No slippers on her feet were seen;
> Yet every step display'd a mien
> As if she might in courts appear,
> Though placed by wayward fortune here.

But this was a single exception, almost lost among the traditional, now even almost old fashioned pieces that he wrote. During this last period at sea Freneau was only half-heartedly concerned with verses, and only two of his poems of Madeira and the Canary Islands were published at this time. "Stanzas Written at the Island of

Madeira in April Last, on the Fatal and Unprecedented Torrents of Water which . . . Destroyed a Considerable Part of the City of Funchal" appeared in the Charleston *City Gazette* on July 2, followed one week later by the "Stanzas Written at Oratava, in View of the Peak or Teneriffe." They must both have been interesting to contemporary readers as topical poems, descriptive of far-away and romantic scenes. But Freneau had done the same thing much better when he was younger.

Late in July the Brig *Washington* cleared for Malaga under the command of Captain Edward Slocum. The vessel was still owned by Peter Freneau and made regular voyages in the wine trade during the next few years.[78] Philip Freneau's career as a seaman, however, was over. He returned to Monmouth, and from there he sent the stanzas "Written at Oratava," to be published on August 24 in the New York *Weekly Museum*, signed "P. Freneau."

4

Throughout the late summer and the autumn of 1804 a series of letters signed by various members of the "Bunker" family appeared in the Philadelphia *Aurora*. "Joe Bunker" began the correspondence on August 25 with a caustic attack on Tench Coxe, an active politician who sought control of the Pennsylvania democratic party and who now supported the candidacy of William Penrose for the Congress of the United States. William Duane, editor of the *Aurora*, had thrown his influence to the side of a second democratic faction dominated by Dr. Michael Leib and for several months had been active in opposition to Coxe and the "tertium quids," as the latter's followers were called. Soon after "Joe Bunker" opened his barrage, a second correspondent who signed himself "Joe Bunker, Jun." entered the discussion. Then, on August 30, "Jonathan Bunker," introducing himself as a nephew of the original contributor, presented the first of a series of letters. He was joined by "Polly Bunker," his wife, and by "Tomo Cheeki" who, though he claimed no relationship with the garrulous Bunker family, seconded each attack against Coxe and Penrose.

The "Bunker" letters, particularly those of "Jonathan Bunker"

and "Polly Bunker," are very much like the "Robert Slender" letters which had appeared in the *Aurora* several years before. They
are witty and perverse, and often gain their point by a pretended
naïve acceptance of some argument put forward by their opponents.
The contributions by "Tomo Cheeki" present double evidence, in
style and signature, that Philip Freneau had once again ventured
upon the turbulent waters of Pennsylvania politics.[79]

Indeed, the supporters of Tench Coxe thought they recognized the
hand of Robert Slender in some of the letters. The editor of the
Aurora, however, issued a vigorous, though ambiguous denial: [80]

Poor *Robert Slender*, quiet, peaceable, and silent as he has been for a long
time, will not be suffered to remain quiet—his poor head has surely enough
to bear, without being burthened with the sins of the *Bunkers*—but the
quids are about as *discerning* in *criticism* as honest in politics—and no more.

Whatever the extent of his contribution to the Philadelphia quarrel, controversy on political questions now had little place in Freneau's scheme of living. At fifty-two he was content in the quiet of
his country home. If now and again he submitted letters to the newspapers, it was as a bystander who offered suggestions, not as a
participant with a plan of attack. In May, 1805, he acted as agent
for his brother in the acquisition of five hundred acres in western
Kentucky.[81] His own financial situation, however, continued to be
precarious, and three months later he was forced to mortgage a portion of his land in Monmouth County for three hundred dollars.[82]
During the next year he made a last visit to Charleston, where his
"Lines, Occasioned by Reading the First Number of Doctor Shecut's
Flora Carolinaensis" were printed as an appendix to the volume
which they praised, "from the pen of Capt. Philip Freneau, who was
lately in this city." Freneau "left Charleston finally, June 6,
1806." [83] His days of wandering were over.

The first extended review of Freneau's poems appeared in a series
of four articles published in the New York *Port-Folio* between October 17 and November 28, 1807. The criticism, both fulsome and
inadequate, praised Freneau for his versatility, his sensitiveness to
nature, and his understanding of the Indian character. It placed
him on a level with such writers of the sea as William Falconer and

Captain Edward Thompson. It compared him with Collins, Cowper, and Swift. But it censored him severely for his Jacobism and for the vulgarity of his language. Finally, the critic made a list of seventy-five poems from the edition of 1795 which, in his opinion, were worthy of preservation. Neither "The House of Night" nor "The Wild Honey Suckle" was included among the poems selected. Freneau was commended, but with reservations, for he was still best remembered as a party writer. But now that the poet was in retirement and his pen innocent of intrusion into contemporary affairs, even so stalwart a Federalist as Joseph Dennie, editor of the *Port-Folio*, could say:

For the *politicks* of the author it is pretty well known that we have no peculiar partiality, but of the *poetry* of this versatile bard we must say that, by the impartial, it will be at length, considered as entitled to no ordinary place in a judicious estimate of American genius.[84]

On public occasions when the American Revolution was remembered, Freneau was still the poet whose works could be ransacked for lines commemorative of great national events. So, when the New York *Public Advertiser* wished to call attention to the "Grand Procession to the Tomb of the Martyrs" on May 26 (a pilgrimage in homage to the unknown soldiers whose "mouldering bones" had been gathered for interment on the shores of Wallabout Bay), it printed on May 19 over the signature "F." the "Stanzas Written Several Years Ago, on the Long Island Shore where Vast Numbers of Americans Were Interred, or Sunk in the River, from the Prison and Hospital Ships." Five days later the same newspaper published extracts from *The British Prison-Ship*, "an elegant poem by Capt. Philip Freneau, who was one of the few prisoners that survived several months confinement on these hulks."

"Now again," Freneau confessed to Thomas Jefferson a year later, "I fear, I am reverting to the folly of scribbling verses." [85] He sent his former employer a copy of the "Lines Addressed to Mr. Jefferson, on his Approaching Retirement from the Presidency of the United States," which had appeared on March 2 in the Trenton *True American* and on March 3 in the New York *Public Advertiser*. Also printed in the *True American* on April 24 were "Verses Handed to the Editor of This Paper, in Manuscript Written at Fundeal [*sic*], in the Island of Madeira, by Capt. P. Freneau, July, 1803."

Freneau himself recognized the ephemeral quality of his productions. Were he allowed to have his own way, he told Madison, he would leave "these old scribblings to float quietly down the stream of oblivion to their destined element the ocean of forgetfulness." When early in 1809 he learned, however, that a new edition of his poems had been projected in Philadelphia without his "knowledge or approbation," he immediately set out for the city to supervise the publication. In April he sent subscription papers to James Madison, who had just been elected President of the United States, and to Thomas Jefferson, who had retired to his estate at Monticello. On May 12 he wrote to the former from Philadelphia: [86]

I hope you will credit me when I say that the republication of these Poems, such as they are, was not a business of my own seeking or forwarding. . . . However, I have concluded to remain here this Summer, and have them published in a respectable manner, and free as possible from the blemishes imputable to the two former Editions, over which I had no controul, having given my manuscripts away, and left them to the Mercy of chance.

The edition was to be issued in two volumes from the press of Lydia M. Bailey, the widow of Francis Bailey's son Robert, who had recently inherited her father-in-law's old printing establishment on Market Street. One of the reasons, Freneau later said, that he had been induced "to pay some attention" to the edition was that it was published "for the benefit of, and to assist Mrs. Bailey." [87] Nonetheless, he was determined that it should be a representative collection and carefully edited. John Eckstein, "formerly historical painter and statuary to the King of France," [88] was commissioned to engrave a frontispiece for each volume. Circulars announced that the edition bound in sheep would detail for two dollars, in calf for twenty-five cents more; dealers, were, of course to be offered a satisfactory discount. The response was immediately satisfactory. Jefferson and Madison each subscribed for ten sets. Mathew Carey ordered two hundred for his bookstore in Philadelphia, and Peter Freneau undertook to distribute more than one hundred and fifty in Charleston.[89] "1500 copies are to be printed, only; but I have a certainty, from the present popular frenzy," the poet wrote Madison, "that three times that number might soon be disposed of." By the end of the first week in August Freneau was able to inform his friends that the edition would be ready for delivery within a very few days.[90]

The text of the *Poems Written and Published during the American Revolutionary War* was divided into four books: translations from the ancients and the juvenile poems; original poems relative to the early events of the Revolution; poems written and published during the Revolution; and miscellaneous poems on moral, satirical, and political subjects. Except for this rough grouping, however, little attempt was made to follow any chronological order as to date of composition. Of the verses omitted from the 1795 volume, only the "Song on Captain Barney's Victory" was resurrected. Some forty-six poems which had been included in the former collection were omitted, including many relating to the events of the French Revolution, most of the New Year odes, and such fine pieces as "Neversink," "The Pilot of Hatteras," "The Country Printer," and "Slender's Journey." The text of individual poems, except for minor changes in details of punctuation, was essentially that of the 1795 edition. "The Wild Honey Suckle," "The British Prison-Ship," and the fragmentary version of "The House of Night" were left as they had appeared fourteen years before. Although "To a Night-Fly Approaching a Candle" and "On a Honey Bee, Drinking from a Glass of Wine, and Drowned Therein" were both rewritten, most of the editorial emendation consisted in the addition of footnotes, the expansion of titles, and the prefacing of individual poems by Latin mottoes, quotations from Shakespeare, and aphorisms from such modern writers as Voltaire and Mirabeau.

Fifteen new poems and twenty-two poems which had been published between the years 1795 and 1801 were included, "but not so as to materially interrupt the general tenor of the Poems that arose from the incidents of the American revolutionary contest." [91] Most significant of these additions are the translations from Ovid's *Tristia* and from Lucretius's *De Rerum Natura* [92] which indicate that Freneau, in retirement, had returned to his former preoccupation with classical literature. Also important in reference to the poet's growing concern with philosophic contemplation are the poems "Science, Favourable to Virtue," "Reflections on the Constitution and Frame of Nature," and "On the Powers of Human Understanding." [93] Not since he had left Princeton had Freneau offered so clear an expression of his gropings toward religious and philosophical truth. He still questioned:

> Where ends this world, or when began
> This spheric point displayed to man?—

Now that he had put behind him the distracting scene of political squabbles and petty ambition, he pondered again on the eternal scheme of nature, "vast, undivided, and supreme":

> Here beauty, order, power behold
> Exact, all perfect, uncontrouled;
> All in its proper place arranged,
> Immortal, endless, and unchanged.[94]

Yet how vain was the wish to fathom her mysteries, for

> The mind, though perch'd on eagle's wings,
> With pain surmounts the scum of things.[95]

Beyond all power of man to understand existed the God

> Who life through all creation spread,
> Nor left the meanest atom dead.[96]

And man, might attain only to an approximation of eternal truth. Reason was a ladder which reached high into the empyrean. Man, drugged by brutal passions, slept at the foot of the ladder which, awaking, he might climb.

Fundamentally, however, the 1809 edition of Freneau's poems was planned "justly to record the deeds of fame" and "tell the conflicts of the stormy days" of America's struggle for independence. The poet dedicated the volume "to his Countrymen, the real *Patriotic Americans*, the *Revolutionary Republicans*, and the rising generation who are attached to their sentiments." The contents were intended "to expose vice and treason, their own hideous deformity" and "to depict virtue, honour, and patriotism in their native beauty." "Whether the following verses," submitted Freneau, "have any real claim to the attention of the citizens of the United States, who may honour them with a reading, is left to the Public to decide." [97]

That portion of the public which subscribed to republican principles approved of the new volumes. Joseph Lloyd, liberal young
editor of the *Pennsylvania Democrat,* wrote:

We hope the work will meet with that liberal patronage which it so justly
deserves, and that the works of so celebrated *an American poet* might be expected to obtain from his countrymen. The Americans have been accused
by Europeans of a poverty of genius, and reproached as having given little
or no encouragement to the few among them who possess any. The evidence
to prove the falsehood of the first charge is accumulating with vast rapidity,
and we hope the spirit of the Americans will ere long rescue their country
from the stigma of the latter. They could not have a better opportunity of
contributing towards this rescue than by purchasing and giving general circulation to the works of one of our best poets. That Mr. Freneau ought to
stand in the first rank of the Columbian poets no person qualified to judge
will dispute. . . . Mr. Barlow has been called, perhaps with some degree of
propriety, the American Homer; and although he is a great poet, he certainly does not possess that versatility of genius which is so peculiar to Mr.
Freneau. Barlow's poetic genius is confined to one style, one measure, one
subject, and one solemn tone; but Freneau can accommodate his genius to
any subject, any measure, or any style. . . . The favourite subject of his
Muse is satire. . . . It may truly be said that he contributed more towards
the success of the Revolution by his pen than did a great majority of those
who commanded in the field of battle. . . . In short, Mr. Freneau is entitled to the respect and applause of every American as a man, as a poet, and
as a patriot. I do not know that I have ever seen the term useful applied to a
poet, but Mr. Freneau is in the true sense of the word, a useful poet. His
works ought to be universally read by Americans, and every true born son
of Columbia ought to feel proud that his country has given birth to Philip
Freneau.[98]

The Federalist press, on the other hand, was silent on the edition
of 1809. A year later, however, the editors of the *Monthly Anthology*
of Boston published a "Retrospective Review" [99] of Freneau's 1786
volume, in which they admitted:

It is pretty good for the time and circumstances under which it was written,
tolerably good for American poetry, and would be very good if we possessed no better poetry. But in these days of refinement, while the poetical
market is glutted with delicacies of every description, a bard of the middling class can hardly expect his produce to be sought after with the greatest
avidity, or that the pampered taste of our literary epicures should indulge in
a coarse and unsavoury, though perhaps a wholesome morsel.

Freneau's political sins had found him out. His partisan songs created a cacophony unpleasant to conservative ears, and his poetry went unnoticed amid the noisy reverberation of his satirical verse.

5

While resident in Philadelphia during the summer of 1809, Freneau entered mildly into republican activities. He wrote verses to the memory of Thomas Paine.[100] Lines "For the Fourth of July," which had first been published in 1797, were refurbished and read at Crosby's tavern as part of the celebration of the anniversary of American independence.[101] "The Rival Suitors of America" was rewritten and on September 15 printed in the *Pennsylvania Democrat* as "The Political Courtship." Factional rivalry was rife among the republicans of Philadelphia, and Freneau, veteran of many controversies and master of the telling phrase, was welcomed by members of the less conservative party, who embodied lines from his satirical poems in editorials directed against their opponents.[102] When he wasn't quarreling, he got along with people very well. "He was a small man," Mrs. Bailey remembered many years later, "very gentlemanlike in his manners, very entertaining in his conversation, and withal a great favorite with the ladies." [103]

In such an atmosphere of newspaper bickering Freneau might well have found a place. "I feel much in the humour of remaining here about two years to amuse myself, as well as the Public," Freneau wrote to Madison.[104] Nevertheless, by the middle of October he was back in Monmouth, busy again with the management of the family acres.[105] Even in retirement he was a "useful poet," keeping abreast with the times. His "Lines Occasioned by the Late Disaster of One of the Paulus Hook Passage-boats' Upsetting" appeared simultaneously on November 11 in the *New York Journal*, the *Commercial Advertiser*, and the *Evening Post*, and four days later in the *New York Herald*. He wrote with the authority of his years at sea when he advised:

> Let Fulton's art, unrivall'd art, prevail,
> Nor trust existence to the treacherous sail.

This was still only newspaper verse, topical and inconsequential. But whatever America seemed to lack in the appreciation of native poetry, she made up for by her instantaneous approval of native humor. Two years earlier young Washington Irving, in collaboration with his brother William and with James Kirk Paulding, had issued the *Salmagundi* papers in New York. They were lightly satirical and uproariously funny, and succeeded in amusing the public in a way that the letters of poor, politically-minded Robert Slender had never done. Now Irving created Diedrich Knickerbocker, who, like Tomo Cheeki many years before, left a manuscript behind in his city lodgings. The result of the purported discovery of his papers was the publication of Irving's facetious *History of New York, from the Beginning of the World to the End of the Dutch Dynasty*. America chuckled over the book and a new literary career was launched.

If his countrymen, then, wanted only burlesque, Freneau had plenty of that commodity to offer. Nine of his lighter pieces were included in *The Cabinet of Momus: A Choice Selection of Humorous Poems*, which Mathew Carey published early in December.[106] Freneau was now in that company with which he best belonged, with "Peter Pindar," Jonathan Swift, the deftly humorous Francis Hopkinson, and the incomparably popular Dibdin. None of Freneau's contributions are weighted with grave philosophical content or with political dogma, and they supply much of the zest and sparkle of the volume. Later in December Thomas Neversink, another Philadelphia bookseller, issued a new edition of *A Laughable Poem; or Robert Slender's Journey from Philadelphia to New York*. The text was essentially as Freneau had revised it for the edition of 1795: the indelicate allusions and the coarseness which had marred the poem on its first appearance in 1787 were deleted, and minor corrections were made in rhyme and punctuation.

After this small splurge of activity in 1809, Freneau continued to live quietly at Monmouth. "Robert Slender," the letter writer, was still remembered in Philadelphia, and his name was used to cast odium upon victims of newspaper controversy in that city.[107] But Freneau was through with public affairs. "Since . . . quitting the hustle and distraction of active life," he wrote to Madison a few

years later, "my walks have been confined . . . to the neighbourhood of the Neversink hills, and under some old hereditary trees,
and on some fields which I well recollect for sixty years." [108] His
mother, Agnes Kearny, now nearly eighty years old, joined him at
Mount Pleasant when Mary Freneau and the Hunns moved up the
Hudson from New York to Newburgh.[109] His older daughters were
becoming young ladies; at least one of them showed signs of inheriting her father's talent for making verses.[110]

But his property in Monmouth became gradually less extensive.
Freneau was obliged to sell a portion of it in 1812 and to mortgage
another tract of fifty-three acres the next year.[111] The old trees beneath which he had wandered as a boy became associated with
many memories. Freneau was fond of his trees and loved to senti-
mentalize about them. "Here lies Watch," he wrote after he had
buried a favorite dog at the foot of one of them; "Living he wanted
for all things. Dead he wants for nothing. May he have a speedy
Resurrection into this Poplar." [112]

Hardly more than a year later the poet had occasion to write
another epitaph, more poignantly personal. On November 9, 1813,
his brother Peter died in Charleston in his fifty-seventh year.[113] The
end had come suddenly and there had been no opportunity for him
to put his estate in order. His land and his buildings were sold to
satisfy his creditors. They "who had never pushed him in life,"
wrote a friend in South Carolina, "had the sheriff in the house before his remains were carried out of it." [114] Like his father, his
grandfather, and each of his uncles, Peter Freneau left little behind
him except his reputation as an active and ambitious man.

6

While thus living quietly with his family in Monmouth, Philip
Freneau followed political affairs with a detached, but with hardly
a disinterested and certainly not an unprejudiced eye. Of the quarrels among the American republicans, of the last attempts of the
New England Federalists to regain national power, of the expansion
and development of the West, or of the series of domestic crises
which marked the early years of the nineteenth century he has, how-

ever, left no comment. He must have followed with intense personal interest the trial and conviction of his old college mate Aaron Burr. He must have rejoiced that the common man of the frontier was raising his voice with increasing effect in the national councils. In spite of internal dissension, the principles of freedom for which Freneau had fought for forty years were abroad among his country-men. Only the tyranny of monarchial interference from Europe seemed to hinder their consummation.

While France and England struggled for supremacy in Europe, the foreign commerce of the United States was caught helpless be-tween the restrictions imposed by each of the belligerent nations. To Freneau, Napoleon Buonaparte, though misled by ambition, was the enemy of hereditary despotism and, therefore, the friend of human rights. British tyranny, on the other hand, ruled the seas.[115] British greed was responsible for the seizure and search of American vessels and the impressment of American seamen into service in His Majesty's navy:

> Not a ship, or a barque, that departs from our shore
> But her cargo is plunder'd, her sailors are slain,
> Or arriving in England, we see them no more,
> Condemn'd in the court of deceit and chicane,
> Where their wicked decrees
> And their costs and their fees
> Have ruin'd the merchant—mechanics half fed,
> And sailors uncaptured are begging their bread.

This Freneau had written in 1809 in "On the Symptoms of Hos-tilities." [116] War was irrational, but war was inevitable if American independence was to be maintained in fact as well as word. So much had been sacrificed for freedom that the citizens of the United States could not now surrender even a portion of their rights to foreign tyranny. The spirit of the American Revolution quickened in Fre-neau as he exhorted:

> Then arouse from your slumbers, ye men of the west,
> A war is approaching, there's room to suppose;
> The rust on your guns we abhor and detest,
> So brighten them up—we are coming to blows
> With the queen of the ocean . . .

After President James Madison issued a proclamation of war in 1812, Freneau's early verses of the Revolution were resurrected to arouse public opinion against England. The first ten lines of "On the Conqueror of America Shut up in Boston" were printed on July 14 in the New York *Public Advertiser* as a "Patriotic Appeal" for volunteers for the Canadian campaign. "On the Departure of the British from Charleston" and "To the Memory of the Brave Americans under General Greene" were published in the Charleston *Investigator* on October 12 and 14 to remind the citizens of South Carolina that they again faced an ancient and detested foe.

During the first two years of the war, however, Freneau apparently wrote little that was new. There was not much to write about. England was hard pressed in Europe and could ill afford to send reinforcements to her army in Canada or to concentrate large naval forces along the American coast. And the loss of Detroit did little to inspire faith in their own army among the citizens of the United States. On the seas, however, the prospect was more encouraging. Two articles calling for an immediate increase in the American navy appeared in the Philadelphia *Aurora* on December 22 and 25 over Freneau's old signature of "Hawser Trunnion," and when the United States frigate *Constitution* defeated the British *Guerriere*, he composed a stirring ballad in celebration of the victory.[117] He wrote an elegy "In Memory of James Lawrence," to commemorate the hero who had fallen in a naval action.[118] He chronicled the conquests of the American fleet on Lake Erie [119] and, when England sent over new vessels to institute a rigorous commercial blockade, he wrote heatedly "To America: On the English Depredations on the American Coast." [120]

When Napoleon was defeated in the spring of 1814, and England was able to concentrate on her American opponents, Freneau became more active. The courageous battles and amazing victories of the impromptu naval units with which his countrymen dared defy British command of the seas inspired some of his most tuneful patriotic songs, such as "On the Launching of the Seventy-four Gun Ship Independence, at Charlestown," "On the Brigantine Privateer Prince de Neufchatel," and "On the Capture of the United States

Frigate Essex." [121] And again he wrote in praise of the gallant American squadrons on Lake Erie and Lake Champlain.[122]

When the British forces landed in Maryland and marched on Washington, Freneau's old hatred of the "Goths" and "butchers" from England became again articulate. He wrote bitterly "On the British Invasion" [123] and, after the capital had been destroyed, gave voice to his wrath and detestation of the enemy in verses "On the Conflagrations at Washington" and "On the English Devastations at the City of Washington." [124] The death of General Robert Ross, who had led the enemy against the capital, seemed to Freneau an omen that freedom would triumph over ambition and avarice, and he rejoiced in the brave defense which the citizens of Baltimore made against the naval attack upon their city.[125] He prophesied the downfall of all tyranny. He called on his countrymen to take revenge on their oppressors. He sang clearly, as he always had sung, the ultimate victory of every force which made for human freedom.

Sometimes, as he had so often done during the Revolution, he ridiculed the enemy for cowardice or ineptitude. In "Sir Peter Petrified" he told of the death of a gluttonous English officer who risked his life in order to satisfy an appetite for roast goose.[126] In "The Terrific Torpedoes" he presented a soliloquy supposed to have been spoken by Sir Thomas Hardy, a general who suffered loss of sleep because of his fear of being blown to bits by American "submarine bombs." [127] But Freneau did not ridicule only the enemy: in "The Pardae and Sham Fight"; he satirized the inept officers of the United States army; in "The Suttler and the Soldier," [128] he called attention to the low morale of the American volunteer. And he wrote heatedly against clergymen who loaded their sermons with British propaganda.[129] In fact, every stop which Freneau had opened during the Revolution was again opened during the War of 1812. He played old tunes new written, and held steadfastly to his conviction that freedom would prevail.

Yet apparently none of the poems mentioned above was printed until the war was over. They were the patriotic jottings of a veteran who had retired from service, but who still thrilled to every exploit of his younger compatriots. "My pen," he confided to Madison, "could not be entirely idle, and for amusement only now and then I had recourse to my old habit of scribbling verses." [130] When occasionally he did submit patriotic songs for publication, they were widely copied among Eastern newspapers. "The Volunteer's March," paraphrased from Robert Burns's rendering of the stirring words which Robert Bruce addressed to his army before the battle of Bannockburn, appeared in the New Brunswick *Fredonian* on August 11, 1814, and was immediately reprinted in the New York *Columbian*, the Newark *Centinel of Freedom*, and the Trenton *True American*. More than a month later, on September 24, "The Battle of Stonington" was published in the *Columbian*, and subsequently appeared in the *New-Jersey Journal*, the Philadelphia *Aurora*, the Morristown *Palladium of Liberty*, and the *Centinel of Freedom*.

On September 29 Freneau's congratulatory ballad "To the Squadron on the Lakes" was printed in the *Columbian*. On the same day "A Dialogue at Washington's Tomb. Between the Genius of Virginia and Virginia" and "The Prince Regent's Resolve" appeared in the *Fredonian*. Almost two weeks later, on November 10, "A Royal Dialogue" relative to the disposal of Lord Wellington's army was published in the same newspaper. Nor were Freneau's patriotic contributions limited to verse. On August 25 "Robert Slender" once again appeared in the *Aurora* with an appeal "To the Members of the General Ward Committee" of Philadelphia to put an end to their quarreling. With his country oppressed by war Freneau had little patience with small political bickerings.

From Monmouth he followed the conflict sorrowfully. Freedom still was the end for which men fought with blind and courageous vigor. Yet human greed and the assertion of individual human needs seemed to rise continually as barriers to man's progress toward any rational goal. Older now and able to see, perhaps, that the end for which he had striven was beyond any man's reach, Freneau wrote in "The Brook in the Valley":

> The world has wrangled half an age,
> And we again in war engage,

While this sweet, sequester'd rill
Murmurs through the valley still.

.   .   .

Emblem, thou, of restless man;
What a sketch of nature's plan!
Now at peace, and now at war,
Now you murmur, now you roar;

Muddy now, and limpid next,
Now with icy shackles vext—
What a likeness here we find!
What a picture of mankind! [131]

TWELVE

THE VETERAN POET

1815–1832

"I THINK after the age of fifty, or thereabouts, the vanity of authorship ought to cease," Freneau wrote to Madison early in 1815. "At least," he added, "it has been the case with myself." This was both an explanation and something of an apology. because the poet had learned that a new collection of his verse was to be published in New York by bookseller David Longworth. "The work cannot be very tedious," Freneau assured Madison, "for in two small volumes there will be upwards of one hundred and thirty Poems on different subjects . . . and not a few upon the events of the times since May 1812." At sixty-three Freneau admitted that he considered his poems "mere trifles." "I do not know," he said, "that the verses are of any superior or very unusual merit; but . . . the Town will have them: and of course, have them they will, and must." [1]

The volumes would be ready for distribution by the middle of February. "Finding, however, that the business went on slowly," and "a little vexed to be under the necessity of leaving" the "solitude and the wild scenes of nature in New Jersey," Freneau set out for New York late in January to supervise the undertaking. He arrived "unnoticed and almost unknown," and "seriously out of humour" at the delay. He complained of the unremitting cold. He was unhappy amid the "noise and observation" on the "ever execrated streets" of the city. But he boasted that, in spite of his age, he abounded in "all the powers of health and vigour," and early in March was able to report, "By my incessant exertions in spurring on the indolence of typography, the work, such as it is, is now finished." [2]

A Collection of Poems, on American Affairs, and a Variety of Other Subjects, Chiefly Moral and Political contained many of the verses which had first been printed in the *Time-Piece,* and all of the poems which had appeared in various periodicals since Freneau's retirement, as well as a number which had never before been published. "None of my effusions in these volumes," Freneau told Madison, "much exceed two hundred lines, and several do not reach more than the fourth part of that number." [3] Outstanding, of course, were the songs and ballads of the War of 1812, but perhaps equally important was the series of contemplative poems—"Belief and Unbelief," "On the Uniformity and Perfection of Nature," and "On the Religion of Nature"—in which Freneau presents a summation of his mature deliberation on the "ways of God to man." Though there was much that could never be understood of her plan, Nature, benign, perfect, and pervading all things, moved steadily along her predestined way, in spite of, even making a place for man's chicanery, his superstitions, and his irrational hypocrisies. Freneau struggled no longer against discrepancies between things as they were and things as they should be. He was now satisfied that

> All, nature made, in reason's sight
> Is order all, and *all is right.*[4]

Such a philosophy of optimistic resignation, comforting as it may have seemed among the "shades and solitudes" of Monmouth, proved to be of little practical value when faced with the bitter and disappointing truth that the public would not purchase the new collection of poems. Freneau returned to Mount Pleasant "not a little out of humour" because the edition had "fallen nearly dead born from the Press." He blamed its failure on the "enmity of some, the politics of others, and the general inattention of all." "Had I written a Volume of psalms, hymns, and Spiritual Songs," he grumbled, "I believe the success would have been infinitely greater."

A "strange manoeuvering" of partisan readers deprived him of "almost two hundred dollars" which he had expected from the sale of the work. Democrats refused to purchase because the volumes had been published by Longworth, a Federalist. Conservative men "smelt out dirision" in stanzas to the memory of Thomas Paine and objected to the republicanism evident in verses addressed to Thomas Jefferson. Pious readers took exception to what seemed to them a profane interpretation of Biblical story in "Pythona: or, the Prophetess of En-dor." "In short," Freneau complained,

I have reason to believe there is scarcely a solitary trifle through the two volumes but has its personal enemy, all combining in damning the works and sending the author, publisher, printer, bookseller and even the binder to the devil. I almost wonder at there not being people who have enquired what were the politics of the paper maker. . . . These party men have done the work much harm, God reward them according to their works!

"All this," Freneau said, "has rather disgusted me with author-ship." Even the booksellers proved to be uncooperative: "They are either very poor, or will risque nothing at present even to the value of ten copies at $33\frac{1}{3}\%$ discount." The chief fault, however, re-mained with the public. "I suppose . . . the truth is," Freneau ad-mitted, "that almost every person in your city has other and more serious matters to think of than mine, or at least such poetry as mine happens to be." Again, it was not the proper time for poetry:

After all, as I take it, the genius of the city of New York is so entirely com-mercial, that I suspect it swallows up all ideas of poetry . . . further than what is calculated for the fly market stalls, or to be sung at some Tammany Convivial meeting or Bacchanian Sons of the Hotels. A drop of water might exist, merely as such, in a furnace, as poetry, where all the ideas of people seem to be devoted to Commerce, Speculations, Bank Shares, &c. &c. . . . What use for poetry where men have no idea of its efficacy and influence over the human mind.[5]

Even those most friendly to American letters found little good to say of the collection. Gulian C. Verplanck temporized when he reviewed the volumes in the *Analectic Magazine:* [6]

The veteran bard . . . depicts land battles and naval fights with much animation and gay colouring; and being himself a son of old Neptune, he is never at a loss . . . when the scene lies at sea. . . . His martial and politi-cal ballads are by no means contemptible; they are free from bombast and affectation, and often have an arch simplicity in their manner, that renders them very poignant and striking. If the ballads and songs of Dibdin have cheered the spirits and excited the valour of the British tars, the strains of Freneau, in like manner, are calculated to impart patriotic impulses to the hearts of his countrymen, and their effect in this way should be taken as the test of their merit, without entering into a very nice examination of the rhyme or reason.

Even this faint praise was qualified with a note of condescension:

Readers of a very refined taste will not, probably, relish the general style of Mr. Freneau's composition, for it is marked with a certain rusticity of expression and phraseology, that can only be palliated by the wit and humour of which it may be the vehicle, or the influence it may exercise in kindling patriotic and heroic feelings in the bosom of the peasant or common soldier. Mr. Freneau has considerable merit in this way; and as he makes no high pretensions to classic grace or elevation, he should not be judged by the severe rules of criticism, and condemned because he is not splendid in diction, mellifluous in cadence. . . . For our own part, we have no inclination to dwell on his defects; we would rather

> With full applause, in honour to his age
> Dismiss the veteran poet from the stage;
> Crown his last exit with distinguished praise,
> And kindly hide his baldness with the bays.

2

In New York Freneau was cordially welcomed by David Hosack and John Wakefield Francis, both physicians on the faculty of the College of Physicians and Surgeons and both leaders in the cultural life of the city. With them he visited the New York Academy of Fine Arts, where canvases by Gilbert Stuart and Rembrandt Peale were on display. He browsed among the curiosities of the New York Historical Society and among Francis's own fine collection of pamphlet and manuscript material. He borrowed books from the latter's personal library, but "had not leisure, or rather was not in a humour to read them through with attention." He considered applying himself to historical research, but had to admit, "I am now so entirely out of the Literary World, that I can only muse upon such things, without the opportunity of taking an active part in the Business."

When conversation among his friends turned to natural history, however, Freneau's participation became more active. He told them of a neighbor in Monmouth who had made scientific observations in Italy and on the Barbary coast, and he promised to bring a particularly interesting specimen of spermaceti with him when next he came to New York. He read Dr. Hosack's pamphlets and examined

engravings on botanical subjects. Returning to Mount Pleasant, he
confessed:

I feel a strong inclination to write 4 or 500 flowing lines in the poetical style
of *Darwin,* on the Elgin Garden, as soon as I can get materials into my
hands sufficient for the ground work of the Poem, and that I may go to work
merely on imagination, without any semblance of reality.[7]

For, in spite of his disappointment at the reception of his last
volumes, Freneau still contemplated new literary projects. He had
been at work for several months on a poem celebrating the repulse
of the British army at New Orleans. "There is a subject indeed! far
above my powers, I fear," he wrote to Madison in March. "If there
be any thing in inspiration, it will be needful for such a theme." [8]
By the middle of May the poem was finished, fourteen hundred
lines in heroic measure. It was to be published at once. Freneau
informed Dr. Francis of his plans:

To this will be appended some shorter poems generally on light subjects.
This Work makes a half dollar volume. Mr. Longworth, or rather Nicholas
Van Riper, will set about printing it in three weeks. Heaven prosper the
poor Bantling; it has a dramatic air; as I thought the subject demanded
something like progressive action, and not the Monotony of Addison's celebrated *Campaign* and Glover's *Leonidas.*[9]

The volume never appeared, for Longworth, perhaps, was unwilling to send a second venture too closely on the heels of the unsuccessful collection he had issued so few months before. Nor does
Freneau ever seem to have published the heroic lines on the Battle
of New Orleans which were to have formed the major portion of the
book. A year later, however, he did contribute a group of poems to
the New York *Weekly Museum* over the initials "P.F." [10] Slight,
scarcely more than doggerel, there were probably some, perhaps
all, of the "shorter poems generally on light subjects" which he had
planned to include in the projected "half dollar volume."

The first of this group, "Stanzas Written in September 1811, on
the Great Comet, Which Had Passed Its Perhelion, and Was Travelling Rapidly to the Southward," was printed on August 10, addressed "To Ismenia." It was followed on August 31 by playfully
satirical lines "On Madam Charity Careless, a Disconsolate Widow,"
whose husband, a bookish man, died of neglect while she "flirted

away to the ball." Next, on September 7, came "Stanzas Written for a Boy about Eight Years of Age, Who, in Walking with His Parents through a Forest of Pine Trees, Very Narrowly Escaped Being Bitten by an Uncommonly Large and Venomous Rattle Snake." Finally, on September 21 appeared "Stanzas Addressed Several Years Ago to Mr. Blanchard, the Celebrated Aeronaut in America." Like "The Progress of Balloons," which Freneau had published in the *Freeman's Journal* more than thirty years before, and the "Reflections on Balloons," which had been printed in the *National Gazette* in 1793, this poem considered the possibilities of aerial traffic to unknown regions; but, unlike the former poems, it cautiously warned of "Phaeton's sad fate" in venturing too close to the sun.

During the autumn of 1816 seven more poems appeared in the *Weekly Museum*, these over the signature "F." "The Fortunate Blacksmith," on September 28, told of the conquest over "fair Priscilla's *iron* heart" made by "young Vulcan" when he won a cash lottery prize. The "Salutary Maxims, Derived from the Old Cynic Philosophy," printed on October 5, contained the reflections of a veteran controversialist:

> Would you peace and safety find?
> To live in quiet with mankind,
> Do not quarrel with their notions,
> Let each have his own devotions,
>
> . . .
>
> Meddle not with satire's pen
> Make no friendship with *cross* men;
> More than all I would advise
> Always act with some disguise.
>
> . . .
>
> To command the pure good will
> Of human kind remember still,
> *This* is the secret, *this* the charm,
> *Do them neither good nor harm.*

On October 12 appeared both an "Epitaph upon a Spanish Horse Called Royal-gift, Sent Over and Presented to General Washington by the King of Spain in the Year 1785," and "Stanzas on an Ancient Burying Ground in Maryland, One Corner of Which Was Appropriated to the Interment of Suicides, or Self-murderers." In the latter poem, the author pondered again the encroachment of time and the disappointments of age:

> Life is probation, human life a task,
> A task of toil, but with it we should bear—
> When this world's winter and its storms are past
> Spring, in its beauty, will no doubt appear.

"The Tye-Wig, Lines on an Old Dotard, Who Had Cut Away the Blossoms of *Sixty-Eight,* and Upwards, to Put on a Fashionable Tye-Wig," printed on October 19, and "Letitia; or, the Fortunate Spinning Girl," printed on November 2, were both facetious caricatures of the sort that Freneau had often written before when he considered the foibles of his countrymen. "A Dialogue between a News-Printer and His Cash-Collector," November 9, is written in the colloquial style that Freneau had made familiar in such poems as "Slender's Journey" and "The Country Printer."

In addition to these contributions in verse, an article in prose "On the Spots in the Sun" was printed in the *Weekly Museum* on September 7 over the initials "P.F." It discussed circular spots, clearly visible to the naked eye, which appeared on the surface of the sun during the spring and summer of 1816, spots which the author concluded had been caused, not by any planetary bodies "that transit the sun's disk," but which were "exhalations from the globular surface of the sun . . . condensed in his atmosphere, where they remain stationary until dissipated by some cause or causes unknown to us." He suggested that, in time, the spots might "gain such an ascendancy as to obscure, or incrust the whole solar orb." Then, "a whole system of primary and secondary planets perishes, and all that exist thereon!" The moral seemed clear:

Thus, these brilliant solar orbs, the blazing suns of the firmament, like the systems of government contrived by men, seem to contain the seeds of their own dissolution. Nature will take her time; I should rather have said, the God of nature, either to renovate, or to leave their place a blank in the creation, as best suits the will of supreme wisdom.—*Intellect* alone, that emanation from Deity, is secure from the effects of these changes in the material world; and *Mind*, we have powerful reason to conclude, will survive when matter is no more.

Freneau had, indeed, become resigned to the inscrutable ways of Nature's God. The astronomical disquisition was introduced with the quotation from *Hamlet*:

> There are more things in heaven and earth, Horatio,
> Than is dreamt of in your philosophy.

Now that he was older, Freneau seemed to center all his conviction on the certainty that the God of Nature would somehow work all things together toward his own unchangeable ends, and that the ideal of human perfection might be realized, man yet knew not how, as human reason plumbed the mysteries which Nature spread before him. If Freneau ever bridged the "mechanical separation between deity and humanity" which has been said to have been maintained in America until the time of Emerson,[11] it was now as he realized that his own failures, even the struggles of his country and the disruptions which threatened Europe, were all results of man's failure intelligently to adjust himself to the great and harmonious scheme of which he was a part. Nature, the manifestation of God, worked as a "vast machine" which "scorns to change her wonted course."[12] Man, in spite of his self-willed struggles for individual liberty, was caught in her onward sweep. Only in intellect was he akin to God— and free.

3

During the next five years Freneau sold three more tracts, almost twenty-four acres, from the homestead in Monmouth and mortgaged an additional thirty-two acres.[13] In the winter of 1816 his two eldest daughters were married—Helena Denise Freneau to John Hammell, and Agnes Watson Freneau to Edward Leadbeater, both merchants of New York.[14] Some months later Agnes Kearney died in her ninety-first year and was interred in the family burying ground at Locust Grove.[15] On Sunday afternoon, October 18, 1818, "precisely one year after my mother's death," Freneau noted in the family Bible, the old house at Mount Pleasant burned to the ground "with a large part of property therein." Books were destroyed and papers, including "some of his best poems," said Freneau, "which had never been published." [16] Luckily, however, a second residence had already been erected—perhaps, as tradition suggests, built by Edward Leadbeater and his wife for a summer home at Mount Pleasant.[17] On the day after the fire Philip Freneau, his wife, and their two younger daughters "began to move into the new house," beside the charred remains of the old.[18]

When he made an infrequent visit to New York, Freneau was noticed as a curious old-fashioned character who still wore small clothes, but whose deep-set eyes flashed brightly and whose mind was keen and elastic. John W. Francis described him [19] as

somewhat below the ordinary height; in person thin yet muscular, with a firm step, though a little inclined to stoop; his countenance wore traces of care, yet lightened with intelligence as he spoke; he was mild in enunciation, neither rapid nor slow, but clear, distinct, and emphatic. His forehead was rather beyond the medium elevation, his eyes a dark grey . . . his hair must have once been beautiful, it was now thinned and of an iron grey. He was free of all ambitious displays; his habitual expression was pensive.

Among his acquaintances, who are said to have included the "most prominent and patriotic New Yorkers"—such men as Samuel Latham Mitchell, DeWitt Clinton, Cadwallader Colden, and Gulian Verplanck, Freneau was admired for the breadth of his knowledge and his frank, but genially tolerant expression of opinion. Like many other veterans he was fond of recounting his experiences, refighting old battles, and drawing liberally on his fund of anecdotes of the American Revolution. "His private worth, his courteous manner, and his general bearing," said Dr. Francis, "won the admiration of all parties." Even those who disagreed with him politically forgave Freneau his former "indiscreet zeal as an advocate of the rational doctrines of his day" and esteemed him as a true patriot whose "pen was more acrimonious than his heart." [20]

As a poet, however, Freneau belonged to an era that was past. A new literary generation was risen in America, a generation that drew inspiration from new sources and appealed to a new public. American literature grew more voluble, more ambitious, and more nationally self-conscious. American writers struggled valiantly to produce distinctively native works, yet clung to the literary models of England with a tenacity which must have seemed an evil augury to Freneau, who more than a quarter century before had scornfully condemned the influence of "that damnable place." The measure of literary excellence was now, more than it had ever been before, an English measure. The writings of Lord Byron, Thomas Moore, Thomas Campbell, and William Wordsworth were standards against which Americans judged the excellence of their own works. American booksellers entered fierce and active competition for the first American publication of the popular novels of Walter Scott and Maria Edgeworth.[21]

Among native writers, American readers of 1819 admired the sweetly moralistic verse of Lydia Huntley Sigourney and the earnestly sensitive strains of young James Gates Percival. The publication of "Thanatopsis" had established William Cullen Bryant as the morning star of a new literary day. In New York the "Croaker" papers by Fitz-Greene Halleck and Joseph Rodman Drake were the talk and wonder of the town. Samuel Woodworth, known then as he is now for "The Old Oaken Bucket," and James Kirk Paulding, whose narrative poem on American frontier life, *The Backwoodsman*, received attention, if not applause from his countrymen, were both recognized as solidly established men of letters. All eyes were on Washington Irving, who hob-nobbed with the literary great of England and whose *Sketch Book* was achieving unprecedented success on both sides of the Atlantic.

"I am frequently importuned in N. York, as well as in this State for my Poems and Miscellanies," explained Freneau when late in 1818 he wrote Mathew Carey to ask whether the collected edition of 1809 "be disposed of or not" in Philadelphia. "If it be," Freneau suggested, "how would a new and more complete and enlarged Edition take with the Public?" [22] Carey did not encourage him. The old collection of Freneau's poems was sold out, after nine years: "The demand here has ceased." [23] Though Fitz-Greene Halleck later expressed his admiration for "many life long remembered lines," [24] Freneau was not recognized among the literary contemporaries of his later years, except as a popular versemaker who had lived beyond his time. Many, like Dr. Francis and Washington Irving, re-

membered his patriotic poems, because they had memorized them as
schoolboys.[25] Some, however, like William Cullen Bryant, did not
even realize that the old poet still lived. When he contributed an
essay on American poetry to the *North American Review* in 1818,
Bryant dismissed Freneau with a few contemptuous lines:

A writer of inferiour verse was Philip Freneau, whose pen seems to have
been chiefly employed on political subjects, and whose occasional productions, distinquished by a coarse strength of sarcasm, and abounding with
allusions to passing events, which is perhaps their greatest merit, attracted
in their time considerable attention.[26]

More tolerantly, but in a tone of condescension which relegated
Freneau no less definitely to the past, another critic wrote:

> Nor let that "veteran poet" be forgot,
> Simple in tongue, but eloquent in thought,
> Who rose in ages, when the wheels of war,
> Trod letters down beneath her fiery car:
> Let FRENEAU live! though Flattery's baleful tongue
> Too early tuned his youthful lyre to song,
> And ripe old age, in ill-directed zeal,
> Has made an enervated last appeal:
> His song could fire the sailor on the wave,
> Raise up the coward,—animate the brave,
> While Wit and Satire cast their darts around,
> And fools and cowards tremble at the sound:
> Although Ambition never soar'd to claim
> The meed of polish'd verse, or classic fame,
> And caustic critics honour, but condemn,
> A strain of feeling, but a style too tame,
> Let the old Bard, whose patriot voice has fann'd
> The fire of Freedom that redeem'd our land,
> Live on the scroll with kindred names that swell
> The page of history, where their honours dwell . . .[27]

Even "The Dish of Tea," which had so long been associated with
Freneau's name, now dropped into anonymity. "I know not who is
the writer," confessed a correspondent in the New York *Weekly
Visitor* [28] on requesting a republication of the poem. "It has," he
continued with naïve good judgment, "the merit of morality to
make amends for the want of sublimity."

4

But in spite of his earlier protestations, Freneau even at seventy
was not ready to admit that his career was over. Often in the past
he had put poetry behind him; just as often he had returned to make
one more bid for literary fame. On May 14, 1822, he asked Dr.
Francis to see what the latter could accomplish in circulating proposals for a "new, correct, and elegant edition of the Poems and
Miscellanies of Philip Freneau." "Very sure I am," the old poet
wrote, "that from 500 to a thousand copies could be sold at the City
of Washington toward the conclusion of the next session of Congress—and I think New York and South Carolina would not be
backward in forwarding the Publication."

Recalling one of the sources of opposition to his former collection, Freneau admitted, "I can expect nothing from the Bible
Societies—and so much the worse." Nevertheless, he promised to
appease his critics by writing no more about the Witch of Endor,
and he enclosed a provisional prospectus in his letter to Francis,
suggesting:

Should you disapprove of it in general, you can correct, change or modify
it as you see proper. In fact, I have ever found that, after all is said and
done, a Judicious Bookseller, well hackneyed in business, such for instance
as Mathew Carey, and some others I might mention, brothers of the craft,
can always draw up a Paper of this kind to better advantage than any mere
Author of a Book. Generally speaking, they have a better knack at so word-
ing and managing a thing of this kind as to produce a respectable subscription from a publication, when every man seems to set his face against the
whole Subscription System.

The proposed edition would include "those pieces which were
written previously to, during the American Revolutionary War,
and at different times since that Event, down to the Year 1822." The
first three editions, those of 1786, of 1795, and of 1809, "being all
sold off, disseminated, and long since out of print, the Author,"
Freneau explained, "has been induced . . . to issue Proposals
for printing an entire new Edition . . . more complete, interesting
and extensive than any of the former." He rested his chief claim
to attention on the patriotic poems:

The writings of that Memorable period of Seventy-Six, and the seven Revolutionary Years will ever, it may be presumed, be particularly interesting to the American readers of the present day, and to the generations that are to succeed, more especially when they accompany, and have reference to the historical Events of those times, which now seem to bid fair in no small degree to influence the future destinies as well as Moral and political character of mankind at large.

The plan for a new collection was apparently not an inspiration of the moment, for Freneau had kept his manuscripts by in preparation for just such a contingency. "Should the Matter go on as you seem to think it would," he wrote to Dr. Francis, "be so good as to let me know, when convenient. . . . I shall be ready with the copy when I have information." [29]

During the previous year poems by Freneau had been occasionally printed in the Trenton *True American*. On June 30, 1821, he published "Stanzas Written on the Grand Western Canal of the State of New-York, Contemplated to Connect the Atlantic Ocean with the Interior Lakes of North America," a rough first draft of which is found on the inside rear cover of one of the books from Freneau's library.[30] On September 8 the same newspaper published an "Address, Presented at the Re-opening of the Park Theatre in New York, Sometime Since Destroyed by Fire, and Now Completely Repaired, and Rebuilt in a Superior Style. (Said to be written by P. Freneau, of Monmouth, New Jersey)." [31] As he had done thirty-five years before in "Literary Importation," Freneau again complained of his country's lack of literary independence:

> To pass the amusing hours, that all desire,
> New *Plays*, new *subjects*, justly you require;
> For *these*, on *Europe* still our Stage relies,
> And *Europe*, *Europe* every want supplies.
> Why sleeps COLUMBIA's genius for the stage—
> Can not one *Bard* arise to glad the age,
> Not one be found to abandon flimsey rhymes,
> And rise the *Shakespeare* of our modern times?
>
>   .   .   .
>
> Arise, young Authors, on COLUMBIA's soil,
> And give us SOMETHING NEW, to cheer our toil,
> Thus shall the Muse re-animate the Stage,
> And more than *Shakespeare* glow through every page.

This was followed three weeks later by "Jersey City, Lines Written in the Churchyard on Bergen Heights, Near the Village of Hoboken." [32] Looking across the Hudson to New York, the poet begs the London of the New World to extend river rights to her smaller sister-city in New Jersey. The poem is of so little merit that there seems no reason for exhuming it from the files of the old newspaper in which it has been buried for more than a century.

More characteristic of Freneau and more worthy of reproduction is "The City Poet" [33] which appeared in the *True American* on October 6. Its cynical resignation is reminiscent of "The Epistle to Sylvius, on the Folly of Writing Poetry," which had been printed by Freneau in Charleston more than thirty-five years before. Even his familiar lightness of touch cannot conceal his disappointment at the failure of his contemporaries to appreciate poetry "such as mine happens to be." Perhaps, he even suggested now, there could be no poets in a democracy:

> Let such on custards and fine cakes be fed
> And we, plain country Bards, eat barley bread.
>
> You court the favours of the town,
> You carry verses up and down,
>   You scribble for the stage—
> Who would pursue so poor a trade,
> Such *debts of honor*, badly paid
>   For many a labored prize?
>
> To steer a boat, or drive a cart,
> To practice some mechanic art,
>   Yields something for your pain;
> But poems are in no demand,
> Few read them, fewer understand
>   The visions of your brain.
>
> Let Poets choose some gainful trade,
> And not depend on Clio's aid—
>   With all the muse's skill,
> With all the drama in his scull
> *Shakespeare* was bred *to combing wool*,
>   And *Plautus* turned a mill.
>
> Of all the Poets dead and gone,
> I cannot recollect but ONE

That throve by writing rhyme—
If *Pope* from *Homer* gained rewards,
Remember, statesmen, kings and lords
    Were poets, in his time.

A poet where there is no king,
Is but a disregarded thing
    An atom on the wheel;
A second *Iliad* could he write
His pockets would be very light,
    And beggarly his meal.

The SHERIFF, *only* deals in prose,
And *prisons* have a hundred woes;—
    With *debts*, you have no *dues*—
You have no thousands in the Bank,
You float upon a rotten plank—
    —Go home, and mend your shoes.

"Hezekiah Salem," under whose name Freneau had contributed a series of informal essays to the *Time-Piece* twenty-five years before, reappeared as a character in "Elijah, the New England Emigrant," a long burlesque poem which was printed in four installments in the *True American* from October 13 to December 15. It tells the story of a young Massachusetts farmer who had the misfortune to be son-in-law of Hezekiah Salem, now characterized as a wily and parsimonious Yankee deacon. Onions, barley, even pumpkins, did so poorly in Elijah's rocky fields that the young man decided to emigrate with his wife to the newly opened Western country. But he reckoned without the deacon. Hezekiah, representing an older and more conservative generation, resolved to restrain the young couple by argument if possible, by coercion if necessary. The rambling and discursive poem comes to no logical end: after four hundred and eighty-four lines the young farmer is still only thinking of setting out for the West. A satire was evidently intended, but it lost its effectiveness as it descended to farce. Freneau seldom had written so badly as when he said of Elijah's wife:

Were you as homely as a squaw,
And wore a bonnet made of straw,
Still for the virtues of the mind,

Such *Spirit* with *discretion* joined;
Were I a single man again
I would be headmost in your train;

.   .   .

God help us, if you had a nose
As long as what I might suppose,
Still I would swear from *mental* charms,
I clasped a Goddess in my arms.

On April 13, 1822, lines "To a Young Friend, with Some Maple Sugar" appeared in the *True American*. They were composed, said the editor,

by a venerable Patriot, who will neither eat, drink, nor wear any thing of foreign producture, from a belief that we can raise and make all that we need, and that we ought to give *our own* the preference. They were not written for publication; but we have been permitted to transcribe them by a friend to whom a copy of them was transcribed.

There could have been few "venerable Patriots" in New Jersey who wrote poetry, even fewer who could have produced such facile and felicitous lines as:

Fond of her country—will my Mary please
To taste her sweets produced from Maple trees.

Such, then, it may be supposed, were some of the poems [34] which Freneau planned to include in his new and complete edition. They add little to our knowledge of Freneau except to show that the poet was not idle during his later years. He refused to grow old. On May 14, the same day on which he addressed the letter to Dr. Francis regarding the republication of his collected poems, lines on "The Youth of the Mind" [35] appeared in the *True American* over the signature "F." After considering the example of Benjamin Franklin, active in old age, Freneau wrote:

And hence an argument I draw
That *mind* can never die:
The Body yields to nature's law,
But that which animates the frame
Forever lives, and is the same;

.   .   .

'Tis young to all Eternity.

Freneau also remained active. On May 18, 1822, the editor of the *True American* published a "Prologue to Kotzebue's Play, entitled 'The Stranger,' Acted for the Celebrated Mrs. Baldwin's Benefit at Washington Hall, New-York, April 15, 1822. Said to be Written by P. Freneau, of N. Jersey." [36] An excursion to the home of his brother-in-law, John S. Hunn, at Newburgh is suggested by the "Stanzas Written on a Visit to a Field Called 'The Military Ground,' near Newburgh, in the State of New-York, Where the American Army Was Disbanded by General Washington, Almost Forty Years Ago." The poem first appeared in the *True American* on June 9, and three days later was reprinted in the *New York Statesmen*, the editor of which announced:

The following effusion is from the pen of a poet and patriot of the Revolution, who is now in his seventy-second year, but whose body and mind, owing to a life of temperance and exercise, are still vigorous. His poetry, like that of Humphrey, often nerved the arm of the revolutionary soldier; and it is not strange that his muse still loves to dwell on themes, and to linger around scenes associated with other times and other men. There are few instances in which Fancy lives to the age of three score and ten. . . . The venerable author of the following lines has our warmest wishes, that the pleasures of literature may smooth the declivity of age, and that he may be blest with frequent visitations of the muse.

Encouraged, perhaps, by the attention thus gratuitously given in the New York newspaper, Freneau on June 15 contributed "On the Loss of the Packet Ship Albion" to both the *Statesman* and the *True American*. The former paper attributed the poem to "the veteran bard whom we mentioned a few days since," and the latter identified the author as "Capt. Philip Freneau . . . whose patriotic and harmonious pen has amused and interested his country for more than half a century." News of the wreck of the *Albion*, which had struck a reef off the Irish coast two months before, had been reported in detail by the American press and had "awakened the melancholy tones of many a lyre, both in this country and Europe." [37] "No subject for many years has excited poetic sensibility so deeply," said the editor of the *True American*, "as the melancholy catastrophe commemorated by Mr. F. with the sympathy of a seaman and the easy skill of a veteran in poesy." [38]

5

It must soon, however, have become apparent to Freneau that the projected new edition of his poems would never appear. Publishers were wary of works by American authors: they did not sell, especially when English books were so readily acquired and so universally popular. One New York bookseller had recently remarked that Fitz-Greene Halleck and Washington Irving were the only native authors in whose writings he would risk an investment.[39] Even the publication of James Fenimore Cooper's *The Spy* in 1821 was frankly an attempt to capitalize upon the American success of Walter Scott's *Waverley Novels*.[40]

But Freneau had a batch of poems on hand—old poems, never published, now rewritten and corrected, and new poems composed during his retirement at Mount Pleasant. If they were not to appear in a volume, they could at least be sent to the newspapers. Therefore, during the next two years he contributed a succession of poems to the *True American* in Trenton and to the *Fredonian* in New Brunswick. It was a literary house cleaning, a systematic assembling of odds and ends of verse which had, for one reason or another, not appeared in any of the collected editions. Most of them were signed with one of the initials "F.," "R.," "E.," "N.," "A.," or "U.".[41]

Like those which he had published during 1821, they add little to the poet's literary stature. Many are simply restatements of themes which Freneau had often expressed before. For example, the advice "To a Young Farmer, or Agriculturist, Being Taken from the Plough, and Sent to College," which was printed in the *True American* on July 6, 1822, over the signature "R.," emphasizes the inadequacy of collegiate education in much the same way that "The Pilgrim" essays and "The Indian Student" formerly had done. Freneau reminded the young farmer that unpolished diamonds were always valuable, but that pebbles, no matter how brightly burnished, would never sell at high prices. He recalled the career of George Washington, who, though he knew no language but his own, attained to highest success. The arts of agriculture and navigation, Freneau warned, are not mastered from books; only effeminate fripperies re-

sult from too much learning. Similarly, the "Stanzas Addressed to a
Young Person of Condition, Much Addicted to the Gambling Table,"
which appeared in the same newspaper signed "F." on July 13, playfully satirizes human folly, as Freneau had often done before. And
"On the Civilization of the Western Aboriginal Country," published
in July 20 over the signature "A.," is a repetition of the refrain that
had been implicit in many of Freneau's verses on the Indian:

> Take all, through all, through nation, tribe or clan,
> The child of Nature is the *better* man.

Sometimes, as he had done the year before in "On the Loss of the
Packet Ship Albion," Freneau turned his attention to more timely
subjects. Such were the "Stanzas on General Lefevre Denouette,"
which appeared in the *True American* on July 20, and the "Lines
Written at Demarest's Field, near Tappan, on the Disinterment and
Transportation of Major Andre's Bones to England," in the same
paper on August 24, both over the signature "R." More often, however, Freneau's later poems dealt with old themes and familiar speculations. In "Philosophical Fortitude," printed in the *Fredonian* on
July 18 over the signature "F.," he accepted life courageously and
looked forward to death without fear:

> The Wise at Nature's Laws will ne'er repine,
> Nor think to scan, or mend the grand design.
> Ills from ourselves, and not from Nature flow,
> And true Religion never leads to woe:
> What Nature gives, receive—her laws obey,
> *If you must* live *tomorrow, live today:*
>
> .   .   .
>
> The *fools* in life, the *wise*, in death depend,
> Waiting, with sweet reverse, their toils to end.

"Recollections of Past Times and Events," in verse and prose, appeared in four installments in the *True American* during the summer
of 1822. Freneau first on July 6 discussed the depreciation of currency during the Revolution. The reminiscences were illustrated by
a humorous prose dialogue between Squire Sandby and Dick Sharp-
skins, the latter a debtor who insisted upon settling his accounts with
continental currency which was worth only a fraction of its original

value. The second installment, on July 27, contained recollections of the colonial boycott on tea and of the homemade substitutes with which housewives had been forced to make shift during the war, to which was added in verse the "colloquial conference" entitled "A Boston Dialogue." On August 10 Freneau pictured the situation of Bermuda during the Revolution, particularly the quarrels between American sympathizers there and the loyal British governor of the islands. A "little Poem . . . founded on the Tradition that these islands, or some one of them, was the scene of one of Shakespeare's finest and most forceful Plays called the Tempest" concluded the discussion. The last of the "Recollections," on August 17, told of liberty poles, their history, and their prevalence in early Revolutionary New York, and contained stanzas which had been read in 1775 at the dedication of the new iron-covered and destruction-proof pole.

Many of these later poems by Freneau were apparently contributed both to the *True American* and to the *Fredonian*. "Lines, Written on Leaving an Elegant New Mansion House, called Beaurepaire (Pleasant Retreat) not an Hundred Miles from Lake Cayuga" appeared in the former paper on August 24 over the signature "N." On September 2 the same poem was printed in the *Fredonian* over the signature "R." as "Verses Written on Leaving a Great House of Much Ceremony, but Little Sincerity, or Hospitality." Its sequel, on the other hand, appeared first in the latter paper on September 26 over the signature "E." as "The Arrival at Indian Sam's (or, Wee-Quali's) Wigwam" and, secondly, in the *True American* over the signature "N." on September 28 as "Beaurepaire, the Arrival at Wee-quali's, or Indian Sam's Wigwam." This poem, quite the most ambitious of Freneau's later writings, tells of a traveler who, after leaving the artificial gaiety and splendor of a pretentious mansion, finds true hospitality and peace in the simpler forest home.

Freneau's poems continued to appear in both newspapers all through the summer of 1822. "Verses on an Upper Street Physician who Deserted a Populous City on the Approach of Malignant Fever," first printed in the *Fredonian* on August 29, must have been written at the time of one of the frequent epidemics in New York or Philadelphia.[42] The "Lines to a Lady Engaged in Manufacturing an Elegant Carpet, Intended to be Forwarded as a Present to Nadir Shah,

Despot of Persia," signed "F." in the *True American* on August 31, ridiculed the custom of "making presents to the Great" who, in a more rationally conceived situation, might themselves be expected to be donors. The "Lines Written near an Elegant and Romantic Garden, Adjacent to Passaick River, in Essex County," by "A." in the same newspaper a week later, complained of roisterers from nearby taverns whose noisy orgies made a quiet enjoyment of nature impossible.

The most denunciatory of Freneau's poems published during this later period is that "written at the time the intelligence first arrived in America that Bonaparte, from the first consulship, had ascended the throne of France." The lines appeared over the signature "E." in the *True American* on September 14, 1822. "Dogs unnumber'd growl," "distant wolves still louder howl," "vultures scream," and "tigers roar" when Napoleon forfeits his right to be considered a friend to the common man. Freneau's attitude toward monarchy had not changed:

> O, grand mistake! what can atone
> For mischiefs thus so rashly done!
>   Now Europe hugs her chains:
> Had France remained *republican*
> And sanctioned, *there,* the RIGHTS OF MAN
> All would have been secure and free
> From tyrants and from tyranny
>   That soon may rise again.

"A Midnight Storm in the Gulph Stream, Written on an Outward Bound Voyage from Charleston to the Canary Islands" was printed in the *Fredonian* on September 19, and in the *True American* on September 21 over the signature "E.," and dated "Brig Washington, January 25, 1804." This graphic account of the perils of the sea was followed in the same issue of the *True American* by "Lines to a Lady Remarkably Fond of Sleep Preparing for a Voyage to Europe," printed over the signature "A.," and republished in the *Fredonian* on October 5 over the signature "R." Take to your bed immediately upon embarking, Freneau advised the fair voyager. Thus, you may "sleep the danger all away." Or, better yet, remain at home, because

> Who would slumber on the deep
> That on shore might sounder sleep?—
> Take your choice of sea or land,
> *Both* are *yet* at your command;
>
> *Both* have ever, plagues and care,
> And, on land, *you have your share*
> Be the choice as you incline,
> *Terra Firma* shall be mine.

Freneau's poems appeared less frequently during the autumn. "Circumnavigation," printed in the *True American* on October 19 over the signature "E.," was introduced by a note explaining that the poem had been inspired by the fact that the "United States Seventy-four gun ship Franklin is now in the Pacific Ocean, supposed to be upon a voyage round the globe." Rather than celebrate the naval achievement, however, Freneau stressed the circumstance that the "commanding officer has his lady with him":

> The Franklin, with her sails unfurled,
> Wafts the *first lady* round the world.

Then, addressing the lady directly, he offered a final good-natured gibe at the beaus and belles of urban America:

> You will return with *Indian Teas*
> And *porcelain* from the famed *Chinese,*
> The rarest products ever known,
> And MONKIES purchased at Ceylon,
> That will in every street appear,
> And rival half our *Dandies* here.

But why, he asked in gentle raillery, are not American products good enough for Americans?

The "Ode Written on a Remote Perspective View of Princeton College (or Nassau Hall) from a Remarkably Woody Eminence in Monmouth, Commonly Called Pine Hill," which appeared in the *True American* on October 26 over the signature "R.," and in the *Fredonian* on October 31, signed "N.R.," recalled the scenes which Freneau had known half a century before.[43] In "Lines on a Transient View of Monticello," by "E.," in the *Fredonian* on November

7, the poet once more expressed his admiration for Thomas Jefferson, "the patriot, sage, philosopher." As he reviewed incidents of the past, Freneau realized that he had lived beyond the span allotted to most men. It must, then, have been with some special care that he wrote "On the Continuance of a Red-Streak Apple on the Tree in the Month of January," a poem which appeared over the signature "A." in the *True American* for November 9 and over the signature "E." in the *Fredonian* five days later:

> Alas! small pleasure can there be
> To dwell a hermit, on the tree—
> Your old companions, all, are gone,
> Have dropped, and perished, every one;
> You only stay to face the blast,
> A sad memento of the past.

Yet Freneau remained a cheerful, chatty, and alert old man. In the "Answer to a Letter of Despondency from an Invalid in the North," printed over the signature "F." in the *Fredonian* for December 5, he exhorted:

> Rouse up your spirits—and if here
> You choose to meet on Shrewsbury plains
> Your friend—sound cyder—and strong beer.[44]

At last he apparently yielded to the verdict of his contemporaries and was "content with mediocrity." Now that the rigors of active life were past, he admitted in lines "Translated from a Fragment of Bion," published in the *Fredonian* on November 28 over the signature "R.":

> To write was my sad destiny,
> The worst of trades, we all agree.

Other writers were succeeding where Freneau had failed—but few in America. In verses addressed "To a New-England Poet" in the *True American* of January 4, 1823, Freneau presented a final indictment of the "damnable place," the literary favor of which so many of his American contemporaries courted still:

> See, IRVING, gone to Britain's court
> To people of *another sort*,
> He will return, with wealth and fame
> While Yankees hardly know *your name*.

Lo! he has kissed a Monarch's—hand!
Before a Prince I see him stand,
And with the glittering nobles mix
(Forgetting times of seventy-six,)
While you will turn to meet the frown
Of *Bank Directors* of the town,
    The home-made *nobles* of our times,
    Who hate the bard, and spurn his rhymes.

Why pause? Like IRVING, haste away,
To England your addresses pay;
And England will reward you well,
When you some pompous story tell
    Of British feats, and British arms,
    To maids of *honor*, and their *charms*.

Dear Bard, I pray you, take the hint,
In England what you write and print,
Republished here in shop and stall,
Will perfectly entrance us all.

On February 1 two more poems by Freneau appeared in the Trenton paper—"On a Widow Lady, (Very Rich and Very Penurious)," signed "R.," and "Lines Written Several Years Ago on the Death of Robert Fulton," signed "E." and dated "June, 1816." Your money, Freneau admonished the rich widow, can do many things, but "it cannot make me fond of you." But Fulton he addressed as "the *Archimedes* of America, who by his inventions, discoveries, and improvements in machinery, acted upon by his *aquatic* steam, introduced a new system of river and coast navigation, for which the civilized world at large, and North America in particular, should pay . . . respect to his memory."

Then it was more than a year before verses addressed to "General de la Fayette, on his expected visit to America," appeared on July 31, 1824, in the *True American*, and in the *Fredonian* over the signature "F." on August 18. They were followed by "Stanzas Made at the Interment of a Sailor on the Island of Tortuga, near the North Side of Hispaniola, or Hayti, as now Called. (Written Many Years ago, but never Published)," in the *True American* on August 21 and in the *Fredonian* on September 8. During the next three months more poems in Freneau's familiar idiom appeared in both newspapers, but none of these is identified by any of his familiar signatures.[45]

6

Freneau's last years were darkened by an ever lengthening shadow of poverty. When he was an old man past seventy, he worked on the public roads of Monmouth in order to pay his taxes.[46] Later, lands which he had mortgaged at Mount Pleasant were sold at auction to meet the demands of his creditors.[47] Local tradition recalls that Freneau went from house to house as a tinker, mending clocks and doing other small jobs of repairing. It has been suggested that more than once he had to ask friends in New York for financial assistance.[48] In Monmouth he was regarded with suspicion by his more industrious neighbors.[49] By 1826 he had removed his family from the old homestead to a farmhouse eight miles away on land which belonged to Eleanor Freneau's brother, Denise Forman. There at least one of Freneau's grandchildren was born, and there the poet, whom his sister described as "atho' an old, a happy man," spent the remainder of his life.[50]

It seems appropriate that the last of Freneau's poems which has survived is entitled "Winter," for the analogy between the seasons of the year and the periods in the life of man had always been a favorite with him. The poem, found only in manuscript, is dated "November 28, 1827." [51] Freneau was seventy-five years old when he wrote:

> The Sun hangs low!—So much the worse, we say,
> For *those* whose pleasure is a Summer's day;
> Few are the joys which stormy Nature yields
> From blasting winds and desolated fields;
> *Their* only pleasure in that season found
> When orchards bloom and flowers bedeck the ground.
>
> But, are no Joys to these cold months assign'd?
> Has winter nothing to delight the Mind?
> No friendly Sun that beams a distant ray,
> No Social Moons that light us on our way?—
> Yes, there are Joys that may all storms defy,
> The chill of Nature, and a frozen Sky.

> Happy with wine we may indulge an hour;
> The noblest beverage of the mildest power.
> Happy, with Love, to solace every care,
> Happy with sense and wit an hour to share;
> These to the mind a thousand pleasures bring
> And give to winter's frosts the smiles of spring,
> Above all praise pre-eminence they claim
> Nor leave a sting behind—remorse and shame.

Though his verses might be forgotten and his services to his country twisted and turned by those who came after him until each act was made to seem political opportunism, Freneau had watched a new nation grow to life, and he had contributed a poet's share to its development. His dream of literary glory had been early put aside to make place for a greater vision of freedom and happiness for all men. He accepted the ritual and adopted the catchwords which went with service to the new vision, and they colored his poetry until it often became little more than a paraphrase of the radical political philosophies of the late eighteenth century. Now, as these philosophies were taken as a matter of course in America, Freneau's restatement of them in his later verse must have seemed to his contemporaries an old-fashioned and unnecessary repetition of things past. New poets were singing of new themes, drawn from less jaded inspiration. In 1827 Edgar Allan Poe published *Tamerlaine* in Boston, Henry Wadsworth Longfellow was already a young man of fine poetic promise, and John Greenleaf Whittier was soon to publish his *Legends of New England*. America was beginning to recognize, in literature as in politics, that she had a genius of her own. But Freneau was an old man. Occasionally he sent a poem to a Monmouth newspaper, but that was all.[52]

Though he must have been delighted by the election of President Jackson, Freneau apparently did not write a poem about the victory of the liberal cause to which he had devoted his literary talents. During his quiet life on the farm, he did, however, keep a careful family record in the old Fresneau Bible. His son-in-law, Edward Leadbeater, died at Mount Pleasant in 1828. Margaret Hunn, his youngest sister, died at Newburgh during the same year. Mary Freneau was buried by her side early in 1829. John Hunn was fatally stricken a few weeks later.[53] No less attention was given to the births of his grandchildren—ten of them, and after the last was born on August 31, 1830, Freneau listed their names carefully: the Leadbeaters—Jane Grey, Philip Freneau,[54] Edward Henry, Euphemia Kearny, Catherine Ledyard, and Marianna; and the Hammells—Anne Roome, Eleanora Freneau, Sarah, and, the youngest, Mary Freneau.

His financial worries must have been somewhat lightened when, in 1828, his wife's brother, Samuel Forman, deeded to her the right to dispose of all the land in Monmouth County which had been left to them jointly by their father.[55] During the next four years the records of the Monmouth courthouse disclose sale after sale, sometimes only one small lot at a time, by Philip Freneau and his wife.[56] Then, on August 1, 1832, the old poet appeared before the judges of the Inferior Court of Common Pleas to make application for a pension as a veteran of the American Revolution.[57]

The application was granted, but Freneau did not live to receive even the first payment of the thirty-five dollars a year which was awarded him for service to his country. On the evening of December 18, 1832, the old man stayed late in the village of Freehold, some say at the town library,[58] others insist that he was detained by the more convivial delights of the village tavern. He had hardly started the two-mile walk over the fields to the farmhouse where he now lived when a blizzard blew up from over the Navesink Highlands. Attempting a short cut through a bog meadow, Freneau lost his way in the darkness amid the snow. The next morning his body was found beside the pathway.[59] "My Dear Father was buried," wrote his daughter in the family Bible, "by his own particular request in the Locust Grove very near his beloved mother, on Friday afternoon the 21st of December 1832." "He was a staunch whig, a good soldier, and a warm patriot," said his obituary.[60] "Many of his productions will live when much of the fashionable, new-fangled, mawkish verse of modern poets will have sunk into endless oblivion."

NOTES

CHAPTER ONE

1. *The Writings of Thomas Jefferson*, ed. Paul Leicester Ford, New York, 1892, I, 231 and 254; and Washington Irving, *Life of George Washington*, New York, 1869, V, 174.

2. *Specimens of American Poetry, with Critical and Biographical Notices*, ed. Samuel Kettell, Boston, 1829, I, 285.

3. Eugène and Emil Haag, *La France protestante*, Paris, 1888, VI, 716.

4. MS *Archives de la Charente-Inférieure*, La Rochelle, B, 175, 235, 453, 530, and I, 60. I am indebted to *M.* F. de Vaux, l'Archiviste de la Charente-Inférieure, to *M.* Victor Belliard, Officer de l'Instruction Publique, of St. Trojans-les-Bains, and to *M.* L. Robin, Maire de Saint Pierre-d'Oléron, for this and other information concerning the Fresneaus in France. The family is also prominently mentioned in *Noms féodaux ou noms de ceux qui ont tenu fiefs en France . . . depuis le XIIe siècle jusque vers le milieu dè XVIIIe*, Paris, 1867, II, 181.

5. MS *Archives notariales de la Charente-Inférieure* (1688), p. 224.

6. MS *"Extrait de l'estat de liquidation des biens délaissez par ceux de la R. P. R. de La Rochelle et pays d'Aunix, Marenne, Olleron et autre lieux qui ont abandoné le royaume," Archives Nationales*, T.T., 259.

7. "Registers of the French Church, Threadneedle Street, London," *Publications of the Huguenot Society of London* (1899), XIII, 62 ff.; and David C. A. Agnew, *Protestant Exiles from France in the Reign of Louis XIV*, London, 1874, pp. 32, 43, and 69.

8. "Letters of Denization and Acts of Naturalization for Aliens in England and Ireland, 1701–1800," *Publications of the Huguenot Society of London* (1923), XXVII, 68–70.

9. According to a MS notebook which belonged to Philip Freneau's daughter, Mrs. John Hammell, André Fresneau was born in 1672. No further notice of his birth has been found among the MS *Archives de la Charente-Inférieure* or the Fresneau family papers. Mrs. Hammell's notebook, now owned by the Monmouth County Historical Association, Freehold, N. J., will hereafter be designated "Hammell notes."

10. The Fresneau family Bible, owned by Miss Evelyn Drumm, Seattle, Washington, will hereafter be designated "Family Bible."

11. "Letters of Denization and Acts of Naturalization," p. 69.

12. Mary S. Austin, *Philip Freneau, the Poet of the Revolution, A History of His Life and Times*, New York, 1901, p. 52. Miss Austin's biography, edited by Helen Kearny Vreeland, a great-granddaughter of the poet, is often more correct in spirit than in detail.

13. MS conveyances, Office of the Surveyor General of the Proprietors of East New Jersey, Perth Amboy, I, 321 and 412. André Fresneau, with seven other Huguenot émigrés, purchased "42,500 Acres in Bergen county in the Eastern Division of New-Jersey in the Back of New-York." The subsequent history of this tract, which included the present townships of Franklin, Hohokus, and Ridgewood in Bergen County, a small part of Passaic County, and extended into Rockland County in New York, is told in Edward S. Rankin's "The Ramapo Tract," *Proceedings of the New Jersey Historical Society* (1932), L, 377 ff.; and in William Roome's *Early Days and Early Surveys in East New Jersey*, Morristown, 1883, pp. 31–36.

14. MS *Alexander Papers*, New York Historical Society, Box III; see also Austin,

Freneau, p. 53. In Philip Freneau's obituary (*New York Mirror,* January 12, 1833) it is stated, "The house from which his grandfather was buried, was formerly pointed out in Hanover Square."

15. *Collections of the New York Historical Society* (1885), XVIII, 90.

16. According to the family Bible, André Fresneau was married on June 17, 1710. For Pierre Morin, see Charles W. Baird, *History of the Huguenot Emigration to America,* New York, 1885, I, 290 n.

17. See J. R. Brodhead, *Documents Relating to the Colonial History of New York,* Albany, 1855, V, 331; *Collections of the New York Historical Society* (1893), XXVI, 65 and 81; and MS conveyances, Office of the Register of the City and County of New York, XXVIII, 84–86, 250–52, and XXX, 207–08.

18. *Ecclesiastical Records of the State of New York,* Albany, 1902, III, 2023.

19. *Minutes of the Common Council of the City of New York,* New York, 1905, III, 181 and 210. André Fresneau was elected assessor on September 29, 1718, and reelected one year later.

20. MS conveyances of New York, XXVIII, 228, and XXX, 335; MS *Monmouth County Deeds,* Freehold, G, 135–36; and MS deeds, Office of the Secretary of State of New Jersey, Trenton, D3, 113–14.

21. MS Simsbury town records, IV, 219–20. Austin, *Freneau,* p. 52, suggests that André invested in the mines in 1705, before he settled in New York, and that he gave up interest in the enterprise by 1707. The mines were discovered in 1705, but were not worked till 1712, when the proprietors, citizens of the township of Simsbury, gave an eight year lease to a company of capitalists from Boston and New York, who in turn leased to Elias Boudinot of New Jersey, from whom Fresneau purchased his shares in 1718 and 1719. See MS Simsbury town records, II½, 79, 84, and 88; and Lucius I. Barber, *A Record and Documentary History of Simsbury,* Simsbury, 1931, pp. 113 ff.

22. MS *Alexander Papers.*

23. Ann Maury, *Memoirs of a Huguenot Family; Translated and Compiled from the Original Autobiography of the Rev. James Fontaine,* New York, 1853, pp. 296–300. André Fresneau associated as an equal with members of such New York families as the Livingstons, the Jays, the Stuyvesants, the Van Courtlandts, the Roosevelts; see *New York Genealogical and Biographical Record,* XLIX, 372 (October, 1918).

24. Record of the baptism of each of André Fresneau's children is found in "Registers of the Births, Marriages and Deaths of the 'Eglise Françoise à la Nouvelle York' from 1688 to 1804," ed. A. V. Wittmeyer, *Collections of the Huguenot Society of America* (1886), I, 122 ff. André's daughters died, the first in 1736 and the second in 1738, both of heart disease; they were, say the MS Hammell notes, both beautiful girls, each of whom died shortly before the time appointed for her marriage.

25. Marie Fresneau's death is recorded in the family Bible. Mentioned among the communicants of the Church of St. Esprit is Esther Morin, who acted as Godmother to Thomas Louis Fresneau (Wittmeyer, p. 149). Because André Fresneau's widow, Esther, and his father-in-law, Pierre Morin, later shared a house at Simsbury (MS *Connecticut Archives,* Hartford, I, 312a), it may seem reasonable to suppose that André married his first wife's sister.

26. MS Simsbury town records, IV, 254–74; and MS *Connecticut Archives,* I, 287–89 and 305–12.

27. MS *Alexander Papers.*

28. Family Bible. André Fresneau's will (*Collections of the New York Historical Society,* 1893, XXVI, 318–19) was probated August 16, 1725. His estate was left to his wife, to be held in trust for his children until they attained majority. André was buried, say the MS Hammell notes, beside his first wife in Trinity Churchyard "beneath a Tomb Stone the inscription now (1856) scarcely legible." The tombstone no longer exists.

29. MS *Alexander Papers.*

30. MS *Connecticut Archives,* I, 305 and 312a.

31. MS Simsbury town records, V, 5, and VI, 78 ff.

32. Andrew Fresneau was admitted to the Roll of Freemen of New York in 1737 (*Collections of the New York Historical Society,* 1890, XXIII, 90). See also the MS conveyances of New York, XXXIII, 12–14, and Pierre Fresneau's MS letter book, Freneau Collection, Rutgers University Library.

33. See the *New-York Weekly Journal,* August 4, 1740; MS conveyances of New York, XXXIII, 12–14 and 337–38; MS deeds, Office of the Secretary of State of New Jersey, D3, 143; and MS deed, May 29, 1742, Freneau papers, Monmouth County Historical Association.

34. *New-York Gazette,* May 9, 1748.

35. Pierre Fresneau's MS letter book, June 16, 1749.

36. *Calendar of New York Colonial Commissions, 1680–1770,* ed. Edward B. O'Callaghan, New York, 1929, p. 50.

37. *Select Cases of the Mayor's Court of New York City 1674–1784,* ed. Richard B. Morris, Washington, 1935, p. 193.

38. *New-York Gazette,* March 24, 1745.

39. Francis Fresneau married in 1746 or 1747. See Pierre Fresneau's MS letter book, February 10, 1747; and Edwin R. Purple, "Contributions to the History of the Ancient Families of New York City," *New York Genealogical and Biographical Review,* VII, 151 (October, 1876).

40. *New-York Gazette,* January 25, 1748.

41. Pierre Fresneau's MS letter book, September 14, 1748.

42. Helena Provoost Fresneau, the "widow of Francis Fresneau," remarried in 1760 (MS marriage records, Office of the Secretary of State of New York, III, 189). The date of Francis Fresneau's death, however, is not recorded in the letters of administration, dated April 28, 1764, which designated Pierre Fresneau as his executor (*Collections of the New York Historical Society,* 1897, XXX, 448).

43. Unless otherwise indicated all further information in this chapter pertaining to the activities of Pierre Fresneau is drawn from his MS letter book; see Lewis Leary, "Philip Freneau's Father," *Journal of the Rutgers University Library,* II, 48–56 (June, 1939).

44. MS conveyances of New York, XXXII, 338.

45. See John E. Stilwell, *Historical and Genealogical Miscellany: Early Settlers of New Jersey and Their Descendants,* New York, 1932, V, 250–54; F. R. Symmes, *History of the Old Tennent Church,* Cranbury, 1904, p. 367; and the family Bible.

46. MS *Marriage Bonds,* Office of the Secretary of State of New Jersey, F, 29.

47. Family tradition alone reports that Pierre Fresneau and his bride lived on Frankfort Street and that Philip was born there on January 2, 1752. There is no record in the Register's office in the city of New York of any Fresneau having purchased property during this period. David Provoost, Francis Fresneau's father-in-law, was, however, a landholder on Frankfort Street; see *Collections of the New York Historical Society* (1897), XXX, 227–28. It seems possible, therefore, that Pierre Fresneau may have resided in one of the Provoost houses. The date of Philip's birth, attested by the family Bible, the MS Hammell notes, and his obituary notices, is not corroborated by any public record which I have found.

48. *New-York Gazette,* January 13, 1752.

49. *New-York Post Boy,* January 6, 13, and March 14, 1752.

50. Pierre Fresneau and his family moved to Monmouth by July 1, 1752, on which day an account is entered in his name in the MS *Ledger A of us, Rhea & Wickoff Merchants at Middletown Point,* Monmouth County Historical Association, pp. 41–42. Of the Fresneau homestead at Mount Pleasant, Philip Freneau wrote in the family

Bible, "Said old house was built in 1752 by my father—42 feet in length and 24 in breadth."

51. Family Bible.

52. Family Bible.

53. MS *Monmouth County Deeds*, K, 60. *The Poems of Philip Freneau*, ed. Fred Lewis Pattee, Princeton, 1902, I, xv: "The estate at this time contained nearly a thousand acres"; Austin, *Freneau*, p. 65: "In the year of Philip's birth, Pierre bought an estate of one thousand acres in Monmouth County." There is also a persistent tradition among Freneau descendants that the settlement of Mount Pleasant was named for the Fresneau family estate in France (see Austin, p. 65). As a matter of record, Mount Pleasant, New Jersey, existed in 1701, eight years before evidence is found of any Fresneau in America (MS conveyances, Office of the Surveyor General of the Proprietors of East New Jersey, J, 430).

54. *Documents Relating to the Colonial History of the State of New Jersey* (1928), 1st ser., XXXIII, 153–54.

55. MS *Minutes of Council*, Office of the Proprietors of East New-Jersey, A, 536.

56. *Collections of the New York Historical Society* (1897), XXX, 448.

57. *Ibid.*, pp. 417–18.

58. *Minutes of the Common Council*, VII, 32 and 38.

59. *Documents Relating to the Colonial History*, loc. cit.

60. A record of daily prayers and Bible readings for 1756–58 is found in Pierre Fresneau's MS letter book.

61. For a description of these and other volumes in Freneau's library, see the appendix to the present volume.

62. MS *Monmouth County Deeds*, K, 136.

63. Austin, *Freneau*, p. 71.

64. Pattee, in *Poems*, I, xv.

65. *Supplement to the New-York Gazette*, July 22, 1762.

66. *New-York Gazette*, June 3, 1762.

67. The MS Hammell notes, p. 3, report that Philip was placed "on the 14th of February 1766 with the Reverend Alexander Mitchell teacher at the Penelopen Latin School." Situated in that district of Monmouth County which was known variously as Manalapan, Penelopen, or Ponolopon (see William S. Stryker, *The Battle of Monmouth*, Princeton, 1927, p. 120 n.) was the Mattisonian Grammar School, "lately opened" (*New-York Journal*, January 1, 1767), presided over by Alexander Mitchell, and supervised by a committee headed by William Tennent (see James Steen, "*The Presbyterian Church of Freehold, in Middletown*," New Jersey, Freehold, 1907, pp. 11–13). Among the signatures of witnesses to the indenture by means of which Aaron Mattison on July 8, 1767, deeded land and a schoolhouse to the trustees of the Presbyterian church is that of fifteen year old Philip Fresneau (MS *Records of the Old Tennent Church*, Monmouth County Historical Association, II, 36–37).

68. Examination in these subjects was necessary for entrance to Nassau Hall at Princeton (see Varum Lansing Collins, *President Witherspoon*, Princeton, 1925, I, 122).

69. MS Hammell notes, p. 9.

70. *New-York Journal*, September 3, 1767.

71. Pierre Fresneau's death is recorded in the family Bible; see, also, MS wills, Office of the Secretary of State of New Jersey, K, 161.

CHAPTER TWO

1. See John MacLean, *History of the College of New Jersey, from Its Origin in 1746 to the Commencement of 1854*, Philadelphia, 1877, I, 300 ff.; George R. Wallace, *Prince-*

ton Sketches, the Story of Nassau Hall, New York, 1894, pp. 54–57; and Collins, *Witherspoon*, pp. 103–05.

2. MS Hammell notes, p. 7.

3. Wallace, p. 18.

4. Philip Vickers Fithian, *Journal and Letters, 1767–1774*, Princeton, 1900, pp. 7–13.

5. John Witherspoon, *The Works of the Rev. John Witherspoon*, Philadelphia, 1800, IV, 349.

6. *Ibid.*, III, 389.

7. "The Distrest Orator," *The Poems of Philip Freneau*, Philadelphia, 1786, pp. 64–65.

8. Wallace, p. 21; and MacLean, I, 32.

9. On the flyleaf of a volume of Horace owned by Freneau and at one time in the possession of Mr. J. H. Innes, of Ossining, New York. I am indebted to the late Varum Lansing Collins for a transcript of the quatrain and for information concerning the volume (which I have not been able to locate). The Kelsey mentioned by Freneau was Enos Kelsey, merchant and tavern keeper, sometime treasurer of the college, and an active and patriotic citizen of Princeton.

10. Witherspoon, "Lectures on Moral Philosophy," *Works*, III, 321.

11. *Glimpses of Colonial Society and the Life at Princeton College by One of the Class of 1763*, ed. W. Jay Mills, Philadelphia, 1903, p. 94.

12. Fithian, p. 43.

13. "Ode Written on a Remote Perspective View of Princeton College," Trenton *True American*, October 26, 1822; see note 41 of chapter XII.

14. MS *Madison Papers*, Library of Congress, I, 11 (August 10, 1769).

15. "Ode Written on a Remote Perspective View." Morven: "An elegant summer house, retreat of the late Hon. Richard Stockton, Esq., on the western bank of Stoney River" (Freneau's note).

16. Except the record in the MS *Minutes of the Board of Trustees* which approved his graduation in 1771; see note 57 below.

17. Harry Hayden Clark, "The Literary Influences of Philip Freneau," *Studies in Philology*, XXII, 9 (January, 1925).

18. A list of books given in 1755 by Governor Jonathan Belcher to the library at Nassau Hall is printed in *Princeton University Library. American Library Association Visit, June 26, 1916*, Princeton, 1916, pp. 26–28. No other record of the library during Freneau's college years seems to exist.

19. Witherspoon, "Lectures on Eloquence," *Works*, III, 377 ff.

20. Clark, "Literary Influences," p. 6.

21. Elizabeth Nitchie, *Vergil and the English Poets*, New York, 1919, p. 150.

22. Edwin W. Bowen, "Philip Freneau, the Poet of the American Revolution," *Sewanee Review*, XI, 215 (April, 1903).

23. *Works*, London, 1757, VIII, 242.

24. *Ibid.*, p. 159.

25. *Ibid.*, p. 36.

26. Said to be "Done in the year 1768" when printed in *Poems* (1786), p. 1.

27. Clark, "Literary Influences," p. 12.

28. Printed as "The Village Merchant," *National Gazette*, May 17–June 28, 1792; dated "Anno 1768" when reprinted in *Poems* (1795), p. 15.

29. Dated 1769 in *Poems* (1786), p. 35.

30. MS AM.0336, Historical Society of Pennsylvania. Brackenridge's chapter is dated "September 20, 1770"; Freneau finished his portion on October 22. Claude Milton Newlin, *The Life and Writings of Hugh Henry Brackenridge*, Princeton, 1932, pp. 15–21, presents a transcript of Brackenridge's chapter. Freneau's contribution has never been published.

31. Dated in *Poems* (1786), p. 32.

32. *Ibid.*, p. 39.

33. Samuel Marion Tucker, "The Beginnings of Verse, 1610–1808," *The Cambridge History of American Literature*, New York, 1917, I, 181; the poem is dated "1770" in *Poems* (1786), p. 18.

34. See Gay Wilson Allen, *American Prosody*, New York, 1935, pp. 2 ff., for an analysis of Freneau's prosody in this and other poems.

35. Dated 1770 in *Poems* (1786), p. 13; but in *Poems* (1795), p. 23, and (1809), I, 42, dated 1769.

36. Dated 1770 in *Poems* (1786), p. 23.

37. The works of John Locke were in the library at Nassau Hall (see *Princeton University Library. American Library Association Visit, June 16, 1916*, pp. 26–28), and among Freneau's college books was W. B. Martin's *Philosophia Britannia, or a New and Comprehensive System of the Newtonian Philosophy* (see the appendix of the present volume).

38. Woodbridge Riley, *American Philosophy: The Early Schools*, New York, 1907, p. 227.

39. William Butler Yeats in the introduction to *Bishop Berkeley, His Life, Writings, and Philosophy*, by J. H. Hone and M. M. Rossi, London, 1931, p. xxiii; see also Herbert M. Morais, *Deism in Eighteenth Century America*, New York, 1934, pp. 54–56.

40. See "Reflections on the Constitution, or Frame of Nature," *Poems* (1809), I, 262, and "On the Universality and other Attributes of Nature," *Poems* (1815), I, 99.

41. An excellently concise statement of the influence on Freneau of contemporary doctrine and literary tradition will be found in Harry Hayden Clark's introduction to the *Poems of Freneau*, New York [1929].

42. Moses Coit Tyler, *The Literary History of the American Revolution*, New York, 1897, I, 180. For further evidence of Freneau's turning from his earlier eighteenth-century English models in composing this poem, see Thomas P. Haviland, "A Measure for the Early Freneau's Debt to Milton," *Publications of the Modern Language Association of America*, LV, 1033–40 (December, 1940).

43. *Lamia, Isabella, The Eve of St. Agnes, and Other Poems*, London, 1820, p. 122.

44. MS *Madison Papers*, I, 13 (July 23, 1770).

45. Collins, *Witherspoon*, I, 119.

46. *Ibid.*, p. 141.

47. *Notes and Queries*, 5th ser., VI, 81 (July 29, 1876).

48. Henry Clay Cameron, "History of the American Whig Society," *Addresses and Proceedings at the Celebration of the One Hundredth Anniversary of the Founding of the American Whig Society*, Princeton, 1871, pp. 6–23 and 46–141.

49. See note 30 above.

50. MS "Satires against the Tories," pp. 23–24.

51. MS "Satire I against the tories," lines 7–18; compare "MacSwiggen," *Poems* (1786), pp. 95–100, lines 71–85. For further similarities, compare "Satire II," lines 7–11, with "MacSwiggen," lines 107–10; "Satire II," lines 125–29, with "MacSwiggen," lines 125–29, and "Satire III," lines 25–26, with "MacSwiggen," lines 23–24.

52. See Joseph M. Beatty, Jr., "Churchill and Freneau," *American Literature*, II, 127–28 (May, 1930).

53. MS "Satire II," lines 7–16.

54. MS "Satire III," lines 9–14.

55. *A Poem on the Rising Glory of America*, Philadelphia, 1772, pp. 20–21.

56. *Ibid.*, p. 19.

57. A complete program of the commencement exercises is found in the *Pennsylvania Gazette*, October 3, 1771, and in MacLean, *History of the College*, I, 312–13; see also the MS *Minutes of the Board of Trustees of the College of New Jersey*, September 25, 1771, in which "Philip Fresneau" is listed as one of the graduating class.

58. H. M. Brackenridge's "Biographical Notice" in *Modern Chivalry*, Philadelphia, 1856, p. 153.

59. The poem was first published in 1772 at Philadelphia. When Freneau republished his own share, with modifications and additions, in the *Poems* (1786), pp. 42–58, he explained: "This poem is a little altered from the original . . . such parts being only inserted here as were written by the author of this volume. A few more modern lines toward the conclusion are incorporated with the rest, being a supposed prophetical anticipation of subsequent events." Pattee in *Poems*, I, 49–84, prints both versions.

60. *A Poem on the Rising Glory of America*, p. 24.

CHAPTER THREE

1. MS *Monmouth County Deeds*, R. 449.

2. MS *Marriage Bonds*, Secretary of State of New Jersey, K, 364.

3. *Loc. cit.*, p. 365; a MS duplicate of the agreement is owned by Miss Edna M. Netter, Freehold, New Jersey.

4. MS *Croes Papers*, Rutgers University Library. James Kearny's will was made in 1768, the codicil added November 3, 1772, probated August 16, 1773.

5. Samuel E. Forman, *The Political Activities of Philip Freneau, Johns Hopkins University Studies in Historical and Political Science*, XX, 13 (September–October, 1902) ; see, also, Austin, *Freneau*, p. 82. The MS Hammell notes report, "He would have prepared the Law but his Mother persuaded him to comply with the wishes of his Father [to prepare for the ministry]." There is a persistent tradition among Freneau descendants that Philip read law. Whether it was this time or later cannot be determined, nor does it seem particularly important; see note 40 below.

6. "The Miserable Life of a Pedagogue," *The American Village*, New York, 1772, p. 22.

7. Edmund D. Fisher, *Flatbush Past and Present*, New York, 1902, p. 51–52.

8. MS *Madison Papers*, I, 17.

9. Collins, *Witherspoon*, I, 112–13.

10. Brackenridge, "Biographical Notice," p. 154.

11. For a description of this and other publications by Freneau, see the bibliography at the end of the present volume.

12. *New-York Journal*, August 10–September 7, 1772.

13. MS *Madison Papers*, I, 17.

14. H. L. Koopman, introduction to *The American Village*, Providence, 1906, p. xii.

15. II, 578–83.

16. A detailed discussion of possible influences of the "choice" school of poetry on Freneau will be found in Ellen Coyne Masters' typescript Master's essay *The American Village* (1935) in the Columbia University Library.

17. James Thomson, *The Complete Poetical Works* (Oxford edition), London, 1908, pp. 177 and 179.

18. *The American Village*, p. 5; Thomson, *Poetical Works*, p. 26.

19. Alexander Pope, "Discourse on Pastoral Poetry," *The Poetical Works* (Globe edition), London, 1930, p. 10.

20. "Windsor Forest," lines 203–204; "The American Village," lines 345–46.

21. "Windsor Forest," line 106; "The American Village," line 4.

22. "Windsor Forest," line 24; "The American Village," line 171.

23. "Windsor Forest," line 26; "The American Village," line 26.

24. "Windsor Forest," lines 44–46; "The American Village," lines 32–34.

25. "Windsor Forest," lines 409–10.

26. *The American Village*, p. 18.

27. *Ibid.*, p. 21.

28. Reprinted as "The Citizen's Resolve. Written 1770" in *Poems* (1786), pp. 32–34; see Koopman, p. xx.

29. *Freeman's Journal*, May 18, 1785; reprinted in *London Morning Herald*, July 12, 1787.

30. Clark, "Literary Influences," p. 13.

31. *City Gazette*, February 12, 1790.

32. Koopman, p. xx.

33. First published in *Poems* (1786), p. 60, where it is dated 1772.

34. Beatty, "Churchill and Freneau," pp. 122–24.

35. *Princeton University Library. American Library Association Visit, June 26, 1916,* p. 28.

36. *Poems* (1786), pp. 61–62; compare "An Essay on Man," Epistles III, IV, and, particularly, Epistle I, lines 99–109.

37. Brackenridge, "Biographical Notice," p. 154. Somerset Academy, or the "Back Creek School," was established in 1767 as a private institution to prepare for college the sons of Presbyterian Maryland and Virginia families. In 1772 the building was enlarged and the number of students considerably increased. During the Revolution the institution was closed, to reopen in 1779 as Washington Academy. See *Maryland Journal*, November 23, 1784; Bernard C. Steiner, *History of Education in Maryland*, Washington, 1894, p. 39 n.; and J. Thomas Scharf, *History of Maryland*, Baltimore, 1879, II, 514 n. For a complete description of the academy two years before Freneau went there, see "Extract of a letter from a Gentleman, on his travels, to a friend in Williamsburg," *Virginia Gazette*, February 23, 1769.

38. MS *Madison Papers*, I, 17.

39. MS *Forman Papers*, New York Historical Society, I, 41.

40. R.F.R., "A Revolutionary Poet. The Life and Writings of Philip Freneau," *New York Evening Post*, April 15, 1893; Austin, *Freneau*, p. 82; Pattee, in *Poems*, I, xxiv; and Forman, *Political Activities*, p. 12. Freneau's residence in Philadelphia at this time is further attested by the MS Hammell notes; by the obituary notice, "Philip Freneau," *New York Mirror*, January 12, 1833; and by Rufus W. Griswold, *The Poets and Poetry of America*, Philadelphia, 1842, p. 1. The suggestion in the two latter sources that Freneau was at this time associated with Francis Hopkinson is probably, however, an attempt by Freneau's partisans to clear the poet of radical stigma by linking his name with one so eminently respectable as Hopkinson. Professor George E. Hastings, Hopkinson's biographer, informs me (1938) that he has never been able to find evidence of association between the two at this period. In fact, Hopkinson's growing Federalist sympathies led him heartily to disapprove of the boisterous republicanism exhibited by Freneau a few years later (see p. 121 below).

41. R.F.R., "Philip Freneau," p. 13. No record of the *Mary Howe* is found among the newspaper reports of New York or Philadelphia custom house entries for this period. The vessel may have belonged to the port of Amboy or Middletown Point in New Jersey, of which records are few and equally silent. "R.F.R.," however, writes with authority, apparently had access to family records, and mentions facts unknown to other biographers of his time.

42. *Works*, VIII, 228; see the appendix of the present volume.

43. Dated "Anno 1774" in *Poems* (1795), p. 63. The poem was first printed in the *Miscellaneous Works* (1788), pp. 1–30; when reprinted in 1795 and in 1809 (I, 105–29), omitted were Pictures II and III, which detailed Columbus's visit to the enchantress and the forecast of the future by means of a magic and prophetic mirror. In the place of these scenes, for the mixture of truth and fiction in which Freneau apologized to his readers in the 1788 printing, only a few lines at the end of Picture I and the beginning of Picture IV were changed to accomplish the necessary transition.

44. *Massachusetts Centinel Extraordinary*, March 24, 1790.

45. Allen, *American Prosody*, p. 2.

46. In the Freneau Collection, Rutgers University Library.

47. P. 109. The Van Pelts were neighboring landowners in Monmouth (see MS *Asher Holmes Papers*, Monmouth County Historical Association, and MS *Monmouth County Deeds*, R. 465); no record, however, of the marriage to which Freneau refers is found among New Jersey archives. Freneau's poem is here transcribed just as it is written in the notebook, except that at the end of line one, stanza two, "O tell" is deleted with a penstroke and "reherse" written in its place.

48. Pp. 58–59; see Gilbert Burnet, *A Discourse on Pastoral Care*, London, 1736, pp. 143–48.

49. P. 61.

50. Pp. 90–108; see Isaac Watts, *Sermons, Discourses, And Essays*, London, 1752, III, 533–34.

51. P. 96.

52. Pp. 66–67.

53. P. 44.

54. P. 48.

55. P. 96.

56. P. 82.

57. P. 113.

58. On the title page of *Meditations among the Tombs*, New York, 1774. Rivington also issued *The Contemplations on Night* and *The Heavenly Reflections on the Beauties of Nature* as separate publications in 1774. "Hervey's Meditations" was among the books Bishop Burnet recommended to candidates for the ministry.

59. P. 117; compare *Contemplations on the Night*, New York, 1774, pp. 24 and 36.

60. P. 117.

61. P. 115.

62. P. 113.

63. MS *Bradford Papers*, Historical Society of Pennsylvania, October 17, 1774.

64. "Recollections of Past Times and Events, No. II," *True American*, July 27, 1822; see note 41 of chapter XII. No paper entitled *The American Whig* is found for the years 1773–74; however, late in 1769 and "during the whole of 1770, a periodical paper under the signature of the *American Whig* made its weekly appearance" (Thomas Jones, *History of New York during the Revolutionary War, and of the Leading Events in the Other Colonies at that Period*, ed. Edward Floyd DeLancey, New York, 1879, I, 19). Published in New York by John Holt in 1768 and again in 1769 was *A Collection of Tracts from the late Newspapers, &c. Containing particularly the American Whig*. Printed on half-sheets, the collection contained partisan essays and poems. It may be, therefore, that Freneau contributed to a continuation of these papers, copies of which are now, as he suggested, "long since forgotten, and perhaps shot away in cartridges during the Revolutionary war."

65. "Recollections of Past Times and Events, No. IV," *True American*, August 17, 1822. "At this time the Asia Ship of War of 63 guns was stationed before the city. She was then under the command of *George Vandepot*, Esq., a violent Englishman, who on the 8th of August following discharged several broadsides into the Town, and then hauled off to Gibbet Island" (Freneau's note).

66. See Allen French, *The First Year of the Revolution*, New York, 1934, pp. 277–79 and 290–92.

67. Although dated "New York, Sept. 26, 1775" in *Poems* (1786), p. 66, the poem was said to be written "New York, June 1775" when reprinted in *Poems* (1809), I, 161, which was, said Freneau, "the first edition I have in reality attended to" (MS *Jefferson Papers*, Library of Congress, 2d ser., XXXIV, 154).

68. See Vernon Louis Parrington, *The Colonial Mind: Main Currents in American*

Thought, New York, 1927, pp. 372–73; Forman, *Political Activities,* p. 17; and Tyler, *Literary History,* I, 424.

69. *A Voyage to Boston,* New York, 1775, p. 24.

70. The advertisement ran for five weeks, July 2–27, 1775. The poem, a twelve page pamphlet, was apparently hurriedly printed; a copy in the Brown University Library contains (Freneau's?) autograph corrections on nearly every page.

71. Found to be "in the style of Freneau's earlier verse" (Victor Hugo Paltsits, *A Bibliography of the Works of Philip Freneau,* New York, 1903, p. 25), is a broadside of forty-eight lines, *The Last Words, Dying Speech, and Confession of J—s R—g—n, P—t—r, who was executed at New Brunswick, in the Province of New Jersey, on the Thirteenth Day of April, 1775. Supposed to be written by himself the Night preceeding the Day of his Execution.* Though written in the taunting manner of Freneau's later satires and in title reminiscent of "Spring's Soliloquy that morning before he hung himself," composed by one of the members of the collegiate American Whig Society, the poem has only the dubious distinction of "sounding like Freneau" (who we have seen sounded, in turn, like a great many poets from England) ; Freneau never reprinted the poem, nor did he, which is perhaps more significant, ever incorporate any of it in subsequent satires on the Tory printers. *Tom Gage's Proclamation* is also found "in the style of Freneau's verse" (Paltsits, p. 27). Printed first in the *Pennsylvania Journal,* June 28, 1775; reprinted in the *New-York Journal,* July 13, the *Connecticut Courant,* July 17, and as a small folio broadside dated "New York, June 30, 1775," the latter poem has been erroneously attributed to, among others, John Trumbull (see Annie Russell Marble, *Heralds of American Literature,* Chicago, 1907, p. 69). There seems little evidence which allows attribution of either poem to Freneau.

72. See Joseph Sabin, *Bibliotheca Americana,* New York, 1885, XV, 446. Of the second edition only one copy has been found (in the Brown University Library) ; mutilated and wanting a title page, it is more carefully printed than the first, and is corrected according to the autograph notations in the Brown University copy of the earlier edition (see note 70 above).

73. P. 3.

74. Pp. 11–12.

75. Reprinted in *Poems* (1786), pp. 67–71, the poem was said to have been "published in New York, by *H. Gaine,* in August 1775." No copy of the 1775 printing is found, but a transcript in Freneau's hand (Library Company of Philadelphia, Ridgeway Branch) also notes that the poem was "Printed in New York, August, 1775."

76. Reprinted in *Poems* (1809), I, 167–78, as "The Expedition of Timothy Taurus, Astrologer, to the Falls of the Passaick River, in New Jersey: Written soon after an excursion to the village at that place in August 1775 . . . and formerly printed in New-York." No trace of the original printing, as a separate publication or as a contribution to a newspaper, has been found.

77. *New-York Gazette,* October 9, 1775.

78. In this, as in all following instances of the first appearance of Freneau's writings in a newspaper or periodical, see the bibliography at the end of the present volume for subsequent printings and changes in title.

79. *Constitutional Gazette,* October 21–November 28, 1775.

80. November 28, 1775; see also the *Pennsylvania Gazette,* November 15 and 22, and the *Pennsylvania Ledger,* November 18–December 16, 1775.

81. A copy of the *Confession* owned by the Library Company of Philadelphia contains Freneau's autograph notation: "By Gaine, Published October 25: 1775."

82. When printed in *Poems* (1786), pp. 88–94, "Female Frailty," a light and satirical attack on the faithlessness of young ladies whose lovers were called to the war, was dated November, 1775. Also said to be written in 1775 was "The Distrest Shepherdess" (*Miscellaneous Works,* pp. 166–67), which Pattee, in *Poems,* I, 195, suggests is an

earlier version of the former poem. According to the roughly chronological arrangement of the first collected edition of Freneau's poems, the composition of the following also belongs to this period: "The Prayer of Orpheus" (pp. 28–29) ; "The Dying Elm" (p. 38— see also the *United States Magazine*, June, 1779) ; the "Epitaph of Peter Abelard" (pp. 36–37) ; "Retirement," (p. 59) ; "The Desolate Academy" (pp. 82–83) ; "The Sea-Faring Bachelor" (pp. 83–84) ; and "The Vernal Ague" (pp. 86–87).

83. See Cooper's *The Patriots of North America*, New York, 1775.

84. "MacSwiggen," *Poems* (1786), p. 95; when reprinted in *Poems* (1809), II, 22, the satire was said to be "First written, and published 1775."

85. *A Voyage to Boston*, p. 6; see Pattee, in *Poems*, I, 161 n.

86. *American Liberty*, pp. 5 and 7; see Pattee, in *Poems*, I, 143 and 145.

87. *A Voyage to Boston*, p. 23; see Pattee, in *Poems*, I, 181–82 n.

88. "MacSwiggen," *Poems* (1786), pp. 99–100.

89. *Ibid.*

CHAPTER FOUR

1. MS *Alexander Anderson's Diary, for the Year 1794*, Columbia University Library, p. 101.

2. MS pension application W.23069, Veteran's Administration, Washington, D. C.

3. *Poems* (1795), p. 436.

4. *American Liberty*, p. 9.

5. *Ibid.*

6. *A Voyage to Boston*, p. 5.

7. MS *Monmouth County Deeds*, K, 16.

8. Freneau's copy of John Robertson, *The Elements of Navigation* (see the appendix of the present volume) is autographed "David Watson, Sept. 20th 1775" and "Philip Freneau, 1776."

9. MS Hammell notes, p. 7.

10. Forman, *Political Activities*, p. 20.

11. "Account of the Island of Santa Cruz," *United States Magazine*, I, 83 (February, 1779).

12. Though critics have assigned it to the dreamy atmosphere of the Caribbean (see Clark, in *Poems*, p. xvii), there is reason to believe that "The House of Night" was written in 1775, before Freneau's departure for the West Indies. Freneau placed the poem in his collected editions between "MacSwiggen," the valedictory to the paper wars in New York, and "The Jamaica Funeral," which definitely belongs to the later period. "The House of Night" is redolent of the heavy atmosphere which characterized the period of theological study. "Coffins, shrouds, and horrors of a tomb" sung "midst grief in exstacy of woe run mad" remind us of the morbid moralizing of Freneau's "*Innuenda Sermonibus*" and of Hervey's *Meditations* which had been recommended to the student of divinity. More immediate sources of somber inspiration are suggested by Freneau's references in the poem to treatises on death by William Sherlock and Charles Drelincourt. "The House of Night," moreover, seems to spring from a period of intense concern with books; Clark, "The Literary Influences," p. 31, has successfully stormed the "impregnable citadel of originality" which had been built about the poem to expose it as compounded of elements borrowed from Sackville, Gray, Blair, and Young. Finally, it is difficult to neglect the evidence presented in the final stanza of the poem as it was printed in the *United States Magazine*, I, 362 (August, 1779) :

> Enough—when God and nature give the word
> I'll tempt the dusky shore and narrow sea:
> Content to die, just as it is decreed,
> At four score years, or now at twenty-three.

If Freneau had meant twenty-four, he could easily have managed it by reversing the last two phrases of the second line.

13. *United States Magazine*, I, 359 (August, 1779).

14. This and other descriptive passages quoted above are from Freneau's "Account of the Island of Santa Cruz," pp. 81–84.

15. "The Hermit of Saba," dated 1776 in *Poems* (1809), I, 179–86.

16. "The Jamaica Funeral," *Poems* (1786), p. 131.

17. "Account of the Island of Santa Cruz," p. 88.

18. *Ibid.*

19. *Ibid.*, pp. 81–84.

20. MS record of voyages, written by Freneau on the flyleaf of vol. III of his *Pub. Ovidii Nasonis Opera Omnia* (see the appendix of the present volume) ; hereafter designated "record of voyages, *Ovid*."

21. "Account of the Island of St. James; in a Letter to Mr. A. A.," *United States Magazine*, I, 124 (March, 1779).

22. MS record of voyages, *Ovid*.

23. MS record of voyages written by Freneau on the flyleaf of vol. I of John Robertson's *The Elements of Navigation* (see the appendix of the present volume) ; hereafter designated "record of voyages, *Navigation*."

24. The MS Hammell notes, p. 6, tell us that Freneau "wrote many pieces of poetry . . . to Amanda an amiable young Lady, the Governor of Bermuda's daughter at whose Fathers house he remained six months [weeks?]." The Governor of Bermuda at this time was George James Breure, an irascible man who looked on all Americans as "mere rebels" (Wilfred Brinton Kerr, *Bermuda and the American Revolution*, Princeton, 1936, p. 40). He was loyal and conscientious, and fought zealously to keep the islanders faithful to the Ministerial cause. Little can be discovered of the governor's fourteen children—Freneau observed that an excessive diet of fish, together with the "great salubrity of the air," made Bermudians very prolific ("Account of Some of the West Indian Islands," *United States Magazine*, I, 32, January, 1779). Two of Breure's sons served in the British army under General Gage at Boston, one being killed in action at Bunker Hill. It does not seem, therefore, that the governor would have welcomed as a house guest Philip Freneau, the author of *A Voyage to Boston* and *American Liberty*.

One of Breure's daughters married Captain Pendock Neale, master of a British privateer and notorious for his depredations on American shipping. Breure's oldest daughter, Frances, however, was the wife of Henry Tucker, whose family was prominent in island affairs and sympathetic to America. Tucker's brothers, Thomas Tudor of Charleston and St. George of Virginia, made no secret of their approval of the colonial rebellion (Thomas Addiss Emmet, *Account of the Tucker Family*, New York, 1898, pp. 3–4). Another brother, Nathaniel (whose poem *The Bermudian* had been printed in 1774), left the island to study medicine shortly before Freneau's arrival. The former's sister-in-law, Frances Breure Tucker, is said to have been fond of listening to Nathaniel as he read from his own verse, recited passages from Gray or Goldsmith, or talked eloquently of belles-lettres (Kerr, pp. 15–33). May not Frances, then, have been the unfortunate "Amanda" of whom Freneau wrote, and may not Nathaniel Tucker have been playfully transformed by a new rival for her literary affections into the absent lover for whom she mourned? There is no evidence among the parish papers of Bermuda or among the Tucker family papers to support this supposition. The Bermuda episode is clothed heavily in darkness; yet the evidence of the MS Hammell notes which, often erring in particulars, are usually correct in broader outline, must not be neglected.

We must, however, be wary of attributing to this period every poem which Freneau subsequently addressed to "Amanda." As grouped in *Poems* (1809), I, 235–40, the "Amanda" pieces undoubtedly contain some autobiographical reference, but fact and fancy have been so intertwined that it is impossible to separate them. Although "On

Amanda's Singing Bird" (I, 235–36) is elsewhere dated 1778 (see note 25 below), the next poem, "Florio to Amanda" (I, 236–38), was first "addressed to Miss ——, New Jersey" (*Daily Advertiser*, April 15, 1789). "The Fair Solitary" (I, 238–39) was included in *Poems* (1795), p. 293, as "The Mourning Nun." "Amanda in a Consumption" (I, 239–40) was first entitled "On a Young Lady in a Consumption" (*Freeman's Journal*, February 7, 1787), then included in "Light Summer Reading," *Miscellaneous Works*, pp. 259–60, as "To Marcia" and in *Poems* (1795), p. 259, as "Marcella in a Consumption." Freneau used old poems freely to fit new situations.

25. Dated "Bermuda, 1778" in *Freeman's Journal*, July 3, 1782.

26. "Light Summer Reading," pp. 251–65.

27. *Ibid.*, pp. 262–63.

28. MS record of voyages, *Navigation*.

29. *American Independence, an Everlasting Deliverance from British Tyranny*, Philadelphia, 1778, p. 123.

30. "America Independent," *Poems* (1786), p. 154.

31. *American Independence*, p. 124.

32. MS pension application.

33. *Official Register of the Officers and Men of New Jersey in the Revolutionary War*, compiled under orders of Theodore F. Randolph, Governor, by William S. Stryker, Adjutant General, Trenton, 1872, p. 465.

34. MS pension application.

35. "To the Dog Sancho," *Poems* (1809), I, 260–61.

36. *Pennsylvania Magazine*, June 8, 1779, p. 3.

37. Facsimile broadside in Sidney G. Fisher's *The Struggle for Independence*, Philadelphia, 1908, II, 252.

38. *Poems* (1786), pp. 169–71. This, and the next two poems mentioned, though apparently not published at the time, belong in spirit and in relation to the events which they celebrate to the period of Freneau's military and naval service.

39. See the Philadelphia *Independent Chronicle*, August 13, 1778; Freneau's poem was first published in the *New-Jersey Gazette*, December 13, 1780.

40. Dated 1778 in *Poems* (1809), I, 223.

41. MS record of voyages, *Ovid*.

42. MS log, Freneau Collection, Rutgers University Library.

43. MS record of voyages, *Ovid*.

44. MS pension application.

45. MS log, Freneau Collection.

46. MS *Asher Holmes Papers*, Monmouth County Historical Association, Box I.

47. *New-York Gazette*, January 3, 1780.

48. See *New-Jersey Journal*, January 11, 1780; and *New-Jersey Gazette*, January 26, 1780.

49. MS pension application.

50. MS *Madison Papers*, XVIII, 51 (May 20, 1795).

51. September, 1779, p. 402.

52. When Freneau reprinted "The House of Night" in *Poems* (1786), pp. 101–23, he expanded the poem from 73 to 136 quatrains. The last six stanzas of the first printing were deleted, and the ending made less subjective. In subsequent editions Freneau changed the title to "The Vision of Night" and left only a fragment of twenty-one stanzas; see *Poems* (1795), pp. 92–94, and (1809), I, 145–47. The rejected portions were used in "The Hessian Debarkation," *Poems* (1795), p. 215, and (1809) I, 205–6, and (with fragments from "The Jamaica Funeral") in "The Sexton's Sermon at the Burial of a Deist," *Poems* (1809), I, 150–52; see Pattee, in *Poems*, III, 122 n.

53. Frank Moore, *Songs and Ballads of the American Revolution*, New York, 1856, p. 259; I have found no trace of this broadside publication.

54. "Remarks for August, in a Conversation of Ladies," *United States Magazine*, I, 406 (December, 1779).

55. MS pension application.

56. *Royal Gazette*, May 31, 1780.

57. MS *The British Prison-Ship*, Freneau Collection, Rutgers University Library.

58. MS record of voyages, *Ovid*. In spite of Freneau's later protestations to the contrary, it is fairly evident that he did ship as an officer on the *Aurora:* he had his volumes of Robertson's *Navigation* with him, autographed "Philip Freneau 1780—Ship Aurora"; see the appendix of the present volume.

59. MS *Some Account of the Capture of the Ship Aurora*, Freneau Collection.

60. *Ibid.*

61. *The British Prison-Ship*, Philadelphia, 1781, p. 8.

62. MS *Some Account of the Capture*.

63. "The Autobiography of Major Samuel S. Forman," *Historical Magazine*, new ser., VI, 322 (December, 1869).

64. MS *Some Account of the Aurora*.

65. *The British Prison-Ship*, p. 3.

66. See notes 57 and 59 above.

67. *Pennsylvania Packet*, September 30, 1780.

68. MS of Act I–Act III, Sc. 2, and the first lines of Sc. 3 (see Pattee, in *Poems*, II, 39–70) is in the Freneau Collection, Rutgers University Library; one sheet of the MS, containing parts of Sc. 3 and 4, Act III (see Pattee, II, 70–72), is in the Princeton University Library. Paltsits, *Bibliography*, p. 39, mentions a fragment containing lines of Act IV and Sc. 1 of Act V, which "passed into the hands of a collector through Dodd, Mead and Co." Dodd, Mead and Company have (1938) no record of the transaction, nor have I been able to find trace of the fragment.

69. Freneau's MS note on the flyleaf of the *Essay* (see the appendix of the present volume).

CHAPTER FIVE

1. *Freeman's Journal*, April 25, 1781.

2. MS pension application.

3. Pattee, in *Poems*, I, xxxv.

4. In Freneau's annotated file of the *Freeman's Journal*, April 25, 1781–February 9, 1785 (New Jersey Historical Society Library), in addition to an index on the flyleaf of the issues of the newspaper in which his contributions appear, each article and poem by Freneau is either checked or initialed "P. F." There is, of course, room for suspicion that all items checked in this file are not by Freneau; see Philip M. Marsh, "Philip Freneau's Personal File of the Freeman's Journal," *Proceedings of the New Jersey Historical Society*, LVII, 163–70 (July, 1939). But because many so marked are included in his collected editions, I have assumed in the following discussion that, except those which Marsh, p. 166, otherwise identifies, all contributions checked or initialed are Freneau's; for those which Freneau did reprint and for changes of title upon subsequent appearances, see the bibliography at the end of the present volume.

5. August 15, 1781.

6. *Freeman's Journal*, August 28, 1781.

7. September 5, 1781.

8. *Freeman's Journal*, September 5, 1781.

9. *Ibid.*

10. *Freeman's Journal*, October 24, 1781.

11. Evert A. and George L. Duyckinck, *Cyclopædia of American Literature*, New York, 1865, I, 335.

12. In the introduction to the third canto of *Marmion*, the apostrophe to the Duke of Brunswick reads:

> Lamented Chief!—not thine the power
> To save in that presumptuous hour,
> When Prussia hurried to the field
> And snatched the spear but left the shield.

13. *Massachusetts Centinel*, July 13, 1789.
14. See the bibliography at the end of the present volume.
15. *Pennsylvania Packet*, November 10, 1781.
16. *Royal Gazette*, March 2, 1782.
17. J. Thomas Scharf and Thompson Westcott, *History of Philadelphia, 1609–1884*, Philadelphia, 1884, I, 422 n.
18. July 3, 1782.
19. January 2, 1782.
20. January 23, 1782.
21. "Plato the Philosopher to his Friend Theon."
22. "The Pilgrim, No. I," November 21, 1782.
23. *Ibid.*
24. *Ibid.*, No. II, November 28, 1781.
25. *Ibid.*, No. V, December 19, 1781.
26. *Ibid.*, No. II.
27. *Ibid.*, No. VII, January 2, 1782.
28. *A Voyage to Boston*, p. 23.
29. "The Pilgrim, No. II."
30. *Ibid.*, No. I.
31. *Ibid.*, No. VIII, January 9, 1782.
32. *Ibid.*, No. VI, December 26, 1781.
33. *Ibid.*, No. IV, December 12, 1781.
34. *Ibid.*, No. IX, January 16, 1782.
35. *Ibid.*, No. XIX, August 14, 1782.
36. *Ibid.*, No. IX.
37. *Ibid.*
38. *Ibid.*, No. XIV, May 8, 1782.
39. *Ibid.*
40. *Ibid.*, No. III, December 5, 1781.
41. *Ibid.*, No. XVII, June 19, 1782.
42. *Ibid.*, No. XI, January 30, 1782.
43. *Ibid.*, No. III.
44. *Ibid.*, No. XII, February 13, 1782.
45. *Ibid.*, No. XI, January 30, 1782.
46. *Ibid.*, No. XII.
47. *Ibid.*, No. VI.
48. *Ibid.*, No. VIII.
49. *Ibid.*, No. XVI, June 19, 1782.
50. *Ibid.*, No. VI.
51. See Burton Alva Konkle, *George Bryan and the Constitution of Pennsylvania*, Philadelphia, 1922, pp. 219 ff.
52. See the *Freeman's Journal*, March 26, 1783.
53. "To Those Whom it May Concern," *Freeman's Journal*, September 25, 1782.
54. George E. Hastings, *The Life and Works of Francis Hopkinson*, Chicago, 1926, p. 377.
55. *Ibid.*
56. September 7, 1782.

57. December 14, 1782.

58. December 4, 1782.

59. December 4, 1782.

60. *Independent Gazetteer*, October 19, 1782.

61. Throughout all the series of attacks which Freneau directed against him during 1782, Rivington displayed a calmness and apparent good nature which makes his opponent's perseverance often seem unnecessarily harsh. When the first part of "Rivington's Reflexions" appeared, the loyalist printer inserted it in the *Royal Gazette* for December 14 with the following introduction: "Mr. Rivington having been applied to by many Gentlemen for a pleasant Publication respecting himself, exhibited in the Philadelphia Freeman's Journal . . . takes leave to copy it into this Day's Gazette, and assures the Author that a Column shall at anytime be most cheerfully reserved to convey that Gentleman's lively Lucubrations to the Public."

62. *Calendar of the John Paul Jones Manuscripts in the Library of Congress*, Washington, 1903, p. 242; see also Fred Lewis Pattee, "Philip Freneau as a Postal Clerk," *American Literature*, IV, 61–62 (March, 1932).

63. "The Belknap Letters," *Collections of the Massachusetts Historical Society*, 5th ser., II, 186 and 199.

64. Rufus W. Griswold, "Philip Freneau, the Poet of the Revolution," *Graham's Magazine*, XLVII, 197 (September, 1855). Freneau thought no more highly of Hopkinson. On p. 123 of his copy of Humphreys's *An Essay on the Life of the Honourable Major-General Israel Putnam* (see the appendix of the present volume) Freneau identifies Hopkinson's "Battle of the Kegs" by writing in the margin, "Song by Francis Fiddlestick."

65. Never included by Freneau in any of his collected editions, but very much in his manner of writing is the unsigned poem "Lines formerly Addressed to Mr. Peter Markoe, the Philadelphia Poet, upon Hearing he had Got a New Coat," which appeared during Freneau's residence in New York in the *Daily Advertiser*, February 18, 1790, and during Freneau's residence in Charleston in the *City Gazette*, January 11, 1790.

66. William McCulloch, "Additions to Thomas's History of Printing," *Proceedings of the American Antiquarian Society*, new ser., XXXI, 232 (April, 1921).

67. See the appendix of the present volume.

68. Both of these translations are marked in Freneau's personal file of the *Freeman's Journal* (see note 4 above).

69. Peter Freneau to Philip Freneau, January 9, 1783 (MS owned by Mr. Edmund S. Freneau, Summit, New Jersey).

70. "Lines Occasioned by the Death of Mr. Robert Bell," *Freeman's Journal*, February 28, 1787.

71. The *New Travels* was advertised in the *Pennsylvania Gazette*, July 30–August 27, in the *Freeman's Journal*, July 30–August 6, and was listed among other publications for sale at Bell's bookshop in the *Pennsylvania Packet*, September 27, 1783.

72. "Belknap Letters," p. 259.

73. *New Travels*, p. 28 n.

74. *Ibid.*, p. iii.

75. September 3, 1783.

76. *Freeman's Journal*, December 10, 1783.

77. McCulloch, *op. cit.*, p. 226.

78. See Pattee, in *Poems*, II, 242 n.

CHAPTER SIX

1. MS record of voyages, *Ovid*.

2. Peter Marsden, *An Account of the Island of Jamaica*, Newcastle, 1788, p. 13.

See also the *Pennsylvania Gazette*, September 15, and the *South Carolina Gazette*, September 4, 1784.

3. *Freeman's Journal*, August 20, 1788.

4. *Freeman's Journal*, April 13, 1785.

5. *Columbian Herald*, February 2, 1786.

6. "The Island Field Negro," *Daily Advertiser*, February 1, 1791.

7. *Daily Advertiser*, April 20, 1791.

8. *Ibid.*, February 1, 1791.

9. *Ibid.*

10. MS record of voyages, *Navigation*.

11. *Ibid.* See *Pennsylvania Herald*, November 14, 1784.

12. See the bibliography at the end of the present volume.

13. MS *Franklin Papers*, American Philosophical Society, XXI, 185.

14. MS letter to Thomas Jefferson, March 31, 1784, *Jefferson Papers*, Library of Congress, X, 1656.

15. *Independent Gazetteer*, July 12, 1784.

16. MS letter, February 18, 1784, from the collection of Edmund Hopkinson, Esq.; quoted in Hastings, *Life of Hopkinson*, p. 336.

17. MS Mathew Carey correspondence, Lea and Febiger Collection, Historical Society of Pennsylvania, XII, 2407. Patrick Rice was a job printer in Philadelphia as early as 1777 (Joseph Carson's MS account book, Historical Society of Pennsylvania, Am. 9531). He later entered partnership with his brother Henry Rice, who in 1785 was of the firm Spottswood and Rice, with a shop on Market Street (MS Lea and Febiger Collection, VII, 422; VIII, 431; and XI, 2690). The *Philadelphia Directory* for 1785 does not list Patrick Rice, nor is his name found in any newspaper of the period as an independent printer or bookseller. He probably worked for his brother, whose firm at this time was associated with Carey in the publishing of Abbé Mably's *Remarks Concerning the Government and the Laws of the United States*. In the preparation of this work, translated from the French, Freneau could have given valuable assistance.

18. Note to "The Invalid" in *Poems* (1809), II, 211. In the *City Gazette*, February 9, 1788, the poem is said to have been "written in 1785," and in the *Daily Advertiser*, May 26, 1791, to have been written at Charleston.

19. "Extract of a Letter from a Gentleman at the Healing Springs, Pacolet River," *Columbian Herald*, October 17, 1785. Possibly this letter, which gives highest recommendation to the mineral waters for the cure they have effected on the writer, was by Freneau, who was in Charleston at this time. See, also, Robert Mills, *Statistics of South Carolina*, Charleston, 1826, p. 14.

20. See note 18 above. Also perhaps by Freneau was the "Ode Addressed to the Nymph of Pacelot Spring; by a Young Gentleman, whose Mistress was Recovered from a Dangerous Disease by the Efficacy of its Waters," which appeared, signed "Corydon," in the *Columbian Herald*, September 26, 1785.

21. "The Prospects of America," *The Literary Remains of Joseph Brown Ladd*, New York, 1832, pp. 34–35.

22. *Independent Gazetteer*, October 19, 1782.

23. *Freeman's Journal*, July 8, 1789.

24. MS record of voyages, *Navigation*; see *Columbian Herald*, January 9, 1786.

25. "The Departure (Written at Leaving Sandy Hook on a Voyage to the West Indies)," *Freeman's Journal*, April 18, 1787. The poem is dated November 26, 1785, and was, therefore, written at sea; but Freneau was evidently mistaken in thus later assigning the composition to a voyage to the West Indies, for one week later he landed at Charleston.

26. *Charleston Evening Post*, December 9, and *Columbian Herald*, January 9–19, 1785.

27. Written by Freneau on the margin of p. 166 of his volume of Rousseau; see the appendix of the present volume.

28. *Charleston Evening Post*, January 21 and February 6, 1786.

29. *Columbian Herald*, February 16; *City Gazette*, February 20–March 1; *Charleston Evening Post*, March 1; and *Daily Advertiser*, March 24, 1786.

30. *Columbian Herald*, October 26, 1786, *et seq.*

31. MS *James Muir's, Book Binder, Ledger, 1782–1795*, Historical Society of Pennsylvania, Am. 9119.

32. MS *Jefferson Papers*, 2d ser., XXXIV, 134, May 27, 1809.

33. MS record of voyages, *Navigation.*

34. *Pennsylvania Packet*, July 24, 1786.

35. *Port Folio*, IV, 352 (November 28, 1807).

36. *Daily Advertiser*, July 20, 1786.

37. *Ibid.*, October 11, 1786.

38. Bailey published Swedenborg's *Summary View of the Heavenly Doctrines of the New Jerusalem Church* in 1787, after running proposals irregularly from September 13, 1785. Also appearing in the newspaper since the beginning of the year was a series of advertisements for Ramsay's *History of the Revolution in South Carolina*, published by Isaac Collins in Trenton, but for sale at Bailey's bookstore. That Freneau's poem was used by at least one other printer to advertise the book is attested by the fact that when the poem was reprinted in the *New-Jersey Journal*, November 6, 1786, the editor of that paper noted: "Several copies of this History may be had of the Printer."

39. *Pennsylvania Journal*, April 4–July 7; *Independent Gazetteer*, April 4–5; *Pennsylvania Packet*, April 4–11; and *Pennsylvania Gazette*, April 4–11, 1787.

40. *Independent Journal*, May 5–19, 1787.

41. *Charleston Morning Post*, May 20–26, 1787.

42. *Columbian Herald*, June 7, 1787.

43. First published in the *Miscellaneous Works*, pp. 170–71.

44. "The Seasons Moralized," *Charleston Morning Post*, August 9, 1786, and "The Royal Adventurer," *State Gazette of South Carolina*, November 9, 1786. "The Progress of Balloons" appeared in the *Charleston Morning Post*, August 3, 1786, as "From a collection of poems written by Mr. Philip Freneau, and lately published in Philadelphia," and "Stanzas Occasioned by the Departure of the British from Charleston" in the *Columbian Herald*, August 7, 1786, "From Freneau's Poems." Most of the newspaper reprints in Charleston and other cities along the Atlantic seaboard, however, were apparently poems copied from the *Freeman's Journal*, rather than from the edition of 1786.

45. *Connecticut Courant*, June 25, 1787.

46. "Columbus to Ferdinand" appeared on pp. 362–64 and "Verses Occasioned by General Washington's Arrival in Philadelphia" on pp. 368–71 of the *Grammatical Institute of the English Language*, Part III, Philadelphia, 1787.

47. See T. P. Cross, "Joseph Ritson, a Critical Biography," *Studies in Philology*, XV, 59 (August, 1919); and F. E. Farley in *Anniversary Papers by the Colleagues and Pupils of George Lyman Kittredge*, Boston, 1913, pp. 251–60.

48. *Pennsylvania Herald*, August 15, 1787.

49. MS Gratz Collection, Historical Society of Pennsylvania; see C. T. Hallenbeck, "A Note for Future Editors of Freneau's Poems," *American Literature*, IV, 392 (January, 1933).

50. MS Lea and Febiger Collection, XVI, 4214.

51. The Virginia newspaper in which the poem appeared has not been found; see the bibliography at the end of the present volume.

52. James L. Onderdonk, *History of American Verse, 1610–1897*, Chicago, 1901, p. 79.

53. See Pattee, in *Poems*, II, 370 n.

54. MS Lea and Febiger Collection, XVI, 4214. Freneau was in Monmouth on November 13, 1787 (see MS *Monmouth County Deeds*, I, 396).

55. *Columbian Herald*, December 17, 1787.

56. See *Miscellaneous Works*, p. 393.

57. *Columbian Herald*, December 20, and *Gazette of the State of Georgia*, December 27, 1787.

58. *Columbian Herald*, January 3 and 7, 1788.

59. *City Gazette*, January 21, 1788.

60. Louie M. Miner, *Our Rude Forefathers*, Cedar Rapids, 1937, p. 203, says, "A voice very like Freneau's spoke out plainly in Charleston" in opposition to the proposed federal constitution with verses "On the New Constitution," *State Gazette of South Carolina*, January 28, 1788. The poem is in Freneau's manner and he was in Charleston at the time; but Freneau never acknowledged it, nor did he at any other time, so far as I know, submit original poems to the *State Gazette*. All during February verse in the *City Gazette* was more vigorous than usual, but none of it can with surety be attributed to Freneau. From February 25 a series of essays on local affairs appeared in the same newspaper signed "Pilgrim"; they are in no way up to the standard of "The Pilgrim" essays in the *Freeman's Journal* during the Revolution: it is worth noting, however, that one day after the last essay appeared, Freneau sailed from Charleston.

61. *City Gazette*, February 21–26; *Daily Advertiser*, March 24–29; and *State Gazette of South Carolina*, April 24, 1788.

62. The advertisement in the *Freeman's Journal* ran continuously till July 1.

63. Robert Hodge advertised the *Miscellaneous Works in the Daily Advertiser*, May 28–July 12, 22–September 15; in the *Impartial Gazetteer*, May 31–June 21; and in the *New-York Journal*, May 29, 1788–August 6, 1789.

64. *Pennsylvania Mercury*, June 28, 1788.

65. "Advice to Authors," *Miscellaneous Works*, p. 42 n.

66. Pp. 87–91.

67. "Advice to Authors," pp. 42–48.

68. "The Sick Author," pp. 197–98.

69. Pp. 49–53.

70. *City Gazette*, May 5, and *Daily Advertiser*, May 15, 1788.

71. *City Gazette*, June 17, 1788.

72. *City Gazette*, June 26, and *Daily Advertiser*, July 7, 1788.

73. *Freeman's Journal*, August 20, 1788.

74. *Independent Journal*, September 20, 1788.

75. *State Gazette of South Carolina*, November 6, 1788.

76. *Federal Gazette*, December 26, 1788.

77. "Polydore to Amanda," *Daily Advertiser*, February 10, 1791.

78. W. J. Mills, "The Poetic Courtship of Philip Freneau," *Through the Gates of Old Romance*, Philadelphia, 1903, pp. 123–55.

79. *Daily Advertiser*, April 15, 1789.

80. *Maryland Journal*, January 2, 1789.

81. "Stanzas Written at Baltimore, in Maryland, January, 1789," *Freeman's Journal*, January 29, 1789.

82. *Ibid.*, February 6, 1789.

83. *City Gazette*, February 27, and *Georgia Gazette*, March 12, 1789.

84. *Freeman's Journal*, July 8, 1789.

85. *City Gazette*, March 19, April 2–7, 1789.

86. *Ibid.*, April 14, 1789.

87. *Daily Advertiser*, April 24, 1789.

88. *Daily Advertiser*, March 4, and *City Gazette*, March 21, 1789.
89. *City Gazette*, June 1, and *Daily Advertiser*, June 9, 1789.
90. *New-York Daily Gazette*, June 16–18, and *Daily Advertiser*, June 16–19, 1789.
91. *New-York Daily Gazette*, June 23, 1789.
92. "Written at Cape Hatteras, June, 1789," *Daily Advertiser*, September 19, 1790. When he reprinted the poem in the *National Gazette*, March 19, 1792, Freneau dated it "Castle-Island, Bermuda, Jan. 20, 1789." The later attribution is obviously a literary affectation, for the poet was in Baltimore at that time.
93. Said to have been "Written off the cape, July, 1789," when printed in the *Daily Advertiser*, November 14, 1789.
94. *New-York Packet*, August 6, 1789.
95. *Daily Advertiser*, September 5–19, 1789.
96. *City Gazette*, October 6 and 28, 1789.
97. "Stanzas Written at St. Catherines, an Island upon the Coast of Georgia, Nov. 1789, By Captain Freneau," *Daily Advertiser*, January 2, 1790.
98. *City Gazette*, November 25, 1789.
99. *Daily Advertiser*, December 21, 1789–January 9, 1790.
100. See note 41 of chapter XII.
101. Also appearing in the *City Gazette* during Freneau's residence in Charleston are the following contributions, each of which was reprinted in the *Daily Advertiser* (see note 5 of chapter VII) after he moved to New York: a humorous essay on the use of words, December 30, 1789; "Lines formerly Addressed to Mr. Peter Markoe, the Philadelphia Poet, upon Hearing he had Got a New Coat," January 11; and "The Demolish'd Church," February 9, 1790.
102. MS record of voyages, *Navigation*; also see the *City Gazette*, January 29, 1790.
103. *New-York Gazette*, February 12, 1790.

CHAPTER SEVEN

1. *Daily Advertiser*, November 23, 1789.
2. *New-York Magazine*, I, 133 (March, 1790).
3. Thomas E. V. Smith, *The City of New York in the Year of Washington's Inauguration*, New York, 1889, pp. 20–23.
4. *Daily Advertiser*, December 19, 1789.
5. On February 18 the "Lines formerly Addressed to Peter Markoe" appeared over the signature "M."; in the same issue over the same signature, appeared a humorous essay on the origin of words which had been printed in the *City Gazette*, December 30, 1789. When the "Lines Descriptive of a Tavern in Log Town" were contributed by "M." to the *Advertiser* on February 19, they were said to describe a hostelry "in the pine barrens of South Carolina," rather than "in the pine barrens of New Jersey." "The Demolish'd Church" was published in the New York paper on February 20 as "The Ruins of a Country Church"; the stanzas which had been printed without title in the *City Gazette* appeared as "The Bird at Sea" on March 4; and "A Characteristic Sketch of the Long Island Dutch," also March 4, was copied, said the editors, "from a late Charleston paper."
6. March 5, 1790. Though unsigned when first printed and never subsequently collected, the poem is found in an undated (*ca.* 1833) clipping from the *Monmouth Inquirer* (owned by Mrs. George Yates Gilbert, Ridgewood, New Jersey), attributed to the "late Philip Freneau" and introduced with this note: "The following lines were addressed to Miss Fanny Ledyard, sister of the celebrated John Ledyard, and Miss Eleanor Forman, who were detected cutting in scollops the bottom of an old over coat belonging to the author shortly before his marriage." No file of the *Inquirer* for this period has been found.

7. Not collected by Freneau, but unmistakably in his manner; printed in the *City Gazette*, April 13, 1790, as "By Captain Freneau."

8. Affidavit made by Eleanor Freneau, August 7, 1838; filed with the MS pension application.

9. *Heads of Families at the First Census of the United States taken in the United States in the Year 1790, New York*, Washington, 1908, p. 118.

10. MS ledger, 1789–91, New York Society Library, p. 244. Freneau sold his membership to Francis Childs on May 20, 1791. Before that time, he withdrew the following volumes (dates indicate withdrawal and return of the books) : *Political Magazine for 1783*, March 8–19; Tobias Smollet, *Travels through France and Spain*, March 19–April 7; one volume of Etienne Savary, *Letters on Egypt*, April 7–26, and two volumes of the same, April 26–May 21, 1791.

11. "The Country Squire's Exit," April 10, 1790, when reprinted in the *City Gazette*, June 3, 1790, was "Supposed to be written by Capt. Freneau"; "The Origin of Lee Boards," March 16, 1791, when reprinted in the New York *Diary*, November 9, 1797, was said to be "By Philip Freneau." In addition to these poems, and the "Lines Addressed to Some Young Ladies" and the "Epistle to Peter Pindar," already mentioned, the following poems in the *Daily Advertiser*, though never collected by Freneau, are unmistakably in his manner: "A Meditation among Some Old Books Belonging to Capt. Peacock, at Sunbury in Georgia," April 2; "Rhode Island Conversion," June 12; "Lines Addressed to a Dull Country Parson," June 15; "Stanzas . . . Written some Years Ago to a Lady Going to Live in the Western Country," June 18; "On George's Square, a Rural Walk between the State House and the New Jail, in Philadelphia," June 23; "The River Delaware to the River Hudson," July 5; "On the Prisoners in Albany Jail Celebrating the Fourth of July," July 17; "Lines Occasioned by a Visit to Federal Hall," August 30; "The City Lady to her Husband, Fond of the Country," August 31; "The Complaint of the Burling Slip Boatmen," November 16; "Lines . . . Addressed to a Gay Young Lady that was Courted by a Grave Religious Lover, and Far Advanced in Years," November 24, 1790; "Humanity at Sea," January 29; "The Physician and his Patient (Translated from the French)," February 15; "On Leaving a Dutch House in the Western Parts of Pennsylvania (Written in 1776)," February 16; "Occasioned by the late Theatrical disturbances in Philadelphia," March 5; "The Island Savage," March 11; "The Potatoe Orator," April 16; "The Southern Jaunt," April 26; "The Morning Walker," April 27; "The Sciota Indian's Complaint," May 5; and "To a Young Lady, who Sent to the Author for 'The Rights of Man,' Written by Mr. Paine," June 9, 1791.

12. Prose written in Freneau's familiar manner in the *Daily Advertiser* includes "A Brief Account of the Ugly Club, Held in One of the Southern States, and Their Usual Mode of Procuring New Members" (reprinted by Freneau in the *Monmouth Almanac*, 1795), April 5; "Description of New-York One Hundred Years Hence," June 12 and 14; "Lady Bab's Soliloquy" (in which Miss Baboon discourses on hair dye, facial lotion, tooth powder, and other such fripperies), June 17; "An Oration in Commendation of Tobacco" (by "A.B."), June 30; an article by "Hop, Skip, and Jump" on the liberty of the press to call a knave a knave, July 15; "The Old Soldier and his Dog," July 5; "Hint to the Public" (On the need of parks along the Hudson shore), July 12; "Funeral Oration" (reported by "Toby Pickle," and on the text, "He died, and now stinketh"), July 19; descriptions of "Nootka Sound," August 10, and "The Great Dismal," August 13; "Commencement Lecture" (in which the author advises encouragement of the coarse, rather than the fine arts), April 25; "On the Advantages of Steadiness" (an introduction to the "Opay Mico" essays—see p. 174 below), August 31; "Magistrates" (a plea for able men in public office), September 29; "On Patriotism" (and world brotherhood), September 30; "Letter . . . Sometime Ago Written to a Young Printer in One of the Southern States" (by "A.B."), October 15; "Of the

Florida Gulph Stream," October 16; a letter by "Henrietta Lively" on the balls of the coming winter season, October 21; "Letter to a Newly Elected Young Member of the Lower House" (by "A.B."), October 22; "A Discourse on Barber's Poles" (reprinted by Freneau in the *Monmouth Almanac*), November 1; "On the Propriety of Situation of Public Buildings and Public Places" (particularly against graveyards in cities), November 5; "Description of a North Carolina Ordinary" (the prose counterpart of "Log Town Tavern"), November 10; "Rules How to Complement Great Men in the Proper Manner" (by "A.B."), November 11; "On the Liberty of the Press in England" (there isn't any!), November 12; "On Epic Poetry," November 16; "On the Power of Chance in the Production of Great Characters," November 27; articles by "D. Doubtful" (see p. 182 below), December 9–19, 1790; and "On Notions," February 11, 1791.

13. Hodge, Allen, and Campbell advertised the *Poems* and the *Miscellaneous Works* in the *Daily Advertiser* for twelve weeks, beginning May 18, 1790.

14. July 23, 1790.

15. *Annals of Congress*, Washington, 1834, II, 1716 and 1735.

16. See the *Daily Advertiser*, July 22, 23, and August 16, 1790.

17. *Annals of Congress*, I, 178–79, and II, 1850 and 1893.

18. A facsimile of the broadside is found in Paltsits, *Bibliography*, p. 5.

19. April 9, 1791; see, also, *Gazette of the United States*, April 27, and *General Advertiser*, April 28, 1791.

20. *The Journal of William Maclay*, ed. Edgar S. Maclay, New York, 1890, p. 385.

21. February 11, 1791. The "Extract" is dated "Nov. 30." No mention of such a production is found in the London newspapers, in the dramatic lists in the London magazines, or in extant playbills of the period. Though the dialogue (see "Report of a Law Case," *Miscellaneous Works*, pp. 216–27) may have been used as a curtain-raiser or after-piece, we suspect that Freneau, in the heat of controversy and anxious to forward the subscription for his projected new volume, may have been not over-careful in verifying the report of appearance on the British stage.

22. Philadelphia, 1791, pp. 237–38.

23. *Writings of Jefferson*, VI, 104.

24. MS *Madison Papers*, XIV, 8.

25. February 22, 1791.

26. "The Useful only in Vogue at Court," *Daily Advertiser*, February 26, 1791.

27. MS *Madison Papers*, XXIII, 14; see, also, Gaillard Hunt, "Office Seeking during Jefferson's Administration," *American Historical Review*, III, 280 (January, 1898).

28. *The Writings of James Madison*, ed., Gaillard Hunt, New York, 1908, VI, 117 n.

29. MS *Jefferson Papers*, 1 ser., IV, 153.

30. *City Gazette*, January 5, 1801.

31. MS letter owned by the New Jersey Historical Society; see Rankin, "The Ramapo Tract," pp. 377–79.

32. MS *Madison Papers*, XIV, 8.

33. MS *Trist Papers*, Library of Congress, XVI, 16.

34. MS *Madison Papers*, XIV, 8.

35. *Ibid.*

36. MS *Jefferson Papers*, 1st ser., IV, 186.

37. *Ibid.*, p. 191.

38. *Daily Advertiser*, May 25 and 28, 1791.

39. *Gazette of the United States*, June 4, 1791.

40. *Writings of Jefferson*, VI, 107.

41. *City Gazette*, January 5, 1801.

42. MS *Jefferson Papers*, 1st ser., IV, 207.

43. MS *Madison Papers*, XIV, 28.

44. *Ibid.* The business which detained Freneau was the purchase, with his mother,

of fifty-five acres adjoining the homestead at Mount Pleasant (MS *Monmouth County Deeds*, R, 486).

45. *City Gazette*, January 5, 1801.

46. MS *Jefferson Papers*, 2d ser., XVIII, 47.

47. The *National Gazette* was advertised extensively; see *Pennsylvania Gazette*, November 16, 1791; Boston *Argus*, September 6, 1791; *Maryland Journal*, September 20, 1790; *Virginia Gazette*, November 23, 1791; and *Augusta Chronicle*, September 22, 1792.

48. Family Bible.

49. *City Gazette*, January 5, 1801.

CHAPTER EIGHT

1. Maclay, *Journal*, p. 387.

2. *The Works of Alexander Hamilton*, ed. Henry Cabot Lodge, New York, 1904, I, 411, and IX, 534.

3. "First Report of the Public Credit," *Works of Hamilton*, II, 254–55.

4. Maclay, *Journal*, p. 179.

5. *Maryland Journal*, February 11, 1791.

6. George Gibbs, *Memoirs of the Administration of Washington and John Adams, edited from the Papers of Oliver Wolcott*, New York, 1846, I, 62.

7. Maclay, *Journal*, p. 364.

8. *Writings of Jefferson*, I, 254.

9. *Letters of Mrs. Adams, the Wife of John Adams*, ed. Charles Francis Adams, Boston, 1848, p. 352.

10. Maclay, *Journal*, p. 151.

11. Isaac Weld, Jr., *Travels through the United States of America, and the Provinces of Upper and Lower Canada, during the Years 1795, 1796, and 1797*, London, 1799, I, 21.

12. François René Chateaubriand, *Voyages en Amérique et en Italie*, Paris, 1837, I, 94.

13. Samuel Eliot Morison, *Life and Letters of Harrison Gray Otis*, New York, 1888, I, 126.

14. Weld, *Travels*, I, 7–8.

15. Noah Webster, *A Collection of Essays and Fugitive Writings*, Boston, 1790, p. 217.

16. Duc de la Rochefoucault Liancourt, *Travels through the United States of North America, the Country of the Iroquois, and Upper Canada, in the Years 1795, 1796, and 1797*, London, 1799, IV, 97.

17. Henry Wansey, *An Excursion to the United States of North America in the Summer of 1794*, Salisbury, 1798, pp. 118–20.

18. *Ibid.*, p. 117.

19. Benjamin Henry Latrobe, *The Journal of Latrobe*, New York, 1905, p. 83.

20. Gibbs, *Memoirs*, I, 62.

21. *Writings of Madison*, VI, 62 n.

22. *Ibid.*, p. 69 n.

23. Matthew L. Davis, *Memoirs of Aaron Burr, with Miscellaneous Selections from his Correspondence*, New York, 1869, I, 305.

24. *Writings of Jefferson*, VI, 106.

25. *National Gazette*, October 31, 1791.

26. March 5, 1792.

27. *Writings of Madison*, VI, 69 n.

28. *Ibid.*, p. 84 n.

29. February 27, 1792.

30. March 19, 1792.
31. March 22, 1792.
32. March 26, 1792.
33. April 5, 1792.
34. "Vid. The House of Night—a poem by Sinbat— It is presumed this must have been the fact, for otherwise it is inconceivable why he should kill Death." (Original note in "The Echo.")
35. *Annals of Congress*, III, 484.
36. *Columbian Centinel*, May 5, 1792.
37. *National Gazette*, May 7, 1792.
38. *Gazette of the United States*, May 11, 1792.
39. May 10-24, 1792.
40. May 31, 1792.
41. *Ibid*. Extracts from Paine were printed May 31, June 4, June 7, and July 7, 1792.
42. *Gazette of the United States*, June 9, 1792.
43. *National Gazette*, June 11, 1792.
44. *Gazette of the United States*, June 13, 1792.
45. *National Gazette*, June 14, 1792.
46. *Gazette of the United States*, June 20, 1792.
47. *National Gazette*, June 21, 1792.
48. *Ibid*.
49. *Gazette of the United States*, June 23, 1792.
50. *National Gazette*, June 25, 1792.
51. *Gazette of the United States*, June 23, 1792.
52. *National Gazette*, June 25, 1792.
53. *Gazette of the United States*, June 27, 1792.
54. *Ibid*., July 7, 1792.
55. *National Gazette*, July 9, 1792.
56. July 11, 1792.
57. July 18, 1792.
58. In addition to these poems, all of which were subsequently included by Freneau in one or more of his collected editions, the *National Gazette* contained occasional verses which the editor never acknowledged, but which evidence his authorship in style and subject. Such was the "Address to the Citizens of Holland," April 5, an expression of sympathy "on considering the accounts of the Periodic Inundations, which have destroyed that Country." "An Old Story New Dressed," six lines which told of the happy release of Poor Joe, whose termagant wife had recently died, was printed on April 19. The quatrain on the funding system, appended to an editorial paragraph on speculators, May 3, was certainly by Freneau:

> Public debts are public curses
> In *soldier's* hands! then nothing worse is!
> In *speculator's* hands increasing
> Public debt's a public blessing!

Few of Freneau's contemporaries could create a rhyme as informal as that in the first couplet quoted above. Finally, the "Lines Written on a Back Country Parson, whose Custom it Was to have his Neighbours Cows Milked, whenever They Broke into his Pasture," May 4, treated just the perverse sort of subject in which Freneau delighted:

> Parson adieu!—how can you hope applause
> From efforts of your lungs or holy paws,
> If thus you plunder what poor outcasts need
> And starve the wretches whom you ought to feed.

59. *Works of Hamilton*, IX, 519.
60. *Ibid*., X, 14.

61. *The Works of John Adams*, ed., Charles Francis Adams, Boston, 1856, VIII, 514.

62. *Gazette of the United States*, July 28, 1792.

63. *Works of Hamilton*, X, 14.

64. August 15, 1792.

65. August 18, 1792.

66. August 25, 1792.

67. August 27, 1792.

68. August 27, 1792.

69. September 6, 1792.

70. September 12, 1792.

71. *National Gazette*, September 5 and 11, 1792; *Works*, III, 28 ff.

72. *National Gazette*, September 8, 1792.

73. *National Gazette*, September 22, 1792. It seems fairly evident that he of the "mutton fist" was intended to be John Fenno, he of the "breadth of belly," John Adams, and he of the "length of nose," Alexander Hamilton.

74. *Writings of Washington*, XII, 174.

75. *Ibid.*, p. 178.

76. *Writings of Jefferson*, VI, 105–08. Jefferson's connection as adviser to the editor of the *National Gazette* must necessarily be suspected when we read this paragraph in a letter from Freneau to the Secretary of State (MS *Jefferson Papers*, Coolidge Collection, Massachusetts Historical Society, January 27, 1792); "I have just glanced over Mr. Nenno's last essay, you were so kind as to send. It is much like the others, generally superficial, tedious and too little of argumentative discussion for the subject, to please the generality of readers—however, there are here and there some good things interspersed, which we will give the public when nothing more interesting offers." On the other hand, for a discussion of Freneau's "perfect independence in the management of his paper" see Forman, *Political Activities*, pp. 69–72.

77. *Works of Hamilton*, VI, 30.

78. *National Gazette*, August 25, 1792.

79. "An Old Heathen Story Adapted to Modern Times," *National Gazette*, August 29, 1792.

80. September 8, 1792.

81. September 12, 1792.

82. September 14, 1792.

83. *Dunlap's Daily American Advertiser*, September 15, 1792.

84. September 15, 19, 29, and October 17, 1792.

85. September 15, 1792.

86. *Writings of Jefferson*, VIII, 411.

87. *Writings of Madison*, VI, 118 n.

88. September 22 and October 10, 1792.

89. October 3, 1792.

90. October 3, 1792.

91. October 20, 1792.

92. October 20, 1792.

93. October 24, 1792.

94. October 20, 1792. Ten years later Freneau said, "Before the conclusion of the first year's publication of the National Gazette I had acquired nearly, if not quite, seventeen hundred subscriptions to that paper, in different parts of the United States" (*City Gazette*, January 5, 1801).

95. October 18, 1792.

96. *Writings of Madison*, VI, 84.

97. *Writings of Jefferson*, VI, 134.

98. October 31, 1792.

99. November 10, 1792.

100. *National Gazette*, December 12, 1792.

101. *Letters of John Adams, Addressed to His Wife*, ed. Charles Francis Adams, Boston, 1861, II, 134.

102. *Ibid.*, p. 119.

103. "Governmental Combinations and Abuse (From Mr. Paine's Rights of Man)," July 7, and "Paine's Letter to Dundas," September 1, 1792.

104. August 4, 1792.

105. "Thoughts on the Constitution," December 5, 1792; and "Reflections on the English Revolution of 1688, and that of France on the 10th of August, 1792," February 6, 9, and 20, 1793.

106. January 2, 1793.

107. *Works of Hamilton*, V, 207, and VI, 274.

108. *Letters of John Adams*, II, 119.

109. "On the Royal Portraits, in the Senate Chamber," *National Gazette*, December 22, 1792.

110. Gibbs, *Memoirs*, I, 85.

111. *Letters of Mrs. Adams*, p. 361.

112. "Address to the Boy who Carries the American Mercury to its Subscribers," *American Mercury*, January 7, 1793.

113. December 29, 1792.

114. "Balloons," January 2, 1793.

115. *Letters of John Adams*, II, 119.

116. Burton Alva Konkle, *Thomas Willing and the First American Financial System*, Philadelphia, 1937, p. 149.

117. *Annals of Congress*, III, 753.

118. *Ibid.*, pp. 757–58.

119. *Ibid.*, p. 840.

120. January 12, 1792.

121. *Annals of Congress*, III, 899.

122. February 27, 1793.

123. *Annals of Congress*, III, 934.

124. March 20, 1793.

125. *National Gazette*, March 27, 1793.

126. *General Advertiser*, January 3; *National Gazette*, January 12, 1793.

127. February 4, 1793.

128. February 12, 1793.

129. *National Gazette*, January 12, 1793.

130. *Ibid.*, January 17, 1793.

131. January 21, 1793.

132. *General Advertiser*, February 7, 1793.

133. *Works of Fisher Ames, With a Selection from His Speeches and Correspondence*, ed. Seth Ames, Boston, 1854, I, 128.

134. February 11, 1793.

135. February 13, 1793.

136. February 20, 1793.

137. "The Echo, No. XI," *American Mercury*, February 25, 1793.

138. February 27, 1793.

139. February 27, 1793.

140. Gibbs, *Memoirs*, I, 91.

141. *National Gazette*, March 16, 1793.

142. See March 20, April 13, and May 18, 1793.

143. *Writings of Jefferson*, VI, 192.

144. *Works of Hamilton*, VI, 371–86.

145. *Writings of Jefferson*, III, 226–43.

146. *Ibid.*, III, 230.

147. *Works of Hamilton*, IV, 371.

148. *Gazette of the United States*, April 24, 1793.

149. *National Gazette*, May 18, 1793.

150. Griffith J. McRee, *Life and Correspondence of James Iredell*, New York, 1858, II, 387.

151. *National Gazette*, April 27, 1793.

152. *New-Jersey State Gazette*, May 8, 1793.

153. *National Gazette*, May 4, 1793.

154. *Writings of Jefferson*, VI, 179.

155. *Writings of Madison*, VI, 127.

156. *National Gazette*, May 18, 1793.

157. *Writings of Jefferson*, VI, 260.

158. *National Gazette*, May 22, 1793.

159. *Gazette of the United States*, May 22, 1793.

160. To the often alleged accusation that Freneau was not capable of translating French this action of the French citizens of Philadelphia should be sufficient reply. We have already seen that in the *Freeman's Journal* and the *Daily Advertiser* he translated verse and prose; however one George Taylor, a disappointed applicant for Freneau's position in the State Department, attests (MS *Pickering Papers*, Massachusetts Historical Society, XXIX, 50) : "Before the Government removed from that city [New York], having french treaties to collate, and he being employed by Childs & Swaine, who were printing them, I asked him to assist in the collation and he declined it, alleging that he did not sufficiently understand the language, but from its affinity to Latin made out to read it. However, he soon after came to this city [Philadelphia], received the appointment and in some cases I have assisted a Dutch gentleman then an inmate of my family to translate french documents put into his hands by Mr. Freneau."

161. *Federal Gazette*, May 22, 1793.

162. *National Gazette*, May 15, 1793.

163. *Ibid.*, May 25, 1793.

164. *Ibid.*, June 5, 1793.

165. *Writings of Jefferson*, I, 231.

166. *General Advertiser*, June 4, 1793. A version of the song had already been printed in the *New York Journal*, May 11, 1793, in which the first and fourth stanzas were identical with the first and second stanzas presented by Freneau. Subsequent reprintings (see the bibliography at the end of the present volume) followed the latter version with only minor changes. It was sung again at a celebration held in New York on November 24, 1793, on the anniversary of the British evacuation (*Daily Advertiser*, November 25, 1793).

167. June 10, 1793.

168. "To Jonathan Pindar, Poet Laureate to the National Gazette," August 24, 1793.

169. September 4, 1793.

170. *Writings of Jefferson*, VI, 328. Freneau apparently considered publishing "The Probationary Odes" in a volume; when they did appear from the press of Benjamin Franklin Bache in 1796, Tucker explained (p. 53) :

> That rogue Freneau has left me in the lurch,
> Or, I'd been with you early in the winter;
> Bishops could better do without a church
> Than lofty poets can without a printer.

As an introductory note to Ode VI, the author further attested: "Jonathan hereby

... exculpateth the Editor of the National Gazette from the horrid and damning charge of writing the Probationary Odes."
171. June 1, 1793.
172. June 5, 1793.
173. June 8, 1793.
174. June 12, 1793.
175. June 11 and 15, 1793.
176. June 29–July 20, 1793; see *Works*, II, 432–89.
177. *Writings of Jefferson*, IV, 338.
178. August 24–September 18, 1793; see *Writings*, IV, 138–88.
179. *National Gazette*, July 3, 1793.
180. *Writings of Washington*, XII, 312.
181. *Writings of Jefferson*, I, 254.
182. *The Writings of John Quincy Adams*, ed. W. C. Ford, New York, 1913, I, 147.
183. August 19, 1793.
184. Gibbs, *Memoirs*, I, 107.
185. July 24, 1793.
186. August 3, 1793.
187. *Works of Hamilton*, X, 50–52.
188. *Writings of Jefferson*, VI, 393.
189. *Virginia Gazette*, July 9, 1793.
190. *Works of Fisher Ames*, I, 129.
191. *Writings of Jefferson*, VI, 197.
192. August 14, 1793.
193. Gibbs, *Memoirs*, I, 108; and *Writings of Jefferson*, VI, 418.
194. *Connecticut Courant*, December 9, 1793; and McRee, *Life of Iredell*, II, 401.
195. *Porcupine's Gazette*, September 6, 1797.
196. See Benjamin Rush, *An Account of the Bilious Remitting Yellow Fever as It Appeared in the City of Philadelphia in the Year 1793*, Philadelphia, 1794, pp. 12–22.
197. September 18, 1793.
198. September 25, 1793.
199. September 4, 1793.
200. August 15, 1793; see *The Life and Correspondence of Rufus King*, ed. Charles R. King, New York, 1894, I, 459.
201. September 4, 1793.
202. September 11, 1793.
203. *Works of Hamilton*, V, 574; and *Life of King*, I, 462.
204. "The American's Prayer," though popularly attributed to Freneau by his contemporaries, is first found in the Baltimore *Daily Repository*, from which it was copied in the *Virginia Gazette*, September 2, 1793. After its publication by Freneau, it was reprinted "From the National Gazette" in the *Federal Gazette*, September 25; *Newark Gazette*, October 2; *New Brunswick Guardian*, October 2; *Augusta Chronicle*, November 2, and *Boston Gazette*, November 25, 1793.
205. October 4, 1793.
206. October 14, 1793.
207. July 20, 1793.
208. August 18, 1793.
209. *Writings of Madison*, VI, 84.
210. September 11, 1793.
211. *City Gazette*, January 5, 1801.
212. *National Gazette*, October 2, 1793.
213. *City Gazette*, January 5, 1801.
214. MS *Jefferson Papers*, 2 ser., XXXIII, 48.

215. *City Gazette*, January 5, 1801.

216. October 19, 1793.

217. Gibbs, *Memoirs*, I, 111.

218. November 4, 1793.

219. *Writings of Jefferson*, VI, 438.

220. *Ibid.*, p. 443.

221. *Life of King*, I, 501–02.

222. Freneau to William B. Giles, December 2, 1793 (MS owned by Historical Society of Pennsylvania).

CHAPTER NINE

1. MS *Madison Papers*, XVIII, 51.

2. MS Hammell notes, p. 3.

3. *American Daily Advertiser*, August 15, 1792, and MS *Monmouth County Deeds*, K, 153.

4. Family Bible.

5. To Samuel S. Forman, 1795; quoted in "The Wife of Philip Freneau," *New York Evening Post*, May 6, 1893, p. 14.

6. *Ibid.*

7. MS *Madison Papers*, XVII, 92.

8. MS letter, dated April 6, 1795, Rutgers University Library.

9. *Miscellaneous Works, Prose and Poetical, By a Young Gentleman of New York*, New York, 1795, pp. 90–91.

10. *American Poems, Original and Selected*, Litchfield, 1793, p. 239.

11. New York, 1794, pp. 80, 125, and 173.

12. MS *Alex. Anderson's Diary, for the Year 1794*, pp. 101–03. During the next ten months Anderson executed several small engravings for Freneau; see *loc. cit.*, pp. 116, 118, 241, and MS *A. Anderson's Journal for 1795*, Columbia University Library, p. 72. Among his boyhood friends in Monmouth, the poet was apparently still known as "Philip Fresneau," for his name is so spelled in the MS *Aaron Longstreet's Book to Take Acct of the Rateables of Middletown for the year 1794*; see William S. Horner, *This Old Monmouth of Ours*, Freehold, 1932, p. 239.

13. Broadside proposals, dated July 4, 1794, Monmouth County Historical Association; see Lewis Leary, "An Unlisted Item in the Bibliography of Philip Freneau," *American Literature*, VI, 331–34 (November, 1934).

14. *Daily Advertiser*, May 4, 1795.

15. The edition was advertised in the *Diary*, April 18–May 9, 1795; *New York Journal*, May 6; *Daily Advertiser*, May 6, 17, June 23, 29; *Argus*, May 13–November 7, 1795.

16. MS inscription by Freneau in a copy of the 1795 edition owned by the Monmouth County Historical Association.

17. MS *Jefferson Papers*, 2d ser., XXXVI, 134.

18. *Jersey Chronicle*, May 2, 1795; see also May 30, 1795.

19. *Ibid.*, May 2, 1795.

20. *Ibid.*, May 9, 1795.

21. MS day book of Francis and Robert Bailey, Historical Society of Pennsylvania, p. 14.

22. *Jersey Chronicle*, September 12, 1795. Freneau's *Poems* (1795) had also been advertised separately as "Just published and for sale" on July 15 and 25, 1795, three months after they had been announced in the New York newspapers.

23. MS *Madison Papers*, XIX, 101.

24. *Jersey Chronicle*, July 11, 1795.

25. *Ibid.*, August 22, 1795.

26. "To the Public," *Jersey Chronicle*, May 2, 1795.
27. MS *Madison Papers*, XVII, 51.
28. *Supplement to the Jersey Chronicle*, May 2, 1795.
29. "Observations on the Treaty with Great Britain," May 2, 1795.
30. May 9, 1795.
31. May 16, 1795; reprinted in the *Time-Piece*, March 13, 1797.
32. May 16, 1795.
33. May 23, 1795.
34. "On the Branch of Government Denominated Executive," May 30, 1795.
35. May 30, 1795.
36. Each of the "Extracts" was reprinted in the *Time-Piece* two years later. None of them, as far as I have been able to discover, had been printed previously. If by Freneau, they constitute his most sustained serious prose.
37. July 4, 1795.
38. July 11, 1795.
39. June 6, 1795.
40. June 13, 1795.
41. June 27, 1795.
42. August 22, 1795.
43. August 29, 1795.
44. September 5, 1795.
45. July 25, 1795.
46. August 1, 1795.
47. August 8, 1795.
48. September 5, 1795.
49. September 5–December 5, 1795.
50. October 3, 1795.
51. October 10, 1795.
52. February 6, 1796.
53. *Spectator*, No. 50, April, 1711. The same theme had been treated by Steele in the *Tatler*, No. 171, May 13, 1710.
54. *Journal to Stella*, New York, 1901, p. 203.
55. *Gentleman's Magazine*, IV, 449 (August, 1734).
56. October 1–15, 1734.
57. London, 1735; see Charles C. Jones, *Historical Sketch of Tomo-Chi-Chi, Mico of the Yamacraws*, Albany, 1868, p. 63 n., and Clark, "Literary Influences," pp. 24–27.
58. *Monthly Review*, appendix to Vol. VIII (1758), p. 648.
59. *Jersey Chronicle*, May 23, 1795.
60. *Ibid.*
61. "Tomo Cheeki, No. I," May 30, 1795.
62. *Ibid.*, No. II, June 6, 1795.
63. *Ibid.*, No. III, June 13, 1795.
64. *Ibid.*, No. XIII, September 12, 1795.
65. *Ibid.*, No. V, July 4, 1795.
66. *Ibid.*, No. VI, July 11, 1795.
67. *Ibid.*, No. VII, July 18, 1795.
68. *Ibid.*, No. VIII, July 25, 1795.
69. *Ibid.*, No. X, August 8, 1795.
70. *Ibid.*, No. XII, August 29, 1795.
71. *Ibid.*, No. XIII, October 17, 1795.
72. *Ibid.*, No. XIII, continued, October 31, 1795.
73. "Political Extracts," *Jersey Chronicle*, March 12, 1796.
74. "Reflections on Several Subjects," *ibid.*, March 19, 1796.

75. April 30, 1796.
76. April 30, 1796. The verses are only slightly altered from Pope's "Epigram" on Dennis, beginning "Should D[enni]s print, how once you robb'd your brother."
77. May 9, 1796.
78. April 23 and 30, 1796.
79. MS *Clinton Papers*, Columbia University, I, 35.
80. MS *Madison Papers*, XIX, 101.
81. MS *Clinton Papers*, I, 35.
82. MS *Madison Papers*, XIX, 101.
83. MS *Clinton Papers*, I, 35.
84. MS *Madison Papers*, XIX, 101. Verses much like Freneau's had been appearing in the *Argus* (see, particularly, "On the Federal City," May 13, and "On a Very Old Bachelor, who Met with an Angry Repulse on Attempting to Snatch a Kiss from a Young Lady," June 2, 1796) ; perhaps, therefore, the poet was for a time associated with Greenleaf in New York.
85. MS *Livingston Papers* (Bancroft transcripts), New York Public Library.
86. *Time-Piece*, March 13, 1797.

CHAPTER TEN

1. "To the Public," *Time-Piece*, March 13, 1797.
2. "Proposals for Publishing a New Paper," *Time-Piece*, March 13, 1797.
3. *Ibid.*
4. "To the Public."
5. *Time-Piece*, April 14, 1797.
6. "Proposals."
7. Timothy Dwight, *Travels in New-England and New-York*, London, 1823, III, 450.
8. Wansey, *Excursion*, p. 57.
9. *New-York Gazette*, May 20, 1797.
10. Wansey, p. 79.
11. Jedidah Morse, *American Geography*, London, 1794, p. 384.
12. New York *Diary*, May 11, 1797.
13. *Ibid.*, January 17, 1797.
14. *Ibid.*, January 12, 1797.
15. *Ibid.*, May 11, 1797.
16. *New-York Gazette*, April 19, 1797.
17. *Diary*, March 6, 1797.
18. *New-York Gazette*, May 6, 1797.
19. George C. D. Odell, *Annals of the New York Stage*, New York, 1927, I, 424.
20. John Bernard, *Retrospections of America, 1797–1811*, New York, 1887, p. 52.
21. Dwight, *Travels*, p. 453.
22. Morse, *American Geography*, p. 384.
23. John Davis, *Travels of Four Years and a Half in the United States of America during 1798, 1799, 1800, 1801, and 1802*, New York, 1909, p. 204.
24. *Time-Piece*, May 5, 1797.
25. *Time-Piece*, October 13, 1797.
26. MS *Miscellaneous Works, Verse and Prose, Serious and Comic of Madam Scriblerus*, Rutgers University Library, p. 881.
27. Reprinted from the *Freeman's Journal:* "Stanzas Written on Ireland in the Year 1781" (July 3) ; from the *National Gazette:* the untitled lines composed in 1793 to celebrate M. Blanchard's ascension in Philadelphia (May 15) ; from the *Poems* of 1795, "On the First American Ship (Empress of China, Capt. Green) that Explored the Route to the East Indies and China after the Revolution" (April 17) ; and from the *Jersey*

Chronicle: "The Rival Candidates for the Favours of America," "Lines Written soon after the Death of General Charles Lee," "Stanzas to the Memory of Miss Field" (March 20), and "The Republican Genius of Europe" (July 3).

28. Dr. Patrick Brydone had suggested in his *Tour through Sicily and Malta*, London, 1773, II, 27, that "a lady who has her head surrounded with a wire cap, and her hair stuck full of metal pins, is to all intents and purposes an electrical conductor isolated. . . . Suppose that every lady should provide herself with a small chain or wire, to be hooked on at pleasure during thunderstorms . . . in the same manner as conductors on the tops of steeples."

29. Elisha Perkins (1741–1799) manufactured his instruments with great secrecy. Leading physicians and laymen, such as Pierpont Edwards, Samuel Willard, and Jedidiah Morse, believed so firmly in the "tractors" that they contributed to a collection of public testimonies (*Evidences of the Efficacy of Dr. Perkins Patent Metallic Tractors*, Philadelphia, 1797). In 1797 Perkins was expelled from the Connecticut Medical Society as a "Patentee and user of nostrums" (*Medical Repository*, 1798). The doom of Perkinism was sounded with the publication of John Haggarth's *On the Imagination as a Cause and as a Cure of Disorders*, London, 1800, and in spite of Thomas Green Fessenden's satirical *Terrible Tractoration!!* London, 1803.

30. *Columbian Centinel*, April 12, 1797.

31. See the *Poems by the Late Josias Lyndon Arnold, Esq.*, Providence, 1897, pp. 46–49.

32. The *Aurora* from March 14, 1797, to the end of the year carried a series of small advertisements for the *Poems* of 1795.

33. "Lines on Being Presented with a Volume of Poems by an American Author, in Which Was a Description of Pennsylvania, my Native Place," *Time-Piece*, July 24, 1797. The 1795 volume was the first collected edition of Freneau's poems in which "A Description of Pennsylvania" appeared. "Caroline's" verses were reprinted by Freneau as an introduction to his 1815 edition, however, with the following announcement: "The Following Lines addressed to the author, were sent to the publisher of these volumes, by a lady, who had read them in manuscript, together with Poems, &c. formerly written during the Revolutionary war, and published in Philadelphia, in 1809." Either Freneau's memory was faulty or he purposely changed the title of these verses in order to increase the prestige of his two final volumes.

34. MS "To Mr. Philip Freneau, on Reading his very Poetical Description of Santa Cruz.—See his Poems," in the MS *Miscellaneous Works of Madam Scriblerus*, p. 901.

35. MS *Miscellaneous Works of Madam Scriblerus*, *passim*.

36. MS Hammell notes, p. 11.

37. *Poems* (1809), II, 34.

38. *Time-Piece*, April 3, 1797, and *Longworth's American Almanack, New York Register, and City Directory*, New York, 1797, p. 183.

39. *Time-Piece*, September 13, 1797.

40. MS *Minutes of the Common Council of the City of New York*, June 26, 1797, City Clerk's Record Office, File No. 18.

41. July 24–26, 1797.

42. See September 8, 1797, *et seq.*

43. John Wood, *A Full Exposition of the Clintonian Faction, and the Society of the Illuminati*, Newark, 1802, p. 28.

44. In the photostatic copy of the MS *Constitution and Roll of Members of the Tammany Society, or Columbian Order, 1789–1816*, in the New York Public Library, Freneau's signature appears as member 503. The only indication of the date of his admission is that member 491 is listed as having joined on May 10, 1797. It may be assumed that Freneau became a member at that time or shortly thereafter.

45. Edwin P. Kilroe, *Saint Tammany and the Origin of the Society of Tammany or Columbian Order*, New York, 1913, p. 136.

46. *New-York Journal*, July 5, 1797.

47. The pamphlet was advertised in the *Time-Piece* from July 31 to November 1, 1797. Greenleaf discontinued advertisements for the publication in the *Argus* and the *New-York Journal* by the middle of August.

48. July 26, 1797.

49. *Daily Advertiser*, July 27, and *New York Gazette*, July 28, 1797.

50. *New-York Journal*, July 13, 1797.

51. July 18, 1797.

52. *Time-Piece*, September 13, 1797.

53. *Ibid.*, September 18, 1797.

54. *Time-Piece*, September 13, 1797.

55. *Porcupine's Gazette*, September 8, 1797.

56. *Minerva*, January 17, 1797; see also Harry R. Warfel, *Noah Webster: Schoolmaster to America*, New York, 1936, pp. 234–38.

57. C. D. H. Cole, *Life of William Cobbett*, New York, 1924, pp. 51–64.

58. Maclay, *Journal*, p. 383.

59. *American State Papers, Naval Affairs*, I, 25–28.

60. *Annals of Congress*, VI, 363–84.

61. September 29, 1797.

62. *Gazette of the United States*, September 22, 1797.

63. *Time-Piece*, September 27, 1797.

64. *Aurora*, September 28, 1797.

65. *Gazette of the United States*, September 29, 1797; see *Porcupine's Gazette*, September 30, 1797.

66. *Time-Piece*, October 6, 1797. The accusation Freneau made against Fenno was probably false. There are no lines in *McFingal* readily applicable to Fenno, who at the time the satire was written was a young man scarcely important enough to have deserved praise or recrimination from Trumbull.

67. *Ibid.*, September 27, 1797.

68. The poem was advertised in the *New-York Journal* and the *Argus* from September 13, in the *New-York Gazette*, from September 15, and in the *Time-Piece* from October 9, 1797. "The Columbiad" here advertised and from which extracts were later printed in the *Time-Piece* (June 8, 13, 15, 18, July 11 and 30, 1798) was neither the poem by that name published by Richard Snowden in 1795 nor the poem which Joel Barlow later published in 1807. It was in blank verse and written "by a gentleman from Europe now resident in this country" (*Time-Piece*, October 9, 1797). The author may have been John Daly Burk, the Irish journalist and playwright whose drama "Bunker Hill" had been presented at the John Street Theater on February 17, 1797 (Brander Matthews, introduction to *Bunker Hill, or the Death of Warren*, New York, 1891) and who succeeded Freneau as editor of the *Time-Piece*. On August 30, 1799, the following announcement appeared: "Those who hold subscription papers for the Columbiad, are requested to send them in to the office of the *Time-Piece*, as Mr. Burk is about putting it to the press immediately." The poem was apparently never published as a volume.

69. *Time-Piece*, September 27, 1797.

70. *Ibid.*, October 9, 1797.

71. *Ibid.* As first printed, this article was unsigned; when it was reprinted on August 10, 1798, after Freneau had left the *Time-Piece*, it was identified as "Written by Mr. Freneau."

72. *Poems* (1809), II, 3; the poem "To the Americans of the United States" is said

to have been "First Published November, 1797." I have found no trace of it in the *Time-Piece* or in other periodicals of the period.

73. December 18, 1797.

74. December 22, 1797.

75. *Time-Piece*, October 25, 1797.

76. According to the MS Hammell notes, p. 11, "While editor of the Time Piece his office was often thronged with visitors mostly wanting favors of one kind or another. One day he came in to dinner and told Mrs. Freneau that there had been rather an eccentric character in the office that morning, telling him that she had served through the revolutionary war in man's attire and had received several wounds and showed the scars. All he could do for her, he said, was to send her to Washington with a Petition which he did. Her name was Deborah Gannet. She went to Congress, presented her Petition and received her pension. Tho he did not put his name to it, it was immediately known, as there were many of the members were his correspondents." On November 28, 1797, Harrison Gray Otis, of Rhode Island, presented the petition of Deborah Gannet to Congress (*Annals of Congress*, VII, 644). Freneau in *Poems* (1815), I, 70 n., notes that the petition was presented on December 28, 1797; Pattee, in *Poems*, III, 182 n., has given the date as December 23, 1797.

77. Philip Freneau to Seth Paine, August 12, 1800 (MS owned by the Library of Congress).

78. *Time-Piece*, May 11, 1798.

79. MS Hammell notes, p. 9.

80. MS letter to Paine, August 12, 1800.

81. *Columbian Centinel*, December 23, 1797.

82. MS record of voyages, *Navigation*.

83. Family Bible.

84. MS record of voyages, *Navigation*.

85. The materials to which Freneau had access were later used in part by Jared Sparks in *The Life of John Ledyard, the American Traveller*, New York, 1828.

86. Baltimore, 1798, pp. xxv–xxvi.

87. *American State Papers, Foreign Affairs*, II, 158–60.

88. *Porcupine's Gazette*, June 7 and 12, 1798.

89. *Annals of Congress*, VII, 573–88.

90. *Independent Chronicle*, April 6 and August 9, 1798.

91. *Time-Piece*, May 11, 1798.

92. *Writings of Jefferson*, X, 36.

93. *Time-Piece*, June 13, 1798.

94. *Albany Centinel*, July 10, 1798.

95. See *Commercial Advertiser*, September 5, 1798, and Frank M. Anderson, "The Enforcement of the Alien and Sedition Laws," *Annual Report of the American Historical Association for 1912*, p. 116.

CHAPTER ELEVEN

1. See the *Independent Chronicle*, October 25 and November 5, 1798; the *Aurora*, October 22; and the *Commercial Advertiser*, December 8, 1799.

2. Francis Wharton, *State Trials in the United States during the Administrations of Washington and John Adams*, Philadelphia, 1849, pp. 658–81.

3. MS letter to Paine, August 12, 1800.

4. MS *Monmouth County Deeds*, L, 336 (March 23, 1799).

5. March 29, 1799.

6. April 23, 1799.

7. May 3, 1799.

8. May 7, 1799.
9. May 16, 1799.
10. May 20, 1799.
11. MS record of voyages, *Navigation*.
12. William L. King, *The Democratic Press of Charleston*, Charleston, 1872, pp. 38–39.
13. MS *Pickering Papers*, Massachusetts Historical Society, VIII, 124.
14. MS records of the Probate Court, Charleston, I6, 274; I7, 35; T5, 336; and Z5, 495.
15. E. S. Thomas, *Reminiscences of the Last Sixty-five Years*, Hartford, 1840, I, 76–82; see, also, the MS Hammell notes, p. 14, and Austin, *Freneau*, pp. 139–40.
16. MS record of voyages, *Navigation*.
17. June 11 and 19, 1799.
18. June 18, 1799.
19. July 31, 1799.
20. August 17, 1799.
21. August 24 and September 3, 1799.
22. October 2, 1799.
23. November 6, 9, 23, and 30, 1799.
24. December 4, 1799.
25. MS Hammell notes, p. 10.
26. See the appendix of the present volume.
27. January 30, 1800. The stanzas are dated January 27, 1800, three days after Rutledge's death.
28. MS letter to Paine, August 12, 1800.
29. August 5, 1800.
30. September 10 and October 9, 1800.
31. October 2, 1800.
32. November 17, 1800.
33. November 18, 1800.
34. From March 6 through the autumn of 1800 the *Poems* and *Miscellaneous Works* were advertised among books to be purchased at Greenleaf's bookstore.
35. From August 16 to October 25, 1800, and from May 9 to October 31, 1801.
36. *The School of Wisdom: or, American Monitor, Containing a Copious Collection of Sublime and Elegant Extracts, from the most Eminent Authors, on Morals, Religion, and Government*, Philadelphia, 1800, p. 123.
37. MS letter to Paine, August 12, 1800.
38. Peter Freneau to Seth Paine, November 28, 1800 (MS owned by the Library of Congress).
39. *Ibid.*, December 3, 1800.
40. *Ibid.*
41. Claude Bowers, *Jefferson and Hamilton*, New York, 1926, pp. 474–82.
42. See Philip Marsh, "Freneau and Jefferson: The Poet-Editor Speaks for Himself about the *National Gazette* Episode," *American Literature*, VIII, 180–89 (May, 1936).
43. Philip to Peter Freneau, March 1, 1801 (MS in the Freneau Collection, Rutgers University).
44. MS *Madison Papers*, XXIII, 127.
45. *Ibid.*, XXVI, 36.
46. Austin, *Freneau*, p. 173.
47. Philip Freneau to Seth Paine, June 26, 1801 (MS owned by the Library of Congress).
48. MS Hammell notes, p. 11.
49. MS, Eleanor Freneau to Samuel Forman, February 28, 1803, *Forman Papers*, New York Historical Society.

50. May 29, 1802.

51. See the *Georgia Republican*, December 17, 1805; the *New-Jersey Journal*, March 4 and September 30, 1806; and the Newark *Centinel of Freedom*, July 29, 1800.

52. March 28, 1799. The poem appeared in the *Time-Piece*, May 7, 1798, under the heading "Selected Poetry"; so we judge it was not Freneau's.

53. September 19, 1800.

54. London, 1802, pp. 98 and 125.

55. New York, 1803, pp. 111–25.

56. December 11, 1801.

57. December 28, 1802.

58. *Travels*, p. 156.

59. New York, 1803, II, 230–33.

60. July 10, 1804. "Freneau's Poems" (probably the edition of 1795) were still advertised; see *The Library; or, Philadelphia Literary Reporter*, May 19, 1804.

61. MS Hammell notes, p. 11.

62. Pattee, in *Poems*, I, lxxix.

63. MS letter to Peter Freneau, March 1, 1801.

64. *True American*, November 20, 1802; see also the Charleston *Times*, April 26, 1803.

65. MS record of voyages, *Navigation*.

66. Dated "Monmouth, February 28, 1803."

67. *City Gazette*, April 25, 1803.

68. MS record of voyages, *Navigation*; see also the *City Gazette*, May 11, August 22, and September 10, 1803. While Freneau was still at sea, his brother wrote to their sister Mary in New York that Mrs. Peter Freneau was ill and would come north to recuperate: "I was in hopes Philip might be back in time to take her, but *it is very uncertain when he will be here.*" (MS letter, July 23, 1803, owned by Mrs. George Yates Gilbert, Ridgewood, New Jersey.)

69. Charleston *Times*, October 15 and *New York Evening Post*, October 29, 1803.

70. *City Gazette*, December 28, 1803.

71. *Ibid.*, January 22, 1804.

72. When printed in the Trenton *True American*, September 21, 1822, the stanzas were dated "Brig Washington, January 25, 1804"; see note 41 of chapter XII.

73. MS record of voyages, *Navigation*.

74. "Stanzas Written at the Island of Madeira," *City Gazette*, July 2, 1804.

75. MS record of voyages, *Navigation*; and *City Gazette*, June 20, 1804.

76. *Poems* (1815), I, 167 and 169.

77. *Ibid.*, pp. 171–88.

78. See *City Gazette*, July 23, 1804; March 20, April 22, and May 18, 1805; and January 14, 1807.

79. "Joe Bunker," whose arguments are calm, caustic, and rather too straight to the point to have been written by Freneau, contributed letters on August 25, 28, 30, 31, September 4, 5, 7, 25, and 27. The contributions of "Joe Bunker, Jun." are short and do little more than approve the arguments set forth by his father. "Jonathan Bunker," whose letters appear on August 30, September 1, 3, 6, 8, 27, and October 4, is distinctly different in personality. He is frightened by the controversy; he warns Duane not to say what he thinks lest he find himself in trouble (August 28); he derides "Connecticut intruders" to Pennsylvania politics (September 3); he pretends to be terrified at a threat of tar and feathers (September 8); and, like Robert Slender, he depends for his information on tavern conversations, which he frequently misinterprets (September 27). Mr. Philip Marsh, who is preparing an edition of Freneau's prose, describes in a letter to the writer the "Jonathan Bunker" articles as "almost exact parallels of the Robert Slender letters in manner." The contributions by "Polly Bunker" (September 29 and

October 5) are marked by the same style as the "Jonathan Bunker" letters, and those of "Tomo Cheeki" are very much in Freneau's manner.

80. September 4, 1804.

81. MS indenture, June 5, 1805 (owned by Mrs. George Yates Gilbert, Ridgewood, New Jersey), by which Philip Freneau in Freehold on the afternoon of May 21, 1805, acquired title to 500 acres of land on the Cumberland River to secure payment of a mortgage held by Peter Freneau, of Charleston, against the property of Richard Throckmorton, insolvent debtor.

82. MS *Monmouth County Deeds*, H, 331, and *Monmouth County Mortgages*, E, 27; in 1808 Freneau sold still another parcel from his land at Mount Pleasant (see MS *Monmouth County Deeds*, L2, 412, and R, 451).

83. MS record of voyages, *Ovid*.

84. October 31, 1807.

85. MS *Jefferson Papers*, 2d ser., XXXIV, 134.

86. MS *Madison Papers*, XXXVII, 78.

87. *Ibid.*, LVIII, 14.

88. *American Daily Advertiser*, February 19, 1806.

89. See Lydia Bailey's MS waste book, Historical Society of Pennsylvania. According to Mrs. Bailey's records, 568 copies were sold by October 6, 1809, and 55 more between 1810 and 1814; to this number may be added the 1026 copies which were ordered in advance of publication by 403 subscribers whose names were listed at the end of the second volume of the *Poems*. Of the subscribers 136 were from Philadelphia, 122 from elsewhere in Pennsylvania, 71 from South Carolina, Virginia, and Maryland, 59 from New Jersey, 12 from New York, and 3 from Wilmington.

90. MS *Madison Papers*, XXXVII, 78.

91. *Ibid.*

92. I, 5–18, and 62–65.

93. I, 261–65.

94. "Reflections on the Constitution, or Frame of Nature," I, 262–63.

95. "Science, Favourable to Virtue," I, 261.

96. "Reflections on the Constitution, or Frame of Nature."

97. "Advertisement," *Poems* (1809), I, iii–iv.

98. September 8, 1809.

99. VIII, 203 (September, 1810).

100. "Stanzas on the Decease of Thomas Paine, who Died at New-York, on the 8th of June, 1809," *Poems* (1815), II, 28–29. In a letter on May 15, 1815 to John W. Francis (see Charles Heartmann, *Unpublished Freneauana*, New York, 1918, pp. 13–14) Freneau says the poem was "first published in Philadelphia near six years ago." I have found no trace of it in the newspapers of that city. Nor, so far as I have discovered, did Freneau ever know Paine personally.

101. *Aurora*, July 7, 1809.

102. See *Pennsylvania Democrat*, September 8, 22, October 20, 1809, and February 9, 1810.

103. Reported by Rufus W. Griswold, "Philip Freneau," *Graham's Magazine*, XLVII, 197 (September, 1855).

104. MS *Madison Papers*, XXXVII, 78.

105. On October 11, 1809, Freneau witnessed in Monmouth the transfer of two parcels of land from Agnes Kearny to her daughters, Mary Freneau and Margaret Freneau Hunn (see MS *Monmouth County Deeds*, W, 344).

106. "The New England Sabbath Day Chace," p. 17; "Humanity and Ingratitude," p. 26; "The Almanac Maker," p. 43; "The Pettifogger, or Fee Simple, Esq.," p. 50; "On the Crew of a Certain Vessel," p. 54; "The Forest Beau," p. 59; "Matrimonial Dialogue," p. 67; "A College Story," p. 132; and "The Indian Convert," p. 135.

107. *Pennsylvania Democrat*, August 9, 1810.

108. MS *Madison Papers*, LVIII, 14.

109. John S. Hunn, notary public and surveyor (*Time-Piece*, April 7, 1797), became in 1809 Street Commissioner of New York (*New York Evening Post*, July 14, 1809). In 1811 he, his wife, and Mary Freneau moved to Newburgh, where Hunn became cashier of the newly incorporated Bank of Newburgh (see E. M. Ruttenber, *History of Newburgh*, New York, 1911, p. 232).

110. Austin, *Freneau*, p. 227.

111. MS *Monmouth County Deeds*, X, 251, and *Mortgages*, E, 341.

112. "Epitaph on a Dog," dated "Nov. 19, 1812," written in Freneau's autograph on p. 685 of his copy of the *London Magazine for 1733* (Freneau Collection, Rutgers University Library).

113. *City Gazette*, November 15, 1813. The epitaph which Philip Freneau composed for his brother in the family Bible appears on Peter Freneau's tombstone in the cemetery of the Huguenot Church in Charleston.

114. Thomas, *Reminiscences*, p. 82. Peter Freneau left his property in trust to David Mazyck, of Charleston, enjoining him "that he do by Sale or other ways raise money sufficient to pay all the Notes of Hand which he has endorsed for me" (see MS *Record of Deeds*, Charleston County, Vol. XXXII, Book B, 1807–1818, p. 769, Charleston Free Library).

115. See "On the Dismission of Bonaparte from the French Throne," *Poems* (1815), II, 102–04.

116. Dated 1809 in *Poems* (1815), II, 20–23.

117. "On the Capture of the Guerriere," *Poems* (1815), II, 40–42.

118. *Loc. cit.*, pp. 141–42.

119. "To the Lake Squadrons" and "On the Lake Expeditions," *loc. cit.*, pp. 51–52 and 87–88.

120. *Loc. cit.*, pp. 64–67; see, also, "On the British Commercial Depredations," pp. 39–40.

121. *Loc. cit.*, pp. 73–75, 113–15, and 148–52.

122. "On the Battle of Lake Erie" and "On the Battle of Lake Champlain," *loc. cit.*, pp. 105–11.

123. *Loc. cit.*, pp. 61–63.

124. *Ibid.*, pp. 68–72 and 124–25. President Madison's copies of the *Poems* of 1809 were destroyed when the British burned Washington. Some years later Freneau wrote to his friend: "A copy or two of the Revolutionary Poems will be forwarded to your Direction—I am sorry the copies you had were doomed to the blazes, but the author had nearly suffered the same fate in 1780. Hoping that all health will attend you and that your Libraries may in future escape the ravages and flames of Goths and Barbarians . . ." (MS *Madison Papers*, LVIII, 14, January 12, 1815).

125. "On the Death of General Ross, Who Had Principal Command of the English Army at the Attack upon Baltimore, in which he Fell, While Out with a Reconnoitering Party," and "On the Naval Attack near Baltimore, September 14, 1814," *Poems* (1815), II, 112–13, and 90–91.

126. *Loc. cit.*, pp. 135–37.

127. *Ibid.*, pp. 116–23.

128. *Ibid.*, pp. 55–60 and pp. 92–95.

129. "On Political Sermons," *loc. cit.*, pp. 97–100.

130. MS *Madison Papers*, LXIII, 14. He had recourse, too, we suspect, to his habit of publishing occasional verse so inferior in quality that even he would not include it in a collected edition. Very much in Freneau's lighter manner are the songs, "The Voice of America" and "To the Soldiers of America," which appeared in the Trenton *True American* over the signature "A Citizen of Monmouth" on June 29 and July 12,

1812; also in his style is a ballad entitled "The Navy" which appeared in the same newspaper on November 23, dated "Monmouth, Nov. 15, 1812."
131. *Poems* (1815), II, 81–83.

CHAPTER TWELVE

1. MS *Madison Papers*, LVIII, 14 (January 12, 1815).
2. *Ibid.*, LVIII, 74 (March 3, 1815).
3. *Ibid.*, LVIII, 14.
4. "On the Uniformity and Perfection of Nature," *Poems* (1815), I, 95.
5. Philip Freneau to John W. Francis, May 15, 1815 (MS owned by Mr. Harold E. Pickerskill, Perth Amboy, New Jersey); see Charles F. Heartman, *Unpublished Freneauana*, New York, 1918, pp. 12–17.
6. June, 1815, pp. 518–19.
7. Heartman, pp. 16–17.
8. MS *Madison Papers*, LVIII, 74.
9. Heartman, pp. 15–16. Nicholas Van Riper, New York printer of the *Military Monitor*, from November 6, 1813, was associated in business with David Longworth (see Clarence S. Brigham, "Bibliography of American Newspapers, 1690–1820. Part VIII: New York City," *Proceedings of the American Antiquarian Society*, n.s., XXVII, 501, October 17, 1917. Both Addison's *Campaign* and Glover's *Leonidas* were in Freneau's library; see the appendix to the present volume.
10. See note 41 below.
11. I. Woodbridge Riley, *American Thought from Puritanism to Pragmatism*, New York, 1915, p. 147; quoted by Clark, in *Poems*, p. xxxvii.
12. "On the Uniformity and Perfection of Nature," *Poems* (1815), I, 94.
13. MS *Monmouth County Deeds*, Y, 317, 520, and 583; *Mortgages*, E, 509.
14. Trenton *True American*, December 23, 1816.
15. Freneau wrote in the family Bible: "She survived her first husband, Pierre Freneau, fifty years and one day; her second, James Kearny, nearly forty-five years."
16. Reported by Rufus W. Griswold, *Curiosities of American Literature*, New York, 1859, p. 25.
17. W. Jay Mills, *Historic Houses of New Jersey*, Philadelphia, 1902, p. 172.
18. Family Bible; on October 26 Freneau wrote Mathew Carey (MS Lea and Febiger Collection, XXV, 11633), "About a week ago I was burnt out and lost considerable property, but fortunately no lives. I have however a new House—partly finished, into which I have moved."
19. In E. A. and G. W. Duyckinck, *Cyclopædia of American Literature*, New York, 1855, I, 333; see, also, the personal reminiscences of the poet's granddaughter, Mrs. Marianna Harris (*Monmouth Inquirer*, July 31, 1884): "In person he was somewhat below the medium height, stooped slightly and was a little bow-legged, yet muscular and of firm step, being a great walker. His forehead was very high, shaded by iron grey hair, the caste of his countenance intellectual; his deeply set dark eyes brightened with intelligence when he spoke, but when in repose his expression was slightly melancholy. He wore 'small clothes' and cocked hat as long as he lived, was plain and unostentatious in his dress, and scorned display of any kind."
Tradition insists that Freneau would never sit for his portrait. "He was once waited upon by an artist, Rembrandt Peale," says Edwin Salter, *Old Times in Old Monmouth*, Freehold, 1887, pp. 110–11, "with a request for this purpose by a body of gentlemen in Philadelphia; but he was inexorable on the subject. On another occasion, the elder Jarvis, with a view of securing his likeness was smuggled into a corner of the room at a dinner party at Dr. Hosack's, to which the poet had been invited; but the latter detected the design and arrested its accomplishment. In late years the neglect has been

in a measure repaired. The portrait prefixed to the volume of his Poems with a memoir by Evert A. Duyckinck, published in 1865, was sketched by an artist, at the suggestion and dictates of several members of the poet's family, who retained the most vivid recollection of his personal appearance. It was pronounced by them a fair representation of the man in the maturity of his physical powers, previous to the inroads of age. His daughter, Mrs. Leadbeater, and his grandson and adopted son, Mr. Philip L. Freneau [see note 54 below] were among those who pronounced it a satisfactory likeness."

In 1902 Mary S. Austin came upon an engraving supposed to be of Freneau "in his nautical attire, and in the cabin of his ship," "an antiquary having found it in Philadelphia years ago" (Mary S. Austin to Warren C. Crane, March 12, 1902, MS in the Freneau Collection, Rutgers University Library). A photostat of the portrait (now owned by Mrs. Betty Rush of Washington, D. C.) was used by Crane in a specially illustrated two-volume "edition" of Austin's *Freneau* (Freneau Collection). The opinion of modern experts is that the engraving represents a sailor in the uniform of a British naval officer of the early nineteenth century.

Another "Freneau portrait," listed in the Frick Art Reference Library, 121 14Q, as by Copley, represents a young man dressed in the attire of a dandy of about 1770. It is not mentioned by Barbara Neville Parker and Ann Bolling Wheeler, *John Singleton Copley, American Portraits in Oil, Pastel, and Miniatures with Biographical Sketches*, Boston, 1938. The portrait is at present part of the George A. Plimpton Collection, Columbia University Library. "I cannot find," says Mrs. Plimpton in a letter (June 24, 1938) to the writer, "that we have anything but the dealer's word for the authenticity of the Freneau portrait." I have been convinced that it is neither by Copley nor of Freneau.

20. Duyckinck, I, 333.

21. See *The North American Review*, V, 98 (May, 1817); William Ellery Leonard, *Byron and Byronism in America*, Boston, 1905, pp. 20–25; Annabel Newton, *Wordsworth in Early American Criticism*, Chicago, 1928, pp. 66–70; and Earl L. Bradsher, *Mathew Carey, Editor, Author, and Publisher*, New York, 1912, p. 129. On August 16, 1822, the *New York Evening Post* recorded: "The report that a copy of Sir Walter Scott's last novel had arrived, set the city in an uproar. . . . It has already been struck off in three editions and set the publishers at Philadelphia, New York, and Boston, by the ears."

22. MS Lea and Febiger Collection, XXV, 11633.

23. *Ibid.*; see Bradsher, p. 82.

24. Halleck to E. A. Duyckinck, May 13, 1866 (MS in the Duyckinck Collection, New York Public Library).

25. See Stanley T. Williams, *The Life of Washington Irving*, New York, 1935, I, 13; Rufus W. Griswold, "Philip Freneau," *Graham's Magazine*, XLVII, 198 (September, 1855); Henry T. Tuckerman, "Memoir of Dr. Francis," in John W. Francis, *Old New York*, New York, 1866, p. xlv; and William B. Wood, *Personal Recollections of the Stage*, Philadelphia, 1855, pp. 187–88.

26. VII, 200–01 (July, 1818). So little was Freneau remembered that Solyman Brown could publish *An Essay on American Poetry* (New Haven, 1818) without once mentioning his name; six years later John Neal in his articles on "American Writers" in *Blackwood's Edinburgh Magazine*, was equally silent.

27. Robert Waln, Jr., *American Bards. A Satire*, Philadelphia, 1820, pp. 16–17.

28. July 29, 1820.

29. Freneau to Francis, May 14, 1822, with which were enclosed two trial prospectuses of the proposed edition (MS owned by Mr. Harold E. Pickerskill; also see Heartmann, pp. 20–21).

30. *Miscellanies for Sentimentalists*, Philadelphia, 1778; see Lewis Leary, "Philip Freneau at Seventy," *Journal of the Rutgers University Library*, I, 2–6 (June, 1938).

Work on the Erie Canal was started July 4, 1811, and was completed October 26, 1825. Dr. Francis, in Duyckinck's *Cyclopædia of American Literature*, I, 333, said of Freneau's later interests: "With Dewitt Clinton and Cadwallader D. Colden he debated the projects of internal improvement and artificial navigation, based on the famous precedent of the Languedoc canal."

31. The Park Theater was destroyed by fire in May, 1820. When the building was repaired a year later, a competition was announced "for the most appropriate and best written Poetic Address" to be spoken on the first night (New York *American*, May 21, 1821). Poems were to be "submitted to a committee of literary gentlemen," and the author of the address selected, if a resident of New York, was to be "entitled to the *freedom of the theatre*; if a resident of any other part of the State or Union, to a Gold Medal of the value of fifty dollars." Sixty poets entered the competition, which was won by Charles Sprague, of Boston, whose prize address was delivered from the stage on the night of September 1, 1821 (*New York Evening Post*, September 2, 1821). At the next performance an "Address written by Mr. [Samuel] Woodworth of this city" (perhaps the second prize poem) was read. (See Odell, *Annals of the New York Stage*, III, 597.) It may be supposed that the verses which Freneau published in the *True American* represent his unsuccessful contribution to the competition.

32. The first draft of lines from this poem are found in Freneau's autograph on the flyleaf and inside rear cover of his copy of Benjamin Rush's *Address to the Inhabitants of the British Settlements in America upon Slave-Keeping*, Philadelphia, 1773, in the Princeton University Library. The manner in which Freneau worked over his verses is illustrated by a couplet written on the inside rear cover (words in parenthesis have been deleted with a penstroke in the manuscript):

line of genuine   shows

Whether that (high), (celestial) beauty (glows)

From

(On) Margerys cheek or *Knickerbocker's* nose.

which lines are printed in the *True American* as

Whether the flush of blooming beauty glows

On Margery's cheek or *Knickerbocker's* nose.

33. The complete poem, in essentially the same form in which it appears in the *True American*, was scribbled by Freneau on the flyleaf and inside covers of his copy of Rush's *Address* (see note 32 above), from which it was printed under the title of "A Poet's Advice" by Varum Lansing Collins in "A Poem by Philip Freneau, Class of 1771," *Nassau Literary Magazine*, LV, 448–50 (February, 1900).

34. In addition to the poems mentioned above, all of which seem readily attributable to Freneau, the following, which appeared in the *True American* during the summer of 1821, are written very much in his manner and idiom: "On the Cession of East and West Florida, from Spain to the United States," July 21; "The Exile of St. Helena," in three parts, on August 4, September 1 and 15; and "The Dotage of Royalty," August 11.

35. May 11, 1822. A first draft of lines from this poem are found in Freneau's handwriting on the flyleaf of his copy of Rush's *Address*.

36. Mrs. Baldwin, noted as a tragedian, advertised the benefit in the *New York Evening Post*, April 15, 1822. No playbill of the performance seems to have survived nor is any mention of a prologue written by Freneau to be found in the New York newspapers of the day.

37. *Statesman*, July 15, 1822.

38. June 29, 1822.

39. See Nelson Frederick Adkins, *Fitz-Greene Halleck, An Early Knickerbocker Wit and Poet*, New Haven, 1930, p. 87.

40. Henry Walcott Boynton, *Annals of American Bookselling*, New York, 1932, pp. 139 and 160.

41. In attributing poems published after 1815 to Freneau, it has been assumed that the authorship of any one poem over a signature having been established, all other poems which appear over the same signature in the same periodical are by the same author. Following are the key poems; that is, those whose authorship by Freneau can be established and which, therefore, authenticate all other poems published over the same signature in the *New-York Weekly Museum* for 1816, and the Trenton *True American* or the New Brunswick *Fredonian* from 1821 to 1824:

1. "P.F.," *Weekly Museum:* "Stanzas Written for a Boy about Eight Years of Age, Who . . . Very Narrowly Escaped Being Bitten by a Large and Venomous Rattle Snake." September 7, 1816, appears in the *Fredonian* on September 12, 1822, over the signature "F" as "Lines Written for a Lad . . . Who Almost Miraculously Escaped the Bite of an Uncommonly Large Rattlesnake." Because another poem signed "F." in the *Fredonian* is found in manuscript (see 4 below), it is assumed that all poems over the same signature in the same periodical are by Freneau; hence, all poems signed "P.F." in the *Weekly Museum* are also by Freneau.

2. "F.," *Weekly Museum:* "Stanzas Written in an Ancient Burying Ground in Maryland, One Corner of Which was Appropriated to the Interment of Suicides," October 12, 1816, appears in the *Fredonian* on February 27, 1823, over the signature "R." (see 6 below).

3. "F.," *True American:* An autograph first draft of "The Youth of the Mind," May 11, 1822, is found in Freneau's copy of Rush's *Address to the Inhabitants of the British Settlements in America* (Princeton University Library).

4. "F.," *Fredonian:* An autograph first draft of the "Stanzas Written on the Great Western Canal," August 8, 1822, is found in Freneau's copy of *Miscellanies for Sentimentalists* (Rutgers University Library) ; see Leary, "Freneau at Seventy," pp. 2–6.

5. "R.," *True American:* "General Lefevre Denouette," July 20, 1822, appears in the *Fredonian* on July 25, 1822, over the signature "F." (see 4 above).

6. "R.," *Fredonian:* "Verses Written on Leaving a Great House of Much Ceremony," September 2, 1822, appears in the *True American* on August 24, 1822, over the signature "N." (see 9 below).

7. "E.," *True American:* "Lines Written for a Lad . . . Who Almost Miraculously Escaped the Bite of an Uncommonly Large Rattlesnake," October 12, 1822, appears in the *Fredonian* on September 12, 1822, over the signature "F." (see 4 above).

8. "E.," *Fredonian:* "A Midnight Storm in the Gulph Stream," September 19, 1822, appears in the *True American* on September 21, 1822, over the signature "E." (see 7 above) and dated "Brig Washington, January 25, 1804."

9. "N.," *True American:* "Beaurepaire. The Arrival at Indian Sam's," September 28, 1822, appears in the *Fredonian* on September 26, 1822, over the signature "E." (see 8 above).

10. "A.," *True American:* "Lines to a Lady, Remarkably Fond of Sleep," September 21, 1822, appears in the *Fredonian* on October 5, 1822, over the signature "R." (see 6 above).

11. "U.," *True American:* "Recollections of Past Times and Events, No. II"; numbers I and IV of the same title appear, July 6 and August 17, 1822, over the signature "R." (see 6 above), and number III, August 10, 1822, over the signature "F." (see 3 above).

42. Published over the signature "R." in the *True American*, December 28, 1822, as "Verses on a Physician who Deserted a Great Commercial City on the Approach and Symptoms of the Yellow or Malignant Fever." It is such changes in signature and title (see the bibliography at the end of our present volume) which suggest that Freneau contributed the poems to both the *Fredonian* and the *True American*, rather than that either newspaper simply reprinted the poems from the other.

43. Rudolf Kirk, "Freneau's 'View' of Princeton," *Journal of the Rutgers University*

Library, III, 21 (December, 1939) finds the poem, though "without slavish imitation," "clearly inspired" by Thomas Gray's "Ode on a Distant Prospect of Eton College."

44. Freneau was still bound to Pope. This poem is an extended paraphrase of the English poet's "Verses to Mr. C.," *Poetical Works*, p. 488.

45. Poems in Freneau's manner, but which cannot be identified by any of his signatures, in the *Fredonian:* "The Dying Prophecy of Tecumseh," January 30, 1823, and "Lines to the Memory of John Nathan Hutchins, who, for more than Fifty Successive Years, Published an Almanac in this Country," September 29, 1824 (reprinted in the *True American*, October 9, 1824) ; and in the *True American:* "On National Prospects and Improvements," May 25; "The Alleghany Beer-House (Written Several Years ago) Addressed to a Man in Power," June 8; "On the New York Claims to the Exclusive Navigation and Use of the Waters Bounding on the Eastern Coasts of New Jersey, as far as High Water Mark," June 15; "The Promenade; or, Walks of Art and Nature," June 29; "The Female Astrologer (A New England Story)," June 29; stanzas following an account of Eleuthra in the Bahamas, "written on the aforementioned spot in 1786, but have not appeared in print," July 13, 1822; "On the Reign of Peace, and Improvements in Arts, Science, with Some Lines Commemorative of Gen. James J. Wilson, Deceased," August 24 (reprinted in the *Fredonian*, September 22) ; "On Signora Crachami, the Sicilian Dwarf Lady, about Eighteen and One Quarter Inches in Height; and, for Several Years, Past, Exhibited as a Curiosity, or *Lusus Naturae*, in London," September 4 (reprinted in the *Fredonian*, September 15) ; "Submarine Taxation. A Voice from the Sea-Coasts of New Jersey," September 11; "Extract of a Letter from Cadet George to his Cousin Jonathan," September 25; "A Village Dialogue, between Madan Fly-About and Dorothy Doolittle, her Female Companion," October 1; "The Portrait Painter. On Several Ill Drawn Pictures of Men Celebrated in and since the Revolutionary War in America, Suspended from the Wall of a Certain Country Hotel, or Tavern," October 16 (reprinted in the *Fredonian*, November 8, as "The Groupe. At a Certain Tavern in Long Island, a Number of Celebrated Revolutionary Personages, and Others are Displayed on a Wall Drawn by a Portrait Painter, by No Means Master of his Business") ; "On General La Fayette's Approach to York, in Virginia," October 24 (reprinted in the *Fredonian*, November 10) ; and "Stanzas, Written at a Small House in Chestnut Street, Philadelphia, Occupied Some Years Ago, as a Tavern or Beer House; and Erected by the Famous William Penn about the Year 1769, Being the First House Built on the Spot where Philadelphia now Stands," November 13, 1824.

46. MS *Old Town Book of the Township of Middletown, containing the records of the Town Beginning with the year 1699 and ending November 5, 1823*, Monmouth County Historical Association, March 16, 1822.

47. A writ, dated October 7, 1823, from the Court of Chancery of the State of New Jersey to Richard Lloyd, Sheriff of Monmouth County, ordered that all lands belonging to Philip Freneau be offered for sale to satisfy a mortgage given April 29, 1805 (MS *Monmouth County Deeds*, H2, 331). A "Sheriff's Sale" was advertised in the *Trenton Federalist* from November 4 to December 29, 1823, and took place at the house of William Johnson, innkeeper, in Middletown, February 10, 1824. At this time John Crawford, Sr., "by his friend Catherine Freneau," purchased the tract for $275—in 1927 a plot of seven acres from the Freneau homestead was sold for $16,000 (*New Brunswick Times*, September 11, 1927) ; in 1939 the owner refused an offer of $17,000 for the same seven acres (*New York Herald-Tribune*, July 2, 1939).

48. Tuckerman, "Memoir of Dr. Francis," p. xlv.

49. Horner, *This Old Monmouth of Ours*, p. 166, say, "In his youth the present writer knew men who knew him well, men like Captain Haddock Whitlock, born 1800 . . . and Asbury Fountain, born 1800 . . . who lived just north of the Freneaus. Men like these had no very high opinion to express of him as a man."

50. Mary Freneau to Margaret Freneau, February 23, 1827 (MS owned by the Rutgers University Library). Philip Freneau apparently moved from Mount Pleasant to the farm on the outskirts of Freehold after the sale of his property in February, 1824 (see note 47 above). According to the family Bible, a granddaughter, Eleanor Freneau Hammell, was born at Mount Pleasant, November 30, 1823, while her younger sister, Sarah Hammell, was born at Freehold, October 26, 1826. The location of Freneau's last home has long been pointed out by informed citizens of Monmouth County; see, however, Philip Marsh and Milton Ellis, "Freneau's Last Home," *Proceedings of the New Jersey Historical Society*, XVII, 2 (April, 1939). After her husband's death, Mrs. Freneau and her daughters sold in 1835 land held in their names at Mount Pleasant (MS *Monmouth County Deeds*, M3, 38) and in September, 1838, sold the farm near Freehold to John Buck (see MS *Monmouth County Deeds*, V3, 181 and 187, and deed of sale now in the possession of Mr. Howard Buck, the present owner of the farm). Thereafter, until her death on September 1, 1851, Eleanor Freneau lived in New York with the Hammells. She was buried in the Forman family burial ground on the highroad between Mount Pleasant and Middletown Point (MS Hammell notes, p. 3; see, also, the MS pension application for record of Mrs. Freneau's persistent and eventually successful attempts to collect her husband's pension of thirty-five dollars a year).

51. See the appendix to the present volume.

52. Years later the *Monmouth Inquirer*, December 16, 1880, reported that "John Connolly, an employee in the Inquirer office for over half a century, knew Freneau well, and has frequently put in type in the Inquirer office, poems from his manuscripts." Only scattering numbers of the *Inquirer* have been found for the period before Freneau's death; but see note 6 of chapter VII.

53. See, also, Peter F. Hunn to Philip Freneau, March 12, 1829 (MS owned by the Rutgers University Library).

54. After Freneau's death (perhaps, as tradition suggests, before), his oldest grandson, Philip Freneau Leadbeater, became Philip Leadbeater Freneau, but died in 1880 (*Monmouth Inquirer*, December 16, 1880) without male issue.

55. MS indenture, November 20, 1828 (owned by Mrs. George Yates Gilbert, Ridgewood, New Jersey), and MS *Monmouth County Deeds*, V3, 180.

56. MS indenture, November 22, 1830 (owned by the New Jersey Historical Society), and MS *Monmouth County Deeds*, T2, 11 and 46; and A3, 438.

57. MS pension application. As no records existed, it was necessary for several of his acquaintances in Monmouth to sign affidavits that Freneau had been a soldier.

58. The MS receipt of Freneau's purchase of one share in the Freehold Library Company, September 30, 1830, is in the Freneau Collection, Rutgers University Library.

59. *Monmouth Inquirer*, December 19, 1832; see, also, the account of David Vanderveer Perrine (*Monmouth Democrat*, August 1, 1935), whose father was one of the last to see Freneau alive, and of John Connolly (*Monmouth Inquirer*, December 16, 1880), who is said to have met Freneau that evening as he walked home over the fields.

60. *New York Mirror*, January 12, 1833; other more perfunctory obituaries of Freneau appeared in the *Boston Advertiser*, December 26; the *United States Gazette, Boston Transcript*, and *New York Evening Post*, December 27; the *New Jersey Gazette* and *Gazette of the United States*, December 29; the *New York Spectator*, December 31, 1832; and the *New Jersey Journal*, January 1, 1833.

APPENDIX

I. Freneau Manuscripts

So little manuscript material by Freneau exists that it seems proper to list it all. The first of his autographs which can be dated is his signature, July 6, 1767, in the Records of the Old Tennent Church, Monmouth County Historical Association; the last, his signature, August 1, 1832, on his application for a pension. Between these dates the following manuscript items are found:

1770. "Father Bombo's Pilgrimage to Mecca in Arabia. Volume II. Wherein is given a true account of the innumerable and surprizing adventures which befell him in the course of that long and tedious Journey, Till he once more returned safe to his native Land as related by his own Mouth. Written by H.B. and P.F. 1770. . . . Satires against the Tories. Written in the last War between the Whigs & Cliosophians in which the former obtained a compleat Victory." This volume, in the Historical Society of Philadelphia, represents juvenile prose and verse by Hugh Henry Brackenridge and Philip Freneau, together with three doggerel burlesques signed "J. Maddison."

1772–1822. Letters written by Freneau are among the Madison Papers, the Jefferson Papers, and the miscellaneous manuscripts in the Library of Congress; the Freneau Collection in the Rutgers University Library; the Gratz, the Giles, and the Lea and Febiger Collections in the Historical Society of Pennsylvania; the DeWitt Clinton Papers in the Columbia University Library; the Collidge Collection in the Massachusetts Historical Society; the miscellaneous manuscripts in the New Jersey Historical Society; and the private collection of Mr. Harold E. Pickerskill, as follows:

November 22, 1772	To James Madison	(Madison Papers, I, 17)
August 28, 1787	To Mathew Carey	(Gratz Collection)
November 10, 1787	To Mathew Carey	(Lea and Febiger, XVI, 4214)
April 20, 1791	To Mr. Rutherford	(New Jersey Historical Society)
July 25, 1791	To James Madison	(Madison Papers, XIV, 28)
N. d., *ca.* 1792	To Mathew Carey	(Lea and Febiger, VI, 1381)
January 2, 1792	To Mathew Carey	(Lea and Febiger, VI, 1379)
January 27, 1792	To Thomas Jefferson	(Collidge Collection)
October 11, 1793	To Thomas Jefferson	(Jefferson Papers, 2d ser., XXXIII, 48)

December 2, 1793	To William B. Giles	(Giles Collection)
November 2, 1794	To James Madison	(Madison Papers, XVII, 92)
May 20, 1795	To James Madison	(Madison Papers, XVIII, 51)
November 8, 1796	To DeWitt Clinton	(Clinton Papers)
December 1, 1796	To James Madison	(Madison Papers, XIX, 101)
August 12, 1800	To Seth Paine	(Library of Congress)
March 1, 1801	To Peter Freneau	(Freneau Collection)
June 26, 1801	To Seth Paine	(Library of Congress)
April 8, 1809	To James Madison	(Madison Papers, XXXVII, 73)
May 12, 1809	To James Madison	(Madison Papers, XXXVII, 78)
May 27, 1809	To Thomas Jefferson	(Jefferson Papers, 2d. ser., XXXIV, 13)
August 7, 1809	To James Madison	(Madison Papers, XXXVIII, 67)
January 12, 1815	To James Madison	(Madison Papers, LVIII, 14)
March 3, 1815	To James Madison	(Madison Papers, LVIII, 74)
May 10, 1815	To James Madison	(Madison Papers, LIX, 51)
May 15, 1815	To John W. Francis	(Harold E. Pickerskill)
October 26, 1818	To Mathew Carey	(Lea and Febiger, XXV, 11633)
May 14, 1822	To John W. Francis	(Harold E. Pickerskill)

1773–74. A manuscript volume containing Freneau's notes on his reading in theology, lists of books to be read, "What a Deacon should have studied in order to his ordination," "Proper texts for Sermons," etc., in the Freneau Collection, Rutgers University Library.

1775. "General Gage's Soliloquy. Printed in New York, August, 1775. By Gaine." A transcript in Freneau's handwriting of one of his pre-Revolutionary satires, in the Library Company of Philadelphia, Ridgeway Branch.

1779–80. Notebook in the Freneau Collection, Rutgers University Library, containing:

1. Log of the brig *Rebecca*, October 15 to November 7, 1779.

2. "Accounts of cash and Sundries Supply'd the Hands of the Brig Rebecca in Santa Cruz in the Island of Teneriffe in the months of November and December, 1779."

3. "The Spy," Acts I and II, with part of Act III. (One sheet from this manuscript, containing the end of Act III, Scene 3, and the beginning of Scene 4, is in the Princeton University Library. Another, containing the eight concluding lines of Act IV and Scene 1 of Act V, was sold, *ca.* 1902, by Dodd, Mead and Company to a private collector—see Paltsits, *Bibliography*, p. 39—and has not since been located.)

4. "Some Account of the Capture of the Ship Aurora."

5. "The Prison Ship."

1779–1804. Records of voyages made by Freneau are found in his autograph on the end pages and inside covers of his copy of the second volume of *Pub. Ovidii Nasonis Opera Omnia* (Monmouth County Historical Association) and of *The Elements of Navigation* (Freneau Collection, Rutgers University Library).

Ca. 1822. Manuscript drafts of poems or parts of poems in Freneau's hand are found on the end papers, flyleafs, or inside covers of his copies of the *Miscellaneous for Sentimentalists, The Elements of Natural Philosophy*, and *The History and Adventures of Don Quixote* (Freneau Collection, Rutgers University Library); in *Pub. Ovidii Nasonis Opera Omnia* (Monmouth County Historical Association); in *An Address to the Inhabitants of the British Settlements in America* and *The Works of J. J. Rousseau* (Princeton University Library).

1827. The first thirty-two lines of a poem entitled "Winter" are found in Freneau's autograph in the New York Public Library: the last four lines have been removed and are found pasted on extra page 14740, opposite page 330, of volume II, part 2, of the specially illustrated, large paper edition of Philip Freneau's *Poems Relating to the American Revolution*, ed. Evert A. Duyckinck, New York, 1865, in the same library. A facsimile of the title, the last ten lines, and the signature from the "Winter" manuscript is used as frontispiece to the trade edition of the same 1865 collection.

II. Freneau's Reading

WE have seen (note 10 of chapter VII) that as a practical journalist, Freneau had apparently little time for reading. When he needed a volume for reference, he borrowed from the well-stocked shelves of his bookseller friend, Mathew Carey (see the MS Lea and Febiger Collection, VI, 1381). As a student, however, he had been most happy in an atmosphere of belles-lettres. Many years later Dr. John W. Francis found it "remarkable how tenaciously Freneau preserved the acquisitions of his early classical studies, notwithstanding he had for many years, in the after portion of his life, been occupied in pursuits so entirely alien to books" (in Duyckinck, *Cyclopædia of American Literature*, I, 334). We have seen in chapter II with what avidity the younger Freneau studied Horace. Professor Harry Hayden Clark, in "The Literary Influences of Philip Freneau," has further indicated the breadth of the student's collegiate reading in the classics. Moreover, as a student of divinity, Freneau studied, analyzed, or quoted many books in his theological notebook. In listing these books below, I have marked with an asterisk those which were among the books given in 1755 by Governor Belcher to the library of Nassau Hall and which, therefore, are books Freneau might have used if he read theology at Princeton. The particular editions here cited, however, are not necessarily those which Freneau used but are at any rate editions in which I have been able to verify the notes he made: his short-title references in the notebook are seldom to pages, but to subjects; where it has been possible to indicate the exact pages which Freneau studied, I have done so.

Guilielmi Bucani, *Institutiones Theologicæ* (Geneva, 1609), pp. 622–23 and 651 ff.

Gilbert Burnet, *A Discourse on Pastoral Care** (London, 1736), pp. 123 ff. and 143–48.

Gilbert Burnet, *An Exposition of the Thirty-nine Articles of the Church of England** (London, 1736), pp. 271 ff.

Matthew Henry, *An Exposition of the Old and New Testaments* (London, 1721).

Robert Jenkin, *The Reasonableness and Certainty of the Christian Religion** (London, 1734), pp. 145 ff.

Daniel Neal, *History of the Puritans** (London, 1732), I, 33.

John Norris, *A Philosophical Discourse concerning the Natural Immortality of the Soul* (London, 1708).

Simon Patrick, *The Christian Sacrifice, A Treatise Shewing the Necessity End and Manner of Receiving the Holy Communion** (London, 1713), pp. 180 and 205–08.

Simon Patrick, *Mensa Mystica: or, a Discourse concerning the Sacrament of the Lord's Supper*, in *Works* (Oxford, 1858), I, 65 ff.

John Pearson, *An Exposition of the Creed* (London, 1801), pp. 41, 112, 236–38, and 368.

Thomas Salmon, *The Chronological Historian, Containing a Regular Account of all Material Transactions and Occurrences, Ecclesiastical, Civil, and Military, Relating to English Affairs, from the Invasion of the Romans to the Death of George I* (London, 1733).

John Selden, *The Table Talk of John Selden* (London, 1689).

Francisco Turrettino, *Institutio Theologicæ* (London, 1696).

James Usher, *A Body of Divinity, or the Summe and Substance of Christian Religion, Catechistically Propounded* (London, 1658), III, 459 ff.

Isaac Watts, *Sermons, Discourses, and Essays on Several Subjects** (London, 1752), III, 552 ff.

Wollebius, *Theologica Latina* (Amsterdam, 1637).

A study of Freneau's poetry reveals the extent of his dependence on the books he read. I have discussed in chapters II and III his debt to Pope, Horace, Churchill, and Goldsmith. At one time or another, however, the whole panorama of ancient and modern literature seems to have passed before him. Professor Clark in "The Literary Influences" has examined in much detail the influence of Ovid, Lucretius, Seneca, Vergil, Juvenal, Shakespeare, Waller, Sackwell, Joseph Warton, Young, Blair, Collins, and Gray. Edward G. Ainsworth, "An American Translator of Ariosto: Philip Freneau," *American Literature*, IV, 4 (January, 1933); Joseph M. Beatty, Jr., "Churchill and Freneau," *American Literature*, II, 121–30 (May, 1930); A. B. Benson, "Misconception in Philip Freneau's Scandinavian War Song," *Journal of English and German Philology*, XXVIII, 111–16 (January, 1929); Thomas P. Haviland, "A Measure for the Early Freneau's Debt to Milton," *Publications of the Modern Language Association of America*, LV, 1033–40 (December, 1940); and S. B. Hustvedt, "Philippic Freneau," *American Speech*, IV, 1–18 (October, 1928), each touch on a phase of Freneau's literary indebtedness. Miss Ellen A. Ganey, *The Satires of Philip Freneau*, typescript Master's essay, 1928, in the Columbia University Library, lists each reference made by Freneau to Shakespeare and to the Bible.

The authors mentioned or quoted most often by Freneau are Vergil, Horace, Shakespeare, and Pope. But in casual reference or quotation the following also appear in his writings: among the ancients, Aesop, Bion, Cicero, Diodorus, Homer, Lucian, Martial, Plato, Pliny, Plutarch, Pythagoras, and Sappho; among modern European writers, Beaumarchais, Boileau, Boulanger, Cervantes, Condorcet, Erasmus, Fénelon, Mirabeau, Molière, Montesquieu, Petrarch, Rabelais, Racine, Rousseau, and Voltaire; among English writers not already mentioned, Addison, Blackmore, Bolingbroke, Bunyan, Burns, Butler, Chaucer, Chesterfield, Darwin, Defoe, Dryden, Fielding, Gay, Glover, Johnson, More, Ossian, Otway, Percy, Raleigh, Ramsay, Spenser, Swift, Thomson, Whitehead, and Wolcot; and among American writers, Barlow, Carey, Dwight, Franklin, Humphreys, Irving, Markoe, Cotton Mather, Paine, and Trumbull.

The Freneaus were proud of their own library at Mount Pleasant. It was the accumulation of many years. When Peter died at Charleston in 1813, many of his volumes were added to it. When the old house burned in 1818, some of the books were rescued and for a long time were among the prized possessions of Freneau descendants. Eventually, however, the library became scattered, and for several years disappeared. A few books have been found in the Huntington Library, in the Princeton University Library, the library of the Monmouth County Historical Association, and in the private collection of Mr. Harold E. Pickerskill. Recently, thanks to the foresighted perseverance of Mr. George A. Osborn, a number have been gathered together in the Freneau Collection in the Rutgers University Library. Unless otherwise indicated, the volumes listed below are part of the latter collection.

ADDISON, JOSEPH. Miscellaneous Works in Verse and Prose of the Late Right Honourable Joseph Addison, Esq; with Some Account of the Life and Writings of the Author, by Mr. Ticknell. In Four Volumes (Edinburgh, 1759), Vol. I.

Autographed on flyleaf "P. Freneau his Book" and on p. 104 "Philip Freneau."

ANSON, GEORGE. Voyage au tour de monde, fait dans les années 1740, 41, 42, 43 & 44 (Paris, 1764).

Autographed on title page, flyleaf, and p. 74 "Pierre Freneau 1781" and on rear flyleaf "Pierre Freneau June 7, 1787."

BRADY, NICHOLAS, and TATE, NAHUM. A New Version of the Psalms of David Fitted to the Tunes Used in Churches (London, 1757).

Autographed opposite p. 1 "Andrew Freneau his Book 1758" and on the rear flyleaf "Agnes Fresneau her Book June the 10 1761 Book of Common Prayer Mount Pleasant Dec 3d 1776."

BROOKE, HENRY. The Fool of Quality, or, the History of Henry, Earl of Moreland. In Five Volumes. The Second Edition (Dublin, 1771), Vol. I.

Autographed on flyleaf "Philip Freneau" and on title page "Philip Freneau 1785." *Huntington Library*.

BECCARIA, MARQUIS DE. An Essay on Crimes and Punishments. With a Commentary Attributed to Monsieur de Voltaire (Philadelphia, 1778).

Autographed on flyleaf "Philadelphia December 10, 1781 Bot of Robert Bell, price 8/specie" and on p. 3 "Philip Freneau 1780." *Pickerskill.*

CERVANTES, MIGUEL DE. The History and Adventures of the Renowned Don Quixote. In Four Volumes (London, 1761), Vol. I.

Autographed on title page "P. Freneau 1795."

DEFOE, DANIEL. The Life and Most Surprising Adventures of Robinson Crusoe (Edinburgh, 1773).

Autographed on flyleaf and on p. 1 "P. Freneau 1795."

DERHAM, GUILLAUME. Théologie physique ou démonstration de l'existence de Dieu (Rotterdam, 1726), Vol. I.

Autographed on flyleaf "Philip Freneau Bought three Volumes of this work at Bell's Auction—February 1783 Philadelphia—Physico-Theology —2 vols 6/ Astro-Theology 1 do 2/6." *Pickerskill.*

DERHAM, GUILLAUME. Théologie physique ou demonstration de l'existence de Dieu. (Rotterdam, 1726), Vol. II.

Autographed on title page "Philip Freneau 1783." The third volume bought at this time, *Astro-Théology: or a Demonstration of the Being and Attributes of God from a Survey of the Heavens*, has not been found.

FIELDING, HENRY. The History of Tom Jones, a Foundling (London, 1750), Vol. IV.

Autographed title page "Peter Freneau 1777."

FIELDING, HENRY. The Works of Henry Felding, with a Life of the Author. In Twelve Volumes (London, 1783), Vol. VI.

Autographed on flyleaf "Philip Freneau's Book."

GLOVER, RICHARD. Leonidas: a Poem (Dublin, 1737).

Autographed on flyleaf "Philip Freneau 1784."

GRANVILLE, GEORGE. The Dramatic Works of the Right Honourable George Granville (Glasgow, 1752).

Autographed on title page "Peter Freneau, 1778" and on the flyleaf "Peter Freneau his Book Bought in Reading in Pennsylvania June 16 1778. Price 10/."

HORACE. The Odes, Epodes, and Carmen Seculare, Translated into English Prose (London, 1760), Vol. I.

Autographed on flyleaf "1768 Nassau Hall Nova Ceasarea Philip Freneau his Book." *Monmouth.*

HUMPHREYS, DAVID. An Essay on the Life of the Honourable Major-General Israel Putnam (Hartford, 1787).

Autographed on p. 7 "P. Freneau, 1792."

The London Magazine for 1733.

Autographed on p. 1 "P Freneau 1784" and "Philip Freneau his Book 1768."

MARTIN, W. B. Philosophia Britannica, or a New and Comprehensive System of the Newtonian Philosophy (London, 1747), Vol. I.

Autographed on verso title page "Philip Freneau 1770" and on p. 1 "Philip Freneau his Book 1768." *Monmouth.*

Miscellanies for Sentimentalists: containing, 1. Life of David Hume, written by himself, II. Travels of a Philosopher, by Le Paivre. III. Principles of Politeness and of Knowing the World, by Lord Chesterfield. IV. Maxims and Moral Reflections, by the Duke de la Rochefoucault. V. Travels of the Imagination; a True Journey from Newcastle to London, by J. Murray. VI. American Independence, by Philip F——u. VII. The Humble Confession, Declaration, Recantation, and Apology of Benjamin Towne, Printer in Philadelphia. (Philadelphia, 1778.)

Autographed on flyleaf "Philip Freneau his Book A present from Mr. Rob. Bell Philadelphia 1778," and the title page of every section contains the signature "Philip Freneau"; a rough draft of a poem on the Erie Canal (see the *True American*, June 30, 1821) is written on the inside cover, and the rear flyleaf contains a draft of a deed executed (1813) between Philip Freneau and Felix Herbert.

OVID. Pub. Ovidii Nasonis Opera Omnia. In Très Tomes Divisa. Accuranté Cornelie Schrevelio (London, 1662), Vol. I.

Autographed on flyleaf "Philip Freneau—a present from Aedanus Burke Esq. Charleston, S. C. Jany 8th 1800."

Ovid. Pub. Ovidii Nasonis Opera Omnia. In Très Tomes Divisa. Accuranté Cornelie Schrevelio (London, 1662), Vol. III.

Autographed on flyleaf "Philip Freneau a present from Aedanus Burke Esq. Charleston, S. C. Jany 8th 1800" and contains a record of Freneau's voyages from 1770 to 1804. *Monmouth.*

Ovid. Ovid's Art of Love, in Three Books. Together with his Remedy of Love. Translated into English Verse by Several Eminent Hands. To which are Added, The Court of Love: A Tale of Chaucer; and the History of Love (London, 1757).

Autographed on title page "Peter Freneau, 1778" and on flyleaf "Peter Freneau his Book 1778."

Parke, John. The Lyric Works of Horace, Translated into English Verse: to which are Added, a Number of Original Poems (Philadelphia, 1786).

Autographed on flyleaf "Peter Freneau 1787."

Pope, Alexander. The Works of Alexander Pope. Volume VIII. Being the First of his Letters (London, 1757).

Autographed on p. 3 "Peter Freneau 1761" and on p. 75 "Catherine L. Freneau March 20 1848" and "Peter Freneau 1761." *Princeton.*

Pope, Alexander. The Works of Alexander Pope. Volume IX. Being the Second of his Letters (London, 1757).

Autographed on flyleaf "Philip Freneau his Book 1780" and on p. 3 "Peter Freneau 1761." *Monmouth.*

Robertson, John. The Elements of Navigation (London, 1772), Vol. I.

Autographed on flyleaf "Philip Freneau 1780" and contains a record of Freneau's voyages from April 1, 1778, to August 9, 1799.

Robertson, John. The Elements of Navigation (London, 1772), Vol. II.

Autographed on flyleaf "David Watson Sept 20th 1775" and "Philip Freneau his Book of Navigation 1776" and on the second flyleaf "Philip Freneau 1780—Ship Aurora." *Monmouth.*

Rousseau, Jean Jacques. The Works of J. J. Rousseau. Translated from the French. In ten volumes. Volume the Eighth (Edinburgh, 1774).

Autographed on flyleaf "Ph. Freneau 1786." A draft of a poem on General Jackson appears on the rear flyleaf. *Princeton.*

Rush, Benjamin. An Address to the Inhabitants of the British Settlements in America, upon Slave Keeping (Philadelphia, 1773).

Autographed on flyleaf "Ex Libris Philippi Freneau, Jan. 25: 1775," and the end papers contain rough drafts of several of his later poems. *Princeton.*

Shakespeare, William. The Complete Works of Shakespeare. Volume the Eighth, containing Romeo and Juliet, Hamlet, Othello, a Glossary, an Index (Edinburgh, 1753).

Autographed on inside rear cover "Philip Freneau."

The Spectator. Volume the First (London, 1767).

Autographed on inside front cover "Ph. Freneau Spt. 2d 1817" and on title page "Peter Freneau 1782." *Pickerskill.*

The Spectator. Volume VIII (London, 1767).

Autographed on inside rear cover "Philip Freneau." *Pickerskill.*

THOMSON, JAMES. *The Seasons* (London, 1768).

Autographed on title page "Peter Freneau 1778."

VERTOT, ABBÉ DE. The History of the Knights Hospitallers of St. John of Jerusalem (Edinburgh, 1757), Vol. III.

Autographed on flyleaf "Philip Freneau—1784." *Pickerskill.*

WATTS, ISAAC. The Works of the Late Reverend and Learned Isaac Watts (London, 1753), Vol. V.

Autographed on title page "Philip Freneau" and "Peter Freneau his Book Bought at New York Anno Domini 1760" and "Agnes Kearny her Book."

BIBLIOGRAPHY

The Writings of Philip Freneau

Freneau's writings appear over a variety of pseudonyms, a few of which, such as "Robert Slender," "Hezekiah Salem," and "Sinbat," are peculiarly his own, but most of which were the common property of many other eighteenth-century newspaper correspondents. In addition to the three mentioned above, he uses the following signatures:

A.	Hermes	R.
A.B.	Justitia Fiat	R.R.
Adam Bluebeard	K.	Rusticus
Cassibilan	K.V.	Serjeant Major
Catholicus	Lucullus	Simon Simple
Christopher Clodhopper	M.	Sinbat the Sailor
per	Martinus Scriblerus	Sylvius
Alexander Dismal	A Monarchist	T.B.
Dobbins	Myrtilla	Tantalus
E.	N.	Timothy Taurus
F.	N.R.	Tory
A Foe to Malice	Orestes	U.
G.	Philomeides	Virginius
G.C.	The Pilgrim	W.H.
Harpax	Plus Ultra	W.S.
Hawser Trunnion	Priscilla Tripstreet	
Heraclitus	Pylades	

Freneau's writings are listed below in chronological order of first appearance, with a detailed notation of subsequent reprintings and changes in title of each separately printed poem or essay. Although files of more than three hundred newspapers and periodicals published between 1774 and 1832 have been examined, every republication of every item has undoubtedly not been discovered. The results below, however, fairly indicate both the extent to which Freneau's writings were copied throughout the United States during his lifetime and the relative popularity of each poem and essay. In compiling this bibliography I have built with gratitude on foundations firmly laid by Dr. Victor Hugo Paltsits and Professor Fred Lewis Pattee.

418

During the period of his editorship of the *Freeman's Journal* (1781–84), the *Daily Advertiser* (1790–91), the *National Gazette* (1791–93), the *Jersey Chronicle* (1795–96), and the *Time-Piece* (1797–98), Freneau undoubtedly wrote many short unsigned articles and editorial notices. Except in the case of the *Freeman's Journal*, a specially marked file of which is in the New Jersey Historical Society Library, I have not attempted to identify any such contributions. In general, I have omitted all doubtful attributions. I have, however, listed uncollected articles and poems published over familiar pseudonyms and, in a few cases, unsigned contributions which have seemed to me undeniably by Freneau. Throughout I have followed the spelling and capitalization of titles as they appeared in the first printing; when significant change was made in subsequent printings, I have indicated the change.

Short titles have been used for newspapers in which Freneau's contributions appeared or were reprinted. I have not given the town or city in which a newspaper was published, except when duplication of title made a complete citation necessary: this information will be found in the index. For location of newspaper files, see Charles S. Brigham, "Bibliography of American Newspapers, 1690–1820," *Proceedings of the American Antiquarian Society*, new ser., *passim*. In locating copies of separately printed items, the following abbreviations are used:

AAS	American Antiquarian Society, Worcester, Mass.
BA	Boston Athenæum, Boston, Mass.
BM	British Museum, London, England
BPL	Boston Public Library
BU	Brown University Library, Providence, R. I.
CLC	Charleston Library Company, Charleston, S. C.
CU	Columbia University Library, New York, N. Y.
HC	Harvard College Library, Cambridge, Mass.
HL	Henry E. Huntington Library, San Marino, Calif.
HSP	Historical Society of Pennsylvania, Philadelphia, Penna.
LC	Library of Congress, Washington, D. C.
LCP	Library Company of Philadelphia
MHA	Monmouth County Historical Association, Freehold, N. J.
MHS	Massachusetts Historical Society, Boston, Mass.
NJHS	New Jersey Historical Society, Newark, N. J.
NJSL	New Jersey State Library, Trenton, N. J.
NYHS	New York Historical Society, New York, N. Y.
NYPL	New York Public Library
NYSL	New York State Library, Albany, N. Y.
PU	Princeton University Library, Princeton, N. J.
RU	Rutgers University Library, New Brunswick, N. J.

1772

A/ Poem,/ on the/ Rising Glory/ of/ America;/ being an/ Exercise/ Delivered at the Public Commencement at/ Nassau-Hall, September 25, 1771./
[*Quotation, six lines from Seneca.*]/ Philadelphia:/ Printed by Joseph
Crukshank, for R. Aitken,/ Bookseller, opposite the London-coffee-/ house,
in Front-street./ M,DCC,LXXII./

 12mo; 28pp. Written in collaboration with Hugh Henry Brackenridge, 1771; advertised, *New-York Journal,* August 10–Setember 7,
1772. Copies: BU, HL, HSP, LC, MHS, NYHS, NYPL, PU. Reprinted:
Poems (1786), pp. 42–58, "a little altered from the original . . .
such parts being inserted here as were written by the author of these
Volumes. A few more modern lines towards the conclusion are incorporated with the rest, being a supposed prophetical anticipation
of subsequent events"; *Poems* (1795), pp. 36–46, and (1809), I, 66–78,
"Being part of a Dialogue pronounced on a public occasion." Charles
Evans, in *American Bibliography,* VIII, 32, lists A poem, on the rising
glory of America; being an exercise delivered at the public commencement at Nassau-Hall, September 25, 1771. Philadelphia: Printed
by R. Aitken & Son, in Market Street, 1790. I have not seen this edition.
The/ American Village,/ a Poem./ To which are added,/ Several other
original Pieces in Verse./ By Philip Freneau, A.B./ [*Quotation, two lines
from Horace.*]/ New-York:/ Printed by S. Inslee and A. Car, on Moor's
Wharf./ M,DCC,LXXII./

 12mo; 28pp. Copies: BU, LC. Reprinted: The American Village/ A
Poem by/ Philip Freneau/ Reprinted in facsimile from the original/
edition published at New York/ in 1772, with an introduction/ by/
Harry Lyman Koopman/ and/ Bibliographical Data/ by/ Victor Hugo
Paltsits/ . . . / Providence, Rhode Island/ 1906./

1773

"Margery and Patty, A Boston Dialogue."
 Printed "in a New York Half sheet weekly Paper . . . called *The
American Whig,* now long since forgotten, and perhaps shot away in
cartridges during the Revolutionary war" (*True American,* July 27,
1822; see note 64 of chapter III).

1775

"The New Liberty Pole.—Take Care!"
 Printed in New York, April, 1775, "in a hand-bill, and circulated in

all directions, and carried thro' every street, and thrown into every door in the city" (*True American*, August 10, 1822).

American Liberty,/ A/ Poem./ [*One line from Vergil*]/ [*Two lines from Pope*]/ New-York:/ Printed by J. Anderson, at Beekman-Slip./ MDCCLXXV./

> 12mo; 12pp. Copies: BU, LC, LCP. Reprinted as The Present Situation of Affairs in North-America. A Poem. Philadelphia: B. Towne, 1775. 8vo; 8pp. Copy: BU (see note 72 of chapter III).

General Gage's Soliloquy. New York: Printed by Hugh Gaine, 1775.

> No copy of the original printing is found. The Library Company of Philadelphia has a manuscript copy in Freneau's hand, upon which is written, "Printed in New York August 1775. By Gaine." Reprinted: *Poems* (1786), pp. 67–71; (1795), pp. 106–09; and (1809), I, 163–66.

The Expedition of Timothy Taurus, Astrologer, to the Falls of the Passaick River, in New Jersey: Written soon after an excursion to the village at that place in August 1775, under the character of Timothy Taurus, a student in Astrology; and formerly printed in New-York.

> Title from *Poems* (1809), I, 167–78; no copy of an earlier publication is found.

A/ Voyage/ to/ Boston./ A/ Poem./ [*Quotation, five lines from Shakespeare*]/ By the Author of American Liberty, a Poem: General/ Gage's Soliloquy, &c./ New-York: Printed by John Anderson,/ at Beekman's Slip./

> 12mo; 24pp. Copies: LC, LCP, NYHS, RU. Another edition: Philadelphia:/ Sold by/ William Woodhouse,/ in Front-street./ M,DCC,LXXV./ 12mo; 24pp. Copies: AAS, HL, HSP, NJHS, NYHS, NYPL, PU. Reprinted as "The Midnight Consultations, or, a Trip to Boston. Published in New York, September 1775, by J. Anderson," *Poems* (1786), pp. 72–81; (1795), pp. 115–22; and (1809), I, 187–95.

"Reflections on Gage's Letter to General Washington, of Aug. 13," *Constitutional Gazette*, October 18, 1775.

> Reprinted as "On the Conqueror of America Shut up in Boston," *Poems* (1786), pp. 85–86; as "The Misnomer," (1795), pp. 211–12; as "To the Americans on the Rumoured Approach of the Hessian Forces, Waldeckers, &c (published 1775) . . . Occasioned by General Gage's Proclamation that the Provinces were in a State of Rebellion, and out of the King's Protection," (1809), I, 204–05; and, the last twelve lines only, without title in the *Public Advertiser*, July 14, 1812.

General Gage's/ Confession,/ Being the Substance of/ His Excellency's last Conference,/ With his Ghostly Father, Friar Francis./ [*Quotation,*

one line from Vergil]/ By the Author of the Voyage to Boston./ A Poem,
&c./ Printed in the Year, 1775./
,   8vo; 8pp. Copies: LCP, RU.
MacSwiggen; a Satire. Written 1775.

> Title from *Poems* (1786), p. 95; no copy of an original printing is
> found. Rewritten from "Satires against the Tories" (1770)—see note
> 51 of chapter II. Reprinted as "To Shylock Ap-Shenkin," *Poems*
> (1795), pp. 392–93, and as "A Satire in Answer to a Hostile Attack.
> (First written, and published 1775)," (1809), II, 22–26.

1778

The/ Travels/ of the/ Imagination;/ a true Journey from/ Newcastle to
London./ To which are added,/ American Independence,/ an/ everlasting
deliverance/ from/ British Tyranny:/ a Poem./ Philadelphia:/ Printed,
by Robert Bell, in Third-Street./ M DCC LXXVIII./

> 8vo; 126pp. Copies: HSP, LC, PU, RU. *The Travels of the Imagina-
> tion* was also issued from the same sheets as No. IV of Miscellanies/
> for/ Sentimentalists:/ . . ./ Philadelphia./ Printed and Sold by
> Robert Bell, in Third-street./ M.DCC.LXXVIII./ Copies: HL, HSP,
> RU. Freneau's poem, pp. 113–26, has its own title page: American/
> Independence,/ an everlasting/ Deliverance/ from/ British Tyr-
> anny./ A Poem./ By Philip F——, Author of the American Village,/
> Voyage to Boston, &c./ [*Quotation, six lines from Shakespeare*]/
> Philadelphia: Printed, by Robert Bell, in Third-Street./ M DCC
> LXXVIII./ Reprinted: as "America Independent," *Poems* (1786), pp.
> 153–65; (1795), pp. 139–46; (1809), I, 241–50; and, without title,
> in *The School of Wisdom; or, American Monitor*, Philadelphia, 1800,
> p. 123.

1779

Sir Henry Clinton's Invitation to the Refugees. Published as a ballad sheet,
1779.

> Frank Moore, *Songs and Ballads of the American Revolution*, New
> York, 1856, p. 359, states, "We have it in a ballad sheet, dated 1779."
> No copy of the ballad sheet has since been found. Reprinted as "Sir
> Harry's Call," *Freeman's Journal*, April 17, 1782, and *Poems* (1786),
> pp. 261–62; as "Sir Harry's Invitation," *Poems* (1795), pp. 212–13;
> and as "Sir Henry Clinton's Invitation," (1809), II, 101–02.

"Account of some of the West-India Islands, by a young American Philosopher and Bel Esprit, just returned from several small Voyages amongst
those Islands. Account of the Island of Bermuda, in a Letter to R.H. Esq.,"
United States Magazine, I, 31–34 (January, 1779).

"Account of the Island of Santa Cruz: Containing an original Poem on the Beauties of that Island. In a Letter to A.P. Esq.," *United States Magazine*, I, 81–88 (February, 1779).

"The Beauties of Santa Cruz," pp. 84–88, is reprinted: *Poems* (1786), pp. 133–52; (1795), pp. 129–39, as "Santa Cruz"; and (1809), I, 207–19.

"Account of the Island of St. James; in a Letter to Mr. A.A.," *United States Magazine*, I, 124 (March, 1779).

"King George the Third's Soliloquy," *United States Magazine*, I, 230–31 (May, 1779).

Reprinted: *Pennsylvania Packet*, June 5, 1779; *Poems* (1786), pp. 171–74; (1795), pp. 153–54; and (1809), II, 12–14.

"The Dying Elm. An Irregular Ode," *United States Magazine*, I, 280–81 (June, 1779).

Reprinted: *Poems* (1786), p. 38; (1795), p. 51; and (1809), I, 90.

"Columbus to Ferdinand," *United States Magazine*, I, 282–83 (June, 1779).

Reprinted: *Poems* (1786), pp. 39–41; (1795), pp. 24–25; (1809), I, 47–49; and *Grammatical Institute of the English Language*, Philadelphia, 1787, III, 362–64.

"The Loyalists," *United States Magazine*, I, 315–16 (July, 1779).

Not reprinted, but lines 1–9 were used by Freneau in *The British Prison-Ship* (1781), canto II, lines 11–19.

"The House of Night; Or, Six Hours Lodging with Death. A Vision," *United States Magazine*, I, 355–62 (August, 1779).

Reprinted as "The House of Night: a Vision," *Poems* (1786), pp. 101–23; and, very much shortened (see note 52 of chapter IV), as "The Vision of Night. (A Fragment.)," *Poems* (1795), pp. 92–94, and (1809), I, 145–47. Portions of "The House of Night," as printed in *Poems* (1786), were used in "The Hessian Debarkation," (1795), p. 215, and (1809), I, 205–06. Other portions of the poem, together with portions of "The Jamaica Funeral," *Poems* (1786), pp. 124–33, were used in "The Sexton's Sermon, at the Burial of a Deist," *Poems* (1809), I, 250–52.

"Psal. cxxxvii. Imitated, By Philip Freneau, a young Gentleman to whom in the course of this Work, we are greatly indebted," *United States Magazine*, I, 402–03 (September, 1779).

Reprinted as "Psalm CXXXVII Versified," *Poems* (1786), pp. 151–52; and as "The Jewish Lamentation at Euphrates," (1795), pp. 150–51, and (1809), I, 229–30.

"The Sea Voyage," *United States Magazine*, I, 435–36 (October, 1779).

"Unique in the October number of the *United States Magazine*," Pattee, in *Poems*, I, 293 n.

"A Dialogue between his Britannic Majesty and Mr. Fox. Supposed to have passed about the time of the approach of the combined Fleets of

France and Spain to the British Coasts, August 1779," *United States Magazine*, I, 495–501 (December, 1779).

> Reprinted: *Poems* (1786), pp. 177–85; (1795), pp. 155–59; and (1809), II, 14–20.

1780

"Verses to the Memory of Capt. Nicholas Biddle, of the Randolph Frigate of 32 guns, blown up in an engagement with Yarmouth, a British Man of War of 64 guns," *New-Jersey Gazette*, December 13, 1780.

> Reprinted as "A Poem on the Death of Capt. N. Biddle, who was blown up, in an Engagement with the Yarmouth, near Barbadoes," *The British Prison-Ship* (1781), pp. 21–23; and as "On the Death of Nicholas Biddle," *Poems* (1786), pp. 166–68; (1795), pp. 148–49; and (1809), I, 225–27.

1781

The British Prison-Ship:/ A/ Poem,/ in Four Cantoes. – – – –/

Viz. Canto
1. The Capture,
2. The Prison-Ship,
3. The Prison-Ship, continued,
4. The Hospital-Prison-Ship.

To which is added,/ A poem on the Death of Capt. N. Biddle,/ who was blown up, in an Engagement with the/ Yarmouth, near Barbadoes./ [*Quotation, thirteen lines from Milton*]/ Philadelphia:/ Printed by F. Bailey, in Market-Street./ M.DCC.LXXXI./

> 12mo; 24pp. Copies: BU, LCP, NYHS. Reprinted: *Independent Ledger*, June 25 and July 1, 1781; as an undated folio broadside, Description/ of the sufferings/ of those who were on board/ the Jersey and other prison ships in the harbour of New-York,/ during the struggle for our glorious independence,/ By an American who was a prisoner on board of one of them./ (Copy: HL—see Philip Marsh and Milton Ellis, "A Broadside of Freneau's *The Prison Ship*," *American Literature*, XI, 4 (March, 1939); *Poems* (1786), pp. 186–205; (1795), pp. 162–75, as "Canto's from a Prison Ship": (1809), II, 36–52; in *An Historical Sketch to the End of the Revolutionary War, of the Life of Silas Talbot, Esq.*, New York, 1803, pp. 111–25; and, excerpts only, in the *Port-Folio*, November 7, 1807, and the *Public Advertiser*, May 24 and 25, 1809.

"A Poem on the memorable victory obtained by the gallant capt. Paul Jones, of the Good Man Richard, over the Seraphis, &c. under the command of capt. Pearson," *Freeman's Journal*, August 8, 1781.

> Reprinted: *Poems* (1786), pp. 207–11; (1795), pp. 175–78; and (1809), II, 52–56.

"To his Excellency General Washington," *Freeman's Journal*, September 5, 1781.

Reprinted: *New-Jersey Journal*, September 19, 1781; *American Museum*, September, 1787, pp. 309–10; *Poems* (1786), pp. 212–14; and as "An Address to the Commander in Chief, Officers, and Soldiers of the American Army," (1795), pp. 183–84, and (1809), II, 58–60.

"Copy of an intercepted Letter from a New-York Tory, to his Friend in this city," *Freeman's Journal*, September 5, 1781.

Reprinted: *Poems* (1786), pp. 214–16; and as "A New-York Tory, to his Friend in Philadelphia," (1795), pp. 184–85, and (1809), II, 60–61.

"Reflection of an American on the above lines," *Freeman's Journal*, September 12, 1781.

Not reprinted, but marked in Freneau's file of the *Freeman's Journal* (see note 4 of chapter V).

"Dialogue between Lords Dunmore and Mansfield," *Freeman's Journal*, September 19, 1781.

Reprinted: *Poems* (1786), pp. 217–18; and as "A London Dialogue, Between My Lords Dunmore and Germaine," (1795), pp. 186–87, and (1809), II, 62–63.

"To Lord Cornwallis," *Postscript to the Freeman's Journal*, October 8, 1781.

Reprinted: *Poems* (1786), pp. 216–17; (1795), pp. 185–86; and (1809), II, 61–62.

"An Epistle from Lord Cornwallis to Sir Henry Clinton," *Freeman's Journal*, October 17, 1781.

Reprinted: *Poems* (1786), pp. 219–20; (1795), pp. 187–88; and (1809), II, 64–65.

"A Moral Thought," *Freeman's Journal*, October 24, 1781.

Reprinted: *Poems* (1786), p. 221; and as "The Vanity of Existence. To Thyrsis," (1795), pp. 95–96, and (1809), I, 148–49.

"On the fall of general earl Cornwallis, who, with above eight thousand men, surrendered themselves prisoners of war to the renowned and illustrious general George Washington, commander in chief of the allied armies of France and America, on the memorable 19th of October, 1781," *Freeman's Journal*, November 7, 1781.

Reprinted: Poems (1786), pp. 222–28; (1795), pp. 189–92; and (1809), II, 66–70.

"To the memory of the brave Americans, under general Greene, who fell in the action of Sept. 8, 1781," *Freeman's Journal*, November 21, 1781.

Reprinted: *Poems* (1786), pp. 229–30; (1795), pp. 192–93; (1809), II, 70–71; and *Investigator*, October 14, 1812.

"The Pilgrim, No. I," *Freeman's Journal*, November 21, 1781.
> Reprinted as "The Philosopher of the Forest. Numb. I. Written, and first printed in the Freeman's Journal, Nov. 1781," *Miscellaneous Works* (1788), pp. 281–88.

"The Pilgrim, No. II," *Freeman's Journal*, November 28, 1781.
> Reprinted in part as "Sentiments of a Traveller. Written 1780," *Miscellaneous Works*, pp. 311–13; and in part as "The Philosopher of the Forest, No. V.," *loc. cit.*, pp. 314–20.

"The Pilgrim, No. III," *Freeman's Journal*, December 5, 1781.
> Reprinted as "The Philosopher of the Forest, Numb. IV," *Miscellaneous Works*, pp. 305–11.

"The Pilgrim, No. IV," *Freeman's Journal*, December 12, 1781.
> Reprinted as "The Philosopher of the Forest, Numb. VI," *Miscellaneous Works*, pp. 320–25.

"The Pilgrim, No. V," *Freeman's Journal*, December 19, 1781.

"The Pilgrim, No. VI," *Freeman's Journal*, December 26, 1781.

1782

"The Pilgrim, No. VII," *Freeman's Journal*, January 2, 1782.

"Plato the Philosopher to his friend Theon," *Freeman's Journal*, January 2, 1782.
> Reprinted: *Poems* (1786), pp. 230–34; and as "To an Old Man," (1795), pp. 193–95, and (1809), II, 71–74.

Untitled verses, *Freeman's Journal*, January 9, 1782.
> Reprinted as "Prologue. Written to a Theatrical Entertainment in Philadelphia," *Poems* (1786), pp. 234–35; (1795), pp. 195–96; and (1809), pp. 74–75.

"The Pilgrim, No. VIII," *Freeman's Journal*, January 9, 1782.
> Reprinted as "The Philosopher of the Forest, Numb. X," *Miscellaneous Works*, pp. 360–67.

"The Pilgrim, No. IX," *Freeman's Journal*, January 16, 1782.

"Stanzas occasioned by the ruins of a country Inn, unroofed and blown down in a storm," *Freeman's Journal*, January 23, 1782.
> Reprinted: *New-York Daily Gazette*, June 12, 1789; *City Gazette*, August 1, 1789; *Poems* (1786), pp. 235–37; (1795), pp. 196–97; and (1809), II, 75–77.

"The Pilgrim, No. X," *Freeman's Journal*, January 23, 1782.
> Reprinted as "A Discourse upon Whigs and Tories, by Mr. Slender," *Miscellaneous Works*, pp. 367–75.

"The Pilgrim, No. XI," *Freeman's Journal*, January 30, 1782.

"The Royal Adventure," *Freeman's Journal*, January 30, 1782.
> Reprinted as "The Royal Adventurer," *New-Jersey Gazette*, February

6; *New-Jersey Journal*, February 6; *Connecticut Courant*, February
12; *Boston Gazette*, February 18, 1782; *State Gazette of North Caro-* ✓
lina, November 6, 1786; *New-York Journal*, August 16; *Independent
Gazetteer*, August 28, 1787; *New-York Journal*, March 4, 1795; *Poems*
(1786), pp. 237–39; (1795), pp. 198–99; and (1809), II, 77–78.

"Lord Dunmore's Petition to the Legislature of Virginia," *Freeman's Journal*, February 13, 1782.
> Reprinted: *New-Jersey Journal*, February 20, 1782; *Poems* (1786),
> pp. 239–41, (1795), pp. 199–200; and (1809), II, 79–80.

"The Pilgrim, No. XII," *Freeman's Journal*, February 13, 1782.

"Epigram occasioned by the title of Rivington's Royal Gazette being
scarcely legible," *Freeman's Journal*, February 13, 1782.
> Reprinted: *Royal Gazette*, March 2; *New-Jersey Journal*, March 27,
> 1782; *Poems* (1786), pp. 241–42; (1795), p. 200; and (1809), II,
> 80–81.

"A Speech that should have been spoken by the king of the island of Britain
to his Parliament," *Freeman's Journal*, February 20, 1782.
> Reprinted: *New-Jersey Journal*, February 27; *Connecticut Courant*,
> March 5, 1782; *Poems* (1786), pp. 244–46; (1795), pp. 202–03; and
> (1809), II, 83–84.

"The Pilgrim, No. XIII," *Freeman's Journal*, February 20, 1782.

"Rivington's Last Will and Testament, (A true copy from the Records),"
Freeman's Journal, February 27, 1782.
> Reprinted: *New-Jersey Journal*, April 10, 1782; *Poems* (1786), pp.
> 247–50; (1795), pp. 204–05; and (1809), II, 85–87.

"Lines occasioned by Mr. Rivington's new titular Types to his Royal
Gazette, of Feb. 27. (See an Epigram on the worn out Types of Said Title,
in No. XLIII. of this Journal)," *Freeman's Journal*, March 13, 1782.
> Reprinted: *New-Jersey Journal*, April 3, 1782; *Poems* (1786), pp.
> 242–43; (1795), p. 201; and (1809), II, 81–82.

"On Mr. Rivington's new engraved King's Arms to his Royal Gazette,"
Freeman's Journal, March 27, 1782.
> Reprinted: *New-Jersey Journal*, April 10; *Boston Gazette*, May 6,
> 1782; *Poems* (1786), pp. 243–44; (1795), pp. 201–02; and (1809),
> II, 82.

Untitled verses, *Freeman's Journal*, March 27, 1782.
> Reprinted: *New-Jersey Journal*, April 10, 1782; as "A Prophecy,"
> *Poems* (1786), pp. 250–51, and (1795), p. 178; and as "An Ancient
> Prophecy," (1809), II, 56.

"The Political Balance; or, the Fates of Britain and America compared, A
Tale," *Freeman's Journal*, April 3, 1782.
> Reprinted: *Poems* (1786), pp. 251–61; (1795), pp. 206–11; (1809),

II, 89–96; and rewritten as "The Case is Altering. Stanzas written on Ireland in the year 1781; extracted from a poem, entitled The Political Balance," *Time-Piece*, July 3, 1797.

"Sir Harry's Call," *Freeman's Journal*, April 17, 1782.

See *Sir Henry Clinton's Invitation to the Refugees* (1779) on p. 79 above.

Untitled article, *Freeman's Journal*, April 17, 1782.

Signed "Pylades." Reprinted as "Reflections, Narratives, and Ideas of the late Robert Slender," *Miscellaneous Works*, pp. 352–60.

"A Dialogue at Hyde-Park Corner," *Freeman's Journal*, April 24, 1782.

Reprinted: *Poems* (1786), pp. 263–64; (1795), p. 214; and (1809), II, 102–03.

Untitled article, *Freeman's Journal*, April 24, 1782.

Signed "Orestes." Not reprinted, but marked in Freneau's file of the *Freeman's Journal*.

"On the late royal sloop of war Gen. Monk (formerly the Washington) mounting six quarter deck wooden guns," *Freeman's Journal*, April 24, 1782.

Reprinted: *Poems* (1786), pp. 264–65; (1795), p. 215; and (1809), II, 103–04.

Untitled verses, with a short prose introduction on Captain Barney's victory, *Freeman's Journal*, May 8, 1782.

Reprinted without introduction as "Song on Captain Barney's victory over the ship General Monk, April 26, 1782," *Poems* (1786), pp. 271–74, and (1809), II, 6–8.

"The Pilgrim, No. 14," *Freeman's Journal*, May 8, 1782.

"On Sir Henry Clinton's Recall," *Freeman's Journal*, May 22, 1782.

Reprinted: *Poems* (1786), pp. 275–78; (1795), pp. 218–20; and (1809), II, 107–09.

"The Pilgrim, No. 15," *Freeman's Journal*, May 29, 1782.

"Sir Guy Carleton's Address to the Americans," *Freeman's Journal*, June 5, 1782.

Reprinted: *New-Jersey Journal*, June 12; *Connecticut Courant*, September 17, 1782; *Poems* (1786), pp. 278–81; (1795), pp. 221–22; and (1809), II, 109–11.

"The Pilgrim, No. 16," *Freeman's Journal*, June 19, 1782.

Reprinted as "The Philosopher of the Forest, Numb. XI," *Miscellaneous Works*, pp. 375–80; included in the essay is the "Scandinavian War Song," reprinted in *Poems* (1795), p. 268, and (1809), II, 165.

"The English Quixote of 1778; or, Modern Idolatry," *Freeman's Journal*, June 26, 1782.

Reprinted: *Poems* (1786), pp. 281–83; and as "Modern Idolatry,

or English Quixotism," (1795), pp. 222–24, and (1809), II, 111–13.
Untitled article, *Freeman's Journal*, June 26, 1782.
> Signed "Hermes." Not reprinted, but initialed "P.F." in Freneau's file of the *Freeman's Journal*.

"The Projectors," *Freeman's Journal*, July 3, 1782.
> Signed "Cassibilan." Reprinted: *Poems* (1786), pp. 284–85; (1795), pp. 224–25; and (1809), II, 113–14.

"On a Lady's Singing Bird, a native of the Canary Islands, confined in a very small cage: Written in Bermuda, 1778," *Freeman's Journal*, July 3, 1782.
> Reprinted: *Poems* (1786), pp. 285–87; (1795), pp. 180–81; and (1809), I, 235–36.

"The Pilgrim, No. 17," *Freeman's Journal*, July 3, 1782.
> Reprinted as "A Discourse upon Law," *Miscellaneous Works*, pp. 245–51.

"A Dialogue of the Dead," *Freeman's Journal*, July 3, 1782.
> Signed "K.V." Not reprinted, but marked in Freneau's file of the *Freeman's Journal*.

Untitled verses, appended to a transcript of General Robertson's Proclamation, *Freeman's Journal*, July 10, 1782.
> Reprinted as "Lines occasioned by General Robertson's Proclamation, New-York, June 22, 1782," *Poems* (1786), pp. 287–89; and as "On General Robertson's Proclamation," (1795), pp. 225–26, and (1809), II, 114–16.

"The tenth Ode of Horace's Book of Epodes, imitated. Written in December 1781, upon the departure of gen. Arnold from New York," *Freeman's Journal*, July 10, 1782.
> Reprinted: *Poems* (1786), pp. 290–91; and as "Arnold's Departure," (1795), p. 227, and (1809), II, 116–17.

Untitled article, *Freeman's Journal*, July 10, 1782.
> Signed "Christopher Clodhopper." Reprinted as "Interesting Thoughts, designed for the public good; By Christopher Clodhopper, Yeoman," *Miscellaneous Works*, pp. 380–84.

"Philosophical Reflections," *Freeman's Journal*, July 17, 1782.
> Reprinted: *New-Jersey Journal*, July 24, 1782; *Poems* (1786), pp. 291–94; and, as "A Picture of the Times," (1795), pp. 228–29, and (1809), II, 117–19.

Untitled article, *Freeman's Journal*, July 17, 1782.
> Signed "Priscilla Tripstreet." Reprinted as "Priscilla Tripstreet's Answer to Christopher Clodhopper," *Miscellaneous Works*, pp. 384–90.

"Prince William Henry's Soliloquy," *Freeman's Journal*, July 24, 1782.
> Reprinted: *New-York Journal*, August 23, 1787; *Poems* (1786), pp. 294–96; (1795), pp. 229–30; and (1809), II, 119–20.

"The Pilgrim, No. XVIII," *Freeman's Journal,* July 24, 1782.

Untitled article, *Freeman's Journal,* July 24, 1782.

> Signed "C. Clodhopper." Reprinted as "A Short Reply to the Above," *Miscellaneous Works,* pp. 390–91.

"The Flagellators," *Freeman's Journal,* July 31, 1782.

> Reprinted: *Poems* (1786), pp. 296–97.

"Satan's Remonstrance. (Occasioned by Mr. Rivington's late Apology for Lying.—See the Royal Gazette of the 10th ult, and our last.)," *Freeman's Journal,* August 7, 1782.

> Reprinted: *New-Jersey Journal,* August 14, 1782; *Poems* (1786), pp. 298–99; and as "Beelzebub's Remonstrance," (1795), p. 231, and (1809), II, 122–23.

"The Pilgrim, No. XIX," *Freeman's Journal,* August 14, 1782.

"A short Catechism, for those whom it may suit," *Freeman's Journal,* August 14, 1782.

> Reprinted as "A Political Catechism, for those whom it may suit," *Miscellaneous Works,* pp. 391–93.

"The Refugees Petition to Sir Guy Carleton," *Freeman's Journal,* August 28, 1782.

> Reprinted: *Connecticut Courant,* September 17; *New-Jersey Journal,* September 25, 1782; *Poems* (1786), pp. 303–04; (1795), p. 232; and (1809), II, 123–24.

"Sir Guy's Answer," *Freeman's Journal,* August 28, 1782.

> Signed "G.C." Reprinted: *New-Jersey Journal,* September 25, 1782; *Poems* (1786), pp. 304–05; (1795), pp. 232–33; and (1809), II, 124–25.

"The following lines are addressed to the Foe of Tyrants, in the Independent Gazetteer of Saturday by a Foe to Malice," *Freeman's Journal,* August 28, 1782.

> Reprinted as "To a writer who subscribes himself 'A Foe to Tyrants'," *Poems* (1786), pp. 299–300; as "To Shylock Ap-Shenkin: (An abusive Court-Writer)," (1795), p. 389; and as "To a Concealed Royalist: on a virulent attack," (1809), II, 186–87.

Untitled article, *Freeman's Journal,* August 28, 1782.

> Signed "Hawser Trunnion." Not reprinted, but marked in Freneau's file of the *Freeman's Journal.*

"To the Foe to Tyrants," *Freeman's Journal,* September 4, 1782.

> Reprinted: *Poems* (1786), pp. 300–01; as "To Shylock Ap-Shenkin," (1795), pp. 393–94; and as "To the Concealed Royalist, in answer to a second attack," (1809), II, 187–88.

"The Midnight Soliloquy in the Market House of Philadelphia," *Freeman's Journal,* September 4, 1782.

Signed "W.H." Not reprinted, but marked in Freneau's file of the *Freeman's Journal*.

"A short account of the Bermuda or Summer islands, and some hints for reducing them to the obedience of the United States," *Freeman's Journal*, September 4, 1782.

Signed "Harpax." Not reprinted, but marked in Freneau's file of the *Freeman's Journal*.

"To the Foe to Tyrants on his Farewell in the Independent Gazetteer of the 7th inst.," *Freeman's Journal*, September 11, 1782.

Reprinted: *Poems* (1786), pp. 302–04; as "To Shylock Ap-Shenkin (On his Farewell)," (1795), p. 406; and as "To the Concealed Royalist; on his Farewell," (1809), II, 188–89.

Untitled article, *Freeman's Journal*, September 11, 1782.

Signed "A.B." Not reprinted, but marked in Freneau's file of the *Freeman's Journal*.

"To those whom it may Concern," *Freeman's Journal*, September 25, 1782.

Reprinted: *Poems* (1786), pp. 305–06; as "To Shylock Ap-Shenkin," (1795), p. 405; and as "To the Royalist Unveiled; (and addressed to all whom it may concern)," (1809), II, 189–90.

Untitled article, *Freeman's Journal*, November 20, 1782.

Signed "Catholicus." Not reprinted, but initialed "P.F." in Freneau's file of the *Freeman's Journal*.

Untitled article, *Freeman's Journal*, November 20, 1782.

Signed "Martinus Scriblerus." Not reprinted, but marked in Freneau's file of the *Freeman's Journal*.

Untitled article, *Freeman's Journal*, November 20, 1782.

Signed "G." Reprinted as "A Discourse on Esquires, with a short narrative. By his honor the President of the Debtor's Club," *Miscellaneous Works*, pp. 395–402.

"Rivington's Reflexions" in two parts, *Freeman's Journal*, December 4 and 25, 1782.

Reprinted: *New-Jersey Journal*, December 11, 1782, and January 1, 1783; *Poems* (1786), pp. 310–16; (1795), pp. 235–38; (1809), II, 125–30; and part 1 only, *Royal Gazette*, December 14, 1782, and *Virginia Gazette*, January 18, 1783.

"The Prophecy of King Tammany," *Freeman's Journal*, December 11, 1782.

Reprinted: *Poems* (1786), pp. 308–10; (1795), pp. 233–34; and (1809), I, 269–70.

Untitled article, *Freeman's Journal*, December 11, 1782.

Signed "R." Reprinted as "On City Burying Places. A Speech, By a Member of the Lower House," *Miscellaneous Works*, pp. 403–08.

Untitled article, *Freeman's Journal*, December 11, 1782.

Signed "Plus Ultra." Not reprinted, but marked in Freneau's file of
the *Freeman's Journal.*
Untitled verse, *Freeman's Journal,* December 18, 1782.
> Reprinted as "To Those Whom It May Concern," *Poems* (1786), p.
> 307.

1783

New Year Verses,/ Addressed to those Gentlemen who have been pleased
to favour Francis Wrigley, News Car-/ rier, with their Custom./ January
1, 1783./
> Bsd. Copy: LC. Reprinted: *Poems* (1786), pp. 381–82; and as "A
> News-man's Address," (1795), pp. 249–50.
New Year's Verses addressed to the Customers of the Pennsylvania Evening
Post, by the Printer's Lad who carries it. January 4, 1783.
> Title from *Poems* (1786), pp. 383–85.
New Year's/ Verses/ Addressed to the Customers of/ The Freeman's Jour-
nal,/ By the Lad who carries it./ January 8th. 1783./
> Bsd. Copy: LC. Reprinted: Poems (1786), pp. 385–87.
Untitled article, *Freeman's Journal,* January 8, 1783.
> Signed "Heraclitus." Not reprinted, but marked in Freneau's file of
> the *Freeman's Journal.*
"Hugh Gaine's Life," in three parts, *Freeman's Journal,* January 8, 29,
and February 12, 1783.
> Reprinted: *New-Jersey Journal,* January 15, February 3, and 19; *New-
> York Packet,* January 23, February 6, 27, and March 6, 1783; without
> title, *Poems* (1786), pp. 317–28; as "Political Biograph. Gaine's
> Life," (1795), pp. 239–47; and as "Political Biography. Hugh Gaine's
> Life," (1809), II, 130–40.
"Stanzas, occasioned by the departure of the British from Charlestown,
Dec. 14, 1782," *Freeman's Journal,* February 19, 1783.
> Reprinted: *South-Carolina Weekly Gazette,* May 13, 1783; with
> "Charlestown" corrected to "Charleston," *Poems* (1786), pp. 329–30;
> (1795), pp. 247–48; (1809), II, 141–42; *Columbian Herald,* August
> 7; *Massachusetts Centinel,* August 30, 1786; and *Investigator,* October
> 12, 1812.
"A few Reflections on reading the King's most gracious speech to his Parlia-
ment, on the 5th of Dec. 1782," *Freeman's Journal,* March 5, 1783.
> Signed "Lucullus." Not reprinted, but initialed "P.F." in Freneau's
> file of the *Freeman's Journal.*
Untitled verse, *Freeman's Journal,* March 12, 1783.
> Reprinted: *New-Jersey Journal,* March 19, 1783; as "Stanzas, occa-
> sioned by the King's Speech, recommending Peace with the American

States—March, 1783," *Poems* (1786), pp. 331–33; and as "On the British King's Speech . . ." (1795), pp. 250–51, and (1809), II, 144–45.

"A New York Tory's Epistle to one of his Friends in Pennsylvania—Written previous to his departure for Nova Scotia," *Freeman's Journal*, May 7, 1783. Reprinted: *South-Carolina Weekly Gazette*, June 14, 1783; *Poems* (1786), pp. 333–37; and as "A Renegado Epistle," (1795), pp. 253–55, and (1809), II, 147–50.

New Travels/ through/ North America:/ In a Series of Letters;/ Exhibiting, the History of the Victorious Campaign of the/ Allied Armies, under his Excellency General Washington,/ and the Count de Rochambeau, in the Year 1781./ Interspersed with political, and philosophical Observations, upon/ the genius, temper, and customs of the Americans; Also,/ Narrations of the capture of General Burgoyne,/ and Lord Cornwallis, with their Armies;/ and a variety of interesting particulars, which occurred,/ in the course, of the/ War in America./ Translated from the original of the Abbé Robin;/ one of the Chaplains to the French Army in America./ [*Quotation, six lines from Young*]/ Philadelphia:/ Printed and Sold by Robert Bell, in Third-Street./ M,DCC,LXXXIII.—Price Two Thirds of a Dollar./

8vo; 112pp. Copies: HL, HSP, LC, LCP, NJHS, NYPL, PU. Translated by Freneau, and advertised in the *Freeman's Journal* from July 30, 1783 (see note 71 of chapter V). Another edition: New Travels/ through/ North-America:/ In a Series of Letters;/ Exhibiting the History of the Victorious Campaign of the Allied Armies,/ under His Excellency General Washington, and the/ Count de Rochambeau, in the Year 1781./ Interspersed with political and philosophical Observations upon the/ genius, temper, and customs of the Americans:/ Also, Nar-/ rations of the capture of General Burgoyne, and Lord/ Cornwallis, with their Armies; and a variety of interesting/ particulars, which occurred in the course of the/ War in America./ Translated from the Original of the Abbé Robin:/ One of the Chaplains to the French Army in America./ [*Quotation, six lines from Young*]/ Boston:/ Printed by E. E. Powars and N. Willis, for E. Battelle,/ and to be sold by him, at his Book-Store, State-Street./ M,DCC,LXXXIV./ 8vo; 96pp. Copies: BA, BPL, BU, MHS, NYHS, NYPL. Reprinted in twenty-two installments in the *Time-Piece*, March 15 to May 3, 1797, with this introductory note: "About fourteen Years Since, the Editor of this Paper translated from an original Epistolatory Journal; the travels of M. Abbé Robin, a chaplain in Count Rochambeau's army; giving a general account of the progress of the French army from Rhode Island, the place of their landing, to York town in Virginia; and of

some other occurrences. As but a small edition was printed off, & the work is now in the hands of very few, the republication, at this period, especially as it is short, may not be un-acceptable to our readers."
"New-York," *Freeman's Journal*, September 10, 1783.

> Reprinted: *Poems* (1786), pp. 341–44; in part, as "Manhattan City: A Picture," (1795), p. 252, and (1809), I, 146–47; and, in part, as "The American Siberia," (1795), pp. 216–62, and 1809), II, 157–58.

"Verses occasioned by General Washington's arrival in this city, on his way to his Seat in Virginia," *Freeman's Journal*, December 10, 1783.

> Reprinted: *New-Jersey Gazette*, December 23, 1783; *Maryland Gazette*, January 2, 1784; *Poems* (1786), pp. 356–59; (1795), pp. 262–64; (1809), II, 158–61; as "Verses on General Washington's Retirement," *Bailey's Pocket Almanac* for 1784, *American Museum*, August, 1787, pp. 201–02; *Grammatical Institute*, III, 368–71; and, excerpts only, with a critical introduction, *Massachusetts Centinel*, August 1, 1789.

"Rivington's Confessions Addressed to the Whigs of New-York" in two parts, *Freeman's Journal*, December 31, 1783, and January 7, 1784.

> Reprinted: *Independent Journal*, January 7 and 14; *New-Jersey Gazette*, January 25 and February 3, 1784; *Poems* (1786), pp. 337–49; (1795), pp. 255–61; and (1809), II, 150–57.

1784

New-Year/ Verses,/ For those who carry the/ Pennsylvania Gazette/ To the/ Customers./ January 1. 1784./

> Bsd. Copy: HSP. Reprinted: *Poems* (1786), pp. 387–88; and as "A News-man's Address," (1795), p. 265, and (1809), II, 161–62.

New Year's Verses, addressed To the Customers of the Freeman's Journal, by the Lad who carries it. January 7, 1784.

> Title from *Poems* (1786), pp. 389–90. Reprinted as "A News-Carrier's Petition," (1795), pp. 278–79; and as The News-Lad's Address,/ To the Readers of the Troy Farmer's Oracle/ Wishing them a Happy New-Year./ Jan. 1, 1798./ Bsd. Copy: NYHS.

"The Dying Indian; or the Last Words of Shalum," *Freeman's Journal*, March 17, 1784.

> Reprinted: *Poems* (1786), pp. 350–52; (1795), pp. 59–60; (1809), I, 100–02; *American Museum*, February, 1788, pp. 190–91; *Columbian Centinel*, January 26, 1791; *Poems by the late Josias Lyndon Arnold, Esq.* (Providence, 1797), pp. 46–49; and *Specimens of American Poetry* (Boston, 1829), pp. 286–87.

"Lines intended for Mr. Peale's Exhibitions, May 10, 1784," *Freeman's Journal*, May 19, 1784.

Reprinted: *Poems* (1786), pp. 352–55; and as "The Triumphal Arch,"
(1795), pp. 266–67, and (1809), II, 162–64.
"Humanity and Ingratitude; A Common Case (Translated from the Mercure
de France)," *Freeman's Journal*, December 8, 1784.
  Signed "K." Reprinted: *American Herald*, December 24, 1784; *Poems*
  (1786), pp. 360–63; (1795), pp. 54–56; (1809), I, 94–96; and *The
  Cabinet of Momus* (Philadelphia, 1809), p. 26.
"Sketches of American History" in two parts, *Freeman's Journal*, December
15 and 29, 1784.
  Signed "K." Reprinted *New-York Packet*, December 20; New Bruns-
  wick *Political Intelligencer*, December 28, 1784; *Columbian Herald*,
  January 10, 1785; *Poems* (1786), pp. 398–407; (1795), pp. 383–90;
  (1809), I, 271–79; *The Beauties of Poetry, British and American*
  (Philadelphia, 1791), p. 237; and *The Columbian Muse* (New York,
  1794), p. 80.
"The Progress of Balloons," *Freeman's Journal*, December 22, 1784.
  Signed "K." Reprinted: *Political Intelligencer*, January 8; *Massachusetts Centinel*, January 15, 1785; *Charleston Morning Post*, August 3,
  1786; *Poems* (1786), pp. 368–71; as "Balloons," (1795), pp. 367–70,
  and (1809), I, 227–30; and as "On Balloons," *National Gazette*,
  January 2, and *New-York Daily Gazette*, Jan. 5, 1793.

1785

"Stanzas on the Emigration to America, and peopling the Western Country," *Bailey's Pocket Almanac* for 1785, pp. [67–68].
  Reprinted: *Columbian Herald*, March 7; *Pennsylvania Packet*, May
  24, 1785; *Pennsylvania Packet*, June 23, 1786; *American Museum*,
  February, 1787, pp. 159–60; *Kentucky Gazette*, July 18, 1788; *Penn-
  sylvania Packet*, November 30, 1790; *State Gazette of South Carolina*,
  January 6; *Brunswick Gazette*, February 8, 1791; *New-Jersey Journal*,
  September 14, 1796; *Kentucky Gazette*, February 1, 1797; *Poems*
  (1786), pp. 378–80; (1795), pp. 276–77; (1809), II, 174–76; *The
  Beauties of Poetry*, p. 192; and *The Columbian Muse*, p. 173.
"The Seasons Moralized," *Bailey's Pocket Almanac* for 1785, p. [2].
  Reprinted: *Columbian Herald*, March 10, 1785; *Charleston Morning
  Post*, August 9, 1786; *Massachusetts Centinel*, February 28; *Pennsyl-
  vania Packet*, April 25, 1787; *American Museum*, February, 1788, pp.
  185–86; *Maryland Journal*, August 11, 1789; *Poems* (1786), pp.
  380–81; (1795), p. 126; and (1809), I, 200.
New Years Verses, addressed to the Customers of the Freeman's Journal,
by the Lad who carries it. January 1, 1785.

Title from *Poems* (1786), pp. 391–93. Reprinted as "On the Vicissitudes of Things," (1795), pp. 279–80, and (1809), II, 179–80.

"The Literary Plunderers," *Freeman's Journal*, January 19, 1785.

Signed "K." Reprinted: *Poems* (1786), pp. 393–97; as "Devastations in a Library," (1795), pp. 280–83; and as "On Devastations Committed in a booksellers library, by rats, mice, &c.," (1809), I, 265–69.

"Elegiac Verses on the Death of a favourite Dog," *Freeman's Journal*, February 16, 1785.

Reprinted: *Poems* (1786), pp. 366–68; as "To a Deceased Dog," (1795), pp. 361–62; and as "On a Deceased Dog," (1809), II, 219–20.

"Pewter Platter Alley: A Poem," *Freeman's Journal*, February 23, 1785.

Reprinted: *Poems* (1786), pp. 363–64; (1795), pp. 269–70; and (1809), II, 166–67.

Untitled verse, *Freeman's Journal*, March 9, 1785.

Reprinted as "Lines occasioned by The Death of General Joseph Reed —March, 1785," *Poems* (1786), pp. 372–73; as "On the Death of a Republican Patriot & Statesman," (1795), pp. 271–72; and as "On the Death of the Republican Patriot and Statesman, General Joseph Reed," (1809), II, 169.

"The Four Ages," *Freeman's Journal*, March 23, 1785.

Reprinted as "The Five Ages," *Poems* (1786), pp. 373–74; (1795), pp. 272–73; (1809), II, 170–71; and *Specimens of American Poetry* (Boston, 1829), pp. 293–94.

"To the Great—the Warlike—the United—the Independent Americans," *Freeman's Journal*, March 30, 1785.

Reprinted: *Poems* (1786), pp. 375–78; and as "A Renegado Epistle to the Independent Americans," (1795), pp. 273–75, and (1809), II, 171–74.

"Verses, made at Sea, in a Heavy Gale," *Freeman's Journal*, April 13, 1785.

Reprinted: *Poems* (1786), pp. 365–66; *American Museum*, August, 1787, p. 202; *Pennsylvania Packet*, January 12; *New-Jersey Journal*, January 16; *Freeman's Journal*, August 20; *Independent Gazetteer*, August 21; *Pennsylvania Packet*, August 21; *Massachusetts Centinel*, September 13; *State Gazette of South Carolina*, September 18, 1788; *Federal Gazette*, November 15, 1790; *City Gazette*, June 9, 1792; *American Poems* (Litchfield, 1793), p. 239; *The Columbian Muse*, p. 125; *Specimens of American Poetry*, p. 292–93; and as "The Hurricane," *Poems* (1795), pp. 270–71, and (1809), II, 168.

"Epitaph intended for the tombstone of Patrick Bay, an Irish Soldier and Inn-holder, killed by an ignorant physician," *Freeman's Journal*, May 18, 1785.

Reprinted: *Daily Advertiser*, May 23; *Pennsylvania Packet*, May 30; *Independent Gazetteer*, June 18; *Massachusetts Centinel*, June 22; *Co-*

lumbian Herald, July 6, 1785; *Farmer's Journal,* May 16, 1791; *State Gazette of South Carolina,* March 6, 1793; *Poems* (1786), p. 35; (1795), pp. 49–50; and (1809), I, 82–83.

"The Deserted Farm House," *Freeman's Journal,* May 18, 1785.

Rewritten from "Upon a very ancient Dutch House on Long-Island," *American Village* (1772), pp. 26–27. Reprinted: *European Magazine,* July, 1787; *London Morning Herald,* July 12; *Independent Gazetteer,* November 5; *Freeman's Journal,* November 14; *Massachusetts Centinel,* November 21, 1787; *American Museum,* November, 1788, pp. 478–79; *Herald of Freedom,* January 6, 1789; Albany *Argus,* November 3, 1796; *Poems* (1786), pp. 30–31; (1795), pp. 26–27; and (1809), I, 49–50.

"The Monument of Phaon," *Freeman's Journal,* May 25, 1785.

Reprinted: *State Gazette of South Carolina,* May 8, 1793; *Poems* (1786), pp. 18–20; (1795), pp. 30–31; and (1809), I, 55–56.

"To the Author of some extraordinary poetical pieces," *Columbian Herald,* September 14, 1785.

Signed "K."

"To Satiricus," *Columbian Herald,* September 30, 1785.

Signed "K."

1786

New Year's Verses,/ for 1786./ (Written for the Carriers of the Columbian Herald.)/

Bsd. Copy: NYHS. Reprinted as "A Newsman's Address," *Poems* (1795), pp. 303–04.

"The Poetaster," *Columbian Herald,* January 12, 1786.

Signed "K." Reprinted as "On the Folly of Writing Poetry," *Poems* (1786), pp. 38–41; as "Epistle to Sylvius: (On the folly of writing Poetry)," (1795), pp. 426–28; and as "To Sylvius: On the Folly of Writing Poetry," (1809), II, 278–80.

"Literary Importation," *Columbian Herald,* January 19, 1786.

Signed "K." Reprinted: *Massachusetts Centinel,* February 3, 1790; *Poems* (1786), pp. 145–46; (1795), p. 305; and (1809), II, 207.

"Lines written at the Pallisades, near Port-Royal, in the Island of Jamaica— September, 1784," *Columbian Herald,* February 2, 1786.

Reprinted: *Poems* (1786), pp. 176–79; as "Port Royal," (1795), pp. 295–97; and as "Written at Port Royal, in the Island of Jamaica— September, 1784," (1809), II, 194–97.

"The Prisoner," *Columbian Herald,* February 16, 1786.

Signed "K." Reprinted: *Pennsylvania Packet,* March 9; *Daily Advertiser,* March 23; *Charleston Morning Post,* April 18; *Political Intelligencer,* May 3, 1786; *American Museum,* January, 1787, pp.

71–72; *General Advertiser*, May 29; *Daily Advertiser*, June 5, 1792; *New-York Weekly Museum*, June 28, 1794; *Kentucky Gazette*, January 10, 1798; *Poems* (1786), pp. 72–73; (1795), p. 86; and "By H. Salem," (1809), II, 134–35.

"The Newsmonger," *Columbian Herald*, February 20, 1786.

Signed "K." Reprinted: *Pennsylvania Evening Herald*, March 29; *Charleston Morning Post*, April 11, 1786; *American Museum*, February, 1787, p. 160; *Freeman's Journal*, February 21; *Pennsylvania Packet*, February 22; *Daily Advertiser*, March 8; *Massachusetts Centinel*, March 10, 1787; *Poems* (1786), pp. 147–49; (1795), pp. 310–12, and (1809), II, 184–86.

"The Lost Adventurer," *Columbian Herald*, March 6, 1786.

Signed "K." Reprinted as "The Lost Sailor," *Poems* (1786), pp. 14–15; as "Argonauta: Or the Lost Adventurer," (1795), pp. 299–301; and as "The Argonaut: or, Lost Adventurer," (1809), II, 201–02.

The/ Poems/ of/ Philip Freneau./ Written chiefly during the late war./ Philadelphia:/ Printed by Francis Bailey, at/ Yorick's Head, in Market Street./ MDCCLXXXVI./

Small 8vo; 208pp. Copies: BM, BPL, BU, CU, HC, HL, HSP, LC, LCP, MHA, NJHS, NYPL, NYHS, NYSL, PU, RU. Advertised in the *Freeman's Journal* from June 7, 1786. For possible second edition, Poems on several occasions, chiefly written during the late war, see pp. 146–48 above.

"The Wild Honey Suckle," *Columbian Herald*, July 6, 1786.

Signed "K." Reprinted: *Pennsylvania Packet*, July 22; *Freeman's Journal*, August 2, 1786; *Massachusetts Centinel*, February 10, 1790; *Miscellaneous Works*, p. 152; *Poems* (1795), p. 95; (1809), I, 148; *New-York Weekly Museum*, May 21, 1814; and in *Specimens of American Poetry*, pp. 287–88.

"The Drunken Soldier," *Columbian Herald*, July 10, 1786.

Signed "K." Reprinted: *Freeman's Journal*, July 26; *Massachusetts Centinel*, August 9; *New-York Journal*, August 10; *American Herald*, August 21; *Connecticut Courant*, August 21, 1786; *Gazette of the State of Georgia*, February 14, 1788; *Philadelphia Museum*, May 26, 1798; *Miscellaneous Works*, pp. 154–55; and *Poems* (1795), pp. 317–18.

"The Roguish Shoemaker, In Imitation of Watts's Indian Philosopher," *Columbian Herald*, July 13, 1786.

Signed "K." Reprinted as "Few Honest Cobblers," *Miscellaneous Works*, pp. 79–80; and as "Parody on Dr. Watts's Indian Philosopher, or, Few Honest Cobblers," *Columbian Herald*, April 24; *New Hampshire and Vermont Journal*, May 2; *Newark Gazette*, May 14, 1794; and *The Tickler*, December 16, 1807.

"On the Honourable Emanuel Swedenborg's Universal Theology," *Freeman's Journal*, October 4, 1786.

Reprinted: *Pennsylvania Packet*, October 7, 1786; *Miscellaneous Works*, pp. 76–77; *Columbian Centinel*, September 20, 1794; in *A Compendius View and Brief Defence of the Peculiar and Leading Doctrines of the New Jerusalem Church* (Baltimore, 1798), pp. xv–xvii; as "On the Book called Unitarian Theology," *Poems* (1795), pp. 149–50, and (1809), I, 227–28.

"On the legislature of Great Britain prohibiting the sale, in London of Doctor David Ramsay's History of the Revolutionary war in South-Carolina," *Freeman's Journal*, October 11, 1786.

Reprinted: *Daily Advertiser*, October 17; *New-York Journal*, October 19; *Massachusetts Centinel*, October 25; *New-Jersey Gazette*, November 6, 1786; *American Museum*, February, 1787, p. 167; *Miscellaneous Works*, pp. 144–45; *Poems* (1795), pp. 304–05, and (1809), II, 206.

Untitled verse, *Freeman's Journal*, October 11, 1786.

Reprinted as "The author and the critic, By Mr. Freneau," *American Museum*, May, 1787, pp. 406–07; as "The Pamphleteer and the Critic," *Miscellaneous Works*, pp. 140–41; and as "To Zoilus, (A Severe Critic)," *Poems* (1795), pp. 387–88.

1787

"A Short Account of the West Indies," containing untitled verse by Freneau, *Bailey's Pocket Almanac* for 1787, pp. 50–52.

Reprinted: "The Following Verses, wrote by Mr. Freneau, are subjoined to a short and accurate account of the West Indies, in the printer's Pocket Almanac for the present year," *Freeman's Journal*, January 31; ". . . are subjoined to a short and accurate account of the West Indies," *Virginia Gazette*, February 15; *American Herald*, February 16; *Massachusetts Centinel*, February 17, 1787; *New-York Weekly Museum*, September 1; *Centinel of Freedom*, October 30; *New-Jersey Journal*, November 6, 1804; as "Stanzas written In a blank leaf of Burke's History of the West India Islands," *Miscellaneous Works*, pp. 155–57; as "Carribbiana," *Poems* (1795), pp. 318–20; and as "Stanzas written at the foot of Monte Souffriere, near the Town of Basseterre, Guadaloupe," (1809), II, 213–15.

"Stanzas on a Young Lady in a Consumption," *Freeman's Journal*, February 7, 1787.

Reprinted as "To Marcia," *Miscellaneous Works*, pp. 259–60; as "Marcella in a Consumption," *National Gazette*, October 13, 1792, and *Poems* (1795), pp. 359–60; and as "Amanda in a Consumption," (1809), I, 239–40.

"The Almanack Maker," *Freeman's Journal*, February 4, 1787.

Reprinted: *American Herald*, March 5, 1787; *Massachusetts Herald*, January 30, 1790; *Miscellaneous Works*, pp. 150–52; *Poems* (1795), pp. 90–91; (1809), I, 142–44; and *The Cabinet of Momus*, p. 43.

"Thomas and Susan. An Irish-town dialogue.—(Suitable to the times)," *Freeman's Journal*, February 28, 1787.

Reprinted, with a critical introduction, *Massachusetts Centinel*, March 24, 1790; as "Picture IX" of "The Pictures of Columbus," *Miscellaneous Works*, pp. 16–17, and *Poems* (1809), I, 105–07.

"The following lines were occasioned by the death of Mr. Robert Bell, the celebrated humorist, and truly philanthropic bookseller, of this city:— they were written more than two years ago, and are now sent for insertion in your journal," *Freeman's Journal*, February 28, 1787.

Reprinted: *Independent Journal*, March 7; *Massachusetts Centinel*, March 14; *Charleston Morning Post*, April 9, 1787; *Miscellaneous Works*, pp. 187–88; as "Elegy," *Poems* (1795), pp. 306–07; and as "Elegy on Mr. Robert Bell. The celebrated humourist, and truly philanthropic bookseller, formerly of Philadelphia, written, 1786," (1809), II, 209.

"The Insolvent's Release, or Miseries of a Country Jail," *Freeman's Journal*, April 11, 1787.

Reprinted: *Miscellaneous Works*, pp. 157–59; *Poems* (1795), pp. 124–25; and "By H. Salem" (1809), I, 195–96.

"St. Preux to Eloisa," *Freeman's Journal*, April 11, 1787.

Reprinted: *Miscellaneous Works*, pp. 159–60; *Poems* (1795), pp. 123–24; and (1809), I, 197.

"The Departure (Written at Leaving Sandy-Hook on a voyage to the West-Indies," *Freeman's Journal*, April 18, 1787.

Reprinted: *Miscellaneous Works*, pp. 163–65.

"May to April," *Freeman's Journal*, April 18, 1787.

Reprinted: *Fairfield Gazette*, May 10; *Charleston Morning Post*, May 11; *Pennsylvania Packet*, May 24, 1787; *New-York Journal*, May 18, 1790; *Newark Gazette*, May 15, 1793; *New-York Weekly Museum*, May 7; *Delaware and Eastern Shore Advertiser*, May 30, 1796; *Centinel of Freedom*, May 22, 1798; *American Farmer*, May 23; *New-Jersey Journal*, June 11, 1799; *Miscellaneous Works*, p. 78; *Poems* (1795), p. 96; and (1809), I, 149.

A/ Journey/ from/ Philadelphia/ to/ New-York,/ by Way of Burlington and South-Amboy./ By/ Robert Slender, Stocking Weaver./ Extracted from the Author's Journals./ [*Two lines from Horace*]/ Philadelphia:/ Printed by Francis Bailey, at Yorick's Head, in/ Market street./ M DCC LXXXVII./ 12mo; 28pp. Copies: BU, NYHS, LC, PU. Advertised in the *Freeman's Journal* from April 25, 1787. Reprinted: *Miscellaneous Works*, pp.

409–29; as "Slender's Journey," *Poems* (1795), pp. 338–50; and as A Laughable Poem;/ or/ Robert Slender's/ Journey/ from/ Philadelphia to New York,/ by/ Way of Burlington and South Amboy./ By Philip Freneau,/ Author of Poems written during the American Revo-/ lutionary War, and lately published in this City/ by Lydia R. Bailey, in two Volumes, Duodecimo./ Persons of the Poem./ [*Nine lines for nine characters*]/ Philadelphia:/ Printed for Thomas Neversink./ December 20, 1809./ 12mo; 24pp. Copies: BA, BM, BPL, BU, HL, LC, LCP, NJSL, NYHS, NYPL, NYSL.

"The Indian Student, or Force of Nature," *Pennsylvania Packet*, June 9, 1787.

Reprinted: *Freeman's Journal*, June 20; *Massachusetts Centinel*, June 27; *New-York Journal*, July 5; *American Museum*, October, 1787, p. 413; *City Gazette*, December 17, 1796; Baltimore *Federal Gazette*, February 8, 1797; *Port-Folio*, October 24, 1807; *Pennsylvania Democrat*, August 11, 1809; *Miscellaneous Works*, pp. 69–71; *Poems* (1795), pp. 80–82; (1809), I, 127–29; *The Columbian Songster* (New York, 1796), p. 66; William Priest, *Travels in the United States of America* (London, 1802), p. 98; *Specimens of American Poetry*, pp. 290–92; and, in part, *Port-Folio*, December 12, 1807.

"Address to Misfortune," *Freeman's Journal*, July 18, 1787.

Reprinted as "To Misfortune," *Miscellaneous Works*, pp. 160–61; and *Poems* (1795), p. 407.

"The Scornful Lady," *Freeman's Journal*, August 29, 1787.

Reprinted: *Miscellaneous Works*, pp. 66–67; *Poems* (1795), pp. 91–92; (1809), I, 144–45; and, without title, *Port-Folio*, October 24, 1807.

"Horace, Lib. II. Ode 16. Imitated, and addressed to Governor Parr," *Freeman's Journal*, September 5, 1787.

Reprinted: *Miscellaneous Works*, pp. 67–68; as "The sixteenth Ode of the second book of Horace's Odes, imitated. To Pomponius Atticus," *National Gazette*, October 24, 1792; and as "To Cracovius Putridus," *Poems* (1795), pp. 398–99.

"The subsequent lines were written two or three years after the event that occasioned them, but have never been printed. If you think them in any degree worthy of the memory of the patriotic young officer they attempt to celebrate (and whose death has been so deeply regretted throughout America) I must request you to insert them in your journal. A.B.," *Freeman's Journal*, October 17, 1787.

Reprinted as "To the Memory of the brave, accomplished and Patriotic Col. John Laurens, Who in the 27th year of his age was killed in an engagement with a detachment of the British from Charleston, Aug. 1782," *Massachusetts Centinel*, October 31; *Columbian Herald*, November 5; *American Museum*, November, 1787; *Miscellaneous Works*, pp. 288–89; and as "On the Death of Colonel Laurens," *Poems* (1795), p. 294; and (1809), II, 177–78.

"Lines occasioned by a visit to an old Indian burying ground.—By Philip Freneau," *American Museum*, November, 1787, pp. 515–16.

Reprinted: *City Gazette*, February 22, 1788; *Massachusetts Centinel*, January 27, 1790; *Port-Folio*, October 17, 1807; *Miscellaneous Works*, pp. 187–88; and as "The Indian Burying Ground," *Poems* (1795), pp. 89–90; (1809), I, 141–42; and William Priest, *Travels in the United States*, p. 125.

1788

Verses, for the New Year's Day, 1788. Addressed to the customers of the Freeman's Journal. By the Lad who carries it.

Title from *Massachusetts Centinel*, February 1, 1788. Reprinted as "New Year's Verses for 1788 (Supposed to be written by the Printer's lad, who supplies the customers with his weekly paper.)," *Miscellaneous Works*, pp. 393–95; and as "A News-man's Address," *Poems* (1795), pp. 336–38.

"A Parody on Sappho's Ode: Blest as the immortal Gods is he, &c. Addressed to Old England," *City Gazette*, January 28, 1788.

Reprinted as "Rinaldo's Complaint: To the fair Shopkeeper," *National Gazette*, August 22; Philadelphia *Mail*, August 23; *Diary*, August 27; *Weekly Museum*, November 17, 1792; as "To Clarissa: A handsome Shop-keeper," *Poems* (1795), pp. 364–65, and (1809), II, 224; and as "To a handsome Milliner," *Port-Folio*, October 31, 1807.

Untitled verse, *City Gazette*, January 30, 1788.

Reprinted with the following note: "Mr. Printer, The following copy of Verses came accidentally into my hand:—I am told it was written by Captain Freneau, and addressed to a Young Quaker Lady, that went passenger in his vessel to Georgia, to reside in the Western parts of that State. A.B.," *Daily Advertiser*, August 26; *Impartial Gazette*, August 30; *Pennsylvania Packet*, September 2; *Freeman's Journal*, September 3; *Brunswick Gazette*, September 9; *Independent Gazetteer*, October 23, 1788; and as "To Lydia," *Poems* (1795), pp. 297-99, and (1809), II, 198–201.

"The Exile (Several of the thoughts in the following stanzas are taken from lord Bolingbroke's Reflections on Exile, written about the time of his banishment to France in 1715.)," *City Gazette*, February 2, 1788.

Reprinted as "The Banished Man," *Daily Advertiser*, September 1, 1790; *National Gazette*, December 1; *Daily Repository*, December 6, 1791; *Poems* (1795), pp. 23–24; and (1809), II, 46–47.

"The Invalid. Written in 1785," *City Gazette*, February 9, 1788.

Reprinted: *Daily Advertiser*, May 26, "written at Charleston"; *Columbian Centinel*, June 8, 1791; *Poems* (1795), p. 317; (1809), II, 211–12, "occasioned by his visit to Pacolet Springs in South-Carolina, for the recovery of his health."

The/ Miscellaneous/ Works/ of/ Mr. Philip Freneau/ containing his/ Essays,/ and/ additional Poems./ Philadelphia:/ Printed by Francis Bailey, at Yorick's/ Head, in Market Street./ M DCC LXXXVIII./ 12mo; 430pp. Copies: BM, BPL, BU, HL, LC, LCP, MHA, MHS, NJHS, NYHS, NYPL, NYSL, PU. Advertised in the *Freeman's Journal* from April 23, 1788.

"Modern Devotion," *City Gazette*, June 23, 1788.

Reprinted: *National Gazette*, December 5; *Freeman's Journal*, December 7; *Federal Gazette*, December 7; *Daily Advertiser*, December 12; *Connecticut Courant*, December 19, 1791; Boston *Argus*, January 13; *Kentucky Gazette*, January 28, 1792; *Columbian Museum*, August 16, 1796; *New-York Weekly Museum*, May 19, 1798; *Poems* (1795), p. 100; and, "By Hezekiah Salem," (1809), I, 154–55.

"The Virtue of Tobacco," *City Gazette*, June 25, 1788.

Reprinted as "On Tobacco," *Maryland Journal*, January 2; *Massachusetts Centinel*, February 14, 1789; *Daily Advertiser*, July 31; *Freeman's Journal*, September 8; *City Gazette*, September 13, 1790; as "Lines written upon a paper of Tobacco," *National Gazette*, November 7; *Daily Advertiser*, November 10; *City Gazette*, December 5, 1791; *New-York Weekly Museum*, September 15, 1792; and as "Tobacco," *Poems* (1795), p. 125, and (1809), I, 199-200.

"Extract of a letter from Capt. P. Freneau, of the schooner Columbia, dated Norfolk, Virginia, July 29, 1788," *Daily Advertiser*, August 13, 1788.

Letter to Francis Bailey, dated "Norfolk, August 6, 1788," and signed "Philip Freneau," *Freeman's Journal*, August 20, 1788.

Reprinted: *Independent Gazetter*, August 21, and *Gazette of the State of Georgia*, August 28, 1788.

1789

"Stanzas written at Baltimore in Maryland, January, 1789. By Capt. P. Freneau. To Cynthia," *Freeman's Journal*, January 29, 1789.

Reprinted: *Freeman's Journal*, January 20; *Daily Advertiser*, August 25, 1790; *Poems* (1795), pp. 378–89; and (1809), II, 251–52.

"To John Dickinson, Esq.," *City Gazette*, April 10, 1789.

Reprinted as "Epistle to the Patriotic Farmer," *Poems* (1795), p. 324; and (1809), II, 217–18.

"Lines Written at Sea. Addressed to Miss ―――, New Jersey," *Daily Advertiser*, April 15, 1789.

Also printed as "A Yankee Epistle Written at sea, December, 1788,"

City Gazette, April 16, 1789. Rewritten as "Polydore to Amanda (Written at Sea)," *Daily Advertiser,* February 10, 1791. Reprinted: *Freeman's Journal,* July 6; *General Advertiser,* February 15, 1791; as "Philander to Amanda," *Poems* (1795), pp. 181–82; and as "Florio to Amanda," (1809), I, 236–38.

Letter, dated "Yamacraw, Savannah, March 14th, 1789," signed "P. Freneau," *Freeman's Journal,* July 8, 1789.

Reprinted: *Daily Advertiser,* July 11; and *Massachusetts Centinel,* July 18, 1789.

"The Pilot of Hatteras. By Capt. P. Freneau," *Daily Advertiser,* November 14, 1789.

Reprinted: *Pennsylvania Packet,* November 19; *Massachusetts Centinel Extraordinary,* November 25, with a critical introduction; *City Gazette,* December 1; *Freeman's Journal,* December 9; *Pennsylvania Mercury,* December 10; *Virginia Gazette,* December 24, 1789; as "The Pilot of Hatteras. Written off the Cape, July, 1789, on a voyage to South Carolina, being detained sixteen days with strong gales," *National Gazette,* January 16; *Freeman's Journal,* January 18; Boston *Argus,* January 31, 1792; and as "Hatteras," *Poems* (1795), pp. 308–10.

"A View of Columbia," *City Gazette,* November 28, 1789.

Reprinted: *Daily Advertiser,* December 30, 1789; as "Lysander's Retreat," *Poems* (1795), p. 320; and as "The Pilgrim's Progress," (1809), II, 218–19.

"To Harriot," *City Gazette,* November 30, 1789.

Reprinted: *Daily Advertiser,* January 3; *Pennsylvania Mercury,* January 19, 1790; and as "To Cynthia," *Poems* (1795), p. 365; and (1809), II, 224–25.

"Lines formerly written in a tavern at Log-Town in the Pine barrens of New-Jersey," *City Gazette,* December 8, 1789.

Reprinted as "Lines descriptive of a Tavern in Log-Town, a small place in the Pine Barrens of North Carolina," *Daily Advertiser,* February 19; *Massachusetts Centinel,* April 7; *Freeman's Journal,* May 26; *City Gazette,* September 9, 1790; as "Stanzas Written at Leaving an Inn, in North Carolina. By Philip Freneau," *New-York Journal,* September 17; Boston *Argus,* September 30, 1791; as "Log Town Tavern (The following was composed some years ago at a small Inn, situated in a remote and desart part of Carolina. A very incorrect copy having appeared in a Northern Newspaper, the subsequent Stanzas are now published as written by the Author)," *National Gazette,* November 7; *Daily Advertiser,* November 12, 1791; as "Log-Town Tavern," *Poems* (1795), pp. 301–03; and "By Hezekiah Salem," (1809), II, 203–06.

Untitled verse, *City Gazette*, December 10, 1789.

Reprinted as "The Bird at Sea," *Daily Advertiser*, February 21; *Massachusetts Centinel*, March 6; *Pennsylvania Packet*, March 24, 1790; and as "The Wanderer," *Poems* (1795), pp. 354–55.

"The Procession to Columbia," *City Gazette*, December 14, 1789.

Reprinted: *Daily Advertiser*, December 30, 1789; and, as "The Procession to Sylvania," *Poems* (1795), p. 321.

"Translated from the Greek of Bion," *Daily Advertiser*, December 16, 1789.

Reprinted as "From the Greek of Bion," *National Gazette*, October 16; *Boston Gazette*, November 18, 1793; and *Kentucky Gazette*, October 4, 1797. Rewritten as "Translated from a fragment of Bion, an ancient Grecian philosopher and poet," signed "R.", *Fredonian*, November 28, 1822.

1790

"Stanzas written at St. Catherine's, an island upon the coast of Georgia, Nov. 1789," *Daily Advertiser*, January 2, 1790.

Reprinted: *Independent Gazetteer*, January 8; *Pennsylvania Packet*, January 8; *Pennsylvania Mercury*, January 9, 1790; as "Lines written at St. Catherine's, on the coast of Georgia," *National Gazette*, February 16, 1792; and as "St. Catherine's," *Poems* (1795), pp. 358–59.

"On the present situation of the theatre in Charleston," *City Gazette*, January 8, 1790.

Also printed as "The following Stanzas were lately written in Charleston, (S.C.) on the situation of their theatre—all diversions of the stage being now prohibited by law, within the limits of the city," *Daily Advertiser*, January 8, 1790. Reprinted: *Pennsylvania Mercury*, January 26, 1790; as "The Distrest Theatre," *National Gazette*, November 21; *Daily Advertiser*, November 28, 1791; *Poems* (1795), pp. 351–52; and (1809), II, 240–41.

"Father Dobbin's Complaint," *City Gazette*, January 15, 1790.

Reprinted: *Daily Advertiser*, February 6; *Connecticut Courant*, February 11; *Pennsylvania Packet*, February 11; *New-York Journal*, February 18; *Freeman's Journal*, February 24; *New York Magazine*, February, 1790, p. 117; *Massachusetts Centinel Extraordinary*, March 10, 1790; *Poems* (1795), p. 19; (1809), I, 41–42; *The Columbian Songster*, p. 42; and as "Farmer Dobbins to the Buck-Suitors," *National Gazette*, August 25; *General Advertiser*, August 27, 1792.

Untitled verse, *City Gazette*, January 16, 1790.

Reprinted as "A Columbian Dialogue. Supposed to have been written by Capt. Freneau," *Daily Advertiser*, February 11; *Pennsylvania Mercury*, February 13, 1790; and as "Sangrado's Expedition to Sylvania," *Poems* (1795), pp. 321–22.

"A characteristic sketch of the Long Island Dutch (From the Rising Empire, a poem)," *City Gazette*, February 2, 1790.

Reprinted: *Daily Advertiser,* March 4, 1790; *New-York Weekly Museum,* May 20, 1795; and as "A Batavian Picture," *Poems* (1795), pp. 18–19, and (1809),I, 40–41.

"A View of Rhode Island (Extracted from a new Poem, entitled the Rising Empire, not yet published.)," *Daily Advertiser*, February 4, 1790.

Reprinted: *Federal Gazette*, February 8, 1790.

"Lines Addressed to some Young Ladies, who were detected in attempting to cut pieces from an Old Great Coat of the Authors, that he might be under the necessity of buying a new and more genteel one," *Daily Advertiser*, March 5, 1790.

Reprinted as "By the Late Philip Freneau," *Monmouth Inquirer, ca.* 1833 (see note 6 of chapter VII).

"On the American and French Revolution," *Daily Advertiser*, March 7, 1790.

Reprinted: *Pennsylvania Packet*, March 12; *New-York Daily Gazette*, March 16, 1790; and as "On the Prospect of a Revolution in France," *Poems* (1795), p. 323, and (1809), II, 216–17.

"On the proposed demolition of Fort George, in this city," *Daily Advertiser*, March 9, 1790.

Reprinted: *City Gazette*, April 3, 1790; *Poems* (1795), pp. 412–13; (1809), I, 68; and, with a prose introduction, *National Gazette*, June 21, 1792.

"A Descriptive Sketch of Maryland," *Daily Advertiser*, March 10, 1790.

Reprinted: *City Gazette*, April 15, 1790; and as "Maryland," *Poems* (1795), pp. 255–56, and (1809), II, 246–47.

"Federal Hall," *Daily Advertiser*, March 12, 1790.

Reprinted: *City Gazette*, April 1; *Federal Gazette*, April 20; *Pennsylvania Mercury*, April 20; *Freeman's Journal*, April 28; *American Museum*, May, 1790, p. 40; *Columbian Centinel*, June 16, 1790; *Poems* (1795), pp. 394–95; and as "Congress Hall, N.Y.," (1809), II, 258–59.

"Philosophical Sketch of America," *Daily Advertiser*, March 13, 1790.

Reprinted: *City Gazette*, May 31, 1790; and as "On American Antiquity," *Poems* (1795), pp. 17–18, and (1809), I, 38–40.

"Epistle to Peter Pindar, Esq.," *Daily Advertiser*, March 15, 1790.

Reprinted: *Massachusetts Centinel*, March 27; and "By Captain Freneau," *City Gazette*, April 13, 1790.

Untitled verse, with a prose introduction, *Daily Advertiser*, March 16, 1790.

Reprinted: *City Gazette*, June 5, 1790; as "The Sabbath-Day Chace," *Poems* (1795), pp. 28–29; as "The New England Sabbath-Day Chace,"

The Cabinet of Momus, pp. 17–18; and "Written under the character of Hezekiah Salem," *Poems* (1809), I, 52–54.

"A Description of Pennsylvania," *Daily Advertiser*, March 17, 1790.

Reprinted: *Massachusetts Centinel*, March 31; *City Gazette*, June 18, 1790; *Daily Advertiser*, February 21, 1797; and as "Pennsylvania (A Fragment)," *Poems* (1795), p. 376, and (1809), II, 237–38.

"On the Sleep of Plants (A curious new discovery.)," *Daily Advertiser*, March 20, 1790.

Reprinted: *City Gazette*, May 12; *Pennsylvania Mercury*, May 29; *Pennsylvania Packet*, July 5; *Herald of Freedom*, July 9, 1790; *National Gazette*, November 14; *Federal Gazette*, November 15, 1791; *New-Jersey Journal*, October 23, 1798; *Poems* (1795), p. 84; and (1809), II, 132–33.

"On the Demolition of Dartmouth College," *Daily Advertiser*, March 22, 1790.

Reprinted: *City Gazette*, July 9, 1790; as "On the Demolition of a Log-College," *Poems* (1795), pp. 374–75; and "On the Demolition of an Old College," (1809), II, 235–37.

"A View of Massachusetts," *Daily Advertiser*, March 29, 1790.

Reprinted: *Massachusetts Centinel*, April 17; *City Gazette*, June 17, 1790; and as "Massachusetts," *Poems* (1795), pp. 383–84, and (1809), II, 256–58.

"A brief account of the Ugly Club, held in one of the southern States, and their usual mode of procuring new members," *Daily Advertiser*, April 5, 1790.

Reprinted: *Monmouth Almanac* (1795).

"The Country Squire's Exit," *Daily Advertiser*, April 10, 1790.

Reprinted: *City Gazette*, June 3, 1790, "Supposed to be written by capt. Freneau."

"Stanzas Occasioned by the Death of Dr. Franklin," *Daily Advertiser*, April 28, 1790.

Reprinted: *Pennsylvania Packet*, May 3; *Federal Gazette*, May 4; *Freeman's Journal*, May 5; *New-York Daily Gazette*, May 5; *Burlington Advertiser*, May 11; *Maryland Journal*, May 11; *Pennsylvania Mercury*, May 20; *Augusta Chronicle*, June 5, 1790; and as "On the Death of Doctor Benjamin Franklin," *Poems* (1795), p. 417, and (1809), II, 271.

Untitled verse, *Daily Advertiser*, May 1, 1790.

Reprinted: *City Gazette*, May 20; *Freeman's Journal*, July 7; *Augusta Chronicle*, July 10; *Farmer's Journal*, July 22; *Columbian Centinel*, July 31, 1790; and as "Constantia," *National Gazette*, August 8; *Connecticut Courant*, August 20; *Diary*, August 23, 1792; *Columbian*

Museum, July 23, 1799; *Poems* (1795), pp. 381–83; and (1809), II, 255–56.

"Description of Connecticut," *Daily Advertiser,* May 10, 1790.

Reprinted: *Farmer's Journal,* June 3; *Connecticut Courant,* June 14; *Freeman's Journal,* June 30, 1790; and as "Terra Vulpa," *Poems* (1795), pp. 307–08, and (1809), II, 210–11.

"Verses From the other World, by Dr. Fr—k—n," *Daily Advertiser,* May 24, 1790.

Reprinted: *Burlington Advertiser,* June 1; *Pennsylvania Mercury,* June 1; *Freeman's Journal,* June 2; *Maryland Journal,* June 11; *Massachusetts Centinel,* June 12, 1790; and as "Epistle from Dr. Franklin (deceased) to his poetical Panegyrists," *Poems* (1795), pp. 417–18, and (1809), II, 271–72.

"A Descriptive Sketch of Virginia," *Daily Advertiser,* June 11, 1790.

Reprinted as "Virginia. (A Fragment.)," *Poems* (1795), pp. 380–81; and as "Old Virginia," (1809), II, 253–54.

"Lines Occasioned by the Skeletons dug up in Fort George," *Daily Advertiser,* June 17, 1790.

Reprinted as "Stanzas Occasioned by Lord Bellamont's, Lady Hay's, and other Skeletons, being dug up in Fort George (N.Y.) 1790," *Poems* (1795), pp. 409–10, and (1809), II, 262–63.

"A Speech on a New Subject," *Daily Advertiser,* June 29, 1790.

Reprinted as "Tomo Cheeki, No. XI," *Jersey Chronicle,* August 15, 1795 (see below).

"The Orator of the Woods (Occasioned by hearing a very elegant Discourse preached in a mean Building, by the Parson of an obscure Parish," *Daily Advertiser,* June 29, 1790.

Reprinted: *National Gazette,* November 10; *Daily Advertiser,* November 15; *Columbian Herald,* November 23, 1791; *Poems* (1795), pp. 82–83, and (1809), I, 130.

"Nanny, the Philadelphia House Maid, to Nabby, her friend in New-York," *Daily Advertiser,* July 1, 1790.

Reprinted: *New-York Weekly Museum,* July 3; *Columbian Centinel,* July 17; *City Gazette,* July 28, 1790; *Poems* (1795), pp. 414–15, and (1809), II, 268–69.

"The Bergen Planter," *Daily Advertiser,* July 12, 1790.

Reprinted: *American Museum,* October, 1791, pp. 21–22; *Poems* (1795), pp. 418–19; (1809), II, 273–74; and as "The Pennsylvania Planter," *National Gazette,* October 3, and *Diary,* October 8, 1792.

"Nabby, the New York House-Maid, to Nanny, her friend in Philadelphia," *Daily Advertiser,* July 15, 1790.

Reprinted: *New-York Weekly Museum,* July 17; *City Gazette,* August 20, 1790; *Poems* (1795), p. 415; and (1809), II, 269–70.

"The Removal," *New-York Daily Gazette*, August 10, 1790.
> Reprinted as "On the removal of Congress from New-York to Philadelphia. Supposed to have been written by Captain Freneau," *City Gazette*, September 11, 1790; as "On the Departure of the Grand Sanhedrin," *Poems* (1795), pp. 419–20; and as "The Departure," (1809), II, 276–77.

"On the advantages of Steadiness," *Daily Advertiser*, August 31, 1790.
> Introduction to the "Opay Mico" essays.

"A short discourse upon Drunkenness (By Opay Mico one of the Indian Kings from the little Tallasee country, lately departed from this city)," *Daily Advertiser*, September 1, 1790.
> Reprinted as "Tomo Cheeki, No. IV," *Jersey Chronicle*, June 20, 1795 (see below).

"Reflections on my Journey from the Tallassee towns to the settlements of the river Hudson. By Opay Mico, one of the Indian Chiefs, lately departed from this city," *Daily Advertiser*, September 8, 1790.

"A Discourse upon Horse Shoes," *Daily Advertiser*, September 17, 1790.
> Reprinted as "Tomo Cheeki, No. IX," *Jersey Chronicle*, August 1, 1795 (see below).

"Tormentia's Complaint. Written at Cape Hatteras, June 1789," *Daily Advertiser*, September 7, 1790.
> Reprinted: *Pennsylvania Mercury*, September 11, 1790; dated "Castle-Island, Bermuda, Jan. 20, 1789," *National Gazette*, March 19, 1792; and as "Amanda's Complaint," *Poems* (1795), pp. 179–80, and (1809), I, 233–34.

"A Discourse upon Barber's Poles," *Daily Advertiser*, November 1, 1790.
> Reprinted: *Monmouth Almanac* (1795).

"Palemon to Lavinia," *Daily Advertiser*, November 17, 1790.
> Reprinted: *Federal Gazette*, November 19; *Columbian Centinel*, December 4, 1790; *New-York Daily Gazette*, February 14, 1791; *National Gazette*, January 26; *City Gazette*, May 11, 1792; *Poems* (1795), pp. 83–84; and (1809), I, 131–32.

"The Blessings of the Poppy," *Daily Advertiser*, November 18, 1790.
> Reprinted: *Poems* (1795), p. 104; and (1809), I, 159–60.

"Reflections on Sundry Subjects," *Daily Advertiser*, December 16, 1790.
> See above, p. 183.

Untitled prose, continuation of "Reflections," *Daily Advertiser*, December 18, 1790.

1791

"The American Soldier (A Picture from the Life,)," *Daily Advertiser*, January 24, 1791.
> Reprinted: *Burlington Advertiser*, February 8; *New-Jersey Journal*,

February 9; *Farmer's Journal*, February 22; *City Gazette*, March 21; *State Gazette of South Carolina*, April 11, 1791; *Minerva*, April 13, 1797; *Pennsylvania Democrat*, February 16, 1810; *Poems* (1795), p. 379; and (1809), II, 253.

"Stanzas Written on the Hills of Neversink, near Sandy Hook, 1790," *Daily Advertiser*, January 26, 1791.

Reprinted: *Pennsylvania Mercury*, January 29; *Freeman's Journal*, February 2, 1791; as "Written on the Hills of Neversink, near Sandy-Hook, July, 1791," *National Gazette*, November 28, 1791; and as "Neversink," *Poems* (1795), pp. 386–87.

"The Market Maid," *Daily Advertiser*, January 28, 1791.

Reprinted as "The Market Girl (A real Character.)," *National Gazette*, May 28; *Diary*, May 31; *Mail*, June 2; *Daily Advertiser*, June 8, 1792; *Poems* (1795), pp. 58–59; and (1809), I, 99–100.

"The Island Field Negro (Written some years ago, on a Sugar Plantation in Jamaica.)," *Daily Advertiser*, February 1, 1791.

Reprinted: *Freeman's Journal*, March 2, 1791; *New-York Weekly Museum*, June 16; *National Gazette*, July 21; *New-York Daily Gazette*, July 26; *American Museum*, July, 1792, p. 3; and as "To Sir Toby, A Sugar-Planter in the interior parts of Jamaica," *Poems* (1795), pp. 391–92, and (1809), II, 192–93.

"Lines on the failure of Mr. Churchman's scheme of going to Baffin's Bay to ascertain the truth of his Variation Chart," *Daily Advertiser*, February 2, 1791.

Reprinted: *Brunswick Gazette*, February 15; *City Gazette*, March 11, 1791; and as "To Mr. Churchman; On the rejection of his Petition to the Congress of the United States, to enable him to make a voyage to Baffin's Bay, to ascertain the truth of his Variation Chart," *Poems* (1795), pp. 428–29.

"The Tea-Drinker," *Daily Advertiser*, February 5, 1791.

Reprinted: *Burlington Gazette*, February 15; *State Gazette of South-Carolina*, March 17, 1791; *New-York Weekly Museum*, July 2, 1792; as "The Dish of Tea," *National Gazette*, July 7; *Diary*, August 28; *Boston Gazette*, September 10, 1792; *Merchant's Daily Advertiser*, September 20, 1797; *Time-Piece*, January 29; *Carey's United States Recorder*, February 1; *Newark Gazette*, February 6, 1798; *Centinel of Freedom*, July 29, 1800; *New-Jersey Journal*, September 30; *True American*, November 10, 1806; *Weekly Visitor*, July 29, 1820; *Poems* (1795), p. 99; and (1809), I, 151–52.

"The Shelbourne Threat (A true Story.)," *Daily Advertiser*, February 8, 1791.

Reprinted: *General Advertiser*, February 11; *New-York Journal*, February 24; *Herald of Freedom*, March 1, 1791; *National Gazette*, April

5, 1792; as "The Menace," *Poems* (1795), p. 352; and as "The Nova-Scotia Menace," (1809), II, 242.

"The Jug of Rum," *Daily Advertiser*, February 1, 1791.

Reprinted: *American Mercury*, February 21; *Burlington Advertiser*, March 1; *City Gazette*, March 16; *New-Jersey Journal*, March 16; *Brunswick Gazette*, March 22; *Farmer's Journal*, April 5, 1791; *Connecticut Courant*, January 6; *National Gazette*, January 23, with a prose introduction "On Country Taverns"; *Freeman's Journal*, January 25; *Weekly Museum*, February 4; *Kentucky Gazette*, April 28; *American Museum*, August 1792, p. 6; *General Advertiser*, October 9, 1792; *New-Jersey State Gazette*, January 5; *South Carolina State Gazette*, February 10, 1796; *Newark Gazette*, December 30, 1797; *Columbian Museum*, November 5; *Newark Gazette*, November 26, 1799; *New-Jersey and Pennsylvania Almanac* (1805), p. 13; *Georgia Republican*, December 17, 1805; *New-Jersey Journal*, March 4, 1806; *Port-Folio*, October 24, 1807; *New-York Weekly Museum*, September 10, 1808, an abbreviated version; *Pennsylvania Democrat*, August 18, 1809; *Centinel of Freedom*, May 10, 1810; *New-York Weekly Museum*, November 27; *Olio*, December 4, 1813; *Trenton Federalist*, February 28, 1814; *New-Jersey Mirror*, September 8, 1824; *Poems* (1795), p. 61; as "The Jug of Whiskey," *General Advertiser*, October 9, 1792; and as "Lines Written on a Puncheon of Jamaica Spirits," *Poems* (1809), I, 102–03.

Proposals/ For a Monmouth Newspaper./ . . ./ The/ Monmouth Gazette,/ or,/ General Magazine of Information and Amusement./ [*Several lines.*]/ New-York, February 15th, 1791./ Philip Freneau./ . . ./

See Paltsits, *Bibliography*, pp. 4–7.

"On the proposed taxation of News-Papers," *Daily Advertiser*, February 18, 1791.

Reprinted: *Maryland Journal*, March 1; *Freeman's Journal*, March 6; *Brunswick Gazette*, March 15; *General Advertiser*, March 19; *State Gazette of South Carolina*, April 7, 1791; and as "Occasioned by a Bill Proposing a taxation upon News-Papers," *Poems* (1795), p. 377, and (1809), II, 250.

"The Useful only in Vogue at Court," *Daily Advertiser*, February 26, 1791.

Reprinted: *General Advertiser*, March 3, 1791; and as "To Memmius," *Poems* (1795), pp. 385–86.

Untitled verse, *Daily Advertiser*, March 4, 1791.

Reprinted as "To Sylvius. On his preparing to leave the town," *Poems* (1795), pp. 433–34, and (1809), II, 283.

"To the Author of the Above," *Daily Advertiser*, March 10, 1791.

See p. 185 above.

"Marriage A-la-Mode," *Daily Advertiser*, March 22, 1791.

Reprinted: *National Gazette,* February 6; *Freeman's Journal,* February 8; *Poems* (1795), p. 102; and (1809), I, 156–57.

"On Putting a Dog ashore at the island Sapola for Stealing: written 1778," *Daily Advertiser,* March 24, 1791.

Reprinted: *General Advertiser,* March 29; *National Gazette,* November 3, 1791; and as "To a Dog: Occasioned by putting him on shore at the island of Sapola, for theft," *Poems* (1795), p. 364, and (1809), II, 223.

"On the prohibition of Spirituous Liquors in the New-York and Albany Jails," *Daily Advertiser,* April 13, 1791.

Reprinted: *General Advertiser,* April 16, 1791; and as "On a Legislative Act, Prohibiting the use of Spirituous Liquors to Prisoners in certain jails in the United States," *Poems* (1795), p. 416.

"Kay-Grove," *Daily Advertiser,* April 15, 1791.

Reprinted as "Hermit's Valley," *Poems* (1795), pp. 248–49, and (1809), II, 233–34.

"Charity A-La-Mode," *Daily Advertiser,* April 16, 1791.

Reprinted: *General Advertiser,* April 25; *Virginia Gazette,* May 12, 1791; *National Gazette,* February 20; *Diary,* February 22; *Freeman's Journal,* February 22; *Independent Chronicle,* March 8, 1792; *Poems* (1795), pp. 312–13; and as "Mercantile Charity: A Genuine Story," (1809), II, 212–13.

"To the Keeper of the King's Water-Works, near Rock-Fort, in Jamaica; on being refused a Puncheon of Fresh Water, Written, August 1784," *Daily Advertiser,* April 20, 1791.

Reprinted: *General Advertiser,* April 23, 1791; *National Gazette,* January 12, 1792; *Poems* (1795), p. 380; and (1809), II, 191.

"Written on a Beau drowned in a Mill Pond," *Daily Advertiser,* April 29, 1791.

Reprinted: *General Advertiser,* May 3; *City Gazette,* July 4; *Columbian Centinel,* August 3; as "Fopling Flutter (Unfortunately drowned in a Mill-pond about a week before his intended marriage, April, 1787)," *National Gazette,* November 24; *New-York Daily Gazette,* November 28, 1791; as "Elegiac Stanzas on a young gentleman drowned in a Mill-Pond," *Poems* (1795), p. 88; and as "Elegiac Stanzas on a young gallant . . ." (1809), I, 140.

"Lines written some years ago on the death of a Fiddler. Addressed to Mrs. ——," *Daily Advertiser,* May 2, 1791.

Reprinted: *General Advertiser,* May 5; *Columbian Centinel,* June 4, 1791; as "Epistolary Lines On the Death of a Fiddler," *Poems* (1795), pp. 15–16; and as "Elegiac Lines On the Death of a Fiddler, called Blind Jacob," (1809), I, 36–38.

"The Rural Bachelor. A Real Character," *Daily Advertiser,* May 13, 1791.

Reprinted: *General Advertiser*, May 16; *Mail*, October 6; *City Gazette*, November 21, 1791; *Poems* (1795), pp. 366–67; and (1809), II, 226–27.

"The Origin of Lee-Boards," *Daily Advertiser*, May 16, 1791.

Reprinted: *General Advertiser*, May 19; *Newark Gazette*, June 2, 1791; and "By Philip Freneau," *Diary*, November 9, 1797.

"Stanzas to the memory of Mrs. Gertrude Burnet, who died at Newark, in Essex county, New-Jersey on the 4th of May, 1791," *Daily Advertiser*, May 17, 1791.

Reprinted as "To the Memory of a Lady," *Poems* (1795), pp. 363–64; and as "To the Memory of Mrs. Burnet, of Elizabeth-town, N.J. (by Request.)," (1809), II, 222–23.

"On the Crew of a certain Vessel, several of whom happen'd to be of the same name with celebrated clergymen," *Daily Advertiser*, May 20, 1791.

Reprinted: *Maryland Journal*, May 27; *City Gazette*, July 21; *American Museum*, September, 1791, p. 16; *American Apollo*, September 27; *New-York Weekly Museum*, October 12, 1793; *Columbian Centinel*, August 23, 1794; *Columbian Museum*, February 3, 1797; *Columbian Museum*, April 23, 1799; *Port-Folio*, November 7, 1807; *The Cabinet of Momus*, p. 54; *Poems* (1795), p. 161; and (1809), I, 132.

"Lines Occasioned by reading Mr. Paine's Rights of Man," *Daily Advertiser*, May 27, 1791.

Reprinted: *General Advertiser*, May 30; *Freeman's Journal*, June 1; *City Gazette*, July 20, 1791; as "To a Republican, With Mr. Paine's Rights of Man," *Poems* (1795), pp. 396–97; and as "On Mr. Paine's Rights of Man," (1809), II, 294–95.

"The Landlord's Soliloquy," introduced by a long article on the destruction of trees, signed "Civis," *Daily Advertiser*, May 31, 1791.

Reprinted: *Federal Gazette*, June 1, 1791; as "On Trees in Cities," introduced by another long article on the subject, *National Gazette*, March 8, 1792; and as "Lines Occasioned by a Law passed by the Corporation of New-York in 1790, for cutting down the trees in the streets of that city, previous to June 10, 1791," *Poems* (1795), pp. 410–12, and (1809), II, 264–66.

"The Drunkard's Apology," *Daily Advertiser*, July 9, 1791.

Reprinted: *City Gazette*, September 12; *National Gazette*, December 15, 1791; *Carey's Daily Advertiser*, July 29; *Columbian Museum*, September 5, 1797; *Poems* (1795), p. 100; and as "An Apology for Intemperance. By Hezekiah Salem," (1809), I, 154.

"Minerva's Advice," *Daily Advertiser*, August 4, 1791.

Reprinted: *Mail*, August 6, 1791; *Poems* (1795), pp. 104–05; and (1809), I, 160–61.

"On a Painter, who was endeavouring to recover from memory the features

& portrait of a Lady, who died at sea. Written 1788," *Daily Advertiser*, August 24, 1791.

> Reprinted: *Poems* (1795), p. 101; and (1809), I, 155–56.

"The Parting Glass. Written at an Inn," *Daily Advertiser*, September 17, 1791.

> Reprinted: *National Gazette*, May 10; *Federal Gazette*, May 11; *Diary*, May 15; *State Gazette of South Carolina*, May 28; Boston *Argus*, June 22; *Catskill Packet*, August 2, 1792; *New-York Weekly Chronicle*, February 19, 1795; *Poems* (1795), pp. 85–86; and "By Hezekiah Salem," (1809), I, 133–34.

"To the Public," *National Gazette*, October 31, 1791.

> Introductory editorial of Freneau's newspaper.

"Political Address to the Public of the United States," *National Gazette*, October 31, 1791.

> Reprinted: *Freeman's Journal*, November 2; *Daily Advertiser*, November 4; *Burlington Advertiser*, November 15; *Columbian Centinel*, November 16; *Newark Gazette*, November 17, 1791; *Kentucky Gazette*, January 7; *City Gazette*, February 18, 1792; and as "To the Public," *Poems* (1795), p. 395.

"A Mistake Rectified," *National Gazette*, November 14, 1791.

> Signed "Sinbat the Sailor." Reprinted: *Daily Advertiser*, November 19, 1791; *City Gazette*, February 10, 1792; as "Epistle to a Desponding Seaman," *Poems* (1795), p. 335; and as "Lines, by H. Salem, on his return from Calcutta," (1809), II, 299.

"The Prudent Philosopher (Occasioned by the conduct of some gentlemen at the conflagration of a certain Southern Court-House, during the sessions," *National Gazette*, November 17, 1791.

> Reprinted: *Poems* (1795), pp. 353–54; and ". . . Occasioned by the Conflagration of the State House at Charleston, 1786," (1809), II, 244–45.

"The Debtor's Soliloquy," *National Gazette*, December 8, 1791.

> Reprinted: *Connecticut Courant*, December 13; *New-York Daily Gazette*, December 31, 1791; *Poems* (1795), pp. 27–28; and "Written under the Character of Hezekiah Salem," (1809), I, 51–52.

"The Country Printer," *National Gazette*, December 19, 22, 29, 1791, and January 5, 1792.

> Reprinted: *Daily Advertiser*, December 22, 26, 1791, January 2, and 14; part 3 only, *Independent Chronicle*, January 12; part 1 only, *Connecticut Courant*, January 23; parts 1–3, *Columbian Centinel*, January 28 and February 1; *City Gazette*, April 14, 16, 17, 18, 1792; *Poems* (1795), pp. 421–24; and in The Village Merchant:/ A/ Poem. To which is added the/ Country Printer./ . . ./ Philadelphia:/ Printed

by Hoff and Derrick,/ M,DCC,XCIV./ pp. 11–16. 8vo; p. 16. Copies: BU, HSP.

1792

"On the present state of Rivers," *National Gazette*, February 23, 1792.

> Reprinted: *Freeman's Journal*, February 29, 1792; and as "The Bridge of Delaware," *Poems* (1795), p. 103, and (1809), I, 158.

"Receipt to make an Echo Writer," *National Gazette*, March 29, 1792.

"Ode to the Echo Writer," *National Gazette*, April 2, 1792.

> Reprinted: *Diary*, April 10; *American Mercury*, April 30, 1792; and as "To Shylock Ap-Shenkin," *Poems* (1795), pp. 404–05.

"The Village Merchant," *National Gazette*, May 17, 24, 31, June 7, 14, and 28, 1792.

> Reprinted: *Aurora*, May 25, June 1, 8, 16, July 2, and 6; *Daily Advertiser*, May 28, June 4, and July 6; *Farmer's Journal*, June 4, 11, 18, July 14, and 28; *Connecticut Courant*, July 2, 9, 16, 23, and 30, 1792; *The Village Merchant, A Poem*, pp. 3–11 (see December 19, 1791, above); *Poems* (1795), pp. 9–15; and as "The Adventures of Simon Swaugum, A Village Merchant. Written in 1768," (1809), I, 27–36.

"The Fair Buckle-Thief," *National Gazette*, June 4, 1792.

> Reprinted: *Diary*, June 7, 1792; and *Poems* (1795), pp. 35–36.

Untitled verse, with prose introduction, *Diary*, June 27, 1792.

> Reprinted: *Federal Gazette*, July 24; *National Gazette*, July 28; *Gazette of the United States*, August 1; *Boston Gazette*, August 27; and, the verse only, as "Stanzas to the Memory of two young persons (twin-brothers) Robert Sevier and William Sevier, who were killed by the Savages on Cumberland River, in North-Carolina, in attempting to assist a new settler, who was then passing the river with a numerous family," *Poems* (1795), p. 103, and (1809), I, 158–59.

"Independence," *National Gazette*, July 4, 1792.

> Reprinted: *Diary*, July 7; *New-York Journal*, July 7; *Daily Advertiser*, July 9; *Weekly Museum*, July 12, 1792; and as "A Warning to America," *Poems* (1795), pp. 430–31, and (1809), II, 282.

"Odes on Various Subjects. Ode I. On the Fourteenth of July," *National Gazette*, July 14, 1792.

> Reprinted: *Columbian Centinel*, July 28; *American Museum*, July, 1792, p. 4; and as "On the Fourteenth of July, A Day ever Memorable to Regenerated France," *Poems* (1795), pp. 431–32, and *Time-Piece*, September 25, 1797.

"Ode II. Addressed to Crispin O'Conner, Esq. a backwoods Planter," *National Gazette*, July 18, 1792.

Reprinted: *Diary*, July 21; *Federal Gazette*, September 10, 1792; *Poems* (1795), pp. 159–60; and "Supposed to be written by Hezekiah Salem," (1809), II, 20–21.

"Ode III," *National Gazette*, July 23, 1792.

Reprinted: *Gazette of the United States*, August 4, 1792; and as "To Shylock Ap-Shenkin," *Poems* (1795), pp. 397–98.

"Ode IV," *National Gazette*, August 4, 1792.

Reprinted, almost completely rewritten, as "To My Book," *Poems* (1795), pp. 394–95.

"To the Public," *National Gazette*, August 8, 1792.

Editor's statement after six months of publication.

"A Curious Dialogue (Occasioned by the Emblematical Devices on a certain Travelling-Coach.)," *National Gazette*, August 11, 1792.

Reprinted: *City Gazette*, October 24; *New-York Journal*, November 28, 1792; and as "A Matrimonial Dialogue," *Poems* (1795), pp. 401–02; (1809), II, 261–62; and *The Cabinet of Momus*, p. 67.

"An Old Heathen Story Adapted to Modern Times," *National Gazette*, August 29, 1792.

Reprinted as "To a Persecuted Philosopher," *Poems* (1795), p. 393.

"The Speculator," *National Gazette*, September 19, 1792.

Reprinted: *Diary*, September 22; *Weekly Museum*, September 29; *Catskill Packet*, October 1, 1792; as "On Pest-Eli-Hali, The Travelling Speculator," *Poems* (1795), pp. 429–30; and as "On a Travelling Speculator," (1809), II, 280–81.

Untitled verse, *National Gazette*, September 26, 1792.

Reprinted as "To an Angry Zealot: (In Answer to Sundry Virulent Charges.)," *Poems* (1795), p. 390.

"Advice to Ladies Not to Neglect the Dentist," *National Gazette*, September 29, 1792.

Reprinted: *Diary*, October 5; *Weekly Museum*, October 13, 1792; *Poems* (1795), pp. 52–53; and (1809), I, 92.

Translation of "Stanzas . . . addressed to the Americans of the United States, by the French patriotic society of Charleston, S.C.," *National Gazette*, December 8, 1792.

Reprinted: *Diary*, December 12; *New-York Journal*, December 22, 1792; and as "On the French Republicans," *Poems* (1795), pp. 432–33.

Translation of "Latin Verses in our Last," *National Gazette*, December 15, 1792.

Reprinted: *Gazette of the United States*, December 18; *Diary*, December 20, 1792; *City Gazette*, January 19, 1793; and as "The Pyramid of the Fifteen American States," *Poems* (1795), pp. 435–36, and (1809), II, 284–85.

"Present View of France and her Combined Enemies," *National Gazette*, December 19, 1792.

Reprinted: *American Daily Advertiser*, December 21; *Diary*, December 24; *New-York Journal*, December 29, 1792, and January 2, 1793; *American Apollo*, January 11; *City Gazette*, January 18; *Augusta Chronicle*, January 19, 1793; and as "On the Demolition of the French Monarchy," *Poems* (1795), pp. 453–54, and (1809), II, 291–92.

"On the Royal Portraits, in the Senate Chamber," *National Gazette*, December 22, 1792.

Reprinted: Boston *Argus*, January 8, 1793; and as "On the Portraits, of Louis and Antoinette, in the Senate Chamber," *Poems* (1795), p. 433.

1793

Untitled verse, *National Gazette*, January 12, 1793.

Reprinted as "To a Noisy Politician," *Poems* (1795), p. 402.

Untitled prose, *National Gazette*, January 12, 1792.

Rewritten as "Tomo Cheeki, Number VIII," *Jersey Chronicle*, July 25, 1795.

Untitled verse, introduced by prose "Reflections on Balloons," *National Gazette*, January 19, 1793.

Reprinted: prose and verse, *New-York Daily Gazette*, January 22; verse only, *Columbian Centinel*, January 30, 1793; as "Stanzas written some years ago on Mr. Blanchard's 45th ascension from the jail yard in Philadelphia—January 3, 1793," *Time-Piece*, May 15, 1797; and as "To Mr. Blanchard; the Celebrated Æronaut: on his ascent in a Balloon, from the jail-yard in Philadelphia: 1793," *Poems* (1795), pp. 446–47, and (1809), II, 286–87.

Untitled verse, *National Gazette*, February 2, 1793.

Reprinted as "Lines Written in a severe February on a Shad, &c. caught in a mild January," *Poems* (1795), p. 360.

"A New Song," *New-York Journal*, May 11, 1793.

Reprinted: Boston *Argus*, May 21; *Federal Gazette*, June 3; *American Daily Advertiser*, June 4; *Gazette of the United States*, June 5; *Diary*, June 5; as "New Ode. To a popular tune," *National Gazette*, June 5; *American Apollo*, July 26; *Daily Advertiser*, November 26; *New-York Weekly Museum*, November 30, 1793; as "Song to the tune of Great Washington," *New-York Journal*, June 28, 1794; as "A New Song," *A Tribute to the Swinish Multitude* (New York, 1795), pp. 11–13; as "Hymn to Liberty," *Jersey Chronicle*, July 11, 1795; *Poems*

(1795), pp. 445–46; and as "The Rights of Man," *North Carolina Gazette*, March 11, 1797.

"Ode to Liberty," *National Gazette*, May 29, 1793.

> Reprinted: *Poems* (1795), pp. 339–40.

"Reflections On the death of a Country Printer. (By his Successor.)," *National Gazette*, July 6, 1793.

> Reprinted as "On the Death of a Country Printer: (By his Partner and Successor.)," *Poems* (1795), pp. 434–35; and as "On the Death of a Country Printer," *Time-Piece*, September 22, 1797.

"Patriotic Stanzas On the Anniversary of the Storming of the Bastille, at Paris, July 14, 1789," *National Gazette*, July 17, 1793.

> Reprinted: *Kentucky Gazette*, November 2, 1793; and as "On the Anniversary of the storming of the Bastille . . ." *Poems* (1795), pp. 438–39.

"To Justice. An abusive Scribbler," *National Gazette*, July 31, 1793.

> Reprinted: *Gazette of the United States*, August 3, 1793; and as "Addressed to a Political Shrimp, or, Fly upon the wheel," *Poems* (1795), pp. 425–26.

"A Dialogue between Whaacum and Whiffle," *National Gazette*, August 3, 1793.

> Reprinted as "A Dialogue between Shadrach and Whiffle," *Poems* (1795), pp. 362–63, and (1809), II, 221–22.

"To Justice (A Writer in the Gazette of the United States)," *National Gazette*, August 7, 1793.

> Reprinted as "To Shylock Ap-Shenkin. (In Reply to Big Looks and Menaces.)," *Poems* (1795), p. 403.

"On a late memorable naval engagement," *National Gazette*, August 17 and 24, 1793.

> Reprinted: *Independent Chronicle*, September 2, 1793; and as "On the Memorable Naval Engagement Between the French Republican Frigate *L'Ambuscade*, Captain Bompard; and the Royal British Frigate *Boston*, Captain Courtney; off the coast of New-Jersey," *Poems* (1795), pp. 450–52, and (1809), II, 296–98.

"Orlando's Flight," *National Gazette*, September 4, 1793.

> Reprinted as "On Dr. Sangrado's Flight," *Poems* (1795), p. 448, and (1809), II, 288.

"Elegy On the Death of a Blacksmith," *National Gazette*, September 18, 1793.

> Reprinted: *Virginia Gazette*, September 26; *Newark Gazette*, October 23; *New Hampshire Journal*, October 25, 1793; *Times*, June 13, 1805; *Poems* (1795), pp. 449–50; and (1809), II, 290.

"Lines Addressed To a very little Man, who was fond of walking with a very large Cane," *National Gazette*, September 25, 1793.

Reprinted: *New-York Journal*, October 26, 1793; and as "To a very Little Man . . . ," *Poems* (1795), pp. 365–66, and (1809), II, 225–26.

"Quintilian to Lycidas," *National Gazette*, September 28, 1793.
Reprinted: *Poems* (1795), pp. 87–88; and (1809), I, 136.

1794

Monmouth News-Paper./ . . ./ The Monmouth Gazette, and East-Jersey Intelligencer/ [*Several lines.*]/ Philip Freneau/ Mount-Pleasant, July 4, 1794./ . . ./
Bsd. prospectus. Two mutilated copies, together forming a complete text, are in the Monmouth County Historical Association Library; see Lewis Leary, "An Unpublished Item in the Bibliography of Philip Freneau," *American Literature*, VI, 330–34 (November, 1934).
The/ Monmouth/ Almanac,/ for the/ Year M,DCC,XCV:/ Being the third after Leap Year; and the/ XIXth of American Independence/ ('Till the Fourth of July.)/ Calculated for the Meridian of New-Jersey./ (Longitude 35 Minutes, East from Philadelphia,)/ and Latitude of 40 Degrees, 20 Minutes North./ Number 1./ [*30 stars*]/ Middletown-Point./ Printed and Sold by P. Freneau, near the above place;/ and may be had of most of the Store-keepers in/ Monmouth, and the adjacent Counties./
12mo; 48pp. Copies: LC, NJHS (mutilated).

1795

Poems/ Written between the Years 1768 & 1794,/ by/ Philip Freneau,/ of/ New Jersey:/ A New Edition, Revised and Corrected by the/ Author; Including a considerable number of/ Pieces never before published./ [*Fifteen stars for the states of the Union, with Latin quotation to p. 435.*]/ Monmouth/ [N.J.]/ Printed/ At the Press of the Author, at Mount-Pleasant, near/ Middletown-Point; M,DCC,XCV: and, of/ —American Independence—/ XIX./
8vo; 446pp. Copies: AAS, BA, BM, BPL, BU, HL, HSP, LC, LCP, MHA, MHS, NJHS, NJSL, NYHS, NYPL, NYSL, PU, RU. Notice of copyright, April 17, 1795, published in *Daily Advertiser*, May 4, 1795. Advertised in New York from April 18, 1795 (see note 15 of chapter IX).

"To the Public," *Jersey Chronicle*, May 2, 1795.
"On the Approaching Dissolution of Transatlantic Jurisdiction in America," *Jersey Chronicle*, May 16, 1795.
Reprinted: *Poems* (1795), pp. 437–38; and (1809), II, 285–86.
"Tomo Cheeki, The Creek Indian in Philadelphia," *Jersey Chronicle*, May 23, 1795.

The "Tomo Cheeki" essays were reprinted in slightly different order in the *Time-Piece*, March 15–June 16, 1797 (see below). As published in the *Jersey Chronicle*, they were reprinted: complete, *New-Jersey State Gazette*, June 23–December 1, 1795; *Newark Gazette*, September 9, 1795–January 6, 1796; Introduction–No. VII, *New-Jersey Chronicle*, June 10–August 16; Introduction–No. III, *Argus*, June 2–18; Nos. I–III, *Aurora*, June 8–July 1; No. XIV, *Independent Gazetteer*, October 28 and November 14; and No. III, *Columbian Herald*, June 27, 1795.

"The Republican Genius of Europe," *Jersey Chronicle*, May 23, 1795.

Reprinted: *Time-Piece*, July 3, 1797; and, almost completely rewritten, as "On the Royal Coalition against Republican Liberty," *Poems* (1815), I, 108–09.

"Tomo Cheeki, The Creek Indian in Philadelphia. Numb. I. (Translated from the original Talassee or Creek Language," *Jersey Chronicle*, May 30, 1795.

Reprinted: *Time-Piece*, March 17, 1797.

"The Rival Suitors for America," *Jersey Chronicle*, May 30, 1795.

Reprinted as "The Rival Candidates for the Favours of America," *Time-Piece*, March 20; Baltimore *Federal Gazette*, March 31; Philadelphia *Daily Advertiser*, April 6, 1797; as "The Political Rival Courtship," *Pennsylvania Democrat*, September 15, 1809; and as "The Political Rival Suitors. Occasioned by the detection of certain foreign schemes for exclusive privileges in American Commerce," *Poems* (1815), I, 46–54.

"Tomo Cheeki, The Creek Indian in Philadelphia. Numb. II. Consolatory advice to my brother Nantounawaw (of the embassy) who had applied to be made a member of a Philosophical Society," *Jersey Chronicle*, June 6, 1795.

Reprinted as "Tomo Cheeki, No. IV," *Time-Piece*, March 29, 1797.

"Lines written several years ago, and intended to have been engraved on a Tomb Stone under an Oak Tree, where a despairing Lover had hanged himself," *Jersey Chronicle*, June 6, 1795.

Reprinted: *Columbian Centinel*, June 20, 1795; and as "Love's Suicide," *Poems* (1809), I, 61.

"Tomo Cheeki, The Creek Indian in Philadelphia. Numb. III. A Piece written in the night—to which is added a short Dream," *Jersey Chronicle*, June 13, 1795.

Reprinted: *Time-Piece*, March 24, 1797.

"Tomo Cheeki, The Creek Indian in Philadelphia. Numb IV. A short talk on Drunkenness," *Jersey Chronicle*, June 20, 1797.

Rewritten from "A short discourse on Drunkenness, by Opay Mico,"

Daily Advertiser, September 1, 1790. Reprinted as "Tomo Cheeki, No. VII," *Time-Piece*, April 17, 1797.

"Tomo Cheeki, The Creek Indian in Philadelphia. Numb. V. (Containing certain Indian Notions and Reflections.)," *Jersey Chronicle*, July 4, 1795.

Reprinted as "Tomo Cheeki, No. IV," *Time-Piece*, April 3, 1797.

"Tomo Cheeki, The Creek Indian in Philadelphia. Numb. VI. To the Big Loom, a white man of this Village," *Jersey Chronicle*, July 11, 1795.

Reprinted as "Tomo Cheeki, No. IX," *Time-Piece*, May 5, 1797.

"Tomo Cheeki, The Creek Indian in Philadelphia. Nummber [*sic*] VII. (Written about Midnight.)," *Jersey Chronicle*, July 18, 1795.

Reprinted as "Tomo Cheeki, No. II," *Time-Piece*, March 29, 1797.

"Tomo Cheeki, The Creek Indian in Philadelphia, Number VIII," *Jersey Chronicle*, July 25, 1795.

Rewritten from *National Gazette*, January 12, 1792. Reprinted as "Tomo Cheeki, No. XIII," *Time-Piece*, June 2, 1797.

"Tomo Cheeki, The Creek Indian in Philadelphia. Numb. IX," *Jersey Chronicle*, August 1, 1795.

Rewritten from "A Discourse on Horse Shoes," *Daily Advertiser*, September 17, 1790. Reprinted as "Tomo Cheeki, No. XII," *Time-Piece*, May 29, 1797.

"Tomo Cheeki, The Creek Indian in Philadelphia. Numb. X," *Jersey Chronicle*, August 8, 1795.

Reprinted: *Time-Piece*, May 12, 1797.

"Tomo Cheeki, The Creek Indian in Philadelphia. Numb. XI," *Jersey Chronicle*, August 15, 1795.

Reprinted from "A Speech on a New Subject," *Daily Advertiser*, June 29, 1790.

"Tomo Cheeki, The Creek Indian in Philadelphia—Number XII," *Jersey Chronicle*, August 29, 1795.

Reprinted as "Tomo Cheeki, No. V," *Time-Piece*, April 7, 1797.

"Tomo Cheeki, The Creek Indian in Philadelphia—Number XIII. To Hopiniyabie, an Indian Woman on the south side of the river O-conee," *Jersey Chronicle*, September 12, 1795.

Reprinted as "Tomo Cheeki, No. VI," *Time-Piece*, April 12, 1797.

"Mr. Jay's Treaty Disclosed by Stephens Thaddeus Mason," *Jersey Chronicle*, September 12, 1795.

See Pattee, in *Poems*, III, 132.

"Tomo Cheeki, The Creek Indian in Philadelphia—Number XIV," *Jersey Chronicle*, October 17, 1795.

Reprinted as "Tomo Cheeki, No. VIII," *Time-Piece*, April 21, 1797.

1796

Editorial note announcing the end of the newspaper, *Jersey Chronicle*, April 16, 1796.

"Parody On the attempt to enforce the British Treaty on the People of the United States," *Jersey Chronicle*, April 23, 1796.

> See Pattee, in *Poems*, III, 133.

"To Subscribers," *Jersey Chronicle*, April 30, 1796.

> The editor's farewell to his readers.

1797

Megara to Altvola. To a female satirist (an English actress) on receiving from her No.1 of a very satirical and biting attack.

> Title from *Poems* (1809), II, 30–34, where Freneau states: "Six copies only, of this little Poem were printed and sent to the satirist."

"To the Public," *Time-Piece*, March 13, 1797.

> Introductory editorial, signed "Philip Freneau."

"Poetical Address," *Time-Piece*, March 13, 1797.

> Reprinted as "Prefatory Lines to a Periodical Publication," *Poems* (1815), I, 55–57.

"Tomo Cheeki, The Creek Indian in Philadelphia: Translated from the original in the Talasse or Creek language," *Time-Piece*, March 15, 1797.

> Reprinted from *Jersey Chronicle*, May 23, 1795.

"Tomo Cheeki, the Creek Indian in Philadelphia. No. I. Reflexions on my first entering the great city of the white men," *Time-Piece*, March 17, 1797.

> Reprinted from *Jersey Chronicle*, May 30, 1795.

"Tomo Cheeki, the Creek Indian in Philadelphia. No. II," *Time-Piece*, March 20, 1797.

> Reprinted from "Tomo Cheeki, No. VII," *Jersey Chronicle*, July 18, 1795. Reprinted in *New World*, June 22, 1797.

"Tomo Cheeki, the Creek Indian in Philadelphia. No. III," *Time-Piece*, March 24, 1797.

> Reprinted from *Jersey Chronicle*, June 13, 1795.

"On the too Remote Extension of American Commerce," *Time-Piece*, March 24, 1797.

> Reprinted: *Aurora*, April 17; *Independent Gazetteer*, April 21; *Centinel of Freedom*, June 21, 1797; and as "Commerce: That internal commerce only, promotes the morals of a country situated like America, and prevents its growth of luxury, and its consequent vices," *Poems* (1815), I, 66–68.

"Tomo Cheeki, the Creek Indian in Philadelphia, No. IV," *Time-Piece*, March 29, 1797.

Reprinted from "Tomo Cheeki, No. II," *Jersey Chronicle*, June 6, 1795.

"To the Americans," *Time-Piece*, March 29, 1797.

Reprinted as "On the War, Projected with the Republic of France," *Poems* (1815), I, 60–61.

"Tomo Cheeki, the Creek Indian in Philadelphia, No. IV [*sic*]," *Time-Piece*, April 3, 1797.

Reprinted from "Tomo Cheeki, No. V," *Jersey Chronicle*, July 4, 1795.

"Warning to the Western Fiddling General," *Time-Piece*, April 3, 1797.

Reprinted: *Columbian Centinel*, April 12; *Delaware and Eastern Shore Advertiser*, April 24; *Merchant's Daily Advertiser*, April 28, 1797; and as "On a Celebrated Performer on the Violin," *Poems* (1815), I, 81–84.

"Tomo Cheeki, the Creek Indian in Philadelphia, No. V," *Time-Piece*, April 7, 1797.

Reprinted from "Tomo Cheeki, No. XII," *Jersey Chronicle*, August 29, 1795.

"On a young lady who wore in her cap, iron wire conductors, on the plan of Dr. Brydone, to guard against the effects of lightning," *Time-Piece*, April 7, 1797.

Reprinted as "To Myrtalis, on her Lightning Wires, or Conductors," *Poems* (1809), II, 27.

"Thetis: or the Heroine; a character," *Time-Piece*, April 10, 1797.

Reprinted as "Nereus and Thetis," *Poems* (1809), II, 28.

"Tomo Cheeki, the Creek Indian in Philadelphia, No. VI," *Time-Piece*, April 12, 1797.

Reprinted from "Tomo Cheeki, No. XIII," *Jersey Chronicle*, September 12, 1795.

"Reflections on Dr. Perkins Metallic Rods," *Time-Piece*, April 12, 1797.

Reprinted as "Reflections on Dr. Perkin's metallic points, or tractors," *Poems* (1815), I, 84–87.

"Tomo Cheeki, the Creek Indian in Philadelphia, No. VII," *Time-Piece*, April 17, 1797.

Reprinted from "Tomo Cheeki, No. IV," *Jersey Chronicle*, June 20, 1795.

"Tomo Cheeki, the Creek Indian in Philadelphia, No. VIII," *Time-Piece*, April 21 and 28, 1797.

Reprinted from "Tomo Cheeki, No. XIV," *Jersey Chronicle*, October 17, 1795.

"On the Progress of the French Armies in Italy," *Time-Piece*, April 26, 1797.

Reprinted as "On the Invasion of Rome," *Poems* (1815), I, 106–07.

"Equestrian Exercises at Mr. Rickett's Circus," *Time-Piece*, May 1, 1797.

Reprinted as "Lines Written for Mr. Ricketts, on the Exhibitions at his Equestrian Circus," *Poems* (1809), II, 143–44.

"Tomo Cheeki, the Creek Indian in Philadelphia, No. IX," *Time-Piece*, May 5, 1797.

Reprinted from "Tomo Cheeki, No. VI," *Jersey Chronicle*, July 11, 1797.

"Lines written on a passage from New-York to the island of Madeira, addressed to Calista on shore," *Time-Piece*, May 10, 1797.

Reprinted as "Publius to Pollia. Supposed to have been written during a cruising expedition," *Poems* (1815), I, 87–91.

"Tomo Cheeki, the Creek Indian in Philadelphia, No. X," *Time-Piece*, May 12, 1797.

Reprinted from *Jersey Chronicle*, August 8, 1795.

"On hearing a remarkably dull discourse, of near two hours in length, from a rambling lay-preacher in the back woods of North-Carolina," *Time-Piece*, May 17, 1797.

Reprinted as "The American Demosthenes. Occasioned by a very weak and insipid discourse on a Fourth of July, indirectly reprobating the democratic representative system. (By Hezekiah Salem)," *Poems* (1809), II, 197–98; and as "On Hearing a Political Oration, Superficially composed on an important subject," (1815), I, 128–29.

"Tomo Cheeki, the Creek Indian in Philadelphia, No. XI," *Time-Piece*, May 22, 1797.

"Tomo Cheeki, the Creek Indian in Philadelphia, No. XIII," *Time-Piece*, June 2, 1797.

Reprinted from "Tomo Cheeki, No. VIII," *Jersey Chronicle*, July 25, 1795.

"On the Proposed American Negociation with the French Republic," *Time-Piece*, June 7, 1797.

Reprinted: Philadelphia *Daily Advertiser*, June 9; *Centinel of Freedom*, June 14; *Morris County Gazette*, June 21; *New-Jersey State Gazette*, June 27; *Boston Gazette*, July 3; *Kentucky Gazette*, July 22, 1797; and as "On Proposed Negotiation with the French Republic, and Political Reformation—1799," *Poems* (1815), I, 103–04.

"Tomo Cheeki, the Creek Indian in Philadelphia, No. XV," *Time-Piece*, June 16, 1797.

"On a Sea Captain that Shot Himself," *Time-Piece*, June 23, 1797.

Reprinted: *Connecticut Courant*, July 17, 1797; and as "Suicide: The Weakness of the Human Mind. A Marine Anecdote," *Poems* (1809), II, 88.

"Ode for the Fourth of July. To be Sung Tuesday next at the New Dutch Church, by the Uranian Society," *Weekly Museum*, July 1, 1797.

Reprinted: *New-York Journal*, July 5; *Diary*, July 5; *Aurora*, July 7;

and as "Ode for the Fourth of July, 1797. Performed by the Uranian Society of the city of New York," *Time-Piece*, July 10, 1797; *Means for the Preservation of Public Liberty. An Oration delivered in the New Dutch Church, on the Fourth of July, 1797* (New York, 1797), pp. 20–21; *Aurora*, July 7, 1809; and as "Ode for July the Fourth—1799," *Poems* (1815), I, 100–02.

"On a very Small Garden Belonging to a Citizen of N.Y." *Time-Piece*, July 19, 1797.

Reprinted: Philadelphia *Daily Advertiser*, July 21, 1797; and as "Lines written on a very small garden," *Poems* (1809), II, 10–11.

"Stanzas occasioned by some illiberal reflections in Fenno's Gazette of the United States of the 18th ult of the Feast of Reason, given by upwards of one hundred patriotic citizens of New-York, to Citizen Munroe, in testimony of their esteem of his character, public as well as private," *Time-Piece*, July 24, 1797.

Reprinted: *Diary*, July 24, 1797; and as "The Republican Festival: In Compliment to Colonel Munroe, on his Return to America. 1797," *Poems* (1815), I, 121–22.

Untitled verse on John Ledyard, included in proposals for an edition of his *Travels*, *Time-Piece*, August 30, 1797.

Reprinted as "Panegyric Lines On the late Mr. John Ledyard, a celebrated Philadelphia Traveller. Supposed to be written by Mr. Philip Freneau," *Columbian Centinel*, September 13; and *Albany Centinel*, September 22, 1797.

"On a Bee Drinking from a Glass of Water," *Time-Piece*, September 6, 1797.

Reprinted: *Carey's United States Recorder*, April 14, 1798; and as "On a Honey Bee, Drinking from a Glass of Wine, and Drowned Therein. (By Hezekiah Salem)," *Poems* (1809), II, 97–98.

"To the Public," *Time-Piece*, September 13, 1797.

Freneau's journalistic creed; see Frank Smith, "Philip Freneau and *The Time-Piece and Literary Companion*," *American Literature*, IV, 275 (November, 1932).

Untitled prose and verse directed against "Peter Porcupine," *Time-Piece*, September 13, 1797.

"Address to the Republicans of America," *Time-Piece*, September 13, 1797.

Reprinted: *Centinel of Freedom*, October 4, 1797; and *Poems* (1809), I, 280.

"Melancholy reflections in passing by a burying ground in the neighbourhood of Philadelphia," *Time-Piece*, September 15, 1797.

Reprinted as "On Passing by an Old Churchyard," *Poems* (1815), I, 137.

Untitled prose and verse directed against "Peter Porcupine," *Time-Piece*, September 18, 1797.

Untitled prose and verse on the rumor that printers in America were bribed by the French, *Time-Piece*, September 25, 1797.

  The verse is reprinted, greatly changed, as "To the Democratic Editors, on a Charge of Bribery," *Poems* (1809), II, 274–76.

"Reflections on the General Debased Conditions of Mankind," *Time-Piece*, September 25, 1797.

  Reprinted: *Constitutional Gazette*, September 30, 1797; rewritten as "False Systems of Government," *City Gazette*, December 24, 1800; *New-York Weekly Museum*, October 16, 1802; and as "On False Systems of Government, and the Generally Debased Condition of Mankind," *Poems* (1809), I, 253–56.

Untitled prose and verse on the first attempted launching of the frigate *Constitution*, *Time-Piece*, September 29, 1797.

  Reprinted: *Newark Gazette*, October 4, 1797; and, the verse only, as "On the Launching of the Frigate Constitution," *Poems* (1815), I, 141–42.

Untitled prose and verse condemning American materialism, *Time-Piece*, September 29, 1797.

  The verse, rewritten, is reprinted as "A Usurer's Prayer," *Poems* (1809), II, 57–58.

Untitled prose and verse on the conduct of social classes, *Time-Piece*, October 2, 1797.

  The verse is reprinted as "The Political Weathercock," *Poems* (1809), II, 121–22.

Untitled prose and verse directed against John Fenno, *Time-Piece*, October 6, 1797.

Untitled criticism of "The Columbiad," *Time-Piece*, October 9, 1797.

  Reprinted, "Written by Mr. Freneau," *loc. cit.*, August 10, 1798.

"The Book of Odes. No. I," *Time-Piece*, October 16, 1797.

  Reprinted: *Morris County Gazette*, November 1, 1797.

"The Book of Odes. No. II. To the Frigate Constitution," *Time-Piece*. October 18, 1797.

"The Book of Odes. No. III. To Duncan Doolittle, A 'Half-starved democrat,' " *Time-Piece*, October 20, 1797.

"The Book of Odes. No. IV. To Pest-Eli-Hali, A democratic Printer, on the western banks of the Hudson," *Time-Piece*, October 23, 1797.

  Reprinted as "To a Democratic Editor," *Poems* (1809), II, 11–12.

"On the Culture of Pumpkins. By Hezekiah Salem, late of New England," *Time-Piece*, October 25, 1797.

"A Sketch of Biography, By Hezekiah Salem, late of New England," *Time-Piece*, October 25, 1797.

"The Book of Odes. No. V. To Peter Porcupine," *Time-Piece*, October 25, 1797.

"The Book of Odes. No. VI. To the Learned Pig," *Time-Piece*, October 27, 1797.

> Reprinted as "Address to a Learned Pig of Particular Eminence, who, in a Certain Great City, Was Visited by Persons of the First Taste and Distinction," *Poems* (1809), II, 99–100.

"The Book of Odes. No. VII. On the Federal City," *Time-Piece*, October 31, 1797.

"Rules how to get through a crowd. By Hezekiah Salem, late of New England," *Time-Piece*, October 31, 1797.

To the Americans of the United States.

> Title from *Poems* (1809), II, 3, where it is said to have been "First published November, 1797."

"From Hezekiah Salem's Last Basket," *Time-Piece*, November 1, 1797.

"The Book of Odes. No. VIII. To Thos. Swawcum, a Wharf Builder," *Time-Piece*, November 1, 1797.

> Reprinted: *New-Jersey State Gazette*, December 26, 1797; and as "On the City Encroachments on the River Hudson," *Poems* (1815), I, 147–48.

"The Book of Odes. No. IX. On the Frigate Constitution," *Time-Piece*, November 6, 1797.

"A Few Words on Duelling. By Hezekiah Salem, late of New England," *Time-Piece*, November 10, 1797.

"The Book of Odes. No. X. To Santone Samuel, the Millennial Prophet, on his System of Universal Pacification," *Time-Piece*, November 10, 1797.

> Reprinted as "The Millennium—To a Ranting Field Orator," *Poems* (1815), I, 32–34.

"The Howling House. By Hezekiah Salem, late of New England," *Time-Piece*, November 13, 1797.

"The Book of Odes. No. XI. To the Philadelphia Doctors," *Time-Piece*, November 13, 1797.

> Reprinted as "On the Free Use of the Lancet, in Yellow Fever," *Poems* (1815), I, 146–47.

"The Book of Odes. No. XII. To the Philadelphia Doctors," *Time-Piece*, November 15, 1797.

> Reprinted as "The Crows and the Carrion: A Medical Story," *Poems* (1809), II, 8–9.

"A Scrap from a Keg of Hezekiah Salem's Sermons (Being a Specimen of my former manner of preaching.)," *Time-Piece*, November 17, 1797.

"Elegiac Verse on a Man that was killed by a Cow," *Time-Piece*, November 29, 1797.

> Reprinted as "On a Man Killed by a Buffaloe (or Wild Cow)," *Poems* (1809), I, 257.

"On Deborah Gannet, The American Heroine, who on Tuesday last presented a petition to Congress, for a pension in consideration of services rendered during the whole of the late war, in the character of a common soldier, in the regular armies of America," *Time-Piece*, December 4, 1797.

Reprinted: *Centinel of Freedom*, December 12, 1797; *South Carolina State Gazette*, August 24, 1798; and as "The heroine of the Revolution," *Poems* (1815), I, 70.

Untitled prose and verse attacking royalty, *Time-Piece*, December 4, 1797.

"The High-Minded Apprentice, A Tale," *Time-Piece*, December 6, 1797.

Reprinted as "The Royal Apprentice. A London Story," *Poems* (1815), I, 30–32.

"On a Fly, fluttering round a Candle," *Time-Piece*, December 8, 1797.

Reprinted as "To a Night-Fly, Approaching a Candle," *Poems* (1815), I, 75–76.

"Of Thomas Swaugum, an Oneida Indian, and a Missionary Parson," *Time-Piece*, December 11, 1797.

Reprinted: *Columbian Centinel*, December 23, 1797; and as "The Indian Convert," *Poems* (1809), I, 252; *The Cabinet of Momus*, p. 135; and *Aurora*, February 7, 1812.

"A Modern Tale," *Time-Piece*, December 13, 1797.

Reprinted: *Connecticut Courant*, December 25, 1797; and as "The Pettifogger, or, Fee Simple, Esquire," *Poems* (1809), I, 222–23; and *The Cabinet of Momus*, p. 50.

"A College Story (Appertaining to Secret History)," *Time-Piece*, December 18, 1797.

Reprinted: *United States Recorder*, February 27, 1798; *Poems* (1809), I, 256–57; and *The Cabinet of Momus*, p. 132.

1798

The Carrier of the Time Piece, Presents the following Address to his Patrons with the Season. New-York, January 1st, 1798.

Broadside, bound with the NJHS file of the *Time-Piece*.

"To the Americans. That the progress of liberty in the world, considering the present state of things, cannot be impeded, or its complete establishment prevented," *Argus*, June 15, 1798.

Reprinted: *New York Journal*, June 16, 1798, and as "Ode to the Americans," *Poems* (1815), I, 39–44.

"The Republic and Liberty," *Argus*, June 16, 1798.

Reprinted: *New York Journal*, June 16, 1798; *Centinel of Freedom*, February 5, 1799; and as "On the Prospect of War, and American Wrongs," *Poems* (1815), II, 9–13.

"Democracy," *Argus*, June 25, 1798.

Reprinted: *New York Journal,* June 27, 1798, and as "The Royal Cock-neys of America—1797," *Poems* (1815), I, 37–39.

"On the Causes of Political Degeneracy," *Argus,* July 7, 1798.

Reprinted: *New York Journal,* July 7; *Centinel of Freedom,* July 31, 1798; and as "Reflections on the Gradual Progress of Nations from Democratical States to Despotic Empires," *Poems* (1815), I, 13–16.

"To an Alien," *Time-Piece,* July 13, 1798.

Reprinted as "Stanzas to an Alien, who after a series of Persecutions Emigrated to the South Western Country," *Poems* (1815), I, 100.

"Botany Bay. Lines occasioned by Federal threats to take up and send off certain Patriotic characters to Botany Bay," *Time-Piece,* July 16, 1798.

Reprinted as "The Serious Menace; or Botany Bay and Nootka Sound: In Answer to the Comminations of a Persecuting Royalist," *Poems* (1815), I, 91.

1799

"To the Editor of the Aurora," *Aurora,* March 25, 1799.

Signed "A Monarchist." Reprinted as No. 1, *Slender's Letters* (1799), pp. 9–14.

"For the Aurora," *Aurora,* March 29, 1799.

Signed "Robert Slender." Reprinted as No. 2, *Slender's Letters* (1799), pp. 15–18.

"For the Aurora," *Aurora,* April 23, 1799.

Signed "Robert Slender." Reprinted as No. 3, *Slender's Letters* (1799), pp. 19–25.

"For the Aurora," *Aurora,* May 3, 1799.

Signed "Robert Slender." Reprinted as No. 4, *Slender's Letters,* pp. 25–31.

"For the Aurora," *Aurora,* May 7, 1799.

Signed "Robert Slender." Reprinted as No. 5, *Slender's Letters,* pp. 31–40.

"For the Aurora," *Aurora,* May 16, 1799.

Signed "Robert Slender." Reprinted as No. 6, *Slender's Letters,* pp. 40–48.

"For the Aurora," *Aurora,* May 20, 1799.

Signed "Robert Slender." Reprinted as No. 7, *Slender's Letters,* pp. 48–54.

"For the Aurora," *Aurora,* June 11, 1799.

Signed "Robert Slender." Reprinted as No. 8, *Slender's Letters,* pp. 54–57.

"For the Aurora. To Mr. Robert Slender," *Aurora,* June 18, 1799.

Signed "Simon Simple." Reprinted as No. 9, *Slender's Letters,* pp. 57–60.

"For the Aurora," *Aurora*, June 19, 1799.
> Signed "Robert Slender." Reprinted as No. 11, *Slender's Letters*, pp. 64–69.

Untitled verse, *Aurora*, July 6, 1799.
> Reprinted: *Centinel of Freedom*, July 16, 1799; and as "Fourth of July —An Ode," *Slender's Letters*, pp. 71–72.

"To Mr. Simon Simple," *Aurora*, August 1, 1799.
> Signed "Robert Slender." Reprinted as No. 10, *Slender's Letters*, pp. 60–63.

"For the Aurora," *Aurora*, August 8, 1799.
> Signed "Robert Slender." Reprinted as No. 13, *Slender's Letters*, pp. 72–78.

"For the Aurora," *Aurora*, August 9, 1799.
> Signed "Robert Slender." Reprinted as No. 14, *Slender's Letters*, pp. 79–83.

"For the Aurora," *Aurora*, August 16, 1799.
> Signed "Robert Slender." Reprinted as No. 18, *Slender's Letters*, pp. 101–07.

"For the Aurora," *Aurora*, August 17, 1799.
> Signed "Robert Slender." Reprinted as No. 15, *Slender's Letters*, pp. 83–89.

"For the Aurora," *Aurora*, August 20, 1799.
> Signed "Robert Slender." Reprinted as No. 16, *Slender's Letters*, pp. 89–94.

"For the Aurora," *Aurora*, August 23, 1799.
> Signed "Robert Slender." Reprinted as No. 17, *Slender's Letters*, pp. 95–101.

"For the Aurora," *Aurora*, August 24, 1799.
> Signed "Robert Slender." Reprinted as No. 19, *Slender's Letters*, pp. 107–16.

"Robert Slender," *Aurora*, September 3, 1799.
> Signed "Robert Slender." Reprinted as No. 20, *Slender's Letters*, pp. 116–23.

"For the Aurora," *Aurora*, September 11, 1799.
> Signed "Robert Slender." Reprinted as No. 22, *Slender's Letters*, pp. 128–31.

"For the Aurora," *Aurora*, September 27, 1799.
> Signed "Robert Slender." Reprinted as No. 23, *Slender's Letters*, pp. 131–38.

"For the Aurora," *Aurora*, September 28, 1799.
> Signed "Robert Slender."

"Oyez!!," *Aurora*, October 2, 1799.
> Signed "Robert Slender." Reprinted as No. 24, *Slender's Letters*, pp. 138–42.

"Robert Slender to the Editor of the Aurora," *Aurora,* November 6, 1799.
  Signed "Robert Slender."
"For the Aurora," *Aurora,* November 9, 1799.
  Signed "Robert Slender."
"For the Aurora," *Aurora,* November 23, 1799.
  Signed "Robert Slender."
"For the Aurora," *Aurora,* November 30, 1799.
  Signed "Robert Slender."
"For the Aurora," *Aurora,* December 4, 1799.
  Signed "Robert Slender."
Letters/ on/ Various interesting and important Subjects;/ many of which
have appeared/ in the/ Aurora./ Corrected and much enlarged./ By Rob-
ert Slender, O.S.M./ [*Two lines from Pope.*]/ Philadelphia:/ Printed for
the Author./ From the Press of D. Hogan—/ And sold at his Store, No. 222,
South Third-street, and at/ the Office of the Aurora./ December 30. 1799./
  12mo; 142pp. Copies: BM, HSP, LC, NJHS, NYHS, NYPL, NYSL,
  PU. Advertised in the *Aurora* from December 28, 1799.

1800

"Stanzas Occasioned by the Death of General George Washington," *City
Gazette,* January 10, 1800.
  Signed "Myrtilla." Reprinted: *Argus,* February 12; *New York Journal,*
  February 15; and as "Stanzas upon the same subject with the preced-
  ing," *Poems* (1815), I, 156–58.
"To the Memory of General George Washington," *City Gazette,* January 15,
1800.
  Signed "Sylvius." Reprinted as "Stanzas to the memory of Gen. Wash-
  ington, who died Dec. 14, 1799," *Poems* (1815), I, 154–56.
"Elegiac Stanzas To the Memory of Edward Rutledge, Esq. late Governor
of the State of South-Carolina," *City Gazette,* January 30, 1800.
  Reprinted: *Poems* (1815), I, 26–28.
"For the Aurora," *Aurora,* August 5, 1800.
  Signed "Robert Slender."
"For the Aurora," *Aurora,* September 10, 1800.
  Signed "Robt. Slender."
"For the Aurora," *Aurora,* October 2, 1800.
  Signed "Robert Slender."
"Robert Slender Argueth with the Parson," *Aurora,* October 7, 1800.
  Signed "Robert Slender."
"For the Aurora," *Aurora,* November 14, 1800.
  Signed "R. Slender."
"For the Aurora," *Aurora,* November 18, 1800.
  Signed "Robert Slender."

"Lines on the Federal City," *City Gazette*, December 18, 1800.
> Reprinted as "On the Federal City," *Poems* (1815), I, 34–35.

"On a View of the Planet Jupiter and his Moons through a large telescope," *City Gazette*, December 20, 1800.
> Reprinted as "On a Nocturnal View of the Planet Jupiter, and Several of his Satellites, through a Telescope," *Poems* (1815), I, 221–22.

1801

New-Year's Address./ From the carriers of the City Gazette,/ to their generous customers./ January 1, 1801./
> Bsd. in Freneau's manner; bound with College of Charleston file of *City Gazette*.

"To the Citizens of South-Carolina," *City Gazette*, January 5, 1801.
> Detailed defense of Freneau's relations with Jefferson; signed "Philip Freneau, Charleston, Dec. 31, 1800." Reprinted: *American Citizen*, August 11; and *Aurora*, August 14, 1801.

"For the Aurora," *Aurora*, February 19, 1801.
> Signed "Robert Slender."

"Stanzas on South Carolina. Said to have been written by P. Freneau," *New-York Weekly Museum*, August 1 and 9, 1801.
> Reprinted as "On Arriving in South Carolina, 1798," *Poems* (1815), I, 22.

"The Third Epistle of the First Book of Ovid's Tristia. Translated from the original Latin," *New-York Weekly Museum*, October 24, 31, and November 1, 1801.
> Reprinted as "Translation of the Third Elegy of the First Book of Ovid's Tristia," *Poems* (1809), I, 5–10.

1803

"On Walking over the ground on Long Island, near New-York, where many Americans were interred from the Prison Ships, during the war with Great Britain. Written July 1802," *New-York Weekly Museum*, April 16, 1803.
> Reprinted as "Stanzas Written some years ago, on the Long Island shore, near the city of New York, where vast numbers of Americans were interred, or sunk in the river, from the prison and Hospital ships during the revolutionary war with Great Britain," *Public Advertiser*, May 19; *L'Oracle*, May 20; *Palladium of Liberty*, June 6, 1808; and as "Stanzas Published at the Procession To the Tomb of the Patriots, in the Vicinity of the Former Stations of the Prison Ships, at New-York," *Poems* (1809), II, 300–02.

1804

"Stanzas written at Ortava, in view of the Peak of Teneriffe, 1804," *City Gazette*, July 9, 1804.

Reprinted: *New-York Weekly Museum*, August 25, 1804; and as "On the Peak of Teneriffe, 1804," *Poems* (1815), I, 177–78.

"Stanzas Written at the Island of Madeira in April last, on the fatal and unprecedented torrents of water which collected from the Mountains, on the 9th of October, 1803, destroyed a considerable part of the city of Funchal, and damaged, to a great amount, several plantations, towns, and villages in that neighbourhood," *City Gazette*, July 2, 1804.

Reprinted: *Poems* (1815), I, 171–76.

"Bunker" letters, *Aurora*, August 25–October 8, 1804.

Signed "Joe Bunker," "Joe Bunker, Jr.," "Jonathan Bunker," "Polly Bunker," and "Tomo Cheeki"; see note 79 of chapter XI.

1806

"Lines occasioned by reading the first number of Doctor Shecut's Flora Carolinaensis, lately published in this city," in John L. E. W. Shecut's *Flora Carolinænsis; or, a Historical, Medical, and Economical Display of the Vegetable Kingdom; according to the Linnaean, or Sexual System of Botany.* (Charleston, 1806), I, [581–82].

Said to be "from the pen of Capt. Philip Freneau, who was lately in this city" and to have "appeared in the City Gazette." I have been unable to find the poem in any Charleston newspaper of the period.

1809

"Lines Addressed to Mr. Jefferson, On his Approaching Retirement from the Presidency of the United States," *True American*, March 2, 1809.

Reprinted: *Public Advertiser*, March 3, 1809; and *Poems* (1815), II, 24–27.

"The following Verses were handed to the Editor of this paper, in manuscript written at Fundeal, in the Island of Madeira, by Capt. P. Freneau, July, 1803," *True American*, April 24, 1809.

Reprinted as "A Bacchanalian Dialogue. Written 1803," *Poems* (1815), I, 169–70.

Stanzas on the decease of Thomas Paine, who died at New-York on the 8th of June, 1809.

Title from *Poems* (1815), II, 24. Freneau, on May 15, 1815, wrote to John W. Francis of "a few stanzas insignificant enough, to the Memory of poor Tom Paine, first published at Philadelphia near six years ago" (*Unpublished Freneauana*, pp. 13–14). I have been unable to find the poem as a separate publication or as a contribution to a newspaper. Poems/ written and published during the/ American Revolutionary War,/ and now/ republished from the original Manuscripts;/ interspersed/ with Translations from the Ancients,/ and other Pieces not heretofore in/ Print./ By Philip Freneau./ [*Four lines in verse.*]/ The Third Edition, in two Volumes./ Vol. I [II]./ Philadelphia:/ From the Press of Lydia R. Bailey, No. 10,/ North-Alley./ 1809./

Two vols.; 12mo; vol. I, 280pp.; vol. II, 302pp. Copies: AAS, BM, BU, HSP, LC, LCP, NYHS, NYPL, NYSL.

"Lines Occasioned by the late disaster of one of the Paulas Hook passage-boat's upsetting from which accident one of our citizens was drowned and the remainder on board narrowly escaped," *Public Advertiser*, November 11, 1809.

Also printed in the *New York Evening Post* and the *New York Journal*, November 11, 1809. Reprinted: *New York Herald*, November 15, 1809, and as "The Blasts of November: Occasioned by a fatal accident on the Hudson," *Poems* (1815), II, 29–30.

1812

Untitled article on shipbuilding and coastal defense, *Aurora*, December 22 and 24, 1812.

Signed "Hawser Trunnion."

1814

"The Volunteer's March," *Fredonian*, August 11, 1814.

Reprinted: *True American*, August 16; *Columbian*, September 7; *Centinel of Freedom*, September 13, 1814; and *Poems* (1815), II, 43–44.

"To the Members of the General Ward Committee," *Aurora*, August 11, 1814.

Signed "Robert Slender."

"The Battle of Stonington," *Columbian*, September 24, 1814.

Reprinted: *New-Jersey Journal*, September 27; *Aurora*, September 29; *Palladium of Liberty*, October 6; *Centinel of Freedom*, November 15, 1814; and *Poems* (1815), II, 45–47.

"To the Squadrons on the Lakes," *Columbian*, September 29, 1814.

Reprinted as "To the Lake Squadrons," *Poems* (1815), II, 51–52.

"A Dialogue at Washington's Tomb. Between the Genius of Virginia and Virginia," *Fredonian*, September 29, 1814.

Reprinted: *Poems* (1815), II, 76–78.

"The Prince Regent's Resolve," *Fredonian*, September 29, 1814.

Reprinted: *Poems* (1815), II, 53–54.

"A Royal Dialogue," *Fredonian*, November 10, 1814.

Reprinted as "Royal Consultations; Relative to the Disposal of Lord Wellington's Army," *Poems* (1815), II, 78–81.

1815

A/ Collection of/ Poems,/ on/ American Affairs, and a variety of other Subjects,/ chiefly moral and political;/ written between the Year 1797 and the pres-/ ent Time./ By Philip Freneau,/ Author of Poems written during the Revolutionary/ War, Miscellanies, &c. &c./ In two Volumes./ [*Four lines of verse.*]/ Vol. I [II]./ New-York:/ Published by David Long-worth,/ At the Dramatic Repository,/ Shakespeare-Gallery./ 1815.

2 vols; 12mo: vol. I, 188pp.; vol. II, 176pp. Copies: BA, BM, BPL, BU, CU, HL, LC, LCP, NJHS, NYPL, NYSL, PU.

1816

"Stanzas Written in September 1811, on the great Comet, which had passed its perhelion, and was travelling rapidly to the southward," *New-York Weekly Museum*, August 10. 1816.

Signed "P.F." For identification of contributions after 1815, see note 41 of chapter XII.

"On Madam Charity Careless. A Disconsolate Widow," *New-York Weekly Museum*, August 31, 1816.

Signed "P.F." Reprinted as "The Neglected Husband," signed "E.," *Fredonian*, September 5; signed "A.," *True American*, December 28, 1822.

"On the Spots in the Sun," *New-York Weekly Museum*, September 7, 1816.

Signed "P.F."

"Stanzas Written for a Boy about eight years of age, who, in walking with his parents through a forest of Pine Trees, very narrowly escaped being bitten by an uncommonly large and venomous Rattle Snake. The Snake, which was killed with some difficulty, measured more than 13 feet long," *New-York Weekly Museum*, September 7, 1816.

Signed "P.F." Reprinted, signed "F.," as "Lines written for a lad of about eight years of age, who almost miraculously, escaped the bite of an uncommonly large rattlesnake," *Fredonian*, September 12; and, signed "E.," as "The following Stanzas were written for a lad about eight years of age, who, walking a small distance before his parents through a forest of pine trees, in those solitary deserts, very narrowly escaped being bitten by an uncommonly large and venomous snake of this species. The Serpent, when with some difficulty and risque, killed by the father, measured upward of nine feet in length, and had thirteen rattles on his tail," *True American*, October 12, 1822.

"Stanzas Addressed several years ago to Mr. Blanchard, the celebrated

Aeronaut in America," *New-York Weekly Museum*, September 21, 1816.
Signed "P.F."
"The Fortunate Blacksmith," *New-York Weekly Museum*, September 28, 1816.
Signed "P.F."
"Salutary Maxims Derived from the old Cynic Philosophy," *New-York Weekly Museum*, October 5, 1816.
Signed "F."
"Stanzas Written in an ancient Burying Ground in Maryland, one corner of which was appropriated to the interment of Suicides, or self-murderers," *New-York Weekly Museum*, October 12, 1816.
Signed "F." Reprinted, signed "R.," *Fredonian*, February 27, 1823.
"Epitaph Upon a Spanish horse called Royal-Gift, sent over and presented to General Washington by the King of Spain in the year 1785," *New-York Weekly Museum*, October 12, 1816.
Signed "F."
"The Tye-Wig. Lines of an old Dotard, who had cut away the blossoms of Sixty-Eight, and upwards, to put on a fashionable Tye-Wig," *New-York Weekly Museum*, October 19, 1816.
Signed "F."
"Letitia: or, the Fortunate Spinning Girl," *New-York Weekly Museum*, November 2, 1816.
Signed "F."
"A Dialogue Between a News-Printer and his Cash-Carrier," *New-York Weekly Museum*, November 9, 1816.
Signed "F."

1821

"Stanzas written on the Grand Western Canal of the State of New York, contemplated to connect the Atlantic Ocean with the Interior Lakes of North America," *True American*, June 30, 1821.
Reprinted, signed "F.," as "Stanzas on the Great Western Canal of the State of New York," *Fredonian*, August 8, 1822.
"Address Presented at the re-opening of the Park Theatre in New-York, sometime since destroyed by fire, and now completely repaired, and rebuilt in a superior style. (Said to be written by P. Freneau, of Monmouth, New Jersey)," *True American*, September 8, 1821.
"Jersey City. Lines written in the Church-Yard on Bergen Heights, near the village of Hoboken, on the Hudson," *True American*, September 29, 1821.
See note 32 of chapter XII.
"The City Poet," *True American*, October 6, 1821.
See note 33 of chapter XII.

"Elijah, The New England Emigrant," *True American*, October 13, November 3, December 1, and 15, 1821.

1822

"To a Young Friend, with some Maple Sugar," *True American*, April 13, 1822.

See pp. 353 above.

"The Youth of the Mind," *True American*, May 11, 1822.

Signed "F."

"Prologue To Kotzebue's Play, entitled 'The Stranger,' acted for the celebrated Mrs. Baldwin's Benefit at Washington Hall, New-York, April 15, 1822. Said to be written by P. Freneau, of N. Jersey," *True American*. May 18, 1822.

"Stanzas Written on a visit to a field called 'The Military Ground,' near Newburgh, in the State of New-York, where the American Army were disbanded by General Washington, almost forty years ago," *True American*, June 8, 1822.

Reprinted, "from the pen of a poet and patriot of the Revolution, who is now in his seventy-second year," *New York Statesman*, June 11; *Times*, June 20; and, signed "F.," *Fredonian*, July 18, 1822.

"Lines On the loss of the ship Albion, Capt. Williams, Wrecked near Kinsale Harbor, in Ireland, on the 22d of April last. By Captain Freneau," *True American*, June 15, 1822.

Also appeared, "from the pen of the veteran bard whom we mentioned a few days since," *Statesman*, June 15, 1822. Reprinted as "On the Loss of the Packet Ship Albion, Captain Williams," *Fredonian*, June 27, 1822.

"Recollections of Past Times & Events, No. I," *True American*, July 6, 1822.

Signed "R."

"To a young Farmer, or Agriculturist, being taken from the Plough, and sent to College," *True American*, July 6, 1822.

Signed "R."

"Stanzas Addressed to a Young Person of Condition, much addicted to the Gambling Table," *True American*, July 13, 1822.

Signed "F."

"Philosophical Fortitude," *Fredonian*, July 18, 1822.

Signed "F."

"General Lefevre Denoutte," *True American*, July 20, 1822.

Signed "R." Reprinted, signed "F.," as "Stanzas On General Lefevre Denoutte, who perished in the wreck of the Albion, April 22d. 1822," *Fredonian*, July 25, 1822.

"On the Civilization of the Western Aboriginal Country," *True American*, July 20, 1822.

Signed "A."

"Lines written at Demarest's field, near Tappan, on the disinterment and transportation of Major Andre's Bones to England, 1821," *True American*, August 24, 1822.

> Signed "R."

"Lines, written on leaving an elegant new mansion House, called Beaurepaire (pleasant retreat) not an hundred miles from Lake Cayuga," *True American*, August 24, 1822.

> Signed "N." Reprinted, signed "R.," as "Verses written on leaving a great house of much ceremony, but little sincerity, or hospitality," *Fredonian*, September 2, 1822.

"Recollections of Past Times and Events, No. II," *True American*, July 27, 1822.

> "Signed "U."

"Verses on an Upper Street Physician who Deserted a Populous City on the Approach of Malignant Fever," *Fredonian*, August 29, 1822.

> Reprinted, signed "R.," as "Verses on a Physician who deserted a great Commercial City on the approach and symptoms of the Yellow or Malignant Fever," *True American*, December 28, 1822.

"Recollections of Past Times and Events, No. III," *True American*, August 10, 1822.

> Signed "F."

"Recollections of Past Times and Events, No. IV," *True American*, August 17, 1822.

> Signed "F."

"Lines to a lady engaged in manufacturing an elegant superfine Carpet, intended to be forwarded, as a present to Nadir Shah, despot of Persia," *True American*, August 31, 1822.

> Signed "E."

"Lines written near an elegant and romantic Garden adjacent to Passaick River, in Essex county," *True American*, September 7, 1822.

> Signed "A." Reprinted, signed "E.," as "The Passaick Garden, in Essex County, July, 1820," *Fredonian*, October 17, 1822.

"The following verses were written at the time the intelligence first arrived in America that Bonaparte, from the first consulship, had ascended the throne of France," *True American*, September 14, 1822.

> Signed "E."

"A Midnight Storm in the Gulph Stream. Written on an outward bound voyage from Charleston to the Canary Islands," *Fredonian*, September 19, 1822.

> Signed "E." Reprinted, signed "F.," and dated "Brig Washington, January 25, 1804," *True American*, September 21, 1822.

"Lines to a lady, remarkably fond of sleep, preparing for a voyage to Europe," *True American*, September 21, 1822.

> Signed "A." Reprinted, signed "R.," *Fredonian*, October 5, 1822.

"The Arrival at Indian Sams (or, Wee-quali's) Wigwam," *Fredonian*, September 22, 1822.

 Signed "E." Reprinted, signed "N.," as "The arrival at Wee-quali's or Indian Sam's Wigwam," *True American*, September 28, 1822.

"Circumnavigation," *True American*, October 19, 1822.

 Signed "E."

"Ode Written on a remote perspective view of Princeton College (or Nassau Hall) from a remarkably woody eminence in Monmouth, commonly called Pine Hill," *True American*, October 26, 1822.

 Signed "R." Reprinted, signed "N.R.," as "Ode on a remote perspective view of Princeton College, or Nassau Hall, from a remarkably woody Eminence in Monmouth county, called by the Neighbourhood, Pine Hill," *Fredonian*, October 31, 1822.

"Lines on a Transient View of Monticello, in Virginia," *Fredonian*, November 7, 1822.

 Signed "E."

"On Observing a Large Red-Streak Apple Hanging on the Tree in January, 1822," *Fredonian*, November 14, 1822.

 Signed "E." Reprinted, signed "A.," as "On the continuance of a Red-Streak apple on the Tree in the month of January," *True American*, November 9, 1822.

"Answer to a letter of despondency from an Invalid in the North," *Fredonian*, December 5, 1822.

 Signed "F." Reprinted, signed "R.R.," *True American*, February 8, 1823.

1823

"To a New-England Poet," *True American*, January 4, 1823.

 Signed "N."

"On a widow Lady, (Very rich and very penurious.)," *True American*, February 1, 1823.

 Signed "R."

"Lines Written several years ago on the death of Robert Fulton," *True American*, February 1, 1823.

 Signed "E." and dated "June, 1816."

"General De la Fayette," *True American*, July 31, 1823.

 Reprinted, signed "F.," as "General De La Fayette. On his expected visit to America," *Fredonian*, August 18, 1824.

1824

"Stanzas Made at the interment of a Sailor on the Island of Tortuga, near the north side of Hispaniola, or Hayti, as now called. (Written many years ago, but never published)," *True American*, August 24, 1824.

 Reprinted, signed "F.," *Fredonian*, September 8, 1824.

1899

Some Account/ of the/ Capture of the/ Ship "Aurora"/ By/ Philip Freneau/ [*Cut of ship*]/ M. F. Mansfield & A. Wessels/ New York/
8vo; 50pp. Copies: BA, BPL, BU, LC, NYHS, NYPL, NYSL.

INDEX

Although no separate source bibliography is given, all book-sources directly used are listed in the index under author or short title. Reference to full documentation is placed first in the sequence of page numbers which follow the short title.